TESTING IN COUNSELING PRACTICE

VOCATIONAL PSYCHOLOGY

Samuel H. Osipow, Series Editor

Gilbert: Men in Dual-Career Families: Current Realities and Future Prospects

Vondracek, Lerner, & Schulenberg: Career Development: A Life-span Developmental Approach

Watkins & Campbell: Testing in Counseling Practice

TESTING IN COUNSELING PRACTICE

C. EDWARD WATKINS, JR.
VICKI L. CAMPBELL
University of North Texas

LEA LAWRENCE ERLBAUM ASSOCIATES, PUBLISHERS
1990 Hillsdale, New Jersey Hove and London

Lawrence Erlbaum Associates, Inc., Publishers
365 Broadway
Hillsdale, New Jersey 07642

Library of Congress Cataloging-in-Publication Data

Testing in counseling practice / [edited by] C. Edward Watkins, Jr., Vicki L. Campbell.
p. cm.
Includes bibliographical references and indexes.
1. Psychological tests. 2. Personality tests. 3. Vocational interests—Testing. 4. Counseling. I. Watkins, C. Edward. II. Campbell, Vicki Lynn.
BF176.T425 1990
150'.28'7—dc20 90-36947
CIP

Printed in the United States of America
10 9 8 7 6 5 4 3

To our respective sources of support
and encouragement:

Wallene and my parents
and
Alan and Keith

Contents

Preface

Testing has long been regarded as an important role of the counselor. Counselors traditionally have provided a variety of testing services, including personality, vocational, intellectual, and aptitude testing. In this book, we hope to consider further the role that tests play in the counseling process. Specifically, the purposes of this book are: (a) to provide important information on tests that are of value to counselors, (b) to provide information on how counselors think about and use tests, and (c) to illustrate how counselors can use different types of test information in counseling.

The book is designed to *introduce* readers to important theoretical, research, and practical information about the tests included here; it is oriented toward counselors, psychologists, and other mental health and education professionals. The book is suitable for graduate students who want to learn about different types of tests and for professionals who wish to get a comprehensive introduction about a test or tests. This book is appropriate for both master's-level and doctoral-level training courses that teach students about tests and their place in counseling.

In considering the tests covered here, an important point to remember is as follows: The tests were included because they focus more on a "normal" or "relatively normal" clientele. The tests presented in sections one and two are suited most appropriately for clients who could be described as psychologically healthy or relatively healthy, nonpathological, and psychiatrically non-disturbed. The clients who use these tests may be mildly to moderately distressed, experiencing some type of developmental issue or concern (e.g., deciding on a career), and in need of facilitative information. For the most part, these tests are designed to help individuals who are well-functioning or, at least, functioning adequately in their life roles.

A number of books that focus on using tests with a more pathological or psychologically disturbed clientele are available. However, there seems to be a real dearth of books that focus on using tests with a more healthy clientele. Counselors do need to be familiar with psychological disturbance, but they also need to know that there are many psychologically non-disturbed clients who can profit from counseling (Watkins & Peterson, 1986). We hope this book will demonstrate how tests can be used effectively for counseling healthy or well-functioning clients.

Although we regard the chapters as a comprehensive introduction to certain tests, two points about this book are important to keep in mind. First, a basic knowledge of test and measurement concepts (e.g., reliability, validity) is assumed of the reader. Therefore, to be able to use and understand the information included here, such knowledge is requisite. This book on testing would logically follow a basic testing/measurement course or, if used in the same course, would logically follow source material (e.g., Anastasi, 1988; Walsh & Betz, 1985) that provides an understanding of basic measurement concepts. Second, even though the test chapters are excellent and provide much rich information, they are not meant to replace study of the test manuals and other more specific, indepth sources. We believe the material that follows provides the reader with a sound beginning knowledge base, which will then need to be further reinforced and refined by more specific study of the particular tests the counselor wishes to learn.

As indicated previously, each of the test chapters contains a blend of theory, research, and practice material. The theoretical portion provides the conceptual foundations for the test under consideration, whereas the research portion provides information supporting the test and considers directions in which future research efforts should move. The practice material focuses on the different ways in which counselors can use the test and also includes a case example. We thought it was important to include a case example, to enable the reader to gain a better understanding of how the tests could actually be used in practice. In developing the case example, we gave the contributors two options: (a) Drawing on a counseling case, present test information and show how to integrate it into the work of counseling; or (b) provided work with the client did not proceed beyond the assessment phase, indicate how to integrate the test information into the counseling process if you were to be seeing this client for counseling. Thus, a major purpose of the book is to show how tests can be used to facilitate the counseling process.

To assist the contributors in developing their chapters, an outline for them to follow was developed. We hoped the outline would provide some continuity within and across chapters and insure that a number of important areas would be addressed. Although we recommended that contributors examine our outline and use it as they deemed appropriate, it was presented more as a tool to use in chapter development rather than a fixed, inflexible format to which everyone had to adhere. So, some continuity can be expected between chapters, but some variation can be expected also.

The idea of using a chapter outline is certainly not unique to our effort here. Previous works that have used a basic outline to organize chapters include Greenburg and Pinsof's (1986) *The Psychotherapeutic Process: A Research Handbook,* Gurman and Kniskern's (1981) *Handbook of Family Therapy,* and Norcross' (1986) *Handbook of Eclectic Psychotherapy.* In each case, the outline seemed useful in rendering the chapter material more effective. We hope our outline, presented at the end of this preface, worked similarly.

The book consists of three sections. Section I presents a model for using tests in counseling and considers five different tests that provide personality, cognitive, and behavioral assessment information. Section II considers various tests and methods that provide vocational assessment information. Section III considers issues and innovative applications in using tests in counseling. The last chapter presents some integrative postulates about the place of tests in counseling.

The decision about which personality and vocational tests to include in the book was given considerable thought and deliberation. In making our decision, three general criteria were used: (a) that the tests be used frequently by counselors; (b) that the tests have a solid history in the counseling profession; and (c) if relatively new in origin, that the tests show much promise for use in counseling. We made our final selection decisions based on test surveys of counselors (Bubenzer, Zimpfer, & Mahrle, 1990; Watkins & Campbell, 1987, 1989; Watkins, Campbell, & McGregor, 1988), readings of the professional literature in counseling, and personal observations about the types of tests counselors use and consider useful in counseling. Although some degree of arbitrariness may have been involved in our decision-making process, we tried to make our decisions in as informed a manner as possible.

Most of the chapters, of course, deal with a specific test. In a case or two (e.g., Chapter 6 on cognitive and behavioral assessment), we chose to include assessment material that technically could not be called a "test," but which seemed of much potential value to counselors. In these cases, the word "test" can be applied loosely to the assessment material. However, for all practical purposes, the best way to refer to such assessment methods is to just call them that: assessment methods.

Like most books, this one is not without its limitations. Perhaps the primary limitation is that, although the chapters that follow contain some highly valuable information on some highly valuable tests, there are other important personality and vocational tests not covered. Also, there are other types of tests beyond the scope of this book (e.g., intellectual, projectives) about which the counselor should have knowledge. Although all books generally have restrictions on their scope of content, it seems important to be aware of these restrictions and the manner in which they limit the reader's knowledge base.

In closing, as we reflect on our development of this book, there are a number of people who deserve thanks. First, we express our appreciation to our respective spouses, Wallene Watkins and Alan Wilson, for the support they provided us regarding this book project and for their continuing support of our careers. Second, we give a hearty thanks to all of the individuals who agreed to provide the chapters that compose this book. Their hard work helped us to bring our idea to realization, and we are indeed appreciative of their efforts. Third, we thank Lawrence Erlbaum for the assistance he provided us from a publishing perspective. Fourth, we express a deeply felt thank you to Sam Osipow for all the assistance and guidance he provided us on this project and for helping us bring it to final form.

C. Edward Watkins, Jr.
Vicki L. Campbell

REFERENCES

Anastasi, A. (1988). *Psychological testing* (6th ed.). New York: Macmillan.

Bubenzer, D. L., Zimpfer, D. G., & Mahrle, C. L. (1990). Standardized individual appraisal in agency and private practice: A survey. *Journal of Mental Health Counseling, 12,* 51–66.

Greenburg, L. S., & Pinsof, W. M. (Eds.). (1986). *The psychotherapeutic process: A research handbook.* New York: Guilford Press.

Gurman, A. S., & Kniskern, D. P. (Eds.). (1981). *Handbook of family therapy.* New York: Brunner/Mazel.

Norcross, J. C. (Ed.). (1986). *Handbook of eclectic psychotherapy.* New York: Brunner/Mazel.

Walsh, W. B., & Betz, N. E. (1985). *Tests and assessment.* Englewood Cliffs, NJ: Prentice-Hall.

Watkins, C. E., Jr., & Campbell, V. L. (1987, September). Counseling psychologists and psychological testing: Practices, applications, and attitudes. In C. E. Watkins, Jr. (Chair), *Contemporary perspectives on and uses of tests in counseling psychology.* Paper presented as part of a symposium at the annual meeting of the American Psychological Association, New York.

Watkins, C. E., Jr., & Campbell, V. L. (1989). Personality assessment and counseling psychology. *Journal of Personality Assessment, 53,* 296–307.

Watkins, C. E., Jr., Campbell, V. L., & McGregor, P. (1988). Counseling psychologists' uses of and opinions about psychological tests: A contemporary perspective. *The Counseling Psychologist, 16,* 476–486.

Watkins, C. E., Jr., & Peterson, P. (1986). Psychiatric epidemiology: Its relevance for counselors. *Journal of Counseling and Development, 65,* 57–59.

Chapter Outline for *Testing in Counseling Practice**

I. Background of the Test

Aim: To describe the development of the test and place it in historical perspective

1. What were the primary influences that contributed to the development of the test (e.g., people, experiences, research, books, conferences)?
2. What were the direct antecedents of the test?
3. How was the test originally conceptualized?
4. What type of construction was used in developing the test?

II. Conceptual Foundations of the Test

Aim: To describe the uses, guiding principles, and current status of the test

1. What are the guiding principles and tenets of the test?
2. What is the basis for electing to use the test in counseling?
3. What are the different ways in which the test can be used in counseling?
4. What major client and/or environmental variables are assessed by the test?
5. At which *unit* levels (e.g., individual, dyadic, system) are assessments made with the test?
6. At which *psychological* levels (e.g., intrapsychic, behavioral) are assessments made with the test?
7. For what populations or types of clients is the test designed?

III. Test Administration and Scoring

Aim: To describe the composition of the test and how the instrument is administered and scored

1. Of what do the test materials consist (e.g., item types, stimuli, booklets, answer sheets, forms, etc.)?
2. How is the test administered (e.g., group, individual, special instructions)?
3. What types of scores result and how are they obtained?
4. Are there alternate scoring systems?
5. What scales or subtests comprise the test and how are they obtained and reported?
6. Are scores presented normatively, and if so, what norm groups are available?

*Several of the questions in this outline were taken or adapted from Norcross (1986).

IV. Test Information

Aim: To describe how the tester understands and interprets the test information

1. What constructs do the scales or subtests measure?
2. How is the meaning of particular scores understood or interpreted for the test's scales or subtests?
3. Are there different methods or systems for interpretation?
4. What are the author's views regarding the interpretive process (e.g., involvement of clients, presenting information to clients)?
5. Do different strategies exist for approaching the interpretive process?
6. Are there special issues or cautions related to the interpretive process that need to be described?

V. Case Example

Aim: To illustrate how the test can be used and interpretive strategies can be applied in working with clients who seek counseling services

1. Who is the client (e.g., age, sex, other relevant demographic variables, presenting problem)?
2. What is the setting in which the counseling occurred (e.g., counseling center, mental health center, private practice)?
3. What prompted you to use the test with this client?
4. What questions were you (and the client) hoping to have answered through giving the test?
5. What results did you obtain from the test and what do they mean?
6. How did you go about integrating the test information into a cohesive picture?
7. How did you go about interpreting the results to the client?
8. How were you and the client able to use the test results in counseling?

VI. Research on the Test

Aim: To briefly summarize the clinical and empirical research on the test

1. What evidence exists to support the psychometric and technical properties of the test?
2. How does the existing evidence support the test's usefulness in counseling practice?
3. Is there any evidence suggesting that certain cautions or reservations need to be maintained about the test's usefulness in counseling?

VII. Evaluation and Future Directions

Aim: To conclude by offering some evaluative comments about the test and considering its future directions and needs

1. What are the advantages/disadvantages and strengths/weaknesses that accompany the test (e.g., applied uses of the instrument, psychometric and technical properties)?
2. How does the test compare with other instruments that are similar in nature?
3. What is your overall evaluation of the test?
4. What are the most important issues surrounding the test that need to be addressed?
5. What further work (clinical, research, theoretical) is needed to improve the test or its usefulness in counseling?
6. In what directions (clinical, research, theoretical) do you see the test moving in the next decade?

1 A Model for Using Tests in Counseling

Vicki L. Campbell
University of North Texas

A major focus of test use in counseling is the test taker, who "is viewed as the primary user of test results" (AERA, APA, NCME, 1985, p. 55). This contrasts with the use of tests for assessment, where the focus is on the counselor's understanding of the client and their functioning. These differences in the focus and goals of testing are important, because they result in different practices. The common view of tests as assessment tools, for example, results in thinking of testing as an enterprise separate from the counseling process. In contrast, when the client is seen as the primary user of results, it follows that it is important to integrate testing with other counseling goals.

The tests that are used in counseling cover a wide range of content. Although certain types of instruments are typically associated with counseling applications (e.g., vocational testing), many tests provide information that could be useful to clients. Although content is a primary factor when choosing tests, thinking about *how* the information will be used in counseling may bring equally important factors to light. The potential contributions of testing to the counseling process can guide test selection, along with clearly specified goals and a consideration of the steps involved when using test information.

A model that describes options for test use in counseling can help users make informed and intentional decisions. The application of test information in counseling is guided by decisions about the selection of instruments, the meaning of scores, and the reporting and use of results. Practices vary depending on the type of information provided by a test, and also by the way that information is to be used. This chapter will present a model that considers the potential contributions of test information to counseling and the steps involved in using tests within the counseling process. Questions that reflect dimensions of test information and use are presented as a guide to decision making. Thinking about the outcomes, processes, and dimensions of test use may encourage diversity and imagination in practice.

USES OF TEST INFORMATION

It may be helpful to consider different ways that testing can contribute to the counseling process. Clients work on several tasks in counseling—self-exploration, decision-making, and learning about themselves and the environment—and these tasks can be aided by information from testing. The contribution of tests to each of these processes is through providing feedback, new perspectives, or information. Tests are an alternate means of achieving certain counseling goals and can be a valuable addition to counseling practices. A delineation of the functions of testing may help counselors be specific when labeling the goals of testing with clients.

To begin with, tests can be a source of feedback that can serve different functions in counseling, like any type of feedback. One use is to confirm something a client already knows; another use is to provide new information. Feedback may also help clients compare or evaluate aspects of themselves. Comparisons may have a normative focus (compare clients to others), or they may be ipsative (focus on comparisons within clients). Normative feedback may help a client take stock of interests or abilities for decision-making. Ipsative information can be a stimulus to a client's self-exploration. Tests may reflect and clarify issues for clients. They may also help clients confront aspects of themselves that are new or difficult to acknowledge. Broadly, feedback may encourage clients to discuss and explore issues in more depth.

A second function of test information is to provide new perspectives. Test instruments often incorporate information given by the client into a framework provided by the test. The presentation of a framework or cognitive map of a topic can provide a new perspective on information. In relation to this use, "a set of test data adds no *new* information but contributes to the organization of the client's concept of himself in relation to whatever decisions are in focus" (Goldman, 1971, p. 30). The organization of interest inventories, for example, may provide a structure for considering interests and the career decision-making process. A personality inventory may help clients conceptualize aspects of themselves and link those concepts with behaviors, concerns, or future courses of action. Other instruments, rather than providing a specific framework, may instead serve as a methodology for assisting clients in exploring or learning about their own personal framework. Card sorts are an example of a methodology that helps clients describe their own way of thinking about occupations.

A third use of test information is to teach or present new ideas. Many instruments are based on a theoretical viewpoint that provides a way of understanding test results. Responding to the questions on the instrument and learning the concepts necessary to make sense of the results can be an introduction to a theoretical viewpoint. Examples are the Strong-Campbell Interest Inventory as an introduction to Holland's theory of occupational types (Hansen & Campbell, 1985), the Career Development Inventory (Super, Thompson, Lindeman, Jordaan, & Myers, 1981) as an introduction to dimensions of Super's model of vocational maturity, and the way results from the Myers-Briggs Type Indicator familiarize clients with concepts from Jungian theory (Myers & McCaulley, 1985). Theories vary in their focus, and test information may focus on a process (e.g., career decision-making), or it may be a way to expose clients to new information (e.g., unfamiliar occupations).

Finally, the content of tests may be a stimulus for discussion in counseling. The questions or ideas presented in a testing instrument may help clients express themselves, or introduce topics that may be difficult to talk about. The dimensions of a personality inventory or clients' reactions to answering test items may be a starting point for discussions. From this perspective, tests can be a way of giving clients permission to discuss difficult subjects, or a way of presenting the kind of information that is significant to a topic. For example, items that ask questions about decision-making difficulties inform clients that this is an appropriate topic of discussion in career counseling; items that focus on emotional distress may encourage clients to discuss issues of concern. Questions about decision-making difficulties may also help clients express their concerns by adding structure and specific content to a struggle that is vaguely felt.

In this section, tests have been considered in terms of their potential functions within the counseling process. The feedback, new perspectives, or information from tests have a variety of functions within the counseling process. Certain steps and tasks are involved in using tests so they can serve those functions.

COUNSELING SKILLS AND TEST USE

The use of test information in counseling requires attention to all of the communication skills and steps that are important in any type of counseling. Decisions about how to make use of test information occur in relation to goal setting, the selection of tests, the understanding and discussion of results, and the evaluation of the usefulness of testing. There are tasks at each stage of the counseling process that are important for the optimal use of tests.

During initial stages of counseling, the goals of testing need to be clarified and made explicit. "Taking a test" is not a useful goal statement because it doesn't describe the purpose of testing or the information a client hopes to obtain by taking a test. A goal related to testing should state not only what is being measured, but the purpose of measuring it. A useful goal might be to measure aspects of personality style and compare the client's scores to norms for the purpose of checking the client's self-perceptions; another example would be to measure vocational interests for the purpose of learning how the test organizes interests and viewing the client's interests within that framework. The first step in specifying a useful goal is labeling the topics the client wishes to explore. Stating *how* test information may contribute to the overall goals of clients is the second step in specifying a useful goal. Putting the anticipated contributions of testing into words is a way of labeling process goals that will be helpful in guiding the discussion of test results. The functions of test information discussed in the previous section may help frame process goals. For example, a client might take the Kuder Occupational Interest Survey (Kuder & Diamond, 1979) for the purpose of broadening their ideas of potential majors or occupations, *or* for the purpose of validating choices they have already made. Clients may want to take personality tests to clarify conflicts within themselves, *or* to help them compare their own characteristics to those of other people. Thinking about and labeling the specific purpose of testing prior to discussing results is likely to make for more productive applications.

Selecting instruments that can contribute to clients' goals is the second step in using tests. If the purpose of taking a test was clarified in the previous step, then the choice of testing instruments will be simplified. Approaches to testing vary in their views of the extent that clients can be usefully involved in the selection of test instruments. However, if the client is to be optimally involved in the testing process that involvement will have to begin with goal setting and the selection of tests (Patterson & Watkins, 1982). If the appropriate knowledge is provided by the counselor, clients can be effectively involved in choosing tests. Options can be discussed with clients, with the counselor presenting information concerning tests that are available, differences among the instruments, and the contributions that each could make to the goals of the client.

The third step in using test information is helping clients explore the meaning of results and relate them to the purpose of counseling. Traditionally, training in the use of tests has focused on the counselor's understanding or interpretation of test results, without a corresponding emphasis on conveying that information to clients or making use of the information in relation to counseling goals. The use of all of the communication skills of counseling is particularly significant at this phase of the testing process. A first step in helping clients understand test results is to provide information about the structure and content of results. This provides the client with the necessary background to discuss and explore the personal meanings and implications of the results. This task involves careful listening, and relating test information to goals and issues the client and counselor have discussed earlier. Once again, the clear specification of goals is an important precursor to the successful use of test information. The counselor's role in this process may range from providing technical information, to using basic counseling skills to facilitate the exploration and discussion of test material.

Finally, the client and counselor need to evaluate whether the goals of testing were accomplished. This may be a point to end the counseling relationship, or it may lead to establishing new goals. The concept of "exploration validity" (the evaluation of tests on the basis of their ability to stimulate the exploration of issues and questions) may be particularly applicable to the counseling use of tests (Tittle, 1978).

QUESTIONS TO FRAME DECISIONS

The discussion of testing to this point has been to encourage thinking about options available when using tests in counseling. There are questions at each step of the counseling process that frame the choices and decisions that counselors and clients need to make when using tests. These questions consider both the contributions and applications of testing.

First are questions for goal setting and test selection. These questions ask, what are the goals of counseling, and how can testing contribute to those goals?

1. Broadly, what type of information should testing provide? What are topic areas being discussed in counseling where testing might play a useful role? Would it be useful for tests to provide feedback, information, and/or new perspectives? Are the client's goals to learn about how they do things, what they are like, how their characteristics relate to future behavior, or how their characteristics compare to others? In other words, is the purpose of testing to describe, predict, or evaluate?
2. What functions can test information serve in counseling? This question focuses on the process goals of testing. Would the client like to expand the career options being considered? Would the client like to explore the effects of their interpersonal style?

The next set of questions refer to test selection. Broadly, what testing instruments are available that may contribute to the clients goals, and what information about the instruments is important for test selection?

1. What types of testing instruments are available in the content area?
2. How does the testing instrument approach the area, and what type of information will result? What are the advantages and disadvantages of that form of information? Are there other instruments which might add a different perspective on the issue in question?
3. What technical information (e.g., method of test construction, reliability, validity) would be important for test selection?

The third type of question the counselor needs to ask will affect how test information is used within counseling. These questions consider the functions of test information in the counseling process, and also the counselor's skills and actions.

1. What were the process goals that were labeled in relation to the testing?
2. What role does the counselor want to take in facilitating the client's use of test information?
3. What technical information needs to be explained to help the client understand the meaning of test results?
4. What counseling skills will be important to help the client explore and discover the meaning of test results?

Finally, there are questions related to evaluating the effectiveness of using tests.

1. Did the test information effectively cover the content area? Had the client hoped for other types of information? Are there still questions in regard to information about the area?
2. Did the use of test information accomplish the process goals that were labeled prior to testing? For example, did the results stimulate discussion or promote exploration?
3. Are there further goals for counseling which have been labeled as a result of the test results? Are there any further goals related to testing?

Although these questions are not exhaustive, they may be a starting point for the consideration of tests and their application within counseling. Labeling the possible functions of test information may broaden ideas for test-related goals. Specific goals will contribute to appropriate test selection and the usefulness of test results for clients. Thinking about the steps involved in using test information within counseling may encourage counselors to use all of their skills and integrate testing with other goals of counseling. The procedures outlined will make it more likely that clients are involved with the purposes of testing rather than being passive recipients of results.

REFERENCES

American Educational Research Association, American Psychological Association, and National Council on Measurement in Education. (1985). *Standards for educational and psychological testing*. Washington, DC: American Psychological Association.

Goldman, L. (1971). *Using Tests in counseling* (2nd ed.). Santa Monica, CA: Goodyear Publishing.

Hansen, J. C., & Campbell, D. P. (1985). *Manual for the SVIB-SCII* (4th Edition). Stanford, CA: Stanford University Press.

Kuder, F., & Diamond, E. E. (1979). *General Manual: Kuder DD Occupational Interest Survey* (2nd Ed.). Chicago: Science Research Associates.

Myers, I. B., & McCaulley, M. H. (1985). *Manual: A guide to the development and use of the Myers-Briggs Type Indicator*. Palo Alto, CA: Consulting Psychologists Press.

Patterson, C. H., & Watkins, C. E., Jr. (1982). Some essentials of a client-centered approach to assessment. *Measurement and Evaluation in Guidance, 15,* 103–106.

Super, D. E., Thompson, A. S., Lindeman, R. H., Jordaan, J. P., & Myers, R. A. (1981). *The Career Development Inventory*. Palo Alto, CA: Consulting Psychologists Press.

Tittle, C. K. (1978). Implications of recent developments for future research in career interest measurement. In C. K. Tittle & D. G. Zytowski (Eds.), *Sex fair interest measurement: Research and implications*. Washington, DC: National Institute of Education.

2 The Minnesota Multiphasic Personality Inventory

Jane C. Duckworth
Ball State University

BACKGROUND OF THE TEST

The Minnesota Multiphasic Personality Inventory (MMPI), the most widely used personality test in the world, was developed by Starke Hathaway and J. C. McKinley in the late 1930s and published in 1943. The authors designed the test to be used for routine clinical assessment, mostly to help in assigning an appropriate psychodiagnostic label to a patient. Previous inventories developed by Woodworth (1920) and Bernreuter (1933) had attempted to do approximately the same thing. The Woodworth Personal Data Sheet (Woodworth, 1920), a test of 116 items reflecting neurotic symptoms to which a person answered "yes" or "no," was the first inventory. If the person taking the test answered a significant number of items in the scoreable, neurotic direction, he or she was given an individual interview. The test was used during the latter part of World War I to identify those recruits who were emotionally unsuitable for armed service.

The success of the Woodworth inventory led to the development of other inventories such as the Bernreuter (1933). All of these tests were developed on a rational basis, that is, the items on them were selected as being indicative of pathology and the scoring was determined by the test maker to reflect what a neurotic or psychotic person would answer. Several critiques, however, (Landis & Katz, 1934; Page, Landis, & Katz, 1934) showed that these rationally derived tests were inadequate to classify the neurotic and psychotic people being tested.

The authors of the MMPI took these criticisms into consideration when they developed their testing instrument. They gathered a large number of items from psychiatric textbooks, other personality inventories, and clinical experience. After deleting duplicate items they had a sample of items that were then used to develop a number of scales to diagnose various types of psychoses and neuroses. In selecting the items for the various scales, however, Hathaway and McKinley used an empirical approach rather than the discredited rational approach. For an item to be included in a scale, it had to be answered differently by a diagnostic group (e.g. schizophrenic patients) when compared to a group of normals. Because this approach is strictly empirical, it is not always possible to discern why a particular item differentiates between the diagnostic group and the normals. These items have been labeled "subtle" items and are one of the major strengths of the MMPI. It is very difficult for people wanting to fake the test to guess which way these subtle items should be answered to be counted on a particular scale.

The eight clinical scales, which were originally developed by this empirical method, are as follows; Scale 1 (Hypochondriasis), Scale 2 (Depression), Scale 3 (Hysteria), Scale 4 (Psychopathic Deviate), Scale 6 (Paranoia), Scale 7 (Psychasthenia), Scale 8 (Schizophrenia), and Scale 9 (Mania). Two additional scales were added a short time later which are not reflective of either neurosis or psychosis. These are Scale 5 (Masculine-Feminine Interests) and Scale 0 (Social Introversion-Extroversion). These 10 scales comprise the clinical scale profile of the MMPI.

A unique feature of the MMPI is the addition of four Validity Scales to the profile of the individual. These scales were added to provide measures of the test-taker's honesty or frankness in responding to the items on the test. These four scales are the ? Scale (number of items left unanswered), L Scale (Lie Scale), F Scale (Faking Bad Scale), and the K Scale (Correction Scale). The raw score of the K scale, or a fraction of it, is added to Scales 1, 4, 6, 8, and 9 to improve the discrimination of these five scales (McKinley, Hathaway, & Meehl, 1948). The L and K scale were designed to detect trying to look good on the test, and the F scale was designed to detect trying to look bad. The ? scale was included to give an indication of the number of items that the test taker had left unanswered, perhaps in an attempt to keep the individual's personality a secret. The validity scales were not developed by comparing a criterion group to a group of normals. (See Dahlstrom, Welsh, and Dahlstrom (1972) for a description of the methods used to derive these scales.)

It was originally thought that a person taking the MMPI would have an elevated score (above 70 T-score points) on one of the original eight clinical scales, and this would indicate the appropriate diagnosis for that individual. Almost immediately after the MMPI was published, however, it became apparent that many people did not obtain a high score on only one clinical scale but rather had elevations on two or more scales. This development led to a coding system (Hathaway, 1947) that reflected the high points on the profile. It has become common to base MMPI interpretations on the configuration of the two or three highest scales elevated above 70 T-score points (called a codetype) rather than on the single highest scale.

"Cookbooks" have been developed (Gilberstadt & Duker, 1965; Lachar, 1974; Marks & Seeman, 1963; Marks, Seeman, & Haller, 1974) that report the most common codetypes and the corresponding behaviors and personality traits associated with them. These cookbooks are based on empirical data that have been gathered by the respective authors. Other books giving information regarding codetypes based on empirical data, but also using the author's clinical experience, have also been published (Duckworth & Anderson, 1986; Graham, 1987; Greene, 1980).

The MMPI, because of its original development by and for clinical psychologists, was not originally seen as part of a counselor's typical testing battery. Only when a counselor was doing an assessment of a more seriously disturbed individual would the test be used; frequently it was considered inappropriate to use with the more normal counseling population. When it was used for this normal population, most typically in college counseling centers, it was quickly discovered that the usual interpretation of elevated scales as indicating severe pathology was frequently inappropriate. One of the first books about the MMPI and the counseling population addressed this problem. Drake and Oetting (1959) published a book specifically for interpreting the MMPI in college counseling centers. They based their interpretive statements for elevated clinical scales on information found in the casefiles of counseling center clients who had MMPIs with elevated scales. This book led the way for other books and articles to specifically address the question of the use of the MMPI with counseling clients.

The next publication to look at this population was a book by Carkhuff, Barnette, and McCall (1965). These authors surveyed the recent literature and in outline form, presented data on the relevant research found for moderately elevated MMPI scales (60 to 70 T-score points), markedly elevated MMPI scales (70 T-score points and above), and low MMPI scales (45 T-score points and below). They reported not only clinical information but vocational implications for the various scales as well.

Leo Goldman's *Using Tests in Counseling* (1971) was the next major text to be published reporting on the unique usage of the MMPI by counselors. He reported on the possibilities of using the MMPI as part of a counselor's repetoire. This book was followed by one by Duckworth and Duckworth (1975), in which the approach pioneered by Carkhuff, Barnette, and McCall (1965) of reporting on the literature pertinent for moderately elevated, markedly elevated, and low points on the MMPI clinical scales was continued with the addition of selected research scales that were useful for the counseling population. This book has been followed by second and third editions (Duckworth, 1979; Duckworth & Anderson, 1986) in which the research on the counseling implications of the scales has been updated, and chapters on the interpretation of unelevated MMPIs and the interpretation of MMPIs from different races and cultures have been added.

Kunce and Anderson in 1976, in a seminal article entitled "Normalizing the

MMPI,'' proposed that the clinical scales of the MMPI were measuring competencies as well as problem behaviors and that each scale could indicate coping behaviors when they were at the moderate elevations as well as defensive/noncoping behaviors at the marked elevations. Kunce (1979) followed this line of reasoning further in a book chapter in *MMPI: Clinical and Research Trends* (Newmark, 1979), in which he postulates three major personality types that can be categorized on the basis of moderate elevations of the MMPI. These personality types are relatively stable, and indicate long term ways of reacting to others.

There have been many articles written about the MMPI since the Kunce and Anderson article in 1976, but only a few are concerned with the counseling approach to the test. How then do counselors presently see this clinical test as fitting into their work? Watkins and Campbell (1987) in a survey of 630 counseling psychologists employed in counseling centers (20.2%), academic departments (36%), and private practice (19.2%), report that the MMPI is the test most frequently used by the respondents (83%) followed closely by the Strong-Campbell Interest Inventory and the Wechsler Adult Intelligence Scale-Revised. When asked to indicate which tests they would recommend students learn, 80% of the sample indicated the MMPI. Clearly, the MMPI in spite of its clinical origins and the relative paucity of material on its use in counseling is found highly useful by counselors in the field.

CONCEPTUAL FOUNDATIONS OF THE TEST

As was mentioned previously, the original purpose of the MMPI was as an assessment instrument, primarily for assigning a diagnostic label to a client. The original clinical scales of the test reflect this focus. They cover the major neuroses (hypochondriasis, depression, hysteria, and psychasthenia [obsessive-compulsiveness]) and psychoses (paranoia, schizophrenia, and mania) of that time.

Although the test is still an excellent diagnostic tool and can be used as such by counselors who are working with disturbed clients, it also has these other uses for counselors.

1. In medical settings the test can be given to clients in *pain clinics* to show the patient's reaction to the pain and the amount of psychological strain the client is experiencing. In *wellness centers* the test can help evaluate the importance of psychological factors in the overall health profile of the individual.
2. The test is useful in assessing members of a family in *family therapy* or the participants in *marriage counseling*. It is helpful to see how each person is reacting to the current stress as well as the interactions taking place within the family or marital system. In this situation, looking at the MMPI as indicating whether the individual seems to be moving towards others in

the system, indicated by elevations on scales 1, 3, 7, and 9; is moving away from others in the system, as indicated by elevations on scales 2, 8, and 0; or is moving against others in the system as indicated by elevations on scales 4 and 6, can be very helpful.

3. The test can be used as an adjunct to *vocational counseling* when given in conjunction with vocational tests. The MMPI clinical scales are useful to indicate the personal strengths as well as the weaknesses of the individual seeking vocational help. (See Table 2.3 for strengths and weaknesses indicated by each scale.) In addition, the 0 scale (social introversion-extroversion) can be used to indicate how much interaction with others the individual would feel comfortable with in a work setting.
4. The MMPI can be useful in *personnel screening,* especially for sensitive jobs such as police officers. It can indicate potential problems such as alcoholism (the MacAndrew Addiction Scale [MacAndrew, 1965]) or lack of good judgment (elevations on scales 4 and 8).

Although the MMPI is typically used to measure individuals, it can also be used for groups (families and personnel selection). The scales on the test measure both intrapsychic factors (scales 2, depression; 6, paranoia; 7, anxiety; and 8, confusion) and actual behavior (scale 4, self-centeredness; 9, acting out, impulsivity; and 0, introversion). This combination of scales makes the MMPI more difficult to interpret than a test with only one kind of scale; therefore it is highly recommended that counselors intending to use this test have training in its interpretation in order to get the full benefit of its complexity and to insure that the test is not misused or misinterpreted.

TEST ADMINISTRATION AND SCORING

The MMPI is available in two paper-and-pencil forms (the booklet form and Form R), a card sort version, and an audio tape version for clients who do not have the sixth-grade reading ability necessary to take the test in the usual manner or for those people who are blind. In addition, there are a number of short forms of the MMPI in which the client answers fewer than the 566 items that are included in the full MMPI. These shortened forms will not be discussed in this chapter because many of the scales that are useful for working with a normal population can not be scored when shortened forms are used.

All forms of the test are sold by National Computer Systems (NCS), Minneapolis, Minnesota. NCS also sells the answer sheets and scoring keys for the validity, clinical, and selected research scales. The NCS catalog should be consulted for further information regarding ordering the test, answer sheets, and keys and the cost of these items. Care must be taken to ensure that the appropriate scoring keys are obtained for the version of the MMPI that is being used; for example, the Form R keys will not work for the booklet version and visa versa.

Computer scoring is available for the MMPI from a number of sources. Computer scoring is handled in one of four ways. In the first method, after the client has taken the test, the responses from the answer sheet are put into a computer by a clerk. The test is then scored by the computer immediately and the results are printed as a profile. This can be done on either a personal computer or a mainframe computer. In the second method, the MMPI answer sheet is scanned by a machine, the computer scores the test, and the results are printed. Again the results are immediately available. A third method of computer scoring is to send the test to a testing service. The test is scored by them and typically returned within a week. In the fourth method, the client takes the test on the computer, which then scores it and prints a profile.

The test can be administered in either a group setting or individually. Typical instructions to the client are as follows: ''I would like you to take a test, the Minnesota Multiphasic Personality Inventory, to help me learn some things about you in a relatively quick way. The test asks you to answer a number of questions concerning how you feel and behave and the things that are currently on your mind. Because there are many questions to answer, and the first answer is the one most likely to reflect where you are currently, I would ask you to just go ahead and mark down the first answer that comes to your mind. If you should be having difficulty deciding what to answer to a question, I would encourage you to choose your answer as quickly as possible, and then put a question mark by that answer, and we will discuss it when I interpret the test to you. Try not to leave any answer blank. I can get to know you better if you answer all the questions. We can talk about questionable answers later. This is your chance to help me know you. I will be interpreting the test to you at some later date. You will have a chance to discuss any of the test results with me at that time.'' When instructions are given in this manner, most people respond by answering the items as accurately as possible.

Scales and Subscales

As has already been discussed, the MMPI as it was originally developed had four validity scales (?, questions left unanswered; L, Lie; F, Feeling Bad; and K, Correction) and ten clinical scales (1, Hypochondriasis; 2, Depression; 3, Hysteria; 4, Psychopathic Deviate; 5, Masculine-Feminine Interests; 6, Paranoia; 7, Psychasthenia; 8, Schizophrenia; 9, Mania; 0, Social Introversion-Extroversion.) Since the original test was developed, additional scales have been formulated and many of them are now routinely scored, depending upon the particular scoring templates or computer scoring program used. Ten frequently scored scales, (A, Anxiety; R, Repression; Es, Ego-strength; Lb, Low back pain; Dy, Dependency; Do, Dominance; Re, Social Responsibility; Pr, Prejudice; St, Status; Cn, Control) are discussed in Duckworth and Anderson (1986), and Graham (1987), and Greene (1980). Table 2.2 lists these scales and gives a brief interpretation for each of them.) A scale that has become routinely scored because of its usefulness in diagnosing drug and alcohol addiction is the MacAndrew Addiction Scale (1965). It is also listed in Table 2.2 with its interpretation.

Another frequently scored group of scales are the Wiggins content scales (Wiggins, 1966). These are 13 scales that are mutually exclusive, internally consistent, and moderately independent. They are designed to be representative of the major content areas of the MMPI. Because the items that make up these scales tend to be obvious in what they are testing, the scales have been found to be useful as indicators of what the test taker believes his or her problem(s) to be. As such they can be compared to the clinical scales which show what the person's problems are when compared objectively to others. Frequently the two sets of scales provide different information, indicating that the person sees his or her problem(s) differently than the more objectively derived clinical scales do.

Subscales have also been developed for all of the clinical scales except scale 1, Hypochondriasis, and scale 7, Psychasthenia (Harris & Lingoes, 1955; Serkownek, 1975). These subscales can be used to increase the accuracy of the MMPI interpretation (cf. Graham, 1987; Greene, 1980). Two of the ways in which interpretive accuracy can be increased using these subscales are as follows: If there is an elevation on a clinical scale, it is useful to see which of the subscales of that clinical scale are most elevated so that they can be emphasized in the clinical interpretation. Another possibility for using the subscales is when there is no elevation on a clinical scale itself, but one of the subscales of that scale is elevated. This might indicate that there is a significant concern for the individual even though the clinical scale itself is not elevated; this concern may need to be mentioned in the clinical report.

The individual test interpreter will need to examine the many additional scales that are available and work with them for a while to see which ones will be the most useful for his or her clinical situation.

Norms

Raw scores for the MMPI scales are converted into standard scores with a mean of 50 and a standard deviation of 10. Scores are considered in the clinically significant range when they are 70 T-score points or higher. A group of Minnesota normal people tested in the late 1930s and early 1940s form the normative group to which test takers are compared. A study of normal individuals conducted in the late 1970s (Colligan, Osborne, Swenson, & Offord, 1983) indicated that the average person today answers the MMPI differently than the average person did in the 1930s and 1940s. In general, people in the 1970s scored higher on the clinical scales than people did in the original sample. The average person today is answering more items in the deviant direction than was true in the 1930s, perhaps reflecting a greater willingness to admit to problematic feelings and behaviors. It would seem, therefore, that caution is needed in interpreting MMPI scale scores that are borderline, that is, around 70 T-score points, because these scores may not be as "abnormal" as they once were.

Norms have recently been developed for adolescents (Marks, Seeman, and Haller, 1974) in recognition of the fact that normal adolescents tend to have higher scores than normal adults on some of the MMPI clinical scales, typically scales F, 4, 8, and 9. Caution has also been urged in the use of the usual adult norms when Blacks or other minorities are tested (Gynther, 1972; Gynther & Green, 1980). Again, it has been found that scales F, 4, and 8 seem to be elevated for many minority test takers who are not experiencing any psychological difficulties.

The MMPIs of people who have had some college education may also be misinterpreted when the original norms and scale interpretations are used. Three scales, especially, may be interpreted incorrectly. For the original sample, when the 5 scale was elevated above 70 T-score points for men, it was an infrequent score and was interpreted as reflecting excessive passivity and atypical feminine interests. However, men today with some college education frequently score above 70 T-score points on this scale. The 5 scale for them tends to be reflecting aesthetic interests and their educational level rather than passivity and femininity. Therefore this scale can be misinterpreted if the old norms and interpretations are used. The K scale also can be misinterpreted for people with some college education. This scale originally was interpreted as showing defensiveness and wanting to look good when it was close to 70 T-score points. For educated people, the K scale frequently is close to 70 T-score points, but this reflects the better-than-average adjustment the individual has to life rather than defensiveness. The L scale, on the other hand, presents a different kind of interpretation problem. It may indicate unusual personal rigidity and a desire to be seen as "good" for a college-educated person even when it is at 60 T-score points, a level that was not considered to reflect this rigidity and desire when the original norms were established. Other problems for the interpretation of the MMPIs of college students and educated people are discussed in Duckworth and Anderson (1986).

These examples show how important it is when interpreting the MMPI to use the proper norms for comparison and interpretation.

TEST INTERPRETATION

Because of the widespread use of the MMPI and the almost mystical belief by some people in its ability to diagnose people and their problems, caution must be exercised in order not to abuse the test. First and foremost, there is no substitute for a thorough knowledge of the test and its interpretive possibilities. A class or workshop on MMPI interpretation is a must.

Although many books are available covering MMPI interpretation (cf. Dahlstrom, Welsh, & Dahlstrom, 1972; Duckworth & Anderson, 1986; Gilberstadt & Duker, 1965; Graham, 1987; Greene, 1980; Lachar, 1974; Marks, Seeman, & Haller, 1974) there will always be a need for a clinician's evaluation of a profile to ensure the best fit of the interpretation to the person being evaluated. In the next two sections of this chapter are a) interpretations for the MMPI validity and clinical scales and selected research scales, and b) a suggested process that can be used in interpreting the MMPI. These two sections reflect what might be considered a counseling approach to the interpretation of MMPIs, as opposed to a clinical approach. This counseling approach can be summarized as follows:

1. The MMPI is given primarily for the client's knowledge and edification, as opposed to being primarily for the clinician's knowledge and edification.
2. As much as possible, the interpretation is phrased in nonperjorative and nonthreatening language, as free as possible from value-laden words. For example, the words "confused" or "feeling alienated" can be used when interpreting an elevation on scale 8 instead of "schizophrenic," which is value laden and usually frightening for the client to hear.
3. The interpretation of the test mentions personal strengths as well as weaknesses/problems.
4. The interpretation includes the diagnostic implications of low scales and/or moderately elevated scales where appropriate, as well as the more typically interpreted markedly elevated scales.

Table 2.1 shows possible interpretations for the MMPI validity and clinical scales. Table 2.2 has the same information for selected research scales. In as much as possible, these interpretations are given in non-threatening, value free words. Included in these tables are interpretations for elevated scales (above 70 T-score points), moderately elevated scales (between 60 and 70 T-score points), and low scales (below 45 T-score points). Also included in the two tables are some counseling/therapy implications for the scales when they are elevated. Tables 2.3 and 2.4 show the same validity, clinical, and selected research scales but this time indicates the potential client strengths and weaknesses indicated by elevations on each of them. In the next section of this chapter, Case Examples, two MMPIs are interpreted to show one method of using the material in Tables 2.1 through 2.4.

One of the best ways for a client to benefit from taking the MMPI is for feedback to be given regarding the test results. Therefore it is usually beneficial to the client to have a test interpretation at some appropriate time in therapy. The following are guidelines to use when doing this.

TABLE 2.1
MMPI Validity and Clinical Scales—Interpretations and Therapy Implications

	Interpretation			
MMPI Scale	*Low (below 45 T-score pts.)*	*Moderate Elevation (60–70 T-score pts.)*	*Marked Elevation (70 T-score pts. or above)*	*Counseling Implications for Marked Elevations*
L	Willing to admit to common human faults.	Sees things in black and white, there is a wrong and right way to behave. High standards for self and others.	Not usual score.	Fearful of being judged as bad by others.
F	No problems he/she is aware of.	Feeling badly in one area, but not too worried about the problem.	Feeling badly, life is not going along well.	Usually motivated for therapy because of psychological pain.
K	Life is not going well or has not gone well in the recent past.	Life is going along well.	Great emphasis upon life being good.	Inability to see life's negative aspects of personal hurt.
1	Doesn't complain about physical illness as much as the average person.	May have had a cold or not felt well when took the test.	Illness is a main focus of concern for the person.	Person does not see how psychological stress affects his/her bodily complaints. Does not see the need for psychological help.
2	Optimistic.	Feeling blue, may have had a "down" day.	Depressed.	Hurting may motivate person to seek psychological help.

3	Believes others see life as too easy.	Optimistic, cheerful.	Denies the psychological impact of problems. Unaware.	Lacks insights into personal problems.
4	Peaceable.	Assertive.	Self-centered, angry if others don't put client's needs first.	Difficulty seeing need to change own behavior.
5 (men)	Not usual score.	Aesthetic interests.	Educated, does not fit "macho" male role.	May have some behavioral passivity.
(women)	Feminine, accepts feminine role.	Rarely seen. Does not like to be seen as typical woman.	Not usual score.	May have difficulty with appropriate sex role identification.
6	Naive or wishes others to see him/her that way.	Sensitive.	Suspicious of others' motives.	May be suspicious or wary of therapist.
7	Non-anxious. May appear unmotivated.	May be organized and punctual.	Anxious, ruminating about problems.	Anxiety may motivate person to come in for therapy.
8	Likes structure. May be non-imaginative.	Creative.	Confused, typically has poor judgment. May feel "different" than others.	Hard to follow in therapy. May use words idiosyncratically.
9	Lacks energy.	Energetic.	May be hyperactive and take on more than can finish.	May have difficulty keeping to one task and focusing on one topic.
0	Extroverted. May like being in front of people.	Prefers the company of people he/she knows well.	Introverted. Hurts to be around others.	Difficulty in overcoming introversion to come into therapy.

TABLE 2.2
Selected MMPI Research Scales—Interpretations and Therapy Implications

	Interpretation		
MMPI Scale	*Low (below 45 T-score pts.)*	*Elevation (60 T-score pts. or more)*	*Counseling Implications for Elevations*
A	No conscious anxiety	Consciously anxious	Anxiety may be motivation for seeking therapy.
R	Is not saying that certain areas are off limits to counseling.	Does not wish to talk about some area of his/her life.	May have problems in therapy because not willing to talk about all areas of his/her life.
Es	Feels inadequate to deal with personal problems.	Feels capable of dealing with personal problems.	Can be confronted in therapy without deteriorating because feels capable.
Lb	Not known.	May be angry/irritated but believes he/she shouldn't be.	May be angry but is unwilling to do something about it.
Dy	Does not need to psychologically lean on others.	Needs to psychologically lean/depend on others and have them take over life.	May be willing to do what therapist suggests because of need to have someone to depend upon.

Do	Wishes others to take charge of his/her life.	Likes to take charge of own life.	Usually willing to risk new behavior in order to have control over own life.
Re	Is questioning society's values.	Accepts society's values.	Feels comfortable with societal expectations.
Pr	Accepts differing viewpoints.	Cannot accept people who are different.	May have difficulty accepting the therapist if he/she is seen as different (e.g., wrong sex, age, or values.)
St	Does not aspire to a better life, may feel unworthy to have one.	Likes aesthetic things and/or is achievement oriented.	May be willing to change in therapy in order to have a better life.
Cn	If clinical scales are elevated, cannot keep clinical scale behavior from being seen by others.	If clinical scales are elevated, can keep behavior/emotions indicated by scales from being seen by others.	Others may not know of problem behaviors or emotions because can keep them from being seen.
Mac	Not known.	If 24 raw score points or higher, may have addictive behavior, e.g., excessive smoking, alcoholism, or drug addiction.	The higher the raw score points above 24, the greater likelihood of addictive behavior.

TABLE 2.3
MMPI Validity and Clinical Scales—Interpretations, Strengths, and Problems of Elevations (T = 70 T-score Points and Above)

MMPI Scale	*Interpretation*	*Strength(s)*	*Problem(s)*
L	Fears judgment of others	Does not act out	Unwilling to look at own behavior critically
F	Feeling badly	Knows he/she is hurting	Maybe exaggerating psychological pain
K	Feeling competent	Unflappable, appropriate in behavior and dress	Restricts emotions to "good" ones
1	Bodily complaints	Aware of nuances of bodily functions	Overreads physical symptoms
2	Depression	Introspective Willing to look at faults	Non-assertive about own needs/wants
3	Denial	Able to ignore hurtful situations, sensuous	Unrealistic view of world and others' behavior
4	Anger	Assertive, forceful	Lacks regard for others needs/wants
5	Masculine/feminine interests	Empathetic, sensitive (men)	May not fit "masculine" image/vocations (men)
		"Tough", aggressive (women)	Assertive, non-traditional (women)
6	Sensitivity	Sensitive to interpersonal dynamics	"Overreads" others' actions/motives, thin skinned
7	Anxiousness	Organized, prompt	Over-compulsive, rigid
8	Confusion	Creative, sees situations/people in new ways	Alienated, feels "different" and/or flawed
9	Energy	Dynamic, energetic, "up"	Overcommitted, chronically late
0	Introversion/extroversion	Independent	Shy, quiet

When the client is asked to take the MMPI, it is usually best not to set a specific date for the test interpretation. When a specific date is set for interpretation, the client may have a pressing issue or crisis to work on, but may put off dealing with it in order to have the test interpretation that is scheduled. It is usually better, therefore, to tell the client that the test will be interpreted sometime during therapy when it seems the most appropriate time to do so. This allows the counselor to do the interpretation when there is a lull in therapy. This procedure also allows the therapist to look at the MMPI profile to see if the client is in a solid enough position to be able to hear the interpretation without becoming more disturbed. If the profile indicates the client is quite fragile, the interpretation may need to be postponed until the client is in a less vulnerable state.

The MMPI profile can be helpful in indicating a particular approach that would be best to take with the interpretation of the test. For example, if the 3 scale (Hysteria) is elevated indicating a great deal of denial, it is usually best to wait to do the test interpretation until enough examples from the person's life have been gathered to illustrate the problems indicated on the test. Using the clients' own life situations to explain the elevated MMPI scales helps the clients to be able to overcome the denial shown in the elevated 3 scale and helps them to acknowledge that indeed they may be having problems in their lives.

During the interpretation, using nonthreatening language and an approach that conveys a nonjudgmental attitude helps the client feel understood and valued.

TABLE 2.4
Selected MMPI Research Scales—Interpretations, Strengths, and Problems of Elevations (T = 60 T-score Points and Above)

MMPI Scale	*Interpretation*	*Strength(s)*	*Problem(s)*
A	Anxiety	Aware of pain	Anxious
R	Repression	Able to not talk about certain areas of life	Not "open" about self
Es	Ego strength	Able to tolerate stress	Difficulty in seeing others as competent as self
Lb	"Nice" person's anger	Pleasant in upsetting situations	Questions rightness of own anger
Dy	Dependency	Willing to accept help from others	Overdependent
Do	Dominance	Able to take care of self	Domineering (if 4 scale is also elevated)
Pr	Prejudice	Sure of rightness of own viewpoint	Unable to tolerate ideological differences
Re	Social Responsibility	Socially responsible	Tolerates "different" behavior if other person is seen as responsible
St	Status	Achievement oriented	Puts undue emphasis on getting ahead
Cn	Control	Can keep others from seeing personal problems	May seem aloof, unemotional

Tables 2.1, 2.2, 2.3, and 2.4 illustrate some of the nonthreatening language that can be used for various scale elevations. It is also important to give a balanced interpretation and to talk about strengths indicated on the profile as well as problems indicated. Try to give a test interpretation that you would want to receive if you were a client, an interpretation that indicates the problems that may be present but also indicates hope for resolution of those problems with the mobilization of the personal strengths shown.

It is ideal when doing MMPI interpretations with special populations such as Blacks, adolescents, or highly educated people to be able to get feedback from them and/or their counselors regarding the appropriateness of the interpretation being given. Modifications in interpretation then can be made when they seem appropriate.

Another problem for MMPI test interpretation is when a test taker is not coming in willingly to be evaluated. When the test taker is being forced to be evaluated, the question of test bias becomes important and appropriate consideration of it must be made when a test is being interpreted. If the individual being tested has a reason to try to look good on the test, such as when he or she is being ordered by the court to be evaluated for custody of a child, this may bias the way he or she takes the test. There can also be a problem when a person has reason to want to look bad, such as when he or she is being evaluated for a disability claim. Roger Greene in his book, *The MMPI: An Interpretive Manual* (1980) suggests a method for evaluating test bias by looking at other MMPI scales in addition to the validity scales. His book should be consulted if there is reason to believe that there is the possibility of a test bias.

In recent years computer interpretation of the MMPI has become popular. The more popular computer services using mainframe computers are reviewed in Graham (1977). With the growth of the use of personal computers, interpretation systems that individuals can use in their offices with their own computers have proliferated. The advantage of a personal computer interpretation system is its reasonable cost, a one time purchase price as opposed to the mainframe computer systems' fee per test. The disadvantage of a personal computer interpretation system is the lack of storage space for a large number of interpretive statements, limiting the capability of the system to adequately interpret a wide variety of the MMPI profiles. With the growth of the personal computer's storage capacity this disadvantage may soon be eliminated.

Although the use of computer interpretation systems is growing rapidly, there is still the need for an individual to be able to interpret the test. All computer systems are not equally good at interpreting the test. Until there is some type of expert evaluation of the various computer systems, counselors have to make their own judgments regarding the accuracy of the computer interpretation system being used. These judgments can only be made if the counselor knows how to interpret the MMPI. In addition, many computer interpretation systems do well in interpreting the more common profile types but are less accurate in interpreting the unusual profile. In this case, the counselor may need to do his or her own interpretation of the profile in order to get one that is accurate.

As has already been mentioned, another reason for caution in accepting computer interpretations is when a counselor is working with populations that are different from the original MMPI normative group. For these clients, interpretations that are made by computer systems that are derived from adult white clinical populations may not be accurate because appropriate modifications have not been made.

CASE EXAMPLES

To illustrate the usefulness of the MMPI for counseling, two cases will be discussed. The two people involved were a husband and wife who were coming in for marriage counseling. The husband had initiated the counseling because he was unhappy with the way the marriage was going. His initial complaint was that his wife was not meeting his needs. His MMPI is shown in Figure 2.1. Mr. A was 41 years old, had gone to a university for two years taking a business curriculum, and had been married to his wife (his second marriage) for five years. He was a very successful insurance salesman and in many ways tried to run his marriage as he did his business, through a combination of personal

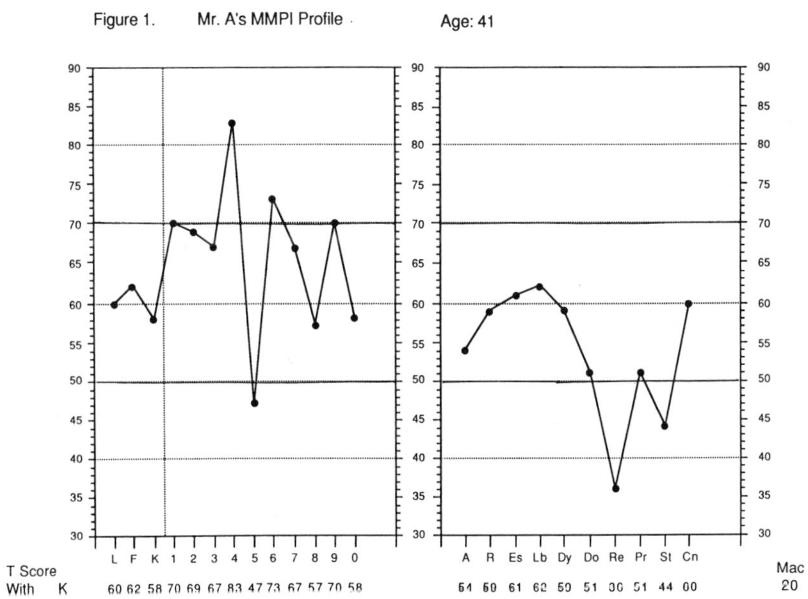

FIG. 2.1. Mr. A's MMPI Profile.

charisma and bullying when he did not get what he wanted. The impression he gave in the intake session was a hail-fellow-well-met heartiness on the surface, but a critical attitude underneath. He initially wanted to enlist the counselor as an ally in getting his wife to change to be more what he wanted. The counselor asked the wife to come in to start marriage counseling, and she agreed to do so. Her MMPI is shown in Figure 2.2. Mrs. A was a 34-year-old woman with an 11th grade education who had been married twice before this current marriage.

The interpretation of each profile will be given first, then the implications of the MMPIs for counseling will be discussed. Finally, there will be discussion of the feedback that was given to the couple.

I start an MMPI interpretation by looking at the validity scales using them as an indication of the general test-taking attitude of the individual. For example, the client may be saying he or she is feeling good (high K) or bad (high F) on the day he or she took the test. The higher these validity scales are above 60 T-score points, the more likely the person is to be emphasizing that particular feeling and maybe even exaggerating it.

After getting a general idea about the mood of the person taking the test, I then proceed to the clinical scales and interpret them individually from the highest scale above 70 for the client down to the scale closest to 70 T-score points. If no clinical scales are above 70 or only the 5 scale is above 70 T-score points for a man, I then interpret the scales that are between 60 and 70 T-score points as well as the 5 scale

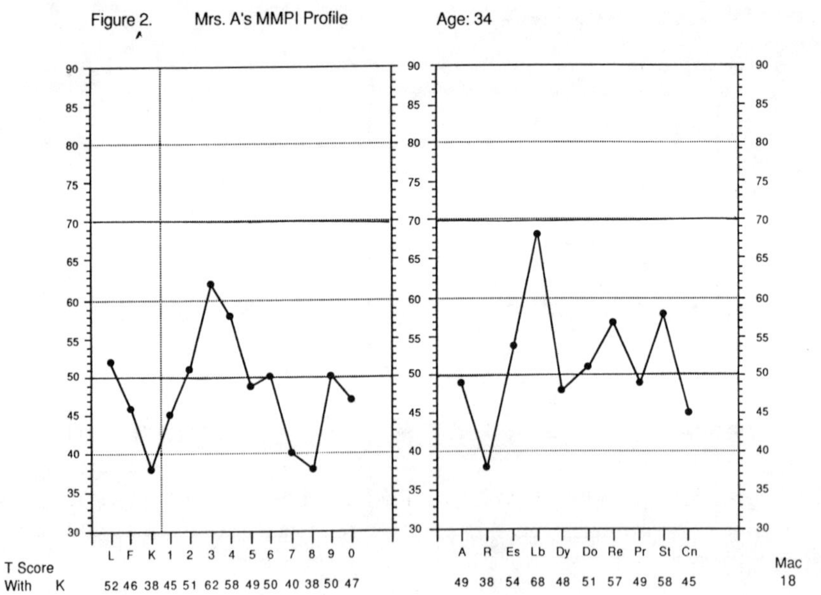

FIG. 2.2. Mrs. A's MMPI Profile.

if it is above 70 T-score points. I look then at the lowest scales and interpret those that are below 45 T-score points, starting with the lowest of these scales and moving up to the one that is closest to 45 T-score points. Brief interpretations of these scales at various levels of elevation have already been presented in Table 2.1.

After looking at the various high and low points of the clinical scales, I move to selected research scales and follow the same procedure that has already been used with the clinical scales, except here I interpret all scales above 60 T-score points. Again I start with interpreting the highest scales and work down to the scales just above 60 T-score points. I then interpret the lowest scales below 45 T-score points and work up to the scale that is just below 45 T-score points. Table 2.2 presents brief synopses of the interpretations that I use for these research scales.

After noting the high and low scales for the clinical and research scales, I then start the much more difficult process of considering the scales in combinations and balancing the information from one scale against the information from another. I do not ignore inconsistencies in the individual scale interpretations but rather try to determine under what conditions these two behaviors could exist in the same person at the same time. This situation is where the research scales are of greatest use. They can help refine the information presented in the clinical scale elevations so that the most accurate interpretation of the clinical scales can be given. A high 2 scale (depression) may not indicate self-deprecation for example, if the Ego Strength scale (Es) is above 50 T-score points. As has already been mentioned, the research scales can also indicate strengths that the individual has.

In addition to considering these refinements of the clinical scale information, I also look at combinations of the clinical scales when they are above 70 T-score points. Duckworth and Anderson (1986) and Graham (1987) are two useful sources for information about various scale combinations.

When all of this information about a profile has been gathered, the interpretation can then be made. When I do an interpretation, I try to say something first about the test-taking attitude of the person so that the rest of the information given in the report can be interpreted in light of how the client was feeling at the time. I then proceed with the body of the report and start by mentioning those behaviors and feelings most likely to be overtly shown and expressed by the client, using the two or three highest clinical scale elevations as my clues.

Next I bring in the refinements to the clinical scales that I may have learned from the research scales or from the clinical scale combinations. After describing as accurately as I can the behavior and feelings shown by the client, I then go to strengths in the profile. These strengths may be revealed by the research scales or sometimes by lower clinical scale elevations. The report is typically ended with some predictions concerning prognosis and implications for therapy.

I advise people using this method of interpretation to make a worksheet for the profile in the following manner. Divide a sheet of paper by drawing a vertical line two to three inches from the left side of the paper. Place the scale number to be interpreted on the left side of the line and the interpretation of it on the right. Do this for all the validity, clinical, and research scales that need to be interpreted. Combinations of scales are considered after the elevations of the clinical scales that make up that combination.

After these interpretations are done, I then write a summary for the profile incorporating the information that has just been listed. The following are the worksheets and summaries for the couple with the profiles shown in Figures 2.1 and 2.2. When the MMPI interpretation is sent to someone, the work sheet material about the individual scales is not sent. Only the summary without the scale identifications (numbers in parentheses in the summary) is sent as the interpretation.

MR. A'S WORKSHEET AND SUMMARY

Validity Scales

All scales are below 70 and above 45 T-score points. Not feeling unduly good or bad.

Clinical Scales

4 = 83	Self-centered, may become angry if others don't put his needs first. Has difficulty seeing a need to change his behavior. Could be charming and charismatic.
6 = 73	Is suspicious of other's motives. This scale may be elevated somewhat because of the marriage problems he is having.
4–6 comb.	Could be angry, resentful, and suspicious. This may be covered by a charming exterior.

Research Scales

Lb = 62	Shows the same tendencies to be angry as is shown by the elevated 4 scale.
Es = 61	Feels capable of dealing with personal problems. Feels good about himself and his abilities.
Re = 36	Questions society's values, may be rebellious.
St = 44	Does not have aspirations for a better life. (I do not include the interpretation "may feel unworthy to have a better life" because the Es is elevated.)

Refinements

Es elevation compared to high 4	Because of the Es elevation, Mr. A would not tend to see as many situations as stressful as he would if his Es were lower. Therefore Mr. A's self-centeredness and anger, which comes out when he is feeling stressed, will not be seen a great deal. Instead he will tend to show the charming exterior.
Es compared to high 6 scale	Again because Mr. A does not usually feel easily threatened, his suspiciousness will tend to be confined to those very close to him.

SUMMARY

When Mr. A took the test he was not feeling either unduly good or bad about his life. He did however, show a great deal of anger and resentment (scale 4) as well as some suspiciousness (scale 6). It could be that these feelings are directed primarily at his wife and the marriage and are not directed at his total life situation. Mr. A is likely to be charismatic, assertive, and forceful; however, this is offset by a self-centeredness and a lack of concern for other's wants and needs. He is confident of his own abilities (Es scale) and is not hurting in ways people sometimes are when they come into counseling, that is, he is not depressed, anxious, or confused. Instead, the overall picture that is presented in Mr. A's profile is one of someone who is blaming someone else for the difficulties that are presently occurring in his life. His typical stance in troublesome situations is to see the other person as needing to change. This type of individual ordinarily comes into counseling because he wants to enlist the counselor as an ally in getting this change to occur. He is most likely to work in counseling if he can see that his needs are going to be met by cooperating in the therapy process.

MRS. A'S WORKSHEET AND SUMMARY

Validity Scales

K = 38	Feels that life is not going well. This may be a reaction to the current marriage problems or the result of long term feelings that her life has been a rough one.

Clinical Scales

3 = 62	Optimistic, cheerful
8 = 38	Likes structure, may be nonimaginative.
7 = 40	Nonanxious, may appear unmotivated.

Research Scales

Lb = 68	May be angry/irritated, but believes she shouldn't be.
R = 38	Is not saying that certain areas are off limits to counseling.

Refinements

3 scale combined with Lb scale	While feeling some anger/irritation is likely not going to do much about it, so she can remain optimistic and cheerful.

SUMMARY

Mrs. A took the test feeling that her life was not going along well at the present time, or she may feel that she's had a rough life in general (K scale). In spite of this feeling, she was not feeling badly nor was she upset (normal level F scale).

The test shows that Mrs. A is an optimistic, cheerful person (3) in spite of having some anger/irritation (Lb). It could be that she has some anger about her marriage but does not want to upset others (her husband) or herself. Her need to be optimistic may outweigh her anger/irritation. Her desire for structure and routine (low 8) may also contraindicate doing something about her anger, because if she did do something her typical routine might be disrupted.

Despite the fact that Mrs. A is currently in marriage counseling, she is not depressed (2), anxious (7), or confused (8). Indeed, she is reporting less anxiety than people do in general (low 3 scale). It could be that Mrs. A is an ignorer of bad feelings, so that in spite of being angry and irritated and feeling that life is not going along well, she still approaches life with optimism and nonanxiety.

In summation then, Mrs. A's MMPI shows her to be someone who is optimistic (3), nonanxious (7), and liking structure and routine (8). This stance seems to be taken at the expense of ignoring her own anger and irritation and the fact that her marriage is in trouble. She seems to be interested in keeping things peaceful and calm at all costs.

In looking at Mr. and Mrs. A's profiles together, it would seem that Mr. A's outlook on life is to blame others for problems that occur, and Mrs. A's outlook is to ignore them. In spite of these stances, which may be causing some of the problems they have, they both have assets as well in that they both have good levels of ego strength (Es above 50) so that they feel and most likely are capable of dealing with the problems that are upon them.

The interpretation of the two profiles was first done individually with the two clients in order to see how each of them reacted to the interpretation. Mr. A was told that his take charge attitude was a real asset in his job as a salesman but not so helpful in his relationship with his wife. Because this way of dealing with others frequently is the result of childhood experiences, family history was explored with Mr. A to see why this style might have been learned and how it was reinforced by his family.

Mrs. A was told that she was a peacemaker, and that while this kept things pleasant, covering over or ignoring did not get at the root of problems but allowed them to fester and recur. Again it was pointed out to her that her method of dealing with life had its origin in her childhood. Her family of origin was talked about and the reinforcement she had received in her family when she was a peacemaker was explored.

After interpreting the MMPIs individually, the couple met with the counselor for a discussion of the tests in light of their current marriage difficulties. Only those things that were pertinent to the marriage problems were discussed. When the tests were interpreted to them individually, it had been emphasized to the two clients that they could choose not to have something discussed in the group session if they wished. Most clients feel more comfortable with this approach because they are then in control of who knows the test information. Eventually most of them reveal the test information to the spouse, at the time each feels most capable of handling this revelation. The purpose of interpreting the MMPIs to the couple in addition to interpreting it individually is to point out to both of them the personal strengths and weaknesses that each has that are operating in their current problems with each other. It is usually important to discuss the personal strengths that each has first, because it is then easier for clients to hear about their personal weaknesses. When personal weaknesses are discussed, it is important to emphasize again in the couple interpretation that these are behaviors that they have learned as they were growing up, that they were reinforced for acting in these ways, and that they can learn new ways of behaving that may not be weaknesses if they so choose.

For Mr. and Mrs. A, the message to each of them is summarized as follows:

> Mr. A you have many strengths shown on the MMPI. You are a capable human being, confident, and charismatic. You have the type of test profile that would indicate that you are well suited to be a salesman. Your difficulties come in trying to understand where your wife is and what her needs are. Most likely in the past, you have had to take care of your own needs or they wouldn't be met, and because of this you have developed a fine sensitivity to what you need and when you are not getting your needs taken care of, but the other side of the coin, sensitivity to others and their needs, has not been as well developed.
>
> Mrs. A you have many fine qualities also. You are confident, serene, and a peacemaker. However, you have become this frequently at the expense of ignoring bad feelings, others' as well as your own. This can come across to others as uncaring at times, even though that is the last thing that you intend to have happen. For both of you, the fine qualities that each of you have will allow you to profit from therapy and will allow you to do some exploration of alternative ways of reacting to each other. I appreciate you both for being willing to take the tests and to come for counseling. Now let's get to work.

When the MMPI is interpreted in the way just described, most people feel nonthreatened and understood in ways that they have not been before. Therefore, giving the MMPI to most clients in this manner helps to establish rapport and gives the counselor insight into the client's strengths and weaknesses, insight that might not ordinarily be obtained until much later in therapy if the test is not used.

RESEARCH ON THE TEST

There are many research studies about the MMPI reported in the literature each year. The studies reporting on the reliability of the MMPI show that there is considerable evidence for the test's reliability depending on the scale being studied. Those scales that reflect mood, such as Scale 2 (Depression), vary considerably over time and therefore do not have high test-retest reliability. Other scales, that are measuring more characterological personality attributes, such as Scale 1 (Hypochondriasis), have relatively high test-retest reliabilities. Split-half reliabilities for some of the scales are relatively low, reflecting the heterogeneity of the items in these scales.

The validity of the MMPI varies with the population being studied and how closely it approximates the original Minnesota normative sample of white, middle-class individuals. In general, similar to other tests, the MMPI shows the most valid results when it is being used for the task for which it was originally developed, that is, the diagnosis of abnormal behavior in people who are highly disturbed. However, as has been already mentioned in other sections of this chapter, the MMPI can be used successfully with other populations if appropriate changes in the scale interpretations and/or norms are made.

The MMPI has become the most widely researched personality inventory. Indeed, except for the major intelligence tests (e.g. the Wechsler Intelligence Scale for Children, the Wechsler Adult Intelligence Scale, and the Stanford-Binet Intelligence Test), it is the most widely researched test in the world. Digesting all of this research and keeping up to date with it is a difficult task. Books such as the *Mental Measurements Yearbook* (Mitchell, 1985), which reviews research and also reports on the current trends for the test being reviewed, are excellent sources of information regarding research on the test's current status. Critical reviews of research on the MMPI are also available in journals such as *Psychological Reports* and *Psychological Bulletin.* Individual research studies on the MMPI are reported in such journals as the *Journal of Clinical Psychology,* the *Journal of Clinical and Consulting Psychology,* and the *Journal of Personality Assessment.*

This abundance of research indicates that the MMPI is alive and well even though it is almost 50 years old. The MMPI research shows, in general, that the more normal the person is being tested with the MMPI, the more modifications should be made in the usual interpretation of the test. The changes in terminology for elevated clinical scales suggested in this chapter, the extension of MMPI interpretation into moderately elevated and low scales, and the use of selected research scales are all attempts that have been made to make the MMPI more applicable to a normal population.

When research studies are reported in the literature, it is always important for the counselor to note how "normal" the subjects are in the studies before applying the research results to the typical counseling population. Any time the subjects of the research study are people with long-term maladaptive behavior, it is unlikely that the results of the research are directly applicable to people in the usual counseling population. Even if the problems are of comparable severity, the very fact of the usual shorter duration of the problem for the counseling population, tends to indicate a better prognosis for therapeutic change than is typically found for people who have long-term maladaptive behavior.

In general then, the problem for a counselor in dealing with the research concerning the MMPI will be keeping up with the volume of studies and evaluating the studies for their relevance for the more normal counseling population.

EVALUATION AND FUTURE DIRECTIONS

Before evaluating the usefulness of the MMPI for the counseling population, an important change which will be occurring for the test must be noted. In response to criticism regarding the applicability of the original MMPI norms for current test takers, and in light of the data found in the normative study done by Colligan et al. (1984), a major research project has been undertaken to renorm the MMPI (Butcher, 1987). In addition to renorming the test, some of the outdated MMPI items are being studied to see if new more relevant items can be substituted for them. The projected result of this project is a major revision of the test, both in items included on the test and the norms that are to be used for comparison of the test results. What the implications of this change will be for how the test is used and interpreted are unknown at this time. Whether both the new form of the test and the old form will be published at the same time is also unknown.

The advantages and disadvantages of the current test for counseling are many. In this brief overview, only a few of them can be mentioned. One of the main advantages of the MMPI is its ability to reflect the tremendous complexity of the individuals being tested while at the same time allowing the individuals to be classified into some kind of diagnostic system. No other personality assessment instrument seems to do this task as well as the MMPI. In addition, the amount of research that has been done with the test on people with many different problems means the test can be used in practically every setting where a counselor practices.

The disadvantages of the test are also many, although not as compelling for most clinicians and counselors as the advantages. Faschingbauer (1979) mentions a few of these disadvantages.

> It's scales are heterogeneous, redundant, and overlapping. From a theoretical perspective, traits seem to be mixed with states in the MMPI code types in a haphazard manner. . . . Some MMPI items are anachronisms of the 1930s, using words with which many patients are unfamiliar. (pp. 374–375)

This is a very complex test, one that is not always easy to understand or interpret. This very complexity creates problems in knowing how best to use and interpret the test for the clients that counselors typically see. In spite of these problems with the test, however, it still remains the *sine qua non* of the personality assessment field, the instrument all others are compared to. When used by a skilled counselor, one who understands and respects its complexity and who knows its applicability to the normal population, the MMPI ranks as the instrument no counselor can do without.

REFERENCES

Bernreuter, R. G. (1933). The theory and construction of the personality inventory. *Journal of Social Psychology, 4,* 387–405.

Butcher, J. (1987). *The revision of the MMPI.* Paper presented to the Twenty-second Annual Symposium on the MMPI, Seattle, WA.

Carkhuff, R. R., Barnette, L., & McCall, J. N. (1965). *The counselor's handbook: Scale and profile interpretation of the MMPI.* Urbana, IL: R. W. Parkinson & Associates.

Colligan, R. C., Osborne, D., Swenson, W. M., & Offord, K. P. (1983). *The MMPI: A contemporary normative study.* NY: Praeger.

Dahlstrom, W. G., Walsh, G. S., & Dahlstrom, L. E. (1972). *An MMPI handbook: Vol. I: Clinical interpretation.* Minneapolis, MN: Univ. of Minnesota Press.

Drake, L. E., & Oetting, E. R. (1959). *An MMPI codebook for counselors.* Minneapolis MN: Univ. of Minnesota Press.

Duckworth, J. (1979). *An MMPI interpretation manual for counselors and clinicians* (2nd ed.). Muncie, IN: Accelerated Development Inc.

Duckworth, J., & Anderson, W. (1986). *An MMPI interpretation manual for counselors and clinicians* (3rd ed.). Muncie, IN: Accelerated Development Inc.

Duckworth, J., & Duckworth, E. (1975). *An MMPI interpretation manual for counselors and clinicians.* Muncie, IN: Accelerated Development Inc.

Faschingbauer, T. R. (1979). The future of the MMPI. In C. S. Newmark (Ed.), *MMPI: Clinical and research trends* (pp. 373–392). NY: Praeger.

Gilberstadt, H., & Duker, J. (1965). *A handbook for clinical and actuarial MMPI interpretation.* Philadelphia: W. B. Saunders Co.

Goldman, L. (1971). *Using tests in counseling* (2nd ed.). NY: Appleton-Century-Crofts.

Graham, J. R. (1977). *The MMPI: A practical guide.* NY: Oxford University Press.

Graham, J. R. (1987). *The MMPI: A practical guide* (2nd ed.). NY: Oxford Univ. Press.

Greene, R. L. (1980). *The MMPI: An interpretive manual.* NY: Grune & Stratton.

Gynther, M. (1972). White norms and black MMPIs: A prescription for discrimination? *Psychological Bulletin, 78,* 386–402.

Gynther, M., & Green, S. B. (1980). Accuracy may make a difference, but does a difference make for accuracy? A response to Protchard and Rosenblatt. *Journal of Consulting and Clinical Psychology, 48,* 268–272.

Harris, R. E., & Lingoes, J. C. (1968). *Subscales for the Minnesota Multiphasic Personality Inventory: An aid to profile interpretation* (rev. version). Berkeley: University of California.

Hathaway, S. R. (1947). A coding system for MMPI profile classification. *Journal of Consulting Psychology, 11,* 334–337.

Kunce, J. (1979). MMPI scores and adaptive behaviors. In C. S. Newmark (Ed.), *MMPI: Clinical and research trends* (pp. 306–327). NY: Praeger.

Kunce, J., & Anderson, W. (1976). Normalizing the MMPI. *Journal of Clinical Psychology, 32,* 776–780.

Lachar, D. (1974). *The MMPI: Clinical assessment and automated interpretation.* Los Angeles, CA: Western Psychological Services.

Landis, C., & Katz, S. E. (1934). The validity of certain questions which purport to measure neurotic tendencies. *Journal of Applied Psychology, 18,* 343–356.

MacAndrew, C. (1965). The differentiation of male alcoholic outpatients from nonalcoholic psychiatric outpatients by means of the MMPI. *Quarterly Journal of Studies on Alcohol, 26,* 236–246.

Marks, P. A., & Seeman, W. (1963). *The actuarial description of abnormal personality.* Baltimore: Williams & Wilkins.

Marks, P. A., Seeman, W., & Haller, D. (1974). *The actuarial use of the MMPI with adolescents and adults.* Baltimore: Williams & Wilkins.

McKinley, J. C., Hathaway, S. R., & Meehl, P. E. (1948). The MMPI: VI. The K scale. *Journal of Consulting Psychology, 12,* 20–31.

Mitchell, J. R. (1985). *The Ninth Mental Measurements Yearbook. Vol. I.* Lincoln, Neb.: The University of Nebraska Press.

Newmark, C. S. (1979). *MMPI Clinical and Research Trends.* NY: Praeger.

Page, J., Landis, C., & Katz, S. E. (1934). Schizophrenic traits in the functional psychoses and in normal individuals. *American Journal of Psychiatry, 90,* 1213–1225.

Serkownek, K. (1975). *Subscales for Scales 5 and 0 of the MMPI.* Unpublished manuscript.

Test Critiques, Vol. I (1984). Kansas City, Mo.: Test Corporation of America.

Watkins, C. E., & Campbell, V. L. (1987). *Counseling psychologists and psychological testing: Practices, applications, and attitudes.* Paper presented to the American Psychological Association, New York.

Wiggins, J. S. (1966). Substantive dimensions of self-report in the MMPI item pool. *Psychological Monographs, 80* (22, Whole No. 630).

Woodworth, R. S. (1920). *Personal data sheet.* Chicago: Stoelting.

3 The California Psychological Inventory

Harrison G. Gough
Institute of Personality Assessment and Research
University of California, Berkeley

BASIC PRINCIPLES

The California Psychological Inventory (CPI) was first published in 1956, followed by the initial manual in 1957 (Gough, 1957). At that time, the inventory contained 480 items to be answered "true" or "false" according to whether the respondent found them to be descriptive of self or nondescriptive. The intentions of the inventory, then as now, were to assess the kind of everyday interpersonal themes in behavior that may be called "folk concepts." Folk concepts refer to human attributes or qualities such as dominance, sense of responsibility, self-control, and flexibility that all people, everywhere, recognize and denominate in their languages.

An inventory scaled for folk concepts, it follows, will by definition be relevant to the description and understanding of persons in any culture or society, although the validity of each scale must be established and not just assumed on the basis of linguistic pertinence. Given this emphasis on cultural universals, it is not surprising to find that many cross-cultural studies of the inventory have been published (see, for example, Abbott, 1976; Gendre, 1974; Lazzari & Gough, 1973; Levin & Karni, 1970; Mizushima & DeVos, 1967; Nishiyama, 1973; Pitariu & Helmine, 1980; Stankov & Kvascev, 1974; and Szalanski & Szymanska, 1977).

In addition to the theoretical decision to scale the inventory for folk concepts, several other basic considerations should be mentioned. One is that the set of scales constitutes an open system, to which variables can be added as the need arises, and from which measures can be removed if and when they no longer serve any useful purpose. Both kinds of changes have been made over the years.

For instance, in its prepublication form the CPI included a scale for neurodermatitis, a measure quite out of keeping with the inventory's focus on folk notions and on positive psychological functioning. After this scale was removed there were 15 measures remaining on the profile sheet. To them were added the scales for Social Presence, Self-acceptance, and Self-control, bringing the total up to 18. In the current edition (Gough, 1987), folk measures for Empathy (Hogan, 1969) and Independence have been added.

A second basic postulate is that the scales of the inventory should be topographically in correspondence with folk usage of the same concepts. That is, if everyday evaluations of self and others generate a relationship between, say, dominance and sociability, then the scales for these two variables should be correlated at precisely the same level. Given this principle of social-psychological mapping, the conventional psychometric desideratum of uncorrelated or orthogonal measures becomes irrelevant. In other words, the folk scales are intended to map the highly intercorrelated contours of folk usage, even if this purpose is unsanctioned by contemporary psychometric dogma.

A third basic postulate is that the scales should possess instrumental rather than definitional validity. The function of the scale for Dominance, for example, is to identify people (a) who will, in specified contexts, behave in dominant ways, and (b) who will be described and evaluated by those who know them well as dominant, forceful, strong, self-confident, and so on. This is the instrumental view of measurement, and from its standpoint any cluster of items that will achieve these two objectives at a high level of accuracy is acceptable. The mandates of the definitional view for systematic domain sampling by the items, intrascale factorial homogeneity, and linkage to trait concepts are inapplicable.

Justification for the decisions to scale folk concepts, in an open system, and with topographical and instrumental intentions, derives from a pragmatic or use-oriented perspective. The scales of the inventory should be of help to the counselor who wants to work with clients as they deal with and attempt to solve the problems of everyday living in a shared, interpersonal world. The depiction of behavioral style, normative internalizations, intellective modes, and role preferences should correspond to what in fact is occurring in the life of the client, rather than to some arbitrary (even if elegant) formal model of personality and social structure.

THE 1987 REVISION

The first review of the 480-item CPI was by Shaffer (1957) and the most recent by Wegner (1988). Landmark publications dealing with the inventory and its full range of implications include an early interpretational syllabus (Gough, 1968), Megargee's *Handbook* in 1972, Rodgers' (1983) manual on configural interpretation, and McAllister's (1988) practical guide. All of these reports pertain to the 18-scale edition of the inventory.

In 1987 a new version of the CPI was brought out (Gough, 1987), in which the test booklet was shortened to 462 items, old-fashioned and sexist language either modified or deleted, and two new folk scales added to the profile. The current version of the inventory contains 20 folk measures (named and defined below), three structural scales for use in classifying respondents in regard to type and level, and a number of special purpose scales and indexes, as, for example, a scale for Managerial Potential (Gough, 1984), and an index for creativity (Weiss, 1981). The two new scales are for Empathy (Hogan, 1969), and Independence.

Scoring templates for the 20 folk and three structural scales are available in a set from the publisher. The *Guide* (Gough, 1987) lists the 13 special purpose and research scales currently available, and gives scoring instructions. Normative data for all 36 scales are furnished in the *Guide* for 39 male and 30 female samples (pages 94–104). The special purpose indices are described in the research papers in which they were introduced. In the computer narrative, and in the scoring offered by the publisher, findings are included for the Weiss (1981) creativity index, the leadership potential index (Gough, 1969), and the social maturity index (Gough, 1971).

The inventory can be administered in from 45 minutes to one hour. The examiner can read the instructions aloud while the respondents read silently, if testing is done in groups; for college students and others with good reading skills, the respondents can simply be asked to read the instructions, to note how reactions are marked on the answer sheet, and then to proceed until finished. In the counseling situation, a student could be asked to take the CPI while waiting for an interview, or could even take a booklet and answer sheet home for return at the time of the next appointment. The existence of algorithms for identifying invalid protocols (see Gough, 1987, pp. 35–42) allows the examiner to detect any answer sheet of questionable reliability.

Once the inventory has been finished and the answer sheet is in hand, scoring can be done either with the transparent templates available from the publisher, or the sheet can be mailed in for processing. There is also a computer narrative that can be requested from the publisher if desired. Later in this chapter a full computer narrative on a college student will be presented.

If handscoring is carried out, the raw scores are entered on the appropriate profile sheet (for males or for females), and then the 20 entries are connected by straight lines in order to define a standard score profile. CPI standard scores have means of 50 and standard deviations of 10, based on large, general population norms. The profile sheet gives an automatic conversion of raw to standard scores.

PROFILE INTERPRETATION

The 20 folk scales are clustered into four groupings on the profile sheet. The first cluster of seven scales pertains to different aspects of interpersonal style, the ways in which people deal with others and the ways in which they conduct themselves in the interpersonal context. The second cluster of seven scales pertains to normative orientations and values, with each scale assessing a particular facet of normative or prescriptive societal rules. Then there is a third cluster of three scales, pertaining to the intellective-cognitive domain, and the ways in which intellectual talents are employed. Finally, there is a fourth cluster of three scales that assess broadly stylistic aspects of behavior, including psychological-mindedness, flexibility, and masculine/feminine role modalities. In reading a CPI profile, the examiner should take note of these groupings and the elevations within each as one of the initial steps in developing a psychological picture of the person tested.

After noting the elevation of scales within groups, particularly in the interpersonal and normative sectors, the interpreter should go on to the individual scales in order to specify nuances and characteristics associated with different profile patterns. The CPI guidebooks by Rodgers (1983) and McAllister (1988) are very helpful in this kind of interpretation. Because the scales assess folk notions—concepts about personality that are in everyday use and recognized by everyone—a good bit of information is conveyed merely by the name of a scale. In addition, the specific emphases reported in Table 3.1 below should be kept in mind.

The 32-item F/M (Femininity/masculinity) scale in Table 3.1 is a bipolar measure. That is, females tend to score higher than males, and within each sex those rated or described as more "feminine" tend to score higher than those rated or described as more "masculine" (Gough, 1987, pp. 72–73). Because folk notions of male/female roles tend to be bipolar in this same way, and because the CPI seeks to map or represent the topography of folk usage, bipolarity of the F/M scale is theoretically justified.

Nonetheless, it is easy to decompose the 32-item scale into its 15 "feminine" and 17 "masculine" items, and to score each subset as a separate. When this is done, the two subscales are unipolar and uncorrelated, and can be used to define sex-role quadrants exactly as recommended by Bem (1974) and by Spence and Helmreich (1979). Publications by Kanner (1976) and Babl (1979) report this kind of subscale treatment of the prior 38-item Fe (femininity) scale for the CPI.

Baucom (1976, 1980) has also developed new separate "MAS" and "FEM" scales for the CPI that are unipolar and independent of each other. The current *Guide* (Gough, 1987) for the CPI gives scoring of the Baucom scales and the F/M subscales, as well as normative data for all four measures.

THE CUBOID MODEL

Over the years at least 50 factor analyses of the old set of 18 CPI scales have been published. In every instance (see Megargee, 1972), these studies have agreed that the two major themes refer to interpersonal and normative orientations. In 1970, Levin and Karni (see also, Karni & Levin, 1972) published the first

TABLE 3.1
The 20 CPI Folk Concept Scales and Their Meanings

Measures of Interpersonal Style and Orientation

Do (Dominance). A 36-item scale focused on prosocial dominance. High scorers tend to be sure of themselves, assertive, task-oriented, and enterprising. Low scorers tend to be unassuming, reserved, and hesitant about taking the initiative.

Cs (Capacity for Status). A 28-item scale that attempts to measure personal qualities that are associated with and that lead to high social status. High scorers tend to be ambitious, interested in many things, and clever. Low scorers tend to be ill at ease in competitive or demanding situations, and uncomfortable with uncertainty or complexity.

Sy (Sociability). A 32-item scale aimed at outgoing and socially affiliative behavior. High scorers are friendly, gregarious, and sociable. Low scorers are shy, often inhibited, and prefer to stay in the background in social situations.

Sp (Social Presence). A 38-item scale seeking to assess poise, spontaneity, and self-assurance. High scorers are versatile, imaginative, and verbally fluent. Low scorers tend to be cautious, subdued, and self-denying.

Sa (Self-acceptance). A 28-item scale addressed to feelings of personal worth and self-esteem. High scorers tend to be self-confident, talkative, and good at making conversation. Low scorers tend to be self-doubting, withdrawn, and taciturn.

In (Independence). A 28-item scale that attempts to measure the twin elements of resourcefulness and distance. High scorers tend to be independent and poised, but somewhat detached. Low scorers tend to seek support from others, to avoid conflict, and to delay or avoid action.

Em (Empathy). A 38-item scale focused on affective insight and resonance to others. High scorers are comfortable with self and accepted by others, perceptive about social nuances, and optimistic. Low scorers are unempathic, skeptical about the intentions of others, and defensive about their own feelings and desires.

Measures of Normative Orientation and Values

Re (Responsibility). A 36-item scale focused on awareness of rules and the ability to conform when appropriate. High scorers are reliable, mature, and ethically perceptive. Low scorers are apt to be self-indulgent, undisciplined, and distractible.

So (Socialization). A 46-item scale seeking to assess the degree to which the respondent has internalized the normative values of the culture. High scorers tend to be conscientious, well-organized, and productive. Low scorers tend to be rebellious, dissatisfied, and nonconforming.

Sc (Self-control). A 38-item scale indicative of the cathexis of normative constraints and suppressive ego defenses. High scorers tend to deny or suppress hostile and erotic impulses, but are not always successful. They are often seen as thorough, painstaking, and conventional. Low scorers have strong emotions and do little to suppress them. They are often seen as impulsive, restless, and pleasure-seeking.

Gi (Good Impression). A 40-item scale with two functions. The first, for raw scores of 31 or above, is to identify protocols too strongly characterized by socially desirable responses. The second is to identify persons whose self-presentational style is to emphasize or even over-emphasize prosocial attributes. Short of the invalidity level, high scorers tend to be conventional, moderate, and formal. Low scorers tend to be individualistic, easily annoyed or irritated, and impatient.

(*continued*)

TABLE 3.1
(Continued)

Cm (Communality). A 38-item scale with two functions. The first, for raw scores of 27 or below, is to identify protocols with too many unusual or random responses. The second is to assss a continuum going from conventionality at the high end to unconventionality at the low. High scorers are often seen as reasonable, organized, and stable. Low scorers are often seen as unconventional, complicated, and changeable.

Wb (Well-being). A 38-item scale addressed to feelings of physical and psychological well-being. Very low scorers (of 20 or below) are indicative of invalid emphasis on problems and worries. Raw scores of 21 or above may be psychologically interpreted. High scorers tend to be optimistic about their own prospects, energetic, and persevering. Low scorers tend to be worrying, complaining, and dissatisfied.

To (Tolerance). A 32-item scale intended to assess attitudes of tolerance, forbearance, and openmindedness. High scorers tend to be clear-thinking, insightful, and fair-minded. Low scorers tend to be distrustful, fault-finding, and extrapunitive.

Measures of Cognitive and Intellectual Functioning

Ac (Achievement via Conformance). A 38-item scale aimed at achievement drives that function well in defined and clearly structured settings. High scorers tend to be ambitious, capable, and well-organized. Low scorers tend to be distractible, undependable, and rule-resistant.

Ai (Achievement via Independence). A 36-item scale focused on achievement drives that function well in open, minimally defined settings. High scorers tend to be intelligent, independent, and clear-thinking. Low scorers tend to be somewhat narrow in interests, easily confused, and indifferent about doing well.

Ie (Intellectual Efficiency). A 42-item scale that seeks to reflect the degree to which intellectual resources are efficiently utilized. High scorers are often seen as capable, resourceful, and logical. Low scorers are often seen as lacking in ability, unsure of self, and inarticulate.

Measures of Role and Personal Style

Py (Psychological-mindedness). A 28-item scale that attempts to measure intraceptiveness or the ability to discern what others feel and think. High scorers tend to be insightful, perceptive, and intelligent, but not necessarily affiliative or nurturant. Low scorers tend to be somewhat conventional, uncomfortable with change, and intellectually shallow.

Fx (Flexibility). A 28-item scale assessing strong resistance to change at one pole versus fluidity and delight in change at the other. High scorers tend to be seen as imaginative, clever, and progressive, but also as careless and loosely organized. Low scorers tend to be seen as conservative, conventional, and stolid, but also as well-organized and hard-working.

F/M (Femininity/Masculinity). A 32-item scale addressed to the social role continuum going from agentic masculinity at one end to communal or nurturant femininity at the other. Among males, high scorers tend to be described as sensitive, high-strung, and esthetically reactive, whereas low scorers are viewed as confident, aggressive, and strong. Among females, high scorers tend to be described as sympathetic, sentimental, and vulnerable to threat, whereas low scorers are viewed as independent, ambitious, and forceful.

Smallest Space Analysis of the CPI, which suggested that in addition to these two axes there was a third component centering on the Wb (Well-being), To (Tolerance), and Ie (Intellectual Efficiency) scales. From their work, it was apparent that if three orthogonal measures could be developed, a geometric cuboid model could be derived to represent the underlying psychometric structure of the inventory.

Prior attempts had been made (see Nichols & Schnell, 1963) to construct scales for the interpersonal and normative factors, but in subsequent applications these scales turned out to be too strongly correlated with each other, and both had undesirable positive correlations with the theme of overall elevation embedded in the three-scale cluster of Wb, To, and Ie. Accordingly, a new program of research was launched to see if uncorrelated measures could be developed for each of the three regions in the Levin and Karni display. After considerable time and effort, this work succeeded in producing three scales possessing the requisite properties.

The first, called v.1 (for vector 1), is addressed to the interpersonal continuum. Low scores refer to engagement in the interpersonal milieu, affective response to the rewards and punishments of the social nexus, and externality in behavior. High scores refer to detachment, libidinization of the private, inner world, and feelings of internality.

The second scale, called v.2, is aligned with the normative dimension. Low scores are indicative of norm-doubting, norm-questioning dispositions, and high scores are associated with norm-accepting and even norm-favoring inclinations. Because v.1 and v.2 are uncorrelated, a conjoint display will classify about 25% of the general population in each quadrant.

In the cuboid theoretical model, these quadrants represent four life styles, or ways of living, or kinds of people. Persons low on v.1 and high on v.2 are designated as *Alphas*. The Alpha life style stresses constructive and sanctioned social behavior. A well-integrated Alpha can be a charismatic leader, someone to be trusted and followed. A poorly-integrated Alpha will tend to be merely invasive, manipulative, and ineffective.

The *Beta* life style incorporates norm-adherence and internality. At their best, Betas are quietly contemplative, inspirational, and exemplary in their goodness and virtue. At their worst, Betas are commonplace, overly conventional, and judgmentally conformist.

The *Gamma* life style involves externality and the valuing of interpersonal rewards, with doubt or skepticism concerning the legitimacy of the ways in which life's benefits are distributed. At their best, Gammas are innovative, quick to discern the flaws and internal contradictions of any social or intellectual system, and skilled in proposing new and better ways. At their worst, Gammas become alienated, unproductively rebellious, and asocial in behavior.

Thc *Delta* life style derives from an inner, private reaction to the shared social structure and from doubt and disbelief concerning the authenticity of conventional imperatives. At their best, Deltas are visionary, working out their own inner conflicts in artistic, literary, or theoretical formulations that synthesize in new and better ways the inconsistencies of prior views. At their worst, Deltas become fragmented and disintegrated, and are prone to psychiatric psychopathology.

The four life styles just described constitute the typological component of the cuboid model. By use of the cutting scores for v.1 and v.2 given in the CPI *Guide*, any person can easily be classified into one of these four ways of living. The question then becomes "How well has the respondent achieved the positive potential of the type, and to what extent have the negative possibilities been avoided?" The answer to this query is furnished by the third scale, called v.3, for sense of realization (as seen by the respondent) or competence (as seen by observers). The v.3 scale is essentially uncorrelated with v.1 and v.2, which means that persons of any of the four types can vary from the lowest level of 1 on v.3 to the highest of 7. Cutting scores on v.3 permit assignment to one of the seven levels of realization. The 1987 *Guide* provides this information, along with extensive interpretational data on all three structural scales. Another important source of information on the v.3 scale is the recent (1987) paper by Helson and Wink.

The full cuboid model generated from the v.1, v.2, and v.3 scales is shown in Figure 3.1. For each of the four life styles there are seven levels of realization or competence, producing, in effect, a 28-cell taxonomy of personality functioning. For each type there are characteristic potentialities and pitfalls, and certain life goals that are deemed to be desirable. Persons at lower levels on v.3 will feel unfulfilled, aware that they are far from achieving their own hopes and aspirations; they will also tend to be judged by others as below average in competence. Counseling can certainly be of help to these individuals, as it can be to persons at higher levels on v.3, but it should be directed to the characteristic problems and to the particular goals associated with each of the type classifications.

In the cuboid model, the v.1 scale for interpersonal orientation and the v.2 scale for normative views conjointly define the four types, and the v.3 scale for realization of potential defines the vertical axis. The planes for Levels 1, 4, and 7 only are given in the figure, to reduce complexity, but the planes for Levels 2, 3, 5, and 6 can easily be visualized.

In interpreting the CPI, the type/level model permits entry into the conceptual system of the 20 folk measures. For instance, if the protocol is from an Alpha-6, then one begins by anticipating an outgoing, entrepreneurial person of considerable effectiveness. Starting from these guidelines one can then move on to the specific and individuating characteristics indicated by the scales in the full profile. In the case illustration to follow at the end of this chapter an interpretation of this kind will be presented.

The *Guide* furnishes type and level data for a large number of educational, occupational, and other samples of each sex. For instance, in a sample of region-

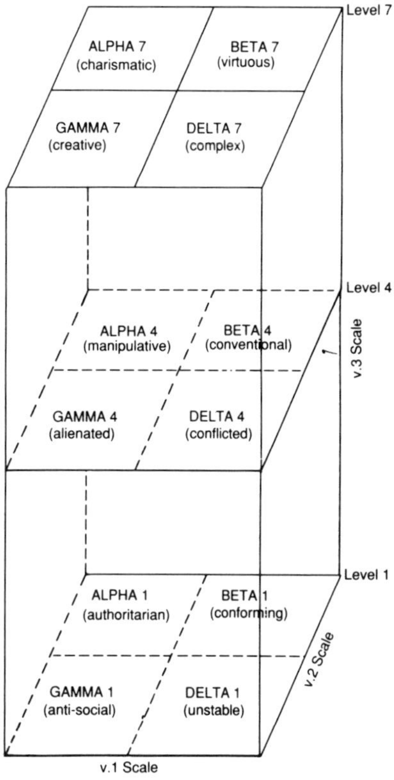

FIG. 3.1. The three-dimensional cuboid model.

al sales managers from a large Midwest company, 61.2% were Alphas. In a sample of Catholic priests, 41.5% were Alphas and also 41.5% were Betas. From the implications of the cuboid model, one would expect the Alpha priests to be primarily interested in the financial and numerical health of the diocese, and the Betas to be principally involved in spiritual and liturgical matters.

Both male and female psychology graduate students tend to be Gammas, with 47.5% of 623 males and 49.9% of 405 females receiving this classification. Juvenile delinquents of both sexes also tend to be Gammas, with percentages of 38.2 for males and 49.1 for females. Among males, psychiatric patients and prison inmates were modal Deltas; among females, prison inmates, pharmacy students, and professional mathematicians had their largest numbers in the Delta category.

In regard to level, high-ranking male samples included research scientists, psychology graduate students, medical school students, and professional mathematicians. Low-ranking male samples included prison inmates, juvenile delinquents, high school students, and psychiatric patients.

Among females, high-ranking samples on v.3 included psychology graduate students, medical school students, college counselors, and professional mathematicians. Low-ranking samples included prison inmates, juvenile delinquents, psychiatric patients, and high school students.

A CPI BIBLIOGRAPHY FOR COUNSELORS

The complete CPI bibliography now carries something over 2,000 titles, far too many for citation in this chapter. Because of this, the references were reviewed for reports that might be of particular interest to counselors. Seventy-five were chosen for inclusion in a "CPI Bibliography for Counselors," presented at the end of this chapter.

These 75 publications deal with topics such as high school and college dropouts, personality variables related to different programs of study, mathematical talent and attitudes toward mathematics, personality changes occurring in college and later life, occupational and career interests as related to personality, academic achievement in general and within certain subgroups, the intellectually and cognitively gifted, counseling effectiveness as related to the counselor's personality, effects on personality of various kinds of educational and treatment experiences, the effect on performance of different kinds of educational environments, stresses associated with medical education, drug use among high school and college students, and contrasts between students who do or do not seek counseling.

In selecting the references, more emphasis was given to current or fairly recent studies than to earlier work in the 1950s and 1960s. There are only two citations from the 1950s, 19 from the 1960s, 33 from the 1970s, and 21 from the 1980s.

A CASE ILLUSTRATION

The subject for this case illustration was a participant in a research study of vocational aspirations and career planning. He came to the Institute of Personality Assessment and Research where he took part in a day-long program of interviews, observational procedures, and psychological testing. He is 19 years old, in his second year of college, majoring in writing. His SAT scores were above 700 on the verbal part, and just under 600 on the mathematical. His grade average was 3.60, to date. He says he has only a few friends, gets drunk occasionally, and uses marijuana sparingly. He feels he has a talent for creative writing, and reported that if he finishes college he will go on to develop this talent further.

As shown in Figure 3.2, his v.1 and v.2 scores of 19 and 10, respectively,

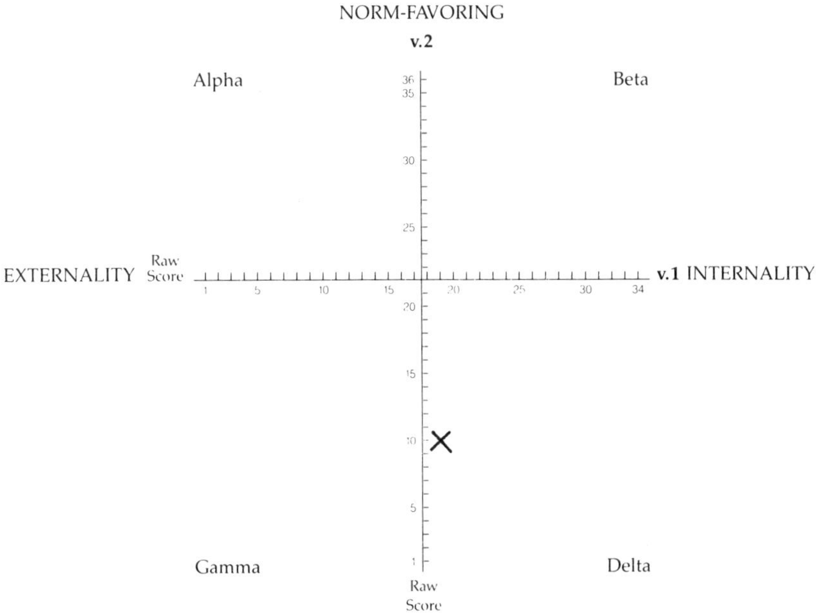

v.1 versus v.2 classificatory grid

FIG. 3.2. Typological classification of Mr. X.

place him in the Delta quadrant, but (because of the 19 on v.1) bordering on the Gamma. His v.3 score of 51, as indicated in Figure 3.3, puts him at level 7. From the type/level model, it can be inferred that in spite of strong internal complexity and contradictory impulses, he has achieved a superior level of integration.

The profile of folk measures, as shown in Figure 3.4, reveals the two highest scores to be Social Presence (Sp) and Flexibility (Fx). From this we can infer spontaneity, verve, and a distinct preference for change and variety. His third highest score is on Empathy (Em), indicating a talent for sensing what others feel and think. On the two achievement scales, Ac and Ai, there is a large differential in favor of Ai. From the studies of Domino (1968, 1971) and others on the Ac/Ai interaction, we can anticipate frustration and below par performance in routinized situations, but an excellent reaction to settings in which he can develop and carry out his own strategies.

Impressionistic analysis of the profile could proceed in this way. However, a more detailed and systematic appraisal is available in the computerized narrative for the CPI developed by the writer and programmed by Kevin Lanning. The computer narrative for this subject is reproduced below.

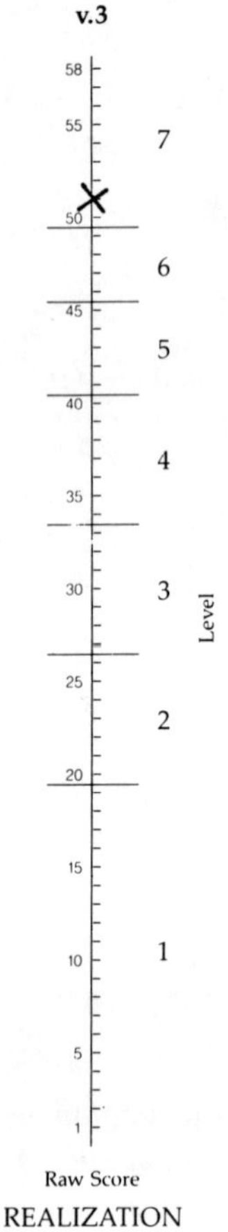

FIG. 3.3. Realization (level) classification of Mr. X.

A COMPUTERIZED INTERPRETATION OF THE CALIFORNIA PSYCHOLOGICAL INVENTORY
by Harrison G. Gough, Ph.D.
Software Editor: Kevin Lanning, Ph.D.

The protocol to be interpreted below is based on the responses given by Mr. X, and scored on 10-16-87.

This program for interpreting the CPI is intended for professional psychologists and others who are qualified to use complex multivariate tools of assessment. In

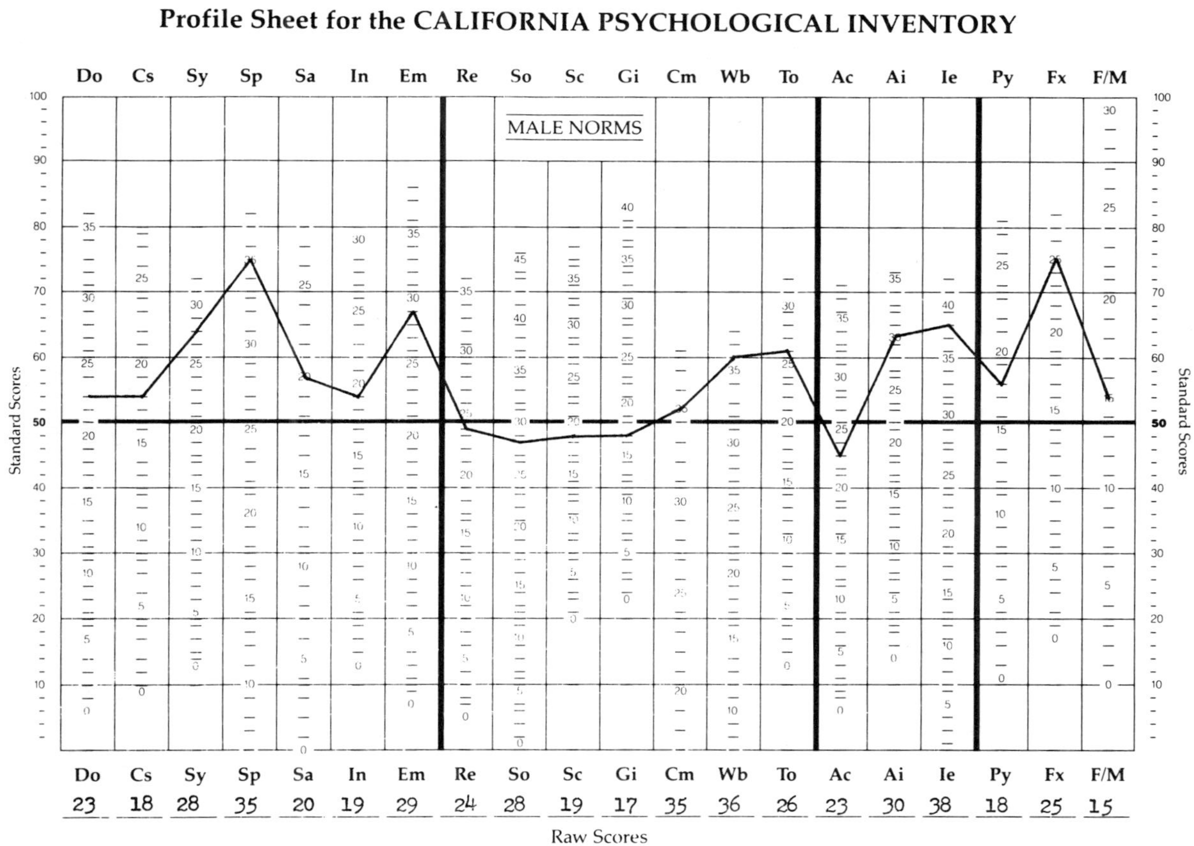

FIG. 3.4. CPI profile for Mr. X.

addition to a general background in personality theory and assessment methodology, as well as supervised experienced in the analysis of individual test data, persons using this program should be familiar with the CPI itself and with major sources of information concerning the inventory. These sources include, in particular, the *California Psychological Inventory administrator's guide* (Gough, 1987), and *California Psychological Inventory handbook* (Megargee, 1972), *Configural Interpretation of the CPI* (Rodgers, 1983), and *A practical guide to CPI interpretation* (McAllister, 1988).

This narrative report is in five parts or sections. In Part 1, the reliability of the protocol is examined. In Part II, the protocol is classified with respect to Type and Level. In Part III, an analysis is presented of the individual's scores on the folk concept scales. In Part IV, special purpose scales and indices are described. In Part V, a CPI-estimate is given of the way in which a benevolent and knowledgeable observer would describe this person on the 100-item *California Q-set* (Block, 1961).

Part I. Reliability of the Protocol

The protocol has been reviewed for unreliability, whether caused by an overly favorable self-portrait, an unduly critical self-representation, or the giving of too many atypical and possibly random responses. The protocol appears to be acceptable by all three criteria.

Part II. Classification in Regard to Type and Level

Type and Level Scores

	Raw	*Standard*
v.1 (internality)	19	53
v.2 (norm-favoring)	10	30
v.3 (realization)	51	65
Classification (type and level): Delta-7		

Two broad themes underlie the scales of the CPI, one pertaining to interpersonal orientation and the other to normative cathexes. The first continuum is assessed by a scale called v.1 (for vector), on which higher scores indicate an internal, introversive orientation and lower scores indicate an external, extraverted stance. The second is assessed by a scale called v.2, on which higher scores indicate a norm-accepting and norm-favoring perspective and lower scores indicate a norm-questioning disposition. The two scales are uncorrelated; because of this, when considered conjointly they define four ways or styles of living.

The scores on v.1 and v.2 obtained by Mr. X place him in the Delta quadrant (see Figure 3.2). The following brief description of the Delta type gives some of the important implications of this classification.

> Deltas' cathexes are centered on a private, internal world and on a personal as opposed to a traditional or sanctioned system of values. Deltas are reflective, idiosyncratic, and detached. At their best, they are imaginative, creative, aesthetically perceptive, and visionary. At their worst, they are fragmented, withdrawn, at odds with themselves and prone to decompensation.

A third major feature of the total profile of scores on the CPI is height or elevation. This facet of level is assessed by the v.3 scale. Level indicates the degree to which the favorable potentialities of the type have been realized, in the viewpoint of the respondent. The higher the classification on level, the greater the individual's sense of self-realization or fulfillment. A score of 1 on level signifies the lowest level of attainment, 4 signifies the average level, and 7 the highest. Mr. X is at Level 7, suggesting an unusually favorable realization of the potentialities of his type. For persons at this level one can expect unusual adeptness in dealing with abstract or complex ideas, originality, broad interests, and a strong sense of individuality or detachment.

Part III. Comments on the Profile of Folk Concept Scales

The type and level classifications given just above furnish initial guidance for interpreting this protocol. The specific comments presented here in Part 3 should be coordinated with the prior Type/Level heuristics. Let us now turn to the profile of 20 folk concept scales, attending to the four regions of the profile sheet, and to the scales within each sector. A professional, individuated interpretation can, of course, go farther than this, taking account of patterns and configurations among the scales. Two excellent sources of information for configural hypotheses are the monographs by Rodgers (1983) and McAllister (1988). Important information can also be gleaned, however, from a sequential reading of the scales on the profile sheet. This analysis of each of the 20 scales will lead to more specific comments than can be derived from Type and Level alone.

The first sector of the profile (see Figure 3.4) contains scales assessing interpersonal style and manner of dealing with others. From an analysis of the seven scales in this region of the profile we can get an impression of how Mr. X approaches others, and of qualities such as self-confidence, poise, and initiative.

The scale standard scores are in parentheses immediately following the scale name. From each of the scales, some inferences about Mr. X may now be proposed:

Scales and Interpretations

Dominance (54)
is not strongly characterized by either dominance or submission; can accept either a leader's role or that of a follower.

Capacity for Status (54)
is resourceful and self-confident; shows ingenuity and versatility in dealing with problems; has moderately strong desire for success and status.

Sociability (64)
enjoys the company of others; is outgoing and talkative; initiates humor.

Social Presence (75)
is spontaneous, versatile, and clever; is verbally fluent and articulate, at ease in nearly any situation; is adventurous, likes excitement.

Self-acceptance (57)
is at ease and comfortable in most situations; is good at avoiding interpersonal friction and conflict; is usually liked and accepted by others.

Independence (54)
is not strongly characterized by either independence or dependence; is moderately ambitious and enterprising; gets along well with others.

Empathy (67)
is insightful concerning how others feel and think; is quick to respond to social nuances; is pleasant to be with; has a wide range of interests; is outgoing and sociable; has progressive views on most issues.

The next sector of the profile contains scales pertaining to the internalization and endorsement of normative conventions, including norms related to self-presentation. From an analysis of scores in this region, we can obtain an impression of how Mr. X views social norms and how his conduct is affected by these considerations.

Scales and Interpretation

Responsibility (49)
is not strongly characterized by either a clear sense of responsibility or its absence; tends to be moderate and reserved in behavior.

Socialization (47)
is not strongly characterized by either social conformity or its opposite; depending on skills and talents, can be creative and independent in seeing things in new ways and suggesting innovations.

Self-control (48)
is not strongly characterized by either over-control or under-control; has a good balance between restraint and spontaneity.

Good Impression (48)
is not strongly characterized by concerns over making a good impression;

behaves in a more or less natural way, claiming some virtues while acknowledging some flaws.

Communality (52)
has given moderately typical replies to a cluster of items characterized by strong consensual agreement or disagreement.

Well-being (60)
feels self to be generally in good health; is industrious, enterprising, and capable of productive effort; is not given to worry or anxiety about personal problems.

Tolerance (61)
values rationality and logic in dealing with others; tries to be fair-minded and tolerant; seen by others as trustworthy, mature, and insightful.

The third sector of the profile sheet contains three scales pertaining to cognitive/intellective functioning and the need for achievement in either structured or open situations. From an analysis of scores in this region we can obtain an impression of how Mr. X behaves with respect to these matters.

Scales and Interpretations

Achievement via Conformance (45)
may have considerable ability, but does not perform well in tightly defined or rule-dominated situations; in high school likely to be an under-achiever; easily distracted and bored.

Achievement via Independence (63)
has a strong drive for achievement, particularly in settings calling for independent work and ingenuity; is capable, clear-thinking; and verbally fluent; can be impatient and easily bored.

Intellectual Efficiency (65)
is an intelligent, resourceful, clear-thinking person; verbally fluent, with a flair for discussion and analysis; feels sure of self, equal to nearly any situation; has a stable, optimistic view of the future.

The final sector of the profile sheet contains three scales that assess broadly stylistic or qualitative aspects of thinking and behavior. The scores on these scales have implications in their own right, but also serve to color or even modify the expectations attached to higher and lower scores on the preceding scales. The inferences proposed for Mr. X from each scale are these:

Scales and Interpretations

Psychological-mindedness (56)
has a certain talent for sensing what others may say or do; has diverse but not necessarily well-integrated interests; probably above average in general abil-

ity; at least moderately ambitious; seen by others as independent, curious, and assertive.

Flexibility (75)

likes change and variety, and responds with frustration and irritation to routine; impresses others as intelligent, but also as complicated and unpredictable; has progressive even avant-garde views, and a wide range of interests.

Femininity/Masculinity (54)

is not strongly characterized by either masculine attributes or their absence; sees self as relatively normal or ordinary in regard to sex-role behavior.

Part IV. Special Purpose Scales and Indices

From time to time, various special purpose scales and indices have been and will continue to be developed. These measures will not always be relevant to the purposes of testing, but in certain settings or circumstances they will be quite important. At the present time, two such scales are included in the narrative report, as well as three indices based on clusters or combinations of scales. The two scales—Managerial Potential (Gough, 1984), and Work Orientation (Gough, 1985)—will be of principal utility for testing carried out in occupational environments. The three indices are for Social Maturity (Gough, 1966, 1971), Leadership (Gough, 1969; Hogan, 1978), and Creativity (Weiss, 1981). The equations for the three indices have been modified from the published versions to accommodate changes in the present revision of the CPI.

Scales and Interpretations

Raw score	*Standard score*	*Special scales and indices*
25	59	Mp (Managerial Potential): somewhat above average in managerial potential
33	57	Wo (Work Orientation): somewhat above average in self-discipline, conscientiousness, and reliability as a worker.
55	59	Lpi (Leadership Potential Index): somewhat above average in leadership potential
51	53	Smi (Social Maturity Index): accepts the rules and regulations of everyday life, but occasionally finds it difficult to do just what he is supposed to do
54	59	Cpi (Creative Personality Index): above average in creative potential.

Part V. A Fully Individuated Reading of the Protocol

From the Type/Level section, certain broad, orienting notions about this person were derived. In the section on the folk concept profile, certain specifically salient personal qualities were inferred. Now, in Part 5, we go on to a fully individuated reading of the protocol, drawing on the 100 descriptive items in Block's (1961) *California Q-set*. From the CPI, an estimate has been made of how each of these 100 items would be Q-sorted by someone in a position to describe the subject, for example a close friend, a parent, a spouse, a counselor, or anyone else who might know the person well and whose inclinations would be to give an accurate and benevolent description.

Block's method calls for placing 100 items in nine groupings, according to relevance or salience. The number of items in each grouping or category, going from most to least descriptive, are 5-8-12-16-18-16-12-8-5. The five most descriptive items are assigned values of "9" for correlational purposes, then the eight in the next category are assigned values of "8," and so on down to the five least salient or descriptive items, which are assigned values of "1." By use of these values, any Q-sort of the Block set can be correlated with any other.

In the presentation below, an estimated Q-sort value has been computed for each of the 100 items. The five highest-rated statements are given in full, as are the five lowest-rated. These 10 statements—5 very likely to be true of this person, and 5 very unlikely to be descriptive—are the most important. All 100 estimates, however, are reported, so that verification of this CPI-based Q-sort formulation can be carried out against a formulation from an observer or panel of observers. Inclusion of the estimates for all 100 items also makes the analysis potentially useful for research involving descriptions inferred from the inventory. (Note: Although all 100 numerical estimates are given in the standard computer narrative, they will not be presented here because of the space the 100 estimates and items would require).

The five highest-rated items (hence most descriptive of this person) are:

8. Appears to have a high degree of intellectual capacity. (7.52)
96. Values own independence and autonomy. (7.21)
80. Interested in members of the opposite sex. (6.75)
67. Is self-indulgent. (6.61)
72. Concerned with own adequacy as a person, either at conscious or unconscious levels. (6.55)

The five lowest-rated items (hence least descriptive of this person) are:

99. Is self-dramatizing, histrionic. (2.51)
37. Is guileful and deceitful, manipulative, opportunistic. (2.59)
63. Judges self and others in conventional terms, such as "popularity," "the correct thing to do," social pressures, etc. (2.63)
78. Feels cheated and victimized by life; self-pitying. (2.76)
61. Creates and exploits dependency in people. (3.16)

Interviewer's Character Sketch

To complete this case illustration, the life history interviewer's character sketch will be quoted verbatim. The sketch is an attempt to capture the essential and differentiating psychology of the subject. Here is what was said about Mr. X:

> This assessee is the most complex, contradictory, and concealed person I have so far encountered in the assessments. Apparent polarities characterize his social demeanor. His marked verbal facility seems crimped by a reluctance to reveal very much about himself. His casual, slouching posture only partially conceals his muscular tenseness. Intense emotions are expressed in a soft-spoken and affectless voice. And a seemingly cool detachment is superimposed on an underlying, anxious involvement.
>
> More than others, he struggled against revealing much about himself, partly because of his feeling, as he himself stated it, of wanting to be on guard. He kept wondering what I was writing down about him, and wanted to escape from the surveillance of the assessment. And although he did not refuse to answer any of the questions I asked, he asserted firmly at the outset that it was his right to do so.
>
> Anxiety and a fundamental lack of deep self-confidence seemed masked by a bemused yet defensive detachment from the flow of events. Perhaps these inner feelings of self-doubt prompted the antagonism he felt towards the assessment staff, which was trying to find out all about him.
>
> His fantasies reflect, at the same time, a desire for public recognition and a wish for anonymity. To the question "What would you do if you could do anything you wished?" he responded "Travel in foreign countries and write books under a pseudonym." Rarely does a single response so clearly reveal the inner ambivalence between involvement with others versus detachment and distance.

Implications for Counseling

Mr. X, it will be recalled, took the CPI as a participant in a research project on vocational planning and career aspirations. The fact that he elected to take part suggests that he had at least minimal uncertainty about his future goals and how to attain them. In addition, in his life history interview various problems and worries were mentioned for which counseling would be helpful. For instance, he described himself as somewhat withdrawn, finding it hard to feel at ease and compatible with others. He also mentioned a number of career possibilities, and stated that it was hard to decide which would be best for him. In this realm, the contrasts were between security and income on the one hand, versus opportunity for personal growth and self-expression on the other.

What contribution can the information from the CPI profile and narrative make to these considerations? First, we should note his typological classification as a Delta, but with borderline Gamma characteristics. As a Delta, X will be an internalizer of the contradictions, imperfections, ambiguities, and illogicalities of the normative milieu. These outer contrasts become inner conflicts, and he will feel himself pulled and pushed in different directions. Also, he will be exquisitely aware of these complexities. Solutions that appeal to others, and that work well for them, will not for these reasons alone appeal to X. He must develop, from within, his own resolution of personal views and the choosing of goals.

At Level 7, he has the strength and inner resources to achieve a rewarding life style, but he has not yet done so. Whereas well-integrated Alphas and Betas might have their life trajectories pretty well established by their early 20s. Deltas will not yet be at this stage of realization. So one can anticipate some false starts, some explorations down blind alleys, and some psychological errors in the next five to ten years. Counseling, if he should seek it, could well be directed towards the development of realistic expectations about the slow pace of personal growth. That is, persons in the Delta category, whose private doubts about normative structures demand a personal resolution, will typically take longer to achieve a sense of personal fulfillment than will those who are more comfortable with societal conventions.

A word should also be said about the Gamma affinity of X. His v.1 score puts him just a few points from the cutoff between Gamma and Delta. This means that to a certain extent the rule-testing and acting-out drives of the Gamma will be moderately present in X. One can anticipate friction in closely defined settings, resistance to the imperatives of academic and professional education, and problems stemming from headstrong and self-indulgent behavior. Again, however, because of his high standing on Level, these dispositions will in all likelihood be assimilated into an effective totality.

Direct, managerial, task-assigning counseling would be inappropriate for X. He would rebel against such treatment, and would devalue anyone from whom it was received. A more reflective, even non-directive approach would be better, to create a context in which X could talk out his ambivalences and inner doubts to his own satisfaction. Best of all would appear to be an insightful counselor, skilled in listening but also adept at offering therapeutic interpretations of the self-defeating and merely provocative maneuvers to which X is prone.

REFERENCES

Abbott, K. A. (1976). Culture change and the persistence of the Chinese personality. In G. A. DeVos (Ed.), *Response to change: Society, culture, and personality* (pp. 74–104). New York: D. Van Nostrand.

Babl, J. D. (1979). Compensatory masculine responding as a function of sex role. *Journal of Consulting and Clinical Psychology, 47,* 252–257.

Baucom, D. H. (1976). Independent masculinity and femininity scales on the California Psychological Inventory. *Journal of Consulting and Clinical Psychology, 44,* 876.

Baucom, D. H. (1980). Independent CPI masculinity and femininity scales: Psychological correlates and sex-role typology. *Journal of Personality Assessment, 44,* 262–271.

Bem, S. L. (1974). The measurement of psychological androgyny. *Journal of Consulting and Clinical Psychology, 42,* 155–162.

Block, J. (1961). *The Q-sort method in personality assessment and psychiatric research.* Springfield, Illinois: C. C. Thomas. (Reprinted, 1978, Consulting Psychologists Press, Palo Alto, California).

Domino, G. (1968). Differential prediction of academic achievement in conforming and independent settings. *Journal of Educational Psychology, 59,* 256–260.

Domino, G. (1971). Interactive effects of achievement orientation and teaching style on academic achievement. *Journal of Educational Psychology, 62,* 427–431.

Gendre, F. (1974). L'évaluation de la personnalité à l'aide de l'inventaire psychologique de Californie (California Psychological Inventory, ou C. P. I.) de H. Gough (Evaluation of the personality be means of the California Psychological Inventory). *Revue de Psychologie Appliquée, 24,* 159–179.

Gough, H. G. (1957). *Manual for the California Psychological Inventory.* Palo Alto, California: Consulting Psychologists Press.

Gough, H. G. (1966). Appraisal of social maturity by means of the CPI. *Journal of Abnormal Psychology, 71,* 189–195.

Gough, H. G. (1968). An interpreter's syllabus for the California Psychological Inventory. In P. McReynolds (Ed.), *Advances in psychological assessment* (Vol. 1, pp. 51–79). Palo Alto, California: Science and Behavior Books.

Gough, H. G. (1969). A leadership index on the California Psychological Inventory. *Journal of Counseling Psychology, 16,* 283–289.

Gough, H. G. (1971). Scoring high on an index of social maturity. *Journal of Abnormal Psychology, 77,* 236–241.

Gough, H. G. (1984). A managerial potential scale for the California Psychological Inventory. *Journal of Applied Psychology, 69,* 232–240.

Gough, H. G. (1985). A work orientation scale for the California Psychological Inventory. *Journal of Applied Psychology, 70,* 505–513.

Gough, H. G. (1987). *The California Psychological Inventory administrator's guide.* Palo Alto, California: Consulting Psychologists Press.

Helson, R., & Wink, P. (1987). Two conceptions of maturity examined in the findings of a longitudinal study. *Journal of Personality and Social Psychology, 53,* 531–541.

Hogan, J. C. (1978). Personological dynamics of leadership. *Journal of Research in Personality, 12,* 390–395.

Hogan, R. (1969). Development of an empathy scale. *Journal of Consulting and Clinical Psychology, 33,* 307–316.

Kanner, A. D. (1976). Femininity and masculinity: Their relationship to creativity in male architects and their independence from each other. *Journal of Consulting and Clinical Psychology, 44,* 802–805.

Karni, E. S., & Levin, J. (1972). The use of smallest space analysis in studying scale structure: An application to the California Psychological Inventory. *Journal of Applied Psychology, 56,* 341–346.

Lazzari, R., & Gough, H. G. (1973). Una applicazione del California Psychological Inventory al problema della stima del Q. I. (An application of the California Psychological Inventory to the problem of estimating the I. Q.). *Bollettino di Psicologia Applicata, n. 118-120,* 49–57.

Levin, J., & Karni, E. S. (1970). Demonstration of cross-cultural invariance of the California Psychological Inventory in America and Israel by the Guttman-Lingoes smallest space analysis. *Journal of Cross-Cultural Psychology, 1,* 253–260.

McAllister, L. W. (1988). *A practical guide to CPI interpretation* (Second Edition). Palo Alto, California: Consulting Psychologists Press.

Megargee, E. I. (1972). *The California Psychological Inventory handbook*. San Francisco: Jossey-Bass.

Mizushima, K., & DeVos, G. (1967). An application of the California Psychological Inventory in a study of Japanese delinquency. *Journal of Social Psychology, 71*, 45–51.

Nichols, R. C., & Schnell, R. R. (1963). Factor scales for the California Psychological Inventory. *Journal of Consulting Psychology, 27*, 228–235.

Nishiyama, T. (1973). Cross-cultural invariance of the California Psychological Inventory. *Psychologia* (Kyoto, Japan), *16*, 75–84.

Pitariu, H., & Helmine, H. (1980). Investigatarea personalitath cu ajutorul inventarului psihologic California (C. P. I.) (Studies in personality with the CPI). *Revista de Psihologie* (Bucharest), *26*, 461–473.

Rodgers, D. A. (1983). Configural interpretation of the CPI. In J. T. Webb, K. M. McNamara, & D. A. Rodgers (Eds.), *Configural interpretations of the MMPI and CPI* (Rev. Edition, 3rd printing, pp. 55–76). Columbus, Ohio: Ohio Psychology Publishing Company.

Shaffer, L. (1957). Review of the California Psychological Inventory. *Journal of Consulting Psychology, 21*, 359.

Spence, J. T., & Helmreich, R. L. (1979). *Masculinity and femininity: Their psychological dimensions, correlates, and antecedents*. Austin: University of Texas Press.

Stankov, L., & Kvascev, R. (1974). Faktora analiza Goughvog CPI i Cattellvog 16 P. F. (Factor analysis of Gough's CPI and Cattell's 16PF). *Jugoslovenska Revija za Psihologiju* (Belgrade), *4*, 35–46.

Szalanski, J., & Szymanska, I. (1977). Personality traits of third year students of psychology and medicine as measured by the CPI. *Przeglad Psychologiczny* (Warsaw), *20*, 757–770.

Wegner, K. W. (1988). The California Psychological Inventory, 1987 revised edition. In D. J. Keyser & R. C. Sweetland (Eds.), *Test critiques* (Vol. 7, pp. 66–75). Kansas City, MO: Test Corporation of America.

Weiss, D. S. (1981). A multigroup study of personality patterns in creativity. *Perceptual and Motor Skills, 52*, 735–746.

A CPI BIBLIOGRAPHY FOR COUNSELORS

Aiken, L. R., Jr. (1963). Personality correlates of attitudes toward mathematics. *Journal of Educational Research, 56*, 476–480.

Albert, R. S. (1980). Exceptionally gifted boys and their parents. *Gifted Child Quarterly, 24*, 174–179.

Becker, S. (1977). Personality correlates of the discrepancy between expressed and inventoried scores. *Measurement and Evaluation in Guidance, 10*, 24–30.

Bohn, M. J. (1973). Personality variables in successful work-study performance. *Journal of College Student Personnel, 14*, 135–140.

Boyle, B. P., & Coombs, R. H. (1971). Personality profiles related to emotional stress in the initial year of medical training. *Journal of Medical Education, 46*, 882–888.

Campagna, W. D., & O'Toole, J. J. (1981). A comparison of the personality profiles of Roman Catholic and male Protestant seminarians. *Counseling and Values, 26*, 62–67.

Cartwright, L. K. (1977). Continuity and noncontinuity in the careers of a sample of young women physicians. *Journal of the American Medical Women's Association, 32*, 316–321.

Cartwright, L. K. (1978). Career satisfaction and role harmony in a sample of young women physicians. *Journal of Vocational Behavior, 12*, 184–196.

Crovitz, E. (1975). Comparison of male and female physician's associate program applicants. *Journal of Medical Education, 50*, 672–676.

Domino, G. (1968). Differential prediction of academic achievement in conforming and independent settings. *Journal of Educational Psychology, 59,* 256–260.

Domino, G. (1971). Interactive effects of achievement orientation and teaching style on academic achievement. *Journal of Educational Psychology, 62,* 427–431.

Freedman, S. A., Antenen, W. W., & Lister, J. L. (1967). Counselor behavior and personality characteristics. *Counselor Education and Supervision, 7,* 26–30.

Garman, L. C., & Plant, W. T. (1975). Personality, academic performance, and educational aspirations of very bright women and men vs. those of high average intelligence. *Journal of Genetic Psychology, 126,* 163–167.

German, S. C., & Cottle, W. C. (1981). The use of the CPI to ascertain differences between more and less effective student paraprofessional helpers. *Journal of the National Association of Women Deans, Administrators, and Counselors, 44,* 11–16.

Gill, L. J., & Spilka, B. (1962). Some nonintellectual correlates of academic achievement among Mexican-American secondary school students. *Journal of Educational Psychology, 53,* 144–149.

Gough, H. G. (1966). Graduation from high school as predicted from the California Psychological Inventory. *Psychology in the Schools, 3,* 208–216.

Gough, H. G. (1968). College attendance among high-aptitude students as predicted from the California Psychological Inventory. *Journal of Counseling Psychology, 15,* 269–278.

Gough, H. G., & Kirk, B. A. (1970). Achievement in dental school as related to personality and aptitude variables. *Measurement and Evaluation in Guidance, 2,* 225–233.

Gough, H. G., & Lanning, K. (1986). Predicting grades in college from the California Psychological Inventory. *Educational and Psychological Measurement, 46,* 205–213.

Gruber, D. L., & Shupe, D. R. (1982). Personality correlates of urinary hesitancy (paruresis) and body shyness in male college students. *Journal of College Student Personnel, 23,* 308–313.

Haier, R. J., & Denham, S. A. (1976). A summary profile of the nonintellectual correlates of mathematical precocity in boys and girls. In D. P. Keating (Ed.), *Intellectual talent: Research and development* (pp. 225–241). Baltimore: The Johns Hopkins University Press.

Helson, R. (1967). Personality characteristics and developmental history of creative college women. *Genetic Psychology Monographs, 76,* 205–256.

Helson, R. (1985). Which of those young women with creative potential became productive? Personality in college and characteristics of parents. In R. Hogan & W. H. Jones (Eds.), *Perspectives in personality* (Vol. 1, pp. 49–80). New York: JAI Press.

Helson, R., Elliot, T., & Leigh, J. (1989). Adolescent personality and women's work patterns. In D. Stern & D. Eichorn (Eds.), *Adolescence and work: Influences of social structure, labor marketing, and culture* (pp. 259–289). Hillsdale, NJ: Lawrence Erlbaum & Associates.

Helson, R., Mitchell, V., & Moane, G. (1984). Personality and patterns of adherence and nonadherence to the social clock. *Journal of Personality and Social Psychology, 46,* 1079–1095.

Helson, R., & Moane, G. (1987). Personality change in women from college to midlife. *Journal of Personality and Social Psychology, 53,* 176–186.

Helson, R., & Wink, P. (1987). Two conceptions of maturity examined in the findings of a longitudinal study. *Journal of Personality and Social Psychology, 53,* 531–541.

Herbert, T. T. (1980). An exploratory investigation into the nature of the part-time MBA student. *Human Relations, 33,* 279–295.

Hersch, P. D., Kulik, J. A., & Scheibe, K. E. (1969). Personal characteristics of college volunteers in mental hospitals. *Journal of Consulting and Clinical Psychology, 33,* 30–34.

Hetherington, E. M., & Feldman, S. E. (1964). College cheating as a function of subject and situational variables. *Journal of Educational Psychology, 55,* 212–218.

Hill, A. H. (1966). A longitudinal study of attrition among high aptitude students. *Journal of Educational Research, 60,* 166–173.

Hogan, R., Mankin, D., Conway, J., & Fox, S. (1970). Personality correlates of undergraduate marijuana use. *Journal of Consulting and Clinical Psychology, 35,* 58–63.

Hogan, R., & Weiss, D. S. (1974). Personality correlates of superior academic achievement. *Journal of Counseling Psychology, 21,* 144–149.

Holland, J. L. (1959). The prediction of college grades from the California Psychological Inventory and the Scholastic Aptitude Test. *Journal of Educational Psychology, 50,* 135–142.

Irvine, R. W. (1979). Structure of school, personality, and high school dropouts. *Journal of Negro Education, 48,* 67–72.

Johnson, D., Shertzer, B., Linden, J., & Stone, S. C. (1967). The relationship of counselor candidate characteristics and counseling effectiveness. *Counselor Education and Supervision, 6,* 297–303.

Johnson, J. A. (1987). Influence of adolescent social crowds on the development of vocational identity. *Journal of Vocational Behavior, 31,* 182–199.

Johnson, R. W., Flammer, D. P., & Nelson, J. G. (1975). Multiple correlations between personality factors and SVIB occupational scales. *Journal of Counseling Psychology, 22,* 217–223.

Kassera, W. J., & Sease, W. A. (1970). Personal change as a concomitant of counselor education. *Counselor Education and Supervision, 9,* 208–210.

Kegel-Flom, P. (1985). Predicting optometry school grades from intellectual and nonintellectual admission variables. *American Journal of Optometry and Physiological Optics, 62,* 901–907.

Kegel-Flom, P. (1988). Women optometry students: How qualified? *American Journal of Optometry and Physiological Optics, 65,* 666–673.

Kipnis, D. (1968). Social immaturity, intellectual ability, and adjustive behavior in college. *Journal of Applied Psychology, 52,* 71–80.

Kurtines, W., & Hogan, R. (1972). Sources of conformity in unsocialized college students. *Journal of Abnormal Psychology, 80,* 49–51.

Leitner, D. W., & Sedlacek, W. E. (1976). Characteristics of successful campus police officers. *Journal of College Student Personnel, 17,* 304–308.

Mason, E. P., Adams, H. L., & Blood, D. F. (1966). Personality characteristics of gifted college freshmen. *Psychology in the Schools, 3,* 360–365.

Megargee, E. I., & Carbonell, J. L. (1988). Evaluating leadership with the CPI. In C. D. Spielberger & J. N. Butcher (Eds.), *Advances in personality assessment* (Vol. 7, pp. 203–219). Hillsdale, NJ: Lawrence Erlbaum Associates.

Mordock, J., & Patterson, C. (1965). Personality characteristics of counseling students at various levels of training. *Vocational Guidance Quarterly, 13,* 265–269.

Murray, S. G. (1981). Personality characteristics of adult women with high and low profiles on the SCII or SVIB occupational scales. *Journal of Applied Psychology, 66,* 422–430.

Musante, L., MacDougall, J. M., Dembroski, T. M., & Van Horn, A. E. (1983). Component analysis of Type A coronary-prone behavior pattern in male and female college students. *Journal of Personality and Social Psychology, 45,* 1104–1117.

Myers, M. B., Templer, D. I., & Brown, R. (1984). Coping ability of women who become victims of rape. *Journal of Consulting and Clinical Psychology, 52,* 73–78.

Ostrand, J. L., & Creaser, J. (1978). Development of counselor candidate dominance in three learning conditions. *Journal of Psychology, 99,* 199–202.

Palladino, J. J., & Domino, G. (1978). Differences between counseling center clients and nonclients on three measures. *Journal of College Student Personnel, 19,* 497–501.

Pfeifer, C. M., Jr., & Sedlacek, W. E. (1974). Predicting black student grades with non-intellectual measures. *Journal of Negro Education, 43,* 67–76.

Picano, J. J. (1989). Development and validation of a life history index of adult adjustment for women. *Journal of Personality Assessment, 53,* 267–277.

Plant, W. T. (1965). Personality changes associated with college attendance. *Human Development, 8,* 142–151.

Reich, S. (1976). California Psychological Inventory: Profile of a sample of first-year law students. *Psychological Reports, 39,* 871–874.

Rapaport, K., & Burkhart, B. R. (1984). Personality and attitudinal characteristics of sexually coercive college males. *Journal of Abnormal Psychology, 93,* 216–221.

Ross, H. G. (1980). Matching achievement styles and instructional environments. *Contemporary Educational Psychology, 5,* 216–226.

Rutkowski, K., & Domino, G. (1975). Interrelationship of study skills and personality variables in college students. *Journal of Educational Psychology, 67,* 784–789.

Scott, N. A., & Sedlacek, W. E. (1975). Personality differentiation and prediction of persistence in physical science and engineering. *Journal of Vocational Behavior, 6,* 205–216.

Shaver, P. R., & Scheibe, K. E. (1967). Transformation of school identity: A study of chronic mental patients and college volunteers in a summer camp setting. *Journal of Psychology, 66,* 19–37.

Smith, S. D., & Smith, W. D. (1979). Teaching the poor: Its effect on student teacher self-concept. *Journal of Teacher Education, 30,* 45–49.

Sprafkin, R. P. (1972). Personal problems versus vocational problems: Personality differences between clients. *Journal of Clinical Psychology, 28,* 114–116.

Steinberg, R., & Shapiro, S. (1982). Sex differences in personality traits of male and female master of business administration students. *Journal of Applied Psychology, 67,* 306–310.

Swisdak, B., & Flaherty, M. R. (1964). A study of personality differences between college graduates and dropouts. *Journal of Psychology, 57,* 25–28.

Tuma, A. H., & Gustad, J. W. (1957). The effects of client and counselor personality characteristics on client learning in counseling. *Journal of Counseling Psychology, 4,* 136–143.

Viernstein, M. D., McGinn, P. V., & Hogan, R. (1977). The personality correlates of differential verbal and mathematical ability in talented adolescents. *Journal of Youth and Adolescence, 6,* 169–178.

Vingoe, F. J., & Autonoff, S. R. (1968). Personality characteristics of good judges of others. *Journal of Counseling Psychology, 15,* 91–93.

Walsh, W. B. (1974). Consistent occupational preferences and personality. *Journal of Vocational Behavior, 4,* 145–153.

Watson, C. G. (1967). The California Psychological Inventory as a predictor of academic achievement in normal and maladjusted college males. *Journal of Educational Research, 61,* 10–13.

Weinstein, N. D. (1978). Individual differences in reaction to noise: A longitudinal study in a college dormitory. *Journal of Applied Psychology, 63,* 458–466.

Weiss, D. S., Haier, R. J., & Keating, D. P. (1974). Personality characteristics of mathematically precocious boys. In J. C. Stanley, R. J. Haier, D. P. Keating, & L. H. Fox (Eds.), *Mathematical talent: Discovery, description and development* (pp. 126–139). Baltimore: The Johns Hopkins University Press.

White, M. S. (1975). Psychological characteristics of the nurse practitioner. *Nursing Outlook, 23,* 160–166.

Widdop, J. H., & Widdop, V. A. (1975). Comparison of the personality traits of female education and physical education students. *Research Quarterly, 46,* 274–281.

Zarski, J. J., Sweeney, J. T., & Barcikowski, R. S. (1977). Counseling effectiveness as a function of counselor social interest. *Journal of Counseling Psychology, 24,* 1–5.

4 The 16 Personality Factor Questionnaire

Samuel E. Krug
MetriTech, Champaign, Illinois

Edgar F. Johns
Human Synergistics, Inc., Plymouth, Michigan

HISTORICAL BACKGROUND OF THE TEST

The 16 Personality Factor Questionnaire (16PF) represents a unique chapter in the history of personality assessment. Most tests were designed to measure human characteristics that had immediate, practical significance. In Woodworth's *Personal Data Sheet* (1917), for example, the emphasis was on *assessing* emotional instability, not understanding its causes or components. Hathaway and McKinley sought in the MMPI an objective method for differentiating among known diagnostic categories.

The 16PF, on the other hand, was constructed by its principal author, Raymond B. Cattell, simply to measure "personality." His approach was first to study the naturally occurring structure of personality and then to develop rating scales and questionnaires to measure what he discovered. It was only later that he turned to study the relevance of his scales to important social criteria.

As an undergraduate in London, Cattell studied chemistry. From this training he developed an analytic orientation and a strong belief that all matter could be most thoroughly understood in terms of an underlying set of definable elements. As a graduate student of Charles Spearman, the inventor of factor analysis, he learned the techniques that would allow him to search for the underlying elements of personality.

Cattell began his personality studies in earnest in the early 1940s. However, he was not the first to apply factor analysis to the study of personality. Guilford had already begun to report his results a decade earlier (Guilford & Guilford, 1933; 1936) and Thurstone published his 7-factor temperament model in 1947. But, Guilford began his studies from the perspective of separating hypothesized components of extroversion–introversion (Guilford, 1975) and Thurstone's goal seems to have been finding a more parsimonious, oblique solution to Guilford's 15-factor model.

Cattell, on the other hand, began by exploring the entire universe of "trait elements" and attempting to identify the "larger unities" that explained the covariation among them (Cattell, 1943). He adopted the position that "all aspects of human personality which are or have been of importance, interest, or utility have already become recorded in the substance of language" (Cattell, 1943, p. 483). As an operational definition of the universe of trait elements, he took the anthology of 17,953 terms that Allport and Odbert (1936) found in *Webster's New Unabridged International Dictionary*. Starting with the 4,504 terms in the group Allport and Odbert called "personal traits" (as opposed to "temporary states," "social evaluations," and "metaphorical or doubtful terms"), he and a colleague began to reduce this list to a more manageable number that could be analyzed by empirical methods.

This first reduction was achieved by logically combining synonyms and eliminating arcane terms. It resulted in a set of 171 variables that included such bipolar terms as "worrying-placid," "reliable-undependable," and "assertive-submissive" but also terms like "agoraphobic," "alcoholic," and "strong in personality." To insure that his list was as complete as possible, Cattell reviewed historical models (e.g., Galen's humoral model) and trait and type patterns postulated by theorists of the past century. His final set of 171 variables included ability and interest variables as well, because Cattell saw both as subspecies within the general class of personality traits.

This list of 171 variables was further reduced to 35 by applying informal cluster-analytic methods to a correlation matrix of peer ratings made by 100 adults. These 35 variables served as the basis for obtaining peer ratings on a sample of 208 adults. The correlations among these peer ratings were subsequently factor analyzed.

Today, the statistical analysis of such a data set requires only microseconds on high-speed computers. In the 1930s and 1940s, however, the effort involved was substantial. Correlations, usually tetrachorics, needed to be read and verified from charts. Factor extraction, even by the simplified centroid method, was a laborious process. And, there was no "little jiffy" (Kaiser, 1970) to handle the rotation process. Rotation to simple structure by visual methods took months.

Cattell next generated a pool of questionnaire items hypothesized to represent the factors he had found in the rating studies. Cattell's insistence on linking personality factors across various "media of observation" (Cattell, 1957)—self report, observer ratings, and objective performance data —undoubtedly contributed to the robustness of the 16PF scales and their predictive utility in many kinds of situations. Although some characteristics were obviously unique to each method of observation, Cattell tried to focus on factors that demonstrated the greatest replicability across all three media. These studies concluded with the definition of 16 scales or "factors" that became the basis for the 16PF.

Since it was first published in 1949 the test has undergone several major and minor revisions, most recently in 1975. In 1952, all items were changed from a second person format (i.e., "*Do you* usually tend to do your planning, alone, without suggestions from, and discussions with, other people?") to a first person format (i.e., "*I like* quiet vacations, away from people"). The 1956, 1962, and 1968 revisions replaced outdated items with new ones. The 1975 revision eliminated sexist language in those that remained. Partly as a function of item replacements, some redefinition of the scales took place after 1949. Since 1956, however, the factors have retained their current, basic meaning.

At the same time, the 16PF became the parent of an entire family of personality tests. New instruments were constructed to fit other age ranges, such as the High School Personality Questionnaire (Cattell, Cattell, & Johns, 1984) for teenagers, the Children's Personality Questionnaire (Porter & Cattell, 1975) for preteens, and the Early School Personality Questionnaire (Coan & Cattell, 1976) for children 6 to 8 years of age. Other instruments, like the IPAT Anxiety Scale (Krug, Scheier, & Cattell, 1976), took a subset of 16PF items to focus on clinically important aspects of the total personality space defined by the 16PF. In a later development, a set of scales designed to measure factorially distinct aspects of depression and cognitive disturbance were added to the basic 16PF to create the Clinical Analysis Questionnaire (CAQ) (Krug, 1980).

A number of secondary or derivative scales were subsequently developed from the basic scales. These are variously titled second-order scores, criterion scores, specification equations, adjustment specification equations, or performance equations. However, each corresponds to a set of weights applied to the primary factors to produce a single new score. Some involve clinical concepts like neuroticism or psychoticism and were validated by contrasting scores of clinical patients and normal examinees. Others, called second-order factors, were found by factor analyzing the correlations among the primary factors. The *16PF Handbook* (Cattell, Eber, & Tatsuoka, 1970) describes approximately 100 such scales.

In this way the 16PF became more a system of personality assessment than a single assessment instrument. Although it is an important and widely used instrument in its own right, the entire system represents an important assessment tradition that evolved over time to meet new needs.

Cattell's original vision was to map and measure the most fundamental dimensions of human personality. He felt that these basic building blocks of personality, which he defined as "that which permits a prediction of what a person will do in a given situation" (Cattell, 1950, p. 2), would have relevance to a wide assortment of socially relevant criteria. That conviction was largely borne out by subsequent research findings, as will shortly be seen.

CONCEPTUAL FOUNDATIONS OF THE TEST

At the present time, the 16PF is best described as an instrument that assesses adult personality in terms of 16 reasonably independent and essentially normal categories or "factors." Test results are useful in predicting occupational preferences and job performance, and in understanding personal adjustment. Because it emphasizes normal characteristics, the 16PF has long been used in counseling settings to complement the information provided by more clinical instruments like the MMPI.

The 16PF has one of the most extensive research foundations of any test currently in use. Numerous studies have verified the basic structure and dimensionality of the test (Cattell & Krug, 1986; Krug & Johns, 1986). Thousands more have studied external correlates of the test's scores.

One such study, by Werner and Pervin (1986), reviewed the content of items used in major personality questionnaires. They found that four categories or domains described the levels of assessment represented by those items. Their analysis revealed that the 16PF item pool was fairly evenly balanced across all four categories as follows: 25% cognitive (beliefs, opinions); 30% affective preferences (likes, dislikes, wishes); 23% affective feelings (emotions); 22% behavioral (activities).

The norms for the standard forms cover three broad classifications for males and females: high school, college, and unselected normal adults. Specialized forms offer convenient administration formats and norms for the visually and aurally impaired and clinical populations. Moreover, its research base offers a wide platform from which to apply the 16PF under varying conditions and in many potential settings.

TEST ADMINISTRATION AND SCORING

The 16PF is published in five forms (A through E). A sixth form, combining items from existing forms—mostly from A—with previously unpublished items, is linked with a set of 12 clinical scales in the *Clinical Analysis Questionnaire* (Krug, 1980).

Forms A and B each contain 187 items, require 40–60 minutes to complete, and have a 7th–8th grade reading level. On the basis of usage, Form A has always been the most popular. Most of the published research to date has worked with it. Form B, when used, is combined with Form A to increase reliability. Under these conditions, the average test-retest scale reliability is .80 for shorter intervals of a week or less and .78 for longer intervals of a month. When Form A is used alone the average scale reliability is .80 for shorter intervals and .52 for longer intervals (IPAT Staff, 1986).

Forms C and D were originally designed for use in settings where testing time was at a premium. Each contains 105 items, requires 25–35 minutes to complete, and has a 6th–7th grade reading level. The average C + D test-retest scale reliability is .77 (IPAT Staff, 1986).

For the counseling setting, two features of the 16PF are particularly pertinent. First, a special version of the 16PF is available (Form E) in which the reading level of the items has been dramatically reduced. It is appropriate for use with adults who read at the 3rd–4th grade level, an important population for which few other self-report instruments are appropriate. Form E has been specifically validated for and standardized on a variety of special populations, including persons with visual and aural handicaps and rehabilitation clients. Despite some major differences in the nature of the item pool and test format, research suggests that Form E measures the same personality characteristics as other forms of the 16PF that were designed for use with unselected adult populations (Bolton, 1977; Burdsal & Bolton, 1979; Hughey & Burdsal, 1982).

Second, for those clients whose reading skills are below the 4th-grade level or for clients with significant visual impairments, Form E of the 16PF can be administered via audiotape cassette. Form A is also available on cassette. A videotaped version of Form A in American Sign Language has been developed for use with hearing-impaired clients (Shafqat, 1983). Braille editions are also available for Forms A and E.

With the exception of Form E[1], the 16PF uses a trichotomous response format, which is somewhat unique among personality questionnaires. Most others use either a forced-choice format (i.e., true/false) or a Likert-type format (e.g., a five-point scale ranging from "strongly agree" to "strongly disagree"). Other questionnaires (e.g., the Guilford-Zimmerman Temperament Survey) regard the uncertain or middle response category as a missing response. In the 16PF, however, the middle response was originally intended to represent a compromise halfway in between two specific alternatives, as in the "I would rather vacation (a) by myself, (b) in between, (c) with my friends/family." Unfortunately, with each revision of the 16PF, fewer items retained this format. About 30% of Form A items now use "uncertain" as the middle choice. Goldberg's (1981) analysis of the uncertain choice in questionnaires described four possible meanings: neutrality, lack of information, lack of understanding, and lack of situational consistency. People can obtain "valid" 16PF profiles by endorsing large numbers of uncertain responses, but it is not always clear what the resulting profiles mean.

Administration

The 16PF can be administered individually or in groups. Most people are able to read the instructions and proceed with the test questions without assistance.

---

[1]The dichotomous or forced choice design of Form E was intended to simplify administration.

Reading problems can be detected, for example, by noticing how long it takes to read the instructions. If reading is a problem, consider using the taped version of Form A. Form E may be used alternatively. However, we feel that Form E should only be used when one wishes to make comparisons to the special populations used in its standardization.

Scoring

The 16PF can be scored by hand or by computer. The hand-score option requires the user to purchase scoring keys, norm tables, and, optionally, a worksheet to facilitate the calculation of commonly used second-order scales. Item responses are differentially weighted, and this may cause confusion at first. With practice, however, raw scores can be obtained in just a few minutes.

Three options are available for the machine-score option: mail-in, teleprocessing, and on site. When utilizing mail-in service, answer sheets are sent to a central location that processes and returns printed reports. This approach limits test usage to those applications that can accommodate a delay of several days to weeks in the use of results. The Institute for Personality and Ability Testing (IPAT), which publishes the 16PF, provides the greatest variety of reporting services for mail-in users, with specialized formats for particular applications, such as marital counseling, vocational counseling, and law enforcement selection. Mail-in scoring of the 16PF is also provided by National Computer Systems (NCS), which offers a flexible report format that can be used in many different applications.

Many applications, however, cannot afford a delay in receiving results. Therefore, teleprocessing and on-site systems were developed to meet the need for immediate or nearly immediate results. Two teleprocessing options are currently available, IPAT and NCS, which link on-site terminals or microcomputers to a central computer through the telephone network. The teleprocessing option adds connect charges to the cost of test processing but provides virtually instantaneous results.

For on-site applications at least six options exist (Krug, 1987b). Two systems exist that administer, score and interpret Form A. These programs integrate the entire assessment process from administration to interpretation of scales. Three other systems require off-line administration and scoring because of copyright restrictions. With these systems the user inputs 16PF standard scores and receives a narrative interpretation in return. In this sense, they do not represent true test scoring options. A sixth option is provided by Psychological Resources, an Atlanta-based firm. It offers a variety of consultative reports that integrate 16PF results with other psychometric data. Psychological Resources has developed custom on-site systems for a variety of settings including law enforcement agencies and correctional systems.

Norms

The 16PF was last standardized in 1968 (Forms A and B), 1969 (Forms C and D), and 1985 (Form E). All forms provide gender-specific and combined norms. In addition, Forms A through D offer norms for high school, college, and unselected adult populations. Form E norms are available for rehabilitation clients, prison inmates, schizophrenics, hearing impaired, and culturally disadvantaged youths.

The 16PF uses a 10-point standard score called the sten scale. Stens range from 1 to 10 and have a mean of 5.5 (SD = 2) in the norm population. Primary scores are presented as integers, whereas secondary scores are normally reported to one decimal place. Some of the automated reports present percentile equivalents for standard scores.

TEST INTERPRETATION

Scale Descriptions

This section provides a brief interpretive guide to the basic 16PF content and validity scales. More extensive discussions can be found in Karson and O'Dell (1976), Krug (1981), and Cattell et al. (1970). Meyer (1983) provides a detailed description of the 16PF, along with the MMPI and Rorschach, in clinical use. Table 4.1 summarizes the personality scales and provides two items, one scored in the positive direction (+) and one scored in the negative direction (−) to illustrate the content of each scale.

Factor A: Warmth

People who score high on this scale describe themselves as warm, personable, and caring. Low-scoring people describe themselves as cool, aloof, and distant. Research shows that this characteristic contributes to success in sales and in jobs that reward interpersonal skills. It is one of four scales in the 16PF that measures components of extroversion, the others being Factors F (Impulsivity), H (Boldness), and Q2 (Self-sufficiency).

The self-reports of high-scoring individuals indicate that they are more likely to share their feelings with others. McClain (1968) found Factor A to be an important element in counselor effectiveness. There are also indications that it contributes significantly to success in teaching.

Karson and O'Dell (1976) have suggested a connection between low scores on Factor A and the "burnt-child" syndrome, indicating a long history of unsatisfying interpersonal relationships. An extremely low score on this scale may signify pathological dislike and avoidance of others.

TABLE 4.1
Sample Items Used to Measure the Primary Personality Characteristics[a]

A	Warmth	My social activities usually take up at least one afternoon or evening each week (+). I don't like work that forces me to be with lots of people (−).
C	Emotional Stability	I think of myself as content and satisfied (+). When I look at what's facing me, I don't know how I'll get through it (−).
E	Dominance	I tell people when they're wrong (+). I'm more comfortable following directions than giving them (−).
F	Impulsivity	People say I'm fun at a party (+). I can't let myself go easily (−).
G	Conformity	I believe in work before play (+). I don't like stories that have a moral (−).
H	Boldness	I like jobs that offer challenge and responsibility (+). I feel self-conscious in groups (−).
I	Sensitivity	I enjoy visiting art museums (+). I like horror movies (−).
L	Suspiciousness	Most people will work harder if they are watched closely (+). I think most people are honest (−).
M	Imagination	I notice the color and decoration of a room when I first come in (+). People say I'm practical (−).
N	Shrewdness	People say I'm tactful (+). When I talk to people, I say just what I feel (−).
O	Insecurity	I'm afraid to try new things for fear of failing (+). I trust my own judgment in most things (−).
Q1	Radicalism	My ideas are ahead of their time (+). I'm slow to try new and unusual foods (−).
Q2	Self-sufficiency	I really feel close to only a few people (+). I enjoy group discussions (−).
Q3	Self-discipline	I like to plan things out ahead of time (+). People call me irresponsible (−).
Q4	Tension	It takes me a long time to calm down when something upsets me (+). I handle stress well (−).

[a]These items are taken from the Adult Personality Inventory (Krug, 1984) and are reprinted here by permission of the copyright holder.

Factor B: Intelligence

This scale differs from others in the 16PF in that it measures intellectual performance, rather than personality characteristics. Cattell originally included it because research had shown general ability or intelligence to be a powerful predictor of many different kinds of behavior. The scale is reasonably reliable and valid. However, it was never intended to supplant the more precise measures that can be obtained from individual intelligence tests.

Low scores on the B scale often hold clinical significance. Most of the items are not terribly difficult. An otherwise capable individual who answers too many of them wrong may not be paying attention. Among depressed patients and patients experiencing severe anxiety, the inability to concentrate may show up most dramatically here.

Factor C: Emotional Stability

High-scoring people describe themselves as emotionally stable, mature, and realistic. They don't become upset or anxious easily. Instead they respond well to stress. Low-scoring people appear to have fewer resources to deal with the demands placed on them daily. As a result, they lose control and perform poorly under stress.

Factor C is one of the six scales in the 16PF that measures components of anxiety, the others being Factors H (Boldness), L (Suspiciousness), O (Insecurity), Q_3 (Self-discipline), and Q_4 (Tension). Higher anxiety is usually reflected in lower scores on Factor C. Perhaps for this reason, Factor C is an important contributor to the prediction of accident proneness.

High-scoring individuals report that they are generally able to reach personal goals without particular difficulty. They can concentrate on activities for long periods.

The low-scoring individual is frequently overwhelmed by the challenges of the day. Low scores on Factor C appear to increase the individual's risk of illness, especially coronary artery disease (Krug & Sherman, 1977; Krug & Johns, 1986; Sherman & Krug, 1977). Calsyn (1979) found the average score on Factor C to be the most significant deviation from the norm for a group of 57 low-back pain patients. Cattell et al. (1970) and Karson and O'Dell (1976) have suggested that the prognosis for therapeutic outcome is poorer when scores on Factor C are low. From a clinical perspective, Factor C is regarded as one of the most important factors to consider (Cattell, 1987).

Factor E: Dominance

High-scoring people on Factor E describe themselves as forceful, assertive, and competitive. They feel comfortable in leadership positions where they can control people and are often direct in their relationships with others. Low-scoring people are more likely to appear conforming, submissive, and humble.

Extremely high scores may be associated with a facade of aggression and stubbornness that masks covert inferiority feelings. On the other hand, Karson and O'Dell (1976) suggest that this scale is related to the individual's ability to externalize hostile feelings. That is, high-scoring people can more readily discharge their anger.

Factor F: Impulsivity

People who score high on this scale describe themselves as impulsive, enthusiastic, and happy-go-lucky. They enjoy parties, shows, excitement, and jobs that offer change, variety, and travel. Low-scoring people describe themselves as serious, introspective, and somewhat unhappy.

This is the second of the 16PF extroversion scales. As would be expected, most sales groups score significantly above average. There also appears to be some positive relationship between scores on Factor F and leaving home early (Cattell et al., 1970).

There is a tendency to equate low scores on Factor F with depression. However, a large-scale factor analysis did not find depression contributing significantly to scores on Factor F (Krug & Laughlin, 1977).

Karson and O'Dell (1976) describe Factor F as one of four superego or behavior-control factors among the 16PF primary scales, the others being Conformity (G+), Guilt (O+), and Compulsivity (Q_3+). Thus, there is a suggestion that Factor F may indicate whether the individual will externalize and "act out" inner conflicts (F+) or internalize them (F−).

Factor G: Conformity

People who are high on this dimension are conscientious, persistent, and respectful of authority. They frequently display good work habits and are concerned about getting things done. Low-scoring people are more self-indulgent and expedient.

In self-reports, high-scoring individuals describe themselves as being disgusted by sloppy people and messy rooms. They prefer to anticipate problems before confronting them. They generally follow rules to the letter. There is a negative relationship between scores on Factor G and number of accidents (Marshall & Wasman, 1959; Suhr, 1953).

There is a certain rigidity associated with extreme elevations on Factor G. High-scoring people may set unrealistic standards for themselves and, as a result, feel guilty and inadequate when they fail. Flexibility is not a part of the high-scoring individual's behavioral repertoire, and this may lower that person's ability to cope with extreme stress. Low scores on Factor G may occasionally signal sociopathic trends. But a low Factor G scores is far from an infallible sign.

Factor H: Boldness

High-scoring people describe themselves as adventurous risk-takers. Karson and O'Dell (1976), with much insight, have referred to this as the "Errol Flynn factor." High-scoring people are competitive and frequently try to control others. They enjoy being the focus of attention in a group. Low-scoring people are shy, timid, and sensitive to threat.

A review of the 16PF literature on physical illness (Sherman & Krug, 1977) suggests that low scores may represent increased medical risk. Early work by Meeland (1953) found a connection between scores on Factor H and activity of the autonomic nervous system. Meeland concluded that the parasympathetic system was dominant in high-scoring individuals, whereas low-scoring individuals tended to be more sympathetic dominant. This suggests an analogy between Factor H scores and the degree of psychological "insulation" the individual possesses. Like a well-designed building, high-scoring individuals are able to resist outside changes without expending much energy. Low-scoring individuals, on the other hand, are more vulnerable and reactive. Constant exposure to external stresses and threatening situations can result in psychological exhaustion.

Factor I: Sensitivity

High-scoring people are described as emotionally sensitive and tender. Low-scoring people are tough-minded and self-reliant.

Trait descriptions associated with high scores include artistic, dependent, overprotected, fidgity, clinging, and insecure. High-scoring individuals say they prefer reason to the use of force. In school, they had a definite preference for English to Math.

Research on physical illness has found scores on Factor I positively and significantly related to the incidence of coronary heart disease, hypertension, and frequency of chronic illness (Sherman & Krug, 1977). There is also a suggestion that high-scoring individuals tend to exaggerate symptoms, while low-scoring individuals are more likely to "tough it out."

Factor L: Suspiciousness

Trait descriptions associated with high scores on this scale include jealous, dogmatic, critical, and irritable. Low-scoring people are more likely to be perceived as trusting and accepting. They relate easily to other people.

Self-reports of high-scoring individuals include the notion that they do not easily forget the mistakes or criticisms of others. They are bothered about what others say behind their backs.

This is the third of four important medical risk factors identified by Sherman and Krug (1977). High scores show consistent relationships to the incidence of illness, in general, and coronary heart disease, in particular. Calsyn (1979) found a significant positive correlation between Factor L scores and number of clinic visits made during a 6-month period.

Factor M: Imagination

This is the "absent-minded professor" factor. High-scoring individuals report that they tend to forget trivial things. They are usually not interested in mechanical activities and mechanics, as a group, score significantly below average on Factor M.

High-scoring people are frequently described as unconventional, impractical, and creative. They sometimes act in ways that suggest they have lost touch with reality. Factor M appears to be an important factor in accident proneness. Low-scoring people, on the other hand, describe themselves as practical and conventional.

Factor N: Shrewdness

High-scoring people are described as sophisticated and polished. They are polite and diplomatic, but also guarded in their interactions with others. They prefer to keep problems to themselves. Low-scoring people are more candid and open.

The work of Krug and Laughlin (1977) suggests that this is not just simply a dimension of sophistication, but also one of behavior control. That is to say, low-scoring people are generally less constrained by rules and standards. This hypothesis is supported by reasonably strong correlations with the Self-control scale on the Adjective Check List and the Need for Order scale on the Edward's Personal Preference Schedule (Krug, 1981).

Research on happily and unhappily married couples point to the importance of Factor N in relationship counseling. Individuals who score extremely high may be too detached and unable to respond appropriately to the emotional needs of their partners.

Factor O: Insecurity

High-scoring people describe themselves as worried, guilty, moody, insecure, and depressed. At the other end of the scale we find people who are more self-confident.

Elevated scores are very common in clinical disorders of all kinds. Self-descriptions associated with high scores on this scale are accident-prone, anxious, brooding, cries easily, depressed, downhearted, fearful, lonely, self-deprecating, self-reproaching, easily upset, and worried.

At first glance it might appear that only high scores on this scale are clinically significant. But, this is the third of four 16PF "superego" factors identified by Karson and O'Dell (1976). They suggest that a very low Factor O score raises questions about the adequacy of behavior controls. Extremely low-scoring individuals often present themselves as too confident, even self-satisfied or smug. As such, they are not likely to be bound by convention or societal standards.

Factor Q_1: Radicalism

People who score high on this dimension tend to be analytic, liberal, and innovative, although somewhat critical and rebellious. They trust logic rather than feelings and prefer to break with established ways of doing things. Low-scoring people describe themselves as conservative and traditional.

Studies of small-group interaction (Cattell & Stice, 1954) showed that high-scoring individuals were very frequently identified as the most effective problem solvers in the group. However, they were not necessarily the best-liked group leaders.

Factor Q_2: Self-sufficiency

People who score high on this scale prefer to be alone. They usually avoid mixing with others, except when necessary. Low-scoring people, on the other hand, are group oriented. They enjoy the company of others and work well in team situations.

High-scoring individuals do not appear to need a great deal of group support. They say they prefer to work alone. Extremely high scores on Factor Q_2 are not sufficient evidence of an underlying problem. However, in the presence of other deviations (e.g., low scores on A (Warmth) and F (Impulsivity) and high scores on O (Insecurity) and Q_4 (Tension), there may be indications of pathological withdrawal from other people.

Factor Q_3: Self-discipline

Factor Q_3 can be thought of as the "odd couple" scale. People who score high on this dimension describe themselves as controlled and compulsive. They have a strong self-image. Low-scoring people lack discipline and appear to have a flexible self-concept.

Karson and O'Dell (1976) speak of this dimension as the ability to bind anxiety. In fact, high-scoring individuals generally have strong control over their emotional life and behavior. At the extreme upper levels, there is some suggestion that individuals may become excessively compulsive and difficult to be around. Cattell (1987, p. 83) describes high Factor Q_3 persons as having "regard for [their] self-concept and self-esteem in preserving [their] social reputation."

Factor Q_3 is a major contributor to anxiety. Low scores, which indicate the individual's inability to keep his or her emotions in order, are, of course, diagnostically important. But, Karson and O'Dell (1976) note that when extremely high scores on Factor Q_3 combine with elevations on Factors O (Insecurity) and Q_4 (Tension), there is a tendency to excessive compulsivity, resulting in obsessional types of behavior.

Factor Q_4: Tension

High-scoring people are tense and frustrated. They become upset easily and take a long time to calm down when they lose control. Low-scoring people are more relaxed and easy-going.

This is one of the principal anxiety indicators in the 16PF profile and a major medical-risk factor. As Cattell and others have pointed out, there is evidence to suggest that higher scores are associated with a history of frustration.

High-scoring individuals report that they take a long time to calm down when they are upset. They are irritated by small things. They have difficulty sleeping and get angry with people too quickly. Karson and O'Dell (1976) point out that high scores on Q_4 are always important. Because it is so easy to deny all of the symptoms covered in the items for this scale, high scores signal an unmistakable "cry for help."

The Validity Scales

In addition to the primary scales just described, the 16PF provides several indexes of test-taking attitude. Form A contains three scales: Faking Good, Faking Bad, and Random. These validity scales provide important information and should routinely be evaluated.

The validity scales differ from the primary scales in the way they were constructed. The Faking Good and Faking Bad scales were developed by the method of contrasted groups rather than by factor analysis. Individuals were instructed to respond to the questionnaire under role playing conditions. Their answers were then compared with unfaked protocols in order to identify items that reliably shifted when faking occurred. The random scale is keyed to responses that are very infrequently endorsed under normal test-taking conditions.

Conceptually, the Faking Good scale involves the same processes that lead to high scores on both the MMPI L and K scales. High-scoring individuals say many positive things about themselves and deny unflattering behavior. However, most item content is rather subtle (e.g., "I have a good sense of direction") and only a few of the items are transparent ("I never make smart, sarcastic remarks to people even if I think they deserve it").

The most common situation in which the Faking Bad scale seems to elevate occurs when underlying symptomology is present. As such, it can be regarded as an indicator of distress. Less frequently, the distortion may be deliberate—perhaps to support a disability claim for compensation purposes. Psychometrically, the faking bad scale is unusually skewed. About 1 in 5 people fail to endorse *any* of the keyed items. More than half only endorse 2 of the 15 possibilities.

The Random Scale was constructed in the same way as the MMPI F scale. The selection criterion for items was infrequent endorsement in a normal population. High scores on the Random scale can mean that the individual was careless or hurried through the testing. But, just as elevated F scales on the MMPI can occur in valid profiles, elevated Random scores may suggest the presence of severe disturbance accompanied by elevated anxiety and impaired cognitive functioning.

A Strategy for Interpreting 16PF Profiles

Establish the Validity of the Protocol. The first step is to check the completed answer sheet for missing and/or multiple responses. In Form A, the answers to items 1, 2, and 187 should be reviewed. They ask whether the respondent understands the instructions, is ready to answer each item truthfully, and skipped or answered items improperly. If the answers to these questions are "no," something may be wrong. An unpublished analysis of 10,091 answer sheets sent in to IPAT for scoring found that the percentage of "no" endorsements was 4.2% for item 1 and 3.7% for item 2. With regard to item 187 ("I am sure there are no questions that I have skipped or failed to answer properly") 12.5% said no, but 16.9% had no missing items. By simple subtraction, almost 1 in 20 people may feel they have "failed to answer properly" one or more of the questions in the questionnaire. This is certainly something that should be explored.

For reasons given earlier, it is also worthwhile to count the number of "b" responses selected. Too many will result in a flat profile. As a guideline, the average number of "b" responses selected in the sample of 10,091 profiles was 40. If there are 70 or more middle responses, placing the respondent in the top 90th percentile, the protocol is suspect.

Next, check the validity scales. Three are provided in Form A. If any of these scales is significantly elevated (i.e., a sten score of 8 or above), question the resulting profile.

Review the Second Order Scales. To get an overall impression of the profile, look at the Extroversion, Anxiety, Tough Poise, Independence, and Control scales. These are known as second-order scales in Cattell's system. The first four, in particular, have been carefully studied and described in *Interpreting 16PF Profile Patterns* (Krug, 1981). This book describes a system for profile coding and provides normative distributions of the 81 code types by gender, psychiatric status, and occupational grouping. The types were formed by clustering 17,381 profiles on the basis of their elevation on the first four second-order scales. In addition, the narrative interpretation for each code type can be used to generate hypotheses for further exploration.

Identify Salient Primary Scales. Start with scales that deviate most from the population mean of 5.5. These represent characteristics on which the examinee is most distinctive and help "flesh out" the general picture provided by the second-order scales.

Because 16PF scales are bipolar, both high and low scores should be interpreted. High scores are defined as sten scores of 8 and 10. Low scores include stens of 1, 2, and 3. More than half of 16PF profiles will have 4 or more scores that fall in this range (Krug, 1981). Scores that fall in the average range are the most difficult to interpret and for that reason are often ignored in practice.

Review Other Secondary Scales. Depending on the application, it may be appropriate to calculate additional scores, such as leadership, creativity, accident proneness, etc. (see Cattell, et al., 1970; IPAT Staff, 1986). From an information theory point of view, these scales are "redundant." That is, none of these scales adds to what we already know about the individual from the primary scales. However, the reliability of these scales is usually much higher than that of the primary scales. They also provide useful alternative ways of looking at the 16PF profile.

CASE EXAMPLE

The principles of 16PF interpretation outlined above are concretely illustrated in the following case study of Mary, a 17-year-old high school senior. Mary's parents divorced when she was 12, and she continued to live with her mother and younger sister. Her father was a very successful physician living in a Western state who taught and conducted research at a University. Mary's mother came from an established, aristocratic family. Mary's mother was very critical and aloof, and her relationship with Mary was strained. The children occasionally became pawns in disputes between the parents.

Mary did well academically in school, although she had occasional problems getting along with authority figures. Mary was referred for assessment to determine whether further counseling was necessary, to help her decide whether to attend college upon graduation, and which academic majors she might consider.

Figure 4.1 shows Mary's profile. A check of the validity scales suggests that there is no reason to suspect distortion. That is, the Faking Good, Faking Bad, and Random scales are within the normal range.

In terms of the overall profile, Mary described herself as being below average in Control, average in Extroversion and Anxiety, above average in Tough Poise, and extremely high in Independence. According to Krug (1981), Mary's profile (which shows the 2233 code pattern) is a common one. The interpretation of the 2233 pattern suggests emotional detachment, a strong need for autonomy and control, aggressiveness, and hostility.

In looking at the primary scales, 8 of the 16 fall outside the normal range and are of immediate interest. Starting with the most deviant scales, Mary scored at

```
   ___________________________________________________________________
   |...A...B...C...E...F...G...H...I...L...M...N...O..Q1..Q2..Q3..Q4...|
10 |       *       *           *                       *               | 10
 9 |                                                                   | 9
 8 |                                                               *   | 8
 7 |---------------------------------------*---------------*-----------| 7
 6 |                   *                                               | 6
 5 |           *           *       *   *                               | 5
 4 |-----------------------------------------------*-------------------| 4
 3 |   *                                                       *       | 3
 2 |                                                                   | 2
 1 |                                           *                       | 1
   |___________________________________________________________________|
       A...B...C...E...F...G...H...I...L...M...N...O..Q1..Q2..Q3..Q4
```

Description	Range
A...Warmth	low
B...Intelligence	high
C...Emotional Stability	average
E...Dominance	high
F...Impulsivity	average
G...Conformity	average
H...Boldness	high
I...Sensitivity	average
L...Suspiciousness	average
M...Imagination	average
N...Shrewdness	low
O...Insecurity	average
Q1..Radicalism	high
Q2..Self-sufficiency	average
Q3..Compulsivity	low
Q4..Tension	high

Faking Good	3.0
Faking Bad	5.0
Random	0.0
Extroversion	6.0
Anxiety	5.7
Tough Poise	7.2
Independence	10.0
Control	3.9

FIG. 4.1. 16PF Case Study Profile

the maximum on Intelligence (Factor B), Assertiveness (Factor E), and Boldness (Factor H). This combination suggests aggressiveness and an overbearing nature. The maximum score on Radicalism (Factor Q_1) coupled with the aggressiveness is further suggestive of hostility. The low Shrewdness (Factor N) and somewhat low Self-Discipline (Factor Q_3) indicate a strong tendency to demonstrate her aggressiveness and hostility, oftentimes without much forethought. Mary is somewhat reserved (low on Factor A) and this may be indicative of a long history of unsatisfactory interpersonal relationships (Karson & O'Dell, 1976). Finally, a relatively high Tension score (Factor Q_4), suggests that she is under pressure and is having trouble calming down. Although this is an important Anxiety component, it is the only component that is above average.

Mary's 16PF profile characterizes her as overbearing, aggressive, and hostile. She appears to be quick to criticize and shows little patience with those who do not pick things up as quickly as she does. It was suggested that supportive counseling would help Mary learn alternative strategies in working and interacting with others.

Although tests like the 16PF are useful for organizing information about clients, occasionally a client will view the information as sterile, artificial, and not immediately relevant (Schuerger & Watterson, 1977). Consequently, the first step to working with the client is to describe the test results in meaningful ways. Especially helpful is trying to relate test results to the client's behaviors that illustrate a particular test score or constellation of scores.

In looking at Mary's profile, the constellation of traits E (Dominance), H (Boldness), N (low Shrewdness), and Q_1 (Radicalism) raise significant concern. Following an overall interpretation of the profile with Mary, we would begin by linking these particular scales above to Mary's everyday behavior.[2] For example, we would be interested in learning how she interacts with teachers, friends, and her mother and sister. We know that Mary's mother is openly critical of her and speculate that this may be the source of her low Warmth and elevated Self-Sufficiency. In working with Mary, we would need to explore what her expectations and goals from counseling would be. Assuming that they include improving interpersonal relationships, we would help her develop strategies to monitor and refocus these behavioral tendencies.

With regard to helping her with vocational choice and exploration, the available evidence suggests that further educational training is viable and the likelihood for success is high. With regard to choosing an academic major, the prediction from the 16PF profile is that she would be better suited to careers that value analytic thought and have a fairly loose structure. Although she describes herself as neither extroverted nor introverted, Mary's profile suggests that she would be better off in an occupation that did not depend on team work, unless

[2]We did not continue beyond the assessment stage with Mary. Consequently, we can only describe the process we would use in working further with her.

she is working with highly capable colleagues. She is not likely to easily accommodate those whom she regards as incompetent.

As a postscript, it has been more than two years since Mary was assessed. She chose to attend the university where her father teaches and is majoring in the Language Arts. She is very successful in her classwork, with an "A" average. She has competed for and won a scholarship to study in Europe. Her relationship with her father improved. However, there has been very little change in her relationship with her mother.

RECENT RESEARCH WITH THE 16PF

Much of the pre-1970 16PF research literature has been summarized in the *16PF Handbook* (Cattell, et al., 1970). Post-1970 research bibliographies are found in the *16PF Research Bibliography* (Hussong, Sherman, & Ferris, 1977) and the *Administrator's Manual to the 16PF* (IPAT Staff, 1986). A recent review that focuses on rehabilitation populations can be found in Krug (1986a). Since the early 1950s, the 16PF has been used in job selection and placement. For that reason, a large literature has accumulated regarding personality correlates of occupational preference, job performance, and worker satisfaction.

More recently, research has focused on personality differences by academic majors, occupational types, and interests (Bolton, 1985a; Johns, 1985; Johns & Wardrop, 1987; Walter, 1985). Some of the consistent findings from this research include the following results. Extroversion and its components (Warmth, Impulsivity, Boldness, and low Self-sufficiency) consistently differentiate those in high person-contact occupations from those occupations that offer limited opportunities for interaction. Using Holland's (1985) taxonomy, individuals in the Social and Enterprising occupations, such as sales, score high on Dominance and Boldness. Members of Conventional occupations, such as bookkeeping, are orderly, persistent, and conscientious (Factors G and Q_3).

Counselors are increasingly being sought for outplacement assessment and counseling, as organizations reduce their labor force. McLoughlin, Friedson, and Murray (1983) studied a sample of recently terminated executives. Compared to adult norms, they were found to be more secure and confident (Factor O), more conscientious (Factor G), more assertive (Factor E), and more self-sufficient (Factor Q_2). This pattern suggests that the terminated executives may not have been good "team players" given their self-described confidence, rigidity, and independence.

Comparing occupational groups among each other is a common research strategy used with the 16PF. For example, Larkin (1983) studied differences among systems engineers, data processing managers, and computer sales representatives. She found systems engineers scored highest on the Intelligence (B) scale, whereas the sales group scored highest on the extroversion components.

Interestingly, all groups scored about equally on Dominance (E), low Suspiciousness (L), Conformity (G), and Radicalism (Q_1).

A large body of empirical data describes the 16PF's relationship with various performance criteria, such as absenteeism, tenure, safety, and job performance. Ferris and Bergin (1984) found that Anxiety was related to absenteeism within a sample of school teachers. This replicates Bernardin's (1977) findings. In addition, Bernardin found that Conscientiousness (Factor G) was negatively related to absenteeism and turnover in a sample of telephone sales consultants.

Another extensive area of research has been substance abuse and its treatment. In a meta-analysis of 60 research articles that investigated addiction (alcohol, drugs, and cigarettes), Tuite and Luiten (1986) found a consistent personality pattern across several demographic variables. In particular, they found addicts to be anxious (low on Emotional Stability, Boldness, and Self-Discipline, and high on Suspiciousness, Insecurity, and Tension), low on control (low Conscientiousness and Self-Discipline), and high on Sensitivity (Factor I), Imagination (Factor M), Shrewdness (Factor N), and Radicalism (Factor Q_1).

Characteristics of battered women have been described as well (Hartik, 1977; Mahon, 1981; Star, 1978). The most salient characteristic across three samples totaling 120 battered women was low Emotional Stability. In addition, these women described themselves as low on Warmth, Impulsivity, and Self-Discipline and high on Insecurity, Self-Sufficiency, and Tension.

Increasing attention is being placed on abusing parents (Engfer & Schneewind, 1982; Hyman, 1977; Hyman & Mitchell, 1975). Although the profiles of abusing parents suggest that they may be described as maladjusted, sex differences appear to be prominent. Noteworthy features describe the women as anxious and undisciplined (low Emotional Stability and Self-Discipline and high Suspiciousness and Tension) and the men as serious and independent (low Impulsivity and high Self-Sufficiency).

In marital counseling, early research focused on adjustment and compatibility (e.g., Barton & Cattell, 1972; Cattell & Nesselroade, 1967). More recent research has looked at more specialized aspects of adjustment. For example, Bhagat (1976) has looked into the personality differences among suicide attempters and their spouses. He found that female suicide attempters resembled their husbands in being anxious and maladjusted. However, significant differences between male suicide attempters and their wives were found, with the wives describing themselves as shrewd, emotionally detached, practical, and self-sufficient.

The literature relating 16PF scales to physical health is substantial. A large portion of it is described in Krug (1977). Recent research is highly diffuse, though much of it has concentrated on cardiovascular disease and stress (e.g., Duckitt & Broll, 1983; Krug & Johns, 1986; Lawrence, 1984). The scales relating most highly to various disease states are the components forming the

Anxiety scale (low Emotional Stability, low Boldness, Suspiciousness, Insecurity, low Self-Discipline, and Tension). The review by Sherman and Krug (1977) also implicates Sensitivity (Factor I: related to the incidence of coronary heart disease), low Impulsivity (Factor F: related to the incidence of coronary heart disease, tuberculosis, and diabetes), Self-Sufficiency (Factor Q_2: related to the incidence of coronary heart disease, hypertension, tuberculosis, and peptic ulcers), and low Dominance (Factor E: related to the incidence of coronary heart disease, hypertension, tuberculosis and asthma).

The Adult Personality Inventory

One of the most important recent developments in the 16PF assessment tradition was the appearance of the Adult Personality Inventory (API) (Krug, 1984), which has been described as a modern version of the 16PF (Bolton, 1985b; Hilgert, 1987; Meier, 1986).

The test consists of 324 items that were written to measure the same primary trait dimensions included by Cattell in the 16PF. The selection of items began by factor analyzing the items currently contained in all published forms of the 16PF designed for use with unselected populations. Items that were found to have the strongest loadings on the first principal axis factor within each set were presumed to describe content most central to the definition of each factor.

On the basis of these results new items were written. The criteria for item construction were as follows. *Content:* Item content was based on what had been empirically shown to be the strongest themes in each factor item pool. *Clarity:* Items were to be specific and unambiguous. *Brevity:* Items were kept as short as possible in order to increase the number of items in the final form, and consequently, the reliability of the test, without increasing testing time.

In addition, a standardized set of response options was introduced ("Generally True," "Uncertain," "Generally False"). Items for Factor B (Intelligence) were separated from the personality items rather than being interspersed as they are in the 16PF. The total number of such items was significantly increased to 30, with 10 sampled from each of the following three domains, verbal ability, numeric ability, and verbal reasoning.

Non-overlapping keys were developed for the Faking Good and Faking Bad scales, which were renamed Good Impression and Bad Impression. An Infrequency scale was developed by keying responses which very few people endorsed under normal testing conditions. However, a high score could be obtained by someone racing through the questions or someone who approached the test with a very unusual perspective or "set."

In one rather significant departure from the existing 16PF, the "uncertain" response option was not longer considered in the calculation of substantive scores. Empirical research had shown that endorsement of this category appeared to increase the reliability and validity of clinical test scales. But, it appeared to have an undesirable effect on the psychometric characteristics of scales designed to measure normal-range personality characteristics (McFadden & Krug, 1984).

The most dramatic departure from the existing 16PF was in the design of the test profile. Although the API is scored for the same elementary scales as the 16PF, these are transformed to a new set of scores in the final test profile. The primary API profile consists of a set of seven personal characteristic scales, eight interpersonal styles, and six career preference factors. The reason for this was to attempt to organize the information conveyed by the 16PF along lines that related more directly to user concerns and presenting questions.

In some ways this development parallels those with respect to the Strong-Campbell Interest Inventory. When it first appeared as the Strong Vocational Interest Blank, the test consisted only of a set of empirically constructed occupational scales. Much later, Clark's (1961) rationale for content homogeneous scales led to the development of a set of 22 "basic interest" scales (Campbell, 1969). Still later, the profile was further expanded by the inclusion of a set of six theory-based general "occupational theme" scales (Campbell & Holland, 1972).

In a further attempt to make the API even more considerate of user needs, a microcomputer software system was developed that administers, scores, and generates narrative reports of test results automatically. The system, called TEST PLUS, also incorporates a unique feature that helps the test user focus and plan testing objectives prior to the actual assessment (Krug, 1985).

Through a series of forced-choice comparisons, TEST PLUS helps the user define assessment objectives. From the user's answers, the system creates a "target model" (Wiggins, 1973) or ideal profile that represents a hypothetical test profile of the individual most likely to succeed in the specified situation. Then, for each individual who takes the test, the ideal profile is plotted next to the individual's profile thereby allowing for direct comparisons between the two.

This process introduces a new facet in the application of expert systems to psychological testing and serves several purposes. First, it tells the user how relevant the API is to a particular assessment objective. If all the scores in the ideal profile fall within the average range, one conclusion is that other characteristics may be more useful to explore than those measured by the API. Second, it helps the user *plan* the assessment. Few people would undertake any business activity without some sort of management plan. Why test without having thought through the process first? Third, since it is unlikely that any individual will exactly match the target, the discrepancies between the ideal and obtained score profile can serve an important function by identifying areas for growth and change.

Because there were so many changes and improvements, the name of the test was finally changed to the API in order to avoid confusion with earlier versions of the 16PF. But, like other tests in the 16PF system that were adapted for use with special populations or special assessment needs, the API retains links with the original 16PF and the underlying personality model on which the 16PF is based. During its standardization, API scales were made statistically equivalent to corresponding 16PF scales in order to maintain continuity between the two instruments.

EVALUATION AND FUTURE DIRECTIONS

In assessing the strengths of the 16PF, we first stress its nonpathological orientation. The test assesses normal characteristics and individuals' behavior in typical kinds of situations. For this reason, the information it conveys is applicable to a broad range of decisions. In counseling, the 16PF may be helpful in clarifying personal preferences that relate to career choice and occupational satisfaction. The 16PF profile has also been found to be helpful in understanding interpersonal dynamics related to marital adjustment (Russell & Madsen, 1985).

A second, major strength of the 16PF lies in the extensive body of research findings that have accumulated with respect to the primary scales. Several thousand published articles and books have provided a rich data base that is equaled by very few instruments. Cattell's own researches have provided a detailed analysis of how the characteristics measured by the test change and develop throughout the life span (Cattell, 1973). Additional studies have explored the relative strength of genetic and environmental factors in shaping and molding the personality factors measured by the 16PF (Cattell, 1982).

But, perhaps the greatest strength of the 16PF lies in the multivariate personality model that underlies the test and, indeed, all of Cattell's work. The test items have been selected primarily on the basis of their relationship to a set of unchanging theoretical constructs, which have been successively refined in a series of empirical studies carried out over three decades (Cattell & Krug, 1986). Because item selection was not initially based on criteria that would be expected to alter appreciably as a function of differences in validation samples, it has been possible to update and improve the test several times since its initial publication. Information obtained with one form or edition of the test can be systematically related to information obtained with subsequent forms and editions, providing the necessary steps are taken. This interchangeability feature has been a significant factor in the accumulation of such an extensive data base.

On the negative side, the 16PF is a challenging instrument with which to work. Much of Cattell's extensive research was directed toward theoretical and psychometric concerns. He paid less attention to practical issues of profile analysis or clinical interpretation. It was not until the 1970s, nearly 30 years after the test was first published that the 16PF began to be used on a very broad scale in applied personality work. This was due principally to the publication in 1976 of Karson and O'Dell's *Guide to the Clinical Use of the 16PF* and, later, to the appearance of *Interpreting 16PF Profile Patterns* (Krug, 1981).

By itself, the 16PF is weak in assessing major affective and cognitive disturbances. Although experienced interpreters of the profile have identified certain score patterns suggestive of depression (Karson & O'Dell, 1976, such a diagnosis from the 16PF alone is usually difficult or impossible to make for the vast majority of test users.

The Future

In some ways, much of the future of the 16PF has already been written, in no small part due to the extraordinary vision and effort of its principal author. In the quarter century he actively worked with the 16PF, it underwent continual development and restandardization. It also became the focus of numerous theoretical and applied research activities.

During this same period Cattell created the first of the derivative instruments that uniquely characterized his systems approach to personality assessment. That is, he did not attempt to accommodate all contingencies simply by stretching the existing item pool. Instead he used the 16PF as a starting point for new instruments that were specifically tailored to particular age ranges or testing needs. This approach involved greater effort and investment. Each new instrument required independent validation and standardization. But the plan appears to have been responsive to the needs of test users. With just one exception, the Contact Personality Factor Questionnaire, all have remained on the market since they were first published.

Given the growth patterns evident in psychological testing and Cattell's withdrawal from test development activity in 1973, it seems probable that the future of the 16PF is most likely to be reflected in two of its "offspring," the Clinical Analysis Questionnaire (CAQ) and the Adult Personality Inventory (API). The CAQ significantly broadened the range of application of the 16PF by including scales to assess affective and cognitive disturbances, two areas of personality assessment in which the earlier 16PF was deficient. The API, on the other hand, anticipated the enormous growth of computerized testing (Krug, 1984; 1987a; 1988a; 1988b) and the need for instruments compatible with this new technology. Its short items, simplified format, and decision model feature make it especially adapted to the new era of "solid state psychology" (Bolton, 1985b; Hilgert, 1987; Krug, 1986b; Meier, 1986; Mercadal, 1987).

Cattell retired from active involvement with the 16PF nearly two decades ago to pursue the theoretical integration of his extensive research (Cattell, 1979; 1980; 1982; 1983; 1987). However, he left a legacy and tradition that is still evolving today, a tradition that is rich in empirical data and psychometric sophistication. The underlying personality model of the 16PF is applicable to a broad range of socially relevant criteria and practical personality assessment issues.

REFERENCES

Allport, G. W., & Odbert, H. S. (1936). Trait-names, a psycho-lexical study. *Psychological Monographs, 47.*

Barton, K., & Cattell, R. B. (1972). Personality factors related to job promotion and turnover. *Journal of Counseling Psychology, 19,* 430–435.

Bernardin, H. J. (1977). The relationship of personality variables to organizational withdrawal. *Personnel Psychology, 30,* 17–27.

Bhagat, M. (1976). The spouses of attempted suicides: A personality study. *British Journal of Psychiatry, 128,* 44–46.

Bolton, B. (1977). Evidence for the 16PF primary and secondary factors. *Multivariate Experimental Clinical Research, 3,* 1–15.

Bolton, B. (1985a). Discriminant analysis of Holland's occupational types using the 16PF. *Journal of Vocational Behavior, 27,* 210–217.

Bolton, B. (1985b). Review of the adult personality inventory. In J. V. Mitchell, Jr. (Ed.), *The ninth mental measurements yearbook* (pp. 55–56). Lincoln, NE: Buros Institute.

Burdsal, C., & Bolton, B. (1979). An item factoring of 16PF-E: Further evidence concerning Cattell's normal personality sphere. *Journal of General Psychology, 100,* 103–109.

Calsyn, D. A. (1979). *Non-pathological personality characteristics of low back pain patients.* Doctoral dissertation, University of Washington.

Campbell, D. P. (1969). The vocational interests of Dartmouth College freshmen: 1947–67. *Personnel and Guidance Journal, 47,* 527–530.

Campbell, D. P., & Holland, J. L. (1972). A merger in vocational interest research: Applying Holland's theory to Strong's data. *Journal of Vocational Behavior, 2,* 353–376.

Cattell, R. B. (1943). The description of personality: Basic traits resolved into clusters. *Journal of Abnormal and Social Psychology, 38,* 476–506.

Cattell, R. B. (1950). *Personality, a systematic theoretical and factual study.* New York: McGraw-Hill.

Cattell, R. B. (1957). *Personality and motivation structure and measurement.* Yonkers-on-Hudson: World Book.

Cattell, R. B. (1973). *Personality and mood by questionnaire.* San Francisco: Jossey-Bass.

Cattell, R. B. (1979). *Personality and learning theory: Volume 1 the structure of personality in its environment.* New York: Springer.

Cattell, R. B. (1980). *Personality and learning theory: Volume 2 a systems theory of maturation and structured learning.* New York: Springer.

Cattell, R. B. (1982). *The inheritance of personality and ability: Research methods and findings.* New York: Academic Press.

Cattell, R. B. (1983). *Structured personality-learning theory: A wholistic multivariate research approach.* New York: Praeger.

Cattell, R. B. (1987). *Psychotherapy by structured learning theory.* New York: Springer.

Cattell, R. B., Cattell, M. D., & Johns, E. F. (1984). *Manual and norms for the High School Personality Questionnaire.* Champaign, IL: IPAT.

Cattell, R. B., Eber, H. W., & Tatsuoka, M. M. (1970). *Handbook for the Sixteen Personality Factor Questionnaire (16PF).* Champaign, IL: IPAT.

Cattell, R. B., & Krug, S. E. (1986). The number of factors in the 16PF: A review of the evidence with special emphasis on methodological problems. *Educational and Psychological Measurement, 46,* 509–522.

Cattell, R. B., & Nesselroade, J. R. (1967). Likeness and completeness theories examined by Sixteen Personality Factor measures on stably and unstably married couples. *Journal of Personality and Social Psychology, 7,* 351–361.

Cattell, R. B., & Stice, G. F. (1954). *The dimensions of groups and their relations to the behavior of members.* Champaign, IL: IPAT.

Clark, K. E. (1961). *Vocational interests of non-professional men.* Minneapolis: University of Minnesota Press.

Coan, R. W., & Cattell, R. B. (1976). *Manual for the Early School Personality Questionnaire.* Champaign, IL: IPAT.

Duckitt, J. H., & Broll, T. (1983). Life stress, personality and illness behavior: A prospective study. *Psychological Reports, 53,* 51–57.

Engfer, A., & Schneewind, K. A. (1982). Causes and consequences of harsh parental punishment: An empirical investigation in a representative sample of 570 German families. *Child Abuse & Neglect, 6,* 129–139.

Ferris, G. R., & Bergin, T. G. (1984). *Personal characteristics, job performance, and absenteeism.* Paper presented at the Annual Meeting, American Psychological Association, Toronto.

Goldberg, L. R. (1981). Unconfounding situational attributions from uncertain, neutral, and ambiguous ones: A psychometric analysis of descriptions of oneself and various types of others. *Journal of Personality and Social Psychology, 41,* 517–552.

Guilford, J. P. (1975). Factors and factors of personality. *Psychological Bulletin, 82,* 802–814.

Guilford, J. P., & Guilford, R. B. (1983). An analysis of the factors present in a typical test of introversion-extroversion. *Journal of Abnormal and Social Psychology, 28,* 377–399.

Guilford, J. P., & Guilford, R. B. (1936). Personality factors S, E, and M and their measurement. *Journal of Psychology, 2,* 109–127.

Hartik, L. M. (1977). *Identification of personality characteristics and self-concept factors of battered wives.* Doctoral dissertation, United States International University.

Hilgert, L. D. (1987). Review of TEST PLUS. *Social Science Microcomputer Review, 5,* 95–97.

Holland, J. L. (1985). *Making vocational choices: A theory of vocational personalities & work environments (2nd ed.).* Englewood Cliffs, NJ: Prentice-Hall.

Hughey, J., & Burdsal, C. (1982). 16PF-E structure using radial parcels versus items. *Journal of General Psychology, 107,* 107–119.

Hussong, M. A., Sherman, J. L., & Ferris, G. R. (1977). *16PF research bibliography: 1971-1976.* Champaign, IL: IPAT.

Hyman, C. A. (1977). A report on the psychological test results of battering parents. *British Journal of Social and Clinical Psychology, 16,* 221–224.

Hyman, C., & Mitchell, R. (1975). A psychological study of child battering. *Health Visitor, 48,* 294–296.

IPAT Staff. (1986). *Administrator's manual for the 16PF.* Champaign, IL: IPAT.

Johns, E. F. (1985). *Holland's occupational taxonomy in terms of personality traits and discriminant functions.* Master's thesis, Cleveland State University.

Johns, E. F., & Wardrop, J. L. (1987). *Using the 16PF for occupational classification within Holland's taxonomy.* Paper presented at the 95th Annual Convention of the American Psychological Association, New York.

Kaiser, H. F. (1970). A second generation Little Jiffy. *Psychometrika, 35,* 401–415.

Karson, S., & O'Dell, J. W. (1976). *A guide to the clinical use of the 16PF.* Champaign, IL: IPAT.

Krug, S. E. (Ed.). (1977). *Psychological assessment in medicine.* Champaign, IL: IPAT.

Krug, S. E. (1980). *Clinical Analysis Questionnaire manual.* Champaign, IL: IPAT.

Krug, S. E. (1981). *Interpreting 16PF profile patterns.* Champaign, IL: IPAT.

Krug, S. E. (1984). *The Adult Personality Inventory manual.* Champaign, IL: IPAT.

Krug, S. E. (1985). *TEST PLUS: A microcomputer based system for the Adult Personality Inventory.* Champaign, IL: MetriTech.

Krug, S. E. (1986a). Self-report measures of personality. In B. Bolton (Ed.), *Handbook of measurement and evaluation in rehabilitation (2nd ed.)* (pp. 91–104). Baltimore: Paul H. Brookes.

Krug, S. E. (1986b). Solid state psychology: The role of the computer in human assessment. In R. B. Cattell & R. C. Johnson (Eds.), *Functional psychological testing: Principles and instruments*. New York: Brunner/Mazel.

Krug, S. E. (1987a). Microtrends: An orientation to computerized assessment. In J. N. Butcher (Ed.), *Computerized psychological assessment: A practitioner's guide* (pp. 14–25). New York: Basic Books.

Krug, S. E. (1987b). *Psychware sourcebook: 1987–1988*. Kansas City, MO: Test Corporation of America.

Krug, S. E. (1988a). *Psychware sourcebook: 1988–1989*. Kansas City, MO: Test Corporation of America.

Krug, S. E. (1988b). Computerized testing in industry. In J. W. Jones, B. D. Steffy, & S. W. Bray (Eds.), *Applying psychology in business: The manager's handbook*. Lexington, MA: Lexington.

Krug, S. E., & Johns, E. F. (1986). A large scale cross-validation of second-order personality structure defined by the 16PF. *Psychological Reports, 59*, 683–693.

Krug, S. E., & Laughlin, J. E. (1977). Second-order factors among normal and pathological primary personality traits. *Journal of Consulting Psychology, 45*, 575–582.

Krug, S. E., Scheier, I. H., & Cattell, R. B. (1976). *Handbook for the IPAT Anxiety Scale*. Champaign, IL: IPAT.

Krug, S. E., & Sherman, J. L. (1977). Psychological trait analysis in preventive medicine. *Journal of the International Academy of Preventive Medicine, 4*, 48–56.

Larkin, J. E. (1983). The psychology of DP professionals: A career planning tool. *Computerworld*, February 21, XVII, 8.

Lawrence, R. A. (1984). Police stress and personality factors: A conceptual model. *Journal of Criminal Justice, 12*, 247–263.

Mahon, L. (1981). *Common characteristics of abused women*. Unpublished Master's thesis, Arizona State University.

Marshall, J. W., & Wasman, B. D. (1959). An empirical study of the relationship between certain personality dimensions and the incidence of accidental injuries. *Connecticut Health Bulletin, 73*, 11.

McClain, E. W. (1968). Sixteen Personality Factor Questionnaire scores and success in counseling. *Journal of Counseling Psychology, 15*, 492–496.

McFadden, L. S., & Krug, S. E. (1984). Psychometric function of the "neutral" response in clinical personality scales. *Multivariate Experimental Clinical Research, 7*, 25–33.

McLoughlin, C. S., Friedson, W. S., & Murray, J. N. (1983). Personality profiles of recently terminated executives. *The Personnel and Guidance Journal, 62*, 226–229.

Meeland, T. (1953). *An investigation of hypothesis for distinguishing personality factors A, F, and H*. Doctoral dissertation, University of Illinois.

Meier, S. T. (1986). Review of TEST PLUS. *Computers in Psychiatry/Psychology, 8*, 21–22.

Mercadal, D. (1987). Review of TEST PLUS. *Psychologists' Software Club Newsletter*, November, 2–3.

Meyer, R. G. (1983). *The clinician's handbook: The psychopathology of adulthood and late adolescence*. Boston: Allyn and Bacon.

Porter, R. B., & Cattell, R. B. (1975). *Handbook for the Children's Personality Questionnaire*. Champaign, IL: IPAT.

Russell, M. T., & Madsen, D. H. (1985). *Marriage Counseling Report manual*. Champaign, IL: IPAT.

Schuerger, J. M., & Watterson, D. G. (1977). *Using tests and other information in counseling*. Champaign, IL: IPAT.

Shafqat, L. A. (1983). Translation of the 16PF into American Sign Language: A rationale. *Proceedings of the 3rd International Conference on the 16PF*. Champaign, IL: IPAT.

Sherman, J. L., & Krug, S. E. (1977). Personality-somatic interactions: The research evidence. In S. E. Krug (Ed.), *Psychological assessment in medicine* (pp. 63–113). Champaign, IL: IPAT.

Star, B. (1978). Comparing battered and non-battered women. *Victimology: An International Journal, 3,* 32–44.

Suhr, V. W. (1953). The Cattell 16PF as a prognosticator of accident susceptibility. *Proceedings of the Iowa Academy of Science, 60,* 558–561.

Tuite, D. R., & Luiten, J. W. (1986). 16PF research into addiction: Meta-analysis and extension. *The International Journal of the Addictions, 21,* 287–323.

Walter, V. (1985). *Personal Career Development Profile manual.* Champaign, IL: IPAT.

Werner, P. D., & Pervin, L. A. (1986). The content of personality inventory items. *Journal of Personality & Social Psychology, 51,* 622–628.

Wiggins, J. S. (1973). *Personality and prediction: Principles of personality assessment.* Reading, MA: Addison-Wesley.

Woodworth, R. S. (1917). *Personal data sheet.* Chicago: Stoelting.

5 The Myers-Briggs Type Indicator in Counseling

Mary H. McCaulley, Ph.D.
Center for Applications of Psychological Type, Inc.

BACKGROUND OF THE MYERS-BRIGGS TYPE INDICATOR

The Myers-Briggs Type Indicator (MBTI) falls into the family of personality assessment instruments based on a specific psychological theory. The theory behind the MBTI is C. G. Jung's theory of psychological types (Jung, 1921/1971), that part of Jung's overall theory which is specifically concerned with the way people consciously use their minds. MBTI users apply Jung's powerful framework for looking at individual differences in many ways. Some use Jung's type theory mainly with groups to develop teamwork, to improve communications, and to show that differences are understandable and valuable. Counselors use the dynamics of type development with individuals for self-understanding of lifelong changes; others use Jung's type theory in even greater depth as part of a Jungian analytical approach, which includes consideration of archetypes, the collective unconscious, animus, anima, the persona, and the road to individuation. Counseling uses are the focus of this chapter.

The MBTI was developed by Isabel Briggs Myers and her mother Katharine Cook Briggs. Katharine Briggs became interested in personality differences when her daughter, Isabel, brought home her future husband, Clarence Myers, to meet the family. She described him later as "an admirable young man, unlike anyone in our family before." As a way of understanding her son-in-law, Mrs. Briggs went to the Library of Congress and read biographies. From her analyses she created her own typology. After Jung's *Psychological Types* was published in English in 1923, she recognized the match between Jung's observations and her own independently-developed types. As her daughter Isabel describes it in her book *Gifts Differing* (Myers with Myers, 1980, p. 23), Briggs' "meditative type" was consistent with Jung's "introverts"; her "spontaneous type" corresponded with Jung's "perceptive extraverts"; her "executive type" corresponded with Jung's "extraverted thinking types"; and her "sociable type" corresponded with Jung's "extraverted feeling" types. Katharine Briggs studied Jung's *Psychological Types* intensively, and introduced the concepts to Isabel Myers. Together, mother and daughter became type watchers for two decades, testing Jung's observations against their experiences of their family and friends. This incubation period was an important first step to creating the MBTI. An insight into Isabel Myers' character comes from her own words about the impetus for her long journey in developing and researching the MBTI.

> In the darkest days of World War II, when the Germans were rolling irresistibly along, and my shoulders ached with trying to hold them back, and a horrible sinking feeling lived in the pit of my stomach, the thought came to me one day (I was making my bed at the time) that by letting them spoil my life that way I was helping them win, bringing destruction to pass by my own doing. So I stopped, just like that. I made up my mind that there was no logical justification for turning possible future unhappiness into certain present unhappiness by being afraid of it. Do what you can to make a better world, but don't throw away one day or one minute of the world you've got. What I did, as it turned out, was the Type Indicator. (I. B. Myers, personal communication, December 21, 1970)

The long process of creating the MBTI by solving a series of technical difficulties to be faithful to the theory, is described in the MBTI *Manual* (Myers & McCaulley, 1985). Myers and Briggs began by creating forced-choice questions that were intended to let people indicate the effects of Jungian preferences in everyday life. Almost at once they discovered type differences in the way people interpreted the question choices. As a result, each choice is presented in the frame of reference of the types for whom it is intended. In this way, questions became a "stimulus to evoke a type response." They understood that type theory was complex and sophisticated; the questions were not intended to tap the theory directly, but to be straws in the wind, showing which way the wind blows.

Working alone at home, with only family financial support, Isabel Myers painstakingly constructed a series of versions of the MBTI. She collected data on more than 9,000 high school students, 5,000 medical students, and 10,000 nursing students, handscoring the answer sheets. She obtained and analyzed data on aptitude and achievement for all three samples, and specialty choice for the medical students. Information about this early research can be found in the *Manual,* and in McCaulley (1977, 1978).

In 1962 Educational Testing Service (ETS) published a *Manual* (Myers, 1962). In preparation, ETS psychologists added the MBTI to other measures in the College Student Characteristics Study, and these data were included in the *Manual.* ETS published the MBTI strictly as a research instrument. Purchasers were required to specify their research plans, and to return answer sheets to the author on request. During the ETS period, a Japanese psychologist discovered the MBTI; the Indicator was translated into Japanese by the Nippon Recruit Center in Tokyo where it is still used for career planning (Ohsawa, 1975; 1979). During this period, Donald MacKinnon at the University of California at Berkeley began including early versions of the MBTI in the creativity studies of the Institute for Personality Assessment and Research (IPAR).

By 1975 MBTI research had reached the point where the current publisher, Consulting Psychologists Press (CPP), published it for professional applications. In that same year, Isabel Myers and Mary McCaulley established the nonprofit Center for Applications of Psychological Type (CAPT) for research, scoring, training and other professional services related to the MBTI. Four years later, in 1979, the Association for Psychological Type (APT) was formed for persons interested in psychological type.

In 1975, the MBTI was relatively unknown. In a little over a decade, use of the Indicator has grown exponentially to the point where it will soon be the most widely-used psychological tool for "normal people." Counselors use it with individuals, groups, couples, and families; for children, young people, and adults; for teaching individual development, for career counseling, and for communications training. Educators use the Indicator with teachers and students to work with type differences in teaching styles, learning styles, academic achievement and motivation, dropout, and college roommate matching. Organizations in business, industry, and government use the MBTI to deal with type differences in communication, teamwork, management styles, and lifelong career planning. In the religious community, the MBTI is used to value type differences in spiritual development and ministry. The MBTI has been or is being translated into languages in every continent and is used worldwide.

In 1980, the year of her death, Isabel Myers' book for the public and for the professional was published. *Gifts Differing* describes Jung's theory, each of the types, and distills a life-time of reflection on type and early learning, learning styles, occupations, marriage, and type development.

CONCEPTUAL FOUNDATIONS OF THE MBTI

What is there about type theory and the MBTI that led to such rapid growth in so many fields where psychological tests are seldom used? In Isabel Myers' words (Myers & McCaulley, 1985, p. 1):

> The essence of the theory is that much seemingly random variation in behavior is actually quite orderly and consistent, being due to basic differences in the way individuals prefer to use their perception and judgment.

Perception involves all the ways of becoming aware of things, people, happenings, or ideas. Judgment involves all the ways of coming to conclusions about what has been perceived. If people differ systematically in what they perceive and in how they reach conclusions, then it is only reasonable for them to differ correspondingly in their reactions, interests, values, motivations, skills, and interests.

Because almost every waking act involves perceiving or decision-making, type differences touch all aspects of life.

Overview of Jung's Theory of Psychological Type

The MBTI cannot be understood without also understanding Jung's type theory.

The MBTI Was Designed to Reflect Jung's Theory

The MBTI is not a "test" in the meaning of a measure of better or worse, right or wrong. It simply lets a person "indicate" preferences between equally valuable opposites described in Jung's theory. The MBTI scales indicate the four bipolar, theoretically dichotomous, preferences.

Extraversion (E) or Introversion (I). Attitude toward the outer or inner worlds.

Sensing Perception (S) or Intuitive Perception (N). The balance between perceiving the present realities or envisioning future possibilities.

Thinking Judgment (T) or Feeling Judgment (F). The balance between reaching judgments through impersonal logic or personal values.

Perception (P) or Judgment (J). The balance between taking in information or drawing conclusions.

Each Indicator question forces choices between the poles of a preference. The 16 types are denoted by the letters for the preferred pole (e.g., ISTJ, ENFP, ESFJ, etc.). To describe a group, the types are arranged in a conventional order known as the "type table", such that every type shares three preferences in common with each neighboring type. Characteristics of groupings of the type are described in the *Manual* (pp. 31–38).

Type is Concerned with the Balance of Opposites

As in other aspects of Jung's theory, the tensions and striving for balance between opposites create the dynamic interplay which leads to growth.

Everyone Uses All Preferences, but Not Equally

Both poles of the four preferences are valuable and necessary. Everyone uses E, I, S, N, T, F, J and P daily. Types sharing letters share those qualities in common. However, in each of the 16 types, the pattern of interests and skills associated with one preference is modified by the other three preferences. For example, the extraverted attitude appears differently in ESTJ (a tough-minded executive type) and in ESFJ (a helpful, sociable type.)

The Functions: Building Blocks of Type

The functions, or mental processes described by Jung and the MBTI, are Sensing (S), Intuition (N), Thinking (T), and Feeling (F). In the theory, conscious mental activity falls into one of these four categories. Sensing and Intuition refer to two different kinds of *perception;* thinking and feeling refer to two different kinds of *judgment.*

Sensing perception (*S*) refers to perceptions of the senses, and brings to awareness what is occurring in the present moment. Development of differentiated skills of sensing is expected to lead to characteristics such as realism, acute powers of observation, memory for details, practical common sense, and the ability to enjoy the present moment. Correlations of sensing scores with constructs from other personality instruments reported in the *Manual* (pp. 207, 212) include: practical outlook, economic interests, conventional, natural, favors conservative values, uncomfortable with complexity, contented. In careers, sensing scores correlate with scores for banker, management, skilled and unskilled trades, clerks, accounting, and any other fields requiring close attention to detail. An *Atlas of Type Tables* (Macdaid, McCaulley, & Kainz, 1987) provides data on type distributions in normative samples and careers.

Intuitive perception (*N*) refers to the perception that sees the intangible by way of insight—future possibilities, associations, meanings, symbolic relationships. Jung described intuition as "perception by way of the unconscious." For example, when a person uses sensing to describe a peanut, words are likely to be "crisp," "rough," "shiny on the inside," "two symmetrical nuts." When a person uses intuition to describe the same peanut, you may hear "peanut butter," "take me out to the ball game," "elephants," or "George Washington Carver." Significant correlations between the N scale and other instruments reported in the *Manual* (pp. 207, 212) include: complexity, academic interests, individualistic, artistic, theoretical, creative, foresighted, resourceful. Occupations significantly correlated with intuition are psychologist, artist, physicist, chemist, reporter, foreign language teacher—all fields requiring skills in dealing with abstractions and patterns of symbols.

Because it is intuition that sees new possibilities and patterns, it is not surprising that creative samples show a large majority of intuitive types (*Manual*, pp. 74, 75).

Thinking judgment (*T*) is the rational process that reaches conclusions through an impersonal process of logic or cause and effect. Differentiation of thinking is, in theory, expected to be associated with objectivity, analytical ability, critical judgment, and concern with justice and fairness. Significant correlations between T and other instruments include masculine orientation, theoretical, distrust. Thinking types significantly choose occupations requiring skills with the inanimate, logical, or mathematical, including engineering, business, sciences, and technical fields.

Feeling judgment (*F*) is the rational process that reaches conclusions by weighing values and the merits of people, things, and ideas. Feeling judges subjectively; thinking, objectively. Differentiation of feeling is, in theory, expected to be associated with appreciation, empathy, desire for harmony, and an understanding of and concern for other people. The distinction in psychology between "tough-minded" and "tender-minded" relates to TF differences. Correlations associated with MBTI feeling scores include nurturance, affiliation, altruism, tender-minded, social, and religious values. Examples of occupations of interest to feeling types include social service, religious activities, teaching, and health care.

The Attitudes: Orientations to the World

Jung described the attitudes of *extraversion* (outward-turning) and *introversion* (inward-turning) as directions of energy flow. Extraversion-introversion describes universal aspects of personality. Most other researchers who have tried to describe human personality comprehensively have measured—or discovered—extraversion and introversion. The MBTI includes a scale for measuring extraversion-introversion (EI).

Extraversion (*E*) describes the attitude in which energy flows out or is drawn out to the environment. The world around us provides stimulation, and we wish to interact with the people and things around us. The characteristics expected to result from preferring the extraverted attitude include sociability, action-orientation, impulsivity, and ease of communication. The largest significant correlations between the MBTI EI scale and other instruments are the extraversion-introversion scales of those instruments, generally in the range of .69 to .79. MBTI extraversion also correlates significantly with scales of sociability, dominance, leadership, expressed inclusion, expressed affection, exhibitionism, and being venturesome. Extraverts tend to be attracted to occupations that have action, outdoors or travel, and contact with people.

Introversion (*I*), in Jung's theory, is an important normal variant of human personality. When a person introverts, energy is drawn from the environment and is directed inward to the world of concepts and ideas. People who habitually take the introverted attitude develop the characteristics associated with introversion: interest in the clarity of concepts and ideas, reliance more on enduring concepts than on transitory external events, a thoughtful, contemplative detachment, and enjoyment of privacy. Correlations showing association with MBTI introversion include self-sufficient introspective, reserved. Occupations that attract introverts tend toward working alone, one-to-one contacts, longer attention span, and work with ideas. Introverts are in the majority among computer programmers, engineers, statisticians, librarians, accountants, or anesthesiologists.

Extraversion-introversion is an important dimension in the therapeutic relationship. Extraverts appear to be the valued majority, so that introverts often report feeling different. They are, in fact, a minority group. In many correlations with personality measures, extraversion is associated with positive qualities—ego strength and emotional stability, personal integration, and self-esteem. Introversion is more likely to be associated on other scales with negative qualities—anxiety, guilt, and neuroticism. Some of this difference comes from the extravert's greater comfort with the environment, but some of the negative descriptions of introverts can stem from a lack of appreciation of the strengths of introversion.

The outward-turning extraverts can lead them to look more to others and less to themselves as the cause of their problems. Counselors often see extraverts who are astonished to find they are themselves important actors in their own drama, not simply respondents to external forces. The inward-turning introverts are likely to blame themselves for all their difficulties. Counselors often see introverts who are amazed at the counselor's suggestion that perhaps others might also be at fault in their problems. For extraverts, a majority in our society, the counselor will try to distinguish the deserved confidence of well-developed extraverts from the over-confidence of the less mature extraverts. For introverts, counselors must distinguish the introspection, anxieties, and need for solitude of healthy introverts from the chronic anxiety and despair of introverts in psychological pain. In any case, it is useful to keep in mind that many personality tests, as well as the larger society, describe extraversion as if it were a more positive attribute than introversion.

Judgment (*J*) and *Perception* (*P*) refer to the orientation to the outer (extraverted) world. The JP scale indicates whether extraverted behaviors are more likely to reflect the perceptive functions (S or N) or the judging functions (T or F). JP is used in two ways in the MBTI. First, it identifies observable behaviors important in their own right. Second, JP helps identify the dynamic pattern for each type by pointing to the dominant and auxiliary functions.

In any new situation it is important to take the *perceptive* attitude—seeing everything, and being curious and interested. At some point, one has seen enough (P) and is ready to reach a judgment (J). Characteristics in scales of other instruments associated with perception are complexity, flexibility, autonomy, change-as-challenge, and happy-go-lucky. Measures associated with judgment include self-control, stronger superego, rule-bound, dependability. Many personality scales describe J characteristics more positively than P characteristics. For example, P scores are positively correlated with scales named impulsivity, rebellious, procrastinating, changeable, and restless. J-types occur in greater numbers than P-types in the general population, and J-types are clearly in the majority in samples of managers in business, government, and education. The term "judgment" is often associated in clients' minds with "judgmental." The MBTI use of the word "judgment" is closer to the meaning when one speaks of exercising good judgment; in MBTI terms, being "judgmental" or "closed-minded" comes from use of judgment without the balance of perception.

Nature and Nurture

Both Jung and Myers believed that nature determined the basis of type, and nurture was important in influencing its development. However, environment is important, because families and cultures can disconfirm natural preferences and lead to a "falsification" of type. Jung commented that falsification can lead to an adult neurosis and counseling may be needed in adulthood to help find the lost path.

Preferences are Dichotomous

The opposite poles of the preference are seen as dichotomies. Preferring one pole over the other is like taking one fork in a road rather than the other. One develops *qualitatively* different interests, motivations, and eventually behaviors and skills. Sometimes MBTI data are displayed *as if* there were an underlying continuum, for convenience in research. The most misunderstood (and debated) aspect of the MBTI is the assumption of bipolarity or that preferences are dichotomous.

Dynamic Interaction of the Preferences

Type theory predicts a life-long developmental pattern for each type. This dynamic pattern for each type predicts the order in which E, I, S, N, T, F, J and P develop to produce the characteristics of the 16 types.

The assumptions for these dynamic patterns are stated briefly below. Some are familiar as they are part of other theories; some are specific to type theory. Counselors working with the MBTI use type theory to understand the reasons for the characteristics of each type, and, more importantly, to plan treatment that builds on the strengths of the type.

The Dominant and Auxiliary Functions. Type theory assumes everyone uses sensing, intuition, thinking, and feeling, but that one of these will be the leading or first function (called the *dominant*) and a second will assist (called the *auxiliary*). The dominant function provides consistency of general direction in life. In normal development, the dominant is the most differentiated function; interests, motivations and skills come from its use.

The personality needs balance; the second or *auxiliary function* develops to provide balance in two ways. The dominant and auxiliary appear in different attitudes—one provides adaptation to the outer world (E) and the other to the inner world (I). The dominant and auxiliary also provide balance between perception and judgment. If the dominant is a perceptive function (S or N) the auxiliary will provide judgment (T or F) (or vice versa). The well-developed type will, therefore, be able to deal comfortably with outer and inner events, and will develop skills to take in information and make decisions.

The Less-Developed Functions. The third and fourth functions are assumed to be necessary but less developed. The opposite of the dominant function is called the fourth or *inferior* function; it is assumed to be nearest to the unconscious, a powerful source for growth. Because the inferior is the least developed, it is also the source of vulnerability. Table 5.1 shows the relationship of the four functions for each of the 16 MBTI types.

TABLE 5.1.
Priorities and Directions of Functions in Each Type

ISTJ	ISFJ	INFJ	INTJ
#1 DOMINANT S (I)	#1 DOMINANT S (I)	#1 DOMINANT N (I)	#1 DOMINANT N (I)
#2 AUXILIARY T (E)	#2 AUXILIARY F (E)	#2 AUXILIARY F (E)	#2 AUXILIARY T (E)
#3 TERTIARY F (E)	#3 TERTIARY T (E)	#3 TERTIARY T (E)	#3 TERTIARY F (E)
#4 inferior N (E)	#4 inferior N (E)	#4 inferior S (E)	#4 inferior S (E)
ISTP	**ISFP**	**INFP**	**INTP**
#1 DOMINANT T (I)	#1 DOMINANT F (I)	#1 DOMINANT F (I)	#1 DOMINANT T (I)
#2 AUXILIARY S (E)	#2 AUXILIARY S (E)	#2 AUXILIARY N (E)	#2 AUXILIARY N (E)
#3 TERTIARY N (E)	#3 TERTIARY N (E)	#3 TERTIARY S (E)	#3 TERTIARY S (E)
#4 inferior F (E)	#4 inferior T (E)	#4 inferior T (E)	#4 inferior F (E)
ESTP	**ESFP**	**ENFP**	**ENTP**
#1 DOMINANT S (E)	#1 DOMINANT S (E)	#1 DOMINANT N (E)	#1 DOMINANT N (E)
#2 AUXILIARY T (I)	#2 AUXILIARY F (I)	#2 AUXILIARY F (I)	#2 AUXILIARY T (I)
#3 TERTIARY F (I)	#3 TERTIARY T (I)	#3 TERTIARY T (I)	#3 TERTIARY F (I)
#4 inferior N (I)	#4 inferior N (I)	#4 inferior S (I)	#4 inferior S (I)
ESTJ	**ESFJ**	**ENFJ**	**ENTJ**
#1 DOMINANT T (E)	#1 DOMINANT F (E)	#1 DOMINANT F (E)	#1 DOMINANT T (E)
#2 AUXILIARY S (I)	#2 AUXILIARY S (I)	#2 AUXILIARY N (I)	#2 AUXILIARY N (I)
#3 TERTIARY N (I)	#3 TERTIARY N (I)	#3 TERTIARY S (I)	#3 TERTIARY S (I)
#4 inferior F (I)	#4 inferior T (I)	#4 inferior T (I)	#4 inferior F (I)

Note: From *Manual. A guide to the development and use of the Myers-Briggs Type Indicator* (p.18) by I. B. Myers and M. H. McCaulley (1985). Palo Alto, CA: Consulting Psychologists Press. Copyright 1985 by P. B. Myers and K. D. Myers. Reprinted by permission.

Building on Strengths

Counseling strategies build on the strengths of the first and second functions. The third and fourth functions are touched on gently at first. They can often be developed in the service of the goals of the favored functions. For example, the INTP type describes an introvert with thinking as dominant, intuition as auxiliary, and feeling as the inferior function. The counselor would not push an INTP early in counseling to describe feeling; at first, the strengths of the dominant thinking would be used to identify unrecognized feelings. "If you found yourself trembling, it is logical to assume you might be angry." The counselor would be alert for challenges to the dominant (T) and auxiliary (N) which require good use of the third (S) and fourth (F) functions. The case of Thomas Brown later in this chapter shows how a challenge to the dominant and auxiliary led to development of the third and fourth functions.

Deficiencies Can Result from Focus on Strengths

When members of any type are developing and focusing on the activities of the dominant process, they cannot *at the same moment* focus on and develop the opposite. Students who have focused on immediate details with dominant sensing can have blindspots about the broad implications or future possibilities of those details. Others whose dominant intuition is differentiated in seeing broad new possibilities and symbolic interrelationships may miss facts which are obvious to a sensing type. Dominant thinking types may discount even their own feeling values, and dominant feeling types may not see the beauty and power of logic. It is easier to accept, and remedy the deficiencies of the third and fourth functions when these deficiencies are seen as the natural consequence having spent more energy on the first and second functions.

Type Development as a Lifelong Process

Type development is a lifelong process. Youth is the time of specialization by developing the dominant and auxiliary functions. Mid-life gives the opportunity to develop the third and fourth functions. The journey toward wholeness seeks individuation—loyalty to one's own type preferences, with an increasing ability to move from one preference to another with ease and skill as the situation demands. (In Jung's larger theory, individuation includes also the assimilation of the contents of the collective unconscious into consciousness and divesting the self of the false wrappings of the persona.)

Electing to Use the MBTI in Counseling

Isabel Myers originally developed the Indicator as a tool for career counseling; it has many other counseling uses. Counselors, educators, and others in organization development use the MBTI to:

increase self-understanding;
understand changes at different stages of life;
improve communications in families and groups;
give a new framework for interpreting diagnostic tests.
speed the establishment of rapport;
show students how to manage their own learning;
help students gain access to the richness of campus life.

When used appropriately, the MBTI helps foster an appreciation of one's own individuality and gifts and a greater understanding of others. Differences are valued and used constructively rather than destructively. When the MBTI is included in a diagnostic battery, type theory can provide an additional framework for interpreting other tests and for putting symptoms in perspective.

TEST ADMINISTRATION AND SCORING

MBTI Materials

The standard form of the MBTI is the 126-item Form G.

A research Form F includes 166 questions, those scored for type plus research questions designed to individualize MBTI reports. Form F is being phased out by the 290-question Form J, which includes all Form F and G questions plus all type-related and research questions used by Isabel Myers during the development of the MBTI. Form J will be the basis for a number of individualized reports, available to clinicians through computer-scoring. The first of these are the Type Differentiation Indicator and the Expanded Analysis Report.

All items are in forced-choice format to permit choices between the desirable opposites in each preferences. Choices are always in the same preference (E or I; S or N; but never E or N; T or J). There are two item types—phrase-questions and word-pairs. Phrase-questions present a stem followed by two choices (''Does following a schedule (a) appeal to you, or (b) cramp you?''). Word pairs simply present two words with the instructions, ''Which word in each pair appeals to you more?'' Phrase questions may reflect more of everyday life and pressures; word-pairs may reflect a truer preference.

Administration

The MBTI is essentially self-administering. Instructions appear on the question booklets and on the answer sheets. Procedures for individuals and groups follow standard professional and ethical practice. For poor readers or sight-impaired persons, the questions can be read aloud; readers must be careful to be even-handed lest they make the responses favored by their own type sound more attractive.

Scoring

The MBTI is scored for four indices—EI, SN, TF, and JP. Each answer to each item is weighted O, 1, or 2; weights take into account the popularity of the item, social desirability, omissions, and sex differences. (*Manual* pp. 146–150). The first step in scoring is to sum the weights for each pole of each preference. These 8 raw score totals are called *points*. Letters are assigned for the pole with the highest number of points. (Example: 15 points for E and 9 points for I would indicate a preference for Extraversion.) A linear formula transforms the points to a *preference score* which takes into account the difference and direction of the two poles, and allows for breaking ties. The 4 preference scores are the important MBTI scores; each consists of a letter and a number (e.g., E 11, T 29, etc.); the greater the difference in points between one pole and the other, the higher the preference score.

MBTI theory assumes a dichotomy for each preference; thus, data are displayed on either side of a midpoint as E 19 on one side or I 19 on the other. For research purposes, the convention is to treat the dichotomies *as if* there were an underlying continuum; the midpoint is set at 100 and scores are subtracted from 100 for preferences E, S, T, or J; preferences are added to 100 for preferences I, N, F, and P. Thus a preference score of E 19 would appear as 81, and a preference score of I 19 as 119. When MBTI continuous scores are correlated with scale scores from other instruments, negative correlations indicate an association between the other measures and E, S, T or J; positive correlations indicate a correlation between the other measures and MBTI I, N, F, or P. Examples of MBTI scores appear in the case studies later in this chapter.

Form G and Form F optical-scanning answer sheets can be scored by computer or using templates. Form G is also available in a self-scoring version. Hand-scoring is accomplished with 5 hand-scoring templates—one each for EI, SN, TF male, TF female, and JP. (During construction of the MBTI, all item analyses examined weights for males and females separately; the TF scale is the only one where item weights require separate male and female keys.) Instructions on the templates show how to transform raw scores (*points*) into *preference scores*. Computer reports (see case studies) provide a number of subscores and interpretive information. Reports for showing hand-scored results are also available.

MBTI Normative Data

The purpose of the MBTI is to indicate types; that is, the four letters. The most useful normative data, therefore, concern the question, "How frequent is my type?" If an INFJ and an ESFJ each tell the counselor "I feel as if I have no kindred spirits," the counselor will interpret the two comments very differently. INFJ is in fact a relatively rare type, whereas ESFJ is the most frequent type among females. The *Manual* (pp. 46–51) provides data on distributions of the types for males and females by age levels, and education levels. Means and standard deviations of each preference by age groups are reported in Appendix C (pp. 239–41). The *Myers-Briggs Type Indicator Atlas of Type Tables* (Macdaid et al., 1987) provides extensive data on normative samples and occupations.

MBTI INTERPRETATION

Initial Explanation

The first important task for the counselor is to help clients discover their best-fit preferences and best-fit type. The *Manual* chapters on Initial Interpretation and Verification (pp. 52–62) and Uses of Type in Counseling (pp. 63–73) describe this process. It is not always possible to identify the best-fit type in one session; sometimes one or more preferences may be in doubt at first. Because a counselor using the MBTI in type development will be helping clients find their unique paths to excellence in their own preferences, it is important to understand what those preferences are. If earlier life has caused true preferences to go underground and be falsified, the counselor would not want to increase falsification. In many cases, the client's reactions to the type description give little doubt about the accuracy of the report. An extreme example was a client who said with astonishment, "I feel as if it X-rayed my soul!" Often there are doubts and questions. These should be taken seriously, especially when the client is being tested during an emotional upheaval or life crisis. As one client described a change in her type report, "My world had fallen in, and ISFJ was my hanging-on-by-my-fingernails type. I wasn't a very good ISFJ, but I was living one day at a time and trying to get my life under control. Now that I'm back on my feet, I came out the spontaneous ENFP where I belong." The *Manual* talks about strategies for resolving these issues.

MBTI reports are very unlike clinical reports written for a professional to integrate with other test data. Myers assumed clients would be told their types and would be taught to use type concepts. The primary resource is *Introduction to Type* (Myers, 1987), a 32-page booklet, available at a reasonable cost. Written for persons who answer the Indicator, it describes the preferences, the dominant and auxiliary, and Isabel Myers' descriptions of each of the 16 types in everyday language. The booklet also briefly describes applications in communications, relationships, career choice, in work situations, and in problem-solving.

When MBTI results are introduced to individuals or groups, the explainer usually creates a blank profile, describes each preference and lets the respondent "Guess how you came out." The client writes down the preferred letter, and may plot the estimated strength of preference on the profile. Sometimes, the "Effects of Each Preference in Work Situations" from *Introduction to Type* are checked off and discussed. The report from the MBTI is then produced. The counselor is careful to say, "You *came out* an ENFP" never "You *are* an ENFP." The type description is read carefully "to see if it fits." If the client earlier guessed another type, the description for that type in *Introduction to Type* is read and compared with the MBTI description.

The MBTI *Manual* describes assumptions about type that are shared with the client and other specific details of the process of explaining type to individuals or groups.

During the initial and later sessions, counselors use type theory in many ways. For example:

> You said when you answered the MBTI that having a constant challenge is important to you (N).
>
> When you made that decision, were you following your head (T) or your heart (F)? Can you tell which gave you better advice?
>
> We agree that you have been really successful with past jobs where your knowledge of details (S) made you a star. This new assignment is uncomfortable—it calls on you to use your imagination and look at the "big picture" (N). You haven't suddenly become incompetent—you are simply moving into an area you haven't developed yet.
>
> In our culture, women are socialized toward feeling—concern with other people, tact, sympathy. It sounds as if you have always thrived on logical analysis and being a tough-minded skeptic (T). Your thinking skills serve you well in being a successful engineer. Your mother taught you the social skills, and you can "turn them on" when you have to. Can you stop feeling guilty that when you use F it seems mechanical to you, and when you use T you "come alive"? That's your way, and its legitimate, even if it is not the way of the majority of women.

MBTI Counseling Used in Different Settings

The MBTI is interpreted at many different levels. Sometimes, the main goal is simply to establish the fact that people indeed are different in predictable ways, and that these differences are interesting and valuable. Sometimes the feedback focuses on a specific use—learning styles, teaching styles, or career choices.

A useful strategy with groups is to put people in "type-alike" groups with instructions to discuss their type descriptions. Groups report their consensus of characteristics others need to know to understand their type. Group leaders often give type-related exercises *before* the members of a group receive their MBTI reports. After group members have received their reports, they see the reasons for their differences in the exercises.

When the MBTI is used with couples, they may be asked to answer for themselves, and then answer as if they were their partner. The counselor faces a very different situation when the couple is different and knows it, from the case when a couple is different but each partner sees the other as like oneself. In couples or families, interpretations focus on communications and type differences in behavior, with the goal of creating a climate with respect for and constructive use of differences. Psychotherapists also use the MBTI as an integral framework for reconstructive therapy. Discussions of these issues from practicing counselors can be found in Jones and Sherman (1979), Newman (1979) and Provost (1984) whose *Casebook* describes cases in each of the 16 types. Quenk (1984) covers issues for psychotherapists.

Counselors often find it useful to share their own type preferences with a client. For example, "You prefer to use sensing, and you have learned to be realistic and practical. I prefer to use intuition; my head keeps popping up with new ideas. You are feeling stuck right now. I'm going to let my intuition pop up with new ideas, and then you can let your sensing see if any of them is practical." Here the counselor is teaching "the constructive use of differences" and demonstrating the use of a function that comes less readily to the client.

Cautions

The MBTI can be seen as deceptively simple. Type descriptions can seem like horoscopes. Type theory is powerful, but of course it is not infallible. The counselor needs to be alert for the danger that the client puts too much weight on the type and type description. This danger is greater with the MBTI than with other instruments where a shift of T-scores from 49 to 55 does not have the significance that a shift of letters from E 7 to I 7 may have.

It is easy also for the client, and the counselor, to assume that a clear preference necessarily means high skill. It is logical to assume that if people are clear about preferences, they will be more likely to follow them and develop the skills that go with the exercise of those preferences. This logical sequence often occurs, but there can be many events—lack of opportunity, competing pressures, lack of basic ability—which can cause a discrepancy between preferences and acquisition of the abilities of those preferences.

The MBTI is a self-report instrument. Like any self-report instrument, validity is increased if the respondent is motivated to answer honestly. Because the MBTI is administered in so many nonclinical settings, the counselor must be especially aware of environmental pressures that interfere with true responses. Especially in organizational settings where respondents are not sure what use will be made of the information, there is a strong motivation to answer "as I think 'they' want me to."

As with any other psychological testing, results should be treated with great caution when the MBTI is answered by persons in severe distress. It is useful sometimes to see if the client can answer "as you are feeling today" and "as you used to feel when you were well." We have found it useful in family conferences in an inpatient setting to engage the family in the early stage of guessing type, before the MBTI reports are given. Insights from the discussion about whether the patient is acting as an introvert now, or has always been an introvert, have opened new communications.

CASE EXAMPLES

A major use of the MBTI in counseling is as a tool to conceptualize the problem and the client–counselor interaction. The four cases that follow show how the counselor uses different strategies and focuses on different aspects of the problem, as a function of the client's type.

A basic strategy when using type in counseling is the familiar "build on strengths to overcome weaknesses." In the context of type, this means:

Assess the development of the dominant and auxiliary functions.

Consider the likelihood that the auxiliary is not providing sufficient balance.

Consider whether the third and fourth functions are available.

Use the motivation of the dominant and auxiliary to develop the third and fourth functions.

If the problem seems to reside in the inferior or fourth function, do not attack the problem head on; the inferior function is the source of the greatest vulnerability, as well as holding the potential for positive change. Von Franz (1971) has discussed these issues in some detail.

Consider issues such as the frequency of the type, the types of others in the environment, whether life history has encouraged falsification of type, and whether there is a match or mismatch between the type and current occupation.

For students, consider the relationship between type and intelligence; note especially unexpected failures or unexpected successes—the "IN academic type" who is failing or not interested in learning or the "easygoing" ESP type who is persisting in studies and meeting all commitments on time.

Be aware of the communication style of the client's type, including pacing, words, use of symbolism and metaphors, and the amount of interaction or quiet for contemplation needed to establish rapport.

Consider the counselor's own type, values and blindspots, and especially communication styles, in the therapeutic interaction. An example may make this point clearer. A dominant thinking type and a dominant feeling type were discussing their attitudes toward family therapy. The feeling type therapist said, "It is so rewarding to bring harmony after strife, but even after all these years, when they yell and scream at each other, my stomach knots up." The thinking type therapist replied, "Not for me. I am so interested in analyzing what remark set off what reaction that I don't react to the screaming at all."

In short, type provides a rich tapestry of hypotheses and expectations to be tested in the therapeutic encounter.

Case A. Thomas Brown (INTP)

Thomas Brown was a 25-year-old brilliant medical student in the second half of his third year in medical school. He was doing very well in a combined M.D.–Ph.D. program, and thoroughly enjoyed his dissertation research. What brought him to the counselor was a very low rating in clinical care during his rotation on obstetrics. He was criticized for his care of a 16-year-old who was expecting her first child within two weeks and was frightened that she would die; he had focused on the need for better contraception to prevent future pregnancies. With another patient, he missed essential facts in the family history because, as she later told the nurse, "he seemed so cold I didn't want to talk to him." Worse, he was frustrated by patients who would not follow his orders, when it was clearly logical that they needed to stay on their diets and take prescribed medication.

Thomas had taken the MBTI with others of his class and knew the counselor from feedback to the group. The MBTI results came out INTP (an introvert with dominant thinking, intuition as auxiliary, and feeling as the inferior function). Table 5.2 shows the first page of the report for Thomas, and Table 5.3 shows the detailed scoring information provided to the counselor. Refer back to section on test scoring as a reminder about points, preference scores, and continuous scores.

INTP is one of the types most attracted to science. His high science and academic grades were expected–the IN types have the greatest intrinsic interest in learning for its own sake. Up to now, Thomas had been succeeding in the world of his strengths–ideas (I), theory and abstractions (N), and logical analysis (T). These matters had consumed his interest, and he found social life dull except when he could talk shop with colleagues. Now, he was confronted with a situation calling on his neglected extraversion (comfort with interpersonal interactions) and feeling (warmth, harmony, and interpersonal understanding). He somewhat reluctantly admitted that he liked to help patients for the intellectual challenge of "solving the case" (NT), but that he didn't seem to get so personally involved (F) as his classmates. As he explored his attitudes toward patients and his concern at his lack of competence in the clinical area, he began to see that he had major blindspots in the human relations area. The counselor commented that this was not infrequently a problem for an INTP, and there was a logical reason for it. Up until now, he had been developing his introversion, thinking, and intuition, which was natural at his stage in life. He hadn't been pressed to develop his extraversion and feeling; they were less important for academic

TABLE 5.2.
Myers-Briggs Type Indicator Report

			*

This report was prepared for
CASE A THOMAS BROWN

Here is the report of the Myers-Briggs Type Indicator (MBTI) which you answered on November 7th, 1984. The MBTI indicates sixteen types of people. Your answers to the MBTI questions came out the type called **Introverted Thinking with Intuition**, also known by the letters **INTP**.

The author of the MBTI, Isabel Briggs Myers, wrote sixteen descriptions of the types at their best; the end of each report describes problems which persons of that type may have when not at their best. This page of your report describes type INTP. Page 2 and 3 give reasons why the sixteen types are different from one another, and tell more about your answers. Some people prefer to read their description first; others prefer to read the reasons first. Whichever way you prefer, be sure to read all three pages to see your full report.

INTP
Introverted Thinking with Intuition

INTP people look for principles that explain outcomes. They rely on thinking to develop these principles. As a result, they become logical, analytical, impersonal, objectively critical, and are not apt to be convinced except by reasoning.

Being introverts, they use their thinking to find the principles underlying whatever they become aware of. They can become so absorbed with an idea that they persevere with it, without depending on external circumstances. They organize ideas and knowledge; they usually do not organize situations or people, unless they must for the sake of their work. In the field of ideas they are decisive and sure. Socially they may be rather shy except with close friends.

INTP's are quiet, reserved, detachedly curious, and quite adaptable so long as their ruling principles are not violated. Then they stop adapting. Their main interest lies in seeing possibilities beyond what is present or obvious or known. Their intuition heightens their quickness of understanding, insight, ingenuity, intellectual curiosity, and their fertility of ideas about problems.

Depending on their interests, **INTP**'s are good at pure science, research, mathematics, or the more complex kinds of engineering; they may become scholars, teachers, or abstract thinkers in fields such as economics, philosophy or psychology. They are more interested in the challenge of reaching solutions to problems than of seeing the solutions put to practical use.

A special problem for **INTP**'s is to make themselves understandable. They want to state the exact truth, but often make it so complicated that few can follow them. If they will scale their points down until they seem too simple to be worth saying, their ideas will be more widely understood and accepted.

INTP's need to check out even their most attractive intuitive ideas against the facts and the limitations the facts impose. They need to be rigorous in checking *all* the facts; they can easily neglect those facts which don't support their idea. Unless **INTP**'s develop their perception, they are in danger of gaining too little knowledge and experience of the world. Then their thinking is done in a vacuum and nothing will come of their ideas.

INTP's may rely so much on the logical approach of thinking that they overlook what other people care about and what they themselves care about. They may decide that something they value is not important, just because it isn't logical to care about it. **IF INTP**'s always let their thinking suppress their feeling values, their feeling will not develop and be manageable. If feeling values are ignored too much, they may build up pressure and explode in most inappropriate ways. Feeling contributes to good personal relationships by stressing that it *does* matter how the other person feels. Small things make a great difference--a word of appreciation where honestly due, or mention of the extent of agreement before any disagreement is spoken. Thinking types are naturally critical and it is harder for them to express appreciation than it is for other types. But if they try, they can develop appreciation and will find it helpful on the job as well as in personal relationships.

TABLE 5.3.
Myers-Briggs Type Indicator Detailed Scoring Information

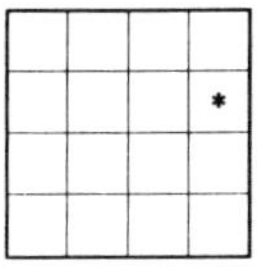

Professional report for
Dr. Mary McCaulley

MBTI results for
CASE A THOMAS BROWN

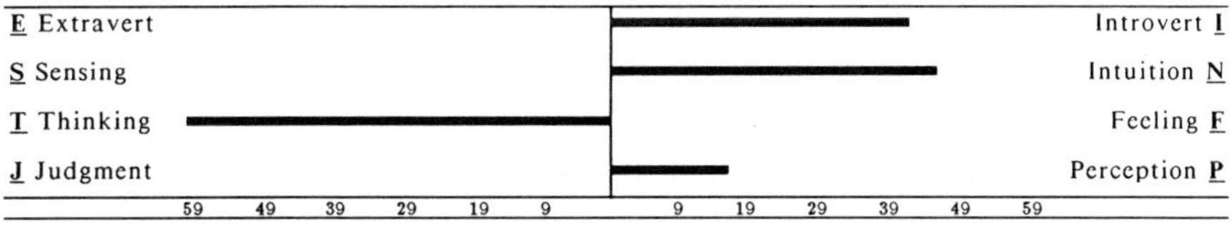

INTP - Introverted Thinking with Intuition

FULL SCALE RESULTS (*Parts I,II and III of the MBTI*)

		E I Direction of Energy	S N Perception Function	T F Judgment Function	J P Extraverted Attitude
INTP	Preference Scores:	I 43	N 47 Auxiliary (Extraverted)	T 61 Dominant (Introverted)	P 17

Total Points

E	0	I	21
S	2	N	25
T	31	F	0
J	11	P	19

PHRASE QUESTIONS (*Parts I and III of the MBTI*).
These questions ask for responses to everyday events and may therefore be more influenced by the demands of these events.

INTP	Preference Scores:	I 31	N 21	T 13	P 23

Phrase Points

E	0	I	15
S	2	N	12
T	7	F	0
J	4	P	15

WORD PAIR QUESTIONS (*Part II of the MBTI*).
Word pairs are less affected by everyday events and may be nearer to true preferences.

INTJ	Preference Scores:	I 13	N 27	T 49	J 5

Word Pair Points

E	0	I	6
S	0	N	13
T	25	F	0
J	7	P	4

Answer Sheet Information

Sex	Male
Computed Age is	25
Highest grade completed	16
Are you a student?	Yes
Likes science best	
Are you working?	No
Date of birth	05/29/59
Form G answered on	11/07/84
Total items available	126
Last item answered was	126

Continuous Scores

	Full Scale	Phrase	Word Pair	X Half	Y Half
EI	143	131	113	117	127
SN	147	121	127	121	127
TF	39	87	51	67	71
JP	117	123	95	111	107

Group Code	4U -88
Case Id	#2292-1
Date Scored	9/16/88

Item Omissions

EI	scored items omitted	5
SN	scored items omitted	1
TF	scored items omitted	1
JP	scored items omitted	1
Subtotal of omissions		8
Research items omitted		11
Total omissions		19

success. Clearly, if his attention had been on I and T, it was not surprising that he had overlooked E and F. Tom now saw a logical (T) reason to develop E and F skills to become the competent doctor he had always imagined he would be. And he intended to be a well-rounded doctor.

Tom and the counselor developed a plan of action. He decided he could not attain and did not need the high levels of empathy that seemed to come so naturally to his classmates with extraversion and feeling, but he *did* need to learn EF skills. Two strategies were set forth. Tom would observe classmates with these skills to learn formulas of comfort and support until he had found his own empathic style. Second, he would use his intuition to see patterns that would help him understand patients better. As he did these experiments, his thinking would, as always, check them out for cause and effect so that he could see if he was on target. With a logical reason to do so, Thomas began to spend more time on extraverted activities and on people-watching. To his surprise, but not that of the counselor, he began to find that not only was he doing better with patients, but somehow his relationships with his peers and superiors became warmer and more satisfying.

In working with Tom, the counselor started with the fact that Tom's MBTI preferences were clear and consistent (see Table 5.3); he was alert for possible conflict over decisiveness or open curiosity (P 23 on phrase questions and J 5 on word pairs) but did not pursue it since Tom's preference for P was clearly evident in his words and behavior. The principle of type dynamics hypothesized to fit Thomas was that he had neglected his third and fourth functions until confronted with the crisis in patient care. His dominant logic told him that if he were to succeed he must be able to manifest more empathy. With the spur from his dominant function, the neglected activities acquired higher valence. His intuition was challenged to find facts about people's values (F) and behavior (S), which he had hitherto missed. Together his N and T made "people watching" intellectually interesting. He forced himself to do more extraverting because it was the logical way to learn. In short, he developed his less-developed preferences in the service of goals desired by his dominant and auxiliary.

Case B. Joyce Black (ENFJ)

Joyce was a 45-year-old married woman with two children—a son who was a freshman in college and a daughter who was a senior in high school. She had been an executive secretary when she married her husband Tom, a civil engineer. She gave up her job when her son was born. During the child-rearing years, she was active in the Parent Teacher Association and other community groups. She met the counselor when he explained the MBTI to a board on which she served. She had come out an ENFJ (extraverted feeling dominant, with intuition auxiliary and inferior introverted thinking).

Mrs. Black appeared for her first appointment, attractive, well-groomed, and confident. She said she came to counseling because she "unaccountably" found herself depressed. Even worse, she was feeling angry at her daughter and her husband "for no reason at all." She took control of the interview, volubly describing her husband, her perfect marriage, her children, and the many demands of her life. As the counselor sought for themes in this deluge of facts, he heard "I try so hard but they don't appreciate me." "I can see so clearly what they need, and I tell them and tell them, but they won't listen to me. In fact, they tell me not to be so bossy." "They hurt my feelings but they don't mean to." Throughout the interview, she watched the counselor carefully. Twice she asked "Am I giving you what you need?"

Between sessions, the counselor found her earlier MBTI report on which she came out an ENFJ. Table 5.4 shows the report for Mrs. Black; Table 5.5 shows detailed scoring information for the counselor.

Based on the interview and his knowledge of ENFJ's, the counselor set his tentative goals and expectations:

> The extraverted feeling type is very sensitive to disharmony and anxious to please. The counselor must be alert that she not hide her real feelings in order to be a "good patient." Transference issues will probably have to be dealt with if her need for affiliation leads to her putting the counselor on a pedestal.
>
> There is probably considerably more friction in the family than she acknowledges to herself. With her dominant feeling, she will probably try to explain away others' behaviors that hurt her.
>
> Extraverted feeling types tend to look outward for validation of their self-worth. Is she working too hard to gain the approval of others? How much has she developed her introverted side with its more independent sense of worth?
>
> As her youngest child leaves the nest, where will she use the nurturance that is so important to an ENFJ? One quiet, self-sufficient engineer husband cannot comfortably absorb all the dynamic, loving energy of an ENFJ.
>
> Is she ready at mid-life to take some "Joyce time," to slow down and develop her own talents? The difference between her scores for phrases (J 17) and for word pairs (P 1) may indicate she is seeking more spontaneity and fewer obligations. Has she been suppressing imaginative or intellectual interests (N on word pairs) because of her need to manage everyday practical affairs (S on phrase questions)?

Counseling sessions lasted some months. Slowly, Joyce Black began to acknowledge the hurt and anger she had been explaining away. Occasionally she was in touch with the desperation of her need to please; slowly she began to separate times of genuine, relaxed helpfulness from the helpfulness forced on others so she could be appreciated. She learned to stop and learn what would be

TABLE 5.4.
Myers-Briggs Type Indicator Report

		*	

This report was prepared for
CASE B JOYCE BLACK

Here is the report of the Myers-Briggs Type Indicator (MBTI) which you answered on December 8th, 1986. The MBTI indicates sixteen types of people. Your answers to the MBTI questions came out the type called **Extraverted Feeling with Intuition**, also known by the letters **ENFJ**.

The author of the MBTI, Isabel Briggs Myers, wrote sixteen descriptions of the types at their best; the end of each report describes problems which persons of that type may have when not at their best. This page of your report describes type ENFJ. Page 2 and 3 give reasons why the sixteen types are different from one another, and tell more about your answers. Some people prefer to read their description first; others prefer to read the reasons first. Whichever way you prefer, be sure to read all three pages to see your full report.

ENFJ
Extraverted Feeling with Intuition

ENFJ people radiate sympathy and fellowship. They are concerned chiefly with people and they place a high value on harmonious human contacts. They are particularly warmed by approval and sensitive to indifference. Much of their pleasure and satisfaction comes from the warmth of feeling of people around them and from their own warm feelings.

ENFJ's enjoy admiring people, and so they tend to concentrate on the admirable qualities of other people. They base their decisions on their personal values and they try to live up to their ideals. They are loyal to respected persons, institutions or causes, often to the point of idealizing whatever they admire.

They are unusually able to see value in other people's opinions. Even when opinions are in conflict, they have faith that harmony can somehow be achieved and they often manage to bring it about. They are friendly, tactful, sympathetic, and can almost always express the right feeling. To bring harmony, they are ready to agree with other people's opinions within reasonable limits; in this process, they need to be careful that they don't concentrate so intensely on other people's viewpoints that they lose sight of the value of their own ideas.

They are mainly interested in seeing the possibilities beyond what is present or obvious or known. Intuition heightens their insight, vision, concern for future possibilities, and curiosity for new ideas as such. They tend to be interested in books and moderately tolerant of theory. They are likely to have a gift of expression, but may like to use it in speaking to audiences rather than in writing.

They are at their best in jobs that deal with people and in any situations where cooperation can be brought about through good will. **ENFJ**'s are found in jobs such as selling, some kinds of direct supervision, teaching, preaching, counseling, face-to-face cooperative work, etc. They are less likely to be happy in work demanding impersonal, factual accuracy, as in accounting.

They think best when talking with people, and enjoy talk. They have to make a special effort to be brief and businesslike and not let sociability slow them down on the job.

They like to have matters decided or settled, but they do not need or want to make all the decisions themselves. They have many definite "shoulds" and "should nots" and may express these freely. They are persevering, conscientious, orderly even in small matters, and inclined to expect others to be the same.

They run some risk of jumping to conclusions before they understand a situation. **IF** they have not taken time to gain first-hand knowledge about a person or situation, their actions may not have the helpful results they intended. For example, **ENFJ**'s beginning a new project or a new job may do things as they judge they *should* be done, instead of taking the pains to find out how the organization works or what is *really* wanted.

ENFJ's find it harder than other types to see things they wish were not true. They find it especially hard to admit the truth about problems with people or things they care about. **IF** they fail to face disagreeable facts, or **IF** they refuse to look at criticisms that hurt, they will sweep their problems under the rug instead of finding good solutions.

TABLE 5.5.
Myers-Briggs Type Indicator Detailed Scoring Information

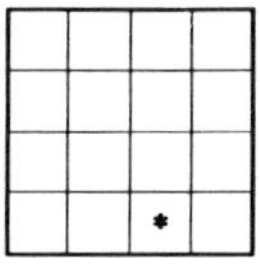

Professional report for
Dr. Mary McCaulley

MBTI results for
CASE B JOYCE BLACK

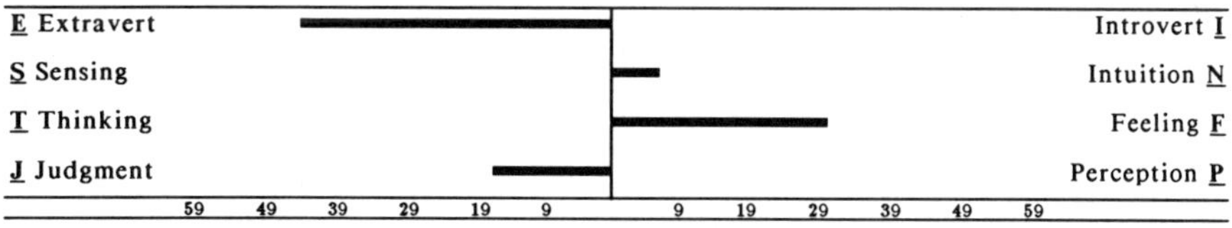

ENFJ - Extraverted Feeling with Intuition

FULL SCALE RESULTS (*Parts I,II and III of the MBTI*)

		EI Direction of Energy	SN Perception Function	TF Judgment Function	JP Extraverted Attitude
ENFJ	Preference Scores:	E 45	N 7 Auxiliary (Introverted)	F 31 Dominant (Extraverted)	J 17

Total Points			
E	23	I	0
S	10	N	13
T	2	F	17
J	19	P	10

PHRASE QUESTIONS (*Parts I and III of the MBTI*).
These questions ask for responses to everyday events and may therefore be more influenced by the demands of these events.

ESFJ Preference Scores: E 35 S 7 F 15 J 17

Phrase Points			
E	18	I	0
S	9	N	5
T	0	F	7
J	13	P	4

WORD PAIR QUESTIONS (*Part II of the MBTI*).
Word pairs are less affected by everyday events and may be nearer to true preferences.

ENFP Preference Scores: E 9 N 15 F 17 P 1

Word Pair Points			
E	5	I	0
S	1	N	8
T	2	F	10
J	6	P	6

Answer Sheet Information

Sex	Female
Computed Age is	45
Highest grade completed	14
Are you a student?	No
Likes art best	
Are you working?	No
Date of birth	10/19/41
Form G answered on	12/08/86
Total items available	126
Last item answered was	126

Continuous Scores

	Full Scale	Phrase	Word Pair	X Half	Y Half
EI	55	65	91	75	81
SN	107	93	115	101	107
TF	131	115	117	111	121
JP	83	83	101	97	87

Group Code	4U -89
Case Id	#1331-1
Date Scored	4/26/89

Item Omissions

EI	scored items omitted	1
SN	scored items omitted	2
TF	scored items omitted	2
JP	scored items omitted	0
Subtotal of omissions		5
Research items omitted		28
Total omissions		33

appreciated before she offered help. She began to explore her own dreams for her future—tentatively because these seemed selfish to her.

The counselor was sensitive to the deep hurts beneath the socially poised facade, and helped her appreciate that she had "got in wrong trying to do right." They processed her feelings of hurt and rejection when the counselor was late or took a vacation, at which times she became superficial and overly "understanding" of his need for time away from "demanding people like me."

At the conclusion of counseling she was more at peace with her family, friends, and with herself. She was planning to return to college, and to prepare herself to teach middle school where she could help children at a critical developmental stage. Some of the insights she shared with the counselor were:

> I was out of touch with how sensitive I am. I didn't know how things hurt me a lot. I used to pretend it didn't happen. I would say "I don't need you!" I learned about feeling my feelings.
>
> It took me 6 months to hear you say "Why do you want to be perfect?" It was such an alien thought. Then I had another insight. If I don't have to be perfect, they don't have to be perfect.
>
> I can make requests now, not demands. Somehow they do more of the things I ask them to. And we feel closer.
>
> I don't push as much. I am able just to be alive. And when I don't try to do everything I get more done.

In terms of type dynamics, Joyce had been so ruled by need for harmony of her dominant feeling that she had not achieved the balance of her auxiliary. She needed the balance of comfortable introversion, and the balance of using her perception before imposing her extraverted feeling on her world. As she learned to slow down and see more around her, she learned to trust her intuition, and her feeling judgments became more appropriate. As she developed her introverted side, she became better able to allow herself to listen to her own needs and became less vulnerable to the demands or criticisms of others.

Case C. Henry Gray (ESTJ)

Henry was a 47-year-old successful businessman who had taken the MBTI with his wife at a parent group conducted by the school counselor. He had come out an ESTJ (extraverted thinking type with sensing). He made a separate appointment to discuss with the counselor his frustration at his son Jim, now a high-school sophomore. In the appointment, he described his attitude toward the responsibilities of parenthood. In brief terms, he listed his duties for being a good parent: (a) make his son tough because it's a tough world out there; (b) make him persistent because no one ever gets anywhere if he gives up; and (c) make him an upright citizen because we need morality in our society.

He listed Jim's misbehaviors. The counselor repeatedly asked variations of "Why do you suppose Jim does that when he knows you don't like it?." The responses were variations of "He mustn't do it. It is wrong for him."

As he described his interactions with Jim, the counselor got a picture of a constant stream of commands, complaints, and corrections. Even when father and son did things together, Henry seemed to use the occasions to correct Jim's every effort. Behind what came across as a barrage of nagging, the counselor began to see great love and concern for Jim.

"Mr. Gray, every time I ask you how the situation may look from Jim's point of view, you tell me how wrong Jim is. I am not there when you talk to Jim, but what you describe is a constant stream of criticism from you. I believe you are doing this because you love Jim and are trying to help him be a good and successful man in a difficult world. I am asking you to stop and think what your interactions seem like *to Jim.*"

Mr. Gray stopped, sat quietly, and shook his head.

"If Jim were here, and I asked him, "Jim, what does your father think of you, what would he say?"

After a pause, Mr. Gray said slowly, "He would probably say, "Dad thinks I'm no good, and I never do anything right."

"If a person feels no good and that he never does anything right, how easy is it for him to motivate himself to try harder?"

"Impossible, I would estimate."

"Mr. Gray, you love Jim and want him to be a strong, good man. You are trying to teach him by showing him whenever he is off track. The result isn't what you want; he is becoming resentful and losing confidence in himself. There are strategies that work better. Let me give you some well-established facts about children his age, so that we can find a strategy that works better."

The counselor briefly outlined research describing that children model after people they admire and by whom they feel loved. He described in practical terms the implications of Jim's developmental level. Together, the counselor and Mr. Gray developed a plan whereby Mr. Gray would (a) work to listen and understand, (b) work to suspend judgment, (c) teach Jim in a relaxed way, with Jim's level in mind, (d) watch for Jim's successes—even small ones—and make an appreciative comment, and (e) schedule activities together that they both could enjoy on a man-to-man basis.

The counselor did not see Mr. Gray again; but she noticed that Jim's grades began to improve, and he seemed better able to stand up for himself with his classmates.

Table 5.6 gives the report given to Mr. Gray; Table 5.7 shows the detailed scoring information in the hands of the counselor. Mr. Gray's preferences were clear and consistent.

In terms of type dynamics, Mr. Gray was using his dominant thinking to comment on what was out of line in Jim's behavior, but was not using his

TABLE 5.6.
Myers-Briggs Type Indicator Report

*			

This report was prepared for
CASE C HENRY GRAY

Here is the report of the Myers-Briggs Type Indicator (MBTI) which you answered on February 23rd, 1987. The MBTI indicates sixteen types of people. Your answers to the MBTI questions came out the type called **Extraverted Thinking with Sensing,** also known by the letters **ESTJ.**

The author of the MBTI, Isabel Briggs Myers, wrote sixteen descriptions of the types at their best; the end of each report describes problems which persons of that type may have when not at their best. This page of your report describes type ESTJ. Page 2 and 3 give reasons why the sixteen types are different from one another, and tell more about your answers. Some people prefer to read their description first; others prefer to read the reasons first. Whichever way you prefer, be sure to read all three pages to see your full report.

ESTJ
Extraverted Thinking with Sensing

ESTJ people use their thinking to run as much of the world as may be theirs to run. They like to organize things and get them done. Reliance on thinking makes them logical, analytical, impersonal, objectively critical, and not likely to be convinced by anything but reasoning.

They focus their thinking on the people and things in the world around them. They organize facts, situations and operations well in advance, and make a systematic effort to reach their carefully planned objectives on schedule. They have little patience with confusion or inefficiency, and can be tough when the situation calls for toughness.

They think conduct should be governed by logic and they govern their own behavior by logic as much as they can. They live their lives according to a definite set of rules that embody their basic judgments of the world. Any change in their ways requires a conscious change in their rules.

They are more interested in seeing present realities than future possibilities. This makes them matter-of-fact, practical, realistic, fact-minded, concerned with here and now. They use past experience to help them solve problems. **ESTJ**'s are more curious about new facts and new things than about new ideas. They want to be sure that ideas, plans and decisions are based on solid fact. As they do not listen to their own intuition very much, they usually need an intuitive around to sell them on the value of new ideas.

They like jobs where the results of their work are immediate, visible and tangible. They have a natural bent for business and industry, production and construction. They enjoy administration, and like to decide what ought to be done next and give the necessary orders. Getting things done is their strong suit.

Like the other decisive types, **ESTJ**'s run some risk of deciding too quickly before they have fully seen the situation. All the decisive types need to stop and listen to the other person's side of the matter, especially with people under them who can't talk back. This is seldom easy for **ESTJ**'s. But **IF** they do not take time to understand, they may judge too hastily, without enough facts or enough regard for what other people think or feel.

ESTJ's may rely so much on the logical approach of thinking that they overlook their feeling values--what they care about and what other people care about. They may decide that something they value is not important, just because it isn't logical to care about it. Thinking and feeling can often lead to different decisions. If **ESTJ**'s always let their thinking suppress their feeling, their feeling will not develop and be manageable. If feeling values are ignored too much, they may build up pressure and explode in most inappropriate ways.

ESTJ's need to find positive ways to take feeling values into account. One useful way to use feeling is to appreciate other people's merits. **ESTJ**'s see what is illogical so they are naturally critical; therefore appreciation comes harder for **ESTJ**'s than for the feeling types. But **ESTJ**'s can learn to make it a rule to mention what is well done, not merely what needs correcting. The results will be worthwhile, both in their work and in their private lives.

TABLE 5.7.
Myers-Briggs Type Indicator Detailed Scoring Information

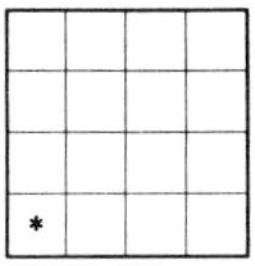

Professional report for **Dr. Mary McCaulley**

MBTI results for CASE C HENRY GRAY

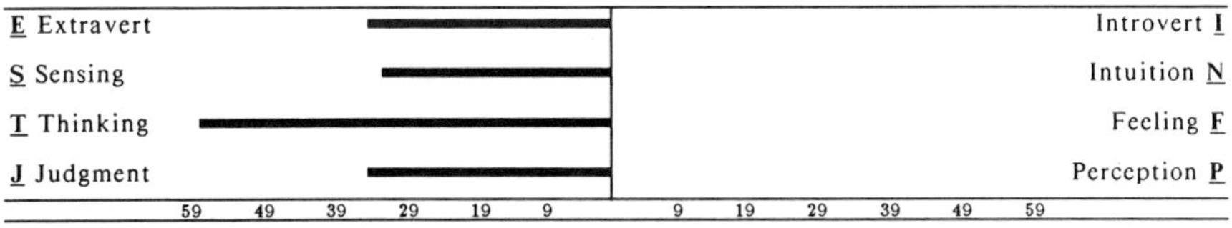

ESTJ - Extraverted Thinking with Sensing

FULL SCALE RESULTS (*Parts I, II and III of the MBTI*)

		E I Direction of Energy	S N Perception Function	T F Judgment Function	J P Extraverted Attitude
ESTJ	Preference Scores:	E 35	S 33 Auxiliary (Introverted)	T 59 Dominant (Extraverted)	J 35

Total Points			
E	23	I	5
S	23	N	6
T	30	F	0
J	22	P	4

PHRASE QUESTIONS (*Parts I and III of the MBTI*).
These questions ask for responses to everyday events and may therefore be more influenced by the demands of these events.

ESTJ Preference Scores: E 27 S 9 T 15 J 17

Phrase Points			
E	18	I	4
S	10	N	5
T	8	F	0
J	12	P	3

WORD PAIR QUESTIONS (*Part II of the MBTI*).
Word pairs are less affected by everyday events and may be nearer to true preferences.

ESTJ Preference Scores: E 7 S 23 T 45 J 17

Word Pair Points			
E	5	I	1
S	13	N	1
T	23	F	0
J	10	P	1

Answer Sheet Information

Sex	Male
Computed Age is	47
Highest grade completed	16
Are you a student?	No
Likes practical skills best	
Are you working?	Yes
Date of birth	01/10/40
Form G answered on	02/23/87
Total items available	126
Last item answered was	126

Continuous Scores

	Full Scale	Phrase	Word Pair	X Half	Y Half
EI	65	73	93	79	87
SN	67	91	77	85	83
TF	41	85	55	67	73
JP	65	83	83	87	79

Group Code	4U -88
Case Id	#2292-3
Date Scored	9/16/88

Item Omissions

EI	scored items omitted	0
SN	scored items omitted	1
TF	scored items omitted	0
JP	scored items omitted	1
Subtotal of omissions		2
Research items omitted		4
Total omissions		6

thinking to look at the logical outcomes of these constant criticisms. The counselor tried to get him to turn off his dominant thinking and use his auxiliary sensing to observe and understand Jim. She gave him specific behavioral guidelines for making these observations of Jim so that he could develop empathy by experience. (Intuition and feeling are the functions most closely associated with empathy and insight; N and F are less accessible to ESTJs.) The counselor tried to convey psychological insight in practical, logical, sequential terms suitable to Mr. Gray's ST style of dealing with the world. His original logical formula for being a good parent was made specific and a more appropriate formula was put in its place. He was also encouraged to suspend judgment (T) and stay more of the time in the perceptive attitude (using his S) so that he could understand Jim more. The counselor was brief, to the point, and factual. The door was open if he wished to discuss other problems, but the counselor did not expect Mr. Gray would seek or see much sense in treatments that involve "just sitting around and talking."

Case D. Allen Green (ISFP)

Allen Green, a 19-year-old college sophomore, came to the University Counseling Center to discuss his career plans. He had taken the MBTI before his freshman year as part of the university's roommate-matching program. His type had come out ISFP, introverted feeling type with sensing. He was completing the basic study requirements and had a solid B average. Allen was tall, solidly built, and sat quietly in the counselor's office, answering specific questions but volunteering little. Table 5.8 gives Allen Green's report, and Table 5.9 shows the counselor's detailed scoring information.

In type theory, ISFPs are most gentle of the types. The counselor started with the hypothesis that Allen would be a gentle man. With ISFPs, feeling is dominant and introverted; they are happiest in careers which let them live out their deepest values. The counselor began by asking Allen to describe any experiences at the university that were especially satisfying. He recalled volunteering at the University Day Care Center where he had supervised the children on the playground. "It's such fun to work with them until they improve their coordination." He had made a few good friends at the dormitory, and they enjoyed bike rides in the country. The dormitory had planned an ambitious float for Homecoming. "They asked me to be in the parade, but I said I would rather work behind the scenes on the float. A bunch of us were up all night working on it. It won second prize." (What was there about it that was especially satisfying?) "We were a really compatible group (F), and it was fun seeing the float come alive under our hands (S)."

Asked about his coursework, Allen said he had liked biology and zoology best. Algebra was hard because he couldn't see any practical use for it, but he liked the teacher and that had helped him get by. English was OK, except when

TABLE 5.8.
Myers-Briggs Type Indicator Report

	*		

This report was prepared for
CASE D ALLEN GREEN

Here is the report of the Myers-Briggs Type Indicator (MBTI) which you answered on January 15th, 1987. The MBTI indicates sixteen types of people. Your answers to the MBTI questions came out the type called **Introverted Feeling with Sensing**, also known by the letters **ISFP**.

The author of the MBTI, Isabel Briggs Myers, wrote sixteen descriptions of the types at their best; the end of each report describes problems which persons of that type may have when not at their best. This page of your report describes type ISFP. Page 2 and 3 give reasons why the sixteen types are different from one another, and tell more about your answers. Some people prefer to read their description first; others prefer to read the reasons first. Whichever way you prefer, be sure to read all three pages to see your full report.

ISFP
Introverted Feeling with Sensing

ISFP people have a great deal of warmth, but they may not show it until they know a person well. They keep their warm side inside, like a fur-lined coat. When they care, they care deeply, but are more likely to show their feeling by their deeds rather than their words.

They have great faithfulness to duties and obligations related to things or people they care about. They take a very personal approach to life, accepting or rejecting everything by their inner ideals and personal values. Their conscious actions are directed toward keeping lesser values subordinate to the greater. They choose their final values with little reference to outsiders, and stick to them with passionate conviction.

ISFP's find their inner loyalties and ideals hard to talk about, though these govern their lives. Their deepest feelings are seldom expressed, and their inner tenderness is masked by reserve and repose.

In everyday activities they are tolerant, open-minded, flexible and adaptable--unless their inner loyalties are threatened. Then they will not give an inch. They usually enjoy the present moment, and do not want to spoil it with undue haste or exertion to get things done. They have little wish to impress or dominate. The contacts they prize are with people who understand their values and the goals they are working toward.

They are mainly interested in the realities shown by their five senses. They are apt to enjoy fields where taste, discrimination, and a sense of beauty and proportion are of value, and they often excel in craftsmanship. **ISFP**'s seem to have a special love of nature and sympathy with animals. The work of their hands is usually more eloquent than their words.

They are twice as good when working at a job they believe in, since their feeling for it puts added energy to their efforts. They see the needs of the moment and try to meet them. They want their work to contribute to something that matters to them, to human understanding or happiness or health, or to the perfecting of something. They want to have a purpose beyond their paycheck, no matter how big the check. They are perfectionists wherever they deeply care about something, and are particularly fitted for work that requires both devotion and a large measure of adaptability.

The problem for **ISFP**'s is that they may feel such a contrast between their inner ideals and what they actually can accomplish that they may burden themselves with a sense of inadequacy, even when they are being as effective as the other types. Anything they do well they take for granted. They are the most modest of all the types, and consistently underrate and understate themselves. It is important for them to find practical ways to express their ideals; otherwise they will keep dreaming of the impossible and accomplish very little.

If they find no actions to express their ideals they can become too sensitive and vulnerable, with dwindling confidence in life and in themselves. Actually, they have much to give, and need only to find the spot where they are needed.

TABLE 5.9.
Myers-Briggs Type Indicator Detailed Scoring Information

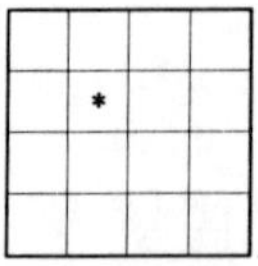

Professional report for
Dr. Mary McCaulley

MBTI results for
CASE D ALLEN GREEN

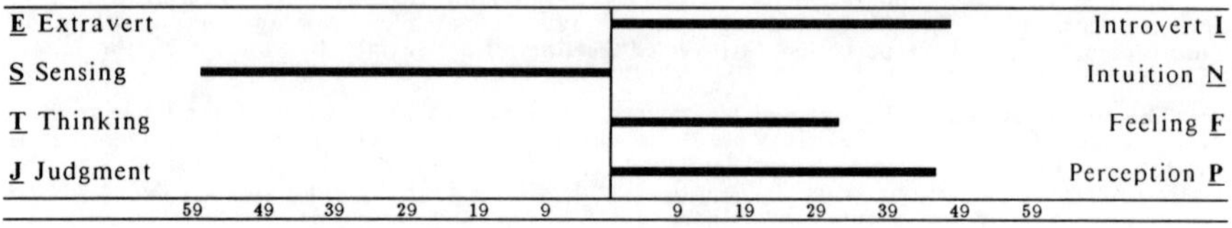

ISFP - Introverted Feeling with Sensing

FULL SCALE RESULTS (*Parts I,II and III of the MBTI*)

		E I Direction of Energy	S N Perception Function	T F Judgment Function	J P Extraverted Attitude
ISFP	Preference Scores:	**I 49**	**S 59** Auxiliary (Extraverted)	**F 33** Dominant (Introverted)	**P 47**

Total Points			
E	2	I	26
S	32	N	2
T	1	F	17
J	3	P	26

PHRASE QUESTIONS (*Parts I and III of the MBTI*).
These questions ask for responses to everyday events and may therefore be more influenced by the demands of these events.

ISFP Preference Scores: **I 43** **S 23** **F 11** **P 27**

Phrase Points			
E	1	I	22
S	14	N	2
T	1	F	6
J	2	P	15

WORD PAIR QUESTIONS (*Part II of the MBTI*).
Word pairs are less affected by everyday events and may be nearer to true preferences.

ISFP Preference Scores: **I 7** **S 35** **F 21** **P 21**

Word Pair Points			
E	1	I	4
S	18	N	0
T	1	F	11
J	1	P	11

Answer Sheet Information

Sex	Male
Computed Age is	19
Highest grade completed	13
Now a Student?	
Date of Birth	11/01/67
Form F answered on	01/15/87
Total items available	166
Last item answered was	166

Continuous Scores

	Full Scale	Phrase	Word Pair	X Half	Y Half
EI	149	143	107	127	123
SN	41	77	65	67	75
TF	133	111	121	111	121
JP	147	127	121	119	129

Group Code	4U
Case Id	#2292-4
Date Scored	9/16/88

Item Omissions

EI	scored items omitted	0
SN	scored items omitted	0
TF	scored items omitted	0
JP	scored items omitted	0
Subtotal of omissions		0
Research items omitted		1
Total omissions		1

they kept asking about the symbolism in the stories (N); he never seemed to see the symbolism the way the professor did.

Allen opened up when talking about home, especially about his two dogs and his cat.

The counselor began to explore career issues more closely. As Allen thought of work he knew about, what occupations would be interesting and fun? They explored occupations with animals—veterinary medicine, animal husbandry, and the university's new dolphin study program. They then explored working with people, health professions, teaching, and sales. Little by little Allen began to define what career characteristics appealed to him: work with animals (SF), work with people if it was one-to-one and hands-on (IS), work that did not require lots of talk and persuasion (I), work where he was free to come and go (P).

They explored his interest in education after college. Allen had not thought of graduate work. College seemed quite a lot for him. (The SP types with sensing and perception are under-represented in college and graduate school.) He talked about the sacrifice of fun and freedom that graduate school would require, but concluded that if it were necessary for work he really cared about (F) he would be able to make himself struggle through graduate training.

The counselor also explored the realism of Allen's expectations of himself. In theory, ISFP and INFP have the greatest discrepancy between their idealistic goals and their perceptions of their own accomplishment. Allen gave a shy smile, and said "My dad tells me that if other people say it is good and I don't think it is good enough, I should believe other people. I never think what I do is as good as it should be, but my dad's advice helps me keep my perspective."

Together, Allen and the counselor set up a fact-finding plan. Allen would look through the college catalog for all the fields that provided work with animals or helping people; he would select a few interesting ones; if he knew anyone in the fields he would visit them and see first-hand what the work was like. Allen hesitated at the amount of extraverting in his plan, but decided to stick to it because he needed the facts. They made an appointment in a month to assess what he had learned.

The particular value of the MBTI in career counseling is the focus on what will be intrinsically interesting and motivating, and the kind of work environment that will be satisfying. How much people contact and action (E) or quiet concentration and long attention span (I)? How much hands on, practical doing (S) or how much imaginative or theoretical work (N)? How much work with the inanimate and mathematical, where logic is important (T), and how much work with the animate world, where love and nurturing are needed (F)? How much pleasure in systems, organization, directed planning, or executive action (J), or how much enjoyment of trouble-shooting or adapting to change (P)? In working with Allen, the plan was to capitalize on his interest in the facts of world around him (extraverted sensing) and his values (introverted F). If he chooses a field requiring heavy coursework in the physical sciences, then a plan will be needed for this easy-going type to survive with constant academic demands for use of his less-preferred intuition and thinking.

All four of these cases can, of course, be conceptualized differently, and all have other dynamic issues not discussed here. The cases showed how type theory provides a framework for looking at counseling issues in a logical and ingenious NT type (Thomas Brown), an enthusiastic and insightful NF type (Joyce Black), a practical and matter-of-fact ST type (Henry Gray), and a sympathetic and friendly SF type (Allen Green).

MBTI RESEARCH ISSUES

Reliability

Internal consistency and test-retest reliabilities are presented to Chapter 10 of the *Manual*. Internal consistency and test-retest reliabilities are reported for EI, SN, TF and JP separately, using correlations of continuous scores. Because type theory postulates underlying dichotomies, not continua, and because the units of measurement for the MBTI are the 16 types, further reliability data are provided on the preferences based on letters, not scores.

Internal Consistency Reliabilities based on split-half correlations of large samples from the MBTI data bank fall between .75 and .88 for EI; .73 and .91 for SN; .76 and .88 for TF; and .80 and .92 for JP. Median split-half correlations reported for smaller research samples from 7th grade through adults are .82 for EI, .82 for SN, .77 for TF and .84 for JP. Lower correlations generally come, as Myers predicted, from younger or underachieving samples.

Test-retest reliabilities reported in the *Manual* for 28 groups with retest intervals from one week to four years showed median correlations of EI .84, SN .81, TF .72 and JP .81. Retest reliabilities showed no consistent patterns of change in two studies with different retest conditions—mood manipulation (Howes, 1977) and career instructions (Parham, Miller, & Carskadon, 1984).

On other self-report instruments, reliability is established from scale scores. With the MBTI, however, scale scores are designed as a way-station to the letters. Test-retest agreement of *type categories* (i.e. letters) for 20 groups including 7th-grade students, college students, medical students, and elementary school teachers retested after five weeks to six years yielded a range of agreement from 68% to 89% for E or I, 64% to 92% for S or N, 69% to 88% for T or F, and 66% to 92% for J or P.

To come out the same MBTI type, all four letters must be the same on retest, an event expected to occur by chance 6.25% of the time. Thirteen studies reported in the *Manual* showed an average of 42% the same on all four letters on retest; 78% of the composite of all samples reported three or four letters the same; less than 1% changed all four letters. Most changes occured when the original preference score was low.

In summary, the test-retest reliabilities of individual scales are comparable to those of other personality instruments. On retest, about three-fourths of a sample will come out with three or four letters the same. Most of the changes occur in one preference only, usually a preference with low scores. Counselors, of course, should be alert to a greater possibility of change, because they are seeing people whose type may have been falsified, or who are reporting preferences clouded by distress.

Validity

The MBTI was designed at every step to represent Jung's theory of psychological types. Construct validity for the MBTI has been demonstrated in the following ways (for specific details, begin with Myers & McCaulley, 1985; Macdaid, McCaulley, & Kainz, 1987; Carskadon, McCarley and McCaulley (1987); and Center for Applications of Psychological Type (1989):

Career choice. The pattern of types selecting specific careers is consistent with predictions from type theory.

Academic success. The more "academic" IN types significantly score higher on aptitude and academic achievement tests. They also seek graduate training in greater numbers.

Learning and teaching styles. Students and teachers report and show differences in preferred modes of learning and teaching that are consistent with type theory (Lawrence, 1984).

Correlations with other personality and interest measures. The *Manual* (pp. 177–206) reports correlations of continuous scores of EI, SN, TF, and JP with scales of personality and interest measures. Some significant relationships appear early in this chapter in the descriptions of the preferences. In general, correlations are in the predicted directions, and MBTI scales do not correlate with measures of unrelated constructs.

Correlations with behavioral ratings. Extensive data from the Institute for Personality Assessment and Research (IPAR) at the University of California at Berkeley (Gough, 1981) are reported in the *Manual* and earlier in this chapter. Trained raters conducted interviews and observed behavior. Researchers at IPAR and elsewhere have reported that preferences for intuition (N) and to a lesser extent for perception (P) are significantly associated with measures of creativity (*Manual, pp. 214–221*).

Individual agreement with MBTI reports. Hammer and Yeakley (1987) interviewed 120 adults to identify the best-fit type; interviews ranged from same day to two years after answering the MBTI. Eighty-five percent agreed with all four MBTI preferences; no subjects disagreed on three or four preferences, and the 15% disagreeing on one preference originally reported preference scores less than seven. Carskadon (1982) and Carskadon & Cook, 1982) found that students chose their type descriptions at rates significantly above chance (35% $p < .001$ and 50% $p < .001$). Kummerow (1988) reported a structured procedures in which 146 retail managers and 241 bank managers compared their "best fit" type to MBTI results; 62% agreed with all four letters and 93% agreed with three or four letters.

Research about Counselors and Clients

Counselors naturally use the communication style of their own type, but need to learn to communicate in the styles of sixteen client types. All 16 types become counselors, but counseling is especially attractive to NF types. In theory intuition is associated with the ability to see patterns and to read between the lines; feeling is associated with motivation to work with and understand people. Table 5.10 shows a type distribution of counselors from the *MBTI Atlas* (Macdaid et al., 1987).

Almost all samples of mental health professionals show a majority of intuitives. The median was 70% N types in 13 samples in the *Manual*. Counselors in the more practical specialties (vocational and rehabilitation counseling) are more evenly divided between S and N types. In contrast to the predominance of intuition among counselors, three-fourths of the general population prefer sensing.

Counselors differ also on the other MBTI preferences. Extraverts outnumber introverts, with school, college, and crisis counselors more E, and with psychiatrists and psychologists more nearly divided between E and I. Although feeling types are in the majority in counselors, more thinking types were found in rational-emotive and behavioral specialties, along with Canadian student counselors reported by Casas and Hamlet (1984).

A few studies (see reviews in Carskadon, 1979; Carskadon, McCarley, & McCaulley, 1987; and research by Coan 1979; Levin, 1978; and Witzig, 1978), mainly with small samples, have addressed counselor preferences for counseling strategies. Extraverts, looking outward, view behavior as affected more by nurture and the environment; introverts, turning inward, see the sources of behavior in biological determinism and nature. Sensing types appear to emphasize factual and quantitative issues; intuitives are more concerned with insight-oriented approaches and the use of fantasy and symbolism. Counselors who prefer thinking tend to choose rational, informational, cognitive, and behavioral approaches, and are more oriented toward objectivism and impersonal causality. Counselors who prefer feeling are more attracted to experiential and affective approaches

TABLE 5.10
Counselors
N = 1803

	SENSING THINKING	SENSING FEELING	INTUITION FEELING	INTUITION THINKING	
	ISTJ N= 121 %= 6.71 ■■■■■■■	**ISFJ** N= 111 %= 6.16 ■■■■■■	**INFJ** N= 109 %= 6.05 ■■■■■■	**INTJ** N= 66 %= 3.66 ■■■■	JUDGMENT / INTROVERSION
	ISTP N= 35 %= 1.94 ■■	**ISFP** N= 52 %= 2.88 ■■■	**INFP** N= 215 %= 11.92 ■■■■■■■■■■ ■■	**INTP** N= 62 %= 3.44 ■■■	PERCEPTION / INTROVERSION
	ESTP N= 28 %= 1.55 ■■	**ESFP** N= 71 %= 3.94 ■■■■	**ENFP** N= 319 %= 17.69 ■■■■■■■■■■ ■■■■■■■■	**ENTP** N= 82 %= 4.55 ■■■■■	PERCEPTION / EXTRAVERSION
	ESTJ N= 129 %= 7.15 ■■■■■■■	**ESFJ** N= 127 %= 7.04 ■■■■■■■	**ENFJ** N= 183 %= 10.15 ■■■■■■■■■■	**ENTJ** N= 93 %= 5.16 ■■■■■	JUDGMENT / EXTRAVERSION

Note: ■ = 1% of sample 8629454

	N	%
E	1032	57.24
I	771	42.76
S	674	37.38
N	1129	62.62
T	616	34.17
F	1187	65.83
J	939	52.08
P	864	47.92
I J	407	22.57
I P	364	20.19
E P	500	27.73
E J	532	29.51
S T	313	17.36
S F	361	20.02
N F	826	45.81
N T	303	16.81
S J	488	27.07
S P	186	10.32
N P	678	37.60
N J	451	25.01
T J	409	22.68
T P	207	11.48
F P	657	36.44
F J	530	29.40
I N	452	25.07
E N	677	37.55
I S	319	17.69
E S	355	19.69
E T	332	18.41
E F	700	38.82
I F	487	27.01
I T	284	15.75
S dom	331	18.36
N dom	576	31.95
T dom	319	17.69
F dom	577	32.00

This table is one of a series of tables from the CAPT-MBTI Data Bank of MBTI records submitted to CAPT for computer scoring between 1971 and June, 1984. This sample was drawn from 59,784 records with usable occupational codes from the total data bank of 232,557. This data bank has 51% Form F cases from 1971 to March, 1978, 35% Form F cases from 1978 to June, 1984 and 14% Form G cases from 1978 to December, 1982. An analysis of Form F and G data banks showed the data banks were comprised of 56% females and 44% males; education level completed: 6% some grade school, 30% high school diploma, 25% some college, 18% bachelor degrees, 11% masters degrees, 3% doctoral or post doctoral work, and 6% unknown. Age group percentages were: 11% under 18, 29% 18 to 20, 12% 21 to 24, 10% 25 to 29, 16% 30 to 39, 10% 40 to 49, 5% 50 to 59, 2% 60 plus, and 5% unknown.

with a focus on personal will and the quality of the relationship. Counselors who prefer the perceptive attitude find it easier to remain open, following the client where the session leads; counselors who prefer the judging attitude find it easier to provide structure, goals, and direction. Counselors include more perceptive types than other health professions (McCaulley, 1977). In Levin's (1978) study of counselors, more than three-fourths of gestalt and experiential counselors were P types; more than 70% of psychoanalytic and rational-emotive counselors were J types. In counseling as in other fields, judging types may gravitate to administrative tasks.

Research on clients is still in the early stages. Research reported in the *Manual* (pp. 73–75) suggests that more intuitives than sensing types seek psychological treatment. Sensing types may be more likely to see psychological problems in physical terms. Intuitive types value or enjoy treatments that involve participation in laboratory learning, fantasy, mental imagery, dreams, and journal keeping. Cann (1979) even found type differences in dream content. Sensing types reported more dreams of everyday life, and intuitives reported more dreams with archetypal content.

Feeling clients, more than thinking types, place high value on affective relationships and the positive regard of counselors. Marital enrichment groups attract more feeling types.

The fact that intuitives are in the majority among counselors and their clients raises questions for the entire field of counseling. Will NF counselors develop appropriate treatment strategies for sensing and thinking clients whose approach to life is so different from their own? One ENFP counselor was caught up short by an ISTJ client. "You keep talking about ways for me to be happy. I am not here to be happy. I am here to solve my problems! Happy is irrelevant." Sensing counselors, a minority in their profession, have a special obligation to interpret the sensing majority in the general population for their colleagues, and to alert intuitive counselors to misperceptions and lost opportunities in reaching the sensing types.

The early evidence shows that both counselors and clients differ in predictable ways in their expectations of counseling and in their preferences for treatment methods. Jung's framework should be increasingly useful as more is known about type differences in diagnosis and effective treatment.

Limitations of the MBTI in Counseling

Type theory and the MBTI are most useful to the counselor in establishing a conceptual framework (a) of possible strengths and weaknesses, (b) of typical and atypical behaviors, (c) of effects of environmental pressures, and (d) of developmental pathways. MBTI reports are usually not directly useful for assessment of psychopathology. MBTI data can, however, alert the counselor to type biases that are reflected on other assessment instruments. For example, "mental health'' measures indicators tend to correlate with MBTI E, T, and J. Type theory alerts the counselor to interpret test scores as true pathology, or as characteristics to be expected from a given type. Personality assessment is complex and we have no perfect personality instruments. The MBTI has the limitations of all self-report instruments. It is essential to consider the motivation of the client in answering the MBTI and to confirm type theory hypotheses with other data.

The fact that MBTI reports are in terms of 16 types, not scale profiles, poses several problems for counselors. Some types (especially ENFP's) resist the entire idea of classification by type; they are slow to see that type describes a developmental pathway, and does not box them in. The type descriptions can be undervalued as horoscopes, rather than as an integrated set of hypotheses, exemplifying a complex theory with considerable empirical support. Some types may reify the descriptions, casting them in concrete. An example is an ISFJ for whom type had become extremely important as part of her identity; she was asked to take the MBTI in a course, and became panicky waiting for the results, fearing that she might not be an ISFJ after all.

EVALUATION AND FUTURE DIRECTIONS

Jung believed his type theory described universal human mental processes. Until recently, Jung's rich and comprehensive theory has been relatively neglected in this country; his work relating to psychological type was little appreciated, even by some Jungians. Isabel Myers' work, carried on apart from academia was also unknown. Her attempt to provide simple explanations of Jung's insights led many to think of her work itself as simple. When I first became acquainted with the MBTI, I consistently underestimated it. After intensive work with Isabel Myers, and after using the MBTI as a counseling tool, a research instrument and a teaching tool, I have come to a much deeper appreciation of its depth and complexity, both in theoretical assumptions, and in psychometric development. In being faithful to Jung's theory, Isabel Myers had to solve many psychometric problems of which we in psychology are seldom aware. These include type differences in interpreting the questions, the assumption of dichotomies, and the consequent need for precision at the midpoint of the scales.

The MBTI descriptions of well-developed examples of each type often provide important self-confirmation. Gifts can be acknowledged; weaknesses can be recognized as blind-spots coming from an overemphasis on gifts. The concept of ''mutual usefulness of opposites'' promotes appreciation for one's own qualities and respect for others. Interactions formerly frustrating can become amusing. The client-counselor process can be a way to experience and honor type differences. The dynamic aspects of the theory provide a useful map for developing and integrating previously unrecognized preferences in a model of lifelong change.

In addition to the type description for the *individual,* a unique feature of the MBTI is the description of *groups* in type tables. Type tables provide a wealth of information for understanding career patterns, family interactions, communications of work groups, and even implications for the larger society. For example, what is the likelihood of one-sided social decisionmaking when managers in business, government, education, the military and the police are 45% to 90% logical, analytical, decisive TJ types? What organizational structures are needed to ensure respectful consideration of value considerations (F) and openness to change (P)?

Future Directions

At the time this chapter is written in 1988, the MBTI has been available for professional applications for only 13 years. The explosion of interest in psychological type points to many future directions:

Type Theory Will Be Known to the General Public

Type is becoming familiar in settings far from the counselor's office. People are learning about type in school, in church, and in the workplace. Popular books are appearing which bring Jung's concepts into everyday language (Brownsword, 1987, 1988; Harbaugh, 1988; Hirsh & Kummerow, 1989; Keirsey & Bates, 1984; Kroeger & Thuesen, 1988, Lawrence, 1982; Mamchur, 1984; Myers with Myers, 1980; Neff, 1988.) The MBTI is being translated into languages worldwide.

Most explanations of type in work and public settings cover the four basic preferences and attempt to create greater respect for differences. Fewer people have been exposed to the dynamic concepts of life-long type development, but their number is growing.

Rapid growth has its costs. Enthusiasts can describe type with such vigor that more skeptical types wonder if type is a cult rather than a body of theory and research. The MBTI is used in organizations, religion, and education by some whose training has not alerted them to the skills caution needed when any psychological instrument is used with complex human beings. Misled by the seeming simplicity of the MBTI, they misinform. People are told their type cannot succeed in the career of their choice; MBTI data do show patterns of types choosing occupations, but rare types often seek out their own niche. People have been told their types are incompatible for marriage, although research shows that all type combinations have produced both successful and unsuccessful marriages.

Growing Focus on Characteristics of the Types

In less than two decades, Jung's theory of psychological types and the MBTI have moved from relative neglect to broad application. This new visibility of course generates challenges, additions and changes. Singer and Loomis question bi-polarity. An extrapolation from classical temperament constructs describes four temperaments, with 16 types as subsets of the temperaments (Keirsey & Bates, 1984). Starting from an abstract systems science model, Lowen (1982) generated types which have characteristics in common with Jungian types.

Specific behaviors associated with the types are being studied and extended (Hobby, Miller, Stone, & Carskadon, 1987; McCarley & Carskadon, 1987; Ware & Yokomoto, 1985). Researchers are studying within-type variations for males and females (Stokes, 1987a, 1987b) and age groups (Kainz, 1985). The future will bring more information on type similarities and differences related to ethnic origin, educational level, work, and intelligence.

Research includes observations by trained judges, laboratory studies of behavior, and life behaviors, such as career choice. The next decade will also show increasing knowledge about type differences in health, illness, and physiology, with brain-behavior a particular interest.

Research on type and behavior is difficult because type theory is general, not specific. The underlying functions and attitudes can be manifested in different ways at the behavioral level. Moreover, good type development leads to the ability to show behaviors appropriate to the situation, whether or not they are preferred.

Type and Children

MBTI users have long asked for an indicator for children. Item analyses for Form G of the MBTI began at fourth grade, but the MBTI is most useful with students in eighth grade or older. Cohen (1981) described research with the Cosiol-Jones-Cohen Children's Personality Scale at Glassboro College in New Jersey. A new instrument, the *Murphy-Meisgeier Type Indicator* for Children (MMTIC) (Meisgeier & Murphy, 1987) was carefully developed and tested at the University of Houston to reflect the Jungian preferences in children from grades 2 to 8. It is now possible to compare the MBTI and MMTIC for children in grades 6 to 8, and to extend the use of type theory to younger ages.

Other Type Instruments

With the growing appreciation of Jung's work, other instruments have been developed to indicate Jungian types. None equals the MBTI in the care in psychometric development nor the empirical research behind it. The Jungian Type Survey or Gray-Wheelright Test (Wheelright, Wheelright, & Buehler, 1964) has scales for extraversion-introversion, sensing-intuition, and thinking-feeling. Most research was published in the 1960s but some still appear occasionally. A newer research instrument by Jungian analysts Singer and Loomis (1984) attempts to identify Jung's basic functions and attitudes, but rejects the assumption that the preferences are dichotomous or bi-polar.

Question lists were developed to give readers of books a way of applying type concepts to themselves. These lists were not intended by their authors to be used as type indicators (Keirsey & Bates, 1984; Lawrence, 1982; Mamchur, 1984).

With or without research, new type descriptions are appearing that include Jung's concepts plus the author's own observations (Brownsword, 1987; DeNovellis 1984a, 1984b, 1985; Grant, Thompson, & Clarke, 1983; Keirsey & Bates, 1984; Neff, 1988).

Future Developments of Interest to Counselors

Research with *clients* will clarify type differences in presenting problems, in diagnostic categories, in most effective treatments, in responses to medication, and in preferred counselor-client interactions. We need to know more about psychological problems and treatment of the sensing types who are less likely to seek counseling. Counselors will discover better strategies to help people develop their preferences. For example, we shall learn how to develop the sensing function (powers of observation, reality-testing, hands-on skills) in those for whom these behaviors are naturally easy, and those for whom they are hard. More attention will be paid to type development in mid-life.

Research with *counselors* will clarify the treatment methods easiest for counselors of different types. How can counselors broaden their repertoire of treatment methods? Are there some methods so alien to any type that counselors of that type are unable to use them therapeutically? What do counselors need to know to talk the ''language'' of each type?

Research into cultural variables may affect the MBTI itself. In her careful work of constructing the MBTI, Isabel Myers took social desirability and gender differences into account in item weights. The world is undergoing many changes that can affect MBTI item weights for age groups (Kainz, 1985) and translations (Inclan, 1985). Changes in language have made some words more difficult, and a few items will be reworded after careful study. Myers' unpublished work using research items not scored for type will generate new interpretative reports. An extended Form J version of the MBTI which includes all items ever used in MBTI development will provide new subscales to supplement the basic scales EI, SN, TF and JP.

New Directions in Practical Applications

Every application of the MBTI leads to requests for more detailed information and for support materials. Information generated by MBTI users in counseling, careers, education, organizations, and religion will need to be integrated into the overall body of knowledge about psychological type. Next steps will discover more facts about type differences in career choices and career satisfaction, in work environments, in learning styles and teaching styles, in academic performance, in stress and burnout, in changes through the life span, and in the effectiveness of teams. The next decade will present more materials for the professional and the public to bring Jung's concepts to life.

In the end, I believe that Jung's insights about the functions and attitudes will prove to be describing human attributes that truly exist, and that the MBTI will remain as a sophisticated instrument for identifying them.

RESOURCES FOR THE MYERS-BRIGGS TYPE INDICATOR

Association for Psychological Type (APT), Gainesville, Florida. A nonprofit membership association for all persons interested in psychological type. APT sponsors biennial international conferences, and through its regions, biennial regional conferences. APT facilitates networking through interest area coordinators for counseling, education, organizations, religion, theory and research, and through local groups in each region of the United states and affiliated international associations. APT publishes a newsletter, *The Bulletin of Psychological Type* and a research journal, *The Journal of Psychological Type.*

Center for Applications of Psychological Type (CAPT), Gainesville, Florida. A nonprofit international organization formed in collaboration with Isabel Briggs Myers in 1975. CAPT provides basic and advanced professional training and consultation for MBTI users and for users of the Murphy-Meisgeier Indicator for Children (MMTIC). The MBTI Data Bank and the Isabel Briggs Myers Memorial Library are at CAPT. In addition to its own research, CAPT provides MBTI research consultation. Other CAPT services include publication or distribution of books and materials about type, the MBTI and MMTIC, computer scoring for the MBTI, and a general information resource for questions about type.

Consulting Psychologists Press (CPP), Palo Alto, California. Publishes both the MBTI and MMTIC as well as many other tests and support materials. CPP provides scoring services and/or software for many of its tests.

REFERENCES

Brownsword, A. W. (1987). *It takes all types.* San Anselmo, CA: Baytree Publication Company.

Brownsword, A. W. (1988). *Psychological type: An introduction.* San Anselmo, CA: Baytree Publication Company.

Cann, D. R. (1979). *Personality structure and the content of dreams.* Unpublished doctoral dissertation, McGill University.

Carskadon, T. G. (1979). Clinical and counseling aspects of the Myers-Briggs Type Indicator: A research review. *Research in Psychological Type, 2,* 2–31.

Carskadon, T. G. (1982). Myers-Briggs Type Indicator Characterizations: A Jungian horoscope? *Research in Psychological Type, 5,* 87–88.

Carskadon, T. G., & Cook, D. D. Validity of MBTI type descriptions as perceived by recipients unfamiliar with type. *Research in Psychological Type, 5,* 89–94.

Carskadon, T. G., McCarley, N., & McCaulley, M. H. (1987). *Compendium of research involving the Myers-Briggs Type Indicator.* Gainesville, FL: Center for Applications of Psychological Type.

Casas, E., & Hamlet, J. (1984). *Psychological types of clients, student-counselors and supervisors in a clinical training center: Study of client-counselor compatibility and therapy internship.* Interim Report: CRHSC, Subvention No. 410 834 0428, University of Ottawa, Canada.

Center for Applications of Psychological Type. (1989). *Myers-Briggs Type Indicator Bibliography.* Gainesville, FL: Center for Applications of Psychological Type.

Coan, R. W. (1979). *Psychologists: Personal and theoretical pathways.* New York: Irvington Publishers.

Cohen, S. R. (1981). Using the MBTI with teachers, supervisors, administrators and students: A program review. *Research in Psychological Type, 3,* 42–47.

DeNovellis, R. (1984a). The Personality Type Preference Indicator. *Journal of Psychological Type, 7,* 29–38.

DeNovellis, R. (1984b). Personality Type Preference Indicator: PTPI Test Manual, First Edition. Claremont, CA: Psychological Research Institute for Business and Education.

DeNovellis, R. (1985). Understanding the Personality Type Preference Indicator. *Journal of Psychological Type, 9,* 34–40.

Gough, H. G. (1981, July). *Studies of the Myers-Briggs Type Indicator in a personality assessment research institute.* Paper presented at the Fourth National Conference on the Myers-Briggs Type Indicator, Stanford University, CA.

Grant, W. H., Thompson, M., & Clarke, T. E. (1983). *From Image to Likeness: A Jungian path in the Gospel journey.* Ramsey, NJ: Paulist Press.

Hammer, A. L., & Yeakley, F. R. (1987). The relationship between "true type" and reported type. *Journal of Psychological Type, 13,* 52–55.

Harbaugh, G. L. (1988). *God's gifted people.* Minneapolis: Augsburg Press.

Hirsh, S., & Kummerow, J. (1989). *LIFETypes.* New York: Warner Books.

Hobby, S. A., Miller, D. I., Stone, J. A., & Carskadon, T. G. (1987. An empirical test of differing theoretical positions of Myers and Keirsey concerning type similarity. *Journal of Psychological Type, 13,* 56–60.

Howes, R. J. (1977). Reliability of the Myers-Briggs Type Indicator as a function of mood manipulation. Unpublished master's thesis, Mississippi State University.

Inclan, A. (1985). Cross-cultural analysis of language in the assessment of personality variables (Doctoral dissertation, University of Florida, 1984). *Dissertation Abstracts International, 46* (04), 896A.

Jones, J. H., & Sherman, R. G. (1979). Clinical uses of the Myers-Briggs Type Indicator. *Research in Psychological Type, 2,* 32–45.

Jung, C. G. (1921/1971). *Psychological Types* (H. G. Baynes, Trans. revised by R. F. C. Hull). Volume 6 of *The collected works of C. G. Jung.* Princeton, NJ: Princeton University Press. (Original work published in 1921.)

Kainz, R. I. (1985). *Myers-Briggs Type Indicator preference scores and age.* Unpublished doctoral dissertation, University of Florida.

Keirsey, D. W., & Bates, M. (1984). *Please understand me.* Del Mar, CA: Prometheus Nemesis Book Company.

Kroeger, O., & Thuesen, J. (1988). *Type Talk.* New York, Delacorte Press.

Kummerow, J. M. (1988). A methodology for verifying type: Research results. *Journal of Psychological Type, 15,* 20–25.

Lawrence, G. D. (1982). *People types and tiger stripes*. Gainesville, FL: Center for Applications of Psychological Type.

Lawrence, G. D. (1984). A synthesis of learning style research involving the MBTI. *Journal of Psychological Type, 8,* 2–15.

Levin, L. S. (1978). Jungian personality variables of psychotherapists of five different theoretical orientations. (Doctoral dissertation, Georgia State University, 1978). *Dissertation Abstracts International, 39,* 4042B–4043B. (University Microfilms No. 79-01, 823)

Lowen, W., with Miike, L. (1982). *Dichotomies of the mind: A systems science model of the mind and personality*. New York: John Wiley and Sons.

Macdaid, G. P., McCaulley, M. H., & Kainz, R. I. (1987). *Myers-Briggs Type Indicator Atlas of Type Tables*. Gainesville, FL: Center for Applications of Psychological Type.

Mamchur, C. M. (1984). *Insights: Understanding yourself and others*. Toronto: The Ontario Institute for Studies in Education.

McCarley, N. G., & Carskadon, T. G. (1987). Findings and strategies leading to empirically based type descriptions. *Journal of Psychological Type, 13,* 9–14.

McCaulley, M. H. (1977). *The Myers Longitudinal Medical Study* (Monograph II). Gainesville, FL: Center for Applications of Psychological Type.

McCaulley, M. H. (1978). *Application of the Myers-Briggs Type Indicator to medicine and other health professions* (Monograph I). Gainesville, FL: Center for Applications of Psychological Type.

Meisgeier, C., & Murphy, E. (1987). *The Murphy-Meisgeier Type Indicator for Children: Manual*. Palo Alto, California: Consulting Psychologists Press.

Myers, I. B. (1962). *Manual: The Myers-Briggs Type Indicator*. Princeton, NJ: Educational Testing Service. (Out of print).

Myers, I. B. (1987). Introduction to type (4th ed.). Palo Alto, CA: Consulting Psychologists Press.

Myers, I. B., & McCaulley, M. H. (1985). *Manual: A guide to the development and use of the Myers-Briggs Type Indicator*. Palo Alto, CA: Consulting Psychologists Press.

Myers, I. B. with Myers, P. B. (1980). *Gifts differing*. Palo Alto, CA: Consulting Psychologists Press.

Neff, L. (1988). *One of a kind*. Portland, Oregon, Multnomah Press.

Newman, L. E. (1977). Counselor characteristics and training as related to the process of empathy and its manifestations (Doctoral dissertation, University of Florida, 1975). *Dissertation Abstracts International, 37,* 4138A–4139A. (University Microfilms No. 77-114)

Newman, L. E. (1979). Personality types of therapist and client and their use in counseling. *Research in Psychological Type, 2,* 46–55.

Ohsawa, T. (1975, October). MBTI experiences in Japan: Career choice, selection, placement, and counseling for individual development. Paper presented at the first National Conference on the Myers-Briggs Type Indicator, Gainesville, FL.

Ohsawa, T. (1979, June). A profile of top executives of Japanese companies. Paper presented at the Fourth Biennial Conference on the Myers-Briggs Indicator, Palo Alto, CA.

Parham, M., Miller, D. I., & Carskadon, T. G. (1984). Do "job types" differ from "life types"? The effects of standard vs. vocationally specific instructions on the reliability of MBTI scores. *Journal of Psychological Type, 7,* 46–48.

Provost, J. A. (1984). *A casebook: Applications of the Myers-Briggs Type Indicator in counseling*. Gainesville, FL: Center for Applications of Psychological Type.

Quenk, A. T. (1984). *Psychological types and psychotherapy*. Gainesville, FL: Center for Applications of Psychological Type.

Singer, J., & Loomis, M. (1984). *Interpretive Guide for the Singer-Loomis Inventory of Personality* (Experimental Edition). Palo Alto, CA: Consulting Psychologists Press.

Stokes, J. (1987a). Exploring the relationship between type and gender Part 1: Anecdotal experiences of MBTI users. *Journal of Psychological Type, 13,* 34–43.

Stokes, J. (1987b). Exploring the relationship between type and gender Part 2: A review and critique of empirical research and other data. *Journal of Psychological Type, 13,* 44–51.

von Franz, M-L. (1971). The inferior function. In M-L. von Franz and J. Hillman (Eds.), *Lectures on Jung's Typology* (pp. 1–72). Dallas, TX: Spring Publications, Inc.

Ware, R., & Yokomoto, C. (1985). Perceived accuracy of Myers-Briggs Type Indicator descriptions using Keirsey profiles. *Journal of Psychological Type, 10,* 27–31.

Wheelwright, J. B., Wheelwright, J. H., & Buehler, H. A. (1964). *Jungian Type Survey: The Gray-Wheelwright test.* San Francisco: Society of Jungian Analysts of Northern California.

Witzig, J. S. (1978). Jung's typology and classification of psychotherapies. *Journal of Analytical Psychology, 23* (4), 315–331.

6 Cognitive and Behavioral Assessment

Thomas V. Merluzzi
University of Notre Dame

Michael D. Boltwood
Stanford University

INTRODUCTION

In contrast to other chapters in this book we will not be discussing a particular test, nor will we be using terminology such as personality or personality assessment. Also, in contrast to traditional approaches to personality assessment, which are trait or *sign* oriented (Mischel, 1968), cognitive and behavioral assessment deal with more discrete phenomena and are *sample* oriented. Although the level of measurement in cognitive and behavioral assessment compared to traditional assessment is less global, and the inferences made in the assessment process far less deep, the issues generally encountered in traditional personality assessment are nonetheless relevant. That is, reliability and validity, particularly ecological validity, are critical issues in cognitive and behavioral assessment.

The distinction between cognitive and behavioral assessment and more traditional assessment methods noted above should not lead one to assume that cognitive and behavioral assessment are based on identical underlying assumptions. Although cognitive and behavioral assessment might share some common assumptions about the scope of the tasks of assessment, strictly speaking, they are not based on the same conceptual presuppositions. On a more practical level, strict adherents of behavior theory might not value self-reported thoughts concomitant with directly observed behavior. For them, overt behavior is considered the most relevant criterion when assessing validity. For example, a measure of validity would be the consistency of the thoughts with the behavior. Conversely, strict adherents of the cognitive perspective might view a behavior as literally meaningless without the context provided by self-reported thoughts. Thus, thoughts might determine the interpretation of behavior.

More recently, the differences between the perspectives have received less and less attention. Current interest in the integration of psychotherapy approaches has promoted the pursuit of discovering what is common and effective in all approaches to psychotherapy and, presumably, assessment.

We hope to accomplish several goals with this chapter. First, we hope to set cognitive and behavioral assessment techniques in context both historically and conceptually. Second, we hope to introduce the reader to the dominant approaches to cognitive and behavioral assessment. Because of the broad scope of the task, we have chosen to focus on one particular problem area, social skills, and will use that problem to illustrate the various approaches to assessment. Finally, we hope to provide information that contrasts cognitive and behavioral assessment with traditional assessment. Our intention in this last goal is *not* to present a case for the superiority of cognitive and behavioral assessment but to illustrate the different assumptions that underlie those approaches and to suggest points of integration.

HISTORICAL PERSPECTIVES

For excellent treatments of the history of cognitive and behavioral assessment the reader is encouraged to read McReynolds (1986) and Sundberg (1981). In both chapters the authors provide ample evidence that behavioral assessment did not simply emerge from behavior therapy and that cognitive assessment did not simply emerge from cognitive therapy.

Behavioral Assessment

The recent emergence of behaviorism and, eventually, behavioral assessment is easily traced to the work of Watson (1913) and Skinner (1951) as well as a number of others whose work was related to the scientific traditions of behavior theory (e.g., Pavlov). The reader is likely familiar with the work of these authors and their direct connection to the development of behavioral perspectives in operant and classical conditioning research.

Direct observation is an integral aspect of behavioral assessment with roots in other fields as well as psychology (McReynolds, 1985). McReynolds (1985) cited the observation methods of Darwin (1859), the direct observation of children (Gesell, 1925; Goodenough, 1949) and groups (Bales, 1951), and the emphasis on role playing in psychodrama (Moreno, 1983) as less than well recognized influences on the emergence of behavioral assessment. Further, the ecological perspective of Lewin and Barker (Barker, 1968) has direct connections to the conceptual bases of behavioral assessment in that the emphasis on environmental influences on behavior was an integral part of Lewin's famous equation: $B = f(p, e)$. Behavior is a function of the person and the environment.

In citing the influence of these authors McReynolds notes that interest in direct observation and on ecological variables was not relegated solely to the behavioral perspective. Also, these authors helped contribute to an intellectual and scientific environment that would support the growth of behavioral assessment.

More recently the work of Lindsley (1956), Skinner (1969), and Ayllon and Azrin (1968) has contributed greatly to the focus on behaviorism. In addition McReynolds noted the work of Bijou and Patterson (1971) as a major contribution to the systematic development of behavior observation systems. Lindsley (1956) used operant technology to assess behavior deficits in schizophrenics. In a classic book on token economies, Ayllon and Azrin (1968) underscored the need for thorough and controlled observation in the assessment of behaviors in a hospital setting.

All things considered, however, the major thrust in behavioral assessment seems to have been a function of the behavioral technology used in single subject designs and the abandonment of traditional assessment and diagnosis by behaviorists. The intention of behavioral assessment was to reduce the inference in assessment and diagnosis and create methods that would be more science than art (Hersen & Bellak, 1976). That thrust was also prompted by the fact that in behavior therapy assessment and treatment are closely tied.

The first major books on behavioral assessment were published in 1976 and 1977 and journals devoted to the topic (*Journal of Behavioral Assessment* and *Behavioral Assessment*) were first published in 1980. Clearly, behavioral assessment, as a well defined area of study, is quite young. The remarkable growth in the field appears to be related to the scientific traditions inherent in the behavioral perspective, the emphasis on single subject research, and the integration of assessment and treatment.

Cognitive Assessment

Cognitive assessment has a more convoluted history. As opposed to behavioral assessment, which emerged primarily from behavior therapy, cognitive assessment is more of a hybrid. Interestingly, some of the methods used in cognitive assessment were derived from treatments or perspectives that have been labeled cognitive-behavioral. The most notable example of this is the Assertive Self-statement Test (ASST; Schwartz & Gottman, 1976). The ASST assesses the degree to which subjects have thoughts that might either inhibit or facilitate an assertive response. This approach to cognitive assessment can be traced to the work of Meichenbaum (1977) whose influence on the field has been enormous. Meichenbaum's treatment studies were primarily based on the premise that thoughts were the final common pathway for information related to a problem area such as a phobia or a skill deficit. Thus, early cognitive assessment measures were based on the belief that one could assess dysfunctional thoughts as well as document change in thoughts as a function of treatment.

Because the background and methods of cognitive assessment are so diverse, it is difficult to narrow the focus of the historical developments leading to present-day methods. Therefore, we will limit our historical analysis to those people and events that had a major impact on cognitive assessment.

Kelly's personal construct theory (1955), with its emphasis on the psychological construction of one's environment and the importance of expectancies and prediction, is very consistent with the present-day approaches to cognitive assessment. Although Kelly would object to being labeled "cognitive," the richness of the theory and its compatibility with cognitive perspectives contribute to its importance in cognitive assessment. Neimeyer and Neimeyer (1981) presented an extended discussion of how assessment is conducted from a personal construct perspective.

The influence of social learning theory is apparent when one considers that cognitive assessment has focused on both behavior and outcome expectancies. Rotter (1954) and Bandura (1986) were essential figures in this area. However, milestones for the cognitive perspective are the publication of Mischel's (1968) book *Personality and Assessment* and, to a greater extent, his 1973 *Psychological Review* article entitled "Toward a cognitive social learning reconceptualization of personality." In that paper he presented what he termed person variables, and in a subsequent paper (Mischel, 1981) he explicated strategies for the assessment of person variables. Finally, Brock (1967) and Greenwald (1968) are deserving of recognition for their work on the elicitation and scoring of thought data in attitude change research.

In spite of the recent emergence of cognitive assessment from the cognitive-behavioral treatment literature, the influence of personal construct theory, social learning theory, and attitude change research, there is a broader context for cognitive assessment, namely, information processing. A recent volume edited by Ingram (1987) illustrates how the clinical and cognitive sciences have been integrated. In that volume Lachman and Lachman (1987) provide an insightful history of the information processing paradigm, whereas other chapters of the book illustrate the importance of the paradigm for the future of clinical cognitive psychology.

CONCEPTUAL FOUNDATIONS

The conceptual underpinnings of behavioral and cognitive perspectives can be best illustrated by contrasting the paradigmatic assumptions that drive each perspective. Some of the major assumptions of the cognitive and behavioral perspectives are presented in Table 6.1. Although we do not want to create what Michael Mahoney has called "science friction," it is important to note that Table 6.1 contains tenets of those perspectives that are "at odds." Also, we have

TABLE 6.1
Paradigmatic Assumptions of Associationism and Information Processing

	Associationism	*Information Processing*
Metascientific assumptions	Mind is passive Behavior is a product of the environment Tabula rasa Behavior is modifiable	Mind is dynamic and active Behavior is a product of mental acts Innate properties Mind is modifiable
Subject matter	Performance Conditioning Testing learning theory	Mental processes Thought and language Comprehension and knowledge
Methodologies	Reversal and multiple-baseline designs Classical and operant research paradigms	Convergent validation techniques Use of reaction time to decouple cognitive processes Computer simulations
Concepts	Stimulus, response, associations, reinforcement, incentives, and so forth	Input, output, encoding, storage, retrieval, competence, executive processor, primary and secondary memory, and so forth
Theories	Mechanistic: S-r-s-R	Computerlike: mind, as a rule governs learning

From Merluzzi, T. V., Rudy, T. E., & Glass, C. R. (1981) The information-processing paradigm: Implications for clinical science. In T. V. Merluzzi, C. R. Glass, & M. Genest, (Eds), *Cognitive assessment* (p. 87). New York: Guilford Press.

chosen to contrast the paradigmatic assumptions that represent neobehaviorism (or associationism) and information processing.

In contrast to the behavioral (or associationistic perspective) and cognitive (or information processing) approach assumes that the mind is a real entity that is acceptable for scientific investigation. Moreover, the cognitive perspective assumes that cognitive systems actually transform input and construct "reality." Some might label the cognitive paradigm rationalist particularly if one only uses the computer metaphor to represent that perspective. However, more recently there has been an attempt to break away from the computer metaphor in order to present cognitivism as constructivist.

By aligning cognitive assessment with the information processing paradigm we need to distinguish between cognitive content or structure and cognitive processes or mechanisms. Content or structure refers to the products of cognitive processes (Martzke, Andersen, & Cacioppo, 1986). An example of content or structure would be to assess the thoughts of socially anxious persons and find that they endorse negative and inhibiting cognitions in social interactions. In further experimentation we also discover that these persons selectively remember information from social interaction or actively distort information such that only negative information is encoded and that positive experiences are minimized. These latter examples are process oriented in that we are dealing with the encoding, retention, and retrieval of information. Although the content-process distinction is important, Martzke, Anderson, and Cacioppo (1986) emphasize that the content or structure analysis may be products or markers of those processes. Thus, we may view the information processing perspective as a relevant overarching paradigm for cognitive assessment.

It is important to note that despite the differences cited in Table 6.1 both the cognitive and behavioral perspective have empiricism as their method of proof, operationism as a way of describing experimental procedures, and adhere to the rational canons of science (Lachman, Lachman, & Butterfield, 1979).

In the following sections we will present basic information about behavioral and cognitive approaches to assessment. For each approach we will present information about administration and scoring, interpretation, and finally, a short case example.

BEHAVIORAL ASSESSMENT

Administration and Scoring

Behavioral assessment measures have been developed for a wide array of problem areas ranging from marital discord to phobias, from school behaviors to sexual dysfunction. These assessment procedures can play an important role in initial problem identification and specification as well as treatment planning, evaluation, and adjustment. The following discussion begins with a brief explanation of various standard types of behavioral assessment. Attention is then focused on a selective review of behavioral assessment of social skills. There has been a great deal of interest in social skills and social skills deficits. In large part, this has been due to the association of social skills deficits with a broad range of clinical problems including depression, juvenile delinquency, marital distress, social isolation, and illness (McFall, 1982). Assessment methods used in the evaluation of social skills are presented as representative of the issues and methods germane to behavioral assessment in general.

Behavioral Interviews. A number of specific guidelines have been developed for behavioral assessment interviews. Well known examples include Kanfer and Saslow (1965), Wolpe (1982), and Goldfried and Davidson (1976). At the core of these formats is the identification of problem behaviors, and the functional analysis of their antecedent conditions and their consequences. This approach serves to identify related events that either function as reinforcers which maintain target behaviors, or as aversive stimuli which decrease them. This type of analysis leads to the formulation of specific hypotheses concerning target problems. Meyer & Turkat (1979) describe this problem formulation as having three components: "1. It identifies the functional relationship among the various presenting problems of the patient. 2. It accounts for the etiology of these behavioral difficulties. 3. It provides predictions of the patient's responses to future stimulus situations" (p. 262). The behavioral interview is an essential first step in comprehensive behavioral assessment. In addition to identifying problems and formulating hypotheses about them, the information generated in the interview should be used to select additional appropriate forms of behavioral assessment.

Self-report Questionnaires. Although self-report questionnaires were once looked upon with disfavor by many behavioral therapists, they are now a common form of behavioral assessment. Unlike projective tests or empirically derived inventories such as the MMPI, behavioral questionnaires place a strong emphasis on specific behaviors and situations, thus giving them strong face validity, and potentially improving predictive validity. Jensen and Hayes (1986) have outlined a number of functions and goals for self-report questionnaires, these include: collection of historic and demographic information; screening and diagnosis; and identification and specification of target behaviors, controlling variables, and alternative behaviors. The use of self-report questionnaires has many advantages. They are inexpensive and relatively easy and quick to complete. They are available in the form of broad inventories that can screen for a wide range of problems. There are also numerous questionnaires that are tailored to very specific behaviors and situations. In the face of the proliferation of behavioral questionnaires, users must be cautioned that the development of a valid and reliable instrument requires complex and extensive psychometric development, testing, and analysis. Before a questionnaire is used to make clinical judgments, the clinician should carefully evaluate its validity and reliability along with its appropriateness for a specific client and/or situation.

Self-monitoring. Self-monitoring refers to the systematic observation and documentation of one's own behavior. Pertinent associated environmental data are often recorded as well. Self-monitoring procedures are a rich source of assessment information and can also serve as an important component of behavioral self-control interventions (Thoresen & Mahoney, 1974). Self-monitoring provides a relatively simple and highly flexible approach to the collection of a variety of behavioral data. Types of information collected can include various forms of individual or group behavior, the antecedents and consequences of such behaviors, and any number of environmental aspects of the settings in which these events occur. Types of measurement can include frequency counts (i.e., how often the behavior occurs in a specified time period), time related measures (i.e., the duration of target behavior) and also qualitative ratings of a variety of internal or external events. Common formats for monitoring include narrative descriptions, rating scales, check lists, and graphs. In addition, a variety of mechanical, timing, and electronic devices have been developed to aid in self-monitoring (Bornstein, Hamilton, & Bornstein, 1986). Ingenious self-monitoring systems, formats, and aids have been developed for almost every conceivable area of behavioral assessment (Mahoney, 1977; Thoresen & Mahoney, 1974). Problems associated with self-monitoring include questions of reliability and reactivity (i.e., the influence of the monitoring process on the behavior being measured). These problems have been the subject of considerable research and discussion and they are reviewed in detail by Bornstein, Hamilton, & Bornstein (1986).

Direct Observation. The direct observation and recording of an individual or group has been called the "hallmark" of behavioral assessment (Ciminero, 1986). Direct observation is usually employed to assess motor and/or verbal behaviors. Target behaviors can range from discrete activities such as arm or eye movements to more complex behaviors such as social interactions. As Kazdin (1981) points out, the selection, operationalization and measurement of target behaviors in an objective, clear, and complete manner may appear deceptively simple, but requires careful planning and execution. Careful training of observers is essential for reliable observational assessment. Factors that must be considered include, interrater reliability, observer drift, observer bias, and interactions between the observer and the observed (Foster & Cone, 1986). Behaviors are usually quantified by using frequency measures or discrete categorizations (e.g., yes/no, correct/incorrect). Recording procedures can be continuous or carried out at specified time units or intervals. Numerous variations and combinations of measurement and sampling procedures have been devised for behavioral observation programs (Gambrill, 1976). Direct observational assessment has been used very successfully with certain populations such as school children and the institutionalized. For general outpatient populations effective observational assessment is more difficult because of the inability to control or standardize the assessment setting. For these populations analogue methods have frequently been used.

Analogue measures. Analogue measures require the subject to respond to a contrived situation that simulates relevant conditions in the natural environment. Analogues provide an alternative form of direct behavioral observation when factors such as cost and difficulties in trying to structure and control stimuli make direct observation in the natural environment impractical. One of the most frequently used forms of analogue assessment is the Behavioral Avoidance Test (BAT). The BAT was originally described by Lang and Lazovik (1963) in the assessment of snake phobia. Since then the BAT has been used in the assessment of a variety of avoidant behaviors (Bernstein & Nietzel, 1973). In a typical BAT analogue, the subject is instructed to proceed as far as possible through a series of progressively challenging approaches to a specified object or situation. For example, in assessing spider phobia the subject may first be instructed to view a picture of a spider and finally progress to letting the spider crawl on his or her hand. A BAT typically includes from 5 to 15 progressive approach behaviors, with scoring based on the number of behavioral steps successfully completed. Role plays are another common form of analogue assessment. A typical role play begins by having a narrator describe a specific stimulus situation. A confederate then initiates an interaction with the subject that approximates a situation that might occur in the subject's natural environment. The behavior of the subject is rated according to specific response criteria. Variations on this format include using a written, audiotape, or videotape stimulus in place of a live actor, or having the subject write out his or her responses rather than state them (Nay, 1977). Analogue procedures provide a flexible format for the assessment of a wide range of behaviors within the practical restrictions of a clinical setting. However, as assessment procedures move away from in-vivo, naturalistic observation toward contrived analogues carried out in clinical or laboratory settings, the validity of the analogue measure must be carefully addressed (Merluzzi & Biever, 1987).

Psychophysiological Assessment. Experimental psychology, behavioral medicine, and biofeedback research have been responsible for the development of a number of physiological measures that are useful in behavioral assessment. Measurement devices have been developed to accurately measure multiple parameters of all major physiological systems (e.g., cardiovascular, respiratory, digestive, central and peripheral nervous systems). Special attention has been given to physiological indices of stress, anxiety, and affective responses such as autonomic nervous system activity, muscular tension, and endocrine functions (Kallman & Feuerstein, 1986). When measures are properly selected and applied psycho-physiological assessment can be very valid and reliable. The major disadvantages are that they often require expensive and elaborate equipment that is often intrusive and restrictive.

Assessment of Social Skills

Since the development of the Wolpe-Lazarus Assertiveness Inventory (Wolpe & Lazarus, 1966), numerous social skills assessment measures have appeared in the behavioral literature. The number and variety of these assessment procedures has been matched by the many, often divergent, definitions of social skills found in the behavioral literature. Assessment has focused on a number of different aspects of social skills including: global sequences of behavior, numerous different molecular response behaviors, anxiety levels, available repertoires of social responses, and the ability to understand and appropriately respond to social cues. In spite of this extensive work in the area of social skills assessment, Conger and Conger (1986) pointed out that there is "no theoretically derived nor empirically established listing of (social) skills" (p. 527). Hersen and Bellack (1977) provided a broad, clinically useful definition for social skills by describing the construct as the "effectiveness of behavior in social interactions" (p. 512). The reader is referred to McFall (1982) for an insightful discussion of current theoretical and assessment issues in the conceptualization of social skills. The formats most frequently used in the behavioral assessment of social skills are self-report questionnaires and analogue measures. An overview of some of the better known social skills assessment measures is provided below. Detailed reviews of social skills measures are provided in Bellack and Hersen (1979).

Behavioral Interviews. Arkowitz (1981) has described an outline for a comprehensive behavioral interview to assess social inadequacy. This interview guide includes a physical description of the patient; behavioral observation of the patient during the interview; patient's description of presenting problems and treatment goals; operational definitions of problems and goals; major problems other than social inadequacy; effects of social dysfunction on the person's life functioning; assessment of social functioning in a number of specific areas along with estimates of social skill, anxiety, and self-evaluations in each area; cognitions relating to social functioning; sexual knowledge, experiences, and fears; current living situation with particular reference to potential social contacts; description of a typical day with particular reference to social contacts; and current employment and educational situation.

Self-Report Questionnaires. Two of the most widely used social skills questionnaires are the Rathus Assertiveness Schedule (Rathus, 1973) and the Galassi College Self-Expression Scale (Galassi & Galassi, 1974). The Rathus Assertiveness Schedule contains 30 descriptive statements to which the subject responds on a Likert scale ranging from "very uncharacteristic" to "very characteristic." On the Galassi College Self-Expression Scale, the subject uses a Likert scale (ranging from "never or rarely" to "almost always") to indicate the similarity of his or her behaviors to each of 50 social behaviors described in the questionnaire. As its title implies this scale is tailored to college students, however the authors have also developed a less frequently used "adult" version. The Gambrill-Richey Assertion Inventory (Gambrill & Richey, 1975) also uses a Likert format, but in contrast to the above measures, each descriptive situation is rated separately for the likelihood of engaging in the behavior and the amount of discomfort associated with carrying it out. The Gambrill-Richey Assertion Inventory also provides separate scales for different types of social situations such as declining requests, engaging in social contacts, and expressing negative feelings.

The Social Avoidance and Distress Scale (SADS) is a measure of general social functioning in which subjects rate the similarity of their behaviors to a range of social situations and responses (Watson & Friend, 1969). A single summary score provides an overall rating of avoidance and distress. The Situational Questionnaire, developed by Rehm & Marston (1968), assesses heterosexual social anxiety in males. Subjects rate the level of anxiety (on a 7-point Likert scale) they would feel in 30 social situations. The Social Performance Survey Schedule (SPSS) is comprised of 100 interpersonal behaviors (Lowe & Cautela, 1978). On the SPSS, subjects use a Likert scale to rate the similarity of their behavior to each item. The SPSS yields two scores, one for positive and one for negative interpersonal behaviors. The Survey of Heterosexual Interactions (Twentyman & McFall, 1975) is a self-report measure of heterosocial skill. It contains 20 items that are scored on 7-point Likert scales ranging from "being able to perform the desired behavior in every case" to "being unable to perform the desired behavior in every case." The Personal Assertion Analysis (Hedlund & Lindquist, 1984) was developed to distinguish between passive, assertive, and aggressive behaviors. It contains 30 behavioral situations, with subjects responding on a Likert scale ranging from "just like me" to "not at all like me." Self-report questionnaires are the most frequently used and most diverse form of behavioral assessment of social skills. As this brief review of different scales indicates, self-report questionnaires demonstrate the many different aspects of social skills that have been addressed in the assessment literature.

Self-Monitoring. Self-monitoring has been used to measure dating frequency and casual heterosexual interactions (Christensen, Arkowitz, & Anderson, 1975). Gambrill and Richey (1985) have developed a social contact recording form in which the recorder documents a number of aspects of social interactions. These include the person contacted along with the setting, nature, and duration of the interaction. In addition, the recorder rates his or her comfort, confidence, and enjoyment concerning the contact. Self-monitoring of behaviors has been used by Peterson (1979) in a study of social interactions. Subjects kept an Interaction Record in which they recorded the most important interaction of the day noting conditions under which the exchange took place, how the interaction started, and a detailed description of the interaction. These records were scored by first breaking the interaction into a sequence of individual acts. These acts were then coded into categories of affect (e.g., affection/affiliation, aggression/disapproval), construal (e.g., positive relationship, negative relationship), and expectation (e.g., compliance, withdrawal).

Direct Observation. Although direct observation is generally considered the most valid form of behavioral assessment, it has been infrequently used in the area of social skills. As Bellack and Hersen (1979) noted, "the special character of interpersonal behavior frequently makes such observations impractical or impossible. Intimate and private interactions generally are not privy to outside observers, and many public interactions (e.g., assertion situations, meeting with a stranger) occur too infrequently and unpredictably to permit easy access'' (p. 87). As a result of these difficulties a great deal of attention has been turned to the development of analogue measures as described below.

Analogue Measures. After self-report questionnaires, analogues or role-plays of various types are the most frequently reported form of behavioral assessment used in the evaluation of social skills. In these analogues a stimulus is presented and the subject is then instructed to respond as he or she would in a real situation. As with self-report questionnaires, a wide variety of designs has been reported. Variations involve time periods (ranging from brief stimuli and responses to extended conversations), different levels of realism in the settings used, different stimulus presentations (ranging from audiotapes to live actors serving as confederates), and differing response modes and restraints. Scoring procedures also vary widely across different analogue assessments. Factors that are scored include perceived anxiety levels, length of responses, use of assertive phrases, and motor behaviors such as eye contact, hand gestures and body language. Scoring methods include, global judgments, likert scales, timing, and frequency counts. Scoring has been conducted by subjects, actors, and trained and untrained judges. (Hersen & Bellack, 1977).

In the Simulated Social Interaction Test (SSIT), a narrator explains a specific social situation and a confederate then provides a verbal prompt to which the subject responds (Farrell, Curran, Zwick, & Monti, 1983). For example: ''Narrator: 'Let's suppose you respond to an ad in the newspaper and go for a job interview. As the interview goes on, the interviewer says': Confederate: 'What makes you think you're a good person for the job?' '' (p. 5). The subject then responds as he or she would in an actual situation. Eight such interactions are videotaped, with the subject responding to examples of disapproval, assertiveness, confrontation, heterosexual contact, interpersonal warmth, rejection by parents, interpersonal loss, and positive feedback. These tapes are then rated by a group of trained judges who use 11-point Likert scales to assess overall assertiveness and overall anxiety. The Behavioral Assertiveness Test (BAT) developed by Eisler, Miller, and Hersen (1973), uses a similar format. For the BAT judges rate verbal responses such as duration of reply, loudness, compliance, and requests as well as nonverbal behaviors such as eye contact and smiles.

In a format similar to the above, Mullinix and Galassi (1981) presented subjects with four audiotaped statements involving work related conflict. Subjects were asked to take the role of a coworker and write down exactly what they would say in response to the taped statement. These statements were then rated by trained judges for level of compliance and presence of annoyance/hostility.

Higgins, Frisch, & Smith (1983) have developed a naturalistic analogue procedure with many of the advantages of direct behavioral observation. In the

Behavioral Assessment Situation (BAS) the subject is confronted by a confederate student who, in the course of a conversation, makes a series of increasingly demanding requests to borrow some important class notes from the subject. The subject is unaware that the fellow student is a confederate and that the interaction is being videotaped. The videotape is then scored for overall social skill, tenseness/uneasiness, number of speech disturbances, frequency of conversational questions and feedback, latency of responses, and level of compliance. The reader is encouraged to consult Merluzzi and Biever (1987) concerning issues related to the validity of analogue methods of behavioral assessment of social skill.

Psychophysiological Assessment. Unfortunately little use has been made of psychophysiological measurements as a component in the comprehensive behavioral assessment of social skills. This most likely is due to the intrusive nature of required instrumentation. Several studies (Kaloupek & Levis, 1980; Monti, Wallander, Ahern, & Munroe, 1984) have used a psychophysiological measure of anxiety (i.e., heart rate) as part of a multi-modal assessment of anxiety and social skills. Although anxiety is often present in individuals with poor social functioning, neither its role in overall social functioning, nor its relationship to social skills behaviors is currently clear (Bellack, 1979).

Summary. Although the sheer number and variety of assessments may appear confusing to the clinician, this broad variety can serve as an asset. The variety of choices currently available allows the clinician to select from a wide range of assessment options and select measures that best suit a specific client's needs. Choice of an appropriate set of assessment measures should be guided by a careful assessment of intervention targets (Kanfer, 1985) and should focus on the individual problems and circumstances of the client. The initial interview should suggest hypotheses about target behaviors that can be clarified and tested using multiple modes of behavioral assessment.

Interpretation

Interpretation of behavioral assessment measures most often focuses on the degree of change between pre-treatment (baseline) measures and those made during and after treatment. This contrasts many other forms of psychological assessment in which client scores are compared to normative data. Normative data are characteristically available for global or molar measures. As a result these measures are useful as screening tools to identify general problem areas (e.g., depression, poor social functioning) but usually do not identify specific problem behaviors. In addition they are less sensitive to change than molecular measures. In contrast, repeatedly administered molecular measures can detect relatively small changes over the course of treatment and also provide important idiographic information.

A second characteristic of behavioral assessment evaluation is an emphasis on single subject designs and visual or clinical analysis rather than group comparisons and analysis of variance (Turner & Ascher, 1985). This is in large part due to the emphasis behavioral therapy places on the empirical evaluation of clinical practice (Barlow, Hayes, & Nelson, 1984). Although group comparisons are often considered the hallmark of psychological research, it should be noted that single subject designs have had an important role in the advancement of both clinical and basic research in psychotherapy (Barlow, Hayes, & Nelson, 1984).

Statistical significance tests are infrequently used in the evaluation of behavioral assessment information. Bergin and Strupp (1972) have argued that clinically effective psychotherapeutic interventions should produce results that are of sufficient magnitude to be clearly apparent without the use of statistical significance tests. In the area of psychological research, Meehl (1978) has similarly stated that statistical significance tests are generally inappropriate and misleading. Significance tests are at best only partly related to the effect size of a therapeutic intervention. Differences in sample size and variance can at times obscure substantial therapeutic effectiveness and other times produce statistically significant results in the face of trivial differences between groups. Although the focus of clinical treatment evaluation is on the individual, statistical significance measures are concerned with group comparisons. As a result, significance tests are not sensitive to important aspects of individual change. Alternative forms of interpretation are discussed below in the context of single subject time series designs.

Single Subject Time-Series Designs

Single subject time series designs can provide effective and practical means for the evaluation of clinical interventions. The utility and accuracy of single subject designs depends on the selection of both an appropriate design and an appropriate set of measures. Measures should be chosen that are specifically related to the client's problem and sensitive to changes in the target behaviors. In addition, multiple types of measurement are superior to a single form of assessment. These measures should be collected as frequently as is feasible before, during, and after treatment. In each phase of the design, collection of information should continue until reasonable estimates of level, trend, and variability (or stability) can be made. The reader is referred to Barlow, Hayes, and Nelson (1984) for a pragmatic and comprehensive guide to the use of time-series methodology in the evaluation of clinical practice.

Basic Designs. Single subject time-series designs involve the collection of assessment data for a single subject at multiple times in each phase of the design.

Assessment information collected in the absence of any intervention provides a reference or baseline measure of the target behavior(s). In single subject designs this is referred to as the baseline phase and is typically represented by the letter "A." The introduction of a treatment is usually described with a letter to indicate each separate treatment. In the simplest single subject design, A–B, a single baseline phase (A) is followed by the introduction of a single treatment (B). A frequent variation of this design is the A–B–A design which includes a second phase of no treatment in order to assess the effect of withdrawing the treatment. Additional treatments can be added and evaluated either separately (e.g. A–B–C, A–B–A–C) or concurrently (e.g. A–B–BC). These basic baseline and treatment components can be combined in an infinite number of design variations.

Complex designs. A large number of more complex single subject time-series designs have also been described (Barlow & Hersen, 1984; Glass, Wilson, & Gottman, 1974). These designs have been developed to control for some of the validity problems that have been noted in the simpler designs described above, and to evaluate special treatment and research situations. Two frequently used designs are alternating treatment and multiple baseline. Alternating treatment designs alternate two or more treatments or conditions. They differ from A–B–C–B–C designs in that the alternation between treatments is relatively frequent and is repeated a number of times. The actual frequency of alternation can range from minutes to weeks depending on the nature of the treatment. The pattern of alternation between treatments can be fixed and regular or random. The multiple baseline design can be seen as two or more baseline/treatment designs carried out concurrently. For each type of treatment, the change from baseline phase to treatment phase occurs at a different time. A withdrawal phase can also be added following each treatment. As with the transitions from baseline to treatment the timing of the phase change is different for each treatment. Finally it should be noted that multiple single subjects are often grouped for both cumulative and counterbalanced evaluation. For the interested reader, Barlow & Hersen (1984); Glass, Wilson, & Gottman (1974); and Barlow, Hayes and Nelson (1984) provide detailed discussions of single subject time-series designs and their implementation.

Evaluating Results of Single Subject Times-Series Design

The three primary methods for evaluating single subject time-series design results are visual analysis, assessment of clinical significance, and statistical analysis (Craighead, Kazdin, & Mahoney, 1981). Each form of evaluation focuses on the comparison of data points within and across different phases of the design. For purposes of clarity and simplicity, these methods will be discussed in relation to a simple A–B design. It should be noted that the use of an A–B design does not control for a number of validity threats that question whether the observed changes are due to the intervention or other factors (Campbell & Stanley, 1963). The repeated withdrawal of treatment, and other more complex design features mentioned above have been used to control for these validity threats (Barlow & Hersen, 1984).

Visual Evaluation. The visual analysis of a graphic representation of assessment data plotted in a graphic display is the most common form of a single subject design evaluation. The clearest indication of significant change is found when there is no overlap in data between the baseline and treatment phase (Kazdin, 1980). This is demonstrated in examples *a* and *b* in Figure 6.1 which show a clear difference in level at the point of change from phase A to phase B. A more frequent, but less compelling situation is a clear change in slope but no change in level as shown in examples *c* and *d* in Figure 6.1. The ability to make a meaningful visual analysis also depends on the magnitude of the treatment effect, the extent of variability within and across phases, and the number of assessment points within each phase. (Craighead, Kazdin, & Mahoney, 1981). Kazdin (1982) provided an extended discussion of criteria for the visual analysis of single subject time-series data.

Clinical Evaluation. Clinical evaluation focuses on the practical significance of the change achieved in the course of treatment. The amount of change that is required in order to be considered clinically significant depends on the nature of the behavior being assessed (Kazdin, 1980). One appropriate method for determining the criteria for clinically significant change is to work with the client at the time of assessment to set clinical goals that specify desired levels of behavioral change (Jayarantne & Levy, 1979). Kazdin (1980) has proposed

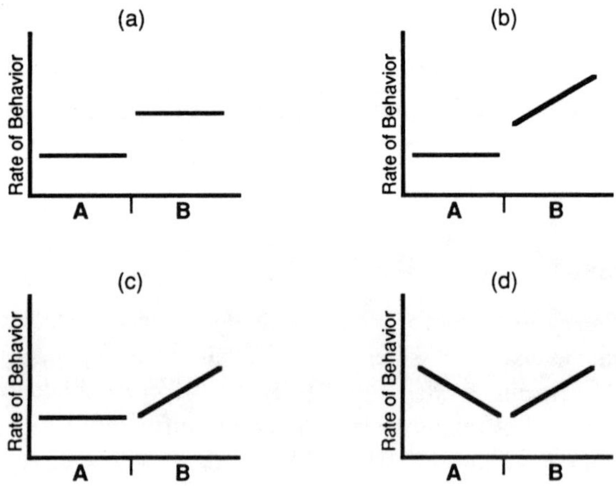

FIG. 6.1. Data patterns in A B designs.

social validation as a criterion for assessing clinically significant treatment effects. This refers to the identification of the normal functional level of others as the criterion for clinical significance. When the target behavior is brought to a level equivalent to the client's social peers who are functioning adequately in society, the effect of the intervention is considered significant.

Statistical Analysis. The use of statistical analysis in the evaluation of single subject time-series designs is somewhat controversial. In addition to a traditional preference for the use of visual and clinical evaluation techniques for the reasons noted above, technical problems have limited the use of statistical significance testing. Although the reliability of interventions used in single subject designs have traditionally been demonstrated through replications across subjects and settings, statistical analysis has several advantages in selected situations. Statistical analysis can be used to demonstrate therapeutic changes when the nature of the baseline data make accurate visual evaluation difficult. In addition, statistical techniques can document subtle but reliable treatment effects not readily seen upon visual inspection of the data. This can be especially important in situations where an intervention results in incremental changes that are individually small but may have important cumulative effects (Kazdin, 1984).

A fundamental problem in the application of statistical significance tests to times series data is the autocorrelation usually found in serially dependent data. This refers to the fact that when such a series of assessment scores are repeated over time, successive scores are usually correlated. This autocorrelation tends to seriously inflate the results of conventional statistical significance tests (Kazdin, 1984). Special time-series analysis techniques have been developed for the statistical analysis of serially dependent data. These time-series analysis procedures take into account changes in both level and slope when comparing baseline and treatment data, while controlling for autocorrelation (Glass, Wilson, & Gottman, 1974).

Other statistical techniques that have been used in the analysis of time-series designs include randomization tests, tests of ranks, and split middle procedures (Kazdin, 1984). The reader is referred to Glass, Wilson, & Gottman (1974), and Edgington (1984) for an extensive presentation and critique of statistical significance tests used in the evaluation of single subject time-series designs.

Case Example

Susan is a 29-year-old woman, referred by a friend to a local community mental health center. Her presenting complaint was dissatisfaction with her current social and personal life. Behavioral assessment techniques used by the psychologist who worked with Susan included a structured interview, several self-report questionnaires, role plays, and self-monitoring procedures.

An outline developed by Arkowitz (1981) was used as a guideline for the behavioral assessment interview. The interview was conducted over several sessions and is briefly summarized below. Susan is presented as an appropriately dressed young woman who appeared her stated age and was of average physical appearance. She displayed little eye contact and tended to respond to questions with short monotonic answers. Susan showed little affect except for a brief period of tearfulness. A review of her current functioning and past history showed no evidence of major psychopathology.

The client related that she had come to feel increasingly socially isolated over the past several years. Three years ago she had broken up with her boyfriend after a 4-year relationship and had not dated since. Susan worked as a registered nurse in a local hospital and had been working a night shift shortly after the breakup with her boyfriend. She had a small group of female friends with whom she felt at ease and saw regularly. In addition she had a close relationship with her family. Areas of difficulty included conversations with men, speaking in front of a group, and situations that called for assertiveness (e.g., making complaints, disagreeing with others).

Susan was taken through a broad overview of her social functioning as a child and adult. This was followed by a detailed review of a number of specific areas of social functioning such as casual relationships, intimate relationships, interactions with authority figures, and relationships with family members. In addition she was asked to review the events in a typical day in her current life. This process was used to help identify specific problem areas and skill deficits. Problematic behaviors were carefully examined in terms of their antecedents and consequences.

The client completed the Social Avoidance and Distress Scale (SADS, Watson & Friend, 1969) and the Gambrill-Richey Assertion Inventory (GRAI, Gambrill & Richey, 1975). Susan's score for the SADS was 19, well above the normative mean of 9. On the GRAI she had a discomfort score of 115 (normative mean = 96, S.D. = 20) and a response probability score of 110 (normative mean = 104, S.D. = 16). A review of the different categories of the GRAI showed that areas of highest discomfort were engaging in social contacts, handling criticism, and disagreeing.

At the close of the first session Susan was instructed in the use of a social contacts recording form, which she was to keep with her and complete throughout the next week. Following any social contact, she was to record the day, time, general nature, and duration of that contact; information on the other person(s) and their responses; who initiated the exchange, and if it was Susan, what she said; and finally, a brief rating of her comfort, satisfaction, and enjoyment of the situation. At the time of her second interview this self-monitoring form was used for further assessment of problem areas and their antecedents and consequences. The information was also used to help identify specific behavioral skills deficits and situations that led to increased anxiety.

Two analogue role-plays were conducted during the second session. In the first a male therapist and in the second a female therapist from the agency volunteered to serve as a confederate. In each analogue, Susan was simply instructed to maintain a conversation for 5 minutes, pretending that she and the confederate were sharing a table during lunch in a cafeteria. Her psychologist served as an observer for both analogues. After each analogue both the psychologist and Susan gave global ratings of her social skill and again for her anxiety on a scale of 1 (lowest possible skill or anxiety level) to 10 (highest level). The observer scores were, male role play social skill 3, social anxiety 7, female role play social skill 5, social anxiety 5. Susan's self-ratings for the male role play were, social skill 3, social anxiety 8. In the female role play her self-ratings were, social skill 5, social anxiety 7.

Although the scoring was subjective, it allowed the psychologist to view the client's behavior with both a male and a female. Observing the role plays gave him the opportunity to later discuss with Susan the relationship of her self-perceptions of her social skill and anxiety with those of an observer. A comparison of observer and self-ratings of anxiety was used to analyze some of her actions that indicated anxiety, and to explore some the fears and self-talk that contributed to Susan's social anxiety in the role plays and at other times. Most importantly, the analogues allowed the psychologist to observe, and later discuss with the client, a number of specific components of her social interactions. These included motor behaviors (e.g., eye contact, nodding, and body posture), speech characteristics (e.g., latencies and volume), conversational style and content (e.g., asking open-ended questions, providing reinforcement, balancing talking and listening).

The information provided by the questionnaires, role plays, and self-monitoring was used to help identify specific problem areas and skill deficits, and in the selection of appropriate treatment strategies. Assessment information was also used to help set treatment goals and priorities. For example, excessive anxiety across a number of social situations served to limit Susan's initiation of conversations and interfered with performance in and enjoyment of social interactions. Selecting anxiety reduction in social situations as an early treatment goal led to instruction in relaxation techniques, and the development and application of coping strategies appropriate to the types of anxiety she was experiencing.

Another goal identified during the initial assessment was the client's desire to increase her social contacts with men and improve her skills and increase her enjoyment in these situations. This led to further assessment of this area, skills training to correct specific behavioral deficits, and exploration of the types of situations that would lead to increased contacts with men in nonthreatening settings. Figure 6.2 graphs the frequency with which Susan initiated social conversations with men. This information was collected by the client in her self-monitoring record. The phase labeled *A* indicates the assessment (or baseline) period prior to beginning any interventions. The *B* phase indicates when she began using relaxation and coping procedures. The *BC* phase represents the use of verbal and nonverbal social skills techniques in conjunction with the continuing use of the relaxation and coping procedures.

Susan was seen weekly for approximately four months. Throughout her treat-

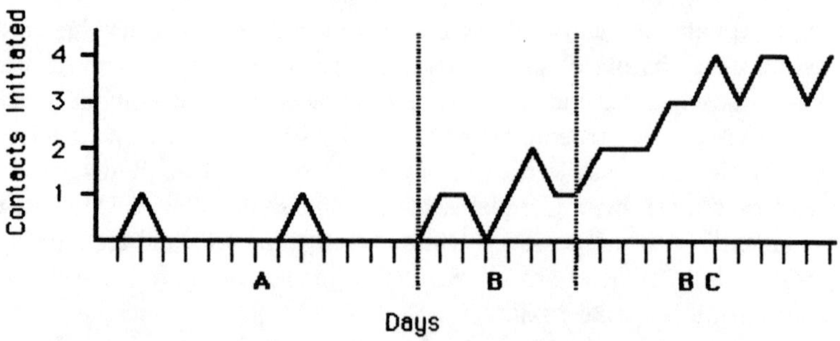

FIG. 6.2. Number of social contacts per day initiated with men.

ment, assessment was seen as an ongoing process. Different forms of self-monitoring were used to help redefine goals and indicate when they had been attained. Occasional role play exercises were used to help identify specific skill deficits in different social settings.

At the next to last treatment session the SADS and GRAI were completed a second time, and the initial two role play analogues were repeated. Susan's SADS score improved from 19 to 10. On the GRAI, her discomfort score decreased from 115 to 95, while her response probability score improved from 110 to 100. The two role play analogues were also repeated. The observer scores were, male role play social skill 6, social anxiety 5, female role play social skill 7, social anxiety 2. Susan's self-ratings for the male role play were, social skill 7, social anxiety 5. In the female role play her self-ratings were, social skill 7, social anxiety 3. All of these scores showed relative improvement since the initial assessment.

By the final session Susan felt that she had met all the specific goals set during the course of counseling. The accomplishment of these various, progressive behavioral goals had been documented through the use of self-monitoring procedures throughout treatment. She felt that the skills she acquired had greatly enhanced her level of social functioning. Of equal importance, Susan felt she now had the skills to shape her own behavior. She planned to continue to use the self-monitoring and behavioral analysis procedures she had learned in treatment. With these skills she felt she could continue to improve her skills and enhance her enjoyment of social situations in the future.

Psychometric Analysis of Behavioral Assessment: Current Trends

A review of the current literature reveals considerable controversy concerning the validity and reliability of behavioral assessment measures of social skills. Areas of criticism include debates about definitions of social skills, the lack of standardized assessment procedures, the proliferation of measures with questionable psychometric properties, and poor correlations among various social skills measures (Conger & Conger, 1986). These issues are representative of current debates throughout the field of behavioral assessment (Strosahl & Linehan, 1986).

A major factor in all of these problems is the lack of a standardized definition of social skills and disagreement as to its basic components (Conger & Conger, 1986). Further, although it is generally recognized that social skills involve multiple components, self-report questionnaires usually yield only a single score. In light of this, it is not surprising that comparisons of different social skills measures show disappointing low correlations (Furnham & Henderson, 1984). Bellack (1979) notes that since different aspects of social skill such as anxiety, skills, and behaviors are often not correlated, it makes little sense to sum them into a single global score.

Although analogue measures are more likely to provide multiple component measures in addition to (or instead of) a single global score, they have been subject to criticism on other grounds. The validity of these components is not clear, especially given the variety of components assessed across studies and the different ways they are measured (Conger & Conger, 1986). In addition, although the behavioral literature stresses the importance of situational specificity in behavioral responses, analogue measures are often very limited in the variety of stimulus situations that they present (Arkowitz, 1981). Galassi and Galassi (1976) have demonstrated that variations in analogue design, (e.g., length of interaction, live model versus videotape versus audiotape) result in significantly different results. Finally, the ecological validity of analogue measures remains unclear in light of research that has shown a lack of correlation between role-plays and more naturalistic measures in some instances (Frisch & Higgins, 1986), while finding adequate correlations in others (Merluzzi & Biever, 1987).

Most social skills assessments have focused on either global (molar) ratings of social skill or molecular frequency counts of specific behaviors. A group of social skills researchers (Farrell, Rabinowitz, Wallander, & Curran, 1985; Wallander, Conger, & Conger, 1985) are currently developing a third approach. They note that while global ratings lack important descriptive information, measures that provide detailed counts of molecular components such as eye contact or speech duration have demonstrated poor discriminant and concurrent validity (Wallander, Conger, & Conger, 1985). As an alternative they have proposed an intermediate level of analysis focusing on the description and measurement of a set of discrete, intermediate level, behavioral components for social skills. This level of analysis would hopefully provide valid and reliable data that would be useful in further understanding the nature of social skills. On a clinical level it would allow the assessment of specific strengths and weaknesses in an individual's social skills. As Farrell, Rabinowitz, Wallander, and Curran (1985) point out, "This approach could enhance simple frequency counts and duration measures by allowing raters to evaluate elements of interactions such as timing and sequencing of behavior, and situational context. At the same time, an intermediate approach could provide more detailed information than global ratings by focusing on more specific behavioral domains'' (p. 156). Wallander, Conger, and Conger (1985) have developed the Behaviorally Referenced Rating System of Intermediate Social Skills (BRISS) as a coding system for measuring an intermediate level of social skills components. The BRISS consists of Likert scales (ranging from ''very inappropriate'' to ''very appropriate'') for 11 component behaviors. These include assessing use of the head, arms and hands, body and legs, and facial expressions as well as ratings for language, speech delivery, conversational structure, conversation content, personal conversational style and partner directed behavior. Ratings were made on videotaped interactions of male subjects who were instructed to initiate and maintain a conversation with a female confederate. Judges were trained to recognize specific behaviors associated with each component. A second format for intermediate level assessment, the Intermediate Level Social Skills Assessment Checklist (ILSSAC) has also been tested (Farrell, Rabinowitz, Wallander, & Curran, 1985). The ILSSAC uses the same intermediate level components as the BRISS, but utilizes a revised scoring system that is easier to score and provides more specific behavioral information than the BRISS. Although the BRISS and ILSSAC are still in the early stages of development and evaluation, they have the promise of addressing some of the validity and reliability problems discussed above while also serving as a useful instrument in the clinical evaluation and treatment of social skills deficits.

COGNITIVE ASSESSMENT

Following the growth of cognitive and cognitive-behavioral therapies interest in cognitive assessment has increased. In addition there is growing interest in framing the cognitive assessment process in information processing terms (Nasby & Kihlstrom, 1987). The information processing approach to cognitive assessment does differ, to some extent, from those that emphasize cognitive products.

In the sections that follow we will review the prevalent approaches to cognitive assessment. Although we will emphasize the cognitive products that the clinician-researcher is likely to use, the reader is encouraged to read Nasby and Kihlstrom (1987) for a treatment of the information processing approach to cognitive assessment. There are, in fact, some practical measures that could be developed from that approach.

By far the most popular approach to assessing cognitive products is the assessment of self-statements and self-talk. Glass and Merluzzi (1981) developed a taxonomy for methods of self-statement assessment that will be used in the following discussion.

Recognition Method of Self-Statement Assessment. In this approach a structured questionnaire is typically used. The client is presented with a number of "thoughts" and is asked to rate (usually on a 5-point scale) how frequently he or she might have had each thought ("hardly ever" to "very often"). These questionnaires are usually used for a specific problem (e.g., assertiveness, initial social encounters) or situation (e.g., cardiac catherization). Typically they include positive and negative self-statements and, therefore, yield at least two scores.

The advantage to this type of assessment is that the questionnaires are usually easy to administer and score. A disadvantage is that the subject may not have thoughts precisely like those contained in the questionnaire. Thus, the idiosyncratic nature of the individual's thoughts is not captured. On the other hand, the thoughts in the questionnaire may be considered prototypes of thoughts the person can endorse as representative of his or her own thoughts. Finally, there is the problem of priming. That is, a subject might endorse a thought that represents typical thoughts he or she might have in a similar situation but, in fact, may not have had that thought in the situation being studied. Thus, for example, that person's "phobic" self-schema may prompt him or her to endorse thoughts that are consistent with that schema.

Although the recognition approach is easy to administer and score, the development of such a measure is no small task if the problem of the prototypicality of the statements is to be handled well (cf., Glass, Merluzzi, Biever, & Larsen, 1982).

Recall Method of Self-Statement Assessment. This approach is commonly referred to as the thought-listing approach (Cacioppo & Petty, 1981). Typically, the subject is asked to list thoughts he or she might have had during a specified period of time (e.g., while waiting for a job interview) or, in the case of social anxiety, while they were interacting with a stranger.

For example, socially anxious clients may be asked to imagine or remember a recent interaction with a stranger and then to "list thoughts that went through your head; whether about yourself, the other person, or the situation; whether positive, negative, or neutral." Usually, the client is given a period of time to complete this task (e.g., 2.5 minutes). The protocols generated from this task are then scored by judges and/or subjects.

In studies on social anxiety (e.g., Cacioppo, Glass, & Merluzzi, 1979) the statements generated have been scored as either positive (facilitating social interaction) or negative (inhibiting social interaction). In addition, intensity ratings have been used to refine the analyses of the thought listing data. For example Huber and Altmaier (1983) had phobic subjects rate (on a 3-point scale) the salience of the thoughts they generated. The authors also had judges rate the degree of threat expressed by each thought after it was cast into a bipolar format.

The combination of judges' ratings of threat and the subjects' ratings of intensity or salience allowed for a highly discriminating measure of thoughts.

The advantage of the recall format is that it can be easily used in a variety of situations for most problems. The disadvantages are that it relies on judges to score the protocol and that the subjects may produce relatively few thoughts.

Prompted Recall Method of Self-Statement Assessment. This method involves eliciting self-statements with the aid of some cues. The most representative example of this method is the videotape prompted recall approach. Subjects view a videotape of their performance and, essentially, dub their thoughts as they watch themselves (Smye & Wine, 1980). Typically, subjects talk into an audiotape recorder while watching the screen. A variation on the "thought dubbing" approach is to have the clients first view their performance and then list their thoughts (Burgio, Glass, & Merluzzi, 1982). The thoughts are then scored much in the same way they are scored in the recall method. In the dubbing approach one can also study the relationship between the action on the screen (e.g., overt behavior or nonverbal behavior) and the thoughts that accompany those behaviors. Additionally, one might be able to apply sequential analysis to the thought and behavioral data.

The advantage of this approach is that one is able to generate a large sample of cognitive data. A disadvantage is that prompted recall of thoughts may be based largely on the post-hoc evaluation of their performance in the situation.

Projective Method of Self-Statement Assessment. This method differs somewhat from those already mentioned in that the client does not state his or her own thoughts but those of a character in a picture or vignette. Sobel (1981) presents an overview of the uses of this technique. It has a great deal of potential; however, validation is especially critical in the development of projective assessment procedures.

Expressive or Concurrent Method of Self-Statement Assessment. In this method subjects are asked to "think aloud" as they are engaged in a situation or as they imagine themselves in a situation. The advantage of this method over the prompted recall method is that the stream of thoughts is captured as the situation progresses. This avoids the problems associated with the prompted recall method in that the person is not as likely to base their ongoing thoughts on a critical post-hoc evaluation of their own behavior. The reader is referred to Genest and Turk (1981) for a review of this technique. One of the problems with this method is that in certain situations (such as those involving social interaction), one cannot interact and simultaneously report thoughts. It is more applicable to situations in which the person does not have to converse. For example, during treatment of a simple phobia such as acrophobia the clinician might have the person think aloud while engaging in desensitization or in-vivo exposure therapy. In their concurrent thought sampling work, Hurlburt (Hurlburt & Melancon, 1987) and Singer (Pope & Singer, 1978) used a sound generator that randomly cues the subject to list or check thoughts. This approach might be an interesting compromise in those situations where one cannot continually express thoughts.

Attributions. The role of causal attributions and attributional style in clinical work has proliferated over the past 5 years. Essentially, causal attribution refers to the causal explanation given to personal or social events. A recent example of the clinical use of causal attribution assessment is a study by Peterson, Luborsky, and Seligman (1985). Those authors combed through verbatim transcript materials and noted events and the causes ascribed to those events by the client.

The term attribution style is now being replaced by explanatory style. For example, the depressive explanatory style for the causes of events is internal, global, and permanent. One can surmise that for negative events seeing one's self as responsible (i.e., internal), seeing the cause as pervasive (i.e., global) and permanent (i.e., stable) would contribute to negative affect.

Expectancies. Self-efficacy (or behavior expectancy) has received much attention in the domain of assessing expectancies. It must be emphasized that efficacy expectations are *behavior expectancies* (i.e., the perceived ability to perform a behavior) and not *outcome expectancies* (i.e., the perceived consequences of performing that behavior). Bandura (1986), who developed efficacy theory, has offered as one of its central tenets that efficacy expectations may be more predictive of behavior than outcome expectancy or previous behavior in the same situation. The reader is referred to Bandura (1986) in which he reviews the research supporting efficacy theory.

Outcome expectancies (Rotter, 1954) assess the perception of the outcome of a particular situation or generalized expectancy about outcomes that may be pervasive across all situations. Thus, an individual may be anxious about cocktail parties and expect that he will have trouble making small talk and, therefore become anxious and have a miserable time. If that pattern were to occur across all situations one would have a generalized expectancy. However, if it occurs in one specific situation it is a more situationally discrete expectancy.

Beliefs. Initially based on Ellis' (Ellis & Harper, 1961) theory, measures of beliefs attempted to assess irrational beliefs. Typically, these measures have been constructed as questionnaires. However, one could assess irrational beliefs by having clients articulate the beliefs they might have in certain situations such as social rejection.

Cognitive Assessment of Social Skill

The cognitive assessment of social anxiety and to a greater extent depression has developed as a function of the increased knowledge concerning the role of cognitive factors in those problems. In essence, however, there have been no coherent principles to organize cognitive assessment methods beyond the taxonomies offered by various authors (Glass & Merluzzi, 1981; Kendall & Hollon, 1981; Martkze et al., 1986). Nasby and Kihlstrom (1987) have presented an organizational framework based on a social information processing or *social intelligence* perspective. However, as noted earlier they focus on cognitive processes and mechanisms and not on cognitive products. Nonetheless, their innovative approach will likely have an impact on the future of clinical-cognitive assessment.

The sections below contain examples of assessment approaches in each of the categories reviewed in the last section. The reader is encouraged to consult the sources cited for a more complete analysis of particular assessment instruments.

Recognition Methods of Self Statement Assessment. The best known recognition measure is the Assertive Self-Statement Test (ASST; Schwartz & Gottman, 1976). This questionnaire is designed to assess self-statements that may facilitate (i.e., positive thoughts) or inhibit (i.e., negative thoughts) one's ability to refuse unreasonable requests. The client rates 17 positive and 17 negative statements on a 5-point scale ("hardly ever" to "very often") indicating how often he or she had a particular thought before, during, or after a situation involving an unreasonable request. This measure has been used with both college student samples and clinical populations (Heimberg, Chiauzzi, & Madraso-Pederson, 1983).

A measure similar to the ASST is the Social Interaction Self-Statement Test (SISST; Glass, Merluzzi, Biever, & Larsen, 1982; Dodge, Heimberg, Hope & Becker, 1982). It is a 30-item measure containing 15 facilitating and 15 inhibiting thoughts that relate to heterosocial encounters. The format is similar to the ASST in that clients rate on a 5-point scale the frequency of occurrence of each thought. Segal & Marshall (1985) used the SISST with a prison population and Merluzzi, Burgio, and Glass (1984) have used it with an outpatient population.

In general, with questionnaires such as these, it appears that negative self-statements are more discriminating and predictive of social anxiety than positive self-statements. We will elaborate on this point in the section on interpretation.

Recall Methods of Self-Statement Assessment. The thought listing method has been used in a number of studies. For example, Cacioppo et al (1979) had male subjects list thoughts prior to an interaction with a woman with whom they were unacquainted. In a group treatment study for socially anxious males Malkiewich and Merluzzi (1980) had participants list their thoughts after an 8-minute conversation with two other group members. Negative (but not positive) self-statements discriminated high and low anxious groups in Cacioppo et al. and negative (but not positive) self-statements changed as a function of treatment in the latter study.

As noted earlier an extension of the typical thought listing protocol was reported by Huber and Altmaier (1983). By taking into account (a) the degree of threat in the thought after it was cast into a bipolar format and (b) the subjects' ratings of salience of each of their self-statements, the authors were able to conduct a more fine-grained analysis of the thought listing protocols. This approach seems very promising in that phobics had a significantly higher overall threat value (salience multiplied by judged threat) than nonphobics. This approach takes into account both the subjective judgments of the client and the objective scoring necessary to accomplish assessment and research.

Prompted Recall Method of Self-Statement Assessment. This method, also called "thought dubbing," is similar to Kagan's Interpersonal Process Recall (Kagan & Krathwohl, 1967). Smye and Wine (1980) had male and female high-school students recall their thoughts after they responded to 26 difficult social situations. Subjects viewed a videotape of their responses and recalled the thoughts they had prior to and after their responses to the situations. Results indicated that while men were more aggressive than women behaviorally, women tended to evaluate others more negatively and to deny the impact of others on them. Thus, the cognitive data seem to indicate that while the women may be less assertive, they had a "cognitive" buffer to lessen the impact of others on them.

Burgio et al (1982) and Chiauzzi and Heimberg (1983) had subjects report their thoughts after they viewed their performance on videotape. However, in these studies the thought list data failed to discriminate groups that were high versus low on social skill, in the former, and high versus low assertiveness, in the latter.

The prompted methods have, on the one hand, a great deal of potential for assessing cognitions, and on the other hand are fraught with conceptual and methodological difficulties. More research will have to be conducted comparing this method to others before it can be confidently used.

Expressive or Concurrent Method of Self-Statement Assessment. Although this approach has the greatest appeal from the perspective of obtaining unbiased data of a quantity that can be used to check consistency, it has limited use in social skills assessment. As noted earlier, it is impossible to interact naturally in a social situation and simultaneously think aloud. Also, Kendall and Hollon (1981) note that there may be a reactive effect that affects the actual flow of self-talk. That is, subjects who are asked to think aloud spend more time on individual thoughts than those who do not think aloud. However, there have been some variations on this technique that have been applied to social anxiety. For example, Goldfried and Sobocinski (1975) and Craighead, Kimball, and Rehak (1979) asked subjects to imagine themselves in a social situation such as social rejection and to report what was going on in their mind during the interaction. In both studies negative thoughts were significantly correlated with anxiety.

Hurlburt (Hurlburt & Melancon, 1987) and Singer (Pope & Singer, 1977) have used a sampling approach to generate thought data. This sampling method has not been directly applied to social anxiety but could be adapted for research on social interaction. If clients were to carry a sound generator that beeps at random intervals they could respond by filling out a brief questionnaire (or list thoughts) and also indicate the setting (i.e., alone or with someone, etc.).

Attributions. The bulk of the work on causal attributions has focused on depression. However, the application of attribution theory to social anxiety may provide a fruitful analysis of the thoughts socially anxious persons have concerning the causes of certain outcomes in social situations. Further, a situational analysis of causal attributions may produce a more complex picture of the causal reasoning of clients.

Expectancies. The distinction between behavior expectancy (e.g., self-efficacy expectations) and outcome expectancies has its counterparts in the assessment process. For example the perceived efficacy one has concerning certain behaviors that contribute to social skill (e.g., friendliness, warmth) is likely related to their social behaviors *in-vivo*. Fichten, Bourdon, Amsel, and Fox (in press) have developed and presented validation data for a self-efficacy measure called the College Interaction Self-Efficacy Measure. An interesting aspect of Fichten's work is that she compares efficacy judgments when the stimulus person is either handicapped or not handicapped.

Outcome expectancy has been assessed by measures of the *subjective expected utility* of certain outcomes. Fiedler and Beach (1978) found that the subjectively judged probability of consequences was related to the intent to behave assertively. Like Fiedler and Beach (1978), Bruch, Hasse, and Purcell (1984) found that scores on the measure of subjective expected utility did not correlate with measures of assertiveness. One can assume that research in this domain may direct the subject's attention to situational variables that account for more of the variance in behavior than dispositional levels of assertiveness. Alternatively, based on Bruch et al. (1984), one might assume that subjective expectancy is tapping another construct or process. The decision making process of socially anxious and nonanxious persons would be an interesting line of research to pursue. For additional information on this subject the reader is referred to Merluzzi, Rudy, and Krejci (1987).

Beliefs. There are two questionnaires that have been used to assess beliefs: the Irrational Beliefs Test (Jones, 1969) and the Rational Behavior Inventory (Shorkey & Whiteman, 1977). It has been our experience that these measures are much too global and likely represent some overarching construct common to many measures, namely anxiety or neuroticism. It would be helpful to develop more specific measures for certain problems, such as a social interaction irrational beliefs test.

Interpretation

The discussion of the interpretation of cognitive assessment data will focus primarily on self-statements. The process of interpreting clients' self-statement data can take many forms. For example, a clinician may attempt to determine the idiosyncratic meaning of a client's self-statements. The difficulties in this approach are similar to those encountered with projective tests; however, in cognitive assessment one assumes a more conscious awareness of the meaning of the statements. In Beck's approach to cognitive therapy, he first elicits what he has termed "automatic thoughts," then has the client explain the meaning of the each thought and, finally, he explores how the thought serves to maintain depression. In this approach the meaning seems less important than the function. A clinician might be able to classify thoughts as depressogenic or nondepressogenic, or anxiety provoking or anxiety inhibiting thoughts. Thus, the depression or anxiety producing function of the thoughts could be emphasized with the client's subjective meaning used to enhance or fine tune the analysis of thoughts.

Although there have been several scoring schemes proposed for self-statement or thought data, the most prevalent categories used to score thought data have been positive and negative. For example, in the Assertive Self-Statement Test and the Social Interaction Self-Statement Test there are two scales: positive (facilitating assertion or social interaction) and negative (inhibiting assertion or social interaction). Interpretation of the scores from these instruments involves evaluating the levels of positive and negative self-statements. Although norms are not available, one could use previously published data comparing anxious or unassertive groups with groups that are not anxious or unassertive.

An alternative to using the positive and negative scales separately in the interpretation of self-statement data, is to use a difference score: the positive score minus the negative score. Merluzzi et al (1984) indicate that this difference score may be a more sensitive measure than either of the scales used separately.

In an intriguing approach to the problem of interpreting cognitive assessment data, Schwartz and Garamoni (1986) have clarified why the difference score noted above may be a more sensitive measure than either score separately. Those authors first present a treatise on the notion that polarity in thought has a rich history in ancient and modern philosophy and in psychology from its infancy to the present day. They conclude that the evaluative dimension (positive versus negative) appears to be a dominant dimension in the construction of information. Although we are capable of using many other dimensions to construe events, the evaluative dimension appears to be at a higher level of abstraction than many others and applicable to a wide variety of information.

Schwartz and Garamoni (1986) offer a model based on the polarity of thoughts. That is, they conceptualize the positive-negative dichotomy as an important feature of what they call internal dialogue. They propose a *states of mind model* that includes five states of mind and is based "on the relative balance between positive and negative cognitions" (p. 17). Those five states are *Positive Dialogue, Negative Dialogue, Internal Dialogue of Conflict, Positive Monologue,* and *Negative Monologue*. Each state of mind (SOM) is associated with a different proportion of positive to negative cognitions. Schwartz and Garamoni suggest that the optimal state, positive dialogue, is characterized by 62% (± 6%) positive self-statements and 38% (± 6%) negative self-statements. They propose that this asymmetry promotes a positive, facilitating approach to life while having a sufficient amount of negative thoughts to remain sensitive to problems and to threatening information. Also, because the dominant state of mind is positive, negative information may stand out when it arises and thus contributes significantly to the cognitive appraisal of a situation. For example, a person who exhibits the positive dialogue (i.e., 62% positive and 38% negative) on a measure such as the Social Interaction Self Statement Test, has positive cognitions that should facilitate social interaction, but also has sufficient negative cognitions to remain interpersonally sensitive.

In contrast to positive dialogue, the negative dialogue pattern is approximately 62% negative and 38% positive self-statements. The dominance of negative cognitions generally would promote inhibition and a tendency to discount positive events even though they may stand out against a backdrop of negative thoughts. The internal dialogue of conflict represents approximately 50% negative and 50% positive self-statements. Finally, the positive and negative monologue have predominantly positive (greater than 62% positive) statements in the former and predominantly negative (greater than 62% negative) in the latter.

In their review of cognitive assessment literature covering a variety of assessment methods and problem areas, Schwartz and Garamoni (1986) present convincing evidence supporting the states of mind model. The consistency of the findings across these studies is impressive. Essentially, one would find optimal adjustment in the positive dialogue state, mild psychopathology in the negative dialogue state and severe pathology in the negative monologue state. The advantage of the states of mind approach is that it provides an interpretive framework for the assessment of self-statements. The reader is strongly encouraged to read Schwartz and Garamoni for an extended treatment of the states of mind analysis of self-statements.

Case Example

Client. Ralph H. is a 28-year-old software developer for a small computer firm. He has managed a successful career by working long hours and thoroughly devoting himself to his work. He has been shy all his life particularly in unstructured situations such as informal social gatherings (e.g., a party at the boss's house) and has managed to avoid them as much as possible. He has sought therapy for his shyness as he would like to date and be able to attend social functions with the office staff.

Recognition Method. In order to get a precounseling assessment of the client's states of mind the counselor asked the client to think of a recent encounter with a woman. He reported that a woman was working temporarily in an adjoining office and that they had a brief conversation one day. He also indicated that she was someone he would like to date. The counselor then asked Ralph to fill out the Social Interaction Self-Statement Test while thinking about the brief interaction with the woman. The Positive (facilitating) Score was 46 and the Negative (inhibiting) Score was 50. This indicated to the counselor that Ralph was exhibiting what Schwartz has characterized as the ''internal dialogue of conflict.'' This conflict was very apparent in the client's description of the client's brief interaction with the woman. He vacillated for a very long time before saying hello to her for the first time. However, overall it seemed that inhibition prevailed. The conflict was fueled by a fear that rejection was evidence of unattractiveness and unlikability.

Recall Method. The counselor also asked Ralph to imagine himself talking to the woman in line at the company cafeteria. He was asked to imagine the situation as vividly as possible and then to write down any thoughts he had during the imagined encounter. This approach was used to assess spontaneous idiosyncratic thoughts that he might have in the actual situation.

For this task Ralph was given a standard thought-listing form, which is a sheet of paper with lines drawn across the page about an inch apart. Ralph was told that he would have about 2 minutes to list his thoughts, writing one thought in each of the sections on the page.

The following is a verbatim transcription of the thoughts Ralph listed on the thought listing form.

1. I was thinking that she's merely patronizing me by talking to me. (2)
2. Maybe she is really interested in me. (1)
3. Nah! She thinks I'm a social nerd—a typical software programmer! (3)
4. I'm a nervous wreck. (3)
5. I hope I don't say something stupid. (2)

6. I'll probably spill my tray and really make a fool of myself. (2)
7. I've got to hang in there. (1)
8. I can't be giving up every time I want to engage a woman in conversation. (2)
9. But it is so hard to be calm and talk. (3)
10. Just relax and take it one step at a time. (3)

As an exercise you may want to try to score these as either Negative (e.g., inhibiting social interaction) or Positive (e.g., facilitating social interaction).

The therapist had Ralph put a "+" or a "−" sign by each statement to indicate whether it was facilitating or inhibiting. The therapist then had Ralph rate the intensity of each statement thereby assessing the subjective importance of each statement for Ralph. That is, how salient was each thought during his imagining of the encounter with the woman. These scores are in the parentheses after each statement.

This type of therapist-client interaction and the participation of the client in the assessment process can produce considerable incidental information that may be useful in treatment. It is interesting to note that at times there is a discrepancy between the therapist's categorizing of the statements and the client's. In this case the therapist and Ralph agreed on the classification of all but one of the thoughts listed by Ralph. He and the therapist agreed that 1, 3, 4, 5, 6, and 9 were negative or inhibiting. They also agreed that 2, 7, and 10 were positive. The disputed item was 8. The therapist categorized it as positive and Ralph categorized it as negative. The therapist assumed that this was a coping statement that might help foster interaction. Ralph, on the other hand saw it as a negative statement that expressed frustration and futility in the imagined situation.

When you take into account the client's subjective ratings of intensity, the relative nature of the statements begins to emerge. Although they are still in the range that Schwartz and Garamoni (1986) call negative dialogue, the client's idiosyncratic negativity emerges more clearly than if the client's subjective ratings were absent. If we use the client's categorizing then the intensity ratings change the Schwartz and Garamoni ratio from 60/40 to 68/32 indicating a slightly more negative pattern.

In the next session the therapist reviewed the individual items on the Negative-SISST that were endorsed at scale values of 4 or 5. The client was encouraged to choose those statements that were most typical of his thinking during interactions with this woman or other women that he was attracted to in the past. These thoughts as well as those derived from the thought listing were used as the basis for interventions in subsequent sessions. Moreover, the counselor obtained information about the idiosyncratic nature of the client's "self-talk." For example, they were used to determine if irrational beliefs (Ellis & Harper, 1961; Beck,

Rush, Shaw, & Emery, 1979) were fostering the statements in potential rejection situations.

In the initial sessions the counselor assisted the client in identifying the thoughts (self-talk or automatic thoughts) and feelings that accompanied social situations. The client was also encouraged to examine the fears associated with rejection. In particular, the counselor introduced the Rational Emotive principle of separating one's intrinsic worth from one's performances or behaviors. Finally, the client was encouraged to anticipate social interactions, actually imagine the situation as it might occur, and to "think out loud" as he imagined the situation. The counselor noted any negative dialogue or inhibiting thoughts. After discussing the situation the client imagined the situation again; however, this time he was encouraged to eliminate the negative or inhibiting thoughts and replace them with facilitating or coping thoughts. This process was repeated several times over the next few sessions.

The client was given homework assignments that were graded from relatively easy to difficult. Easy assignments included behaviors such as smiling and making eye contact; intermediate difficult tasks included initiating and maintaining a conversation with a woman for a few minutes; and difficult tasks included asking someone for a date. As noted above the counselor had the client imagine the task and describe in detail his thoughts during the task. Again, inhibiting self-talk was replaced with positive or coping self-talk.

Counseling continued in this manner for 10 sessions with the client showing marked improvement in his ability to approach women and maintain brief conversations. He continued to report a lot of subjective anxiety in those situations but had seemingly improved in his ability to cope with the anxiety by reducing his anticipatory negative self-talk and coping with his fears of rejection by focusing on his behaviors rather than on global self incrimination.

A post-counseling administration of the SISST indicated that the SISST-Negative score was 38 and the SISST positive was 55. These scores represented a shift from the internal dialogue of conflict state of mind to the low end of the positive dialogue state of mind.

Issues in Measurement, Reliability, and Validity

The issue that is most salient in the cognitive assessment literature is the validity of self-reports. The controversy over the validity of self-report data was fueled by Nisbett and Wilson (1977) who contended that subjects are not able to account for causality based on cognitive self-reports. If subjects happen to be accurate in causal explanations, Nisbett and Wilson claim that it is because the subjects are responding as an observer of their own behavior or they have a predictive model that would be accurate regardless of the specific data. Thus, verbal self-reports are seen by Nisbett and Wilson as lacking accuracy and thus not useful as data.

Genest and Turk (1981) point out in a discussion of the Nisbett and Wilson arguments that "it is important to distinguish between the situations in which it does and does not make sense to use subjective cognitive accounts as data" (p. 239). They suggest that methods of collecting data have an effect on the accuracy of the data. In the experiments that were reported in Nisbett and Wilson the judgments that people made required them to arrive at causal explanations of their behavior. Also, the situations tended to be trivial unlike information gleaned from adjustment problems that may be more personally relevant.

Genest and Turk make an important distinction between data and causality. That is, if one views cognitive reports as data as opposed to causal explanations, then the analysis of the data is the work of the researcher not the subject. Also, under those circumstances, the subject's causal explanation would not be viewed as a failed attempt to find the correct causal model, but data about the subject's causal explanation for that situation. Finally, Mischel (1981) notes that

> "the studies on the comparative utility of direct and indirect personality assessment seem quite consistent: The predictions possible from a person's own simple direct self-ratings and self-reports generally have not been exceeded by those from more indirect, costly, and sophisticated personality tests, from test batteries, and from expert clinical judges. (p. 481)

Based on the work of Ericsson and Simon (1981) and others, Meichenbaum and Cameron (1981) offered the following guidelines for the collection of self-report data.

1. The inquiry should be conducted as soon as possible following the cognitive events of interest, assessing directly for information in short-term memory whenever possible.
2. The amount of probing should be minimized in order to decrease the likelihood that subjects will engage in inferential processes about their own cognitive experience or about the expectancies of the experimenter.
3. Analysis of the internal consistency of such reports should be included in order to assess the validity of the verbal report.
4. Subjects should be asked to describe verbally their cognitive experience. They should not be asked to explain why they behaved as they did or provide motives for their behavior.
5. Subjects should be given a set that motivates them to provide honest and full accounts. In providing such a set, the assessor might emphasize that his or her ability to study the target experience depends entirely upon honest, careful reporting.
6. It may be helpful to provide a set that legitimizes disclosure of cognitions. For example, subjects might be asked to provide their "impressions" or

descriptions of their experience during the experimental task, as opposed to being asked to "recollect" what occurred or to tell what they "did."

7. Providing the subject with retrieval cues immediately after performance may also foster full and veridical reporting. (pp. 6–7)

The intention of this brief discussion is not to lead the reader to conclude that self-report data is valid but to provide information concerning how validity might be enhanced. It is important for researchers and clinicians to be aware of the problems associated with collecting veridical self-report data and the measures one might take to assure that high quality data are being obtained.

CONCLUSIONS

It may be evident to the reader that behavioral and cognitive assessment differ from other forms of personality assessment that are based on assumptions about traits or based on the projective hypothesis. As such behavioral and cognitive assessment methods were devised as systems that were in opposition to the traditional assessment methods. The controversy raised as a function of the development of these alternatives to traditional assessment is parallel to the controversy in personality that pit the trait approach against the situationist position. As that controversy brewed the interactionist perspective (Endler & Magnussen, 1976) emerged and appeared to be the most reasonable perspective to account for the relative stability of certain behaviors as well as the impact of situations. Even Walter Mischel, the most ardent proponent of the situational perspective, can be characterized as an interactionist. His recent work seems to indicate that certain dispositional factors do distinguish people and that certain situations (high demand situations) may exacerbate those initial differences. Essentially, the same process is occurring in assessment in that some behavioral assessors (Hersen & Bellak, 1988) are advocating for an integration of traditional assessment such as the DSM-III diagnostic categories and behavioral assessment. Hersen and Bellak (1988) viewed the integration of DSM-III and behavioral assessment as fostering complementarity in seemingly different assessment systems. Behavioral (and cognitive assessment) may represent an *idiographic* approach within the broader scope of the DSM-III which may be considered *nomothetic*. Moreover, the integration of traditional and behavioral and cognitive assessment will provoke behavioral and cognitive assessors to attend to larger and more abstract patterns of psychopathology. That will, in turn, expand the scope of behavioral and cognitive assessment and foster the inclusion of more specific behavioral and cognitive phenomena in the description and diagnosis of psychopathology.

Future Directions

As noted in the previous section, some advocates of behavioral assessment envision that traditional assessment and behavioral assessment will be complementary systems. Recent developments in the field might strongly support this trend. For example the *Journal of Behavioral Assessment* recently changed its title to the *Journal of Psychopathology and Behavioral Assessment* to reflect a larger domain of issues that may be included in behavioral assessment. Thus, the potential impact of behavioral assessment on the diagnostic system used in psychology and psychiatry is already a reality. In sum, the future of behavioral assessment appears to be in the mainstream of psychological assessment. The scientific rigor that is evident in behavioral assessment will likely stimulate further the improvements in the diagnostic classification system of the DSM.

The future of cognitive assessment appears to be aligned with recent research in cognitive psychology and information processing (Ingram, 1987; Kendall & Ingram, 1987). The rich tradition of methods and research have already made an impact on the assessment of cognitive processes in psychopathology. The most well studied of the disorders from an information processing perspective is depression. However, the practical utility of this research for clinical assessment needs to be clarified. Also, clinical cognitive assessment has yet to develop into a discipline with the maturity of behavioral assessment. There appears to be much work needed in the development of measures of cognitive products with clinical populations. In addition, there needs to be more attention paid to the subjective world of the client in the cognitive assessment methods. The Huber and Altmaier (1983) study mentioned earlier in this chapter is a good example of assessment that may take into account the objective nature of thoughts as well as integrating the subjective experience of the client. However, cognitive assessment is not likely to become as coherent a force in assessment as behavioral assessment as it is not as well defined as a discipline.

REFERENCES

Arkowitz, H. (1981). Assessment of social skills. In M. Hersen & A. S. Bellack (Eds.), *Behavioral assessment: A practical handbook.* NY: Pergamon.

Ayllon, T., & Azrin, N. H. (1968). *The token economy: A motivational system for therapy and rehabilitation.* NY: Appleton-Century-Crofts.

Bales, R. F. (1951). *Interaction process analysis.* Cambridge, MA: Addison-Wesley.

Bandura, A. (1986). *Social foundations of thought and action: A social cognitive theory.* Englewood Cliffs, NJ: Prentice-Hall.

Barker, R. F. (1968). *Ecological psychology: Concepts and methods of studying the environment of human behavior.* Stanford, CA: Stanford University Press.

Barlow, D. H., Hayes, S. C., & Nelson, R. O. (1984). *The Scientist practitioner: Research and accountability in clinical and educational settings.* New York: Pergamon.

Barlow, D. H., & Hersen, M. (1984). *Single case experimental design: Strategies for studying behavior change* (2nd ed.). New York: Pergamon.

Beck, A. T., Rush, A. J., Shaw, B. F., & Emery, G. (1979). *Cognitive therapy of depression.* New York: Guilford Press.

Bellack, A. S. (1979). A critical appraisal of strategies for assessing social skill. *Behavioral Assessment, 1,* 157–176.

Bellack, A. S., & Hersen, M. (Eds.) (1979). *Research and practice in social skills training.* New York: Plenum.

Bergin, A., & Strupp, H. (1972). *Changing frontiers in the science of psychotherapy.* Chicago: Aldine.

Bernstein, D. A., & Nietzel, M. T. (1973). Procedural variation in behavioral avoidance tests. *Journal of Consulting and Clinical Psychology, 41,* 165–174.

Bijou, S., & Patterson, R. F. (1971). Functional analysis in the assessment of children. In P. McReynolds (Ed.), *Advances in psychological assessment* (Vol. 2) (pp. 63–78). Palo Alto, CA: Science and Behavior Books.

Bornstein, P. H., Hamilton, S. B., & Bornstein, M. T. (1986). Self-monitoring procedures. In A. R. Ciminero, K. S. Calhoun, & H. E. Adams (Eds.), *Handbook of behavioral assessment* (2nd ed.) (pp. 176–222). New York: Wiley.

Brock, T. C. (1967). Communication discrepancy and intent to persuade as determinants of counterargument production. *Journal of Experimental Social Psychology, 3,* 269–309.

Bruch, M. A., Haase, R. F., & Purcell, M. I. (1984). Content dimensions of self-statements in assertive situations: A factor analysis of two measures. *Cognitive Therapy and Research, 8,* 173–186.

Burgio, K. L., Glass, C. R., & Merluzzi, T. V. (1982). The effects of social anxiety and videotape performance feedback on cognitions and self-evaluation. *Behavioral Counseling Quarterly, 1,* 288–301.

Cacioppo, J. T., Glass, C. R., & Merluzzi, T. V. (1979). Self-statements and self-evaluations: A cognitive response analysis of heterosocial anxiety. *Cognitive Therapy and Research, 3,* 249–262.

Cacioppo, J. T., & Petty, R. E. (1981). Social psychological procedures for cognitive response analysis: The thought-listing technique. In T. V. Merluzzi, C. R. Glass, M. Genest (Eds.), *Cognitive assessment* (pp. 309–342). NY: Guilford Press.

Campbell, D. T., & Stanley, J. C. (1963). *Experimental and quasiexperimental designs for research.* Chicago: Rand McNally.

Chiauzzi, E., & Heimberg, R. G. (1983). Effect of subjects' assertiveness level, sex, and legitimacy of request on assertive relevant cognitions: An analysis by postperformance videotape reconstruction. *Cognitive Therapy and Research, 7,* 555–564.

Christensen, A., Arkowitz, H., & Anderson, J. (1975). Practice dating as treatment for college dating inhibitions. *Behaviour Research and Therapy, 13,* 321–331.

Ciminero, A. R. (1986). Behavioral assessment: An overview. In A. R. Ciminero, K. S. Calhoun, & H. E. Adams (Eds.), *Handbook of behavioral assessment* (2nd ed.) (pp. 3–11). New York: Wiley.

Conger, J. C., & Conger, A. J. (1986). Assessment of social skills. In A. R. Ciminero, K. S. Calhoun, & H. E. Adams (Eds.), *Handbook of behavioral assessment* (2nd ed.) (pp. 526–560). New York: Wiley.

Craighead, W. E., Kazdin, A. E., & Mahoney, M. J. (1981). *Behavior modification: Principles, issues and applications* (2nd ed.). Boston: Houghton Mifflin.

Craighead, W. E., Kimball, W. H., & Rehak, P. J. (1979). Mood changes, physiological responses, and self-statements during social rejection imagery. *Journal of Consulting and Clinical Psychology, 47,* 385–396.

Darwin, C. (1859). *The origin of the species.* London: John Murray.

Dodge, C. E., Heimberg, R. G., Hope, D. A., & Becker, R. E. (1988). Evaluation of the Social Interaction Self-Statement Test with a socially phobic population. *Cognitive Therapy and Research, 12,* 211–222.

Edgington, E. S. (1984). Statistics and single case analysis. In M. Hersen, R. M. Eisler, & P. M. Monti (Eds.), *Progress in Behavior Modification* (Vol. 16) (pp. 831–119). New York: Academic Press.

Eisler, R. M., Miller, P. M., & Hersen, M. (1973). Components of assertive behavior. *Journal of Clinical Psychology, 29,* 295–299.

Ellis, A., & Harper, R. A. (1961). *A guide to rational living.* Englewood Cliffs, NJ: Prentice-Hall.

Endler, N. S., & Magnussen, D. (1976). *Interactional psychology and personality.* Washington, DC: Hemisphere.

Ericsson, K. A., & Simon, H. A. (1981). Sources of evidence on cognition: A historical overview. In T. V. Merluzzi, C. R. Glass, & M. Genest (Eds.), *Cognitive assessment* (pp. 16–51). New York: Guilford.

Farrell, A. D., Curran, J. P., Zwick, W. R., & Monti, P. M. (1984). Generalizability and discriminant validity of anxiety and social skills ratings in two populations. *Behavioral Assessment, 6,* 1–14.

Farrell, A. D., Rabinowitz, J. A., Wallander, J. L., & Curran, J. P. (1985). An evaluation of two formats for the intermediate-level assessment of social skills. *Behavioral Assessment, 7,* 155–171.

Fichten, C. S., Bourdon, C. V., Amsel, R., & Fox, L. (in press). Validation of the College Interaction Self-efficacy Questionnaire: Interaction between students who have physical disability and their able-bodied peers. *Journal of College Student Personnel.*

Fiedler, D., & Beach, L. R. (1978). On the decision to be assertive. *Journal of Consulting and Clinical Psychology, 46,* 537–546.

Foster, S. L., & Cone, J. D. (1986). Design and use of direct observation. In A. R. Ciminero, K. S. Calhoun, & H. E. Adams (Eds.), *Handbook of behavioral assessment* (2nd ed.) (pp. 253–324). New York: Wiley.

Frisch, M. B., & Higgins, R. L. (1986). Instructional demand effects and the correspondence among role-play, self report, and naturalistic measures of social skill. *Behavioral Assessment, 8,* 221–236.

Furnham, A., & Henderson, M. (1984). Assessing assertiveness: A content and correlational analysis of five assertiveness inventories. *Behavioral Assessment, 6,* 79–88.

Galassi, J. P., & Galassi, M. D. (1976). The effects of role-playing variations on the assessment of assertive behavior. *Behavior Therapy, 7,* 343–347.

Galassi, J. P., & Galassi, M. D. (1974). Validity of a measure of assertiveness. *Journal of Counseling Psychology, 21,* 248–250.

Gambrill, E. D. (1977). *Behavior Modification.* San Francisco: Jossey-Bass.

Gambrill, E. D., & Richey, C. A. (1975). An assertion inventory for use in assessment and research. *Behavior Therapy, 6,* 550–561.

Gambrill, E. D., & Richey, C. A. (1985). *Taking charge of your social life.* Belmont, CA: Wadsworth.

Genest, M., & Turk, D. C. (1981). Think aloud approaches to cognitive assessment. In T. V. Merluzzi, C. R. Glass, M. Genest (Eds.), *Cognitive assessment* (pp. 233–269). New York: Guilford Press.

Gesell. A. (1925). *The mental growth of the pre-school child.* NY: Macmillan.

Glass, C. R., & Merluzzi, T. V. (1981). Cognitive assessment of social-evaluative anxiety. In T. V. Merluzzi, C. R. Glass, & M. Genest (Eds.), *Cognitive assessment* (pp. 388–438). New York: Guilford Press.

Glass, C. R., Merluzzi, T. V., Biever, J. L., & Larsen, K. H. (1982). Cognitive assessment of social anxiety: Development and validation of a self-statement questionnaire. *Cognitive Therapy and Research, 6,* 37–55.

Glass, G. V., Wilson, V. L., & Gottman, J. M. (1974). *Design and analysis of time-series experiments.* Boulder: Colorado Associated University Press.

Goldfried, M., & Davidson, G. C. (1976). *Clinical behavior therapy.* New York: Rinehart & Winston.

Goldfried, M. R., Padawer, W., & Robins, C. (1984). Social anxiety and the semantic structure of heterosocial interactions. *Journal of Abnormal Psychology, 93,* 87–97.

Goldfried, M. R., & Sobocinski, D. (1975). Effects of irrational beliefs on emotional arousal. *Journal of Consulting and Clinical Psychology, 43,* 504–510.

Goodenough, F. L. (1949). *Mental testing: Its history, principles, and applications.* New York: Holt, Rinehart, & Winston.

Greenwald, A. G. (1968). Cognitive learning, cognitive response to persuasion, and attitude change. In A. G. Greenwald, T. C. Brock, & T. M. Ostrom (Eds.), *Psychological foundations of attitudes* (pp. 147–170). New York: Academic Press.

Hedlund, B. L., & Lindquist, C. U. (1984). The development of an inventory for distinguishing among passive, aggressive, and assertive behavior. *Behavioral Assessment, 6,* 379–390.

Hersen, M., & Bellack, A. S. (1988). DSM-III and behavioral assessment. In A. S. Bellack & M. Hersen (Eds.), *Behavioral assessment: A practical handbook* (3rd edition) (pp. 67–84). New York: Pergamon.

Hersen, M., & Bellack, A. S. (1977). Assessment of social skills. In A. R. Ciminero, K. S. Calhoun, & H. E. Adams (Eds.), *Handbook of behavioral assessment* (pp. 509–554). New York: Wiley.

Hersen, M. & Bellack, A. S. (Eds.) (1976). Behavioral assessment: A practical handbook. New York: Pergamon.

Higgins, R. L., Frisch, M. B., & Smith, D. (1983). A comparison of role-played and natural responses to identical circumstances. *Behavior Therapy, 14,* 158–169.

Heimberg, R. G., Chiauzzi, E. J., Becker, R. E., & Madraso-Pederson, R. (1983). Cognitive mediation of assertive behavior: An analysis of the self-statement patterns of college students, psychiatric patients, and normal adults. *Cognitive Therapy and Research, 7,* 455–464.

Huber, J. W., & Altmaier, E. M. (1983). An investigation of the self-statement systems of phobic and nonphobic individuals. *Cognitive Therapy and Research, 7,* 355–362.

Hurlburt, R. T., & Melancon, S. M. (1987). How are questionnaire data similar to, and different from, thought sampling data? Five studies manipulating retrospectiveness, single-moment focus, and indeterminacy. *Cognitive Therapy and Research, 11,* 681–704.

Ingram, R. (Ed.). (1987). *Information processing approaches to clinical psychology.* New York: Academic Press.

Jones, R. G. (1969). A factored measure of Ellis' irrational belief system (Doctoral dissertation, Texas Technological College). *Dissertation Abstracts,* 1969, *29,* 4379B–4380B. (University Microfilms No. 69-6443).

Jayarantne, S., & Levy, R. L. (1979). *Empirical clinical practice.* New York: Columbia University Press.

Jensen, B. J., & Hayes, S. N. (1986). Self-report questionnaires and inventories. In A. R. Ciminero, K. S. Calhoun, & H. E. Adams (Eds.), *Handbook of behavioral assessment* (2nd ed.) (pp. 150–175). New York: Wiley.

Kagan, N., & Krathwohl, D. R. (1967). *Studies in human interaction: Interpersonal process recall stimulated by videotape.* East Lansing, MI: Michigan State University.

Kallman, W. M., & Feuerstein, M. J. (1986). Psychophysiological procedures. In A. R. Ciminero, K. S. Calhoun, & H. E. Adams (Eds.), *Handbook of behavioral assessment* (2nd ed.) (pp. 325–350). New York: Wiley.

Kaloupek, D. G., & Levis, D. J. (1980). The relationship between stimulus specificity and self-report indices in assessing fear of heterosexual social interaction: A test of the unitary response hypothesis. *Behavioral Assessment, 2,* 267–281.

Kanfer, F. H. (1985). Target selection for clinical change programs. *Behavioral Assessment, 7,* 7–20.

Kanfer, F. H., & Saslow, G. (1965). Behavioral diagnosis. *Archives of General Psychiatry, 12,* 529–538.

Kazdin, A. E. (1980). *Behavior modification in applied settings.* (2nd ed.) Homewood, IL: Dorsey.

Kazdin, A. E. (1981). Behavioral observation. In M. Hersen & A. S. Bellack (Eds.) *Behavioral assessment: A practical handbook* (2nd ed.) (pp. 101–124). New York: Pergamon.

Kazdin, A. E. (1984). Statistical analyses for single-case experimental designs. In D. H. Barlow & M. Hersen, (Eds.), *Single case experimental design: Strategies for studying behavior change.* (2nd ed.) (pp. 285–324). New York: Pergamon.

Kelly, G. A. (1955). *The psychology of personal constructs.* New York: Norton Press.

Kendall, P. C., & Hollon, S. D. (1981). Assessing self-referent speech: Methods in the measurement of self-statements. In P. C. Kendall & S. D. Hollon (Eds.), *Assessment strategies for cognitive behavioral interventions* (pp. 85–118). New York: Academic Press.

Kendall, P. C., & Ingram, R. (1987). The future for cognitive assessment of anxiety. In L. Michelson & L. M. Ascher (Eds.), *Anxiety and stress disorders* (pp. 89–104). New York: Guilford Press.

Lachman, R., & Lachman, J. T. (1987). Information processing psychology: Origins and extensions. In R. Ingram (Ed.), *Information processing approaches to clinical psychology* (pp. 23–50). New York: Academic Press.

Lachman, R., Lachman, J. T., & Butterfield, E. C. (1979). *Cognitive psychology and information processing: An introduction.* Hillsdale, NJ: Lawrence Erlbaum Associates.

Lang, P. J., & Lazovik, A. D. (1963). Experimental desensitization of a phobia. *Journal of Abnormal and Social Psychology, 66,* 519–525.

Lindsley, O. R. (1956). Operant conditioning methods applied to research in chronic schizophrenia. *Psychiatric Research Reports, 5,* 118–139.

Lowe, M. R., & Cautela, J. R. (1978). A self-report measure of social skill. *Behavior Therapy, 9,* 535–544.

Mahoney, M. J. (1977). Some applied issues in self-monitoring. In J. D. Cone & R. P. Hawkins (Eds.), *Behavioral assessment: New directions in clinical psychology* (pp. 241–254). New York: Brunner/Mazel.

Malkiewich, L. E., & Merluzzi, T. V. (1980). Rational restructuring versus desensitization with clients of diverse conceptual levels: A test of a client-treatment matching model. *Journal of Counseling Psychology, 27,* 453–461.

Martzke, J. S., Andersen, B. L., & Cacioppo, J. T. (1987). Cognitive assessment of anxiety disorders. In L. Michelson & L. M. Ascher (Eds.), *Anxiety and stress disorders* (pp. 62–88). New York: Guilford Press.

McFall, R. M. (1982). A review and reformulation of the concept of social skills. *Behavioral Assessment, 4,* 1–33.

McReynolds, P. (1986). History of assessment in clinical and educational settings. In R. O. Nelson & S. C. Hayes (Eds.), *Conceptual foundations of behavioral assessment* (pp. 42–80). New York: Guilford.

Meehl, P. E. (1978). Theoretical risks and tabular asterisks: Sir Karl, Sir Ronald, and the slow progress of soft psychology. *Journal of Consulting and Clinical Psychology, 46,* 806–835.

Meichenbaum, D. H. (1977). *Cognitive-behavior modification.* NY: Plenum Press.

Meichenbaum, D., & Cameron, R. (1981). Issues in cognitive assessment. In T. V. Merluzzi, C. R. Glass, & M. Genest (Eds.), *Cognitive assessment* (pp. 3–15). New York: Guilford Press.

Merluzzi, T. V., & Biever, J. (1987). Role-playing procedures for the behavioral assessment of social skills: A validity study. *Behavioral Assessment, 9,* 361–377.

Merluzzi, T. V., Burgio, K. L., & Glass, C. R. (1984). Cognitions and psychopathology: An analysis of social introversion and self-statements. *Journal of Consulting and Clinical Psychology, 52,* 1102–1103.

Merluzzi, T. V., Rudy, T. E., & Glass, C. R. (1981). The information processing paradigm: Implications for clinical science. In T. V. Merluzzi, C. R. Glass, & M. Genest (Eds.), *Cognitive assessment* (pp. 77–126). New York: Guilford Press.

Merluzzi, T. V., Rudy, T. E., & Krejci, M. (1987). Social skill and anxiety: Information processing perspectives. In R. Ingram (Ed.), *Information processing approaches to clinical psychology* (pp. 109–129). New York: Academic Press.

Meyer, V., & Turkat, I. D. (1979). Behavioral analysis of clinical cases. *Journal of Behavioral Assessment, 1,* 259–270.

Mischel, W. (1968). *Personality and assessment.* New York: Wiley.

Mischel, W. (1973). Toward a cognitive-social learning reconceptualization of personality. *Psychological Review, 80,* 252–283.

Mischel, W. (1981). A cognitive-social learning approach to assessment. In T. V. Merluzzi, C. R. Glass, & M. Genest (Eds.), *Cognitive assessment* (pp. 479–502). New York: Guilford Press.

Monti, P. M., Wallander, J. L., Ahern, D. K., & Munroe, S. M. (1984). Multi-modal measurement of anxiety and social skills in a behavioral role-play test: Generalizability and discriminant validity. *Behavioral Assessment, 6,* 15–25.

Moreno, Z. T. (1983). Psychodrama. In H. I. Kaplan & B. J. Sadock (Eds.), *Comprehensive group psychotherapy* (Second Edition) (pp. 158–166). Baltimore: Williams and Wilkins.

Mullinix, S. D., & Galassi, J. P. (1981). Deriving the content of social skills training with a verbal response components approach. *Behavioral Assessment, 3,* 55–61.

Nasby, W., & Kihlstrom, J. F. (1987). Cognitive assessment of personality and psychopathology. In R. Ingram (Ed.), *Information processing approaches to clinical psychology* (pp. 217–239). NY: Academic Press.

Nay, W. R. (1977). Analogue measures. In A. R. Ciminero, K. S. Calhoun, & H. E. Adams (Eds.), *Handbook of behavioral assessment* (pp. 279–328). NY: Wiley.

Neimeyer, G. J., & Neimeyer, R. A. (1981). Personal construct perspectives on cognitive assessment. In T. V. Merluzzi, C. R. Glass, & M. Genest (Eds.), *Cognitive assessment* (pp. 188–232). New York: Guilford Press.

Nisbett, R. E., & Wilson, T. P. (1977). Telling more than we can know: Verbal reports on mental processes. *Psychological Review, 84,* 231–259.

Peterson, C., Luborsky, L., & Seligman, M. E. P. (1983). Attributions and depressive mood shifts: A case study using the symptom-context method. *Journal of Abnormal Psychology, 92,* 96–103.

Peterson, D. R. (1979). Assessing interpersonal relationships by means of interaction records. *Behavioral Assessment, 1,* 221–236.

Pope, K. H., & Singer, J. L. (Eds.). (1978). *The stream of consciousness: Scientific investigation onto the flow of human experience.* New York: Plenum Press.

Rathus, S. S. (1973). A 30-item schedule for assessing assertive behavior. *Behavior Therapy, 4,* 398–406.

Rehm, L. P., & Marston, A. R. (1968). Reduction of social anxiety through modification of self-reinforcement: An instigation therapy technique. *Journal of Consulting and Clinical Psychology, 32,* 565–574.

Rotter, J. B. (1954). *Social learning and clinical psychology.* Englewood Cliffs, NJ: Prentice-Hall.

Safran, J. D., Vallis, T. M., & Segal, Z. V. (1986). Assessment of core cognitive processes in cognitive therapy. *Cognitive therapy and Research, 10,* 509–526.

Segal, Z. V., & Marshall, W. L. (1985). Heterosocial skill in a population of rapists and child molesters. *Journal of Consulting and Clinical Psychology, 53,* 55–63.

Schwartz, R. M., & Garamoni, G. L. (1986). A structural model of positive and negative states of mind: Asymmetry in the internal dialogue. In P. C. Kendall (Ed.), *Advances in cognitive behavioral research and therapy* (Vol. 5) (pp. 1–62). New York: Academic Press.

Schwartz, R. M., & Gottman, J. M. (1976). Toward a task analysis of assertive behavior. *Journal of Consulting and Clinical Psychology, 44,* 910–920.

Shorkey, C., & Whiteman, V. (1977). Development of the Rational Behavior Inventory: Initial validity and reliability. *Educational and Psychological Measurement, 37,* 527–534.

Skinner, B. F. (1953). *Science and human behavior.* NY: Macmillan.

Smye, M. D., & Wine, J. D. (1980). A comparison of female and male adolescents' social behavior and cognitions. *Sex Roles, 6,* 213–130.

Sobel, H. J. (1981). Projective methods of cognitive analysis. In T. V. Merluzzi, C. R. Glass, & M. Genest (Eds.), *Cognitive assessment* (pp. 127–148). New York: Guilford Press.

Strosahl, K. D., & Linehan, M. M. (1986). Basic issues in behavioral assessment. In A. R. Ciminero, K. S. Calhoun, & H. E. Adams (Eds.), *Handbook of behavioral assessment* (2nd ed.) (pp. 12–46). New York: Wiley.

Sundberg, N. D. (1981). Historical and traditional approaches to cognitive assessment. In T. V. Merluzzi, C. R. Glass, M. Genest (Eds.), *Cognitive assessment* (pp. 52–76). New York: Guilford Press.

Thoresen, C. E., & Mahoney, M. J. (1974). *Behavioral self-control.* New York: Holt, Rinehart, & Winston.

Turner, R. M., & Ascher, L. M. (1985). *Evaluating behavior therapy.* New York: Springer.

Twentyman, C. T., & McFall, R. M. (1975). Behavioral training of social skills in shy males. *Journal of Consulting and Clinical Psychology, 43,* 384–395.

Wallander, J. L., Conger, A. J., & Conger, J. C. (1985). Development and evaluation of a behaviorally referenced rating system for heterosocial skills. *Behavioral Assessment, 7,* 137–153.

Watson, D., & Friend, R. (1969). Measurement of social-evaluation anxiety. *Journal of Consulting and Clinical Psychology, 33,* 448–457.

Watson, J. B. (1913). Psychology as the behaviorist views it. *Psychological Review, 20,* 158–177.

Wolpe, J. (1982). *The practice of behavior therapy* (3rd ed.). New York: Pergamon.

Wolpe, J., & Lazarus, A. A. (1966). *Behavior therapy techniques: A guide to the treatment of neurosis.* NY: Pergamon.

7 Interpretation of the Strong Interest Inventory

Jo-Ida C. Hansen
University of Minnesota

The Strong Interest Inventory is the oldest, continuously used interest inventory available today. As was the case with most of the interest inventories developed in the 1920s and 1930s, the Strong Interest Inventory had its beginnings in an item pool created just after World War I. The work was done as part of a seminar, conducted by Clarence S. Yoakum a Carnegie Institute of Technology, which explored the problem of using a paper-and-pencil questionnaire to differentiate people in various occupations. The result of the seminar's effort was a pool of 1,000 items that eventually found their way into several instruments (e.g., Occupational Interest Inventory, Freyd, 1923; General Interest Survey, Kornhauser, 1927; and Purdue Interest Report, Remmers, 1929) only one of which, the Strong Interest Inventory, has survived the changes of time and society to continue in use today. The longevity of the Strong is due primarily to the revisions that have been done periodically throughout its history.

HISTORY OF THE STRONG INTEREST INVENTORY

The predecessor of the Strong Interest Inventory was the Interest Report Blank developed by Karl Cowdery in 1926 under the supervision of E. K. Strong, Jr., who had been an interested observer of the Yoakum seminar at Carnegie prior to joining the Stanford University faculty. Cowdery used a sample of items from the original Carnegie item pool for developing his inventory. For reasons that history has not preserved, Cowdery did not pursue his work in interest measurement research. Strong, however, did continue Cowdery's efforts and improved the Interest Report Blank by adding and deleting items, publishing the first

Vocational Interest Blank in 1927. The instrument later became known as the Strong Vocational Interest Blank and in 1974 it was renamed the Strong-Campbell Interest Inventory, Form T325 of the Strong Vocational Interest Blank (SVIB-SCII; Campbell, 1974).

Each revision of the Strong Interest Inventory resulted in an expansion of the profile, and the instrument now provides information about the similarity of a person's interests to 106 occupations. The Strong also measures interests related to Holland's six global types and 23 basic interests that represent areas commonly recognized as important for understanding the organization and structure of interests as well as the world of work (Hansen & Campbell, 1985).

The development of the Strong Interest Inventory to its current breadth of interest measurement was a gradual process beginning with a rather modest profile of only 10 Occupational Scales representing the interests of men. The first women's form was developed in 1933 (Strong) and revisions of the men's and women's forms took place in 1938 (Strong) and 1946 (Strong), respectively. These revisions provided the opportunity to expand the occupations represented on the profile as well as to improve the item pools.

The next major innovation in the scale construction technology of the Strong Interest Inventory was the development of the Basic Interest Scales in the 1960s (Campbell, Borgen, Eastes, Johansson, & Peterson, 1968). These scales added tremendously to the instrument, supplementing the profile information provided by the empirically derived and atheoretically developed Occupational Scales.

The next series of changes in the Strong Interest Inventory began with the 1974 revision, which featured two major developments: the merger of the men's and women's forms into one item booklet and profile, and the integration of Holland's theory of vocational types with the empiricism of Strong's Occupational Scales. Subsequent revisions of the instrument (Campbell & Hansen, 1981; Hansen & Campbell, 1985) were designed to address questions of sex equity of the instrument, to expand the Occupational Scales to a wider range of professional and non-professional occupations, and to develop better interpretive materials and interpretive aids to accompany the burgeoning profile.

Current Version of the SVIB-SCII

Development of the current version of the Strong Interest Inventory (Hansen & Campbell, 1985) involved sampling over 142,600 people from across the country. From this sample, 48,238 subjects were chosen to use in developing the standardization and criterion samples. Every person used in the development of the current form was an employed adult who indicated that she or he was satisfied with her or his occupation.

Item pool. The Strong Interest Inventory includes a test booklet composed of 325 items that measure interest in or "liking" for occupations, school subjects, work activities, leisure activities, and various types of people, and a short section devoted to estimating self-characteristics. Over the years, the psychometric properties of the items included in the SVIB-SCII booklet have been studied carefully to ensure that the items elicit a wide range of responses among occupations and that they have predictive, as well as concurrent, validity.

In addition, the items are revised periodically to ensure that they are (a) free of sex-role bias, (b) up-to-date, (c) in good taste, and (d) free of cultural bias. The items also are designed to be unambiguous; in other words, most people reading the items should interpret them in the same way. The reading level has been maintained at the 6th-grade level to accommodate the use of the instrument with a wide range of people.

Profile reports. The Strong Interest Inventory is scored by a computer that calculates the scores for the various scales. Then, the results are printed either on a profile form, which emphasizes the scale scores, or as an interpretive report, which includes a narrative with comments tailored to the individual's responses to the inventory items. An interpretive report often is useful in situations that preclude extensive one-to-one interaction between the client and the counselor or in career exploration groups and career development courses.

Appropriate Client Populations. Although the Strong Inventory frequently is used with college-aged young adults, the instrument is appropriate for use with a wide range of ages, for example, high school students, individuals who are reentering the labor force or returning to school, persons who are making midcareer changes, clients in rehabilitation settings, or people who are preparing for retirement. The Strong Interest Inventory also is used as one of several assessment instruments in placement and training situations; in research, as the instrument that measures or operationalizes interests; or with a variety of special populations, such as cross-ethnic or international populations, disabled clients, culturally disadvantaged clients, and people seeking career opportunities or training in vocational-technical areas. Thus, the Strong Inventory is used by a broad cross-section of organizations including secondary and vocational-technical schools, universities, government agencies, mental health centers, hospitals, industry, consulting firms, private institutions, and the military.

Purpose of the Test. People vary in their motivation for engaging in career exploration, and the SVIB-SCII is helpful in reaching a variety of goals. For example, some individuals simply wish to confirm a career choice they already have made; others are trying to narrow their range of possible choices; and still others are hoping to identify new options that they may not have considered in the past.

Psychologists and counselors find the Strong Interest Inventory useful in understanding the unique qualities of each client, and the individual clients find that the Strong helps them to gain insight about their interests and how they relate to the working world. Ultimately, the information can be used by the counselor and client to provide the client with better self-understanding and with the knowledge and information necessary to make better decisions.

The Strong Interest Inventory usually is not administered before the tenth grade. However, the SVIB-SCII can be used as an introduction to the world of work and to career exploration with younger students—eighth and ninth graders. The General Occupational Themes and Basic Interest Scales, in particular, will help 13-, 14- and 15-year olds identify interests that are beginning to develop and give them new directions to explore. Most people's interests begin to solidify by age 17 or 18, and the Strong then can be used to begin long-range educational and career planning.

For younger individuals, or those who may not have the attention span necessary for completing the inventory in one sitting, it is permissible to administer the instrument in two or more shorter sessions. Also, computer administration of the inventory typically takes about one-half the time that paper-and-pencil administration requires.

PSYCHOMETRIC BRIEFING

Three assumptions are basic to the development of any interest inventory. First, interest measurement assumes that a person can give an informed response such as "like," "indifferent," or "dislike" to items that describe activities that are familiar to the person. The second assumption is that the structure of interests underlying these familiar activities is the same structure of interests underlying unfamiliar activities. And, third, the responses to the familiar items then can be used to generalize to interests in the unfamiliar areas.

Based on these assumptions, E. K. Strong, Jr. developed the empirical method of contrast groups for identifying items that differentiated the interests of various occupations from people-in-general. His first effort resulted in 10 Occupational Scales; the current form of the Strong has 207 Occupational Scales for women and men that represent the interests of 106 occupational groups.

Occupational Scale Construction Technique

The method used to construct the Occupational Scales of the Strong Interest Inventory is the empirical method of contrast groups. Essentially, the technique involves the comparison of item responses for two samples, and the identification of the items that differentiate the two groups. This technique has been used in test development with interest inventories and also with personality measures such as the Minnesota Multiphasic Personality Inventory (MMPI; McKinley & Hathaway, 1940) and the California Psychological Inventory (CPI; Gough, 1957).

In the interest measurement field, the two contrast groups typically are a criterion sample representing a specific occupation, such as athletic trainers, and a sample of either women- or men-in-general. The women- and men-in-general samples for the current SVIB-SCII are 300 women and 300 men, all of whom are employed adults selected from a wide range of occupations. Subjects in the two samples are matched on occupational title. In other words, if the women-in-general sample includes one physician, the men-in-general sample includes one physician.

The respondents to each criterion sample collection effort are screened on several criteria, before inclusion in the sample, with the goal of selecting subjects who are typical representatives of the occupation. The final sample consists of a national sample of people who are between the ages of 25 and 60, who have been in their occupation for a minimum of three years, who are satisfied with their occupation, and who pursue their job in a typical fashion for that occupation. The occupational criterion sample generally is composed of about 200 subjects, although a smaller number of subjects will provide a reliable sample if stringent item selection standards are maintained.

Separate-sex scales. Although some interest inventories are available that use one set of scales for females and males (e.g., the Self-Directed Search; Holland, 1985b, or the Career Assessment Inventory; Johansson, 1986), several studies conducted with the Strong Interest Inventory to examine the feasibility of combined-sex scale construction indicate that combined-sex scales are less valid for most occupations and often are less reliable than are single-sex scales (Hansen, 1976; Hansen, 1984; Hansen & Campbell, 1985; Webber & Harmon, 1978). Therefore, the current Strong profile continues to present Occupational Scale scores that are based on separate female and male samples. By using patterns of scores, meaningful interpretations can be provided for both own- and opposite-sex scales.

Weighting the items. Items with large response percentage differences between the criterion sample and the appropriate-sex in-general sample are selected to represent the interests of the occupation on the Occupational Scale. The selected items represent both the "likes," or interests, and "dislikes," or aversions, of the occupation; typically, between 50 and 70 items emerge as those that best differentiate the contrast samples (i.e., occupational criterion sample and in-general sample).

The items that the occupational criterion sample prefers are assigned a unit weight of +1; the aversions of the criterion sample also are weighted +1. The net effect of this weighting system is to provide a scale on which an individual will score high if she or he has the same likes and dislikes as the occupational sample. For example, if a female responds "like" to items such as *inventor* and *calculus,* which are among the preferences of female electricians weighted on the female Electrician Occupational Scale, her score on the female Electrician Scale will increase. Her score also will increase if she responds "dislike" to the items *religious music* and *looking at things in a clothing store* because these are items that female electricians dislike more than do women-in-general. A "like" response to the items *religious music* and *looking at things in a clothing store* would have the opposite effect and would lower her score on the female Electrician Occupational Scale.

Standardizing the Occupational Scales. The Occupational Scales are standardized to allow the scores on various scales to be compared easily and meaningfully. The original criterion sample is used as the standardization sample for its own scale. First, the criterion sample is scored on the Occupational Scale to obtain a raw score; then, the raw scores are used in a raw-score-to-standard-score conversion formula that yields a mean of 50 and a standard deviation of 10 for the criterion sample. Thus, each criterion sample has a mean standard score of 50 on its own scale.

An individual who scores 50 on an Occupational Scale has responded to the items on the scale at a level similar to that of the average member of the criterion sample and, therefore, looks similar to the occupation in terms of her or his interests. The interpretive categories for scores on the Occupational Scales are:

Score	*Interpretive Comment*
14 or below	Very Dissimilar
15–24	Dissimilar
25–29	Moderately Dissimilar
30–39	Average
40–44	Moderately Similar
45–54	Similar
55 or higher	Very Similar

Basic Interest Scale Construction Technique

The Basic Interest Scales (BIS; Campbell, et. al., 1968) first were developed to supplement the Occupational Scales, and to provide a heuristic model for understanding the structure of interests and for identifying the clusters of interests that are relevant to the overall interests of occupations. Currently, there are 23 Basic Interest Scales on the profile. The items on each scale originally were grouped together using a cluster analysis procedure. The item content within each scale, therefore, is highly correlated; the coefficient alphas range from .77 to .96 with a median of .90 (Larkin, personal communication, 1984).

Weighting the Items. The items on the Basic Interest Scales are weighted so that a "like" response is a +1 and a "dislike" response is a −1. Thus, a high score on a particular Basic Interest Scale indicates that the person said "like" to a large number of items included on that scale and representing that cluster of interests.

Standardizing the BIS. The combined women- and men-in-general sample, known as the General Reference Sample (GRS), was used to standardize the Basic Interest Scales. A raw-score-to-standard-score conversion formula was employed that sets the mean for the GRS equal to 50 with a standard deviation of 10. Thus, a score of 50 on any BIS is a score indicating an average interest as compared to people-in-general.

General Occupational Theme Construction Technique

The General Occupational Themes (GOT) were constructed to provide a more parsimonious organization for the Strong Interest Inventory profile (Campbell & Holland, 1972; Hansen & Johansson, 1972). The GOT are based on Holland's theory of vocational types (Holland, 1973) and were developed using a rational-theoretical method to select items that represented each of the six types proposed by Holland: Realistic, Investigative, Artistic, Social, Enterprising and Conventional.

Like the items on the Basic Interest Scales, the GOT items are highly intercorrelated and the coefficient alphas range from 0.90 to .95 with a median of .92 (Larkin, personal communication, 1984). Each scale is composed of 20 items that are weighted +1 for a "like" response and −1 for a "dislike" response. The GOT were standardized using the General Reference Sample (GRS) with the standard score mean set equal to 50 and the standard deviation at 10.

Special Scale Construction Technique

The Special Scales include the Academic Comfort Scale and the Introversion-Extroversion Scale, which were constructed using the empirical method of contrast groups previously explained for the Occupational Scales.

Academic Comfort Scale. The contrast samples for constructing the Academic Comfort Scale (AC Scale) were good and poor students in the University of Minnesota's liberal arts college. The subjects were assigned to the appropriate criterion sample based on a combination of their grade point averages and their academic achievement test scores. Then, the item responses for a sample of the good students were compared to the item responses of a sample of poor students; the items differentiating the two samples were chosen for the AC Scale with the items preferred by the good students weighted +1 (Hansen & Campbell, 1985).

The AC Scale was standardized on a combined-sex sample of subjects (N=815) who all had earned their PhD degrees. The raw-score-to-standard-score conversion formula set the mean for this sample equal to 60 with a standard deviation of 10.

Introversion-Extroversion Scale. The Introversion-Extroversion Scale (IE Scale) was developed using contrast criterion samples whose members were identified as introverted or extroverted based on their scores on the MMPI Social Introversion Scale. Items weighted in the introverted direction are scored +1 and items weighted in the extroverted direction are scored −1. Thus, a high score on the IE Scale suggests an interest in introverted activities such as working with ideas or things; a low score suggests interests in an extroverted direction or those activities that involve working with people (Hansen & Campbell, 1985).

The IE Scale was standardized on a sample of 1,732 females and males using a raw-score-to-standard-score conversion formula with the mean set equal to 50 and standard deviation at 10. Thus, a score of 50 reflects a combination of interests involving both introverted and extroverted activities.

ADMINISTRATION

The Strong Interest Inventory may be administered in either a paper-and-pencil or computer-adapted format. The paper-and-pencil version takes about 25 to 35 minutes for the average individual to complete; the computer administered version takes about half the time or roughly 15 minutes. The SVIB-SCII can be given individually or in groups and is sufficiently robust to be administered in unsupervised settings (e.g., as a take home assignment or through the mail) or during several sittings if an individual cannot complete the entire inventory at one time. Although the reading level has been maintained at the sixth-grade level to ensure that the majority of clients can understand the item content, it is permissible to provide definitions or explanations for items that may be difficult to understand.

Basic instructions for taking the SVIB-SCII should include a standard introduction such as the following:

> The Strong Interest Inventory is designed to help you understand your interests in a general way and to identify some types of activities and work in which you may be interested. The booklet lists a variety of jobs, activities, school subjects, and types of people. You are asked to indicate how you feel about each item—whether you feel you "like" the item, are "indifferent" to it, or "dislike" it. Your answers to the items will be compared to people already employed in a wide variety of occupations to see how similar your interests are to theirs. As you respond to the items in the booklet, remember that the SVIB-SCII is designed to assess only your interests, and it does not measure your abilities. As you think about possible jobs and occupations, you will need to consider both your abilities and interests to make the best decisions.

Additional information and instructions, given to the client prior to taking the SVIB-SCII, will vary according to the situation. Counselors, however, frequently find it helpful to remind the client that most people respond "like" to about one-third of the items, "indifferent" to about one-third, and "dislike" to about one-third of the items. Also, the inventory cannot tell the client what she or he "should do." Rather, the instrument is designed to give some general information that will help the individual to do a thorough self-evaluation of her or his patterns of interests, and the profile is organized to aid the individual in identifying these patterns of interests. Finally, the client should be reminded that career planning is a life-long activity and results on the profile can be used for long-range planning as well as for making immediate educational or career planning decisions.

Scores on the Strong Interest Inventory are used, of course, to explore work-related interests but they also can provide clients with an opportunity to explore other types of interests such as leisure interests, preferences for various types of work, living and recreational environments, and affinity for people with various interests. Although compatibility between interests and work environment is important, compatibility between interests and other life roles also is important. The high and low scores of the General Occupational Themes and the Basic Interest Scales are especially helpful in determining how well a client's lifestyle matches her or his interests. Ultimately, the counseling outcome goal is an integration of the person's various interests into a composite that allows satisfaction through the various roles in her or his life.

INTERPRETATION

The Strong Interest Inventory is used primarily to stimulate respondents to think about activities and occupations that match their interests. The instrument helps them to objectively identify their interests in an efficient manner for a relatively modest expense. The results are organized to provide a framework for relating the interests to career possibilities and for encouraging the individual to consider options that may have been ignored previously.

Several interpretive aids have been developed to assist counselors and clients in understanding and explaining the inventory results including the *User's Guide for the SVIB-SCII* (Hansen, 1984), *Using the Strong in Organizations* (Hirsch & McEvoy, 1986) and the *Manual for the SVIB-SCII* (Hansen & Campbell, 1985). The Strong Inventory results are linked to the world of work to provide generalization to occupations not listed on the profile through the *Strong-Hansen Occupational Guide* (Hansen, 1987), which contains descriptions for the 106 occupations that correspond to the Occupational Scales on the SVIB-SCII.

The purpose of the *Occupational Guide* is twofold: first, to provide a detailed description of the 106 occupations including information about job tasks and responsibilities, work environments, and educational requirements; and second, to suggest occupations that are related to those on the profile. The suggested occupations found in the *Occupational Guide* provide additional options for exploration that are related to an individual's measured interests, but, for one reason or another, are not presented on the profile itself.

The GOT, BIS, and Occupational Scales

The three main sets of scales on the SVIB-SCII profile are the six General Occupational Themes, the 23 Basic Interest Scales, and the 105 female-normed and 102 male-normed Occupational Scales. The Occupational Scales differ from the General Occupational Themes (GOT) and Basic Interest Scales (BIS) in several ways. The GOT and BIS were constructed to measure single interest factors and are composed of items that, within each scale, are highly related to each other. The Occupational Scales, on the other hand, are composed of items that represent several interest factors. As a consequence, the GOT and BIS are somewhat easier to understand and interpret. They provide the best general information about a person's interests and also are useful for exploring non-occupational interests such as avocational interests or preferences for various work and living environments.

The Occupational Scales also are more complicated to interpret than are the other scales because the system assigns positive weights to both the likes and the aversions of an occupation. However, because of their greater length and item complexity, the Occupational Scales are less susceptible to faking than are the GOT and BIS. They also are less susceptible to distortion from extreme response rates and to transient changes in interests. Thus, the Occupational Scales—as they were when Strong first constructed them—are the preferred scales for predicting future occupational choices.

General Occupational Themes. The six General Occupational Themes—Realistic, Investigative, Artistic, Social, Enterprising, and Conventional—were added to the profile to provide a global view of a person's interests; they also provide a useful starting point for the exploration of an individual's occupational interests. And, the GOT contribute to the Strong Interest Inventory in another important way: They are used as part of the procedure for assigning Holland types to the Occupational Scales and the Basic Interest Scales.

Thus, each Occupational Scale is assigned a one to three letter Holland code that is useful in identifying the main clusters of interests of the occupation represented by the scale. For example, the Radiologic Technologist Scale is coded R and I indicating interests that fall in the realistic and investigative areas. Each Basic Interest Scale also has been assigned a primary Holland code based on the BIS scale's highest correlation with the GOT. The Mechanical Activities BIS, for example, has its highest correlation with the Realistic Theme and, therefore, is clustered with other R-Theme BIS on the profile. In turn, the codes assigned to the BIS and Occupational Scales are used to assist in organizing the entire profile; the BIS are clustered together by their Holland type and placed on the profile in Holland's R-I-A-S-E-C order as are the Occupational Scales.

The General Occupational Themes also can be used in interpretation to better understand the type of counseling intervention that may be most effective with the client. Such matching strategies have been shown to improve counseling outcomes and to increase client satisfaction with the counseling process (Kivlighan, Hageseth, Tipton, & McGovern, 1981).

Most people's interests are represented by some combination of the Themes rather than by one pure type, and they find that only some of the descriptors for each type or Theme fit their interests. Definitions for each of the types are presented on the back of the Strong Inventory profile, and often it is a useful exercise during interpretation of the inventory to ask the client to underline the descriptors that seem to fit her or his interests best. For example, Figure 7.1 illustrates the definitions that the client has identified as related to her interests. Her highest GOT scores are on the Realistic and Investigative Themes (scores of 57 and 60, respectively) and her lowest score is on the Conventional Theme. The descriptors that she has underlined reflect this relatively stronger interest in R-Theme and I-Theme activities with significantly fewer underlined definitions for the C-Theme.

Holland's theory of vocational types goes beyond the model of matching people and jobs to also suggest that individuals will increase their satisfaction if they match their interests to learning environments, family environments, leisure activities, and living environments (Holland, 1985a). Scores on the GOT will provide clients with a global view of their interests; once they understand the meaning of the six Themes, it is useful for them to consider where in their lives these interests fit. For some people, their work and leisure activities, as well as the types of people with whom they wish to associate, are quite similar across settings. For others, their interests are very diverse, and they choose to satisfy their many areas of interests by selecting different types of activities for their various roles in life (e.g., family roles, work roles, relaxation roles).

As clients examine their profile scores, it is helpful for them to integrate what they already know about their preferences with their measured interests. They can do this by examining past activities in which they have chosen to engage, past jobs and accomplishments, who their friends have been, where they spend most of their time, and so on. This information, combined with their interest inventory scores, can help them to identify their unique pattern of interests.

Basic Interest Scales. The Basic Interest Scales (BIS) serve as subdivisions for the more global General Occupational Themes. For example, the Science, Medical Science, Mathematics, and Medical Service Basic Interest Scales all are related statistically to the Investigative Theme and measure specific areas of

R-Theme: People scoring high here usually are rugged, robust, practical, physically strong; they usually have good physical skills, but sometimes have trouble expressing themselves or in communicating their feelings to others. They like to work outdoors and to work with tools, especially large, powerful machines. They prefer to deal with things rather than with ideas or people. They enjoy creating things with their hands and prefer occupations such as mechanic, construction work, fish and wildlife management, radiologic technologist, some engineering specialities, some military jobs, agriculture, or the skilled trades. Although no single word can capture the broad meaning of the entire Theme, the word REALISTIC has been used here, thus the term R-Theme.

S-Theme: The pure type here is sociable, responsible, humanistic, and concerned with the welfare of others. These people usually express themselves well and get along well with others; they like attention and seek situations that allow them to be near the center of the group. They prefer to solve problems by discussions with others, or by arranging or rearranging relationships between others; they have little interest in situations requiring physical exertion or working with machinery. Such people describe themselves as cheerful, popular, and achieving, and as good leaders. They prefer occupations such as school superintendent, social worker, high school teacher, marriage counselor, playground director, speech therapist, or vocational counselor. This is the SOCIAL Theme, or S-Theme.

I-Theme: This Theme centers around science and scientific activities. Extremes of this type are task-oriented; they are not particularly interested in working around other people. They enjoy solving abstract problems, and they have a great need to understand the physical world. They prefer to think through problems rather than act them out. Such people enjoy ambiguous challenges and do not like highly structured situations with many rules. They frequently are original and creative, especially in scientific areas. They prefer occupations such as design engineer, biologist, social scientist, research laboratory worker, physicist, technical writer, or meteorologist. The word INVESTIGATIVE characterizes this Theme, thus I-Theme.

E-Theme: The extreme type of this Theme has a great facility with words, especially in selling, dominating, and leading; frequently these people are in sales work. They see themselves as energetic, enthusiastic, adventurous, self-confident, and dominant, and they prefer social tasks where they can assume leadership. They enjoy persuading others to their viewpoints. They are impatient with precise work or work involving long periods of intellectual effort. They like power, status, and material wealth, and enjoy working in expensive settings. Vocational preferences include business executive, buyer, hotel manager, industrial relations consultant, political campaigner, realtor, sales work, and sports promoter. The word ENTERPRISING summarizes this pattern, thus E-Theme.

A-Theme: The extreme type here is artistically oriented, and likes to work in artistic settings that offer many opportunities for self-expression. Such people have little interest in problems that are highly structured or require gross physical strength, preferring those that can be solved through self-expression in artistic media. They resemble I-Theme types in preferring to work alone, but have a greater need for individualistic expression, and usually are less assertive about their own opinions and capabilities. They describe themselves as independent, original, unconventional, expressive, and intense. Vocational choices include artist, author, cartoonist, composer, singer, dramatic coach, poet, actor or actress, and symphony conductor. This is the ARTISTIC Theme, or A-Theme.

C-Theme: Extremes of this type prefer the highly ordered activities, both verbal and numerical, that characterize office work. People scoring high fit well into large organizations but do not seek leadership; they respond to power and are comfortable working in a well-established chain of command. They dislike ambiguous situations, preferring to know precisely what is expected of them. Such people describe themselves as conventional, stable, well-controlled, and dependable. They have little interest in problems requiring physical skills or intense relationships with others, and are most effective at well-defined tasks. Like the E-Theme type, they value material possessions and status. Vocational preferences are mostly within the business world, and include bank examiner, bank teller, bookkeeper, some accounting jobs, mathematics teacher, computer operator, inventory controller, tax expert, credit manager, and traffic manager. The word CONVENTIONAL more or less summarizes the pattern, hence C-Theme.

FIG. 7.1. Client 1. Interpretive Comments for the General Occupational Themes printed on the back of the Strong Interest Inventory profile. Reproduced with permission of the publisher, Consulting Psychologists Press, Stanford University Press.

interest within the global I-Theme. The scale names for the BIS provide an idea of the item content and the appropriate interpretation for each scale; the Adventure Scale, for example, includes items such as *climbing along the edge of a steep cliff* and *taking a chance.*

Thus, scores on the BIS lend themselves to straightforward interpretations about activities that the client likes or dislikes. These scales can be used in the same way as the GOT to help the client identify jobs, environments, activities, and types of people that appeal to them.

GOT and BIS Profile Information. The SVIB-SCII profile presents three types of interpretive information for the GOT and BIS: standard scores, interpretive comments, and interpretive bars. The standard scores are based on a raw-score to standard-score conversion, using the General Reference Sample (300 women- and 300 men-in-general) that was described earlier. The standard score mean for this sample is set equal to 50 with a standard deviation of 10. Therefore, the average score for people-in-general on each scale is 50. The interpretive comments, which appear on the profile next to the standard scores, are based on either the women-in-general subsample or men-in-general subsample of the GRS, and the interpretive bars, shown in Figure 7.2, represent the distribution of women's and men's scores on each scale.

As the interpretive bars in Figure 7.2 illustrate, the distribution of scores on most scales does differ for women and men. Consequently, interpretation based on the client's own sex typically provides the most valid and reliable information and the most options for exploration of interests in areas considered non-traditional for one sex or the other. If women- and men-in-general had the same distribution of scores on the scales, the interpretive comments and the interpretive bars would be unnecessary and the standard scores based on the people-in-general, or General Reference Sample, would be sufficient.

The interpretive comments are assigned to scores based on percentile categories for the client's own sex:

Comment Printed	*In-General Sample Percentile*
Very High	94th and above
High	85th to 93rd
Moderately High	70th to 84th
Average	31st to 69th
Moderately Low	16th to 30th
Low	7th to 15th
Very Low	6th and below

The more similar the distributions of scores for women- and men-in-general are on each of the scales, the more similar the interpretive categories are for each

STRONG-CAMPBELL INTEREST INVENTORY OF THE

STRONG VOCATIONAL INTEREST BLANK

PAGE 1 PROFILE REPORT FOR: Client #1 DATE TESTED:

ID: DATE SCORED:

AGE: 20 SEX: F

SPECIAL SCALES: ACADEMIC COMFORT 60
INTROVERSION-EXTROVERSION 58

TOTAL RESPONSES: 325 INFREQUENT RESPONSES: 6

GOT	
R	HIGH
I	HIGH
A	AVERAGE
S	MOD LOW
E	LOW
C	LOW

REALISTIC

GENERAL OCCUPATIONAL THEME - R: 57 HIGH

BASIC INTEREST SCALES (STANDARD SCORE)

- AGRICULTURE: 50 AVERAGE
- NATURE: 56 MOD HIGH
- ADVENTURE: 63 VERY HIGH
- MILITARY ACTIVITIES: 44 MOD LOW
- MECHANICAL ACTIVITIES: 68 VERY HIGH

INVESTIGATIVE

GENERAL OCCUPATIONAL THEME - I: 60 HIGH

BASIC INTEREST SCALES (STANDARD SCORE)

- SCIENCE: 60 HIGH
- MATHEMATICS: 56 MOD HIGH
- MEDICAL SCIENCE: 64 VERY HIGH
- MEDICAL SERVICE: 54 AVERAGE

ARTISTIC

GENERAL OCCUPATIONAL THEME - A: 52 AVERAGE

BASIC INTEREST SCALES (STANDARD SCORE)

- MUSIC/DRAMATICS: 50 AVERAGE
- ART: 50 AVERAGE
- WRITING: 52 AVERAGE

CONSULTING PSYCHOLOGISTS PRESS
577 COLLEGE AVENUE
PALO ALTO, CA 94306

OCCUPATIONAL SCALES

STANDARD SCORES — VERY DISSIMILAR / DISSIMILAR / MODERATELY DISSIMILAR / MID RANGE / MODERATELY SIMILAR / SIMILAR / VERY SIMILAR (15 25 30 40 45 55)

Realistic	F	M
Marine Corps enlisted personnel	(CRS)	23
Navy enlisted personnel	38	23
Army officer	34	25
Navy officer	46	39
Air Force officer	42	35
Air Force enlisted personnel	(C)	24
Police officer	37	26
Bus driver	43	33
Horticultural worker	48	42
Farmer	21	26
Vocational agriculture teacher	36	16
Forester	56	36
Veterinarian	(IR)	34
Athletic trainer	40	(SR)
Emergency medical technician	33	22
Radiologic technologist	31	30
Carpenter	48	38
Electrician	51	28
Architect	63	(ARI)
Engineer	58	47

Investigative	F	M
Computer programmer	59	49
Systems analyst	61	50
Medical technologist	60	46
R & D manager	66	53
Geologist	59	60
Biologist	54	(I)
Chemist	48	44
Physicist	40	38
Veterinarian	55	(RI)
Science teacher	42	40
Physical therapist	40	44
Respiratory therapist	46	38
Medical technician	37	35
Pharmacist	56	39
Dietitian	43	(CSE)
Nurse, RN	(SI)	29
Chiropractor	32	38
Optometrist	58	61
Dentist	55	50
Physician	36	55
Biologist	(IR)	50
Mathematician	41	35
Geographer	62	58
College professor	56	43
Psychologist	40	35
Sociologist	38	33

Artistic	F	M
Medical illustrator	53	39
Art teacher	10	27
Artist, fine	39	31
Artist, commercial	35	36
Interior decorator	19	28
Architect	(RIA)	55
Photographer	53	53
Musician	46	50
Chef	40	(EA)
Beautician	(E)	30
Flight attendant	27	41
Advertising executive	35	45
Broadcaster	29	40
Public relations director	23	16
Lawyer	46	31
Public administrator	35	27
Reporter	35	39
Librarian	46	40
English teacher	4	24
Foreign language teacher	(SA)	27

FIG. 7.2. Client 1. Strong Interest Inventory profile for a 20 year old female, enrolled as a junior in the biological sciences. In high school she completed a college preparation curriculum with a 3.95 GPA; entered numerous Science Fair competitions; played saxaphone in the band; was active in scouting; played basketball and tennis; and was a camp counselor. In college she continued to work as a camp coun-

STRONG-CAMPBELL INTEREST INVENTORY OF THE

STRONG VOCATIONAL INTEREST BLANK

PAGE 2 PROFILE REPORT FOR: Client #1 DATE TESTED:

ID: DATE SCORED:

AGE: SEX: F

SOCIAL

GENERAL OCCUPATIONAL THEME - S (30 40 50 60 70; F / M)

40 MOD LOW

BASIC INTEREST SCALES (STANDARD SCORE)

TEACHING	46 AVERAGE
SOCIAL SERVICE	38 LOW
ATHLETICS	55 MOD HIGH
DOMESTIC ARTS	29 VERY LOW
RELIGIOUS ACTIVITIES	35 LOW

ENTERPRISING

GENERAL OCCUPATIONAL THEME - E (30 40 50 60 70; F / M)

38 LOW

BASIC INTEREST SCALES (STANDARD SCORE)

PUBLIC SPEAKING	51 AVERAGE
LAW/POLITICS	36 LOW
MERCHANDISING	36 LOW
SALES	30 VERY LOW
BUSINESS MANAGEMENT	42 MOD LOW

CONVENTIONAL

GENERAL OCCUPATIONAL THEME - C (30 40 50 60 70; F / M)

37 LOW

BASIC INTEREST SCALES (STANDARD SCORE)

OFFICE PRACTICES	38 LOW

OCCUPATIONAL SCALES

STANDARD SCORES (F, M) — VERY DISSIMILAR / DISSIMILAR / MODERATELY DISSIMILAR / MID-RANGE / MODERATELY SIMILAR / SIMILAR / VERY SIMILAR (15 25 30 40 45 55)

F	M	Occupational Scale	Standard Score F	Standard Score M
SA	(AS)	Foreign language teacher	6	(AS)
SA	SA	Minister	9	20
SA	SA	Social worker	16	14
S	S	Guidance counselor	10	14
S	S	Social science teacher	6	14
S	S	Elementary teacher	17	19
S	S	Special education teacher	8	13
SRI	SAR	Occupational therapist	34	29
SIA	SAI	Speech pathologist	11	18
SI	(ISR)	Nurse, RN	27	(ISR)
SEI	N/A	Dental hygienist	32	N/A
SC	SC	Nurse, LPN	14	15
(RIS)	SR	Athletic trainer	(RIS)	23
SR	SR	Physical education teacher	26	8
SRE	SE	Recreation leader	39	28
SE	SE	YWCA/YMCA director	20	16
SEC	SCE	School administrator	15	16
SCE	N/A	Home economics teacher	5	N/A
E	ES	Personnel director	13	14
ES	E	Elected public official	14	13
ES	ES	Life insurance agent	11	5
EC	E	Chamber of Commerce executive	6	5
EC	EC	Store manager	11	11
N/A	ECR	Agribusiness manager	N/A	7
EC	EC	Purchasing agent	17	14
EC	E	Restaurant manager	11	12
(AR)	EA	Chef	(AR)	29
EC	E	Travel agent	12	20
ECS	E	Funeral director	14	14
(CSE)	ESC	Nursing home administrator	(CSE)	11
EC	ER	Optician	21	36
E	E	Realtor	1	10
E	(AE)	Beautician	26	(AE)
E	E	Florist	25	24
EC	E	Buyer	-3	11
E	E	Marketing executive	52	50
EC	ECI	Investments manager	56	42
C	C	Accountant	37	28
C	C	Banker	14	25
CE	CE	IRS agent	37	15
CES	CES	Credit manager	12	16
CES	CES	Business education teacher	-5	-1
(CS)	CES	Food service manager	(CS)	16
(ISR)	CSE	Dietitian	(ISR)	24
CSE	(ESC)	Nursing home administrator	12	(ESC)
CSE	CSE	Executive housekeeper	18	22
CS	(CES)	Food service manager	17	(CES)
CS	N/A	Dental assistant	20	N/A
C	N/A	Secretary	10	N/A
C	(R)	Air Force enlisted personnel	22	(R)
CRS	(RC)	Marine Corps enlisted personnel	26	(RC)
CRS	CR	Army enlisted personnel	28	11
CIR	CIR	Mathematics teacher	34	34

ADMINISTRATIVE INDEXES (RESPONSE %)

	L%	I%	D%
OCCUPATIONS	27 L%	17 I %	56 D%
SCHOOL SUBJECTS	42 L%	14 I %	44 D%
ACTIVITIES	31 L%	10 I %	59 D%
LEISURE ACTIVITIES	54 L%	31 I %	15 D%
TYPES OF PEOPLE	38 L%	33 I %	29 D%
PREFERENCES	40 L%	40 I %	20 D%
CHARACTERISTICS	71 L%	0 I %	29 D%
ALL PARTS	37 L%	20 I %	44 D%

CONSULTING PSYCHOLOGISTS PRESS
577 COLLEGE AVENUE
PALO ALTO, CA 94306

selor, took at least one canoeing and camping trip each summer, and began to save her money for a trip to Europe. She maintained a 3.80 GPA, participated in co-ed recreational sports and took the Strong as she began to consider the possibility of graduate or professional school. Reproduced with permission of the Publisher, Consulting Psychologists Press for the Publisher, Stanford University Press.

sex. For example, in Figure 7.2 the distribution of scores for women- and men-in-general on the Realistic Theme differs; the women have a mean score of 47 and the men a mean score of 54; consequently, a score of 57 falls in the high range of scores compared to women-in-general but in the average range compared to men-in-general. Conversely, women and men have similar distributions of scores on the Merchandising BIS, which is located in the profile under the Enterprising category, and a score of 36, for example, is in the low range for females and males.

The interpretive bars provide a visual representation of the score distributions, which can be helpful in explaining the profile to the client. The upper bar, shown in Figure 2, represents the distribution of scores for women-in-general and the lower bar represents the scores of the men-in-general. The vertical line in the middle of each distribution represents the mean or average score for the women- and men-in-general sample. The middle 50% of each distribution (25th to 75th percentile) is represented by the thick portion of the bar, and the area between one end of the thin line and the other is the 10th to 90th percentile.

High and low scores on the GOT and BIS can be used to help clients judge how well their lifestyles match their interests. For example, incompatibility between interests and pursued activities can lead to dissatisfaction with work life if the mismatch is between occupational interests and the chosen job. Conceivably mismatches also can lead to dissatisfaction with personal relationships (Bruch & Skovholt, 1985; Johnson, 1987; Schneider, 1987; Wiggins & Weslander, 1983), living and working environments (Meir, Keinan, & Segal, 1986; Spokane, 1987), or with leisure time (Cairo, 1979), if the incongruence between interests and activities occurs in these domains.

The psychologist's or counselor's role in interpreting the GOT and BIS is to provide plausible hypotheses for high and low scores on the scales, as well as to assist in identifying patterns of interests as they emerge, and to clarify how these interests may relate to a person's educational, work, and personal life. The client must examine her or his own life history to identify what type of interest the scores represent and to determine how best and most fully to satisfy these interests in the future.

Occupational Scales. The most useful scales on the Strong Interest Inventory profile for predicting future occupational choice are the Occupational Scales. They measure the similarity of a person's interests to the interests of people employed in specific occupations. Validity research with the Occupational Scales also has shown that the Strong Inventory can be used to assist clients in their choice of college majors (Hansen & Swanson, 1983).

The Occupational Scales are standardized so that the mean standard score for each occupation on its own scale is 50. Therefore, an individual who scores 50 on a particular scale has responded similarly to the way an average member of that occupation does and looks "similar" to the occupation in terms of interests.

As illustrated in Figure 7.2, the profile reports scores for both female- and male-normed scales for 101 occupations. Five additional Occupational Scales are on the profile that are normed on only female or male samples; they include four scales normed on female samples only—Dental Assistant, Dental Hygienist, Home Economics Teacher, and Secretary—and one scale normed only with a male sample—Agribusiness Manager. These five occupations are dominated by one sex or the other, and therefore, it has been impossible to locate criterion samples sufficiently large to construct scales for both sexes.

As Figure 7.2 illustrates, regardless of the individual's sex, all Occupational Scales are scored on every profile. The standard scores are printed in the column next to the scale name and an asterisk for the person's same sex score is printed at a corresponding point along a preprinted grid to provide a graphic representation of the similarity between the individual's interests and those of the occupation. The lowest scores are plotted in the "Very Dissimilar" column and the highest scores in the "Very Similar" column. Scores in the "Moderately Similar" or higher categories are the most predictive of future choices and should be used in interpretation with clients. The range of scores possible to obtain on the Occupational Scales extends from a low of −53 on female Art Teacher to a high of +92 on male Army Enlisted Personnel. A negative score on an Occupational Scale indicates that the person's interests are very dissimilar to those of the occupation.

Whereas, the General Occupational Themes and Basic Interest Scales help an individual to identify global areas of interests that may be satisfied through a variety of activities, the Occupational Scales tie the individual's interests more directly to the world of work. The main objective in interpreting the Occupational Scales is to assist the individual in identifying patterns of interests, and from those patterns, then, to identify occupations that fit the person's area of interests. As illustrated in Figure 7.2, circling the client's highest scores—those of 40 or above—is a useful exercise for identifying patterns of interests. Although a person usually is quite aware of her or his dislikes, pointing out the lowest scores also may be useful to an individual as she or he examines the profile.

The client and counselor may work together to identify common interests among the occupations represented by the client's highest scores. Eventually, the client will want to focus on a few specific occupations to explore in detail. Initially, however, the exploration may be designed to identify interests highlighted on the profile, as well as to generalize to occupations with related interests that are not represented on the profile by an Occupational Scale.

The codes representing Holland's six types that are assigned to each Occupational Scale are useful both for identifying the areas of interest of the particular occupation and for generalizing to related occupations. Also, the *Strong-Hansen Occupational Guide* (Hansen, 1987) was developed to assist clients in generalizing to occupations not listed on the profile. With the use of the *Occupational Guide,* a list of occupations related to the individual's interests can be developed for the client to explore further. Clients should be encouraged to consider all relevant occupations even though they may not have considered them before because of unfamiliarity with the occupation or because of a perception that an occupation may be closed to them on the grounds of such factors as sex, social class, or ethnic background.

For example, the client whose profile is presented in Figure 7.2 scored in the "Similar" range on the Biologist Scale (located in the Investigative category on the profile). Related occupations for this Occupational Scale include anatomists, bacteriologists, biomedical researchers, ecologists, geneticists, oceanographers, and zoologists. These are occupations that incorporate her interests and are worthy of consideration as career possibilities.

In addition to helping clients identify related occupations, the Holland codes assigned to each Occupational Scale reflect the likes and the aversions of people in the occupation. For example, the Purchasing Agent Scale (located in the Enterprising category on the profile) is assigned the code EC suggesting that items in the enterprising and conventional areas are weighted as "likes" and that investigative and artistic items, which according to Holland's theory of vocational types are least related to interests in the E-Theme and C-Theme areas, are weighted as "dislikes."

Just as the codes can be used to draw attention to the similarities among occupations to aid in generalizing to related occupations, the codes also can be used to help understand how occupations differ from one another. For example, although engineers (RI) and research and development managers (IR) both have realistic and investigative interests, the order of the codes assigned to their respective Occupational Scales suggest that realistic activities are the primary interests for engineers (RI), whereas investigative activities are the primary interests for research and development managers (IR).

Academic Comfort Scale

The Academic Comfort Scale (AC Scale) is not a measure of abilities. Rather, the AC Scale was designed to measure interests that frequently are satisfied through participation in activities that require acquiring knowledge, developing theories, and understanding underlying principles. A low score on the Academic Comfort Scale, say a score of 35, does not indicate that the person does not have the ability to perform college level work. The score does indicate, however, that the person may not have the interests necessary to persist in an academic environment. People with low scores on the Academic Comfort Scale, who do choose to go to college or even on to graduate school, often see a degree as a necessary hurdle for entry into the occupation they are seeking or as a means to an end.

As early as the freshman year in college, those individuals who intend to go on to graduate school score, on the average, 15 points higher on the AC Scale than do those individuals who indicate that they are in college simply to have a good time (Swanson & Hansen, 1985). Graduate-school-oriented freshmen typically will score in the 50s on the AC Scale but those interested primarily in the social activities of college score in the 30s.

People who score 45 or higher on the AC Scale usually are oriented toward getting a college education. Those who score at this level or in the 50s and 60s should be encouraged to develop a plan for satisfying their academic interests in the future. College and graduate education provide one mechanism for satisfying academic interests but other possibilities include continuing or community education courses, entering occupations that require the continual acquisition of knowledge, periodically leaving a well-known job or position to enter a new one that presents a new challenge, or engaging in hobbies and leisure activities that require learning new knowledge and information.

Frequently, individuals who score low on the AC Scale are oriented toward learning and acquiring knowledge for the purpose of the practical application of the knowledge, rather than for the purpose of understanding the underlying principle. People who do score low on the scale should not be discouraged from entering an educational system, but they may wish to participate in internship experiences or to hold part-time jobs to complement their course work and to provide practical experience in their occupational area.

Introversion-Extroversion Scale

The Introversion-Extroversion Scale (IE Scale) of the Strong Interest Inventory correlates with personality measures of introversion-extroversion such as the Social Extroversion Scale of the Omnibus Personality Inventory (Goodyear & Frank, 1977). The higher an individual's score on the IE scale the more interests she or he has in activities that involve ideas and things and working alone. For example, samples of people in occupations such as farming, physics, computer programming, and mathematics have mean scores on the IE Scale of 58 or higher (Hansen, 1984). On the other hand, low scores represent an interest in working with people or working in groups. Samples of people in occupations such as auto sales, politics, life insurance sales, or stock brokerage score, on the average, about 20 points lower on the IE Scale than do farmers, physicists, mathematicians, or computer programmers.

People in occupations that require a combination of introverted and extroverted interests, such as teachers, medical personnel (e.g., nurses, physical therapists, and respiratory therapists), and service occupations (e.g., beauticians, funeral directors, and food service managers) typically score between 46 and 54 on the IE Scale. Scores above that range are in the introverted direction and scores below that range are in the extroverted direction.

Administrative Indexes

The profile for the Strong Inventory reports several administrative indexes that are useful for ascertaining the validity of the profile. These indexes include the Total Responses Index, the Infrequent Responses Index, and the indexes that summarize the "like," "indifferent," and "dislike" response percentages for various sections of the item booklet (LP%, IP%, and DP%).

Total Response Index. The Total Response Index simply indicates the number of items on the inventory to which the individual has responded. Most people respond to all 325 items, but occasionally a few items will be missed. Although a large number of items can be deleted without appreciably affecting the profile scores, the computer scoring program is set to reject an answer sheet that is missing more than 20 items to ensure the validity of the results for each individual.

Infrequent Response Index. The Infrequent Response Index was developed as a very general indicator of profile validity using those items on the Strong Inventory that generally are answered in the same way by most people. For example, most people respond "dislike" to the item *Life insurance salesperson;* therefore, a "like" response to this item would be an infrequent response among people-in-general and would lower an individual's score on the Infrequent Response Index.

Each person is allowed to make several infrequent responses before the computer flags the profile as an unusual one. However, once a large number of infrequent responses have been given, the score becomes a negative number and this should serve as a signal that the profile may be invalid.

When a negative Infrequent Response Index does occur, the best way to determine whether the person has responded honestly to the items is to check with the individual. If the person has understood the instructions, feels positively about taking the Strong Interest Inventory and the career counseling process in general, and indicates honesty in responding to the items, then the interpretation should proceed. In these instances, the person probably does have a valid profile in spite of an unusual pattern of interests, and the profile may be interpreted in the same manner as any other would be.

LP, IP, and DP Indexes. The response percentage indexes are included to provide a mechanism for determining quickly how the person has responded to various sections of the item booklet. For example, the profile illustrated in Figure 7.2 shows that the client indicated "like" to 27% of the items in the occupations section of the item pool and "dislike" to 56% of those items.

The All Parts LP, IP, and DP scores summarize the person's response rate for the entire item pool. People-in-general have an average response rate across these three indexes of 33%, 33%, and 33% and most people respond "like" to somewhere between 20% and 50% of the item pool. If a person has an extremely high (say 60% or higher) or an extremely low (20% or lower) Total LP, the result is likely to be an elevated or depressed profile, respectively. Although the profile is an accurate reflection of the individual's interests, the interpretation may need to be modified to accommodate the extreme response rate. Interpretation of elevated, flat, and depressed profiles will be discussed in the next section.

People with high Total IP Index scores may be indecisive or genuinely confused about their interests and the choices available to them. They may need to accumulate additional experience and to learn more about the world of work before proceeding with the decision-making process.

Flat and Depressed Profiles

Occasionally an individual's profile configuration will appear *flat*—the scores will be primarily in the average interpretive ranges—or *depressed* with scores below average on the General Occupational Themes and Basic Interest Scales and below "Moderately Similar" on the Occupational Scales. A flat or depressed profile usually is the result of a low "like" response rate, say less than 20%.

Flat or depressed profiles may be diagnostic of several different career decision-making situations. For example, people with narrow or well-defined interests may score high on only the one or two scales that correspond to their interests and as a result, their profiles will appear to be flat or depressed. For others, the flat or depressed profile is symptomatic of limited knowledge about the world of work, indecisiveness or unreadiness to make a career commitment, or simply apathy towards the concept of working (Hansen, 1984).

One method for interpreting flat or depressed profiles is to treat the results as ipsative data. Rather than comparing the individual's responses to the normative samples (e.g., "Your interests look average compared to men-in-general."), the individual's scores are rank-ordered from high to low and the exploration concentrates on the highest of the person's scores even if none of the scores are higher than average (e.g., "Instead of comparing your interests to those of other people, let's identify the areas of greatest interest to you.").

The most useful scores will be the GOT and BIS scores closest to the mean for that person's own-sex standardization sample, and the highest of the mid-range Occupational Scale scores—those that are between about 39 and 36. The key to remember during the interpretion of flat or depressed profiles is to continuously assess how much "sense" the emerging patterns of interest make. If the profile appears integrated, if the same patterns of interest emerge across the GOT, BIS, and Occupational Scales, then proceeding with the profile interpretation is legitimate. If the results appear random and the interests from one section of the profile to another are unrelated, then caution is advised.

Elevated Profiles

A profile with many scores above average usually is the result of a high "like" response rate. The GOT and BIS are affected more by an elevated response rate than are the Occupational Scales because only the "like" responses determine high scores on those scales whereas both "like" and "dislike" responses contribute to high scores on the Occupational Scales. Usually an elevated profile reflects diversity in a person's interests or a wide range of interests.

Elevated profiles are less difficult to interpret than are flat or depressed profiles. The general procedure is to focus on the highest of the high scores, for example, the three highest GOT, the eight to 10 highest BIS, and the ''Very Similar'' and ''Similar'' Occupational Scales. People with elevated profiles may find it difficult to make career decisions because of their many interests and they may be reluctant to choose one area over another. They can be encouraged, however, to explore several alternatives such as (a) pursuing a job that provides contact with a diversity of people or a position that incorporates a variety of tasks and responsibilities, (b) engaging in a range of leisure activities and hobbies that may be quite different from their vocational activities, or (c) planning a career path that will allow changes in jobs periodically.

Opposite-Sex Occupational Scale Interpretation

The same-sex normed Occupational Scales on the Strong Interest Inventory are the most valid for all clients. However, the opposite-sex scores can be used as part of the analysis of patterns of interests that emerge on the profile. In the analysis of these patterns, the absolute values of scores become less important and the combination of scores become the primary focus. If, for example, an individual scores high on a same-sex Occupational Scale but scores even higher on the opposite-sex scale for the same occupation, the consistency in level of scores on the two scales is more important than the difference between the scores. (See scores on the female and male Physical Therapist Scales, located in the Investigative category on the profile, which illustrate this point in Figure 7.2.)

If a person scores low on a corresponding sex scale but high on an opposite-sex scale, the high scores can be used as valid indicators of interest if they contribute to the pattern of interests that is emerging from the GOT, BIS, and other same-sex Occupational Scales. A consistent pattern of interests across the three sets of scales provides support for consideration of an occupation even if the individual has not scored high on the own-sex Occupational Scale. The client in Figure 7.2, for example, has a very strong pattern of medical interests appearing on the GOT (above average score on the I-Theme), the BIS (above average scores on Science, Medical Science and Medical Service), and Occupational Scales (high scores on the female Biologist, Physical Therapist, Dentist, Medical Technologist, and Respiratory Therapist Scales). These scores all support the ''Very Similar'' score she received on the male Physician Scale and medicine would be a legitimate occupation for her to consider even though she scored in the ''Mid-range'' on the female Physician scale.

Case Study

One of the most visible changes in the last revision of the Strong Interest Inventory (Hansen & Campbell, 1985) was the expansion of the profile to represent additional nonprofessional occupations among the Occupational Scales. The case study described below illustrates the need for these Occupational Scales; six of the Client's 13 scores in the Moderately Similar or higher category were on Occupational Scales not represented on the profile of the earlier version of the Strong.

Client 2 sought career counseling when he was in his mid-twenties. He worked with his parents running a family agricultural operation in the western part of the U.S. However, problems had developed between them and because of the stress, Client 2 was considering other career possibilities. The ideal career described by Client 2 was for him to remain in farming and ranching; the reality was that the cost of setting up his own spread was prohibitive and he, therefore, felt the need to begin to plan a possible career change.

Client 2's profile is illustrated in Figure 7.3. Notable features include the small number of items to which he responded "Like"; the relatively "flat" scores on the General Occupational Themes and Basic Interest Scales; the high score on the Introversion-Extroversion Scale, and the low score on the Academic Comfort Scale.

On the average, people respond "Like" to about 33% of the Strong items; Client 2 responded "Like" to only 11%. A low "Like" response rate may occur for a variety of reasons (e.g., indifference to career exploration and the world of work; clinical depression; unwillingness to say "Like" to items which an individual has not actually tried, etc.). In this case, client 2 simply had very well defined interests. He described his interests as "narrow" and himself as "opinionated" about various occupations and jobs with a few strong likes and many strong dislikes.

The definition of his interests is reflected on the General Occupational Themes (GOT) and Basic Interest Scales (BIS); he had scores below average on five of the six GOT and on 18 of the 23 BIS. As we discussed each of the scales, however, it was apparent that this relatively flat profile was an accurate reflection of his very dominant interest in agriculture; his tolerance, but not passion, for other activities categorized under the Realistic Theme (average scores on Mechanical Activities, Nature, and Adventure), and his disinterest in all other areas except Athletics (an average score found under the Social Theme).

Client 2 scored in the introverted direction on the Introversion-Extroversion Scale and as one might hypothesize, he found it quite difficult to discuss his thoughts and feelings during the counseling interviews. This reluctance for verbal communication generalized to his interaction with his parents both of whom he described as reserved and quiet. He commented that neither he nor his parents seemed able to discuss future plans or to share information necessary for making decisions about their ranching business.

As often happens to clients who are considering career changes, Client 2 felt that one of his few options was to "go back to school." He had attended a vocational-technical trade school to receive training in large equipment operation and had worked on highway construction prior to joining the family business. However, he discussed returning to school with no enthusiasm, and although he

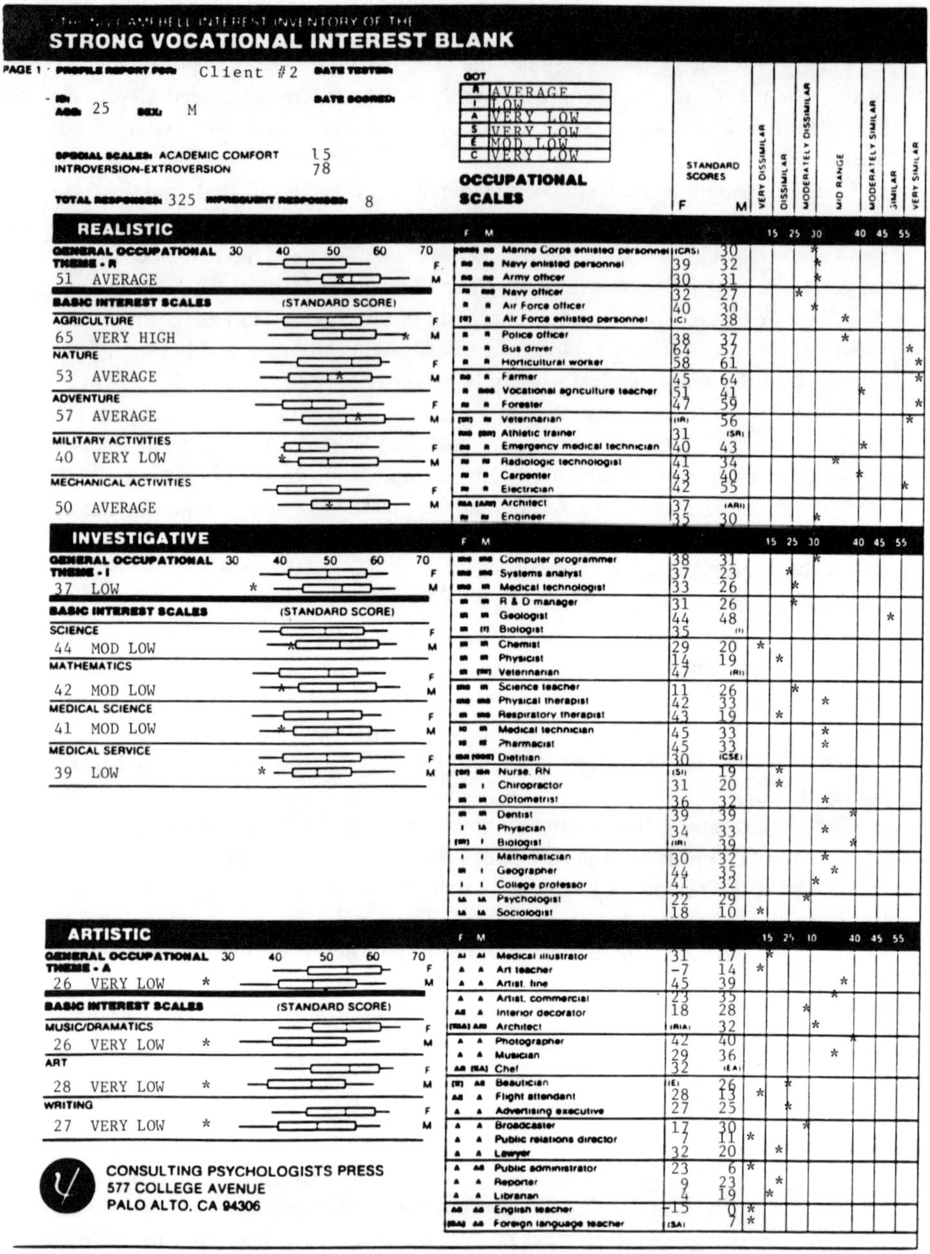
THE 1985 CAMPBELL INTEREST INVENTORY OF THE
STRONG VOCATIONAL INTEREST BLANK

PAGE 1 · PROFILE REPORT FOR: Client #2 DATE TESTED:
ID: DATE SCORED:
AGE: 25 SEX: M

SPECIAL SCALES: ACADEMIC COMFORT 15
INTROVERSION-EXTROVERSION 78

TOTAL RESPONSES: 325 INFREQUENT RESPONSES: 8

GOT	
R	AVERAGE
I	LOW
A	VERY LOW
S	VERY LOW
E	MOD LOW
C	VERY LOW

REALISTIC

GENERAL OCCUPATIONAL THEME - R: 51 AVERAGE

BASIC INTEREST SCALES (STANDARD SCORE)

AGRICULTURE	65 VERY HIGH
NATURE	53 AVERAGE
ADVENTURE	57 AVERAGE
MILITARY ACTIVITIES	40 VERY LOW
MECHANICAL ACTIVITIES	50 AVERAGE

INVESTIGATIVE

GENERAL OCCUPATIONAL THEME - I: 37 LOW

BASIC INTEREST SCALES (STANDARD SCORE)

SCIENCE	44 MOD LOW
MATHEMATICS	42 MOD LOW
MEDICAL SCIENCE	41 MOD LOW
MEDICAL SERVICE	39 LOW

ARTISTIC

GENERAL OCCUPATIONAL THEME - A: 26 VERY LOW

BASIC INTEREST SCALES (STANDARD SCORE)

MUSIC/DRAMATICS	26 VERY LOW
ART	28 VERY LOW
WRITING	27 VERY LOW

OCCUPATIONAL SCALES — STANDARD SCORES (VERY DISSIMILAR, DISSIMILAR, MODERATELY DISSIMILAR, MID RANGE, MODERATELY SIMILAR, SIMILAR, VERY SIMILAR; 15 25 30 40 45 55)

Occupational Scale	F	M
Marine Corps enlisted personnel	(CRS)	30
Navy enlisted personnel	39	32
Army officer	30	31
Navy officer	32	27
Air Force officer	40	30
Air Force enlisted personnel	(C)	38
Police officer	38	37
Bus driver	64	57
Horticultural worker	58	61
Farmer	45	64
Vocational agriculture teacher	51	41
Forester	47	59
Veterinarian	(IR)	56
Athletic trainer	31	(SR)
Emergency medical technician	40	43
Radiologic technologist	41	34
Carpenter	43	40
Electrician	42	55
Architect	37	(ARI)
Engineer	35	30
Computer programmer	38	31
Systems analyst	37	23
Medical technologist	33	26
R & D manager	31	26
Geologist	44	48
Biologist	35	(I)
Chemist	29	20
Physicist	14	19
Veterinarian	47	(RI)
Science teacher	11	26
Physical therapist	42	33
Respiratory therapist	43	19
Medical technician	45	33
Pharmacist	45	33
Dietitian	30	(CSE)
Nurse, RN	(SI)	19
Chiropractor	31	20
Optometrist	36	32
Dentist	39	39
Physician	34	33
Biologist	(IR)	39
Mathematician	30	32
Geographer	44	35
College professor	41	32
Psychologist	22	29
Sociologist	18	10
Medical illustrator	31	17
Art teacher	-7	14
Artist, fine	45	39
Artist, commercial	23	35
Interior decorator	18	28
Architect	(RIA)	32
Photographer	42	40
Musician	29	36
Chef	32	(EA)
Beautician	(E)	26
Flight attendant	28	13
Advertising executive	27	25
Broadcaster	17	30
Public relations director	7	11
Lawyer	32	20
Public administrator	23	6
Reporter	9	23
Librarian	4	19
English teacher	-15	0
Foreign language teacher	(SA)	7

CONSULTING PSYCHOLOGISTS PRESS
577 COLLEGE AVENUE
PALO ALTO, CA 94306

FIG. 7.3. Client 2. Strong Interest Inventory profile for a 25-year-old male employed in agriculture. He took the Strong to consider future career plans, when family conflict and lack of communication became too stressful. Reproduced with permission of the publisher, Consulting Psychologists Press for the Publisher, Standford University Press.

STRONG-CAMPBELL INTEREST INVENTORY OF THE

STRONG VOCATIONAL INTEREST BLANK

PAGE 2 PROFILE REPORT FOR: Client #2 DATE TESTED:

ID: DATE SCORED:

AGE: 25 SEX: M

SOCIAL

GENERAL OCCUPATIONAL THEME - S (30 40 50 60 70)

28 VERY LOW *

BASIC INTEREST SCALES (STANDARD SCORE)

TEACHING	28	VERY LOW *
SOCIAL SERVICE	28	VERY LOW *
ATHLETICS	58	AVERAGE
DOMESTIC ARTS	29	VERY LOW *
RELIGIOUS ACTIVITIES	33	VERY LOW *

OCCUPATIONAL SCALES

F	M	Occupational scale	Standard score F	Standard score M	Very dissimilar (<15)	Dissimilar (15–25)	Moderately dissimilar (25–30)	Mid-range (30–40)	Moderately similar (40–45)	Similar (45–55)	Very similar (55+)
SA	(AS)	Foreign language teacher	-14	(AS)							
SA	SA	Minister	-12	-1	*						
SA	SA	Social worker	7	1	*						
S	S	Guidance counselor	0	8	*						
S	S	Social science teacher	0	9	*						
S	S	Elementary teacher	19	25			*				
S	S	Special education teacher	3	6	*						
SIR	SAR	Occupational therapist	27	11	*						
SIA	SAI	Speech pathologist	-2	0	*						
SI	(ISR)	Nurse, RN	9	(ISR)							
SCI	N/A	Dental hygienist	34	N/A							
SC	SC	Nurse, LPN	30	16		*					
(RIS)	SR	Athletic trainer	(RIS)	36				*			
SR	SR	Physical education teacher	38	20		*					
SRE	SE	Recreation leader	25	20		*					
SE	SE	YWCA/YMCA director	12	10	*						
SEC	SEC	School administrator	0	10	*						
SCE	N/A	Home economics teacher	8	N/A							

ENTERPRISING

GENERAL OCCUPATIONAL THEME - E (30 40 50 60 70)

42 MOD LOW

BASIC INTEREST SCALES (STANDARD SCORE)

PUBLIC SPEAKING	29	VERY LOW *
LAW/POLITICS	30	VERY LOW *
MERCHANDISING	38	MOD LOW
SALES	44	MOD LOW
BUSINESS MANAGEMENT	32	VERY LOW *

F	M	Occupational scale	Standard score F	Standard score M	Very dissimilar (<15)	Dissimilar (15–25)	Moderately dissimilar (25–30)	Mid-range (30–40)	Moderately similar (40–45)	Similar (45–55)	Very similar (55+)
E	ES	Personnel director	9	5	*						
ES	E	Elected public official	-1	17		*					
ES	ES	Life insurance agent	9	7	*						
EC	E	Chamber of Commerce executive	22	5	*						
EC	EC	Store manager	20	26			*				
N/A	ECR	Agribusiness manager	N/A	51						*	
EC	EC	Purchasing agent	22	23		*					
EC	E	Restaurant manager	14	34				*			
(AR)	EA	Chef	(AR)	10	*						
EC	E	Travel agent	20	29			*				
ECS	E	Funeral director	17	32				*			
(CSE)	ECS	Nursing home administrator	(CSE)	14	*						
EC	ER	Optician	37	36				*			
E	E	Realtor	2	26			*				
E	(AE)	Beautician	53	(AE)							
E	E	Florist	50	49						*	
EC	E	Buyer	19	22		*					
E	E	Marketing executive	38	36				*			
EC	ECI	Investments manager	43	37				*			

CONVENTIONAL

GENERAL OCCUPATIONAL THEME - C (30 40 50 60 70)

33 VERY LOW *

BASIC INTEREST SCALES (STANDARD SCORE)

OFFICE PRACTICES	38	LOW *

F	M	Occupational scale	Standard score F	Standard score M	Very dissimilar (<15)	Dissimilar (15–25)	Moderately dissimilar (25–30)	Mid-range (30–40)	Moderately similar (40–45)	Similar (45–55)	Very similar (55+)
C	C	Accountant	36	29			*				
C	C	Banker	38	21		*					
CE	CE	IRS agent	9	32				*			
CES	CES	Credit manager	27	24		*					
CES	CES	Business education teacher	13	7	*						
(CS)	CES	Food service manager	(CS)	15		*					
(ISR)	CES	Dietitian	(ISR)	9	*						
CSE	(ESC)	Nursing home administrator	18	(ESC)							
CSE	CSE	Executive housekeeper	25	21		*					
CS	(CES)	Food service manager	36	(CES)							
CS	N/A	Dental assistant	33	N/A							
C	N/A	Secretary	34	N/A							
C	(R)	Air Force enlisted personnel	36	(R)							
CRS	(RC)	Marine Corps enlisted personnel	34	(RC)							
CRS	CR	Army enlisted personnel	24	37				*			
CIR	CIR	Mathematics teacher	21	36				*			

ADMINISTRATIVE INDEXES (RESPONSE %)

	L%	I%	D%
OCCUPATIONS	4	18	79
SCHOOL SUBJECTS	17	28	56
ACTIVITIES	4	27	69
LEISURE ACTIVITIES	8	33	59
TYPES OF PEOPLE	13	42	46
PREFERENCES	40	30	30
CHARACTERISTICS	36	14	50
ALL PARTS	11	25	64

CONSULTING PSYCHOLOGISTS PRESS
577 COLLEGE AVENUE
PALO ALTO, CA 94306

confirmed a general interest in occupations such as Veterinarian, Forester, Vocational Agriculture Teacher, and Geologist—on all of these scales he scored Moderately Similar or higher—he said he was too restless and action-oriented to engage in a program requiring four or more years of education. His Academic Comfort score, which is low, suggested that he would not be comfortable in an academic environment and that he would prefer to learn in settings that allowed on-the-job training. He confirmed that this was the way in which he had developed many of his skills in the past and noted that he probably was qualified already to work as a bus driver (Very Similar), horticultural worker (Very Similar), farmer (Very Similar), carpenter (Moderately Similar), electrician (Very Similar), agribusiness manager (Similar) and florist (Similar). He also noted that he was quite skilled as an amateur photographer (Moderately Similar) and enjoyed using a piece of machinery to capture nature.

Overall, Client 2's interest profile was very consistent with the Realistic Theme appearing prominently throughout. We used the *Occupational Guide* (Hansen, 1987) to identify additional occupations related to those represented by his high scores on the Occupational Scales. He selected horse trainer, tree surgeon, fire ranger, greenhouse manager, and feedlot manager for further exploration.

Together we pondered his low "Like" response rate to various sections of the Strong item booklet including a 4% "Like" response to various occupations. He stated again that agriculture was his ideal and all other possibilities would be distant second choices. Gradually, he began to talk more about the difficulties of getting started in farming and ranching because of the extraordinary investment it takes. This line of thinking led him slowly to consider whether continuing to work with his parents could possibly be a viable option.

Although the Strong profile in Figure 7.3 served primarily to confirm Client 2's interest in agriculture and ranching, the process of looking at all of his interests in a systematic way helped him to realize how well-defined his vocational interests were and to realize how difficult it would be for him to find satisfaction in any other career. With this realization, he was able to recognize the need for establishing a true working relationship with a line of communication with his parents. Once his interests and career goals and needs were clarified he was able to approach his parents and begin to develop a plan that could accommodate all of their preferences.

Client 2 had never known or realized that his parents were, in fact, eager to have him remain in the family business and even to develop a subsidiary of his own. Over the course of the next year, a collective decision was made to expand the existing ranch, which was primarily beef production, to include a horse breeding operation that Client 2 would direct and manage. They developed a working partnership in which Client 2 assumed the work responsibility, his parents provided initial financing, and a profit-sharing plan was devised that eventually would allow Client 2 to be the major shareholder.

VALIDITY OF THE STRONG

The most important form of validity for the Strong Interest Inventory is predictive validity because the instrument is used to help make decisions that ultimately will affect an individual's future.

Occupational Scale Validity

The predictive validity for the Occupational Scales has been studied using various criteria (e.g., declared major, job entered, stated occupational goal) for prediction. The classic predictive validity design is to collect a sample of subjects, which has completed the Strong Interest Inventory, and store the data for a number of years. After time has passed, the study is reactivated; the original subjects are located, and the criterion questions are asked (usually something like "what is your declared major?" if studying the validity of the Strong for predicting college major, or "what is your occupation?" if the criterion is job entered).

After the follow-up data are collected, the college major or job title is matched to an Occupational Scale as directly as possible. Indirect matches also are made to the Occupational Scales that appear to most closely represent the major or occupation. For example, a major in elementary education would be considered a direct match to the Elementary Teacher Scale; the occupation taxi driver is indirectly matched to the Bus Driver Scale. The hit rate of predictive validity for the sample is computed by determining the percentage of the subjects who scored high on the Occupational Scale that represents their college major or career choice.

Predictive validity studies for the merged-sex SVIB-SCII compare favorably with data collected in the 1930s (Strong, 1935), in the 50s (McArthur, 1954), and in the 60s (Brandt & Hood, 1968). For example, over an 18 year interval between initial testing and criterion data collection, Strong found that 66% of a sample of males had scores of 40 or higher on Occupational Scales that were direct matches to their jobs.

Spokane (1979) found that 71% of a sample of women and 59% of a sample of men had scores of 40 or higher on Occupational Scales, on the first merged-sex version of the SVIB-SCII (Campbell, 1974), that were direct matches to their planned occupation. Two revisions later Hansen (1986) found that 79% of the women and 68% of the men had scores of 40 or higher on Occupational Scales that represented the occupations they were in 12 years after testing with the Strong as freshmen in college.

GOT and BIS Validity

Consistent with the interpretive guidelines that stress the importance of using the Strong Inventory to identify patterns of interests rather than to focus only on the two or three highest scores on the profile, a study by Johnson and Johansson

(1972) has shown that the level of consistency between scores on the Occupational Scales and Basic Interest Scales is important. They analyzed data for students who, 10 years earlier, had scored high on either the Physicist or Life Insurance Agent Scale. Seventy-five percent of these subjects were in occupations related to the scores on their earlier profiles. They also found that the Basic Interest Scales were useful in determining if the subjects would enter occupations represented by their highest scores or if they would enter related occupations. For example, a subject with consistently high scores on both the Sales and Life Insurance Agent Scale would be more likely to enter that occupation than would be a subject who scored low on Sales and high on Life Insurance Agent. The latter subject was more likely to enter a related occupation such as advertising.

Similarly, consistency between the GOT and Occupational Scale scores suggests greater predictive validity of the profile. A study conducted by Varca and Shaffer (1982) showed that the GOT also are useful for predicting the avocational and leisure activities in which an individual will participate.

SPECIAL SETTINGS AND SPECIAL POPULATIONS

The use of interest inventories has increased tremendously over the past 25 years in terms of the sheer volume of answer sheets scored, as well as the variety of settings in which interest inventories are used and the range of populations who are given interest inventories. The use of the Strong Interest Inventory mirrors the increase in use seen elsewhere within the testing industry, and it continues to be the most widely used interest inventory available on the market.

To use the Strong Interest Inventory with various populations and in various settings, the administration and interpretation of the instrument does not need to be altered extensively from the usual procedure. Components of the career counseling sequence, however, may need to be adapted to special circumstances. For example, an outplacement program for high-level executives will be designed differently than will a career exploration course for ninth- or tenth-grade high school students. In each situation, however, an interest inventory may be given to assist the individuals in structuring their career exploration activities, in efficiently and objectively identifying their interests, and in planning activities that match their interests.

Adult Clients

Adult career development intervention has become a major task of human resource professionals in industry and business. One thing to keep in mind for adults who are considering career changes, however, is the distinction between *career* dissatisfaction and *job* dissatisfaction. In some instances, an individual's interests may be matched appropriately with her or his chosen career, but the specifics of the particular job held at that time (e.g., co-workers, salary, level of responsibility, degree of autonomy) may be leading to dissatisfaction. People who are dissatisfied with their particular job often find that the Strong Inventory simply confirms their current occupational choice and offers suggestions for job-situation changes that will produce a better match and greater satisfaction. People who are unhappy with their careers—as opposed to jobs—may find, however, that the Strong profile offers suggestions for new career possibilities.

Cross-cultural Use

In a series of studies conducted during the last few years, the Strong Interest Inventory has been shown to be a useful career guidance tool for minority racial groups and international populations. To enhance the use of the Strong with groups other than the white U.S. majority on whom it was developed, the instrument has been translated into Spanish (Hansen & Fouad, 1984) and French (Chevrier, 1979), and adapted for use in Great Britain (Cook, 1982). Fouad's work with the Spanish version of the SVIB-SCII in Mexico (Fouad & Hansen, 1987; Fouad, Hansen, & Arias, 1986) confirms the cross-cultural validity of the Strong demonstrated by Lonner (Lonner, 1968; Lonner & Adams, 1972), who studied European samples, and Shah (Shah, 1971), who studied the use of the Strong in Pakistan.

Validation studies using the Strong Inventory with American Indian (Hansen & Haverkamp, 1988; Haviland & Hansen, 1987), Black, Asian and Chicano-Latino college students (Hansen & Haverkamp, 1988) have shown the instrument to have validity hit rates equivalent to those found for White college student samples. On the average, about 65% of the subjects scored 40 (moderately high) or higher on the scale representing their chosen college major. Studies conducted with predominantly White college student populations have shown concurrent validity hit rates for college major of about 68% at the moderately high or higher level (Hansen & Swanson, 1983). Among the racial minority groups, the Chicano-Latino sample had the highest hit rate (73%) and the American Indian samples had the lowest hit rate: an average of 56% for females and males in the Haviland and Hansen (1987) and Hansen and Haverkamp (1988) studies. These data, even for the American Indian samples, are sufficiently strong to support the use of the Strong Interest Inventory with racial minority college students.

Vocational-technical Career Exploration

The addition of nonprofessional occupational scales to the 1985 profile of the Strong Interest Inventory should help to ensure its usefulness with noncollege bound populations regardless of race or ethnic origin. On the current version of the instrument, about one-third of the scales represent the interests of vocational-technical and nonprofessional occupations such as carpenters, electricians, florists, food service managers, respiratory therapists, and emergency medical technicians.

Prior to the 1985 revision, the Strong Interest Inventory had become known as an instrument that was oriented primarily towards occupations that required a college education. Although no deliberate effort had ever been made by the publisher, Stanford University Press, or the authors to slant the inventory in this direction, the shift nonetheless had occurred.

The addition of the new nonprofessional Occupational Scales to the profile, combined with the professional Occupational Scales, make the Strong Interest Inventory appropriate for a wide range of occupational and educational goals. The *Strong-Hansen Occupational Guide* (Hansen, 1987) is designed for use with the nonprofessional, as well as professional, scales and assists the counselor and client in generalizing to additional nonprofessional and technical occupations.

Rehabilitation Clients

The SVIB-SCII has a history of use with clients in rehabilitation or educational settings that serve clients with special physical challenges such as hearing impairment (Pressman, personal communication, 1987), spinal-cord injury (Rohe & Athelstan, 1982), or epilepsy (Fraser, Trejo, Temkin & Clemmons, 1982). The work of Rohe and Athelstan, for example, has shown that the mean profile of interests for spinal-cord injured clients can provide useful considerations for treatment. These clients have a tendency toward introversion which, in a medical setting, frequently is misdiagnosed as depression. They prefer practical activities and probably will respond more positively to rehabilitation programs that focus on concrete goal-setting rather than on abstract planning and sharing of feelings.

Use with the Culturally Disadvantaged

Although many of the concurrent and predictive validity studies with the Strong Interest Inventory have used subjects who are college students or college graduates, several studies have shown that the Strong also is appropriate for use with culturally disadvantaged individuals who may not have had extensive educational opportunities. These studies have shown, for example, that the culturally disadvantaged have identifiable interests, show diversity in their interests, and make vocational decisions that are predicted by the Strong (Anderson & Lawlis, 1972; Harmon, 1970).

SUMMARY

The Strong Interest Inventory was under continuous revision between 1971 and 1985; now, the publishers have diverted funds from basic research support to product development. An expanded *Interpretive Report* (Hansen 1988); several guides and aids for improving interpretation (e.g., the *Strong-Hansen Occupational Guide* (Hansen, 1987) and *Using the Strong in Organizations* (Hirsch & McEvoy, 1986); microcomputer software for interactive test administration and in-house answer sheet scoring; and a proposed series of Strong Interest Inventory Topical Reports (personal communication, 1987) all reflect the publisher's effort to assist a wider market of users in their interpretation of the instrument.

As the use of the Strong Interest Inventory expands to new applications and new populations, basic research must be continued to ensure the validity of the instrument for the new applications and populations; the implementation of the Strong with new groups simply must not be allowed to exceed the empirical evidence. Future revisions of the Strong, in turn, will be shaped by the evaluation of the effect of the instrument on users and clients as well as by the moral responsibility of the publisher to make available an instrument that is responsive to social change. The extensive effort expended in the 70s and 80s to ensure the sex fairness of the Strong Interest Inventory must not be negated by subsequent neglect of the technical adequacy of the instrument.

REFERENCES

Anderson, R. P., & Lawlis, F. G. (1972). Strong Vocational Interest Blank and culturally handicapped women. *Journal of Counseling Psychology, 19,* 83–84.

Brandt, J. E., & Hood, A. B. (1968). Effect of personality adjustment on the predictive validity of the Strong Vocational Interest Blank. *Journal of Counseling Psychology, 15,* 547–551.

Bruch, M. A., & Skovholt, T. (1985). Congruence of Holland personality type and marital satisfaction. *Measurement and Evaluation in Counseling and Development, 18,* 100–107.

Cairo, P. C. (1979). The validity of the Holland and Basic Interest Scales of the Strong Vocational Interest Blank: Leisure activities versus occupational membership as criteria. *Journal of Vocational Behavior, 15,* 68–77.

Campbell, D. P. (1974). *Manual for the SVIB-SCII* (1st edition). Stanford, CA: Stanford University Press.

Campbell, D. P., Borgen, F. H., Eastes, S., Johansson, C. B., & Peterson, R. A. (1968). A set of Basic Interest Scales for the Strong Vocational Interest Blank for Men. *Journal of Applied Psychology Monographs, 52,* No. 6, Part 2.

Campbell, D. P., & Hansen, J. C. (1981). *Manual for the SVIB-SCII* (3rd Edition). Stanford, CA: Stanford University Press.

Campbell, D. P., & Holland, J. L. (1972). Applying Holland's theory to Strong's data. *Journal of Vocational Behavior, 2,* 353–376.

Chevrier, J. M. (1979). *Test de preferences professionnelles Strong-Campbell manuel.* (French translation of D. P. Campbell, *Manual for the Strong-Campbell Interest Inventory.*) Montreal: Institut de Recherches Psychologiques.

Cook, M. (1982). *Personal Communication,* July.

Cowdery, K. M. (1926). Measurement of professional attitudes: Differences between lawyers, physicians, and engineers. *Journal of Personnel Research, 5,* 131–141.

Fouad, N. A., & Hansen, J. C. (1987). Cross-cultural predictive accuracy of the Strong-Campbell Interest Inventory. *Measurement and Evaluation in Counseling and Development, 20,* 3–10.

Fouad, N. A., Hansen, J. C., & Arias, F. (1986). Multiple-discriminant analyses of cross-cultural similarity of vocational interests of lawyers and engineers. *Journal of Vocational Behavior, 28,* 85–96.

Fraser, R. T., Trejo, W. R., Temkin, N. R., & Clemmons, D. (1982). *Assessing the vocational interests of those with epilepsy*. Paper presented at the meetings of the American Epilepsy Society, Phoenix, AZ, November.

Freyd, M. (1923). *Occupational Interests*. Chicago: C. H. Stoelting.

Goodyear, R. K., & Frank, A. C. (1977). Introversion-extroversion: Some comparisons of the SVIB and OPI Scales. *Measurement and Evaluation in Guidance, 9,* 206–211.

Gough, H. G. (1957). *Manual for the California Psychological Inventory*. Palo Alto, CA: Consulting Psychologists Press.

Hansen, J. C. (1976). Exploring new directions for Strong-Campbell Interest Inventory occupational scale construction. *Journal of Vocational Behavior, 9,* 147–160.

Hansen, J. C. (1984). *User's Guide for the SVIB-SCII*. Stanford, CA: Stanford University Press.

Hansen, J. C. (1986). *12-Year longitudinal study of the Predictive Validity of the SVIB-SCII*. Paper presented at the meetings of the American Psychological Association, Washington, D.C., August.

Hansen, J. C. (1987). *Strong-Hansen Occupational Guide*. Palo Alto, CA: Consulting Psychologists Press.

Hansen, J. C. (1988). *Strong Interest Inventory Interpretive Report*. Palo Alto, CA: Consulting Psychologists Press.

Hansen, J. C., & Campbell, D. P. (1985). *Manual for the SVIB-SCII* (4th Edition). Stanford, CA: Stanford University Press.

Hansen, J. C., & Fouad, N. A. (1984). Translation and validation of the Spanish form of the Strong-Campbell Interest Inventory. *Measurement and Evaluation in Counseling and Development, 16,* 192–197.

Hansen, J. C., & Haverkamp, B. E. (1988). *Concurrent validity of the SCII for American Indian, Asian, Black and Hispanic college students*. Minneapolis, MN: Center for Interest Measurement Research, University of Minnesota.

Hansen, J. C., & Johansson, C. B. (1972). The application of Holland's vocational model to the Strong Vocational Interest Blank. *Journal of Vocational Behavior, 2,* 479–493.

Hansen, J. C., & Swanson, J. L. (1983). Stability of interests and the predictive and concurrent validity of the 1981 SCII for college majors. *Journal of Counseling Psychology, 30,* 194–201.

Harmon, L. W. (1970). Strong Vocational Interest Blank profiles for disadvantaged women. *Journal of Counseling Psychology, 17,* 519–520.

Haviland, M. L., & Hansen, J. C. (1987). Criterion validity of the Strong-Campbell Interest Inventory for American Indian college students. *Measurement and Evaluation in Counseling and Development, 19,* 196–201.

Hirsch, S. K., & McEvoy, E. (1986). *Using the Strong in Organizations,* Palo Alto, CA: Consulting Psychologists Press.

Holland, J. L. (1973). *Making vocational choices: A theory of careers*. Englewood Cliffs, NJ: Prentice-Hall.

Holland, J. L. (1985a). *Making vocational choices: A theory of vocational personalities and work environments*. Englewood Cliffs, NJ: Prentice-Hall.

Holland, J. L. (1985b). *Professional manual for the Self-Directed Search*. Odessa, FL: Psychological Assessment Resources.

Johansson, C. B. (1986). *Career Assessment Inventory: Enhanced Version*. Minneapolis, MN: National Computer Systems.

Johnson, J. A. (1987). Influence of adolescent social crowds in the development of vocational identity. *Journal of Vocational Behavior, 31,* 182–199.

Johnson, R. W. & Johansson, C. B. (1972). Moderating effect of basic interests in predictive validity of SVIB occupational scales. *Preceedings, 80th Annual Convention, American Psychological Association,* pp. 589–590.

Kivlighan, D. M., Jr., Hageseth, J. A., Tipton, R. M., & McGovern, T. V. (1981). Effects of matching treatment approaches and personality types in group vocational counseling. *Journal of Counseling Psychology, 28,* 315–320.

Kornhauser, A. W. (1927). Results from a quantitative questionnaire of likes and dislikes used with a group of college freshmen, *Journal of Applied Psychology, 11,* 85–94.

Lonner, W. J. (1968). The SVIB visits German, Austrian and Swiss psychologists. *American Psychologist, 23,* 164–179.

Lonner, W. J. & Adams, H. L. (1972). Interest patterns of psychologists in nine western nations. *Journal of Applied Psychology, 56,* 146–151.

McArthur, C. (1954). Long-term validity of the Strong Vocational Interest Blank in two subcultures. *Journal of Applied Psychology, 38,* 346–354.

McKinley, J. C. & Hathaway, S. R. (1940). A Multiphasic Personality Schedule (Minnesota): I, Construction of the schedule. *Journal of Psychology, 10,* 249–254.

Meir, E. I., Keinan, G., & Segal, Z. (1986). Group importance as mediator between personality-environment congruence and satisfaction. *Journal of Vocational Behavior, 28,* 60–69.

Remmers, H. H. (1929). The measurement of interest differences between students of engineering and agriculture. *Journal of Applied Psychology, 13,* 105–119.

Rohe, D. E., & Athelstan, G. T. (1982). Vocational interests of persons with spinal cord injury. *Journal of Counseling Psychology, 29,* 283–291.

Schneider, B. (1987). The people make the place. *Personnel Psychology, 40,* 437–453.

Shah, I. (1971). A cross-cultural comparative study of vocational interests. *Dissertation Abstracts International,* February, 31 (8-B), 5049.

Spokane, A. R. (1979). Occupational preferences and the validity of the Strong-Campbell Interest Inventory for college women and men. *Journal of Counseling Psychology, 26,* 312–318.

Spokane, A. R. (1987). (Ed.). Conceptual and methodological issues in person-environment fit research. *Journal of Vocational Behavior, 31,* 217–361.

Strong, E. K., Jr. (1927). *Vocational Interest Blank.* Stanford, CA: Stanford University Press.

Strong, E. K., Jr. (1933). *Vocational Interest Blank for Women.* Stanford, CA: Stanford University Press.

Strong, E. K., Jr. (1935). Predictive value of the Vocational Interest Test. *Journal of Educational Psychology, 26,* 332.

Strong, E. K., Jr. (1938). *Vocational Interest Blank for Men* (revised). Stanford, CA: Stanford University Press.

Strong, E. K., Jr. (1946). *Vocational Interest Blank for Women* (revised). Palo Alto, CA: Stanford University Press.

Swanson, J. L., & Hansen, J. C. (1985). Relationship of the construct of academic comfort to educational level, performance, aspirations and predication of college major choices. *Journal of Vocational Behavior, 26,* 1–12.

Varca, P. E., & Shaffer, G. S. (1982). Holland's theory: Stability of avocational interests. *Journal of Vocational Behavior, 21,* 288–298.

Webber, P. L., & Harmon, L. W. (1978). The reliability and concurrent validity of three types of occupational scales for two occupational groups. In C. K. Tittle & D. G. Zytowski (Eds). *Sex-Fair Interest Measurement: Research and Implications.* Washington, D.C.: National Institute of Education.

Wiggins, J. D., & Weslander, D. L. (1982). Tested compatibility in first and second marriages. *American Mental Health Counselors Association Journal, 4,* 25–29.

8 The Kuder Occupational Interest Survey

Esther E. Diamond
Educational and Psychological Consultant

BACKGROUND

The history of the Kuder Occupational Interest Survey, Form DD (KOIS) dates back to the depression days of the early 1930s, when, as a graduate student at The Ohio State University, Frederic Kuder undertook some very modest research on the relation between interests and vocations. His research and development work continued, still on his own time and with his own funds, after he joined the University of Chicago. In 1939, after six years of research, the first *Preference Record—Vocational* was distributed by the University of Chicago bookstore. Science Research Associates published it in 1941. Responses yielded scores on seven relatively independent scales: Literary, Scientific, Artistic, Persuasive, Social Service, Musical, and Computational.

Experience with this form suggested the need for more adequate representation of clerical and mechanical interests, and appropriate items for measurement of these interests were compiled and included in the experimental edition of the second *Preference Record—Vocational,* Form B. The problem of including additional items without increasing administration time as well as reading time was solved by using a triad form in which respondents indicated which of three activities in each item they preferred most and which they preferred least. Form B was published in 1943 by Science Research Associates and was subsequently used in the armed forces during World War II.

Form C, published in 1948, was developed in response to a need for a measure of outdoor interests as well as a Verification scale to identify subjects who responded to the *Preference Record* carelessly, insincerely, or without understanding. Form C was superceded in 1956 by the *Kuder General Interest*

Survey, Form E, designed to accommodate younger people. Still another *Preference Record—Personal,* Form A, (also published in the 1940s but no longer in print) measured personal interests that were closely related to preferences for a variety of social and environmental variables in work.

Development of the KOIS

The KOIS had its origin in the Kuder *Preference Record—Occupational,* Form D, in which occupational keys derived from Forms C and A were developed by comparing responses of individuals in an occupational criterion group who had demonstrated satisfaction with their choice of occupation with those of individuals in a general norm or reference group roughly representative of the distribution of occupations in the world of work. This method of scale development was similar to that used for the empirically built scales of the Strong Vocational Interest Blank (SVIB) (Strong, 1943). Items were chosen so as to be well distributed throughout the factorial space pertinent to occupational choice. Criteria for satisfaction were: ages 25 to 65; having been in the same occupation for at least 3 years; and, given a choice, would choose the same kind of work again.

But as Kuder (1966) pointed out, use of a men-in-general or women-in-general base for developing occupational scales implies that the choice is between a single occupation and the composite of all other occupations, thus losing a great deal of sharpness in differentiation. Responses for which there are large differences between the general reference group and the criterion group, he maintained, are not necessarily the same as those that are best for differentiating among the specific occupations in the general reference group. Using actual differences in proportions of two occupational groups marking each response to an occupational interest inventory would result in greater differentiation, an approach suggested by Findley (1956) and adopted by Kuder.

Clemans' lambda

Differences in homogeneity of occupational groups, however, created a problem with use of proportion sums as scores. The more homogeneous a group, the larger the proportion marking the same choice in the *most* and the *least* columns, and the larger the sum of squared proportions. For a group of the lowest possible homogeneity, on the other hand, with one-third marking each of the 3 *most* and each of the 3 *least* response positions, the sum of the squared proportions would be considerably lower. Scores, consequently, would not have the same possible range from occupation to occupation and therefore would not be comparable. If the best cutting point between score distributions for two different occupations—that is, the point at which the two distributions intersect—is other than zero, as it would be in scales of different degrees of homogeneity, then different cutting points have to be computed for the many comparisons that would need to be made.

A solution was to convert proportion scores to Clemans' lambda coefficients (Clemans, 1958). The proportion values for the 600 responses marked by a criterion group represent the continuous variable, and the 200 responses marked by the individual and the 400 not marked represent the dichotomous variable. The lambda coefficient—the ratio of the obtained *r* point biserial to the maximum *r* point biserial—represents the correlation between the individual's responses and the modal responses of the given criterion group. The upper limit of the lambda is 1.00 for all groups, regardless of homogeneity.

Differentiation between occupational groups—an essential characteristic of an occupational interest inventory and the hallmark of its construct validity—improved dramatically over the earlier system in comparison studies. The incidence of members of an occupational group obtaining a higher score on a scale other than their own was 32% less when lambda scores were used, and there was a 36% reduction in errors of classification (Kuder & Diamond, 1979).

In addition to the 104 occupational scales, 39 of which have been developed on women subjects, the 1985 edition of the KOIS contains 39 college major scales, 17 of which have been developed on women subjects. Eight experimental scores are provided for research purposes, and a Verification (V) score gives an estimate of the sincerity and care with which the responses were marked. Vocational Interest Estimates (VIEs) are also provided for the 10 vocational areas corresponding to those in the Kuder *General Interest Survey,* Form E: Outdoor, Mechanical, Scientific, Computational, Persuasive, Artistic, Literary, Musical, Social Service, and Clerical.

CONCEPTUAL FOUNDATIONS

Guiding Principles of Interest Measurement

The major premise in the development of the KOIS was that the purpose of an occupational interest inventory is to help young people discover the occupations they will find most satisfying. Kuder stipulated two fundamental requirements that must be met by such an inventory: (a) It must be valid with respect to the criterion of job satisfaction and (b) it must be suitable for use with young people who may have quite limited backgrounds of training and experience (Kuder, 1977). He cited 12 principles of interest measurement that have guided all of his work in the field:

1. The ability to differentiate well between occupational groups is one of the essential characteristics of an occupational interest inventory.
2. The questions in an occupational interest inventory should be well distributed throughout the domain of interests relevant to vocational choice.
3. The activities described in the questions must be clear and easily under-

stood by the subjects, both by those who answer the inventory for their own guidance and by those who, as members of criterion groups, answer the inventory for the purpose of establishing occupational scoring systems.

4. The use of an interest inventory in occupational counseling rests on the assumption that the domain of interests in generally well-understood activities is essentially the same as the domain of interests in activities that are not generally well understood.
5. A form of item should be used that is known to be affected relatively little by changes in context.
6. The form of question should be as free as possible from the effects of response bias.
7. Occupational titles should not be used in the items in an interest inventory intended for use in occupational counseling.
8. The questions should not be unpleasant or threatening.
9. A means should be available for checking on the confidence that can be placed in the answers to the inventory.
10. The same inventory should be used for both sexes.
11. The set of scores from an occupational interest inventory must have high reliability and stability, and these characteristics should be measured in terms of reliability and stability within the person.
12. The most useful form in which to report scores from an interest inventory is in order of magnitude.

Application of these principles to the KOIS is seen in the studies of differentiation and errors of classification referenced earlier; in the scales available, which represent professional, skilled, white-collar, and service occupations, among others; in the simple descriptions of common activities; in the item format, which minimizes response bias (Cronbach, 1950); in the absence of occupational titles, which might introduce stereotypes into the thinking of respondents; in the existence of the Verification scale; and in the reliability and stability of individual profiles, and differences between pairs of scores (Kuder & Diamond, 1979).

Why Measure Interests?

Holland, Magoon, and Spokane (1981) described interest measurement as possibly the most popular form of vocational assistance. Tyler (1978) saw interest patterns, like value patterns, as structures for processing possibilities: ''What may govern one person's choices, occupational or otherwise, is a value structure in which comfort and security rank very high'' (p. 147). These structures enable the individual to select and develop a unique assortment of possibilities from among those available. Anastasi (1982), discussing recent changes in the goals of interest measurement, pointed to the increasing attention accorded to career decision-making and, as part of that process, self-exploration. Another change she described was the increasing emphasis on expanding the career options open to the individual.

But why measure interests? Why not simply ask a person what his or her interests are and what kind of work he or she would most like to do? These are frequently asked questions. The answer is that people's occupational and educational choices are too often based on irrelevant influences and information rather than critical information about themselves and about the fields they are considering. A famous poet, for example, had in his youth thought he would like to be a naturalist. A course in botany, however, caused him to change his mind; he simply had had a very unrealistic idea of what day-to-day activities the career involved and the kind of educational preparation that it required. As Nunnally (1959) noted, young people are often quite unaware of the specific activities performed in different occupations. Nor do expressed, as opposed to measured, interests provide adequate information; Cronbach (1970) pointed out that a single direct question such as "Would you like to be a teacher?" may prompt a response based on lack of information or on a superficial understanding of the vocation. Darley and Hagenah (1955), who worked with E. G. Strong, found that "claimed interests emerge from different causal factors—factors more associated with prestige, family pressures, aspirational levels, transient considerations, and misconceptions of the world of work—than do measured interests" (p. 75).

Using the KOIS in Counseling

The KOIS, which uses work-related activities rather than occupational titles in its items, minimizes chances for stereotyping such as that described above. Its forced-choice format, which in effect asks the respondent to rank the three activities in each item, greatly reduces response bias or the tendency of respondents to avoid commitment to the extremes of a Likert scale and to choose a safe middle response instead.

The KOIS offers a basis for comprehensive educational and vocational planning and decision-making. It is appropriate for use with individuals in 10th grade and beyond, college students, and adults. It can be administered to individuals or in group settings, but as Zytowski (1981a) has suggested it is best administered when the individual is *asking* for assistance rather than when there is a scheduled wholesale administration. It is also best used "to enhance self-understanding, to reduce too many choices to a manageable few, or to suggest new possibilities to consider" (p. 1). The inventory can be self-administered, but availability of a counselor is helpful in interpreting the profile of scores, helping the inventory-taker discern options he or she might otherwise overlook, and answering related questions or discussing next steps.

As is true of any assessment instrument, the KOIS should be used with pertinent information about an individual's achievements, past work experience if any, scores on measures of ability and other traits, personal goals and values, and other relevant factors. Moreover, as Tittle (1978) found in her review of the research, studies on the effects of interest inventories suggest that by themselves, without supplementary material, interest inventories are not as effective in stimulating exploration as they might be.

Hoffman, Spokane, and Magoon (1981) questioned various studies of the effects of interest inventories and other interventions because of their failure to use multiple short-term outcome measures that had demonstrated validity. In addition, the outcome measures used relied principally on simple recall or on satisfaction with treatment; the treatments lacked equivalence of content or of counselor contact. Hoffman, Spokane, and Magoon used multiple and multimodal measures to study the impact of three conditions—interest profiles only, audiotape in addition to profiles, and counselor contact in addition to profiles. Significantly more subjects in the counselor-contact-plus-profiles group sought occupational information than subjects in the other two groups, and counselor contact was also found to be significantly related to goal attainment.

Whether it is administered on an individual or a group basis, an interest inventory can be most useful if it is part of a series of counseling interventions rather than an isolated event. Only then can it do more than merely confirm existing self-concepts or thinking about occupations. Interest inventory results can suggest exploratory experiences into hitherto unexplored areas. They also can prompt a client to examine his or her value system and its relationship to occupational goals more intensively.

Paving the Way for Interventions

The KOIS facilitates such exploratory experiences and, through its basic and supplementary materials, paves the way for various interventions following administration of the inventory and discussion of the results. For example:

- Items represent all 15 areas of Forms A and C. Areas from A are: preference for being active in groups; for familiar and stable situations; for working with ideas; and for avoiding conflict. From C they are: outdoor, mechanical, computational, scientific, persuasive, artistic, literary, musical, social service, and clerical. In addition, two new areas are represented: preference for working independently and preference for acting spontaneously, in a carefree manner.
- The 2-part report of scores, the counselor's copy and the inventory-taker's copy (discussed on pp. 219–220) provides interpretive information for

each, enabling the inventory-taker to understand much of the report and freeing the counselor to pick up the interpretation at the point where questions arise and assistance is needed.

- In addition to the occupational and college major scores, the Verification, or V, score and the scores on the 8 experimental scales are reported (on the counselor's copy only). The experimental scores provide a very tentative index of the inventory-taker's maturity and of the sincerity of his or her responses.
- Using an interpretive audiocassette that simulates a typical counseling session with individuals who have just received their KOIS results, inventory-takers are stimulated to focus questions about their own scores for a followup counseling session.
- The Vocational Interest Estimates, or VIEs, described earlier, provide information for those counselees who are still uncertain about the general area or areas within which their interests lie. Holland codes—Realistic, Investigative, Artistic, Social, Enterprising, and Conventional—may also be estimated from the percentile ranks of the VIE scales.
- Occupational and college major scores provide counselees with information about how closely their KOIS responses resemble those of men and of women in the various criterion groups. The occupational scales cover a broad spectrum of professional and nonprofessional occupations.
- *Expanding Your Future* (Zytowski, 1981b) helps counselees relate their high-ranking scores to occupations and college-major fields not represented in the KOIS. For each scale, a convenient chart lists the corresponding title in the Department of Labor's *Guide for Occupational Exploration* and the code number and page number in its *Occupational Outlook Handbook.* (The scales are also related to SRA's *Jobs and College Major Charts.*) Graphic examples are given of how to use the chart to obtain pertinent information. Accompanying *Occupational Exploration Worksheets* help the counselee summarize this information in an organized and succinct way.
- *Counseling with the Kuder Occupational Interest Survey, Form DD* (Zytowski, 1981a) deals specifically with analysis and interpretation of the KOIS profile. Two sample profiles are presented, along with the author's analysis of each and forms for the counselor's analysis. A number of typical client/counselor interpretation interviews are also given, with the author's comments alongside the dialog, providing valuable insights into the interaction between the client and the counselor.
- The *General Manual* (Kuder & Diamond, 1979) presents the history of the development of the KOIS and results of the research studies conducted over the years—including studies of accuracy of classification, frequency of differences, predictive validity, interests and job satisfaction, reliability and

homogeneity, and the factor structure. It also contains descriptions of each of the occupational and college major criterion groups.

- A *Manual Supplement* (Zytowski, 1985) provides updated information pertaining to the 1985 revision of the report form. (The report form was revised on the basis of the recommendations of a panel of experienced counselors representing the major settings in which the KOIS is used.)

ADMINISTRATION AND SCORING

Introducing the Inventory

The manner of introducing the KOIS will differ with different settings and with different client needs. In college freshman orientation programs, for example, students will be interested in using the inventory for selection (or confirmation) of a choice of course of study. Some may be looking ahead to possible future occupations. In individual personal or college counseling or in industry, the introduction should be tailored to the individual's needs and level of sophistication. As part of a general testing program in a high school, the KOIS lends itself to several modes of presentation—for example, in the homeroom; in an appropriate club, such as a science, mathematics, or journalism club, or Future Farmers of America; or in an English or social studies classroom.

Many inventory-takers most likely have already been exposed to some discussion of the nature of interests and how they differ from abilities; how they are related to different fields of study and different hobbies and activities; and how they relate to one's self-concept, values, and past experiences. Nevertheless, a brief recapitulation of such discussion before administering and interpreting the KOIS can often be very helpful in understanding and using the results. It's important, too, to discuss how men and women have been socialized in our society and how their interest scores might be affected as a result.

A Word about Ipsativity

The question of ipsativity invariably is raised with regard to forced-choice items. As Anastasi (1982) observed, ipsative scoring applies when the individual expresses preference for one activity over another rather than in absolute terms, and the frame of reference for the scores is the individual rather than a normative sample. But, as Kuder (1975) has pointed out, in the case of the Kuder inventories the intensity of the individual's activity preferences are compared with those of a norm group. That is, the comparison is with the responses of others faced with the same stimulus situation.

Illustrating his point, Kuder (1975) stated that

> "[I]t is not enough to know that an individual strongly likes both 'attending a baseball game' and 'attending an opera.' What is important is which of these he or she prefers to the other when faced with a choice" (p. 6).

Furthermore, decisions in our society are rarely limited to such simple choices but are "complicated by the interaction of various motivations determined by all of our previous experiences." (p. 6)

The 100 forced-choice triads, written at 6th-grade reading level, are contained in a combination survey booklet and optically scanned answer sheet. Because the scoring system requires an enormous amount of computer storage capacity for the table of lambda values for each of the 600 possible response patterns for each scale, as shown in Appendix A, the KOIS cannot be scored locally or by hand. Results are mailed from the publisher within three days of receipt of answer sheets.

The Score Report Form

Two copies of the revised 1985 individualized report form—one for the counselor and one for the inventory-taker—contain interpretive information on the back. One important change from the previous form is that the numerical lambda values are reported only on the counselor's copy, although the inventory-taker should have access to them if desired.

Four different types of scales, accompanied by explanatory comments, are identified on the report form in separate sections. The first section contains a statement of the dependability or the degree of confidence that can be placed in the results, based on the Verification (V) score, the number of missing or invalidly marked triads, the lambda level, and other indices of usability. The second section contains the percentile scores for the VIEs in the same 10 general interest areas as those offered by the Kuder General Interest Survey, Form E, and based on a general population of men and women KOIS users. VIEs are ranked and grouped into high, average, and low interest areas compared with the responses of criterion groups of men and of women.

In the third and fourth sections, respectively, the 143 occupational and college major scores are reported separately in rank order, compared with men and compared with women in each of the criterion groups, in accordance with Title IX guidelines for nondiscrimination on the basis of sex (U.S. Department of Health, Education, and Welfare, 1975). Scores are grouped as indicating interest patterns "most similar to" those of the criterion group—that is, within .06 lambda points of the inventory-taker's highest score, and therefore not significantly different; "next most similar," or between .07 and .12 lambda points of the highest score; and the rest, listed in order of similarity. (Some KOIS scales have been normed only on one sex, but efforts are underway to develop criterion groups for the other sex as subjects become available. There are now 78 "twin" scales—39 pairs of scales—representing 27 occupations and 12 college majors normed on both female and male criterion groups.)

Users of the KOIS sometimes ask why the scales are not grouped by level, industry, job family, broad interest area, or some other classification scheme. Such a system had been considered, but the conclusion was that classification of occupations is seldom clear-cut and usually influences interpretation, implying similarity of occupations in the same classification that may in fact be quite dissimilar in underlying interests and other characteristics. Ranked scores carry no such implications and were deemed best for interpretation (Kuder & Diamond, 1979).

The V score and the scores on the eight experimental scales are shown only on the counselor's copy. The eight experimental scales are just that—experimental; the suggested interpretations should be highly tentative until additional research has been carried out. The M (Men) and W (Women) scores are lambdas derived from comparisons with general norm groups of men and women. The MBI (Men Best Impression) and WBI (Women Best Impression) scores are derived from comparison with responses of the same individuals asked to respond to the KOIS a second time with instructions to make the best impression possible. Differences between the M and MBI scores and the W and WBI scores for the relevant sex provide an additional rough indication of the degree of confidence that may be placed in the individual's scores.

The S (Sons) and D (Daughters) scales are based on the responses of high school boys and girls, respectively, and the F (Fathers) and MO (Mothers) scales are based on the responses of the sons' fathers and the daughters' mothers, respectively. Differences between the two scores of the appropriate sex may serve as a rough index of the maturity of the inventory-taker's interests.

Interpreting the Scores

The extent of the counselor's involvement with the KOIS report of scores depends, again, on the setting and the level of maturity and sophistication of the inventory-takers. In most cases, the explanations of the various scores on the report form are sufficiently explicit for the initial overview without necessitating the counselor's intercession. For younger respondents, however, or those who seem less sure of themselves (or really uncertain about vocational decisions) or those whose profiles contain unexpected high ranks or a confusing array of high ranks, the counselor may be needed to ensure that the information represented by the scores is as meaningful and useful as possible.

If an interpretive session is held, it should be an interactive one, in which the counselor provides a flexible structure and, through his or her own comments and questions, encourages the inventory-taker to take the lead in commenting on the scores, finding relationships among them, noting the extent to which they meet expectations or are surprises, asking appropriate questions, and suggesting next steps.

Dependability. For most adults, dependable results will be indicated in the first section of the score report. Younger respondents are likely to receive more than one of the cautionary messages regarding dependability: more than 15 unreadable responses (in which case the answer sheet is returned to the sender); highest lambda between .31 and .39, indicating that interest patterns may not yet have stabilized; V score between 42 and 44, indicating unusual interests; V score below 42, indicating that results may not be accurate; highest lambda lower than .31, indicating that interest patterns may not be sufficiently developed to score for occupations or college majors (only Section 2 results are printed).

The V score has 60 answer positions for 41 items, based on the number of responses marked significantly more frequently by persons instructed to try to make the best possible impression. When the V score is between 42 and 44, and all other indicators are positive, the interest pattern may truly be unique or nontraditional or representative of values unique to a particular culture. This question can be explored with the respondent and, if the high-ranking occupational and college major scores are in keeping with his or her expectations, the report form should be accepted as reliable. When a caution message appears with a V score below 42, poor reading or inattention is a likely cause, and even though a report of scores is issued, it might be advisable to ask if the inventory-taker understood the content of the survey, and to have him or her retake it if carelessness or inattention appears to have been the problem.

Vocational Interest Estimates. Since the KOIS items were derived from the *Kuder Preference Record—Vocational,* Form C and the *Kuder Preference Record—Personal,* Form A, short scales from those forms are the basis for the VIEs. VIE percentile norms were obtained by selecting answer sheets submitted for scoring from a wide geographic distribution of high school, college, and private agency users (mental health, vocational rehabilitation, military, and private vocational counseling agencies). VIEs are reported in rank order within high, average, and low groupings. The boundaries for high and low percentiles are the 75th and the 25th percentiles, respectively. Scale descriptions are given on the back of the report form. To relate the inventory-taker's KOIS scores to his or her VIEs, the counselor might refer to Appendix B of the *Manual Supplement,* which gives the highest three VIEs for each scale, for the appropriate sex. Page 6 of the *Manual Supplement* also provides a table for converting VIE percentiles to Holland codes, based on data Holland (1979) used to indicate equivalence of Kuder's scales to his six personality types.

Occupational and College-Major Scales. These scales relate to all 12 of the work groups in the U.S. Department of Labor's *Guide for Occupational Exploration* (1979). Inventory-takers should examine the ranks for their own gender first, then look at ranks on the other-gender list for occupations and college majors not on their own-gender list. They may have questions about why the scales are separated by norm-group gender, and the counselor may wish to discuss with them how differences in sex-role socialization and different expectations of males and females traditionally have led to differences in responses to the activities represented by the items. As Kuder (1977) has found, on the average, men obtain higher scores compared with men, and women obtain higher scores compared with women for any occupation for which scales have been developed separately by sex.

The counselor—whose copy of the score report contains the actual lambda values—can also advise the inventory-taker about the magnitude of differences between scores on male-normed and female-normed scales. Because everyone will have *some* highest ranks compared with members of the other sex, those that have considerably lower lambdas than on own-sex norms should be interpreted with caution, especially if there are large differences in scores on "twin" scales—scales for the same occupation or college major that have been developed on both sexes.

Counselors can also help inventory-takers—especially those who are less experienced in occupational and educational exploration—to look for patterns in their top-ranking occupations and college majors and those that are "next most similar." For example, do the ranks show a pattern of interest in health-related occupations, or in mechanical work? Inventory-takers may even find patterns in ranks that are least similar, indicating fields of work and study that they might find dissatisfying. Relating occupational and college major scores to VIEs provides an even broader basis for discovering patterns. More than 10 or 12 "most similar" scales, however, may represent undifferentiated interests and may be confusing for the inventory-taker to interpret. The counselor may want to sound out the inventory-taker as to possible underlying reasons; for example, do the ranks represent leisure-time interests or hobbies, or some deeply hidden aspirations?

As Zytowski (1981a) pointed out, homemakers returning to work often have profiles with a high proportion of high-ranking social service and literary occupations. These usually reflect many of the activities women at home engage in.

The Experimental Scales. Although inferences based on scores on the experimental scales must remain highly tentative until further research has been carried out, the counselor may want to consider the scores in conjunction with other information. For example, if the V score and/or the lambda level are questionable, the counselor may want to look at differences between the M and MBI or the W and WBI scores. If the BI scores are more than 10 points greater, the inventory-taker may have responded insincerely. On the other hand, he or she may be truly social-service oriented or have other interests that are not traditional in our society.

As stated earlier, the difference between the S and F scores and the D and Mo scores may provide some indication of maturity, but there are insufficient data at present to justify such an inference. The difference between M and W scores should never be considered as an indication of masculinity or femininity; at most, it represents differences between general interests of men and general interests of women. For a number of criterion groups (e.g., female physicians and female computer programmers, male clinical psychologists) the difference is very small; for others (e.g., female librarians, male computer programmers, male police officers) the difference is considerably larger (Diamond, 1981).

Further Cautions Regarding Interpretation

Some counselors may be tempted to overinterpret a profile, making clinical or other inappropriate inferences from the scores or the session in which the scores are interpreted. The KOIS is not a clinical or diagnostic instrument and the counselor should not infer attitudes, personality characteristics, or other attributes not specifically measured by the inventory. The occupational exploration implications of the scores should constitute the principal framework for the interpretive session. Even when an inventory-taker brings up feelings, self-doubts, and the like, the discussion should remain within the context of how they affect the occupational exploration and decision-making process.

The KOIS is not recommended for selection for either employment or a program, except in combination with other appropriate measures and validated for that purpose. The counselor should also make it clear to the inventory-taker that the KOIS is not a test of ability, nor does it tell the person what he or she "should" do.

SANDRA HARRIS: A CASE EXAMPLE

Figure 8.1 is the counselor's copy of Sandra Harris's KOIS profile. (The numerical scores do not appear on Sandra's copy; nor do the experimental or V scores.)

Sandra Harris is a 30-year-old "re-entry" woman—returning to work after several years raising a family at home. She is a high-school graduate and held several office and salesclerk jobs until marriage. She now has two very young children in primary school and wants to go back to work, but is not sure of what she wants to do. She has a chance to take an office job again or to take a job in a small neighborhood boutique, but neither option appeals to her very much. She would like to "try something new." She took the KOIS at a community college counseling center and has looked at her score report, but she is now seeking help in interpreting it in depth and in getting answers to a number of questions.

Kuder Occupational Interest Survey Report Form

Name HARRIS SANDRA

Sex FEMALE **Date** 08/14/86

Numeric Grid No. **SRA No.** 00379

1 ***Dependability:*** How much confidence can you place in your results? In scoring your responses several checks were made on your answer patterns to be sure that you understood the directions and that your results were complete and dependable. According to these:

YOUR RESULTS APPEAR TO BE DEPENDABLE.

2 ***Vocational Interest Estimates:*** Vocational interests can be divided into different types and the level of your attraction to each type can be measured. You may feel that you know what interests you have already — what you may not know is how strong they are compared with other people's interests. This section shows the relative rank of your preferences for ten different kinds of vocational activities. Each is explained on the back of this report form. Your preferences in these activities, as compared with other people's interests, are as follows:

Compared with men		**Compared with women**	
HIGH		HIGH	
OUTDOOR	81	MECHANICAL	98
CLERICAL	77	OUTDOOR	87
AVERAGE		AVERAGE	
MECHANICAL	75	MUSICAL	68
MUSICAL	61	CLERICAL	65
SOCIAL SERVICE	45	COMPUTATIONAL	39
LITERARY	31	PERSUASIVE	27
COMPUTATIONAL	29	LITERARY	26
LOW		LOW	
PERSUASIVE	19	SOCIAL SERVICE	17
SCIENTIFIC	04	SCIENTIFIC	06
ARTISTIC	04	ARTISTIC	02

3 ***Occupations:*** The **KOIS** has been given to groups of persons who are experienced and satisfied in many different occupations. Their patterns of interests have been compared with yours and placed in order of their similarity with you. The following occupational groups have interest patterns *most* similar to yours:

Compared with men		**Compared with women**	
AUTO MECHANIC	.43	OFFICE CLERK	.50
CARPENTER	.43	FLORIST	.47
ELEM SCH TEACHER	.42	BOOKKEEPER	.47
INTERIOR DECOR	.42	BANK CLERK	.46
POSTAL CLERK	.42	DEPT STORE SALES	.45
WELDER	.42	ELEM SCH TEACHER	.45
BRICKLAYER	.41	SECRETARY	.45
MACHINIST	.41	VETERINARIAN	.45
ELECTRICIAN	.40	BANKER	.44
PLUMBER	.40	BEAUTICIAN	.44
PAINTER, HOUSE	.39	EXTENSION AGENT	.44
FLORIST	.39		

Compared with men

MOST SIMILAR, CONT.	
FORESTER	.38
TRUCK DRIVER	.37
BOOKSTORE MGR	.37
THESE ARE NEXT MOST SIMILAR:	
BANKER	.36
BOOKKEEPER	.36
PLUMBING CONTRAC	.36
BLDG CONTRACTOR	.36
SUPERVSR, INDUST	.36
FARMER	.36
NURSE	.36
BUYER	.35
PLANT NURSRY WKR	.35
X-RAY TECHNICIAN	.35
TRAVEL AGENT	.34
INSURANCE AGENT	.34
TV REPAIRER	.34
PRINTER	.34
EXTENSION AGENT	.34
LIBRARIAN	.33
CLOTHIER, RETAIL	.33
METEOROLOGIST	.33
FILM/TV PROD/DIR	.33
DENTIST	.32
POLICE OFFICER	.32
ENGINEER	.32
MATHEMATICIAN	.32
AUTO SALESPERSON	.32
PHOTOGRAPHER	.31
VETERINARIAN	.31
THE REST ARE LISTED IN ORDER OF SIMILARITY:	
PHYS THERAPIST	.30
MATH TCHR, HS	.30
REAL ESTATE AGT	.29
COMPUTER PRGRMR	.29
ARCHITECT	.29
OPTOMETRIST	.29
SCIENCE TCHR, HS	.28
AUDIOL/SP PATHOL	.28
PHARMACIST	.27
PHYSICIAN	.27
RADIO STATON MGR	.27
LAWYER	.27
CHEMIST	.26
JOURNALIST	.25
MINISTER	.23
ACCT, CERT PUB	.23
PERSONNEL MGR	.23
SCHOOL SUPT	.23
STATISTICIAN	.22

FIG. 8.1.

Compared with women

THESE ARE NEXT MOST SIMILAR:

NURSE	.42
MATH TEACHER, HS	.41
ACCT, CERT PUB	.41
OCCUPA THERAPIST	.41
DENTIST	.40
PHYS THERAPIST	.40
X-RAY TECHNICIAN	.40
LIBRARIAN	.39
COMPUTR PRGRMR	.38
DENTAL ASSISTANT	.38

THE REST ARE LISTED IN ORDER OF SIMILARITY:

ARCHITECT	.37
BOOKSTORE MGR	.36
FILM/TV PROD/DIR	.36
PHYSICIAN	.36
ENGINEER	.35
INSURANCE AGENT	.35
AUDIOL/SP PATHOL	.33
DIETITIAN	.33
SCIENCE TCHR, HS	.32
INTERIOR DECOR	.32
JOURNALIST	.31
COL STU PERS WKR	.30
NUTRITIONIST	.30
COUNSELOR, HS	.29
RELIGIOUS ED DIR	.28
SOCIAL WORKER	.28
LAWYER	.24
PSYCHOLOGIST	.24

Compared with men

REST, CONT.

COUNSELOR, HS	.22
PODIATRIST	.22
PHARMACEUT SALES	.22
SOCIAL WORKER	.20
PSYCHOLOGIST	.17

Compared with women

4 ***College Majors:*** Just as for occupations, the **KOIS** has been given to many persons in different college majors. The following college major groups have interest patterns *most* similar to yours:

Compared with men

AGRICULTURE	.40
ANIMAL SCIENCE	.40
FORESTRY	.35

THESE ARE NEXT MOST SIMILAR:

MUSIC & MUSIC ED	.32
PHYSICAL EDUC	.32
ELEMENTARY EDUC	.31
ENGINEERING	.31
FOREIGN LANGUAGE	.31
ART & ART EDUC	.30

THE REST ARE LISTED IN ORDER OF SIMILARITY:

ARCHITECTURE	.26
SERV ACAD CADET	.26
MATHEMATICS	.25
BUSINESS ADMIN	.25
PHYSICAL SCIENCE	.24
BIOLOGICAL SCI	.22
SOCIOLOGY	.21
ECONOMICS	.20
ENGLISH	.20
HISTORY	.20
PREMED/PHAR/DENT	.19
PSYCHOLOGY	.17
POLITICAL SCI	.14

Compared with women

PHYSICAL EDUC	.46
HOME ECON EDUC	.44
MATHEMATICS	.43
BUSINESS EDUC	.42
MUSIC & MUSIC ED	.40

THESE ARE NEXT MOST SIMILAR:

ELEMENTARY EDUC	.39
HEALTH PROFESS	.39
NURSING	.38
DRAMA	.37
FOREIGN LANGUAGE	.37
BIOLOGICAL SCI	.36
ART & ART EDUC	.35

THE REST ARE LISTED IN ORDER OF SIMILARITY:

HISTORY	.33
SOCIOLOGY	.30
PSYCHOLOGY	.29
ENGLISH	.28
POLITICAL SCI	.25

Experimental Scales.

V-SCORE 53

M .39 MBI -.12

S .38 F .34

M .46 WBI -.13

D .42 MO .42

7-3881

She is especially curious about her ranks ''compared with men'' and ''compared with women.'' Why is she getting both kinds of scores, and why are they different? For example, on her VIEs she is high in Outdoor and Clerical compared with men and only average in Mechanical, but compared with women she is high in both Mechanical and Outdoor. The counselor explains the rationale for the different norms and points out that her mechanical and outdoor interests are high compared with women because, unlike herself, women in general don't express much interest in work-related mechanical and outdoor activities. In general, however, men are much more interested in mechanical activities than women are, and they mark many such activities in the KOIS more frequently than she did. If Mechanical was only average compared with men, Sandra inquires, why was her rank on Auto Mechanic her highest occupational rank compared with men? Also, her ranks on Office Clerk, Bookkeeper, Secretary, and occupations like that were her highest-ranking scores compared with women, but her VIE Clerical rank was highest compared with men and only average compared with women. Here the counselor has a more difficult explanation to make. She tells Sandra that the VIEs are based on the activities marked most frequently by men in general or women in general, and women in general mark clerical activities much more frequently than men do. The VIE ranks for each scale are based on the percentage of inventory-takers who obtained lower ranks than she did. The occupational ranks, however, represent a direct comparison with the typical responses of a specific group of people in the occupation, regardless of the percentage of inventory-takers who obtained lower ranks. The two types of ranks or scores, then, are not directly comparable. Sandra seems to have some difficulty understanding this, and abandons the effort when the counselor tells her that the important thing to concentrate on is the general idea of how her interests compare with those of men and women, her ranks in each group, and the patterns they suggest.

Why is it, Sandra asks, that compared with men she seems to be interested in jobs she's never even considered, ''mostly things you do with your hands . . . mechanical kinds of things,'' while compared with women she seems to be interested mostly in the kind of work she's always done or could have done, ''women's kind of work.'' The counselor asks Sandra what she thinks of the fact that professional and social-service-oriented occupations are among her lowest-ranking, compared with both men and women. This seems to make sense to Sandra; she's never been interested in that kind of work.

Perhaps, the counselor suggests, Sandra isn't aware of all the choices open to her. They discuss the college major ranks and the outdoor occupations suggested by the top-ranking scales compared with men, as well as the ''next most similar'' engineering rank. The highest-ranking scales compared with women do not appeal to her—especially home economics education and business education; they represent what she has been trying to get away from.

Then, taking a different tack, the counselor asks Sandra if she's ever had a course in home mechanics or industrial arts. Well, she did have a course where she learned to fix mechanical things around the house—"you know, repair a burned-out wire, change washers, learn how the different parts of a sewing machine work, things like that." And yes, she was pretty good at fixing the children's toys and "kind of liked doing that." But auto mechanic, carpenter, welder . . . she gives a little shrug of uncertainty, perhaps tinged with distaste. She has seen a few women construction workers, but she always thought they had to be kind of rough, not very feminine. She has always prided herself on her femininity; it is very important to her, and she thinks it is important to set an example for her daughter. "And I'll bet the men in those jobs give women a hard time." Still, maybe the work is more exciting than being an office clerk or working as a salesperson. And it probably pays better—"It sure is hard to decide."

She seems to be pleading silently with the counselor to tell her what to do. The counselor says Sandra must make the decision herself, but that if there is no pressure to decide immediately, there are a number of things she can do that might help her. To begin with, she might want to find out more about her top rankers compared with women and compared with men in the *Guide for Occupational Exploration.* She might also want to visit some job sites and talk with people working in those jobs; the counselor can help set up those visits. She can also investigate appropriate training at the technician level at the community college. Sandra responds with unexpected eagerness. Yes, it might even be fun to go back to school for a while, and she could get a part-time job to fill in until she really knows what she wants to do. "I guess I really have to do some homework on this," she admits. She realizes that she needs to determine a sequence of next steps and that she needs to obtain more occupational information. A time was set to come back to discuss her progress and to obtain any help she might want with further planning.

Note that the counselor has been very careful not to sanction or disapprove any of the judgments Sandra has expressed. She has acted as a facilitator, enabling Sandra to examine her own values, her experiences, and her feelings about work and about herself, to consider the possibilities open to her, and to outline important next steps. And she has let Sandra know of her support and availability as a resource person.

KOIS RESEARCH

Some of the research on the KOIS was mentioned earlier in this chapter in the context of a particular question or problem. In this section the major relevant research studies will be described more systematically, albeit briefly. (For a complete description of the research see Kuder, 1977, and Kuder & Diamond, 1979.)

Early research on the KOIS was limited to intensive study of the scores of 3000 subjects in 30 core groups selected as being most representative of the spread of occupations and college major fields for which scales had been developed. Where possible, subjects were selected from cross-validation groups whose responses were not used to develop scales; the remainder were chosen at random from the criterion groups. (For the original 148 occupational and college-major scales, the paired comparisons that were basic to much of the research would have amounted to 1,087,000!)

In generalizing from the research on the 30 core groups, one must take into account the fact that all KOIS scales were developed in the same way, with the same standards for membership in a criterion group, and with an acceptable level of homogeneity in criterion group responses. Given these conditions, and on the assumption that the core group scales are representative of the complete set of KOIS scales, differentiation should generally be as good for the other scales. Later studies reported here (follow-up studies and factor analyses, for example) go far beyond the original core research and lend further credence to the inferences drawn on the basis of KOIS results.

Validity

Validity studies included (a) an errors of classification study, an examination of the frequency with which members of an occupational group achieved a higher score on a scale other their own, (b) the rank of scores of the 30 core group members on their own scale, (c) the frequency of differences of varying magnitudes between a person's score on his or her own scale and his or her highest score, (d) predictive validity studies, and (e) factor analyses, which provide evidence of the construct validity of the KOIS.

Errors of Classification: New Scoring System vs. General Reference Group. How did the KOIS scoring system compare with a system that uses a general reference group? Responses for 6 KOIS cross-validation groups consisting of 90 subjects each were scored on all 6 scales, including their own—first, on Form D scales, developed with the use of a general reference group, and then on KOIS scales. That is, there were two sets of five comparisons each for the 540 subjects. Form D scores were converted to standard scores, based on the means and standard deviations of the original criterion groups. For each pair of occupations, the number of persons from one group who obtained a higher score on the scale for the other group than on their own was tallied. A similar tally was made based on the KOIS scoring system.

On the scales developed with a general reference group, subjects scored higher on an occupation other than their own 209 times. When lambdas were used, the number of errors of classification was reduced to 142—a reduction of 32%, and 31% when ties were counted.

In a second errors-of-classification study, the 30 core groups were scored on all 30 scales. The number of errors ranged from 0% to 29% with a mean of 6.2%. Many of the so-called errors occurred in very closely related fields—for example, a number of electrical engineers scored highest on other engineering scales and 16 social workers obtained their highest score on the Clinical Psychologist scale.

Frequency of Differences. The frequency of differences between a score on the person's own scale and that person's highest score was obtained for the 3000 core group members. In 64% of the cases, the score on the subject's own scale was either the highest score or within .009 of the highest. For 71% it was within .019, or one standard error of measurement, of the highest score; and for 90%, it was within .069 of the highest score. Only 10% had a score for their own occupation .070 or more removed from their highest score, indicating a significant difference between the two scores.

Predictive Validity. Zytowski (1976) located more than 1000 men and women 12 to 19 years after they had taken the *Kuder Preference Record—Occupational,* Form D, which contained the same items as the KOIS, in high school or college. Answer sheets were rescored for the KOIS. Data for 882 subjects were available. Of these, 51% were employed in an occupation that would have been suggested to them by scores on the KOIS scales. These results were close to the maximum obtainable concurrent validity in the light of the population, which was extremely variable in socioeconomic status and in consistency of career progression. The college major scales were slightly more predictive than the occupational scales.

Zytowski and Laing (1978) followed up 206 persons from the same population as was used in Zytowski's 1976 study and who were in occupations predictable by one of the 28 KOIS "twin" scales—scales for the same occupation or college major developed on male and female criterion groups. They investigated the predictive validity of own- and other-gender-normed scales, as well as the rank-order correlations between male- and female-normed scales. The predictive validity of scores on the two sets of norms was about equivalent, regardless of the gender of the person taking the inventory. Slightly more than 43% of the sample were in occupations corresponding to their five highest-ranked scales on own-gender norms, and more than 50% were in occupations corresponding to their five highest-ranked scales on other-gender norms.

Interests and Job Satisfaction. Herzberg and his associates (1957) long ago asserted that of all types of tests used in counseling interest tests had the strongest factual justification: " . . . the pattern of interests as measured by objective tests has a demonstrable positive relationship to the satisfaction the individual derives from his job" (p. 215).

In his follow-up study, Zytowski (1976) attempted to learn whether persons in jobs congruent with their measured interests were more satisfied than persons in jobs not congruent with their measured interests. Direct responses to a question about degree of satisfaction showed no relationship, but a question as to whether the respondent would consider changing jobs or occupations if given the chance did show a relationship with congruence, for men only.

Although there have been no other studies relating the KOIS to job satisfaction, data from at least 9 studies involving other forms of the Kuder interest inventories testify to this relationship and appear to be generalizable to the KOIS, particularly because many of the items from those forms are included in the KOIS, the same broad general areas are tapped, and the same principles of interest measurement governed its construction.

The most definitive job-satisfaction study is one by McRae (1959) involving the *Kuder Preference Record—Vocational,* Form C. McRae studied the scores of 1164 young people from 61 secondary schools in 31 states. They had taken the inventory in high school and responded to a questionnaire 7 to 10 years later on how well they liked their work. Analysis of the results showed that 728 persons were in work consistent with their interests as measured in high school, and 436 were in work not consistent with their earlier interests. Of the "consistent" group, 62% were satisfied with their work, as opposed to only 34% in the "inconsistent" group. Also, the proportion of dissatisfied workers in the inconsistent group was about three times as great as in the "consistent" group. These results are in close agreement with a study by Lipsett and Wilson (1954).

Kuder (1977) noted that there are problems with the use of job satisfaction as a criterion, especially because there are great variations in the degree to which people find occupations attractive. Similar observations have been made by Clark (1961) and Strong (1955) among others. For additional studies on job satisfaction and a discussion of job satisfaction as a criterion, see Kuder (1977).

Factor Analyses. Seven factor analyses of KOIS response proportions were conducted between 1963 and 1976 by different researchers. In the first, involving 124 variables, 15 principal factors were extracted: Best Impression, Femininity/Masculinity, Skilled Trades, Behavioral Sciences, Artistic, Scientific-Mathematical, Sales, Youth, Literary, Medical, Religious, Outdoor, and three unidentifiable factors.

In the next three analyses, 13 factors were identified: Skilled Trades, Business-Accounting, Artistic, Social Welfare, Sales, Food, Clerical, Journalism, Physical Sciences, Medical, Nutrition, Library Science, and Young Women.

In the fifth analysis, 20 factors were extracted: Drive, Aggressiveness; Femininity/Masculinity; Mechanical; Medical; Literary; Social Welfare; Artistic; Dietetics; Persuasive; Outdoor; Religious; Engineering; Political Science, Power; Science-Mathematics; Accounting-Clerical; Musical; Physical Education; Library Science; and two unidentifiable factors.

In the sixth analysis, 23 factors were identified, 15 of which were similar to those identified in the fifth analysis. The other 7 were identified as Adult Women; Adult Men; Young Women; Occupational Dissatisfaction; Sales; Typical Responses; Behavioral Sciences; and Journalism.

The last factor analysis was conducted separately for male- and female-normed scales, using lambda scores converted to *z* scores. For male-normed scales, 12 factors emerged: Skilled Trades; Helping; Political Science vs. Language; Medical Service; Mathematic-Numeric; Art; Psychology; Physical Science vs. Language; Physical Science vs. Business; Active, Military; Persuasive vs. Sedentary; and Agriculture. For female-normed scales, 9 factors emerged—7 of them the same as or similar to those for male-normed scales: Lower Level, Easy Access; Helping; Socio-Political Science; Medical Service; Language; Mathematic-Numeric; Art; Psychology; and Homemaking.

For more complete information on the factor analyses and the methodologies employed, see Kuder (1977) and Kuder & Diamond (1979).

Validity of Using Other-Gender Norms. In counseling women or men, the question arises as to how to interpret scores based on data from the other sex. The important consideration is whether scores for occupations based on data from men fall in the same relative order for a woman as would scores based on data from women.

Early in the development of the KOIS, Kuder studied the scores of 99 females on scales for 13 occupations for which both male and female norms had been developed. Subjects were high school girls, college women, and women in a variety of occupations. Median correlation between the two sets of scores was .74 for high school girls, .77 for college women, and .81 for employed women. Scales that yielded the highest scores on one set of norms generally yielded high scores on the other set.

Diamond and Raju (1975) obtained scores on 28 pairs of KOIS scales, male-normed and female-normed, for occupations and college majors with the same or similar names. The sample consisted of 639 males and 353 females who took the KOIS in 1973. Correlations between ranks on the two sets of scales were obtained for each individual. The median correlation was .87 for males and .86 for females, and ranged up to .97. Only 5 of the 982 individual correlations fell below .60, indicating that scales generally rank in the same order for a person on male and female norms.

Zytowski and Laing (1978), in a study mentioned earlier in this chapter, found scores on two sets of twin scales to be highly correlated and approximately equal in predictive validity.

Diamond (1981) investigated the degree of overlap between scores on male-normed and female-normed KOIS scales for KOIS occupational criterion group profiles as an index of sex-typical and sex-atypical interests. The scores of female-normed professional occupational groups exhibited far more overlap with male-normed scores than did the scores of criterion groups for less-skilled occupations, both female-normed and male-normed. In fact, most female-normed professional criterion groups exhibited greater score overlap than did their male counterparts.

Reliability

Several types of KOIS reliability have been investigated and are reported in Kuder and Diamond (1979). The first refers to the reliability of individual profiles, or the consistency of an individual's scores on two administrations (test-retest reliability). The second refers to the stability of individual profiles over time. A third type refers to the consistency of the differences between scores on each pair of scales. Reliability of the VIE scales has also been studied.

Reliability of Individual Profiles. One hundred independent determinations of profile reliability were made for equal proportions of male and female high school seniors and college students, each involving from 25 to 28 pairs of scores. All had satisfactory V scores. The two administrations were approximately two weeks apart. Median reliability for all cases was .90. Fifteen of the 100 reliabilities were below .80, and only 7 were below .75.

In another study, individual test-retest reliabilities were computed for 92 high school senior boys and 50 college senior women on 142 scales. Median correlation for the former was .93, and for the latter .96. Standard errors of measurement ranged from .011 to .052, with a median of .01.

Stability Over Time. Gehman and Gehman (1968) studied the stability of KOIS scores of engineering students over 3 to 4 years. All had taken the KOIS as freshmen and again as seniors. Median reliability was .89.

Consistency of Score Differences. Differences between scores in each possible pair of scores on 4 scales were obtained in two administrations to 92 high school senior boys. Correlations ranged from .84 to .92, demonstrating a high degree of consistency for the scales involved.

Reliability of VIE Scales. VIE scales have KR-20s ranging from .63 to .85, except for the Persuasive scale, which has a KR-20 of only .47. (For more reliable estimates of broad vocational interests, administration of the two earlier instruments is suggested.) All of the scale intercorrelations but one are either negative or below .30, indicating the relative independence of the scales. The highest correlation is .46, between Outdoor and Mechanical.

Homogeneity

The extent to which criterion group members express the same preferences for KOIS activities is a measure of their homogeneity (Kuder & Diamond, 1979). The more homogeneous a group, the larger the proportion marking the same "most" and "least" choices, and the larger the sum of the squared proportions of the 100 combined "most" and "least" responses. For a group with perfect homogeneity, where 100% mark the same choices throughout the inventory (theoretically possible, but highly unlikely), the sum of the squared combined proportions over the 100 triads would be 500. For a group of the lowest possible homogeneity, with one-third of its members marking each of the "most" and each of the "least" response positions, the sum of squared proportions over the 100 triads would be 267.

For each of the KOIS criterion groups, the sum of the squared proportions for the 600 "most-least" patterns of response was found. Values ranged from a low of 329.33 to a high of 363.48. Values were generally higher for social-service-oriented groups and lower for manual workers, who closely resembled the heterogeneous men-in-general group. In general, as Kuder (1977) observed, the greater the degree of specialization in an occupation, the more homogeneous the group is likely to be.

EVALUATION AND FUTURE DIRECTIONS

As Kuder (1977) has commented:

> [I]nterest inventories are fallible and do not furnish all the answers needed for every counseling situation. . . . [W]e now know a great deal more about the role of interests in occupational choice than we knew fifty years ago. It is notable that reviewers do not advocate abandoning the use of interest inventories even in their present imperfect form. The justification for their use in guidance must be essentially the same as that for any psychological instrument: namely, that they contribute to doing a better job of counseling. (p. xi)

KOIS Strengths and Weaknesses

The most notable strength of the KOIS—one that has clearly enhanced the use of interest measurement in counseling—is its innovative method of scale development and scoring. The ability to make direct comparisons between an individual's responses to an interest inventory and the typical responses of various occupational and college major groups is a clear advantage over reliance on items that differentiate between the responses of a general reference group and those of a criterion group. Strong himself (1943) discovered that scales based on a reference group consisting of a sample of the general population did not produce good differentiation between professional groups. He found that no single reference group was satisfactory for the whole range of occupations. The errors of classification and the frequency of differences studies cited earlier (Kuder & Diamond, 1979) affirm the very significant improvement in classification obtained by the use of the KOIS rationale, and consequently in the validity of the inferences drawn from the scores.

Moreover, as both Laime and Zytowski (1964) and Johnson (1978) found, the fact that most women's responses on the Strong Vocational Interest Blank (and, in Johnson's study, the Strong-Campbell Interest Inventory) are unlike those of the Men-in-General group apparently contributes to inflated scores on male-normed scales. Scores on other-gender scales on the KOIS, on the other hand, permit a more straightforward interpretation in counseling.

Another strength of the KOIS is its item content and item type. The KOIS's avoidance of occupational titles and use of easily understood work-related activities discourages the favoring of occupational stereotypes. The forced-choice item format minimizes response bias, or the tendency of some inventory-takers to avoid extreme responses ("like very much," "dislike very much"), or to answer from different reference points, so that the reliability of the responses over respondents is very low.

The availability of materials to help with the counseling uses of the KOIS is still another strength. These include the VIEs; the 2-part report of scores with their comprehensive interpretive sections; a simulation of a typical counseling session on audiocassette; *Expanding Your Future* to help counselees relate high-ranking scores to occupations and college majors not represented in the KOIS; *Counseling with the Kuder Occupational Interest Survey,* which deals specifically with analysis and interpretation of the KOIS profile and presents typical client/counselor interpretive interviews; and the *General Manual* and *Manual Supplement,* which contain the technical information for the KOIS.

The KOIS's main weakness is the relatively limited number of occupational scales and the fact that a number of them are in need of updated norms; most of the scales were developed between 1955 and 1965, the remainder between 1967 and 1981. Although the scales cover a broad range of professional and non-professional occupations, the technology has changed for some of them, some occupations have become outdated, and new occupations have entered the world of work. Also, where possible, more scales normed on women are needed to match scales normed on men. Use of the KOIS cross-culturally has not been systematically investigated. Because of cultural differences, the V score and the lambda score levels tend to be quite low, rendering the results somewhat questionable. For use outside the Western countries and generally with non-English-speaking populations, problems of appropriate translation and of scale development (new criterion group responses would be needed for all scales) are considerable obstacles. Nevertheless, this area is an important one in which to encourage research. Finally, the KOIS can only be centrally scored; turnaround time, in most cases, is 48 hours plus mailing time. What is being done to rectify these shortcomings will be discussed later in this chapter.

Comparison with Other Interest Inventories

Zytowski (1981a) discussed the problem of administering more than one inventory and finding inconsistencies in the profiles for a given individual. He pointed out correctly that some people are not always consistent even when they take the same inventory twice and when the inventory has been shown to be reliable across persons. In addition, inventories that have similar kinds of scales may have very different items and different modes of responding, or the composition of norm groups may differ in such characteristics as age range or specialties within the occupation (e.g., research vs. application). If a client takes two inventories and the results show differences, Zytowski suggested that the counselor present both sets of results, discuss the possible reasons for the inconsistency with the client, and let him or her base next steps on the one that seems to more accurately reflect the client's interests. Or, the information from the two inventories can be used to complement each other, especially if one has scales not represented in the other.

The inventory with which the KOIS can be compared most directly is the Strong-Campbell Interest Inventory (SCII), because both deal principally with occupational interests, as opposed to broad general interest areas, and scales for both are empirically developed rather than internally developed. There are nevertheless a number of major differences. The principal difference is the method of scale construction and scoring. The SCII uses the significant differences between general-reference-group and criterion-group responses to items in the inventory to build a scale. SCII standard scores and percentile bands are based on these differences; the disadvantages of using a general reference group for scale-building and scoring have already been dealt with in detail earlier in this chapter. The KOIS, on the other hand, develops scales directly from the response proportions of the criterion group. Scores are lambdas—correlations between the modal responses of the criterion group and the responses of the individual. Although lambdas are not reported on the student copy of the score report, the scales are rank-ordered on the basis of their lambda values.

Item content and type of response also differ greatly. The KOIS contains 100 groups of three activities each, for which the inventory-taker selects one most preferred and one least preferred, in effect rank-ordering them. No occupational titles are used. The SCII items, on the other hand, include 131 occupational titles, 36 school subjects, 51 work-related activities, 39 leisure activities, 24 types of people, 14 personal characteristics, and 30 activities related to personal characteristics. Most of the responses are Likert-type, for example, Like, Indifferent, Dislike; Yes, ?, No.

A third major difference is type and number of scales. The KOIS has 65 male-normed occupational scales (27 of which are twin scales, also normed on women) and 39 female-normed occupational scales (including the 27 twin scales). There are also 22 male-normed college major scales (12 of which are twin scales) and 17 female-normed college major scales (including the 12 twin scales). The SCII, on the other hand, has 207 male-normed occupational scales and 207 female-normed scales for the same occupations. The SCII has no college major scales.

The KOIS covers a broader range of occupations. There are a number of skilled-crafts scales normed on men—for example, auto mechanic, carpenter, machinist, plumber. In the SCII the skilled crafts are represented by a single skilled-crafts scale. There is also, however, a skilled-crafts scale normed on women.

As mentioned earlier, the KOIS scales were developed mainly between 1955 and 1965, with a number of new scales added and two scales updated between 1967 and 1981. Data for the SCII scales, on the other hand, are more recent: 185 scales were updated between 1981 and 1984, and 22 new scales were added in 1985. The General Reference Groups were also updated. Both inventories include a variety of other scales as well. The KOIS VIEs have a counterpart in the SCII's General Occupational Themes and Basic Interest Scales. The KOIS V scale is somewhat akin to the SCII Infrequent Responses scale. The KOIS has the 8 experimental scales described earlier, and the SCII includes an Academic Orientation scale and an Introversion/Extroversion scale.

Both inventories offer comprehensive manuals, although there is a charge for the SCII manual. Both also offer ancillary materials; the KOIS materials are more extensive. Finally, the KOIS offers centrally-scored reports only, with 48 hours plus mailing time in turnaround time. The SCII, on the other hand, offers three types of scoring services: (a) centrally processed reports with 24-hour turnaround time; (b) microcomputer-based testing on line or in paper-and-pencil format, compatible with a variety of scanners, and with survey scored and results printed locally; (c) interactive video system with students completing survey at a terminal and receiving a videodisc interpretation of results at the terminal. SCII prices for combined booklet/answer sheet and central scoring are slightly less than for the KOIS.

Plans in Progress or Under Consideration

Work is already underway on the development of ten new KOIS scales: female-normed police officers, travel agents, ministers, personnel managers, realtors, business majors, and engineering majors; and both male-normed and female-normed legal assistant majors and data processing majors (community-college level).

Some updating of current scales is also planned, and a revision of the *General*

Manual will include a section on counseling with the KOIS, which is now a separate publication. A new publication, *FastFax,* currently in draft form, will provide occupational descriptions for the KOIS scales that will include the following: skill ratings derived from the Data, People, and Things ratings in the *Dictionary of Occupational Titles;* interests of each occupational group synthesized from the highest interests on the 10 VIE scales; educational requirements for entry, average earnings, and employment outlook. Consideration is also being given to the possible development of a microcomputer version of the KOIS.

Career Matching: A New Concept in Interest Measurement

The traditional task in occupational counseling—matching people to occupations—"really involves person-to-people matching . . . trying to match a specific individual to a group of people in an occupation," Kuder (1977, p. 163) observed. In real life, however, he went on to point out, perfect matching does not occur. "Even the members of an occupational group do not match their group perfectly"; considerable variation exists among them, although the greater the degree of specialization the more homogeneous the group will be.

The original objective, then, of matching people to jobs might be better achieved by matching people to individuals they resemble and who are enthusiastic about their work, Kuder concluded. No longer will the composition of occupational groups be a problem. The task, instead, would be to build a pool of people from as many occupations as possible and from all strata in life with whom to compare the individual. Detailed personal histories of the closest matches would be presented to him or her. New occupations could be represented in the system as soon as data from a few people in the occupation could be obtained.

Some preliminary exploratory work has already been done, but as Kuder pointed out, additional exploratory research needs to be directed at determining the reliability and stability of individual results for a number of persons who have taken the KOIS twice. Eventually, the system could well extend beyond the field of interests and encompass "the whole range of information that can be collected about human beings" (Kuder, 1977, p. 167). Indeed, the future of the KOIS is filled with promise for vastly expanded ways of measuring human characteristics.

ACKNOWLEDGMENTS

The author acknowledges the assistance of Donald G. Zytowski of Iowa State University and Rita K. Bode of Science Research Associates, who provided information about KOIS developments since the author left SRA, and who reviewed the first draft of this chapter.

REFERENCES

Anastasi, A. (1982). *Psychological testing* (5th ed.). New York: Macmillan.

Clark, K. E. (1961). *Vocational interests of nonprofessional men.* Minneapolis: University of Minnesota Press.

Clemans, W. V. (1958). An index of item-criterion relationship. *Educational and Psychological Measurement, 18,* 167–172.

Cronbach, L. J. (1950). Further evidence on response sets and test design. *Educational and Psychological Measurement, 10,* 3–31.

Cronbach, L. J. (1970). *Essentials of psychological testing* (3rd ed.). New York: Harper & Row.

Darley, J. G., & Hagenah, T. (1955). *Vocational interest measurement.* Minneapolis: University of Minnesota Press.

Diamond, E. E. (1981). Sex-typical and sex-atypical interests of Kuder Occupational Interest Survey criterion groups: Implications for counseling. *Journal of Counseling Psychology, 28,* 229–242.

Diamond, E. E., & Raju, N. S. (1977). *Technical supplement, Career development inventory* (rev. ed.). Chicago: Science Research Associates.

Findley, W. G. (1956). A rationale for evaluation of item discrimination statistics. *Educational and Psychological Measurement, 16,* 175–180.

Gehman, W. S., & Gehman, I. H. (1968). Stability of engineering interests over a period of four years. *Educational and Psychological Measurement, 28,* 367–376.

Herzberg, F., Mausner, B., Peterson, R. O., & Capwell, D. F. (1957). *Job attitudes: A review of research and opinion.* Pittsburgh: Psychological Services of Pittsburgh.

Hoffman, M. A., Spokane, A. R., & Magoon, T. M. (1981). Effects of feedback mode on counseling outcomes using the Strong-Campbell Interest Inventory: Does the counselor really matter? *Journal of Counseling Psychology, 28,* 119–125.

Holland, J. L. (1979). *Vocational preference inventory manual.* Palo Alto, CA: Consulting Psychologists Press.

Holland, J. L., Magoon, T. M., & Spokane, A. R. (1981). Counseling psychology: Career interventions, research, & theory. *Annual Review of Psychology, 32,* 279–305.

Johnson, R. W. (1978). Relationships between male and female interest scales for the same occupations. In C. K. Tittle & D. G. Zytowski (Eds.), *Sex-fair interest measurement: Research and Implications* (pp. 95–101). Washington, D.C.: National Institute of Education.

Kuder, F. (1966). *General Manual: Kuder DD Occupational Interest Survey:* (1st Ed.). Chicago Science Research Associates.

Kuder, F. (1975). *Manual: Kuder E General Interest Survey.* Chicago: Science Research Associates.

Kuder, F. (1977). *Activity Interests and Occupational Choice.* Chicago: Science Research Associates.

Kuder, F., & Diamond, E. E. (1979). *General Manual: Kuder DD Occupational Interest Survey* (2nd Ed.). Chicago: Science Research Associates.

Laime, B. F., & Zytowski, D. G. (1964). Women's scores on the M and F forms of the SVIB. *Vocational Guidance Quarterly, 12,* 116–118.

Lipsett, L., & Wilson, J. W. (1954). Do suitable interests and mental ability lead to job satisfaction? *Educational and Psychological Measurement, 14,* 373–380.

McRae, G. G. (1959). The relationships of job satisfaction and earlier measured interests. Unpublished doctoral dissertation, University of Florida.

Nunnally, J. C., Jr. (1959). *Tests and measurements.* New York: McGraw-Hill, 1959.

Strong, E. K. (1943). *Vocational interests of men and women.* Stanford, CA: Stanford University Press.

Strong, E. K. (1955). *Vocational interests 18 years after college.* Minneapolis: University of Minnesota Press.

Tittle, C. K. (1978). *Sex bias in testing: A review with policy recommendations.* Princeton, NJ: Educational Testing Service. (ERIC Document Reproduction Service No. ED 164 623).

Tyler, L. E. (1978). *Individuality.* San Francisco: Jossey-Bass, 1978.

U.S. Department of Health, Education, and Welfare. (1975). Nondiscrimination on the basis of sex. *Federal Register, 40,* 24128–24145.

U.S. Department of Labor. (1979). *Guide for occupational exploration.* Washington, D.C.: U.S. Government Printing Office.

Zytowski, D. G. (1976). Predictive validity of the Kuder Occupational Interest Survey. *Journal of Counseling Psychology, 23:* 221–233.

Zytowski, D. G. (1981a). *Counseling with the Kuder occupational interest survey.* Chicago: Science Research Associates.

Zytowski, D. G. (1981b). *Expanding your future.* Chicago: Science Research Associates.

Zytowski, D. G. (1985). *Manual supplement: Kuder DD occupational interest survey.* Chicago: Science Research Associates.

Zytowski, D. G., & Laing, L. (1978). Validity of other-gender-normed scales on the KOIS. *Journal of Counseling Psychology, 25,* 205–209.

9 A Complete Career Guidance Program: The COPSystem

Lisa Knapp-Lee
Lila Knapp
Robert Knapp
EDITS
San Diego, California

BACKGROUND OF THE COPSystem

The *Career Occupational Preference System Interest Inventory* (COPS) (Knapp & Knapp, 1974, 1982) is designed to assist individuals in the career decision-making process. The COPS is a carefully and systematically developed instrument yielding job activity interest scores based on occupational clusters, which may be used as a first step in career exploration. Using the extensive interpretative material presented with the COPS leads the way to utilization of most occupational information systems and consideration of educational choices, resulting in actual career decision-making. The COPS *Interest Inventory* provides for time-effective administration, scoring and interpretive procedures based on *Career Occupational Preference System* (COPSystem) occupational clusters, which have been established and refined through an extensive series of theoretical and factor analytic studies begun over two decades ago (Knapp, 1967).

The measurement of interests provided by the COPS combined with measurement of abilities, *Career Ability Placement Survey* (CAPS) (L. Knapp & R. R. Knapp, 1976), and measurement of values, *Career Orientation Placement and Evaluation Survey* (COPES) (Knapp & Knapp, 1978), provides a coordinated system for career exploration and decision-making.

For purposes of career exploration, a classification system is clearly needed. There are over 20,000 occupations listed in the *Dictionary of Occupational Titles* (DOT) (1977) which are available for consideration as possible careers. The structural form arrived at for the classification of occupations has great practical implications for career guidance. Clients should be directed to focus their consideration primarily on those occupations consistent with their interests, abilities, and values. Furthermore, this field of focus should broaden their perspective by including all, or virtually all, occupations within such a categorization. With these prescribed goals in mind, appropriate techniques can be chosen to arrive at the most meaningful classification structure.

The structure of interests may be presented from empirically sampling specific occupations or theoretically based on hypothetical groupings demonstrated through a statistical technique known as factor analysis. Among all possible choices, factor analysis is the most efficient tool used to clarify structure and has been used in the development of the COPSystem occupational clusters. In test development, factor analysis is a mathematical technique used to examine the clustering of test items. This grouping or clustering of highly related items defines a factor.

The development of the COPSystem occupational clusters followed closely the work of previous researchers. The early work of Thurstone (1931), who first applied factor analytic techniques to the interest domain, and the more recent work of Guilford, Christensen, Bond and Sutton (1954) led to a clearer understanding of the structure of interests in terms of groups of occupations based on focus of activities performed in the occupations. Kuder (1948) also reported scales including the eight basic group interest factors. During the researching of the structure of occupations, it became apparent that occupational interest could also be clustered by levels based on concepts, such as levels of responsibility, aspiration, and manipulative versus intellectual or planning activities. This distinction was first operationally defined in an inventory developed by Guilford, Shneidman, and Zimmerman (1948) and formally summarized by Roe (1956).

The technique of factor analysis yielded occupational classification systems that laid the groundwork for the development of the COPSystem structure of occupations. The available factor analytic studies presented structures similar enough in content to form a classification system by groups, based on focus of activity, levels, and degrees of responsibility and achievement. This approach, following the work of Guilford et al. (1948), has been empirically demonstrated and refined by Knapp (1967) and Knapp & Knapp (1974,1982). Virtually all available factor analyses have been based on items written to reflect the major focus of activity performed in a wide range of occupations. This categorization by primary focus of activity, which is reflected in the COPSystem (Knapp-Lee, Knapp, & Knapp, 1989b), follows from a long history of research into the structure of occupations guided by theory and empirically confirmed through factor analysis. The milepost stepping stones in the evolution of the structure of occupations can be summarized in Table 9.1.

Factor Analysis and the Group Structure of Interests

In the statistical foundation for a cluster structure of occupations dating back to the pioneering work of Thurstone (1931), four primary factors were identified among professional level occupations, and the direction was set for the scientific

COPS Group Factors Knapp & Knapp	Roe	Guilford	Kuder	Thurstone
Science	Science	Scientific	Scientific	Science
Technology	Technology	Mechanical	Mechanical Computational	Science
Outdoor	Outdoor	Natural	Outdoor	
Business	Business Contact	Mercantile Leadership	Persuasive	People
Clerical	Organization	Clerical	Clerical	Business
Communi-cation	General Cultural	Literary	Literary	Language
Art	Arts and Entertainment	Aesthetic Expression	Artistic Musical	Language
Service	Service	Service	Social Service	People

Table 9.1
Classification of Job Interests by Primary Focus of Activity Summary of Factor Analytic Studies

study of occupational classification. Application of the factor analytic model to the clarification of the interest domain has paralleled developments in the application of this technique in the ability area, both of which were accelerated by advances in computer technology. The technique may be used to demonstrate multiple, lower order factors at the secondary factor level or at the primary factor level, as Thurstone (1938) did in establishing the concept of primary mental abilities. As noted, the necessity of such a classification with multiple broad factors to explain the world of work becomes evident when confronted with a comprehensive list of occupational titles such as that in the Dictionary of Occupational Titles (1977). Although that document is an exemplary compendium of information about specific occupations, its use in occupational exploration is severely limited. Such information is highly useful when keyed to a structure that is based on a primary focus of activity.

Some ad hoc classificatory systems, which have neither been based on empirical nor theoretical research, have been presented. An example of such a classification is one in which occupations are clustered by industry, such as "transportation." Such a cluster groups together occupations involving activities as diverse as a truck driver, ticket agent, accountant, bookkeeper and dispatcher. Similarly, other work group arrangements have categorized together a wide diversity of occupations. One cluster identified as "Leading-Influencing," for example, includes programmer, statistician, teacher, psychologist, lawyer, purchasing agent, radio station manager, business manager, securities trader, newspaper editor, police lieutenant, mine inspector, hotel manager, travel agent, literary agent, and railroad dining car steward. Nonetheless, categorization by the concept of "Leading-Influencing," is perhaps better than no categorization at all.

Other systems of classification, although based on a measurement foundation, provide no information concerning relationship between jobs. Empirically developed scales are illustrative of this approach to interest measurement. Responses of students or other examinees are compared with responses of "seasoned" persons on the job on the assumption that similarity between responses of, for example, a 15-year-old high school sophomore and a 30-year-old Ph.D. psychologist, will indicate a positive prognostication for satisfaction as a psychologist. As Lunneborg and Lunneborg (1978, p. 165) stated, "an outstanding example of an interest measure without a theoretical base lies in the empirically constructed *Strong-Campbell Interest Inventory* (SCII) occupational scales" (Campbell, 1974). Instruments such as the SCII attempt to provide a comprehensive coverage of major occupations by adding occupational scales. Although not directly derived from factor analytic techniques, Kuder (1948) developed and refined his series of scales to the point where the *General Interest Survey Form C,* introduced in 1948, represented all eight of the group interest factors represented in Roe's model. (Actually the *General Interest Survey Form C* presented 10 scales, eight of which parallel those classified by Roe (1956) and are listed in Table 9.1, with the addition of two others, Computational and Musical.)

In that same year, Guilford, Shneidman, and Zimmerman (1948) published an inventory based on Guilford's factor analytic research, which reflected eight interest dimensions but also yielded two social service dimensions, Social Activity and Personal Assistance. The publication of this inventory was the first to present scales representing levels and defined the primary interest structure later elaborated upon by Roe (1956). The first application of a groups-by-levels classification in the measurement of interests thus appeared.

One of the most consequential factor resolutions of this theoretically based classificatory system was a 7-factor resolution published by Guilford et al. in 1954, based on a sample of male air force personnel. Factors obtained in that study were: mechanical, scientific, social welfare, aesthetic expression, clerical, business, and outdoor. The first six of these were among those also hypothesized by Guilford et al. (1954, p. 28). Although clearly emerging in the analysis, outdoor was not among those hypothesized in that study and thus was not listed among the *verified* factors in that study. It was this study which Holland (1973, p. 5) felt represented the "most explicit forerunner" of his typology of personality. Of course, selecting a six category typology omits not only the outdoor work interest factor but also the well-established linguistic or verbal-interest factor, which was apparent in Guilford's other research as well as in most factor analytic studies of occupational interests (Roe, 1956).

Lunneborg and Lunneborg (1975, 1978) have presented data in support of this 8-dimensional structure. The pattern of item correlations against the eight scales and intercorrelations of the scales was interpreted by the authors as supporting this structure. Meir and Barak (1974) have presented a simple inventory using occupational titles to measure the eight group factors. Their data from occupational samples of working adults and intercorrelational data among the scales were interpreted as supporting the validity of that inventory.

The model depicting these eight factors can be conceptualized in a number of ways. Roe and Klos (1969) suggested a circular model and there is some evidence from the use of the COPS *Interest Inventory* which supports this (Knapp, Knapp, & Buttafuoco, 1978).

COPSystem Structure of Occupations

In the development of the COPSystem structure of occupations, factor analysis has been the mathematical procedure chosen as the most appropriate technique for establishing, as well as confirming and monitoring, the theoretical classification of occupations. The resulting structure represents the most parsimonious system for the cluster grouping of occupations.

Early Item Factor Analysis

In the early research (Knapp, 1967) to establish the COPSystem occupational structure, Roe's (1956) classification of occupations (following the work of Guilford et al., 1948) into major groups and then into levels within each group served as the hypothesis. In the model originally presented, the eight groups were based on the primary focus of activity and were identified as: I. Service, II. Business Contact, III. Organization, IV. Technology, V. Outdoor, VI. Science, VII. General Culture, and VIII. Arts and Entertainment. These groups were each further classified by Roe into hierarchical levels reflecting degree of responsibility, training, capacity, and skill. In the study by Knapp (1967), items were written to reflect occupations in each of five of these levels within each of the eight major groups yielding 40 cells in the model. An experimental set of items was developed and administered to a sample of unselected students from the freshmen classes of two colleges and from the junior and senior classes of one high school. The individual item responses were submitted to factor analysis. The factor analyses (Knapp, 1967; Knapp & Knapp, 1974) yielded the eight broad, interpretable factors upon which the occupational clusters in the COPSystem are based. They are defined subsequently in the section entitled "The 14 COPSystem Occupational Clusters." Inspection of the intercorrelational matrix within each of the eight factors suggested high and low level clusters within the areas of Science, Technology, Business, Communication, Arts, and Service.

From this initial development, it was hypothesized that clusters of variables representing professional level occupational interests and skilled level interests would appear. Based on the original logical groupings of items into levels, 14 hypothesized factors were submitted for verification to patterned equamax rotation. All 14 factors emerged in the rotated matrix.

Re-examination of Item Factor Structure

The 1982 revision of the COPSystem *Interest Inventory* was undertaken to update and simplify wording of some items in the inventory, to reflect changes in certain job categories, and to achieve a better sex balance in response to items on certain scales. To determine what effect these changes might have on the structure of the occupational classification, it was necessary to submit the data from the revised instrument to another series of factor analyses.

Professional and Skilled level clusters were confirmed for five groups: Science, Technology, Business, Arts, and Service. The Professional and Skilled levels emerged separately, indicating clusters that were differentiated based on level of responsibility. Separate level clusters did not seem appropriate for the Outdoor, Clerical, or Communication groups. In this and subsequent studies, only five of the eight levels were clearly differentiated at the Professional and Skilled levels. Inspection of item content in the two Technology Skilled clusters suggested two logical groupings which are represented in the COPSystem as

Technology Skilled and Consumer Economics. Although the activities reflect occupations generally confirmed as being in the Technology group, two Skilled level clusters provide better representation for this, the largest occupational group. Confirmatory factor analytic results support these clusters. In terms of focus of activity represented by occupations in the two clusters, the Technology Skilled cluster, as contrasted with the Consumer Economics cluster, might be thought of as a "dirty hands" versus "clean hands" categorization within the Technology group. The Consumer Economics factor has appeared in all recent factor analytic studies and is most clearly defined in the COPS-R analysis (Knapp-Lee, Knapp, & Knapp, 1989a).

Structure of the 1982 COPS items was established through a series of factor analyses based on the new pool of single items. A technique employed to reconfirm the structure at the item level was Bentler's (1971) monotonicity analysis. A second technique using subscores based on highly homogeneous items also confirmed the factors. Although some changes occurred, these analyses generally replicated the results from earlier analyses.

Using the factor analytic techniques to periodically re-examine the structure existing within a given set of job activity items is advantageous because it provides flexibility in revising and updating item content. Items can be rewritten to reflect changing job activities as, for example, the ever increasing application of computer input in the Clerical area. Other examples are application of the technique to a set of sex-balanced items to construct a single sex-normed instrument, COPS *Interest Inventory, Form-R* (COPS-R) (Knapp & Knapp, 1980a, 1980b); application to sets of items at the Professional level only to broaden and refine measurement for the college oriented client, COPS *Interest Inventory, Form-P* (COPS-P) (Knapp-Lee, Knapp, & Knapp, 1982), and confirmation of the appropriateness of the instrument for specialized samples, such as the adult handicapped population (Brookings & Bolton, 1986).

CONCEPTUAL FOUNDATIONS OF THE COPSystem

An assumption underlying development of the COPSystem is that the career guidance process begins by assisting individuals in defining areas for occupational investigation that are specific and appropriate to their personal interests. Investigation of a great many related occupations within a specific area broadens the scope of career exploration, yet supplies an avenue to systematically narrow the choices to consider. Through this process, individuals are more quickly and systematically introduced to those occupations in which they are likely to be employed. Interests, what an individual *likes* to do, along with abilities and temperament play a major role in career selection and also influence the educational preparation that students will consider and select for their career preparation.

Systematic consideration of occupations appropriate to a given individual's personal aspirations and unique characteristics has grown increasingly complex as the number of occupations has multiplied. Test results can help the individual by presenting a wide scope of occupational choices and isolating a smaller segment for consideration in terms of personal interests, abilities, and values. This function of assessment through a testing program is described in the present system as "clustered occupational exploration."

Occupational clusters in the COPSystem are keyed to training and school curriculum. Determination of those clusters representing an examinee's individual interest and ability patterns will help the individual in the choice of curriculum and the selection of particular courses and training available to him or her.

In summary, current trends in career guidance emphasize the broadening of occupational knowledge prior to making a specific vocational choice. Guidance may be most effective if first directed at the identification of occupational clusters or families related to the examinees' interests, abilities, and values rather than focusing on the selection of a particular job or occupation. Identification of the appropriate cluster of similar, interrelated occupations and the obtaining of information on a wide range of occupations within the cluster are prime objectives of the career guidance unit. Thus, the need exists for instruments providing systematic measurement of examinees' interests, abilities and values related to clusters of meaningfully related occupations.

Sample occupations for each of the 14 clusters are presented in the *Self-Interpretation Profile and Guide,* the interpretive booklet accompanying the measurement instruments. These occupations are keyed to occupational information systems. By following this up, examinees are referred to current, detailed information about these and other related occupations in their area of interest. Additional activities are suggested for examinees in evaluating their interests, skills, choice of curriculum, college majors, and job information. The worksheets presented in the *Self-Interpretation Profile and Guide* define the career decision-making guidelines and provide the exercises to put the career decision-making process into action. Examinees are told to identify the areas (for example, Business, Science), the level (either Professional or Skilled) in which they have relatively high or low interests, and to list their three highest interest areas. Examinees then relate their highest interest areas to sample occupations listed under each cluster in the *Self-Interpretation Profile and Guide* by choosing sample occupations to look up in independent sources of information. Selected occupations are chosen and information is provided on the interpretive material or sources consulted from which the examinee lists skills required and tasks performed in these jobs, as well as the courses available and training appropriate to the occupations selected. This research by the examinee, based on measurement scores, results in a clear-cut step-by-step decision-making process.

The COPSystem, thus, provides a career awareness unit based on interest, ability, and value scores keyed to occupational clusters, job information, and curriculum or training programs. Scores used in interpretation are based on instruments providing measurement in three areas: interest, abilities, and values. There are four forms of the interest inventory: the COPS Intermediate Inventory (COPS II) (Knapp & Knapp, 1976); the COPS-R (Knapp & Knapp, 1980a); the COPS (Knapp & Knapp, 1982); and the COPS-P (Knapp-Lee, Knapp, & Knapp, 1982). These four interest inventories may be used with the CAPS (Knapp & Knapp, 1976) ability battery and the COPES (Knapp & Knapp, 1978) work values survey. All of these instruments are keyed to the 8 major occupational clusters measured in the COPSystem. All of the instruments are available in self-scoring format and all but the COPS II may be machine scored.

Description of the Interest Inventories in the COPSystem

COPS II (Career Occupational Preference System Intermediate Inventory)

The COPS II is a self-scoring booklet at the 4th-grade reading level designed to complement the widely used COPS. The COPS II extends measurement to younger, elementary grade students and to those students at higher grade levels for whom reading or language present difficulties or where other motivational considerations interfere with administration of the COPS *Interest Inventory*. The COPS II incorporates graphics and requires less intensive reading than most inventories. With COPS II, measurement is based on a knowledge of familiar school courses and activities, rather than exclusively on knowledge of job-related activities, which may not be familiar to some students. Examinees receive scores in eight areas, five of which are divided into Professional levels and at least one Skilled level. These same 14 occupational clusters are measured in the other forms of the COPSystem. The interpretive material is included in the booklet. The interpretation consists of descriptions of the occupational clusters, sample job titles, lists of skills and abilities, and suggested activities to get experience. The job activity worksheets facilitate career exploration and program planning.

COPS-R (Career Occupational Preference System Interest Inventory, Revised Edition)

The COPS-R is designed to assist individuals in the career decision-making process. Like the earlier COPS *Interest Inventory,* the COPS-R is a carefully and systematically developed instrument yielding job activity interest scores based on occupational clusters. The COPS-R provides a simplified format with sex-balanced items presenting interpretation based on single sex norms.

COPS-R administration, scoring, and interpretation are accomplished through a single, self-contained booklet. Items are written at a 6th-grade level with the whole unit presented in an easy-to-follow programmed booklet. All words in the

COPS-R are at or below a 6th-grade reading level as determined by the vocabulary of Harris and Jacobson (1972).

COPS (Career Occupational Preference System Interest Inventory)

The COPS *Interest Inventory* measures job activity interests in the 8 major occupational clusters. Four of these clusters are divided into Professional and Skilled clusters, three are undifferentiated by these levels and one, Technology, is divided into one Professional level and two Skilled level clusters. The COPS was revised in 1982 with the major goal of eliminating the more difficult words in order to make the inventory conform to a 6th- through 8th-grade vocabulary level. A few of the items were rewritten to achieve greater sex-balance of the scales. Renorming was completed to reflect current attitudes toward the occupational activities in the COPS clusters which would include changes reflecting diminished occupational stereotypes. To lower the reading level of the COPS *Interest Inventory,* 1982 Edition, all words used in the Inventory were at or below a 6th-grade reading level as determined by the vocabulary presented by Harris and Jacobson (1972).

The objective to reduce the sex differences between certain of the scales was achieved, as evidenced by the fact that male–female mean differences for the two editions were reduced in 11 of the 14 scales. Although differences on these scales were reduced, they still were statistically significant and were of such a magnitude as to require separate male and female profile norms. These remaining differences are, of course, due to cultural differences between the sexes in terms of expressed occupational activity preferences on the items which were not revised. For those users who require a single-sex normed profile, a sex-balanced inventory is available in the form of the COPS-R.

Both the COPS and the COPS-R inventories consist of 168 job activity descriptions reflecting work performed in a wide variety of occupations. Examinees respond to these items according to their degree of like or dislike for each activity. Items reflect actual tasks performed in specific occupations rather than being phrased in terms of often unfamiliar occupational titles. Response alternatives allow the examinee to indicate "(L) Like very much," "(l) like moderately," "(d) dislike moderately" or "(D) Dislike very much." This free-choice response format allows examinees to state their degree of like or dislike for each activity without forcing a choice between activities which may be equally appealing or distasteful.

COPS-P (Career Occupational Preference System, Form P)

The COPS-P measures interest within the eight major career clusters and follows the structure of occupations developed by the research with the COPS.

The COPS-P inventory was developed to refine measurement of the eight broad group factors at the Professional level into subclusters for use by college and professionally oriented individuals in the career decision-making process. The further division of the eight clusters into demonstrated subclusters can be used to help in pinpointing an individual's specific areas of interest and choice of college majors and training programs. Persons seeking career changes would be expected to benefit from the specificity of subclusters.

A list of the subclusters measured by the COPS-P is as follows:

SCIENCE	Medical Life Physical
TECHNOLOGY	Electrical Mechanical Civil
OUTDOOR	Agribusiness Nature
BUSINESS	Finance Management Promotion
COMPUTATION	
COMMUNICATION	Written Oral
ARTS	Entertaining-Performing Fine Arts-Design
SERVICE	Instructional Social-Health

ABILITY: CAPS (Career Ability Placement Survey)

The CAPS consists of a battery of eight 5-minute ability tests providing a comparatively brief and time- and cost-effective measure of ability for career development. The battery was developed as a system for ability measurement, which may be used in conjunction with measures of interests and values in terms of the resultant occupational clusters provided in the COPSystem. A complete description of the rationale and development of the battery is presented in the CAPS *Technical Manual* (Knapp & Knapp, 1984).

The CAPS measures abilities in terms of the following eight tests:

Mechanical Reasoning
Spatial Relations
Verbal Reasoning

Numerical Reasoning
Language Usage
Word Knowledge
Perceptual Speed and Accuracy
Manual Speed and Dexterity

Current career development theory indicates that there are many important factors to be considered in career exploration. Perhaps the most important among these are the individual's interests and abilities. There are currently a host of tests available designed to evaluate these areas separately, most of which require several hours of testing time. However, little has been done to integrate the interpretation of measurement in these areas to provide individuals with an overall picture of their interests and abilities, as related to a career choice, in a reasonable length of time. This would seem to be a necessary adjunct to a holistic approach to career counseling. The CAPS is designed as a step in this direction. When interpreted in conjunction with the COPSystem occupational clusters, it provides an individual with a profile or "picture" of his or her abilities in terms of these occupational clusters. Thus, the CAPS is presented as an instrument providing examinees, instructors, and counselors with a powerful tool to aid them in the planning, organization, and evaluation of career development.

The recognition that there are many aspects to mental ability is the basis for defining individual differences in abilities appropriate to jobs in the various clusters. Thus, an individual high in verbal ability and language usage but low in numerical ability and/or manual dexterity may find occupations in the Communication cluster the most satisfying. Another individual who is high in spatial ability, numerical ability, manual dexterity, and low in verbal ability may be most satisfied in jobs in the Technology cluster.

Features of the CAPS include optimal use of testing time, ease of administration, and ease and flexibility of scoring alternatives. The complete battery can be administered in less than one hour and both Machine-Scoring and Self-Scoring Forms are available.

VALUES: COPES (Career Orientation Placement and Evaluation Survey)

Contemporary trends in occupational decision-making theory have placed an increasingly greater emphasis on personality characteristics as they relate to occupational selection. As individuals have become more free to choose how they occupy their time, these characteristics have come to play a greater role in job choice and satisfaction. These characteristics are variously described under such general personality or motivational terms as "work values," "work needs," or "work satisfactions" and all fall within the noncognitive, personality domain.

The perceived importance of the work one chooses has been reiterated by counselors, teachers, therapists, and those actually involved in jobs reflecting all the levels and varied activities represented in the world of work. Dimensions reflected in the COPES have been observed as being related to the type of work a person chooses and the satisfaction derived from the work one does.

Each of the eight COPES dimensions is measured by two-choice, paired comparison items: 20 per scale in the Machine-Scoring Form and 16 per scale in the Self-Scoring Form. A complete description of the development of the COPES may be found in the COPES *Manual* (Knapp & Knapp, 1986).

The eight dimensions measured by the COPES are:

Investigative vs. Accepting
Practical vs. Carefree
Independence vs. Conformity
Leadership vs. Supportive
Orderliness vs. Non-compulsive
Recognition vs. Privacy
Artistic vs. Realistic
Social vs. Self-Concern

The COPES was developed as a measure of work values which may be used in conjunction with measures of interests and abilities and interpreted in terms of the career clusters provided in the COPSystem.

COPSystem ADMINISTRATION AND SCORING

The COPSystem allows the administrator to choose the method of scoring (Machine- or Self-Scoring) and to choose the method of interpreting all three or any one or two of the career units, COPS (Interests), CAPS (Abilities), and COPES (Values). The COPSystem also allows for either group or individual administration.

Scoring of the Instruments

The COPS, COPS-R, and COPS-P *Interest Inventories* can be scored either by hand or by machine. Scoring is accomplished by summing the response weights for the items in each occupational cluster. For hand-scoring, especially where immediate self-scoring by the examinees themselves is desired, the Self-Scoring

Form is used and responses are made directly on the Self-Scoring Booklet. The first step in scoring is done on the booklet and scoring is completed on the *Self-Interpretation Profile and Guide*. Self-scoring by students is usually accomplished in 10 to 20 minutes. Research presented in the COPSystem *Technical Manual* (Knapp-Lee, Knapp, & Knapp, 1989b) regarding the accuracy of self-scoring indicates a very small percentage of error regarding the clusters considered for career exploration.

For machine-scoring, the COPS Machine-Scoring Booklet may be used and can be electronically scored by computer through the use of local optical readers with licensing agreement from EdITS/Educational and Industrial Testing Service. Scoring services are also provided for these forms when returned to EdITS and results are reported in terms of individually plotted profiles for maximum counseling usefulness. See Figure 9.1 for a sample of a computer-generated profile.

The COPS II is available in the Self-Scoring Form only. Responses are reported in terms of raw scores in each of the COPSystem clusters. The COPS II may be used with the CAPS and the COPES and summarized on the COPS II *Summary Guide*.

Description of the Norm Groups

Scores for the COPS, COPS-R, and COPS-P are reported in terms of the COPSystem occupational clusters both as raw scores and percentile scores. The COPS reports scores in two separate interpretive booklets, one for a high-school norm group and another for a college norm group. Norms for the 1982 Edition were based on a national sampling of 6,834 intermediate and high-school students in grades 8 through 12 collected during the 1981–82 school year. Norms for the college level were based on a national sampling of 1,445 students. These norms were updated in 1988. Periodic up-dating of normative data will be continued.

CAPS scores reflect examinees' relative ability in eight major ability dimensions as compared with others at their age and educational level. Scores are interpreted in terms of national norms, which have been established for the tests and are presented in two ways. First, profiles may be plotted on the CAPS Ability Profile based on norms determined separately for each of the eight tests. A second method of scoring and interpreting the scores involves various combinations of the eight stanine scores for each of the COPSystem occupational clusters.

Norms for the CAPS are based on a national sampling of intermediate (grades 8–9), high school (grades 10, 11, and 12) and community college/college students and are presented in separate norm supplements. Norming data were collected in 1981 for a total sample of 5,858 students. A stratified sample was composed of rural and urban samples from five geographical areas, including minority samples in the proportions reported in the 1980 census data. Norming data will be reestablished in the coming years.

Scores on the COPES reflect an individual's work values in terms of the COPSystem clusters. These are interpreted through the COPES profile in such a way as to help examinees identify those work-related values that are most important to them as compared to others in their peer group.

For interpretive purposes, opposite end poles for each major dimension are described on the profile sheet. Because neither pole of the dimension would be interpreted as "good" or "bad," descriptive words and phrases have been chosen to describe both ends of the dimension in a positive way. Examinees should thus be made aware that low scores are not negative attributes, but rather a way of clarifying the dimensions being measured.

The COPES scores are interpreted in terms of a profile which compares the individual's scores with those from the normative sample. Norms for the COPES are based on a national sample of 6,253 intermediate and high school students in grades 7 through 12 and 700 community college students. Means based on the samples for grades 7 through 12 and the separate community college sample were not meaningfully different for interpretive purposes and consequently, were combined to form a single norms sample.

COPSystem INTERPRETATION

Occupational Areas

Statistical results based on factor analysis yielded eight broad interpretable area factors upon which the COPSystem is based. These areas are Science, Technology, Outdoor, Business, Clerical, Communication, Arts, and Service. Occupational activities performed in the jobs represented within each area are seen as being more similar to other jobs in that area than to jobs in the other areas.

The COPSystem occupational clusters group together those occupations which are most similar in terms of activity preference. Interest scores based on such clusters provide a more meaningful basis for career decision-making than scores based on any other set of items because they maximize the use of the psychological relationship among activities performed in the jobs in each of the clusters. For example, when an individual's activity interests (or occupation) change, it is more likely to be to another activity within the same cluster than to an activity or occupation in any other cluster, (Knapp, Knapp, & Buttafuoco, 1978). Such a cluster system is more useful in career exploration than other systems, such as the United States Office of Education (USOE) industry-based job families. In the COPSystem, a truck drive would be grouped with a heavy equipment operator, machine tool operator, welder, etc., rather than with an air traffic controller or travel agent. In the COPSystem, a surgeon would be grouped with occupations such as a chemist, microbiologist, and physicist rather than with a medical records librarian. For user convenience, the COPSystem occupational clusters are also cross-referenced to the USOE job groups. Cross-references from the COPSystem occupational clusters to other job groupings are indicated on the COPSystem career guides. In addition to the keying of clusters to the USOE, DOT, and *Occupational Outlook Handbook* (OOH), cross-references are also available between the COPSystem occupational clusters and many statewide occupational systems (for example, VIEW and OIS).

Professional and Skilled Clusters

Among major considerations in career exploration are questions involving levels of training and of responsibility required by various occupations under consideration. Based on the structure of occupations into groups and levels suggested by Guilford, Shneidman, and Zimmerman (1948) and Roe (1956) and demonstrated by Knapp (1967), the COPSystem organizes occupations into Professional and Skilled level clusters. Such division, of course, has great implications for the interpretive usefulness of the instrument. Measurement of occupational interests provided by the COPS *Interest Inventory* at the Skilled as well as the Professional level will be of assistance equally to the vocationally oriented individual as well as to the college or professionally oriented individual.

Interest scores for five of the eight occupational areas are represented for both Professional level and for Skilled level occupational clusters; these include the Science, Technology, Business, Arts, and Service areas. An examination of the occupations in the two levels suggests certain characteristics which, for interpretive purposes, have been labeled "Professional" or "Skilled." The Technology Skilled cluster is further subdivided into two Skilled level clusters; Technology Skilled, encompassing the so-called "dirty hands" occupations, and Consumer Economics, representing the "clean hands" technology occupations. The clusters of Outdoor, Clerical, and Communication are undifferentiated in terms of Professional and Skilled levels.

In general, occupations in the Professional level typically require college training and often advanced degrees, especially in the areas of Science, Technology, and Service. Occupations at this level are characterized by a high degree of autonomy and responsibility. In addition to interest in these areas, personal qualifications of ability and personality typically will have to be met.

Occupations in the Skilled level usually require specialized training that would be obtained in trade or vocational school and on-the-job training. These occupations may also require little or no specialized training, such as waiter or usher in the Service area; however, some skilled level occupations may require a college degree.

The 14 COPSystem Occupational Clusters

The 14 COPSystem clusters are:

SCIENCE, Professional occupations involve responsibility for the planning and conducting of research and the accumulation and application of systematized knowledge in related branches of mathematical, medical, life, and physical sciences.

SCIENCE, Skilled occupations involve observation and classification of facts in assisting in laboratory research and its application in the fields of medicine and life and physical sciences.

TECHNOLOGY, Professional occupations involve responsibility for engineering and structural design in the manufacture, construction, or transportation of products or utilities.

TECHNOLOGY, Skilled occupations involve working with one's hands in a skilled trade concerned with construction, manufacture, installation or repair of products in related fields of construction, electronics, and mechanics.

CONSUMER ECONOMICS occupations are concerned with the preparation and packaging of foods and the production and care and repair of clothing and textile products.

OUTDOOR occupations are concerned with activities performed primarily out-of-doors involving the growing and tending of plants and animals and the cultivation and accumulation of crops and natural resources in the areas of agriculture and nature as in forestry, park service, fishing, and mining.

BUSINESS, Professional occupations involve positions of high responsibility in the organization, administration, and efficient functioning of business and governmental bureaus in regard to finance and accounting, management, and business promotion.

BUSINESS, Skilled occupations are concerned with sales and promotion and the correlated financial and organizational activities of businesses.

CLERICAL occupations involve recording, posting and filing of business records requiring great attention to detail, accuracy, neatness, orderliness and speed in office work and in resultant contact with customers in regard to compilation of records.

COMMUNICATION occupations involve skill in the use of language in the creation or interpretation of literature or in the written and oral communication of knowledge and ideas.

ARTS, Professional occupations involve individualized expression of creative or musical talent and ability in fields of design, fine arts, and performing arts.

ARTS, Skilled occupations involve application of artistic skill in the fields of graphic arts and design.

SERVICE, Professional occupations include positions of high responsibility involving interpersonal relations in caring for the personal needs and welfare of others in fields of social service, health, and education.

SERVICE, Skilled occupations involve providing services to persons and catering to the tastes, desires, and welfare of others in fields of personal service, social, and health related service, and protection and transportation.

CAPS Ability Areas

The eight CAPS tests are:

MR Mechanical Reasoning measures how well a person can understand mechanical principles and devices and the laws of physics. This ability is important especially in courses in industrial arts and occupations in Technology as well as Skilled level jobs in Science.

SR Spatial Relations measures how well a person can visualize or think in 3 dimensions and can mentally picture position of objects from a diagram or drawings. This ability is important in courses in art and industrial arts and jobs in Science, Technology, and Arts.

VR Verbal Reasoning measures how well a person can reason with words and the facility for understanding and using concepts expressed in words. This ability is important in general academic success and in jobs requiring written or oral communication, especially those Professional level occupations in Communication, Science, and Service involving high levels of responsibility and decision-making.

NA Numerical Ability measures how well a person can reason with and use numbers and work with quantitative material and ideas. This ability is important in school courses and jobs in fields of Science and Technology involving mathematics, chemistry, physics or engineering and in Business and Clerical fields.

LU Language Usage measures how well a person can recognize and use correct grammar, punctuation, and capitalization. This ability is especially important in jobs requiring written or oral communication and in Clerical jobs as well as Professional level occupations in Science, and in all levels of Business and Service.

WK Word Knowledge measures how well a person can understand the meaning and precise use of words. This is important in Communication and all professional level occupations involving high levels of responsibility and decision-making.

PSA Perceptual Speed and Accuracy measures how well a person can perceive small detail rapidly and accurately within a mass of letters, numbers, and symbols. This ability is important in office work and other jobs requiring fine visual discrimination.

MSD Manual Speed and Dexterity measures how well a person can make rapid and accurate movements with the hands. This ability is important in Arts-Skilled and Technology-Skilled occupations and other jobs requiring use of the hands.

COPES Work Values Dimensions

Eight work values are measured by the COPES and are listed below.

Investigative versus Accepting. Intellectual curiosity and the challenge of solving a complex task are major values of persons scoring high on this scale. The need for information is very important to such people. Low scorers value clear-cut activities in which they see the concrete results of their work and do not need to solve many complex problems.

Practical versus Carefree. Showing proper appreciation for one's personal belongings and appreciation of practical and efficient ways of doing things are major values of persons scoring high on this scale. Such persons value activities in which they take good care of their property and work with things to make them more practical and efficient. Low scorers value activities where others take care of equipment and keep things in good working order.

Independence versus Conformity. Independence from rules, regulations, social conventions, and the freedom to work on their own are major values of persons scoring high on this scale. Such persons value activities in which they are relatively free of rules and regulations and are not restricted by social obligations. Low scorers value working under careful supervision where clear directions and regulations can be followed.

Leadership versus Supportive. Making decisions, directing others, and speaking for the group are major values of persons scoring high on this scale. Such persons have a need to be seen as important and usually take positions of leadership. Low scorers value activities in which they can be a good follower and do not need to direct others or tell others what to do.

Orderliness versus Non-Compulsive. Orderliness and keeping things neat and in their proper place are major values of persons scoring high. Such persons value activities in which they keep things tidy and do what they are expected to do. Low scorers value activities in which they can take things as they come and do not need to keep things orderly.

Recognition versus Privacy. To become well-known and famous and to know important people are major values of persons scoring high on this scale. Such persons seek the admiration of others as well as the rewards of honorary degrees. Low scorers value keeping their activities private and are not concerned with being considered a famous person.

Aesthetic versus Realistic. Artistic appreciation and the enjoyment of music and the arts are major values of persons scoring high on this scale. Such persons value activities in which they appreciate beauty, show artistic and emotional sensitivity, and appreciate music and the arts. Low scorers are not involved with appreciation of artistic qualities.

Social versus Self-Concern. Helping others and appreciating the work of charitable service groups are major values of persons scoring high on this scale. Working with people in a friendly situation is important to such persons. Low scorers value activities in which they spend time on their own projects and tend to their own affairs rather than helping others.

Initial Interpretation of COPS, CAPS, and COPES Scores

COPS scores reflect the examinees' degree of interest in 14 occupational clusters. These scores are presented in such a way as to help examinees identify those occupational families in which their interests are greatest compared to others in their peer group. Because items reflect the nature of the activities performed in each occupational family, it is felt the scores more accurately reflect interest independent of considerations of status, salary, and advancement. Instructions are also written to maximize consideration of interest independent of other factors. The Inventory scores, thus, may be thought of as reflecting professed interest to be considered in career selection along with separate indices of abilities, values, and personality characteristics.

A basic concept guiding development of the CAPS was that test results should provide for maximum interpretive usefulness. Use of the test data should initiate activities resulting in greater self-awareness in relation to career development. The CAPS may be interpreted separately as well as in terms of occupational clusters. It may also be used in the COPSystem in conjunction with the COPS and the COPES. Thus, the CAPS scores are presented with interpretive material so that the results of the CAPS can have immediate application for career planning, such as in the selection of school courses and training programs as well as through participation in specific programs and community activities. Every effort has been made in development of the CAPS to maximize the interpretive usefulness of the test results.

Each CAPS occupational cluster score on the career profile is based on a combination of individual ability test stanine scores. This combined score represents the contribution variance for tests measuring those dimensions which historically have been shown to yield the greatest predictive validity for success in the jobs in each cluster.

Some examinees will have satisfactory ability scores in clusters not representing their highest interest. If, however, they have some interest in jobs in those clusters (for example, scores above the 50th percentile) these may represent fields which the examinees may wish to consider further because of ability.

Furthermore, the abilities measured are, of course, not the only factors to be considered in career exploration. Ability may be high in areas for which the examinee does not wish to pursue the vigorous training required to obtain necessary skills for jobs in the cluster. On the other hand, if interest and motivation are high and ability scores are low or fall in the shaded portion of the profile, the examinee may wish to take related courses of study required to improve these skills. Also, it must be remembered that skills other than those measured by the CAPS may be involved in any specific occupation.

When analyzing ability scores in a particular area in which high interest is indicated, the examinee may wish to examine separate ability test scores which comprise the total CAPS Career Profile clusters score. For example, in the Science Skilled area, a stanine score of 5 or above (average or above) may be obtained for Spatial Ability and the remaining tests. However, the Mechanical Reasoning stanine score may be only 1 or 2 (below average). This might indicate that the examinee could benefit from courses or special training in principles of mechanics. The examinee might want to consider occupations within the cluster that do not require a great deal of mechanical skill.

The COPES scores are interpreted by a profile comparing the individual's scores with those from the normative sample. The taxonomy of work values presented in the COPES accounts for eight dimensions which are held to be pervasive work value constructs and are related to the COPSystem occupational clusters.

The concept of work values is sometimes more elusive for examinees to grasp than the concepts of interests and abilities. Once one understands it, however, the importance of values in career planning will become apparent. Reviewing some of the questions from the COPES might help to see what values are being measured. The COPES asks that a choice be made between such pairs of statements as:

work with ideas
work with my hands

team up with others
work on my own

Answers to questions such as these help to identify things considered to be important in work; what rewards an individual needs to get from work in order to be satisfied. Such "satisfiers" are called "values," and they are very strong influences in our lives. Most career researchers feel that people act according to what they feel is important to them. For instance, if "status" or "recognition" are important to you, you are likely to seek out jobs and friends which contribute to meeting that need. If you do not, you will most probably feel unsatisfied and restless.

Full descriptions of the COPES work values appear on the *Self-Interpretation Profile and Guide*. A table relating the COPES work values to the COPSystem occupational clusters is also presented.

Summarization of the COPS, CAPS, and COPES on a Single Profile

The COPS, CAPS, and COPES may be summarized separately on their respective *Self-Interpretation Profile and Guides*. If using all three instruments together or in any combination of two of the instruments, results should be summarized on the *Comprehensive Career Guide*. The *Comprehensive Career Guide* contains individual profiles for each inventory and a means of summarizing the scores from the CAPS and COPES on the COPS *Interest Inventory* profile.

The COPS profile is plotted in the normal manner as described on the *Comprehensive Career Guide*. Below the profile are three rows of boxes, labeled "Interests 1", "Abilities 2", and "Values 3" (see Figure 9.2 for an example). It is suggested for interpreting the COPS that examinees explore their three highest areas of interest, according to percentile score, or peaks on the profile, as opposed to raw score. Three pluses should be put in the row labeled "Interests 1," or perhaps 4 pluses if there is a tie between the third and fourth highest areas of interest. These are the clusters that the examinee should begin to explore in terms of interest.

The CAPS results are plotted on the *Comprehensive Career Guide* in the same manner that they are on the CAPS *Self-Interpretation Profile and Guide*. Any score on the CAPS Career Profile that is in the white portion, or the very upper part of the lightest shaded portion, will receive a plus in terms of ability. These pluses are transferred to row 2 below the interest profile to indicate the COPSystem cluster that should be explored in terms of interest and ability combined. Any cluster that contains a plus for interest and ability would be the direction to explore in the first stages of career guidance.

The COPES results are plotted on the *Comprehensive Career Guide*, once again, in the same manner that scores are plotted on the COPES *Self-Interpretation Profile and Guide*. Examinees are advised to choose their three highest scores on the COPES and record them on their profile. A sample of this summary profile is found in the case study in Figure 9.2. Once the pluses are put in the appropriate boxes on each row of the COPS profile, examinees are ready to explore the clusters in which, first of all, their interests, abilities and values match.

The next step in the career exploration process is to examine the career clusters and the information contained on the profile sheet. On each profile sheet there is information on the definition of the career cluster and related courses of study. Below this information is a list of occupational titles. Each of these occupational titles is keyed to the DOT (1977). The titles are also keyed to the current OOH, the COPSystem *Career Briefs Kit* and the COPSystem *Career Cluster Booklet Kit*. Cross-references between various statewide systems are available, such as VIEW and OIS. Below the selected occupations for each cluster are listed some skills and abilities needed on the jobs in that particular cluster, suggested activities to get experience and college majors.

Once the examinee has studied the individual profile for each instrument, studied the summarized profile for all three instruments combined and briefly examined the clusters that are to be explored, there are additional work sheets to complete which are contained both in the *Comprehensive Career Guide* and the *Self-Interpretation Profile and Guide*. Not only do examinees get a measure of themselves, but they are encouraged to actively use results obtained about themselves. The work sheet entitled "Using your scores in career planning" allows examinees to thoroughly explore the career clusters and the information provided on the profile sheet. Along with this work sheet is one for educational planning, which may be used by the high school student for establishing a 4-year program plan for school. For the college student or adult, this form may be used to outline pertinent classes completed and future schooling and/or training that would be helpful in reaching a desired career goal. A local interview form is the final work sheet that may be used as a structured guide for an informational interview or as a planning guide to conduct an interview.

The COPSystem has major interpretive values that make it extremely useful in the counseling situation. In this system, examinees are guided not to a single specific job title but rather an organized system of exploring the world of work. A cluster of occupations to explore is more useful than a single occupational title. In addition, the COPSystem is a time-effective battery. The entire battery may be administered in 2 hours and self scored in another 2 hours. Also, any one or two of the three instruments may be used to yield results that relate these measured dimensions to clustered career exploration.

Although the COPSystem instruments are administered and interpreted in a group setting, they do not eliminate the need for individual counseling. They are helpful tools for the counselor to guide the examinee in the most productive avenue for the client.

SAMPLE CASE STUDIES

Following are two case studies that are illustrative of the interpretive usefulness of the COPSystem instruments. The COPSystem is effective as a base for communication between the counselor and client. The results are indicators of areas and occupations that the client should explore.

Sample Case: Roger Wu

Roger is a 15-year-old high school sophomore who is enrolled in a career exploration unit as part of his high school curriculum. He has completed the machine scoring version of the COPS, CAPS and COPES as part of the career unit in his English class, and his results are presented in Figure 9.1. His career counselor has brought him in for an individual counseling session to explain the results of the COPSystem. At the meeting, Roger told the career counselor that he wants to be a disc jockey.

In examining his COPSystem results, it can be seen that his three highest interest scores are Communication, Business Professional, and Science Professional, with percentile scores of 95, 89, and 88, respectively. His interest scores are consistent with his desire to be a radio announcer.

However, his ability profile does not match the COPS profile. On the CAPS Career Profile, Roger's probability of success in terms of ability is highest in the clusters of Consumer Economics, Outdoor, Technology Skilled, Service Skilled, Arts Skilled, Science Skilled, Clerical and Business Skilled. Although his percentile scores on the CAPS Career Profile are somewhat low, his scores are still above the printed shaded area on the profile. For example, Roger's ability score in the Business Skilled cluster is at the 20th percentile (percentiles are printed to the left of the cluster title), but his score is above the printed shaded area. The shaded areas are indicators that an individual has a high enough ability level at this time for probable success, if the score obtained is at the top or above this shaded area. If Roger wants to explore the remaining clusters, where his scores fall in the shaded area of the profile, he will probably need to consider ways to improve his ability.

Examination of the CAPS Ability Profile indicates his specific areas of weakness. He has moderate to high scores on all but three of the ability tests. He is in the bottom third of the distribution on Verbal Reasoning (stanine 2), Language Usage (stanine 1), and Word Knowledge (stanine 2). He would thus, seem to have some difficulty in the language areas which might cause problems if he pursues the career of a radio announcer.

His COPES values indicate that he has high values in Orderliness, Practical, Recognition, and Aesthetic. These values seem to indicate that radio announcing meets his value needs. The orderly and practical side allow him to be neat and efficient. He wants to become well-known and appreciates music and the arts, both of which are consistent with his occupational interest.

The Summary section of the printout summarizes Roger's interests, abilities, and values. As can be seen, there is an inconsistency in the profile. In two of the areas, his interests and values match (Business Professional and Communication). However, none of his interests coupled with values correspond to his abilities. The discrepancy is made evident by returning to the CAPS profile. His language skills indicate weakness; language is important to both of these clusters. The career counselor, while interviewing Roger, asks why Roger thinks the CAPS language scores are low and is informed that English is a second language in Roger's home.

There are several options that Roger has, although it is immediately apparent that he should improve his English skills. Private tutoring and additional high school classes should be of help. It is also possible that Roger may become a DJ in his native language, since in large cities there are often many different language stations. He might also consider work in the technical area of radio broadcasting, perhaps becoming a technician as he has a fairly high degree of interest in both Science and Technology. He might do well as a copywriter if his writing skills improve.

After discussing the summary with his counselor, Roger has made some decisions as to immediate steps to be taken to help him reach his future goals. Because Roger is still in high school and has very little work experience, he plans to do further occupational research. He plans to explore careers in the Communication, Business Professional, and Science areas by examining the cluster descriptions and occupational titles on the profile sheet. Roger and his career counselor are planning to outline a high school program with an emphasis on improving language skills. He has been encouraged by the career counselor to get tutoring and to enroll in the journalism class offered at school. Roger has time in his coming high school years to explore a course of study related to occupations which interest him. He now has a better conceptualization of his interests and values as well as areas of strengths and weaknesses.

Sample Case: Kyla Jones

Kyla is a college sophomore who has come to the career counseling center and has indicate that she is uncertain about choosing a college major. She has been encouraged by her parents to pursue a science major, but she feels very uncertain about a particular vocational goal. The COPS-P is usually used for college students when selecting college majors, but Kyla is so uncertain about her professional goals that the career counselor decided to give her the COPS, which will allow her to consider both Professional and Skilled level occupations. At this point in her education, she has completed much of the basic required course work but now wants to know if she should stay in college and continue to seriously consider a science major. Examination of her COPS profile (see Figure 9.2) shows that her three highest interest areas are Service Professional, Business Professional, and Communication, with percentile scores of 93, 90 and 87, respectively. Kyla is guided to explore these three areas.

She has also completed the CAPS ability battery. Scores on the eight tests indicate that she would probably succeed in terms of ability in the following areas where her scores fall into the white or at the top of the lightest shaded

CAREER OCCUPATIONAL PREFERENCE SYSTEM (COPSYSTEM) SUMMARY

ROGER WU   057663913   GR.10

YOU ARE INTERESTED IN AN OCCUPATIONAL TRAINING COURSE AND NEED HELP IN: READING, LANGUAGE, CAREER PLANNING, APPLYING TO A COLLEGE, FINANCIAL ASSISTANCE, FINDING JOB INFORMATION, FINDING A JOB,

SECTION I INTERESTS (COPS)

YOU HAVE RECENTLY COMPLETED THE COPSYSTEM INVENTORIES.
YOUR HIGHEST INTEREST CAREER GROUPS ARE:

COMMUNICATION
BUSINESS PROFESSIONAL
SCIENCE PROFESSIONAL

Your interest profile is plotted below. A percentile number is printed at the end of the row of x's. Each number shows your approximate position on each scale as compared to other people at your educational level who have taken the COPS. If your score is near 50, about half (50%) of others fall below you. The higher your score the greater your interest is compared to others.

COPS INTEREST INVENTORY PROFILE

PERCENTILE SCORES
LOW (20–30)   AVERAGE (40–60)   HIGH (70)
10   20   30   40   50   60   70   80   90

SCIENCE PROFESSIONAL	88
SCIENCE SKILLED	63
TECHNOLOGY PROFESSIONAL	75
TECHNOLOGY SKILLED	32
CONSUMER ECONOMICS	52
OUTDOOR	60
BUSINESS PROFESSIONAL	89
BUSINESS SKILLED	68
CLERICAL	75
COMMUNICATION	95
ARTS PROFESSIONAL	68
ARTS SKILLED	52
SERVICE PROFESSIONAL	55
SERVICE SKILLED	40

SECTION II ABILITIES (CAPS)

Your score is marked with a plus if it is in the white portion or in the lightest shaded portion of each career group. These are groups in which you have measured abilities indicating a high enough level at this point in your career for probable success. Remember, for success it is necessary that you continue to get the training and skills needed in these groups.

In interpreting your profile, concentrate on the distance of your scores from the dark shaded area. Peaks in the profile may not be significant because the shaded areas are different heights. Consider whether other things you know about yourself are consistent with your profile.

In groups where your ability scores are in the dark portion of the career profile, but your interest and motivation are high, you may wish to take related courses of study needed to improve your skills. Your COPSystem Comprehensive Career Guide will help you in these choices.

CAPS CAREER PROFILE

20 SCIENCE PROFESSIONAL
+58 SCIENCE SKILLED
15 TECHNOLOGY PROFESSIONAL
+60 TECHNOLOGY SKILLED
+82 CONSUMER ECONOMICS
+66 OUTDOOR
16 BUSINESS PROFESSIONAL
+20 BUSINESS SKILLED
+38 CLERICAL
15 COMMUNICATION
32 ARTS PROFESSIONAL
+85 ARTS SKILLED
3 SERVICE PROFESSIONAL
+58 SERVICE SKILLED

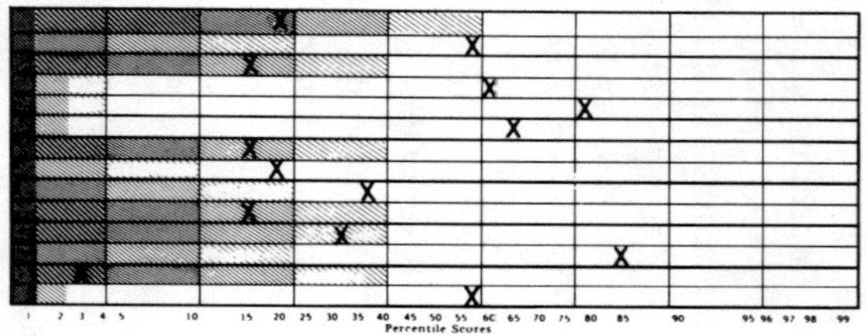

YOUR SEPARATE ABILITY SCORES ARE PLOTTED BELOW.

CAPS ABILITY PROFILE

```
                                                STANINE SCORES
                                   LOW              AVERAGE              HIGH
                          1      2      3      4      5      6      7      8      9

MECHANICAL REASONING      .      .      XXXXXXXXXXX-XXXXXXXXXXX    .      .      .
SPATIAL RELATIONS         .      .      .      .      XXXXXXXXXXX-XXXXXXXXXXX    .
VERBAL REASONING          XXXXXXXXXXX-XXXXXXXXXXX     .      .      .      .      .
NUMERICAL ABILITY         .      .      XXXXXXXXXXX-XXXXXXXXXXX    .      .      .
LANGUAGE USAGE            -XXXXXXXXXXX  .      .      .      .      .      .
WORD KNOWLEDGE            XXXXXXXXXXX-XXXXXXXXXXX     .      .      .      .      .
PERCEPTUAL SPEED AND ACCURACY .  .      .      .      .      .      XXXXXXXXXXX-XXXXXXXXXXX
MANUAL SPEED AND DEXTERITY .     .      .      .      .      XXXXXXXXXXX-XXXXXXXXXXX
                               10    20    30   40   50   60   70    80    90
                                            PERCENTILE SCORES
```

- **Mechanical Reasoning** measures how well a person can understand mechanical principles.
- **Spatial Relations** measures how well a person can visualize or think in three dimensions.
- **Verbal Reasoning** measures how well a person can reason with words.
- **Numerical Ability** measures how well a person can reason with and use numbers.
- **Language Usage** measures how well a person can recognize and use standard English grammar and punctuation.
- **Word Knowledge** measures how well a person can understand the meaning and precise use of words.
- **Perceptual Speed and Accuracy** measures how well a person perceives small detail rapidly and accurately.
- **Manual Speed and Dexterity** measures how well a person can make rapid and accurate hand movements.

Those scores marked as a line of x's show your abilites compared to others at your educational level. Scores extend from the ***middle*** of the score and do not represent a single point. If your score is near the 50th percentile score, about half (50%) of others fall below you. The higher your score, the greater your ability. See your Comprehensive Career Guide for a further description of your results.

SECTION III WORK VALUES (COPES)

COPES WORK VALUES PROFILE

```
                              -  -  -  -  50  -  -  -  -
ACCEPTING      ............................XXXXXXXX-XXXXXXXX........................................ INVESTIGATIVE
CAREFREE       ..........................................  ..........XXXXXXXX-XXXXXXXX............. PRACTICAL
CONFORMITY     ...................XXXXXXXX-XXXXXXXX.....  ........................................ INDEPENDENCE
SUPPORTIVE     .......................................XXXXXXXX-XXXXXXXX............................. LEADERSHIP
NONCOMPULSIVE  ..........................................  ..................XXXXXXXX-XXXXXXXX...... ORDERLINESS
PRIVACY        ..........................................  .......XXXXXXXX-XXXXXXXX.................. RECOGNITION
REALISTIC      ..........................................  .......XXXXXXXX-XXXXXXXX.................. AESTHETIC
SELF-CONCERN   .....................XXXXXXXX-XXXXXXXX...  ........................................ SOCIAL
                                                CENTER
```

Those scores marked as a line of x's show your work values as compared to others who have taken the COPES. Scores falling to the left of center show strength in values described on the left, scores to the right of center show strength in those values given on the right. See your COPSystem Comprehensive Career Guide for a description of these values.

SUMMARY

Those career groups below where your (1) interest, (2) abilities, and (3) values have +'s show you the groups you may wish to explore. First consider those groups where your interests, abilities, and values are high and all three marked with a plus. Next, consider those groups where your interests and abilities are both marked with a plus. Your COPSystem Comprehensive Career Guide will help you in your career exploration.

1 INT	2 AB	3 VAL	Career group
+			SCIENCE PROFESSIONAL Planning and conducting research in math, medical, life and physical sciences.
	+	+	SCIENCE SKILLED Observing and classifying facts in assisting with laboratory research.
		+	TECHNOLOGY PROFESSIONAL Engineering and structural design in the manufacture, construction or transportation of products.
	+	+	TECHNOLOGY SKILLED - Working with one's hands in the skilled trades of construction, installation, repair and manufacturing.
	+	+	CONSUMER ECONOMICS Preparation and packaging of foods, making and care of clothing and textile products.
	+	+	OUTDOOR Activities performed primarily out of doors such as growing and tending plants and animals.
+		+	BUSINESS PROFESSIONAL Positions of high responsibility in organization and administration of business.
	+	+	BUSINESS SKILLED - Sales promotion, marketing and finance in regard to promotion of business.
	+	+	CLERICAL Recording, posting and filing business records with attention to detail, accuracy and speed.
+		+	COMMUNICATIONS Language skill in the written and oral communication of knowledge and ideas.
		+	ARTS PROFESSIONAL Individualized expression of creative or musical talent.
	+	+	ARTS SKILLED - Application of artistic skill in photography, graphic arts and design.
			SERVICE PROFESSIONAL Positions of high responsibility in caring for the personal needs and welfare of others, such as teacher or social worker.
	+	+	SERVICE SKILLED - Providing services to persons and catering to the tastes, desires and welfare of others; examples are flight attendant or taxi driver.

FIG. 9.1. Roger Wu

portion of the profile: Science Skilled, Technology Professional, Technology Skilled, Consumer Economics, Outdoor, Business Professional, Business Skilled, Clerical, Communication, Service Professional, and Service Skilled. In examining the CAPS Career Profile, it is important to focus not only on the scores in the white portion of the profile, but also on the distance from the dark shaded portions to the obtained score. For example, the results indicate a prediction of success, in terms of the measured abilities at a higher probability level for a Service Skilled career than in a career in the Science Skilled cluster, even though the percentile scores are similar in these two career areas. This is because her abilities relating to most Service Skilled professions are considerably greater than the level generally demanded in that cluster (the latter level being defined by the shaded area on the profile.)

The next step in interpreting the CAPS battery is to examine the individual scores from each test. Based on the examination of her stanine scores, her CAPS Ability Profile shows that she is average to strong in Verbal Reasoning, Language Usage, Word Knowledge, and Numerical Ability. Her Mechanical Reasoning and Perceptual Speed and Accuracy are in the mid to low range with Spatial Relations and Manual Speed and Dexterity low. However, considering that her three highest interest areas were Service Professional, Business Professional, and Communication, it is predicted that she will do satisfactorily in terms of ability in those three occupational clusters. Her strong abilities are thus most consistent with her three highest interest areas. However, should she still wish to consider a science career, in which her ability scores fell into the shaded areas, she may need to consider remedial course work or select science careers that require little mechanical reasoning or spatial ability.

Kyla's COPES scores indicate that her three highest value areas are Social, Leadership, and Investigative. She values helping others, working with people and she is not a "loner." Making decisions and directing others are also of importance. Intellectual curiosity and need for information are important to her. She does not need to see practical concrete results in every situation she faces.

In the examination of the complete summary profile, Kyla has best agreement in interest, ability, and value scores for the clusters of Business Professional and Service Professional. In the Service Professional cluster, she might want to consider occupations such as psychologist or counselor, perhaps in private practice, to use her interest, ability, and value in the business area. She also might consider teaching, maybe at a high school or even the university level, as this will match her desire to help and guide individuals and might additionally give her an arena in which to do scientific work which will satisfy her Investigative value and moderate interest in Science. Her ability, however, is not clearly confirmed in this latter area. Teaching is consistent with her interest in Communication and Service and also will be consistent with her high verbal language abilities. In either of these occupations she should do well, if she continues to get the necessary educational training.

The counselor should be able to suggest a course of study in line with her high interest areas that will help her set her goals. This profile should be a confirmation to Kyla to strongly question a science major or a heavy course load of science classes. Kyla might go back to the COPS booklet and circle some of the items that she marked as "(L) Like very much" as they should indicate the specific job activities that most appeal to her. She might then begin to explore these occupations, map out a plan for college, and then declare a college major. It might be of help to Kyla to return to the career counselor at the end of her junior year for follow-up and to take the COPS-P to help pinpoint her educational and occupational goals.

RESEARCH ON THE COPSystem

Reliability and validity of the COPS, CAPS, and COPES will be summarized below. More in-depth information may be found in the Technical Manuals for each of these instruments.

Reliability: COPS

Reliability may be defined as the consistency with which a test measures what it purports to measure. Reliability is an important characteristic, especially for tests designed for use in individual guidance.

Alpha and Test-Retest Reliability

Indices of reliability of the COPS *Interest Inventory,* 1982 Edition, have been determined in terms of alpha coefficients and test-retest data. Alpha reliability coefficients range in magnitude from .86 to .91 and demonstrate the high degree of internal consistency of the scales. Test-retest reliability was established by administering the Inventory twice to a sample of 97 10th-grade students with a 1-week interval and ranged from .80 to .91, which is considered to further demonstrate the high reliability of the Inventory. These reliability coefficients compare favorably with those of other instruments and are not statistically different than reliabilities reported for other basic interest scales.

Long-Term Reliability

Further evidence concerning the reliability of the COPS structure is reflected in the analysis of changes in interests. To examine the nature of changes in major clusters of interests measured in one school year as compared with those obtained in the succeeding school year, Knapp, Knapp, and Buttafuoco (1978) analyzed profiles for 1,243 students tested in grades 7 through 12 for whom test-retest scores were available from successive school years.

After completing Units (2) and (3) copy your CAPS scores below for your files.

CAPS CAREER PROFILE

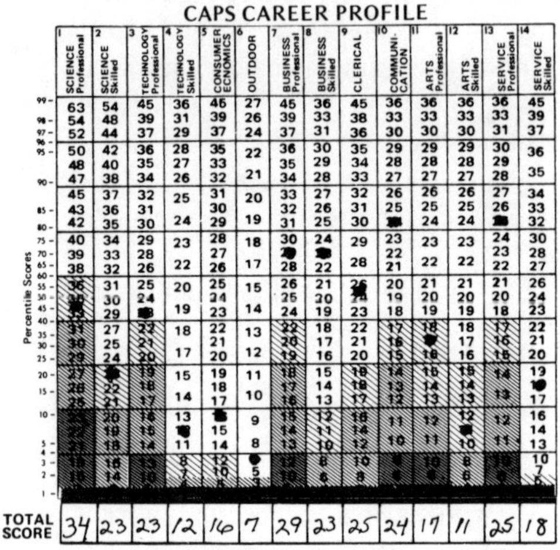

CAPS ABILITY PROFILE

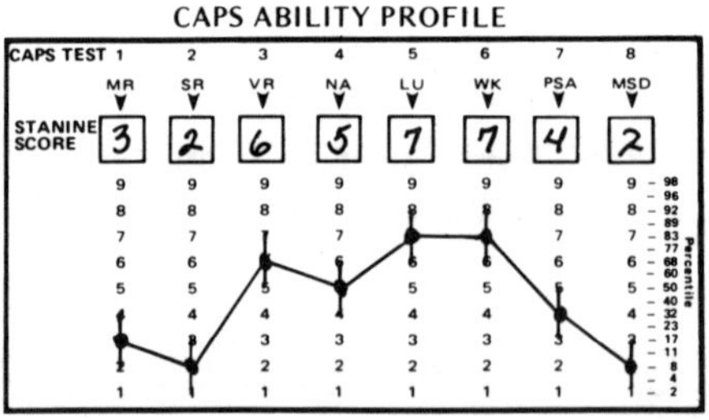

Copy your COPES scores from page 4.

COPES PROFILE OF WORK VALUES

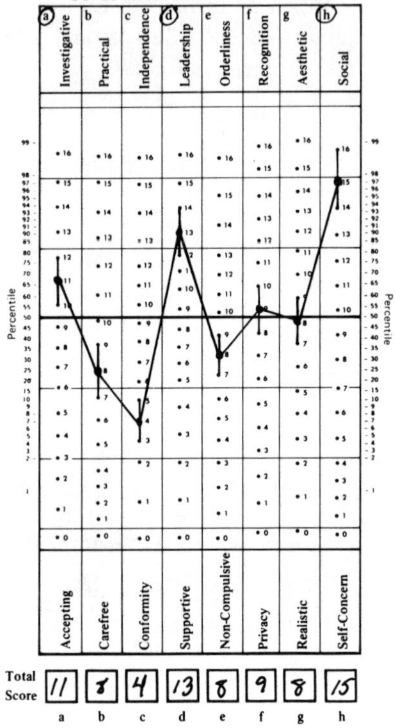

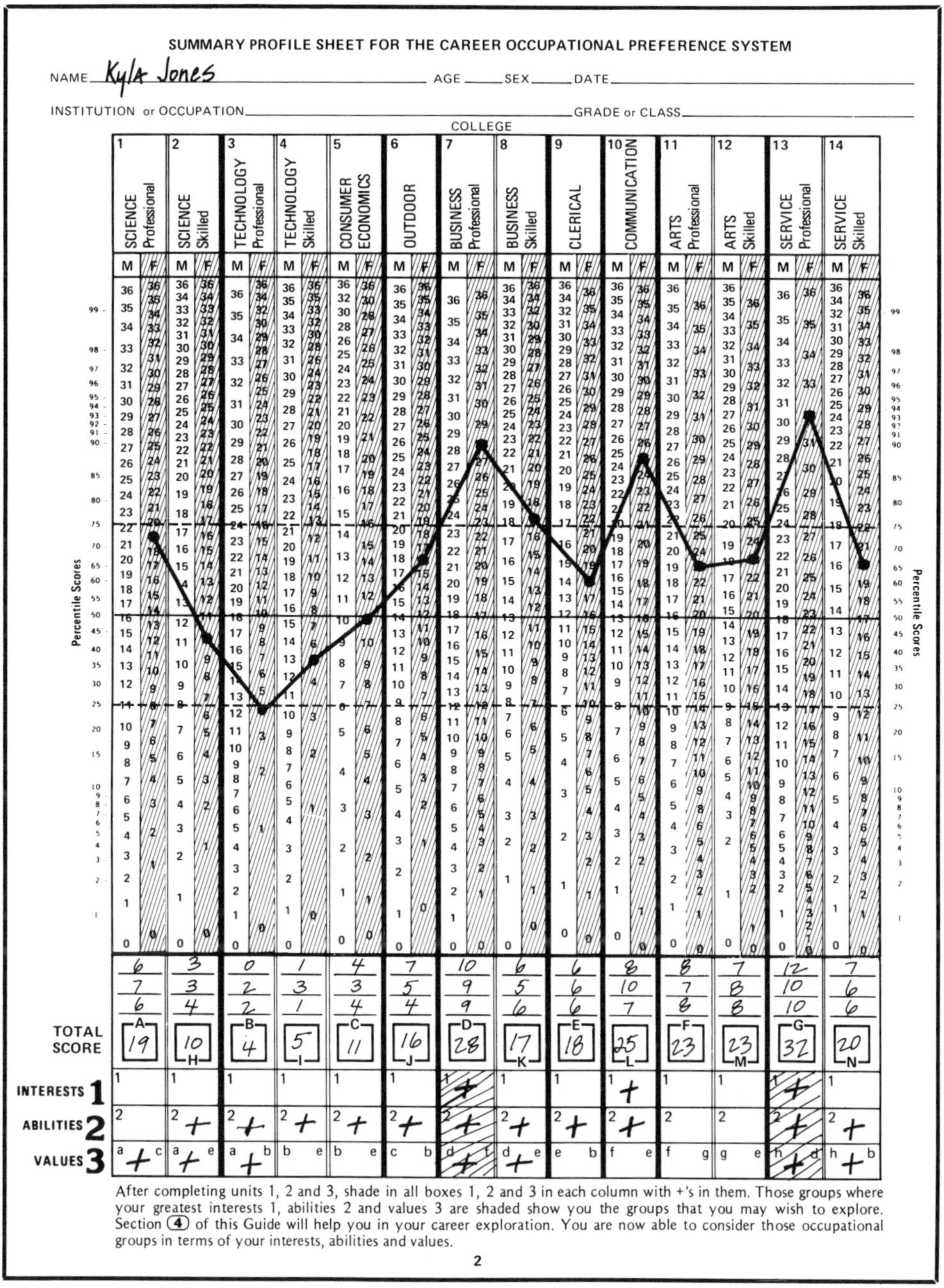

FIG. 9.2. Kyla Jones

Profiles for each student were plotted against the national norms for both administrations of the Interest Inventory and frequencies were plotted for 1st- and 2nd-year peaks (cluster of greatest interest). In comparing 1st-year administration with 2nd-year administration, 565 (45%) of the students had the same highest interest cluster for the two successive years. When the first and second areas of greatest interest are considered, over three-fourths (nearly 80%) of the students had one of their two highest interest areas in common over the period of a year. When the top three areas are suggested for consideration, as is recommended for use in the COPSystem for career exploration, virtually all students (93%) will be considering occupations in those clusters which will still be of greatest interest to them over long periods of time. These data illustrate the effectiveness for most individuals in the clustered career exploration approach for delineating a specific spectrum of the world of work for more detailed exploration.

Reliability: CAPS

To maximize the time effectiveness of a battery, it is far more efficient to provide several unique, short measures than to have a few very long measures. Thus, the trend in modern testing theory is reflected in the CAPS battery, which is composed of many short tests. As Ruch and Ruch (1963) have suggested, it is more efficient to add unique new tests to a battery than to increase the length of the most valid one.

Theoretical and empirical evidence has demonstrated that individual tests in a battery may be considerably shortened without resulting in a serious decrease in the composite validity of the battery. Brokaw (1951) compared the validity of a battery of six predictor tests of different lengths against grades in Aircraft and Engine Mechanics School. Each test was split in half so that validities could be obtained based on full-length and half-length tests. Reliabilities of the full-length tests ranged from .80 to .90 and dropped to .69 to .79 for the half-length tests. The composite validity for the full-length test battery was .57, whereas validities for the half-length tests were .55 for the first half battery and .56 for the second half battery, leading the author to conclude, "previous belief in the necessity for using quite long tests is unfounded when the tests are to be used in a battery." Thus, while increasing *time effectiveness* by shortening the lengths of a number of tests in a battery results in a moderate loss of reliability, it is possible to effect considerable saving of testing time without significant loss of validity.

As Guilford and Fruchter (1973, p. 42) have pointed out, knowing the reliability of a short test makes it possible to determine how long a test would have to be to attain any desired level of reliability simply by using the Spearman-Brown formula in reverse. Thus, based on a 5-minute test with a reliability of .70, doubling testing time to 10 minutes increases reliability only .12 to .82. It should be noted that increases in reliability are also negatively accelerated as a function of test length.

A number of methods are available for estimating test reliability. Because of the highly "speeded" nature of some CAPS tests, wherein many examinees do not complete each test, the split-half method of estimating test reliability is inappropriate. However, it is of interest to note the split-half reliability for the first 6 tests where the speeded nature of the tests is secondary. The coefficients ranged from .76 to .95.

Test-retest reliability coefficients were based on a sample of high school students tested 2 weeks apart. Coefficients ranged from .70 to .95, which may be considered to be further evidence for the high reliability of the CAPS tests. However, test-retest reliability for certain tests may not be the most appropriate index.

In the process of test development, parallel forms of the CAPS tests were utilized. Correlations ranged from .70 to .89 between alternate forms, which were considered promising and well within acceptable ranges based on reported coefficients for available aptitude tests (most of which are of considerably greater length).

Reliability: COPES

To examine the internal consistency of COPES scale scores, alpha reliability estimates were obtained for 2 different samples. Coefficients ranged from .67 to .82, which are considered to represent an acceptable level of reliability commensurate with other values inventories.

Validity: COPS

Evidence of validity, the extent to which an instrument measures what it purports to measure, is available for the COPS, CAPS and COPES in a number of forms. Internal validation techniques concerned with the item content, stability, and factorial structure of the inventories define what the instrument measures. External validation techniques, including correlations with other instruments and relationships to criteria, such as college major choice and occupational choice, provide further evidence of construct validity.

Factorial Validity/Construct Validity

A major source of validity information for the COPS is represented in the extensive factorial data upon which development of the COPS is based. The evidence for factorial validity, a form of construct validity for the structure of the COPSystem clusters and COPS item data, has been previously presented. However, to examine individual item loadings on the 14 scales, a series of clustran item factor analyses was undertaken. Using this technique, the items written to reflect job activities of the occupations in each of the 14 COPSystem clusters were submitted as variables in the factor analysis. For the analysis, each item was hypothesized as belonging to its respective cluster. The factor loadings showed that each item was more highly related to the cluster hypothesized than to any other cluster. Thus, the item "Perform chemical and microscopic tests to determine the causes of disease," has its highest loading (.56) on Factor 1, Science Professional, while "Test urine and make blood counts" is most heavily loaded (.51) on the Science Skilled factor.

The data from the clustran factor analyses confirmed the hypothesized content of each activity item and supported the 14 cluster scales presented in the COPS *Interest Inventory.*

The circularity of the clusters may be used to demonstrate the structure of the interest clusters. In order to statistically test the hypothesis of order (presented on the profile) of the major COPSystem groupings derived from Roe's major groupings, it was necessary to combine the levels within each major area. When combined in this manner and following the procedure used by Roe, Hubbard, Hutchinson, and Bateman (1966), a change from any area to one adjacent to it on either side, such as from 2 to 1 or from 2 to 3, is a 1-step change. A 4-step change is the largest possible for eight areas, such as from area 1 to area 5, or vice versa. The frequency for each step fell in descending order. A test for goodness of fit yielded a chi-square of 25.0, significant beyond the .01 level, indicating that the observed frequencies were not random.

Another requirement for circularity is that shifting should be as likely in one direction as another. Moves from 3 to 2, for example, should be as likely as from 3 to 4. A test of goodness of fit for these data yielded a chi-square value of 5.23, which is not significant. Thus, frequency of change in major areas of interest in one direction is not significantly different from changes in the other direction.

Analysis of data demonstrated that classification and changes with these classifications based on the COPSystem are not random, but are consistent with the model of occupational structure upon which the system is based.

Concurrent Validity: Relationship of the COPS to Similar Instruments

Correlations of inventories, such as the COPS *Interest Inventory,* with other similar inventories provide information concerning the construct validity of the instruments. In particular, in the case of the COPS, correlations with the other interest inventories in the COPSystem series are useful in evaluating validity of the constructs measured by these instruments. The correlation between scales of the COPS and the corresponding scales of the COPS-R, based on a sample of 284 high school students, ranged from .61 to .78 and were held to be of sufficiently high magnitude to support the construct validity of the dimensions measured. To determine the relationship of the COPS to the COPS-P scales, correlations were computed between the inventories based on the responses of 205 entering college freshmen. Correlations between the conceptually similar scales of the COPS-P and the COPS Professional level scales ranged from .70 to .93 with a median correlation of .84. As might be expected, in every instance, the COPS-P scale was more highly correlated to the corresponding COPS Professional level scale than the Skilled level scale.

Relationship of the COPS to the Kuder *General Interest Survey* (GIS) (Kuder, 1975) has been reported based on adult and grade school student samples. Savage (1976, personal communication) reported correlations based on a sample of 57 adult females. As would be expected, correlations were highest between the correspondingly named scales of these instruments. These correlations generally ranged between .5 and .7.

In another study comparing the Kuder GIS with the COPS, Best & Knapp-Lee (1982) reported results based on a sample of 177 unselected 8th-grade students. Similar scales on the two instruments were compared in terms of correlations between the scales. The pattern of correlation wherein the magnitude of positive correlation was higher between conceptually similar scales than between any other scales in the array again provides construct validity for these scales.

As Kuder (1969) has suggested, comparison of the agreement of two interest inventories should be based on the extent to which they lead to similar results in counseling. To examine this, profiles were plotted for each inventory and the three highest areas of interest identified for each subject on both instruments. Results of this analysis indicate that among a sample of 8th-grade students, 25% would be directed to the same top three interest areas for further exploration and 89% would find at least one of their top three interest areas congruent, based on measurement of the two instruments.

Concurrent Validity: Relationship to the Choice of College Major

To examine the validity of the COPS in regard to the choice of college majors made by students, a study was undertaken to determine the relationship between the declared major of entering college freshmen and their measured interests (Knapp, Knapp, & Michael, 1979). The sample consisted of 366 entering college freshmen who took the COPS and who had declared their major. The cluster representing declared major and the peak measured interest clusters were determined for each student. A test of goodness of fit for these clusters gave chi-squares which were significant at the .01 level in all cases. When the three highest interest groups were examined, 71% of the students would have had a correct prediction of the cluster containing their declared major. Analyses of data demonstrate that measured occupational interest clusters are meaningfully related to, and thus predictive of, declared college major upon entry to college.

Predictive Validity, Longitudinal Research

An issue of concern to counselors involves the degree to which a measurement instrument directs individuals to examine occupations in clusters for which they seek training and from which they eventually choose jobs.

To determine the extent to which interpretation of the COPS results directs individuals to explore occupations for which further training or job entry is selected, a follow-up study was initiated based on inventory results obtained between 1974 and 1980.

A follow-up questionnaire was sent to each student from the participating schools for whom COPS scores were available. The follow-up questionnaire included questions about current educational and occupational status. Questions covered present employment and past employment (including job description and title), job satisfaction, colleges attended, major courses of study and future occupational goals.

Of the 1,091 individuals included in the analysis for whom data were available, 660 (61%) were in educational programs or jobs representing occupational clusters consistent with their prior measured interests. When analyzed by sex, 319 of 479 (67%) of the males had jobs or college majors consistent with their prior measured interests and were categorized as hits, and 341 of 612 (56%) of the females were classified as hits. When analyzed by grade in which the students were administered the inventory, 354 of 623 (57%) of the 10th graders had jobs or college majors consistent with their prior measured interests and were classified as hits, 223 of 330 (68%) 11th graders were hits and 83 (60%) of 138 12th graders were hits. Analyses of the data demonstrate that when the COPS was administered during the high school years, the majority of students are correctly directed in their job search to those clusters representing their job or educational goal 2 to 6 years later (Knapp, Knapp, & Knapp-Lee, 1985).

Validity: CAPS

Internal validation techniques concerned with item content, stability, and intercorrelations of the tests define the structure of the CAPS battery. External validation techniques including correlations with other instruments and relationships to criteria such as course grades, vocational course choice, and predictive validity in terms of occupational choice provide further evidence of the construct validity of the CAPS.

Concurrent Validity: Relationship of the CAPS to Similar Instruments

Correlations of the CAPS tests with the *Differential Aptitude Tests* (Bennett, Seashore, & Wesman, 1974) have been obtained for a number of samples (Knapp, Knapp, & Michael, 1977). Illustrative of this are the correlations based on a sample of 160 10th-grade students, in which conceptually similar tests correlations ranged from .47 to .77 and provided evidence of the validity of the CAPS tests.

Correlations of CAPS tests against conceptually similar tests in the *General Aptitude Test Battery* (GATB) (U.S. Employment Service, 1973) provide further evidence of construct validity for these tests (Knapp, Knapp, Strnad, & Michael, 1978). The CAPS Word Knowledge test, which is conceptually the most similar to measures provided by the GATB Verbal Aptitude (vocabulary) subtest, correlated .80 with the GATB. The CAPS Numerical Ability test correlated .67 with the GATB. Correlations between the CAPS Spatial Relations and Perceptual Speed and Accuracy tests and the corresponding tests in the GATB were .63 and .70, respectively.

Correlations between the CAPS tests and the conceptually similar tests of the *Iowa Tests of Educational Development* are in the .70's, which further supports the contention that the CAPS measures abilities important to achievement in various areas.

The CAPS tests were correlated with the *Metropolitan Achievement Tests* (MAT) (Durost, Bixler, Wrightstone, Hildreth, & Lund, 1970) in an 8th-grade sample of 105 students. The correlations of conceptually similar tests ranged from .51 between CAPS Numerical Ability and MAT Total Math to .74 between CAPS Word Knowledge and MAT Total Reading.

Predictive Validity: Relationship to School Marks

Correlation against marks arc presented in the CAPS *Technical Manual.* Generally, the patterns of correlations within particular curriculum areas are consistent with theoretical expectations. In general, Industrial Art classes are significantly related to Mechanical Reasoning with significant correlations ranging from .35 to .63. Also, as would be predicted, Spatial Relations and Manual Speed and Dexterity are, in most instances, significantly related to these courses.

The highest correlations with English marks are against Language Usage and Word Knowledge, as would be expected. Marks in virtually every class are significantly correlated to these two tests in differing degrees. Similarly, marks in math classes are significantly related to Numerical Ability with the exception of the geometry course, which places emphasis on logical proof of theorems. Verbal Reasoning was most highly correlated with geometry classes. Marks in typing classes in most of the schools are significantly correlated with either Perceptual Speed and Accuracy or Manual Speed and Dexterity.

School marks in classes which provide training for many jobs in a given CAPS career cluster, may be used to provide validity criteria for the combined CAPS Career Cluster scores. To examine validity of these scores, correlations were computed against school marks. The resulting relationship of course marks to CAPS career scores supported the predictive validity of the instrument, since high correlations were found between school subjects related to their associated career cluster.

To further examine the predictive validity of the CAPS ability profile, a follow-up study is being conducted on a sample of 2,093 9th- through 12th graders who have graduated from high school, have taken the CAPS in 1979, 1980, and 1981 and for whom home addresses area available. In summarizing the results, a hit was defined as correspondence of a college goal (or the present job, if no college attendance was indicated) with a CAPS career area designated by the subjects' CAPS scores. By chance, a 71% hit rate would be expected. However, the hit rate in this sample was 97%. Although this follow-up study is not complete, it does, at this point, provide evidence for the predictive validity of the CAPS scores.

Validity: COPES

The concept of the effectiveness of using separate measures for the interests and the values domains has received empirical support. For example, Pryor and Taylor (1986) found that when separate measures of values and interests are combined, they provide more information relevant to course choice than each one does separately.

To provide evidence concerning the relationship between measures of the domains of interests and values, a study was conducted by Knapp and Knapp (1979) in which scores obtained from the COPES work values instrument were correlated with occupational activity interests as measured by the COPS. Coefficients ranged in magnitude from .0 to .47. Although correlations between the theoretically similar scales of the COPS and the COPES work values scale are sufficiently low so as to justify use of both instruments, the pattern of greatest magnitude generally is theoretically consistent. These correlations are consistent with the majority of previous studies, which show a generally low order of relationship between measures of the values and of the interest domains. The present results are thus consistent with the concept that it is feasible and desirable to utilize independent measures of the concepts in these two domains.

Evidence of construct validity for dimensions measured by the COPES has been presented in terms of the factor structure in the COPES items. Other evidence of construct validity is available based on correlations with other instruments. Correlations of the COPES with values dimensions presented by Guilford, Christensen, and Bond (1956) and by Allport and Vernon (1970) between like-named, conceptually similar scales are significant and of moderate to high magnitude, thus providing evidence for construct validity of the scales.

In the high school situation, it is interesting to examine the relationship between work values and school achievement, as classes in school can be considered miniature work situations. Subject matter classes correspond to jobs representing occupational clusters. For example, performance in an English class might be considered comparable to performance on a job in the communication area. It is assumed that individuals who do well in scientific laboratory courses will be successful in jobs in the Science area. A study (Knapp & Michael, 1980) was conducted to examine the relationship between work values and academic success in the following courses, which had been shown to be related to performance in actual work situations: Science, English, Social Studies, Arts, Industrial Arts and Typing. These data presented for representative samples of students and vocational groups provide evidence of the validity of the COPES values used in interpreting inventory results in career guidance.

To examine the predictive validity of the COPES work values profile, a follow-up study is being conducted on a sample of 9th through 12th graders who have graduated from high school and had taken the COPES in 1979, 1980, and 1981. The results of a questionnaire requesting the job now held or the course of study now being pursued was analyzed for the 267 students who replied to an initial mailing. Based on this preliminary sample who replied to the questionnaire, 238 (89%) were categorized as hits. By chance, a 64% hit rate would be expected. This preliminary analysis does provide evidence for the predictive validity of the COPES scores in terms of the COPSystem occupational clusters.

EVALUATION AND FUTURE DIRECTIONS FOR THE COPSystem

A primary principle guiding the development of the battery of instruments represented in the COPSystem is to provide the maximum degree of validity per unit of testing time. The COPSystem instruments have been established through extensive theoretical and factor analytic research. The sound theoretical basis with statistical support lends confidence to the counseling usefulness of the instruments.

There is a continual need for the updating and validation of the instruments, as is the case for all measurement instruments. Longitudinal validity studies of the instruments are continuing, and results will be presented as more data become available. In addition to following up examinees to determine if their occupations correspond to their scores on the COPS, CAPS and COPES instruments, research needs to be conducted in terms of concurrent validity. That the COPSystem compares favorably to similar instruments provides substantial concurrent validity support. The COPS Interest Inventory has been correlated to numerous instruments measuring similar concepts, and results support the validity of the COPS scales.

Research into values or the type and level of ability required within specific occupational clusters could be further enhanced by additional studies. CAPS ability tests have been firmly established by past research, but perhaps future studies will yield more specifics on the level of ability required within an occupation. Evidence for the structure of work values is of extreme importance, because it is clear that values are crucial in the career decision-making process. It is impossible to pinpoint all the value aspects that go into making career decisions, yet the COPES contributes to this understanding. Following up more individuals that have completed the COPES and possibly expanding the range of values measured in order to establish the congruence of values and career choice, will be useful.

The COPSystem is valuable in the career counseling process because it is a complete battery of coordinated instruments well established through research, all related to a proven structure of occupations and of very practical relevance to the client and counselor. That the COPS interests, CAPS abilities, and COPES values are time effective and interpreted in terms of clusters of occupations, further enhances the counseling usefulness. Both the self-scoring and machine-scoring options add flexibility for the counselor while yielding the same interpretive information for the examinee. The instruments may also be used individually if some aspects have been previously measured, or if particular measurement aspects are not necessary. Self-scoring for immediate feedback is a major advantage.

The comprehensive measuring of the individual facilitates the counseling process. The measurement of interests, abilities, and values allows both counselor and examinee to interact in a knowledgeable manner about occupational options. Results are presented in such a way to clarify structure and initially expand options rather than immediately presenting the choice of only one or two occupational options. The client may use the inventory results to move forward in a positive direction toward the best suited career goals. The interpretation material accompanying any one or all three of the measurement dimensions is an exceptional strength of the COPSystem. The career decision-making process is thus enhanced by extensive meaningful decision-making exercises that accompany the measurement instruments.

In years hence, the goal is to continue the development and counseling usefulness of the COPSystem. Data will be submitted to factor analysis to reconfirm the cluster of occupations. Just as career exploration is an ongoing changing process, so is the process of test validation and refinement. It may be that the changing world of work will affect the structuring of occupations in terms of interests, abilities, and values. Perhaps the decline in interest in some outdoor occupations will increase, and the now glamorous computer field will continue to sway more interest into computer technology. Factor analyses of items in the development of the COPS-P tend to support this later trend. It may be the case that the gender gap may close, however preliminary new data indicate that this is not happening in all career areas. The 1988 norms revision for the COPS indicates a decline in interest for both males and females in the outdoor area with an increase in interest for both groups in the Business clusters. The gender gap seems to have narrowed in the Technology Skilled and Art Skilled areas. The continued use of factor analytic technique to examine the structure of interests, abilities, and values will make the instruments both more valid and useful.

REFERENCES

Allport, G. W., & Vernon, E. (1970). *A study of values.* Boston: Houghton Mifflin.

Bennett, G. K., Seashore, H. G., & Wesman, A. G. (1974). *Differential aptitude tests, Manual.* Fifth Edition. New York: Psychological Corporation.

Bentler, P. M. (1971). Clustran, a program for oblique transformation. *Behavioral Science, 6,* 183–185.

Best, S., & Knapp-Lee, L. (1982). Relationship of interest measurement derived from the *COPSystem Interest Inventory* and the Kuder *General Interest Survey:* Construct validation of two measures of occupational activity preferences. *Educational and Psychological Measurement, 42,* 1289–1293.

Brokaw, L. D. (1951). Comparative validity of "Short" vs. "Long" tests. *Journal of Applied Psychology, 35,* 325–330.

Brookings, J. B., & Bolton, B. (1986). Vocational interest dimensions of adult handicapped persons. *Measurement and Evaluation in Counseling and Development, 18,* 168–175.

Campbell, D. P. (1974). *Manual for the Strong-Campbell interest inventory.* Stanford, CA: Stanford University Press.

Durost, W. N., Bixler, H. H., Wrightstone, J. W., Hildreth, G. H., & Lund, K. W. (1970). *Metropolitan Achievements Tests.* 1970 Edition. New York: Harcourt, Brace & World.

Guilford, J. P., Christensen, P. R., & Bond, N. A., Jr. (1956). *The DF Opinion Survey.* Los Angeles, CA: Sheridan Psychological Services.

Guilford, J. P., Christensen, P. R., Bond, N. A., Jr., & Sutton, M. A. (1954). A factor analysis study of human interests. *Psychological Monographs, 68,* No. 4.

Guilford, J. P., & Fruchter, B. (1973). *Fundamental statistics in psychology and education.* Fifth Edition. New York: McGraw-Hill.

Guilford, J. P., Shneidman, E., & Zimmerman, W. S. (1948). *The Guilford-Shneidman-Zimmerman interest study.* Beverly Hills, CA: Sheridan.

Harris, A. J., & Jacobson, M. D. (1972). *Basic elementary reading vocabularies.* London: The MacMillan Company.

Holland, J. L. (1973). *Making vocational choices: A theory of careers.* Englewood Cliffs, NJ: Prentice-Hall.

Knapp, L., & Knapp, R. R. (1976). *Career Ability Placement Survey* (CAPS). San Diego, CA: EdITS.

Knapp, L., & Knapp, R. R. (1984). *CAPS technical manual.* San Diego, CA: EdITS.

Knapp, L., & Knapp, R. R. (1986). *COPES manual.* San Diego, CA: EdITS.

Knapp, L., Knapp, R. R., Strnad, L., & Michael, W. B. (1978). Comparative validity of the Career Ability Placement Survey (CAPS) and the General Aptitude Test Battery (GATB) for predicting high school marks. *Educational and Psychological Measurement, 38,* 1053–1056.

Knapp, L., & Michael, W. B. (1980). Relationship of work values to corresponding academic success. *Educational and Psychological Measurement, 40,* 487–494.

Knapp, R. R. (1967, November). *Classification of occupational interests into groups and levels.* Paper presented at the Society of Multivariate Experimental Psychology meeting. Berkeley, CA.

Knapp, R. R., & Knapp, L. (1974). *COPS technical manual. 1974 Edition.* San Diego, CA: EdITS.

Knapp, R. R., & Knapp, L. (1976). *Career Occupational Preference System Intermediate Inventory* (COPS II). San Diego, CA: EdITS.

Knapp, R. R., & Knapp, L. (1978). *Career Orientation Placement and Evaluation Survey (COPES).* San Diego, CA: EdITS.

Knapp, R. R., & Knapp, L. (1979). Relationship of work values to occupational activity interests. *Measurement and Evaluation in Guidance, 12,* 71–78.

Knapp, R. R., & Knapp, L. (1980a). *Career Occupational Preference System Interest Inventory. Revised Edition* (COPS-R). San Diego: CA: EdITS.

Knapp, R. R., & Knapp, L. (1980b). Second-order group interest factors based on sex-balanced items: Factorial validity of the COPSystem occupational structure. *Educational and Psychological Measurement, 40,* 1091–1098.

Knapp, R. R., & Knapp, L. (1982). *Career Occupational Preference System Interest Inventory.* San Diego, CA: EdITS.

Knapp, R. R., Knapp, L., & Buttafuoco, P. M. (1978). Interest changes and the classification of occupations. *Measurement and Evaluation in Guidance, 11,* 14–19.

Knapp, R. R., Knapp, L., & Knapp-Lee, L. J. (1985). Occupational interest measurement and subsequent career decisions: A predictive follow-up of the COPSystem Interest Inventory. *Journal of Counseling Psychology, 32,* 348–354.

Knapp, R. R., Knapp, L., & Michael, W. B. (1977). Stability and concurrent validity of the Career Ability Placement Survey (CAPS) against the DAT and the GATB. *Educational and Psychological Measurement, 37,* 1081–1085.

Knapp, R. R., Knapp, L., & Michael, W. B. (1979). The relationship of clustered interest measures and declared college major. Concurrent validity of the COPSystem Interest Inventory. *Educational and Psychological Measurement, 39,* 939–945.

Knapp-Lee, L. J., Knapp, L., & Knapp, R. R. (1982). *Career Occupational Preference System Interest Inventory, Professional level, Form P.* San Diego, CA: EdITS.

Knapp-Lee, L. J., Knapp, L., & Knapp, R. R. (1989a). COPS-R technical manual. San Diego, CA: EdITS.

Knapp-Lee, L. J., Knapp, R. R., & Knapp, L. (1989b). COPSystem technical manual. San Diego, CA: EdITS.

Kuder, G. F. (1948). *General Interest Survey, Form C.* Chicago: Science Research Associates.

Kuder, G. F. (1969). A note on the comparability of occupational scores from different interest inventories. *Measurement and Evaluation in Guidance, 2,* 94–100.

Kuder, G. F. (1975). *General Interest Survey.* Revised. Chicago: Science Research Associates.

Lunneborg, C. E., & Lunneborg, P. W. (1975). Factor structure of the vocational models of Roe and Holland. *Journal of Vocational Behavior, 7,* 313–326.

Lunneborg, C. E., & Lunneborg, P. W. (1978). Construct validity of four basic vocational interest factors. *Journal of Vocational Behavior, 12,* 165–171.

Meir, E. I., & Barak, A. (1974). A simple instrument for measuring vocational interests based on Roe's classification of occupations. *Journal of Vocational Behavior, 4,* 33–42.

Pryor, R. G. L., & Taylor, N. B. (1986). On combining scores from interest and value measures for counseling. *The Vocational Guidance Quarterly, 34,* 178–187.

Roe, A. (1956). *The psychology of occupations.* New York: Wiley.

Roe, A., Hubbard, W. D., Hutchinson, T., & Bateman, T. (1966). Studies of occupational History. Part 1: Job Changes and the classification of occupations. *Journal of Counseling Psychology, 13,* 387–393.

Roe, A., & Klos, D. (1969). Occupational classification. *Counseling psychologist, 3,* 84–89.

Ruch, F. L., & Ruch, W. W. (1963). *Employee aptitude survey, technical report.* Los Angeles: Psychological Services.

Thurstone, L. L. (1931). A multiple factor study of vocational interests. *Personnel Journal, 10,* 198–205.

Thurstone, L. L. (1938). *Primary mental abilities.* Psychometric Monographs, No. 1. Chicago: University of Chicago Press.

U.S. Employment Service (1973). *General Aptitude Test Battery.* Washington, D.C.

U.S. Department of Labor, Employment and Training Administration (1977). *Dictionary of Occupational Titles* (DOT) Fourth Edition. Washington, D.C.

10 Self-Guided Interest Inventories as Career Interventions: The Self-Directed Search

Arnold R. Spokane
Lehigh University

This chapter covers self-guided career inventories; that is, inventories that are designed to be self-administered, self-scored, and self-interpreted with a minimum of counselor assistance (or none at all). Holland's Self-Directed Search (SDS) (Holland, 1985a), the only one of the "big three" interest inventories (Borgen, 1986) that is self-directing, serves as the benchmark for this discussion of self-guided career inventories. The Strong-Campbell (Hansen & Campbell, 1985) and Kuder Inventory (Kuder & Diamond, 1979) are covered in Chapters 7, and 8, and are excluded from consideration in this chapter. Card sorts or computer systems that require a counseling professional as mediator between the scores and the client are covered in Chapters 11 and 12. Although a distinction is made between counselor-guided and self-guided inventories, the difference is increasingly an artificial one. Most inventories now have computer-generated profiles or "interpretive" report formats that are designed to minimize counselor involvement. The Strong, for example, is available with on-site scoring (the scoring is purchased in batches and metered using a control box) and immediate feedback to the client on a personal computer.

This chapter highlights some of the problems in using these new inventories, traces their history, presents a case example using the SDS, provides guidelines for the optimum use and evaluation of self-guiding inventories, and speculates on the future course of development in the self-assistance area. Those professionals who desire a balanced, scholarly treatment of general trends in vocational interest measurement should read Borgen's (1986) thoughtful chapter on the subject in Volume I of *Advances in Vocational Psychology* (Walsh & Osipow, 1986).

Interest inventories provide preference and personality information in unique ways (Spokane, in press; Zytowski & Borgen, 1983). These inventories unearth new career options, and when skillfully used, can clarify the leading or developing edge of an occupational interest pattern. Interest inventories can also be used to confirm statements of personal orientation or to provide a framework or cognitive structure for understanding occupational preferences and their relation to the world of work (Holland, Magoon, & Spokane, 1981). Interest inventories are, then, useful for designing and structuring career intervention programs (Rayman, 1980).

Interest inventories can reveal conflicts between expressed choices and underlying psychological structures. Such inventories may clarify gender role conflicts, and may be indicators of general psychological adjustment and self esteem. They are useful adjuncts in psychotherapy as well as career counseling, and in personal growth and development classes, workshops and prevention programs (Flamer, 1986). Interest inventories have been an expected and appreciated aspect of career counseling for more than 50 years. The introduction of self-guiding interest inventories mirrors the emergence of self-help strategies in psychotherapy (Mahoney, 1988; Rosen, 1987), and offers the potential for providing career assistance to a much wider client population than otherwise might receive assistance through traditional dyadic encounters with a highly trained professional.

CENTRIPETAL AND CENTRIFUGAL FORCES IN THE DEFINITION OF CAREER INTERVENTION[1]

Two opposing forces exert their influence on our definition of what is (and what is not) a career intervention. The first force is a *centripetal* one that moves the field toward restrictive definitions of career counseling as a variant of psychotherapy (Rounds & Tinsley, 1984). Adherents of this centripetal position argue that researchers should concentrate on career counselling as it has traditionally occurred in dyadic or group interactions with a counselor. Progress in career counseling will result, then, when we develop a psychotherapy-based model for understanding and predicting the change process underlying career treatments. If we achieve this understanding, we can design more powerful psychological interventions to induce desired client gains. Williamson and Bordin (1941) inspired this restrictive influence on vocational treatments when they placed three constraints on their definition of career counseling: (a) that the efforts must be individualized, and (b) that testing alone was not to be considered career counsel-

[1]Several days *after* completion of this section of the chapter, I received the special issue of the *American Psychologist* on training, in which the centrifugal-centripetal analogy was heavily used in reference to the tendency in psychology to move toward or away from basic science as the base for graduate training in Psychology (Altman, 1987; Spence, 1987). I decided to retain the analogy even at the risk of appearing to have imitated it. The analogy is a compelling one in both cases, and I could think of no better illustration of the forces affecting career intervention.

ing, (c) that career counseling was not self-analysis, nor was counseling based upon interview data alone. Bordin's influence continues (Bordin, 1986) in a climate where many Counseling Psychologists are practicing psychodynamically oriented therapy with a wide range of individual clients (including career) with considerable success.[2] Centripetalists assert, with some justification, that a loose definition of career counseling, which includes too many activities, will lead to prolonged confusion about how to improve the delivery of career interventions (Rounds & Tinsley, 1984).

Nonetheless, this restrictive definition faces several serious problems. Career counseling, in the most narrow sense, is practiced almost entirely in college counseling and career development centers or in private practice settings. Counseling centers are overburdened and looking for novel ways to meet service demands (Magoon, 1980), and private practitioners serve only those able to pay hefty fees. Lunneborg (1983) notes that traditional career counseling is not really out of date, but has simply become "out of the question" (Lunneborg, 1983, p. 52). Studies of traditional one-to-one career counseling conducted in college settings may not generalize to other populations nor lead to a clear understanding of the career intervention process for those most in need of assistance (Gottfredson, 1982). Applying psychotherapeutic models to career concerns ignores any differences between personal and career problems, which are considerable.

The second, and opposing influence on the definition of career intervention is a *centrifugal* one. The centrifugal definition uses the term career intervention to refer to any activity designed to enhance an individual's ability to make effective career decisions (Fretz, 1981; Lunneborg, 1983; Myers, 1986; Spokane & Oliver, 1983). Increasingly broad rules for inclusion of techniques and strategies by centrifugalists has resulted in a diverse array of interventions to large that it sometimes defies summary and organization (Lunneborg, 1983; Rounds & Tinsley, 1984). This array includes individual and group counseling, workshops, structured groups, simulations, and counselor-free interventions (Oliver & Spokane, 1988; Spokane & Oliver, 1983). The largest increase in centrifugal activity has occurred in self-directing interest inventories, which are immensely popular.

A broadening of the definition of career counseling to include counselor-free strategies has historical antecedents. In 1925, for example, Douglas Fryer published a book entitled *Vocational Self-Guidance: Planning Your Life Work.* Fryer pressed for a self-help approach to vocational guidance that was directly opposed to the professionally-guided model that was emerging at the time he wrote. Fryer believed that counselors should not meddle, irresponsibly, in the lives of their clients. He had harsh words for what he called "the quack character analyst"

[2]One inescapable conclusion from our review of 58 studies of career intervention with 7311 subjects was that individual counseling, although considerably more costly than counselor-free interventions, was also substantially more effective per hour of treatment (Oliver & Spokane, 1988).

(Fryer, 1925, p. 7), who preyed on the weaknesses of neurotic individuals and gave "exact instructions as to what to make of their lives" (p. vii). The only good guidance, Fryer argued, was self-guidance. "It has been found that in the last analysis the intelligent man can benefit from nothing save vocational *self-guidance*" (p. vii).

Fryer, like John Holland, believed that most clients had the resources to assist themselves in selecting and adjusting to careers. Fryer, no doubt, would have loved the Self-Directed Search (SDS) which initially received a skeptical reaction from many professionals (Crites, 1978). Fryer certainly anticipated the development and popularity of self-guided career interventions, but it was John Holland who captured the professional and public enthusiasm for self-guiding treatments with the Self-Directed Search (SDS).

DIVERSIFYING THE ARRAY OF CAREER INTERVENTIONS

Career intervention is usually distinct from psychotherapy. Career problems are mediated by external social constraints in a more direct manner than interpersonal or intrapsychic concerns. Additionally, the technical and practical sophistication of interest measurement has shaped public expectations about career interventions. Clients anticipate receiving inventories as the principal benefit of career intervention, and interventions designed around inventories appear to accomplish beneficial outcomes without the need for counselor intervention (Hoffman, Spokane, & Magoon, 1981; Holland et al., 1981; Spokane & Oliver, 1983). The continued expansion of the array of career interventions reflects these increasingly sophisticated public expectations about the quality and availability of career interventions. The ameliorative process in a brief, 10-minute intervention is essentially the same as the process in a longer treatment. The difference between brief and extended career interventions is one of magnitude of outcome as opposed to a difference in underlying psychological process. Better understanding of the career intervention process will result from an increased focus on the *client's* process rather than exclusive concentration on the counselor. A centripetal definition that restricts the practice of career intervention to dyadic interactions with a highly trained counselor (Rounds & Tinsley, 1984) will result in only a partial definition of career intervention.

The conflict between opposing definitional forces (centripetal and centrifugal) has been a healthy one for the career counseling field and has refocused attention on the diverse range of career intervention strategies and the processes underlying their effectiveness. Summaries of the entire array of strategies and the place of any one strategy in that array, however, are more difficult than before. Figure 10.1 depicts the possible range of strategies available in a comprehensive counseling center, and is based upon work to strengthen the career offerings several years ago at The University of Maryland Counseling Center. The treatment array depicted in Figure 10.1 was first suggested by Magoon (1980). As the figure implies, interventions can be ordered according to level of counselor involvement on one axis, and level of client investment in time and effort on the other. Treatments which vary in level of counselor and client investment have been found to differ significantly in the degree of client gain they induce (Oliver & Spokane, 1988; Spokane & Oliver, 1983). The complete range of interventions is ordinarily offered in most centers, but the centripetal tendency is to concentrate career intervention effort in counselor-intensive, individual and group strategies (lower right quadrant of Figure 10.1), whereas centrifugalists concentrate on alternative and self-paced interventions (upper left quadrant of Figure 10.1). This balanced array of interventions, although confusing to integrate, is the most commonly employed arrangement in large counseling centers and offers the widest range of options to client and counselor alike. The array is ordered on the basis of treatment intensity, which appears to be the only significant treatment characteristic found to produce differential effects in career intervention outcome research studies (Oliver & Spokane, 1988). The present chapter focuses on Level II in Figure 10.1, with the aim of clarifying a small piece of the array of career interventions available: Self-guiding or self-directing interest inventories. These self-guiding assessment devices are a permanent part of the treatment array in every center this author has seen. The SDS was the first of these inventories to win professional acceptance and significant levels of use. In many of these centers the client completes the SDS without seeing a counselor.

The Self-Directed Search (SDS)[3]

The SDS is unique among interest inventories in three ways. First, the SDS is completely self-administering, self-scoring, and self-interpreting. Holland and Rayman (1986) suggest that the SDS was developed to expand the number of people a counselor could serve, and to provide assistance to those people without access to a counselor. The scoring system, unlike other self-scoring tests, is open to inspection by the respondent, and there are no carbon-paper mechanics to obscure the basis upon which the scales are scored. The scoring itself becomes an informational intervention (Holland, 1985a). Second, the homogeneous (theoretically-derived) scales in the SDS were constructed using Holland's theory, rather than from a direct comparison with reference groups of individuals employed in an occupation. Most criterion-referenced inventories are "blind" or empirical in nature, and are based on an atheoretical model, which may be more difficult for the client to comprehend. Third, and most importantly, the SDS has a large body of data and studies not only of its psychometric characteristics, but also, recently, of the diagnostic and treatment considerations governing its coun-

[3]For a complete account of the development of the SDS see Holland & Rayman (1986).

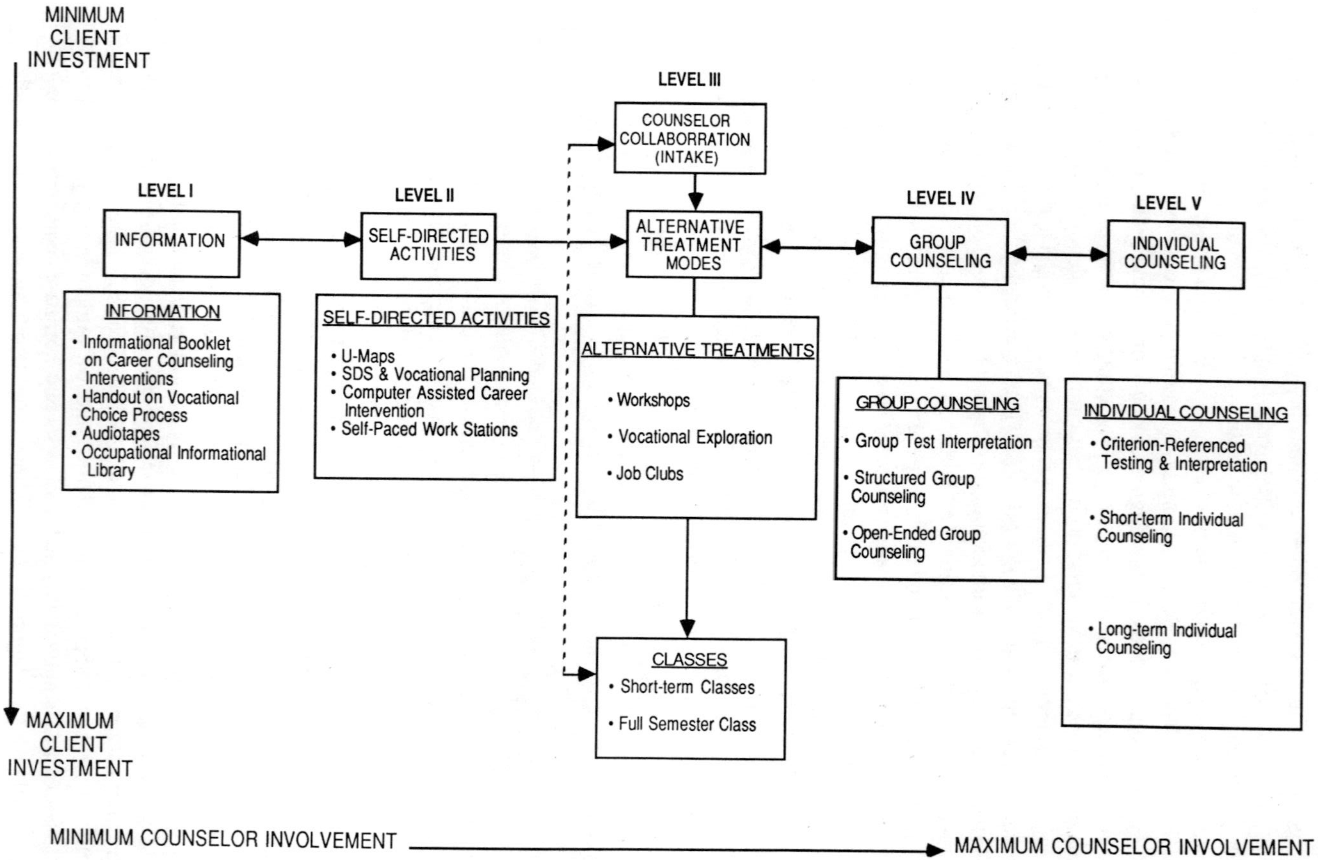

FIG. 10.1. Array of career interventions ordered by level of client investment and level of counselor involvement. Adapted from University of Maryland Counseling Center Report written by Westbrook, Gelso & Spokane.

seling use. This last quality is unique among self-guided interest inventories, and affords an excellent opportunity to evaluate an interest inventory that is appropriate for self-guided use.

The 6 homogeneous, SDS raw scores, are scaled from yes–no, like–dislike items or self estimates for each of the six types in Hollands' (1985b) theory (Realistic, Investigative, Artistic, Social, Enterprising, and Conventional). Table 10.1 contains a description of each of the types taken from the SDS manual. An understanding of Holland's 1985b theory will help to insure a thorough understanding of the SDS profile. The theory contains 7 principal elements, the first 4 of which relate to the types themselves, and the last 3 which relate to the additional diagnostic indicators:

> *Principle 1.* "Most people can be categorized as one of six personality types labeled Realistic, Investigative, Artistic, Social, Enterprising, or Conventional.
>
> *Principle 2.* There are six kinds of environments: Realistic, Investigative, Artistic, Social, Enterprising, and Conventional.
>
> *Principle 3.* People search for environments that will let them exercise their skills and abilities, express their attitudes and values and take on agreeable problems and roles.
>
> *Principle 4.* A person's behavior is determined by an interaction between his or her personality and the characteristics of the environment." (Holland, 1985a pp. 3–5)

The SDS inventory is divided into five sections. The first is the occupational daydreams section wherein the client lists several possible occupations and then checks the Holland code of each occupation in the *Occupations Finder*. The remaining four sections contain items nested within the six Holland types:

> *Activities*- (66 items)- 11 activities listed under each Holland type are endorsed like or dislike (e.g., sketch, draw, or paint)
>
> *Competencies*- (66 items)- 11 competencies listed under each Holland type are endorsed yes or no (e.g., I can use a microscope)
>
> *Occupations*- (84 items)- 14 occupations listed under each Holland type are endorsed yes or no (e.g., bookkeeper).
>
> *Self-Estimates*- (12 self-ratings)- under each Holland type (e.g., managerial skills).

The subtotals for each of the four sections containing items or self-estimates are transferred to a summary page and added to obtain a total score for resemblance to each of the six Holland types. The top three raw scores are used to determine a "three letter code," or the three types the respondent most resembles. Most of the Holland materials then use only this three-letter code for further

TABLE 10.1
Descriptions of the Six Holland Personality Types

The Personality Types

The **Realistic** type likes realistic jobs such as automobile mechanic, aircraft controller, surveyor, farmer, electrician. Has mechanical abilities, but may lack social skills. Is described as :

Asocial	Inflexible	Practical
Conforming	Materialistic	Self-effacing
Frank	Natural	Thrifty
Genuine	Normal	Uninsightful
Hardheaded	Persistent	Univolved

The **Social** type likes social jobs such as teacher, religious worker, counselor, clinical psychologist, psychiatric case worker, speech therapist. Has social skills and talents, but often lacks mechanical and scientific ability. Is described as:

Ascendant	Helpful	Responsible
Cooperative	Idealistic	Sociable
Empathic	Kind	Tactful
Friendly	Patient	Understanding
Generous	Persuasive	Warm

The **Investigative** type likes investigative jobs such as biologist, chemist, physicist, anthropologist, geologist, medical technologist. Has mathematical and scientific ability but often lacks leadership ability. Is described as:

Analytical	Independent	Rational
Cautious	Intellectual	Reserved
Critical	Introspective	Retiring
Complex	Pessimistic	Unassuming
Curious	Precise	Unpopular

The **Artistic** type likes artistic jobs such as composer, musician, stage director, writer, interior decorator, actor/actress. Artistic abilities: writing, musical, or artistic, but often lacks clerical skills. Is described as:

Complicated	Imaginative	Intuitive
Disorderly	Impractical	Nonconforming
Emotional	Impulsive	Open
Expressive	Independent	Original
Idealistic	Introspective	Sensitive

The **Enterprising** type likes enterprising jobs such as salesperson, manager, business executive, television producer, sports promoter, buyer. Has leadership and speaking abilities but often lacks scientific ability. Is described as:

Acquisitive	Energetic	Flirtatious
Adventurous	Excitement-seeking	Optimistic
Agreeable	Exhibitionistic	Self-confident
Ambitious	Extroverted	Sociable
Domineering		Talkative

The **Conventional** type likes conventional jobs such as bookkeeper, stenographer, financial analyst, banker, cost estimator, tax expert. Has clerical and arithmetic ability, but often lacks artistic abilities. Is described as:

Careful	Inflexible	Persistent
Conforming	Inhibited	Practical
Conscientious	Methodical	Prudish
Defensive	Obedient	Thrifty
Efficient	Orderly	Unimaginative

Reprinted with permission from Holland, 1985a.

exploration. Holland offers the "rule of 8," which says that in order for the scores on two types to be considered to be practically different, they must differ by at least 8 score points. The SDS takes from 35–50 minutes to administer, is available in Spanish, Vietnamese, French, Chinese, Japanese, Arabic, Afrikaans, Danish, and Dutch language versions (Kapes & Mastie, 1988). The SDS is appropriate for adolescents over the age of 15, and the hand-scoring by the client or counselor generally takes about five minutes.

There have been four published editions of the SDS (1971, 1975, 1977, and 1985), with minor changes in the scoring and interpretive procedures, and 59 revised items in the 1985 version (Holland, 1985a). Counselors comparing a respondent's scores on the 1977 and the 1985 editions of the SDS in research or practice should take care, therefore, to adjust for altered items and changes in the Occupations Finder.

Five booklets can accompany the test: (a) the *SDS* test booklet, (b) *The Occupations Finder,* (c) an interpretive booklet entitled *You and Your Career* (Holland, 1987), (d) a new *College Majors Finder* (Rosen, Holmberg, & Holland, 1987), and (e) a manual supplement designed to aid interpretation. The SDS is also available in an interpretive format, generated when the SDS booklet is sent back to the publisher for additional scoring, and in a computer-assisted format.

The booklets are attractively produced and easily followed. Taken together they form a simple but complete self-guided exploration system. An expanded version of the *Occupations Finder,* which is published in dictionary form (Gottfredson, Holland, & Ogawa, 1982) but should not be confused with the *Dictionary of Occupational Titles* (DOT) (U.S. Department of Labor, 1977), contains a listing of 12,099 occupations classified by Holland code. This code was derived using multiple discriminant analysis of the DOT position analysis ratings. Holland then "sore thumbed" the 12,099 listing to detect gross misclassifications that are duly noted in the manual. A few "clinkers" remain, and a revision (presently under way) should eliminate most of them. This altered classification of jobs (into Holland types) using job characteristics was employed to construct the revised *Occupations Finder,* and represents a change in the action strategy employed in the SDS. Whereas older editions of the SDS used actual interest inventory data from occupational groups to form the *Finder,* the new system is based on job classification data which presumes that job activities are a better classificatory tool than are the interests of inhabitants in an occupation. This new system allows for a substantial increase in job titles for exploration (there are still a few rare codes that contain no suggested occupations), but strays from the theoretical notion in the Holland system that the people inhabiting a job setting define its nature, and not the activities demanded by the job [see Schneider, (1987), for a discussion of the implications of the position]. The *Occupations Finder* for the 1977 edition and the new *Dictionary* (Gottfredson & Holland, 1989) are based on two somewhat different classification systems.

SUPPLEMENTAL DIAGNOSIS WITH THE SDS

In addition to the six type scores that can be derived from the SDS, the last three theoretical principals in Holland's theory relate to supplemental diagnosis using the SDS.

> *Principle 5.* "The degree of congruence between a person and an occupation (environment) can be estimated by a hexagonal model.
>
> *Principle 6.* The degree of consistency within a person or an environment is also defined by using the hexagonal model.
>
> *Principle 7.* The degree of differentiation of a person or an environment modifies predictions made from a person's SDS profile, from an occupational code, or from their interaction." (Holland, 1985a p 4)

A roughly hexagonal 2-dimensional arrangement has been found to exist among the six types (The hexagon; see Figure 10.2) (Holland, Whitney, Cole, & Richards, 1969), and the hexagon is used to estimate three additional indices (congruence, consistency, and differentiation) of theoretical and practical interest in interpreting the SDS. This additional diagnostic information can be extracted from the SDS scores using the hexagon and a simple calculus. The information needed to calculate these indicators is contained in the manual supplement (Holland, 1987).

The indicators. One primary diagnostic indicator, *congruence,* taps the degree of fit between the respondent's scores and Holland code of the respondent's present occupational environment or an occupation under consideration. An example of a highly congruent individual would be a respondent with a three-letter code of SIA who had selected the occupation of Counseling Psychologist (Classified as SIA). Level of congruence can be calculated using several different methods (Spokane, 1985). Table 10.2 is a summary of the interpretive ideas and indices taken from the SDS manual, and provides references needed to calculate each index. A second indicator, *differentiation,* is a measure of profile shape or crystallization of interests (Gati, 1985), and is the difference between the high and low scores on the profile. To illustrate, a highly differentiated individual might have an Investigative primary or first code score of 41, and a Realistic sixth code score of 3 (Differentiation at the 97 percentile). A third indicator extractable from SDS scores is *consistency,* which is a measure of the coherence of a respondent's scores. Consistency is calculated using the intercorrelations between the first two letters in a three-letter Holland code according to the hexagonal relationship among the six Holland types. The use of the three indicators (congruence, differentiation, and consistency) in combination with

Using the Hexagonal Model to Interpret Person-Environment Relations

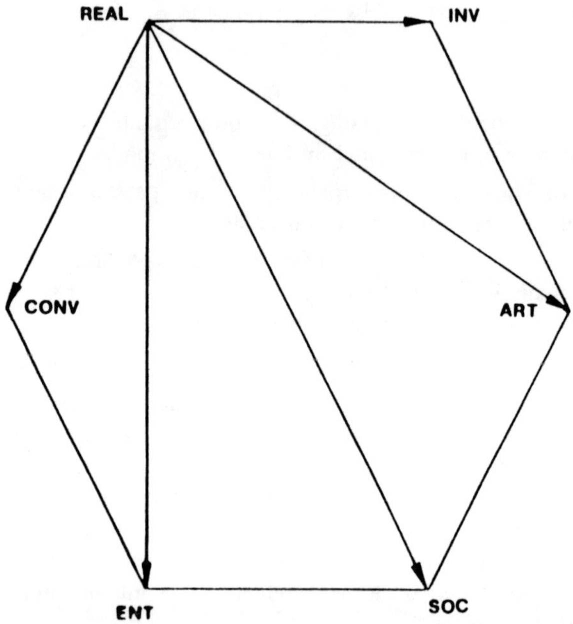

Note R person in an R-environment = 4; in a C- or an I-environment = 3; in an E- or A-environment = 2; and in an S-environment = 1

FIG. 10.2. Hexagonal relationship among the six Holland types. Reprinted with permission from Holland, (1985a).

predominant type information and clinical information from interviews yields considerable material for discussions with the client.

One flaw in this set of indicators is that none of these three indices assesses the absolute elevation of the profile (Swanson & Hansen, 1986), and the interpretation of the degree of overall elevation of the scales is often left to clinical judgment. The extraction process is not incorporated into the routine scoring procedure, presumably because adding these supplemental scales to the inventory itself would require counselor assistance for interpretation, and reduce the self-guiding nature of the SDS. Research is needed to evaluate and improve these indicators and to resolve the debate about which index to use routinely. Norms are provided in the manual for both the type scales and the diagnostic indicators. Iachan's (1984) new procedures for calculating agreement and differentiation are also described. Several recent studies have focused on the calculation (Gati, 1985; Kwak & Pulvino, 1982; Strahan, 1987; Swanson & Hansen, 1986) and use

TABLE 10.2
Summary of Interpretive and Diagnostic Indicators for Use with the SDS

Summary of Interpretive Ideas and Indices

Question	*Diagnostic Construct*	*Indices or Information*	*Source*
		Basic Interpretive Ideas	
Degree of fit between:	Congruency		
Current aspiration or occupation and SDS code?		Zener-Schnuelle Index (7-step—no calculation necessary; use simple table)	SDS Manual, Tables 16 or 18, p. 43
Current occupation and alternative occupation? Any pair of occupations, aspirations, people?		Iachan Agreement Index (28 steps—simple arithmetic calculation)	SDS Manual Supplement. See Table 6 for how to calculate, and Table 5 for norms
Interest/personality Interests, traits Life goals, values	Personality type and SDS profile	Descriptions of the types	SDS Manual Supplement. See Tables 1 and 28, or Holland (1985a)
		Secondary Interpretive Ideas	
Persistence, tenure, or stability of vocational aspiration, choice, or career	Coherence of vocational aspirations	Summary code of aspirations (weighted or unweighted)	SDS Manual Supplement, (pp. 8–11)
		Summary code of work history	SDS Manual Supplement, (same as above)
	Consistency of two-letter code or entire profile	Hexagonal model (adjacent types = very consistent, every other type	SDS Manual, p. 4, or Holland (1985a), pp. 26–28

(*continued*)

TABLE 10.2 (*Continued*)

Summary of Interpretive Ideas and Indices

Secondary Interpretive Ideas			
Question	*Diagnostic Construct*	*Indices or Information*	*Source*
		= moderately consistent, opposite types = inconsistent)	
	Differentiation of entire profile	Highest summary score minus the lowest summary score	SDS Manual, Tables B-1, B-2, pp. 65–66 for norms
		Iachan Differentiation Index	SDS Manual Supplement, see Table 8 for how to calculate, and Table 7 for norms
		Visual inspection: Does the profile of summary scales have high peaks and low valleys or is it relatively flat?	
	Common or rare one-, two-, or three-letter code	Common codes associated with stability; rare codes with change	SDS Manual, Tables B-14–B-19, pp. 71–75

Reprinted with permission from Holland, 1985a.

of these diagnostic indicators in congruence research (Assouline & Meir, 1987; Spokane, 1985).

This set of diagnostic indicators derived from the SDS is one of the few exact and reliable systems of vocational assessment available. Thus, it is curious that Rounds & Tinsley's (1984) review of vocational diagnostic schemas made little mention of the increasingly elaborate operationalization of the Holland diagnostic constructs that meet many of the requirements for a valid diagnostic system. Oddly, also, most studies of Holland's theory in diagnosis for counseling treatment have used resemblance to the six Holland types rather than the diagnostic indicators in designing and evaluating interventions (Fretz & Leong, 1982; Kivlighan, Hageseth, Tipton, & McGovern, 1981; Kivlighan & Shapiro, 1987). Acceptance of these supplemental diagnostic indicators has been slower than approval and use of the six primary Holland types.

The following case is an example of a client who completed some self-directing materials on her own (Bolles, 1988) before seeking counseling, and then requested further assistance in the form of one-to-one counseling. The case history starts after the completion of the Bolles workbook.

Case History Using the SDS

Presenting problem. Jeanette recently resigned from a mid-level management position in the federal government. She describes the paperwork load as unreasonable and overwhelming, and as a result of some errors in this work and general dissatisfaction, she felt pressure to resign and did so. Jeanette is 33 years old, single, with a B.A. in business from a large eastern university. Jeanette circled the following self-descriptors on a vocational history form: realistic about my own ability; anxious about career decisions; don't know my own interests; blocked in my career; using few of my skills; open to new information. Before seeking counseling, Jeanette completed Bolles' (1988) *What Color is Your Parachute,* which she enjoyed. Jeanette still felt uncertain about the direction her career should take after Bolles, and referred herself for counseling. She complained of a mismatch between her aptitudes and her job as the following brief, edited transcription reveals:

cl: Well, yes, I have had my problems with this job, and I think part of it had to do with, you know, a mismatch on my part where I am aptitudinally.

co: What do you mean aptitudinally?

cl: My aptitude for the position as far as my capabilities, you know, carrying out the responsibilities because there are all sorts of different things involved here.

co: You don't strike me as someone without aptitude!

cl: Well, no, I think that given a different position, you know, and maybe some skills, I would be all right. But I think that I'm not a detail person.

Intervention course. The intervention with Jeanette consisted of an initial contracting session and history-taking, followed by a second session using a structured fantasy to imagine a day five years in the future; a third session using a nonsexist version of the Tyler Card Sort, one session devoted to discussion of the SDS, followed by a session on the SCII, and then three sessions devoted to narrowing the expanded options suggested in the inventories to 2–3 possibilities. Jeanette then managed to follow up on a lead from a friend about a job working for a recruiting firm, which she accepted, and two sessions were spent afterward discussing this new position and whether or not it was optimal (10 sessions total). Jeanette at this writing is exploring the possibility of corporate recruiting or recruiting and placement coordinator in a university setting. She reports that she is happy with the progress she is making. Jeanette listed three goals for career counseling:

Goal 1: To become aware of my career interest based on my aptitude and emotional well-being (strengths and weaknesses) (sic).

Goal 2: To be comfortable with the decision I make (sic).

Goal 3: To be responsive to change and possibly a new career field.

SDS results

Occupational Daydreams	*Holland Code*
Recruiter	SEC
Career Counselor	SAE
Personal Shopper	ESR
Entrepreneur	ECS
Lobbyist	ESA
Attourney	ESA
Labor Relations	SEA

Figures 10.3 and 10.4 contain the summary sheets exactly as the client completed them. There were no scoring errors anywhere in the SDS profile (scoring errors affect about 20% of SDS profiles (Holland, 1985a). As can be seen in Figure 10.3, Jeanette's SDS summary code of *ESA,* was both highly consistent (level 1) and well-differentiated. The top three type scores differed by 17 points, and there was a 31-point difference between the lowest and highest score in the summary code, which puts this client at the 81 percentile for high school girls (see Holland, 1985a, p. 64). The Conventional code type appears only once in Jeanette's daydream occupations and not at all in her SDS three-letter code, confirming her feelings of incongruence with the heavy paperwork load on her previous job.

How To Organize Your Answers

Start on page 4. Count how many times you said L for "Like." Record the number of L's or Y's for each group of Activities, Competencies, or Occupations on the lines below.

	R	I	A	S	E	C
Activities (pp. 4-5)	0	1	3	6	9	0
Competencies (pp. 6-7)	1	2	1	7	7	3
Occupations (p. 8)	0	0	7	2	7	0
Self-Estimates (p. 9) (What number did you circle?)	2	1	4	5	6	3
	1	2	3	7	6	4
Total Scores (Add the five R scores, the five I scores, the five A scores, etc.)	4	6	18	27	35	10

The letters with the three highest numbers indicate your summary code. Write your summary code below. (If two scores are the same or tied, put both letters in the same box.)

Summary Code

E	S	A
Highest	2nd	3rd

FIGS. 10.3 and 10.4. SDS summary sheets for case example of a 33 year old female (Jeanette). Reprinted with permission from PAR.

What your Summary Code Means

Your summary code is a simple way of organizing information about people and jobs. It can be used to discover how your special pattern of interests, self-estimates, and competencies resemble the patterns of interests and competencies that many occupations demand. In this way, your summary code locates suitable groups of occupations for you to consider.

It is vital that you search the *Occupations Finder* for every possible ordering of your three-letter code. For example, if you are an ESC, search for all the ESC, ECS, SEC, SCE, CES, and CSE occupations by completing Steps 1 *and* 2.

Step 1. List the occupations whose codes are *identical* with yours. If your code is SEI, occupations with codes of SEI are identical. Go to Step 2, whether or not you find an occupation with a code identical to yours.

Occupation	Education	Occupation	Education
Administrator Soc Welf	6	Alumni Sect'y	5
Dir. Placement	6	Artists Manager	5
Judge	6	Business Rep Lab Union	5
Lawyer	6	Foreign Serv Officer	5

Step 2. Make a list of occupations whose summary codes *resemble* yours. Search the *Occupations Finder* for the five arrangements of your code. For example, if your code is IRE, search for occupations with codes of IER, RIE, REI, EIR and ERI. Start by writing down the five possible letter arrangements of your summary code. (If your summary code includes a tie such as RIEA, you must look up more letter combinations and their arrangements.)

Summary Code	Similar Codes
ESA	EAS SEA AES ASE SAE

	Occupation	Education	Occupation	Education	
EAS	Columnist/Comment	6	Critic	6	AES contd
	Broker & Market Op	5	Editor BK	6	
	Dir Cncl Aging	5	Composer	6	ASE
SEA	Dr Spec Ed	6	Editor Tech & Sci	6	
	Ed Mngng News	6	Humorist	6	
	Arbitrator	5	Career Counselor	5	SAE
AES	Audio Vis Prod Asist	6	Elem Schl Teacher	5	

Go to the Next Page

FIGS. 10.3 and 10.4. SDS summary sheets for case example of a 33 year old female (Jeanette). Reprinted with permission from PAR.

The options taken from the *Occupations Finder* (see Figure 10.3) are congruent with this client's SDS code pattern (ESA) and with her educational level. Several of the options suggested by the finder were nearly identical to those Jeanette listed in the daydream section of her SDS. The Strong-Campbell confirmed this pattern, with a Holland theme code of EAS, and four High or very similar scores (55 or above) (interior decorator, advertising executive, store manager, florist).

Why the SDS?

The SDS made sense for this particular client for a number of reasons. Rayman (1980) offered six reasons for selecting an interest inventory, three of which are relevant to self-guiding inventories. Inventories provide a systematic way of thinking about one's interests, and about the world of work. According to Rayman, this orderly understanding is the first step toward an informed career choice. Secondly, Rayman argued, interest inventories stimulate broad, systematic exploration of options—an outcome which the SDS has repeatedly been shown to do (Fretz & Leong, 1982). Finally, Rayman noted, interest inventories reassure clients of the validity of their choices, thereby releasing energy previously tied up in indecision or ambivalence, and stimulating self-enhancing action on the part of the client. A self-guided inventory can be given to the client to complete as a homework assignment that provides immediate feedback and a sense of accomplishment while the counselor is waiting for other inventories to be machine-scored. Rayman concluded that the SDS is a treatment of choice at several career centers because it is cost effective and convenient, and provides a more powerful educational intervention than the SCII or the Kuder because of its open structure and organization.

For Jeanette, the SDS provided immediate feedback in the form of options that were confirmed by the SCII. Jeanette took the SDS at home after three sessions of clarification and discussion of her goals and while waiting for the SCII and the Kuder to be scored. She brought the SDS with her to the third session, and noted that the results really confirmed her discomfort with all the paperwork (incongruence) in her last job. We discussed the profile and its implications for about 20 minutes of the third session. The options suggested from the SDS appeared to be congruent with her expressed interests, and met her goal of understanding her interests and being comfortable with her choice. In Jeanette's case all of the three letter codes (SDS, SCII, and Daydream) agreed. Had the SDS and the daydreams disagreed, or had the SDS and the SCII disagreed, it would have been necessary to resolve the disagreement and generate a set of options that favored Jeanette's expressed interests. Jeanette could have had access to the SDS without consulting a counselor first, and the outcome would probably have been positive. It is unlikely, however that the SDS alone would have provided sufficient information or a potent enough treatment for Jeanette's choice concerns.

Interpreting Self-Guided Inventories

The SDS and related self-guided inventories are designed to be self-interpreting, and to require minimal assistance from a counselor. There are a few ways to strengthen counselor-mediated interpretations when they occur in individual, group, workshop, or classroom settings, so as to maximize the client's ability to use the information contained in the inventory. An excellent guide to test interpretation prepared by Tinsley (1984) was the source for several of these suggestions. Tinsley's general guidelines for test interpretation are easily adapted to self-guiding inventories if references to the interpretive materials are substituted for references to the counselor. For example, Tinsley cautions that the counselor should understand fully what the test scores mean. Certainly, a self-guided interpretation should have as a goal the client's complete understanding of the test scores. Tinsley offers other suggestions for interpretation, including: (a) integrate test results with other available information, (b) keep the client's goals in mind, (c) consider precision of the test, (d) accentuate positive information, but don't avoid negative, (e) encourage client reaction and feedback, and (f) show the client the test profile. In addition to Tinsley's general suggestions, a self-guiding interpretation should accomplish the following three outcomes:

Provide a cognitive framework for understanding test scores. Holland, et al. (1981) suggested that advance organizers could improve the amount of information the client derived from an inventory. Indeed, Fogg (1983) showed that providing a cognitive framework such as UMAPS depicting all university majors according to Holland's system (see Figure 10.5, Jacoby, Rue, & Allen, 1984) along with the SDS, improved the client's ability to absorb the information presented in the inventory. The UMAPS teach the Holland system as a way of understanding the college majors and academic opportunities available at The University of Maryland. Subjects who were provided this cognitive framework showed significantly higher absorption rates ($F = 5.35$, $df = 1{,}26$, $p < .05$) than those subjects who received no such framework. Those subjects who received the organizer also seemed to need less additional information after the intervention (Fogg, 1983). An additional cognitive framework available for the SDS is the booklet *You and Your Career,* (Holland, 1987). A theoretical framework is also contained in most computer-generated interpretive printouts.

Provide a direct link to a valid job classification system and educational options. The SDS, as stated earlier, contains interpretive booklets which list jobs such as *The Occupations Finder* (Holland, 1985c) and educational possibilities like *The College Majors Finder* (Rosen, Holmberg, & Holland, 1987) which match most profile configurations. These jobs are derived directly from the DOT and the *Occupations Finder* can be used directly with the DOT. The revised APA test standards require that when job possibilities are suggested to a client, the system used to attach these jobs to inventory results must be provided in interpretive materials.[4]

---

[4]APA's test standards encourage but do not *require* a technical manual in all cases, but evidence of validity and reliability for a test must be provided. Additionally, "a test manual may not suggest that an inventory is self-interpreting unless there is evidence supporting the validity of this claim" (APA, 1985).

FIG. 10.5. UMAP for the Artistic Holland type.

Provide referral information. Referral information can be in the form of books or materials for further reading, or suggestions for further professional assistance. At a minimum, a list of references should be included in interpretive materials, or a list of centers where professional help is available (see Bolles, 1988). The SDS contains such a list.

A self-directing interpretation that accomplishes the three outcomes described above would be a useful one for the client. The interpretation framework Tinsley provides can serve as a starting point when a client comes for further counseling after having completed a self-guiding inventory on his/her own.

Maximizing The Benefits of Self-Guiding Vocational Treatments

Two meta-analyses of vocational interventions (Oliver & Spokane, 1988; Spokane & Oliver, 1983) found that seven studies of counselor-free interventions, consisting largely of the SDS or cardsorts, were shorter in duration (mean number of hours of intervention was 2.5, and mean number of sessions was 1.13) and produced less gain (mean effect size = .10) than more intensive counselor-directed treatments. These brief, counselor-free treatments were also less expensive, costing only $1.21 per client hour compared to the nearly $20 cost per hour of individual counseling. Although modest, outcomes for these inventories are consistent across populations and conditions, and seem appropriate for the amount of time and effort the client must invest. The effects of inventories are not, as we once believed (Hoffman, Spokane, & Magoon, 1981; Power, Holland, Daiger & Takai, 1979) equal to those of counselors (Oliver & Spokane, 1988), but these self-guided inventories are modestly effective on a stand alone basis.

Several recent studies (Fretz & Leong, 1982; Kivlighan, Hageseth, Tipton, & McGovern, 1981; Kivlighan & Shapiro, 1987; Krumboltz, Kinnier, Rude, Scherba, & Hamel, 1986; Power et al., 1979; Rayman, Bernard, Holland, & Barnett, 1983; Robbins & Tucker, 1986; Zager, 1982) shed some additional light on the problem of differential benefits from self-help treatments. These studies, which examine the differential effects of career interventions on clients who differ in level of decidedness, sociability, self-esteem, identity or decision-making style, or some other personality variable of interest, generally yield small differences in treatment outcome that are attributable to individual differences. In one case, Kivlighan et al. (1981), a large advantage was found when Holland type matched the nature of the intervention (i.e., for socially-oriented Holland types in group interventions). These individual differences in response to treatments have generally been unstable and difficult to replicate. Rarely do these studies employ the same blocking variable, and some employ no control group; therefore, cumulative conclusions have been slow to surface.

The practical consequences of this line of studies are also troublesome (Holland & Rayman, 1986). If, for example, we discover that some Holland types do better than others with self-guided treatments, do we then withhold such interventions from those persons who would not fare as well? How would we establish their types in advance to screen them out? If harmful effects of some interventions were found for certain individuals, then steps should be taken to prevent deterioration. Presently there is not sufficient evidence to warrant withholding any career intervention. If we could reliably identify individuals who fare well in self-guided interventions, we might reserve more costly one-to-one approaches for those who appear to need more help than a self-directing intervention can provide (Power et al., 1979). There are three conclusions that do seem reasonable to draw from these attribute-treatment interaction studies. Specifically, these recent studies suggest:

1. Self-guided inventories are most effective with high identity, low indecision clients. Fretz and Leong (1982) concluded that highly indecisive students are less satisfied both with the SDS experience and their post-intervention career choice than are more decisive students. Indecisive students are also less likely to have made a congruent choice after intervention with the SDS. Power et al. (1979) found that regardless of client expectations entering treatment, the SDS is evaluated more highly by participants with high identity scores. There is no evidence of deterioration in any group, but the authors speculate that clients with more serious problems need more than a self-guiding inventory can provide.
2. Self-guiding inventories are appropriate for clients wishing to increase or decrease their career options, but will generally result in one additional option that would not otherwise be considered (Fretz & Leong, 1982). Clients who are seeking an increase in information about training also seem more satisfied with the SDS (Fretz & Leong, 1982).
3. Self-guided interventions, which require a certain amount of task orientation, may be more effective in raising identity scores and inducing information seeking for task-oriented individuals (Investigative and Conventional Holland codes) than for socially oriented Holland code types (Social and Enterprising) (Kivlighan, Hageseth, Tipton, & McGovern, 1981; Kivlighan & Shapiro, 1987).

It is important to note that no negative or deterioration effects have been found for a self-guiding career inventory intervention. It is true that some outcomes have been small, and that the diagnostic use of a very few individual differences may increase the gains from self-guiding inventories.

Some New Entries in the Market; Good and Bad

In a recent *Business Week* article, Byrne (1987) reviews a new "mail-in exam," which he says can "provide a real opportunity to take an introspective look at yourself." This new inventory is called *Exploring Career Options* (ECO),

(Andberg & Johansson, 1987). The ECO is, to this author's knowledge, the first interest inventory ever developed specifically for the over-the-counter market and sold directly to the public. ECO is a composite of four tests developed by Charles Johansson, and although available to the general public, must be returned to the publisher for scoring, a procedure that takes 7 to 10 days. The feedback to the client is a 20+ page computer-generated booklet with personalized interpretive sections on Holland themes, workplace attitudes, personal rewards, career commitment, and verbal and math ability. The material is generally clearly presented and includes several suggested options that are selected based on field of interest and verbal and numerical ability. To measure ability, the test taker can choose to complete a timed ability test, or can estimate his/her ability and interests on the basis of personal experience. Most respondents will probably choose the estimation procedure rather than suffer the anxiety of a timed ability test.

The use of ability estimates to generate options in an interest inventory is both a strength and a weakness of the ECO. There is no evidence provided in the ECO report on the accuracy of self-estimates of verbal and math ability. Because the career options suggested in the ECO seem heavily dependent on these ability estimates, and the client is left to his/her own devices, this procedure could be a serious drawback (Lowman & Williams, 1987). At this writing, there was no technical manual available, although a users guide was planned. Scale construction, norming, and validity are thus impossible to ascertain. Another inventory, *IDEAS: Interest Determination, Exploration and Assessment System,* by the same author (Johansson, 1980) is also based upon previous work and is self-scoring and self-interpreting. A brief manual is provided, but technical data are presented in summary rather than detailed form, thus making a complete evaluation of either IDEAS or ECO difficult. A third, and new inventory, currently under development (Campbell, 1986), called the *Campbell Work Orientations Inventory* (CWO), contains sections on working attitudes, working preferences, working skills, self-descriptions and observer descriptions. The CWO has potential for self-interpretation (not self-scoring) and seems wide-ranging and practical for adult workers. Evaluation of the CWO will have to wait until the formal release and construction of a manual.

Interest inventories contained in self-help books. A number of self-help career books are available for over-the-counter use (see Bolles, 1988; Borchard, Kelly & Weaver, 1988; Carney & Wells, 1987; Figler, 1979; Kennedy & Larramore, 1988; Lock, 1988; Otto, 1984). These books contain checklists and inventories of varying levels of sophistication. Whereas Bolles (1988) once contained the party game, and a variant of Holland's system, it now contains a self-estimate skills checklist instead. Borchard et al. (1988), now in its fourth edition, contains skills, thinking styles, and a variant of Holland's interest system. Carney and Wells (1987), probably the best of these volumes, uses a version of the SDS and a college majors finder in a clear and easy to use format. Validity information on the inventory contained in Carney & Wells (1987), however, is not provided in the book itself.

In contrast to these well-written self-help books I found an example of an inventory in a book by Barrett & Williams (1980) that I would not recommend. *Test Your Own Job Aptitude* purports to measure logical reasoning, verbal, numerical and abstract reasoning, technological and clerical skills, personality, and motivation. There is no evidence presented concerning the validity or reliability of the instruments or of the classification system, and the volume claims more than it can deliver.

THE FUTURE EVOLUTIONOF THE DO-IT-YOURSELF MOVEMENTIN INTEREST MEASUREMENT

It is axiomatic in psychology to assume that psychological tests require clinical interpretation to place them in proper context. Interest inventories, which historically have been empirically derived using complex criterion-referenced scoring procedures, are also presumed to need the assistance of a counselor for proper interpretation. As a result, few studies have been conducted of the effects of interests inventories delivered in a self-guided manner (Hoffman, Spokane, & Magoon, 1981); but most of the studies that have been done have used the SDS (see Holland, 1985b for a thorough discussion of these studies).

In the early 1970s several important changes occurred, which challenged the presumption that a counselor was routinely needed in the interest inventory feedback loop. The self-help movement was in full swing by the early 1970s (Craighead, McNamara, & Horan, 1984; Rosen, 1987) and was fueled by increasing demand for psychological services. The perception also emerged in the 1970s that the public had become overreliant upon psychological professionals and would be better served by learning psychological *self*-assistance. At about the same time, the first generation of computer-assisted counseling programs was introduced, and shortly thereafter the first on-site computer-assisted scoring packages became available. John Holland published the SDS, and in 1972 Holland and Campbell collaborated on Holland theme scales for the Strong-Campbell Interest Inventory (Campbell & Holland, 1972). Holland quickly developed a large national and international following among personality and vocational psychologists. Lokan and Taylor's *Holland in Australia,* (1986), is an example of international application.) The first edition of *What Color Is Your Parachute?* appeared in 1970, and in some later editions, Bolles incorporated Holland's themes in the party game assessment.

This movement toward self-assistance in career psychology was accompanied by a shift away from blind empiricism in interest measurement and toward theory-based inventories that were simpler and more understandable. Anastasi (1985) observed that the theory-based shift occurred widely in the field of psychological testing and was the result of the need to provide the client, not just with feedback, but also with a system for understanding themselves in relation to the rest of the world. What followed was a widespread professional and public acceptance of the legitimacy of self-help assistance. In the career field this change was pervasive.

Rosen (1987) dubbed this change toward self-assistance "commercialization," which has a negative tone and implies a cheapening of the quality of psychological assistance. Rosen cautioned that successful therapist-delivered techniques may not be successfully applied in self-help situations and could lead to a worsening of some problems. Rosen also worried that there might be wholesale misdiagnosis and dangerous misapplication of self-help treatments for which exaggerated claims had been made without proper clinical trial. Rosen raises serious questions about psychological self-help that cannot be dismissed lightly. It is not clear, however, whether Rosen's sweeping indictments of self-help interventions apply to all such treatments (Mahoney, 1988). These issues should, however, direct future research on self-help in general and may be helpful in guiding self-help career research.

The general self-help literature and the career self-help literature have some similarities, but the situation in the career area is different than it is in psychotherapy research. There are a few studies that show the effects of a self-guided inventory to be comparable to a counselor-delivered test interpretation, especially when the intervention is a brief one (Krivatsy & Magoon, 1976). Although self-guiding interventions are generally less potent in terms of client gain than counselor-guided interventions (Oliver & Spokane, 1988; Spokane & Oliver, 1983), there is no evidence of deterioration effects associated with self-guided career interventions. The likelihood of dangerous misapplications of self-guiding inventories then, is small in the career area. Rosen's cautions may not be as serious for career self-help but could guide the next wave of research studies on self-guided career interventions.

The Research Agenda on Self-Guided Career Interventions

With respect to Rosen's first question, there is considerable evidence that self-guided career interventions have small but reliable effects that are consistent with the amount of time and effort invested in them by the client and the counselor (Oliver & Spokane, 1988). Generally, the people least in need of assistance (high identity, low indecision) are those who benefit most from the inventories in a self-guided mode. It appears that the SDS is relatively successful whether therapist-delivered or self-guided. In contrast, we have no evidence to counter Rosen's (1987) second claim that there might be large-scale misdiagnosis or misapplication of these inventories because so few of the studies contain any pre-intervention diagnostic procedure, and the inventories are not yet widely available to the public without a counselor as intermediary. Better use could be made of the diagnostic signs in assessing outcomes, especially congruence (see Spokane, 1985), and in designing and evaluating self-guided interventions. Although studies show that some individuals will benefit from self-guided inventories more than others, we do not know what intervention should follow if a self-guiding intervention has been unsuccessful.

We know a fair amount about the concurrent validity of the SDS in adult populations (Spokane & Walsh, 1978) but less about the treatment effectiveness of the SDS and other self-help inventories when applied to adult and midcareer changers whose circumstances and thinking about careers may be different than the adolescent populations on which most of the research has been conducted (Osipow, 1982). More work is needed on the appropriate criteria for evaluating self-help interventions. Should they be the same as for counselor-mediated interventions? The general areas of personal hypothesis testing (Blustein & Strohmer, 1987) and personal agency or self-efficacy (Betz & Hackett, 1987; Lent, Brown & Larkin, 1987; Stumpf, Brief, & Hartman, 1987) seem especially promising as outcome measures for evaluating self-guided interventions.

Studies that pit one delivery mode against another to show superiority have not been helpful in intervention design. What *is* needed are studies that evaluate the cumulative effects of compound treatments in additive or dismantling designs, which will show what aspect of the treatment intervention is responsible for any client gains (Rounds & Tinsley, 1984). These interventions appear more cost effective, but we are rather unsophisticated in our techniques for evaluating and improving cost effectiveness (Yates, 1979). More information is also needed about the use of advanced cognitive organizers that might improve the client's ability to absorb and utilize the information from an inventory in order to make improved career decisions. In the end, more powerful interventions and assessments will improve the effectiveness of all career interventions.

OVER-THE-COUNTER INTERESTS INVENTORIES?

The revised APA standards for psychological tests (American Psychological Association [APA], 1985), acknowledge "that many users of . . . inventories will not have access to a counselor . . ." (APA, 1985, p. 55). The standards require only that the developer of such tests "take into account the likelihood that students will receive little or no professional assistance in interpreting test results . . ." (p. 55). The interpretive materials should be clear and accurate, of course, and a comprehensive test manual for counselors must be available. The principal cautions expressed in the standards are that care should be taken to reduce the possibility of bias (race or gender) in the reports, and that multiple, convergent sources of information should be considered by the user in making a career decision. These revised testing standards imply that the career domain is one appropriate arena for the use and development of self-guided psychological testing.

A subgroup of the APA test standards committee has met several times, and work continues to develop user qualifications that will more tightly control access to psychological tests sold by major publishers (APA, 1986). This constant scrutiny of test publishers by APA has led to reluctance to give direct public access to career inventories. Although direct access is inappropriate for personality inventories, it is the next logical step in the development of career inventories. Most publishers have not made the leap to over-the-counter sales, presumably because they fear that the practice might be inappropriate or unethical. In spite of this pressure, one courageous publisher now sells an interest inventory (ECO) over the counter (National Computer Systems).

Two remaining impediments to widespread, direct public access to interest inventories are the cost and availability of the computer technology needed to score most criterion-related scales. Test authors and publishers are naturally reluctant to release the scoring keys for inventories that might be self-scoring or that could be scored on a home computer. Copyright infringements are a constant concern in test development, and scoring keys are one of the few good ways to protect a product.

Paper-and-pencil inventories such as Holland's Self-Directed Search (Holland, 1985a) have become a popular alternative to traditional criterion-referenced interest inventories because they have no scoring accessibility problems. These self-guided inventories, which serve both as assessment devices *and* instructional treatments, are becoming freely accessible to the public in the same manner that over-the-counter drugs and medical diagnostic tests are now available in most pharmacies. The history of vocational assessment confirms a steadily diminishing professional control of interest inventories. There will surely be some critics and probably a few abuses of this trend toward over-the-counter interest inventories, but the trend is likely to continue into the forseeable future.

CONCLUDING COMMENT

The SDS and related self-guiding career inventories have dramatically altered the shape of career interventions and our thinking about the goals and outcomes of career intervention. These inventories have a firm place in the array of career treatments and will probably become widely available to the public. When self-guiding interpretation materials are properly designed and evaluated, they result in small but reliable gains for most users and substantial gains for more healthy users. There is no reason they should not be available for over-the-counter use. The future of self-guided interventions lies in the improvement of the potency of the materials themselves and the strategies used to employ them for all users. If the same mechanisms are found to underlie self-guiding treatments as underlie traditional counseling, then the broader, more centrifugal definition of career intervention, which includes self-directing inventories, will be accepted. If different client processes are found in traditional and self-guiding treatments, then the more narrow definition of career counseling as a variant of psychotherapy may improve our understanding.

REFERENCES

Altman, I. (1987). Centripetal and centrifugal trends in psychology. *American Psychologist, 42,* 1058–1069.

American Psychological Association. (1985). *Standards for educational and psychological testing.* Washington, DC: Author.

American Psychological Association. (1986). *Test purchaser qualifications: Present practice, professional needs, and a proposed system.* Washington, DC: Author.

Anastasi, A. (1985). Mental measurement: Some emerging trends. In J. V. Mitchell, Jr. (Ed.), *Mental measurements yearbook* (9th ed.) (pp. xxiii–xxix). Lincoln, NE: University of Nebraska Press.

Andberg, M. A., & Johansson, C. B. (1987). *ECO: Exploring career options.* Minnetonka, MN: National Computer Systems.

Assouline, M., & Meir, E. I. (1987). Meta-analysis of the relationship between congruence and well-being measures. *Journal of Vocational Behavior, 31,* 319–332.

Barrett, J., & Williams, G. (1980). *Test your own job aptitude: Exploring your career potential.* Middlesex, England: Penguin Books.

Betz, N. E., & Hackett, G. (1987). Concept of agency in educational and career development. *Journal of Counseling Psychology, 34,* 299–308.

Blustein, D. L., & Strohmer, D. C. (1987). Vocational hypothesis testing in career decision-making. *Journal of Vocational Behavior, 39,* 45–62.

Bolles, R. N. (1988). *What color is your parachute? A practical manual for job-hunters & career changers.* Berkeley, CA: Ten Speed Press.

Borchard, D. C., Kelly, J., & Weaver, N. P. (1988). *Your career: Choices, chances, changes* (4th ed.). Dubuque, IA: Kendall-Hunt Inc.

Bordin, E. S. (1986). The effectiveness of psychotherapy: An introduction. *American Journal of Orthopsychiatry, 56,* 500.

Borgen, F. H. (1986). New approaches to the assessment of interests. In W. B. Walsh & S. H. Osipow (Eds.), *Advances in vocational psychology: Vol. 1: The assessment of interests* (pp. 83–125). Hillsdale, NJ: Lawrence Erlbaum Associates.

Byrne, J. A. (1987, September 21). Getting ahead: This test may tell you to switch careers. *Business Week,* p. 125.

Campbell, D. P. (1986). *Campbell work orientations.* Greensboro, NC: Center for Creative Leadership.

Campbell, D. P., & Holland, J. L. (1972). A merger in vocational interest research: Applying Holland's theory to Strong's data. *Journal of Vocational Behavior, 2,* 353–376.

Carney, C. G., & Wells, C. F. (1987). *Career planning: Skills to build your future* (2nd ed.). Monterey, CA: Brooks-Cole.

Craighead, L. W., McNamara, K., & Horan, J. J. (1984). Perspectives on self-help and bibliotherapy: You are what you read. In S. D. Brown & R. W. Lent (Eds.), *Handbook of counseling psychology* (pp. 878–929). New York: John Wiley.

Crites, J. O. (1978). *Review of the Self-Directed Search.* In O. K. Buros (Ed.), *Mental measurements yearbook* (8th Ed.). Highland Park, NJ: The Gryphon Press.

Figler, H. (1979). *The complete job search handbook.* New York: Holt Rinehart & Winston.

Flamer, S. (1986). Clinical-career intervention with adults: Low visibility, high need? *Journal of Community Psychology, 14,* 224–227.

Fogg, N. J. (1983). *Use of advanced cognitive organizers in the interpretation of interest inventory results* Unpublished Masters thesis. University of Maryland, College Park, Maryland.

Fretz, B. R. (1981). Evaluating the effectiveness of career interventions [Monograph]. *Journal of Counseling Psychology, 28,* 77–90.

Fretz, B. R., & Leong, F. T. L. (1982). Career development status as a predictor of career intervention outcomes. *Journal of Counseling Psychology, 29,* 388–393.

Fryer, D. (1925). *Vocational self-guidance: Planning your life work.* Philadelphia: J. B. Lippincott.

Gati, I. (1985). Description of alternative measures of the concepts of vocational interest: Crystallization, congruence and coherence. *Journal of Vocational Behavior, 27,* 37–55.

Gottfredson, G. D., & Holland, J. L. (1989). *The dictionary of Holland occupational codes: (Rev. ed.).* Odessa, FL: Psychological Assessment Resources.

Gottfredson, G. D., Holland, J. L., & Ogawa, D. K. (1982). *Dictionary of Holland occupational codes.* Palo Alto, CA: Consulting Psychologists Press.

Gottfredson, L. S. (1982). Vocational research priorities. *The Counseling Psychologist, 10(2),* 69–83.

Hansen, J. C., & Campbell, D. P. (1985). *Manual for the SVIB-SCII (4th ed.).* Stanford, CA: Stanford University Press.

Hoffman, M. A., Spokane, A. R., & Magoon, T. M. (1981). Effects of feedback mode on counseling outcomes using the Strong-Campbell Interest Inventory: Does the counselor really matter? *Journal of Counseling Psychology, 28,* 119–125.

Holland, J. L. (1985a). *The Self-directed search: Professional manual-1985 edition* Odessa, FL: Psychological Assessment Resources.

Holland, J. L. (1985b). *Making vocational choices: A theory of vocational personalities and work environments* (2nd ed.). Englewood Cliffs, NJ: Prentice-Hall Inc.

Holland, J. L. (1985c).The *Occupations Finder.* Odessa, FL: Psychological Assessment Resources.

Holland, J. L. (1987). *You and your career.* Odessa, FL: Psychological Assessment Resources.

Holland, J. L., & Rayman, J. R. (1986). The Self-Directed Search. In W. B. Walsh & S. H. Osipow (Eds.), *Advances in vocational assessment: Vol. 1. The assessment of interests* (pp. 55–82). Hillsdale, N.J.: Lawrence Erlbaum.

Holland, J. L., Magoon, T. M., & Spokane, A. R. (1981). Counseling psychology: Career interventions, research and theory. *Annual Review of Psychology, 32,* 279–305.

Holland, J. L., Whitney, D. R., Cole, N. S., & Richards, J. M., Jr. (1969). *An empirical occupational classification derived from a theory of personality and intended for practice and research.* ACT Research Report No. 29. Iowa City, IA: The American College Testing Program.

Iachan, R. (1984). A measure of agreement for use with the Holland classifications system. *Journal of Vocational Behavior, 24,* 133–141.

Jacoby, B., Rue, P., & Allen, K. (1984). UMaps: A person-environment approach to helping students make critical choices. *Personnel & Guidance Journal, 62,* 426–428.

Johansson, C. B. (1980). *Manual for IDEAS: Interest determination, exploration, and assessment system.* Minneapolis, MN.: National Computer Systems.

Kapes, J. T., & Mastie, M. M. (1988). *A counselor's guide to career assessment instruments* (2nd ed.). Alexandria, VA: National Career Development Association.

Kennedy, J. L., & Larramore, D. D. (1988). *Joyce Lain Kennedy's career book.* Chicago: National Textbook Co.

Kivlighan, D. M. Jr., Hageseth, J. A., Tipton, R. M., & McGovern, T. V. (1981). Effects of matching treatment approaches and personality types in group vocational counseling. *Journal of Counseling Psychology, 28,* 315–320.

Kivlighan, D. M., Jr., & Shapiro, R. M. (1987). Holland type as a predictor of benefit from self-help career counseling. *Journal of Counseling Psychology, 34,* 326–329.

Krivatsy, S. E., & Magoon, T. M. (1976). Differential effects of three vocational counseling treatments. *Journal of Counseling Psychology, 43,* 112–118.

Krumboltz, J. D., Kinnier, R. T., Rude, S., Scherba, D. S., & Hamel, D. A. (1986). Teaching a rational approach to career decision making: Who benefits most? *Journal of Vocational Behavior, 29,* 1–6.

Kuder, G. F., & Diamond, E. E. (1979). *Occupational Interest Survey: General manual* (3rd ed.). Chicago: Science Research Associates.

Kwak, J. C., & Pulvino, C. J. (1982). A mathematical model for comparing Holland's personality and environmental codes. *Journal of Vocational Behavior, 21,* 231–241.

Lent, R. W., Brown, S. D., & Larkin, K. C. (1987). Comparison of three theoretically derived variables in predicting career and academic behavior: Self-efficacy, interest congruence, and consequent thinking. *Journal of Counseling Psychology, 34,* 293–298.

Lock, R. D. (1988). *Taking charge of your career direction.* Pacific Grove, CA: Brooks/Cole.

Lokan, J. J., & Taylor, K. F. (Eds.) (1986). *Holland in Australia: A vocational choice theory in research and practice.* Melbourne, Australia: Australian Council for Educational Research.

Lowman, R. L., & Williams, R. E. (1987). Validity of self-ratings of abilities and competencies. *Journal of Vocational Behavior, 31,* 1–13.

Lunneborg, P. W. (1983). Career counseling techniques. In W. B. Walsh & S. H. Osipow (Eds.), *Handbook of vocational psychology: Vol. 2* (pp. 41–76). Hillsdale, NJ: Lawrence Erlbaum Associates.

Mahoney, M. J. (1988). Beyond the self-help polemics. *American Psychologist, 43,* 598–599.

Magoon, T. M. (1980). The eye of a beholder. *The Counseling Psychologist, 8*(4), 26–28.

Myers, R. A. (1986). Research on educational and vocational counseling. In A. E. Bergin & S. L. Garfield (Eds.), *Handbook of psychotherapy and behavior change.* (3rd ed.) (pp. 715–738). New York: John Wiley.

Oliver, L. W., & Spokane, A. R. (1988). Career Counseling Outcome: What contributes to client gain? *Journal of Counseling Psychology, 35,* 447–462.

Osipow, S. H. (1982). Research in career counseling: An analysis of issues and problems. *Counseling Psychologist, 10*(4), 27–38.

Otto, L. B. (1984). *How to help your child choose a career* (New York: M. Evans Inc.

Power, P. G., Holland, J. L., Daiger, D. C., & Takai, R. T. (1979). The relation of student characteristics to the influence of the Self-Directed Search. *Measurement and Evaluation in Guidance, 12,* 98–107.

Rayman, J. R. (1980). *Selecting an interest inventory: A case for the SDS.* Unpublished manuscript. Ames, Iowa, Iowa State University.

Rayman, J. R., Bernard, C. B., Holland, J. L., & Barnett, D. C. (1983). The effects of a career course on undecided college students. *Journal of Vocational Behavior, 23,* 346–355.

Robbins, S. B., & Tucker, K. R. Jr. (1986). Relation of goal instability to self-directed and interactional career counseling workshops. *Journal of Counseling Psychology, 33,* 418–424.

Rosen, D., Holmberg, K., & Holland, J. L. (1987). *The college majors finder.* Odessa, FL: Psychological Assessment Resources.

Rosen, G. M. (1987). Self-help treatment books and the commercialization of psychotherapy. *American Psychologist, 42,* 46–51.

Rounds, J. B. Jr., & Tinsley, H. E. A. (1984). Diagnosis and treatment of vocational problems. In S. D. Brown & R. W. Lent (Eds.), *Handbook of counseling psychology* (pp. 137–177). New York: Wiley.

Schneider, B. (1987). E = f (P , B): The road to a radical approach to person-environment fit. *Journal of Vocational Behavior, 31,* 353–361.

Spence, J. T. (1987). Centrifugal versus centripetal tendencies in psychology. *American Psychologist, 42,* 1052–1054.

Spokane, A. R. (1985). A review of research on person-environment congruence in Holland's theory of careers. [Monograph] *Journal of Vocational Behavior, 26,* 306–343.

Spokane, A. R. (In press). *Career intervention.* Englewood Cliffs, NJ: Prentice–Hall.

Spokane, A. R., & Oliver, L. W. (1983). Outcomes of vocational intervention. In S. H. Osipow & W. B. Walsh (Eds.), *Handbook of vocational psychology,* . Vol. 2. (pp. 99–136). Hillsdale, NJ: Lawrence Erlbaum Associates.

Spokane, A. R., & Walsh, W. B. (1978). Occupational level and Holland's theory for employed men and women. *Journal of Vocational Behavior, 12,* 145–154.

Strahan, R. F. (1987). Measures of consistency for Holland-type codes. *Journal of Vocational Behavior, 31,* 37–44.

Stumpf, S. A., Brief, A. P., & Hartman, K. (1987). Self-efficacy expectations and coping with career-related events. *Journal of Vocational Behavior, 31,* 91–108.

Swanson, J. L., & Hansen, J. C. (1986). A clarification of Holland's construct of differentiation: The importance of score elevation. *Journal of Vocational Behavior, 28,* 163–173.

Tinsley, H. E. A. (1984). *Test interpretation.* Unpublished manuscript revised with permission by B. R. Fretz. University of Maryland: College Park, MD.

U.S. Department of Labor (1977). *Dictionary of occupational titles* (4th ed.). Washington, D.C. U.S. Government Printing Office.

Walsh, W. B., & Osipow, S. H. (Eds.). (1986). *Advances in vocational assessment: Vol. 1. The assessment of interests.* Hillsdale, NJ: Lawrence Erlbaum Associates.

Williamson, E. G., & Bordin, E. S. (1941). The evaluation of educational and vocational counseling: A critique of methodology of experiments. *Educational and Psychological Measurement, 1,* 5–25.

Yates, B. T. (1979). How to improve rather than evaluate cost-effectiveness. *Counseling Psychologist, 8*(1), 72–75.

Zager, J. (1982). *Self-esteem enhancement as an intervention for career indecision.* Unpublished doctoral dissertation. University of Maryland, College Park, MD.

Zytowski, D. G., & Borgen, F. H. (1983). Assessment. In W. B. Walsh, & S. H. Osipow (Eds.). *Handbook of Vocational Psychology.* Vol. 2. Hillsdale, N.J.: Lawrence Erlbaum Associates.

11 The Use of Vocational Card Sorts in Career Counseling

Robert B. Slaney
The Pennsylvania State University

Fiona MacKinnon-Slaney
Bowling Green State University

INTRODUCTION

This chapter will explore the use of vocational card sorts in career counseling and career exploration. The chapter begins by examining briefly the status of career counseling in counseling psychology. The exploration of this issue presents an important backdrop for the chapter, and it emphasizes how the card sort technique may provide at least a partial response to some of the current concerns that seem relevant and somewhat troubling to career counseling. After the introductory exploration of these concerns, the background and development of the vocational card sorts are explored. Available card sorts are briefly reviewed. Then the use of the card sort technique with clients is examined, a description of its administration is provided, and a discussion of some of its effects is presented. A case example is included. Finally the available research is reviewed, the card sort technique is evaluated, and future directions for development and research are explored.

CURRENT STATUS OF CAREER COUNSELING

There is a skit by "Monty Python's Flying Circus" in which a reporter approaches a man on the street to get his opinion on an issue. The man declines to give his opinion because, as he says, "I am an accountant and therefore too boring to be of interest to anyone." It appears that career counselors may be perceived as being in a somewhat similar situation within applied psychology. The results of a number of studies that have been recently reviewed in another context (Slaney & Russell, 1987) seem to be consistent with this possibility. More specifically, the studies seem to suggest that counseling psychologists (especially younger counseling psychologists) who have been trained in and associated with career counseling, are considerably less interested in this endeavor than they are in individual counseling/therapy (Birk & Brooks, 1986; Fitzgerald & Osipow, 1986; Gelso et al., 1985; Pinkney & Jacobs, 1985; Watkins, Lopez, Campbell, & Himmell, 1986).

Fitzgerald and Osipow (1986), for example, concluded that "vocational psychology and its applied arm, vocational/career counseling, long the single most identifiable characteristic of counseling psychologists, appear to be eroding as the foundation of the discipline." Similarly, Watkins et al., (1986) noted that if vocational work "continues to be engaged in minimally and is increasingly unattractive to counseling psychologists, a reevaluation of its place in counseling psychology may be needed." Although these recent studies suggest that concerns about the status of career counseling are particularly widespread at present, it can be legitimately argued that they have been in clear evidence for at least the last 15 to 20 years. There may be some change in the degree to which the importance of career counseling is being questioned, there may be increased openness in discussing this issue, and there may be some additional reasons for this questioning, but the issue itself does not seem to be new.

Whether the issue is new or not, the effect seems evident. Career counseling is perceived, at least by some, as less important than the provision of "personal" counseling or psychotherapy. If this is the case, then a central question that deserves attention is why has this perception developed? This question will only be touched on below. The intent is not to provide an exhaustive discussion of this topic but simply to mention a number of possible issues that seem important. These issues are also seen as forming a backdrop for the presentation of the vocational card sort technique and why the technique seems particularly relevant at present.

There are at least five possible issues related to the perception of career counseling as less important than counseling/psychotherapy:

1. the position of counseling psychology relative to clinical and the other helping professions;
2. the status and isolation of courses on career theories and career development in graduate training;
3. the status of career counseling in practicum training and counseling services;
4. the position of career theories in counseling psychology in particular and in psychology in general; and
5. the techniques and approaches that are used in career counseling.

These will be discussed briefly.

The first hypothesized reason for the current status of career counseling concerns the status of counseling psychology relative to the other helping professions. Although it perhaps oversimplifies issues, there appears to be some truth to the statement that counseling psychologists generally do not wish to be mistaken for the much maligned and stereotyped high school guidance counselor. On the other hand, some counseling psychologists may object very little, if at all, to being mistaken for clinical psychologists. This attitude may suggest syllogistically that: (a) clinical psychologists are better than counseling psychologists, (b) clinical psychologists do therapy and they *do not do* career counseling, and (c) therefore, doing therapy is better. These attitudes, if accurate, seem connected to the pecking order that many perceive in the helping professions in general and in professional psychology specifically. This order places counseling psychologists somewhere between counselors and clinical psychologists. It may be that career counseling, in the minds of many, is more closely related to the tasks appropriate for the counselor than to the tasks appropriate for a psychologist. The acknowledgment of this attitude is often impeded by a closely related second attitude that suggests that it is not in good taste to openly express the first attitude.

A second reason for the secondary status of career counseling relates to the place of courses in career theories or career development in the graduate curriculum. As graduate students, we took a course in vocational behavior. We have also taught such courses for several years, and have observed similar courses being taught for even more years. It seems clear from our admittedly limited sample, that typically, graduate students in counseling psychology enter graduate study with little or no background in this topic. In addition, courses on career development, vocational behavior, career guidance, or whatever they are named, are often perceived as isolated or different from the rest of the courses and curriculum in counseling psychology. In many curricula, this perceived isolation has an element of reality. This isolation does not work in the favor of career counseling because career counseling does not command a central role in most graduate programs. Beyond this, graduate students, despite a lack of background in career courses, frequently expect the course or courses on career topics to be uninteresting.

The status of career counseling in practice and counseling services also has an important effect on its perception. Some programs do not require practicum experience in career counseling, and those that do often find students have less interest and give less attention to their career clients. This is illustrated in the recent study by Gelso et al., (1985). Perhaps this attitude toward career counseling also relates to the pecking order that may determine who actually provides career counseling in particular counseling services. In many centers there is a clear, if often unstated, difference in the status in those who practice career counseling and those who practice "personal" counseling or psychotherapy. At times, there may appear to be a realistic basis for some of these attitudes. It is sometimes suggested that this basis is the repetitive and frustrating nature of a number of the issues that are raised by some of the clients who seek career services. For example, consider the client who, when first seen on Monday, begins by stating, "I have to choose a major by Friday." However,although these clients do exist, a relevant question is whether or not similarly frustrating clients are not seen for "personal" concerns. It appears that the attitudes that are held by the present and future members of the profession and conveyed to students are more central in the determination of the status of career counseling than are the nature of the client concerns that are presented to counselors.

A fourth factor that is suggested is the current lack of activity in the development and expansion of work on theories of career choice and development. This factor also relates to the apparent isolation of theories of career choice and development from other major theories of counseling and psychotherapy. At this point the theories of Super and Holland are the most dominant in the field. Holland's (1985a) recent revision of his theory may or may not breathe new life into a theory that has generated a truly remarkable amount of research but currently seems to be receiving less attention in the professional literature. Only Linda Gottfredson (1981), has added a relatively recent theoretical statement. Her statement has not, thus far, received the attention that it seems to deserve. Overall, the current lack of activity in theorizing about career development may be both a cause and a result of the apparent decline of interest in career counseling.

The final reason for the status of career counseling may also be the most important in considering the provision of career counseling. This reason suggests that the lack of interest in career counseling may be related to the manner in which counselors often approach career counseling. Increasingly the focus is on the use of inventories, computers, career libraries, career information, Holland types, exercises, workshops, and other interventions. The effect often appears to be that a service is provided that seems time-limited, technique oriented, and fragmented. In ways that are perhaps related to the isolation of career courses and theorizing, career counseling often seems to encourage the isolation of career considerations from other aspects of clients' lives.

In looking over the reasons listed above, the striking commonality is that they are all professional issues. That is, the lack of interest in career counseling services does not come from clients. There is and has been a steady and persistent demand for career services over the years, especially on college campuses. The issue, it seems clear, is most centrally a professional one. The effect is that counselors often have a lack of enthusiasm and interest in career counseling relative to "personal" counseling.

The perception by counselors that career counseling is less interesting than "personal" counseling is of great importance. This perception undoubtedly is conveyed to clients, colleagues, and graduate students, and creates a negative attitude toward career counseling. It also suggests that when counselors practice career counseling they may be less than vitally involved and interested in their duties. For counselors, the importance of maintaining interest in the process of counseling, though given very little attention in the literature, seems central. We have both observed occurrences when counselors seemed to discover that their career clients, although not at all certain of their career choices, were also suffering from a lack of self-esteem or some other more "personal" issue. Given the choice between attending to the lack of clarity about career choices and the lack of self-esteem, the tendency we have seen all too frequently is for the counselor to wish to address the lack of self-esteem and put the career issues on hold until the self-esteem issues are "fixed." Such priorities raise the suspicion that the counselor may simply be more interested in self-esteem concerns. Such priorities seem highly arguable to use in terms of the probabilities of positive gains, especially if there are time constraints on counseling, as there often are. However, despite our suspicions, we have never heard a counselor state that the reason that the personal issues were attended to was that the counselor simply found them to be more interesting than career issues.

It is intriguing to speculate about why "personal" concerns are seen as more interesting than career concerns. One reasonable scenario suggests that this is so because the primary reason most counseling psychology students choose this career is because they wish to be intimately engaged with whole persons who are dealing with issues that are of primary concern to them. "Personal" concerns are simply seen as being more intimate and involving than career concerns. This attitude is probably accentuated by the fragmentary approaches that are often passed on to graduate students as appropriate approaches to career counseling. It is also consistent with the striking and almost total lack of research or even speculation about the importance of the counseling relationship in career counseling. These two factors probably have an additive effect. For example, when primary attention is placed on an inventory or a printout, less energy may be devoted to listening carefully and understanding the client. Counselors frequently need time (sometimes months) to build rapport in "personal" counseling. Seldom is such a need heard in career counseling. The sense that career counseling does not call for a full and vital relationship with a client may be extremely influential with persons who choose counseling because they wish to develop those types of relationships. The perception that career counseling does not require a counseling relationship may also explain, partially, how counselors may acknowledge intellectually that career concerns are of vital importance yet respond behaviorally as if these concerns were mundane and uninteresting.

If the above case seems reasonable, then it follows that the lack of interest in career counseling is a problem that the profession needs to address. It also follows that increasing the involvement of counselors in career counseling might be addressed by approaching treatment for career concerns by relating to clients as whole persons who need to be understood and involved in a counseling relationship as an integral part of career counseling. Although this is not a new or a particularly creative idea, it does seem different from what frequently occurs.

We also assume that this approach to treatment will deal directly with the career concerns of the clients who are counseled in a way that is relevant and involves the clients in the process.

VOCATIONAL CARD SORTS AS ONE RESPONSE TO THE ABOVE CONCERNS

This paper develops the theme that the approach to career counseling fostered by the vocational card sort technique is one approach to career exploration that is relevant and involving for both counselors and clients. The card sorts are not suggested as a panacea for all of the concerns about career counseling, but they do seem to get counselors more involved and interested in the process. When counselors are involved, clients have no difficulty getting involved. Having been associated with the vocational card sort for over ten years, as counselors, researchers, and supervisors, we have both come to believe that it is an extremely effective and involving approach to career counseling. When we have introduced students to the approach, they seem to become more interested in their career clients and more interested in career counseling. The process is often described as much more ''clinical'' and interesting than, for example, the use of inventories. It also appears that the counselors who use the vocational card sort know more about their clients, like them better, and actually get excited about the approach. In essence they feel more involved in a relationship with the client. Given the introduction, these effects seem particularly important for career counseling.

Although one should be aware of the limitations of testimonials, we are not alone in our belief that card sorts are an effective, involving, and innovative approach to career counseling. For example, Williams (1978) wrote an article about the potential uses of the card sort approach. He noted that the card sort provided immediate feedback and he examined a variety of means of looking at the sorting procedure, some quite creative, to extract meaningful information from the clients' responses as well as their styles of responding. Cochran (1985) and Crites (1985) reviewed a particular version of the card sort. Although not enthusiastic about the development of the version reviewed, both seemed to suggest that they saw the card sort as potentially useful. Dolliver (personal communication, 1988), the person most identified with the card sort approach, believes that it makes clients more thoughtful about the reasons behind their preferences, including their values. But one of the most thoughtful statements and perhaps the strongest endorsement is provided in a paper by Leo Goldman (1983). Goldman saw the card sort as a technique for counseling as much as an assessment instrument, and he seemed to agree with Dolliver that it was essentially ''a structured interview technique.'' Goldman noted that

> The technique's distinctive and valuable contribution is that it permits—actually requires—each client to project onto a number of occupational titles . . . that individual's idiosyncratic classification of occupations in terms of values, goals, interests, abilities, or whatever the person wants to focus on in answering the question. . . . What results is usually a much richer depiction of the person's self-concept regarding occupations than one obtains from standardized inventories that have already defined the categories or scales into which responses must be placed during the scoring process. . . . Similar to a work sample or a projective test, the card sort thus permits observation of the person's approach to the task-fast or slow, decisive or hesitant, specific or vague, clear or cloudy, simple or complex, informed or uninformed about the world of work. These are many of the components of the concept of career maturity as that concept has been developed in recent years. Leading a client through the card sort in that manner requires time and active, skillful counseling. (p. 108)

In closing Goldman stated

> To understand this kind of use of the card sort technique, [i.e. to understand concepts] a counselor should find it helpful to read the Tyler (1961), Dolliver (1967), Dewey (1974) and Williams (1978) articles. I hope that counselors will do that, because this is perhaps the most valuable single method I have ever found for helping people of almost all ages to examine what they want from their work. (p. 109)

We agree. It is our hope that this chapter will encourage others to examine the potential of the card sort technique in career counseling and in carefully developed research.

BACKGROUND AND DEVELOPMENT OF VOCATIONAL CARD SORTS

Tyler's Research on Choices

The origin of current vocational card sorts can be traced to a paper by Leona Tyler. This paper was, in fact, her 1960 presidential address to APA's Division of Counseling Psychology. Interestingly enough, her focus in the paper was not on career exploration or issues that were particularly related to career choice or career development. Rather, she was pursuing her central concern with the study of individual differences. Tyler had arrived at the idea that "the core of individuality consists of a person's choices and the way he [sic] organizes them" and her address was a description of her research and thoughts in exploring that general hypothesis. Her research combined methods taken from interest measurement, as well as research on concept formation, and used items that were related to four topics: occupations, leisure activities, first names, and community organizations. Of primary interest here, Tyler's approach to research consisted of three steps which will be seen to be the basis for procedures that are still a fundamental part of most card sort techniques. For this reason, they will be presented in some detail as Tyler described them.

First, the subject was seated in front of a board on which 100 cards were arranged in a standard order. Each card had the name of an occupation (leisure activity, first name, or community organization) printed on it, After a short statement about the purpose of the study, these directions were given:

> I would like you to place, in the ''Would Not Choose'' column, all of the occupations you see as out of the question for a person like you and to place in the ''Would Choose'' column those you see as possibilities for a person like you. If you can't make a decision, place the card under ''No Opinion''. (Tyler, 1961, p. 195)

After this preliminary sorting was completed by the subject, the second step was introduced. For this step the ''No Opinion'' items were removed from the board and the following instructions were given:

> Now I would like you to break up these bigger groups into smaller groups of occupations that for some reason go together in your mind. Place those you reject for one reason into one group, those you reject for another reason into a second group, and so on. On the positive side, place those you would choose for one reason in one group, those you would choose for another reason in a second group, and so on. There are no rules for the number of groups you should come out with or about the number of cards in each group (Tyler, 1961, p. 196)

The third step involved interviewing the subject on the topics that were used and the reasoning behind the choices that were made. Tyler described this step by writing that:

> . . . I ask him [sic] to tell me what it is that each of his groups represents. I record on the data sheet the label or explanation he gives for each and the numbers of the items he classifies together under this heading. At this stage it is possible to carry on enough inquiry to make sure that I understand what he means by the distinctions he makes. Finally I ask him which of the negative groups and which of the positive groups he sees as most important for him. We then go through the same procedure with the set of leisure time activities. (p. 196)

It is clear that Tyler thought that this approach to data gathering captured some of the uniqueness of individuals as they were involved in the choice process. At the same time, she was also painfully aware of the difficulty of determining whether this method could be a useful scientific approach to gathering data on the choice process. Tyler's paper is particularly interesting because, in a very real sense, she thought in print about these difficulties. Her attempts at using traditional approaches to measuring reliability and validity are of some interest. But, as she noted, "Dealing with the content or meaning of the responses posed a much more difficult problem. . . ." (p. 198). Her approach to this latter issue is interesting in itself and will be seen later to still have potential relevance.

Tyler began her research by interviewing about 150 subjects using the occupations and the leisure activities items. (It appears from the article that she did all of the interviews and analyses herself). Three months later she conducted a second interview of the subjects who were available. Half repeated the sorting of the occupations and the other half sorted the leisure activities a second time. To make sense of these data, Tyler concealed names and other identifying information and combined and randomized the two sets of interviews. Then for each protocol she wrote down as many statements about the person who had been interviewed as she could generate. When this laborious task was completed, she identified and paired the protocols and compared the two sets of statements she had made to identify "how many of the statements I had made were identical or very nearly so in meaning" (p. 198). For occupations, the percentage of overlapping statements was 61%. For leisure activities, the percentage was 54%. For Tyler these results were encouraging. She then randomly paired some of the protocols and found a noticeably lower percentage of overlap of 24%. It is of relevance that Tyler, although pleased by the data, was more impressed by her sense that protocols for the same person contained "few, if any, real contradictions" while contradictions for the randomly paired protocols were "fairly frequent."

Overall, these results were seen as supportive of the card sort approach and as a reliable method for capturing some of the uniqueness of individual subjects that could be an important addition to more traditional approaches to measurement. Tyler was also aware that the issue of validity was even more important, and she was less optimistic about locating a solution to this problem. The difficulty, according to Tyler, was caused by the fact that "individual differences of many kinds are so large and striking that they outweigh any sort of group differences" (p. 200). Of course, this statement supports the fact that the approach devised by Tyler to get at the uniqueness of individuals in making choices was effective. As Tyler noted, ". . . it is just this 'individual' component that I was after when I set up this procedure. The Strong Blank gets at the common components far better than this" (p. 200).

Finally, toward the end of her address, Tyler made statements that are of particular interest to the development of the card sorts as interventions for career exploration. Tyler wrote:

> One finding that I had not anticipated when I set up the original study was that the process of carrying out this assigned task apparently constituted an important experience for some subjects. Enough of them mentioned spontaneously, "This kind of thing is good for you. It makes you think," and related it to their own plans

> and goals so that I began to see it as possibly a part of the counseling process itself rather than just a way of assessing personality. (p. 200).

Although Tyler mentioned a number of studies on the counseling process in progress that were designed to tell whether the method had something to offer to the counseling process, it does not appear that those studies were published. Indeed, the next apparent attention that was given to the vocational card sort as an intervention for career exploration came from Dolliver who used the card sort in his dissertation (1966). In 1967 Dolliver published an article that described the vocational card sort that he had used. It is clear in this article that Dolliver's card sort, although referred to as an "adaptation of the Tyler vocational card sort", was an important expansion, clarification, and improvement over the basic outline provided by Tyler.

Dolliver's Contributions to the Card Sort Technique

Dolliver noted that although the card sort had some characteristics of a test or inventory, he thought it was best described as a structured interview technique. In administering the card sort, Dolliver used three 4″ × 6″ cards with the categories "Would Not Choose," "Might Choose," and "In Question" printed on them. He used the 51 occupations from the then current men's form of the Strong Vocational Interest Blank which were printed on 3″ × 5″ cards.

Dolliver divided the task into four steps. The first step involved sorting the cards into the three piles. In the second task, the subjects grouped the "Would Not Choose" cards and gave their reasons for not choosing these occupations. Then the "Would Choose" cards were grouped and the basis for choosing these occupations was specified. Step three was Dolliver's addition to the task. Subjects were asked to select and rank-order the ten occupations that were most preferred. Dolliver assumed that the subjects were also choosing and ranking the importance of the values associated with these occupations. Step four also involved an addition to the task by Dolliver. He used the "Requirements for an Ideal Job checklist" (Rosenberg, 1957) to help clients clarify their motives in selecting an occupation. These requirements or motives were also rank-ordered. The client then was asked to add any occupations to the hierarchy that were under consideration but that had not been included in the original cards. The remainder of the task involved a summary and evaluation of the entire procedure. Dolliver estimated that the task took between 15 and 45 minutes depending on how verbal the client was.

Dolliver's (1967) article provided an example of the use of the Tyler Vocational Card Sort (TVCS) and illustrated how the counselor could raise questions and help integrate the information gathered in the process of completing the TVCS. A particular point of emphasis for Dolliver's approach to the card sort involved his use of Kelly's theorizing about personal constructs as a theoretical rationale for making sense of the results. Dolliver concluded by addressing the issues of reliability and validity that had interested Tyler. He noted that

> . . . the method [i.e. of sorting occupational titles] is a structured interview technique that deals mainly with a client's reasons for making the choices. The concepts of validity and reliability have quite a different meaning in relation to an interview than they have in relation to a test. There is often a low "validity" and a low "reliability" between an early counseling interview and a later one, since from early topics of discussion there evolve new, more pertinent topics. To see whether this modified TVCS procedure has validity, one would ask whether its use led more quickly than would a test or a straight interview to the identification of important vocational counseling topics for discussion. (p. 920)

Dolliver continued by noting that reliability would be negatively valued in counseling because clients' reasons and choices change. Dolliver's statements about establishing reliability and validity for the TVCS as a structured interview represent one perspective for considering reliability and validity for the card sorts. This perspective may, however, be most useful in helping us to recall that the TVCS is basically a career intervention and should be studied in terms of its process and outcome effects on clients. Although this perspective is important, it does not deny that the TVCS also contains elements of an instrument that could also be explored in terms of more standard approaches to reliability and validity issues.

With Dolliver's statements about the reliability and validity of the card sort in mind, it may seem ironic that it was Dolliver's work on the predictive validity of expressed vocational choices that provided very important support for the use of expressed vocational interests in counseling. The term "expressed interests" referred to occupations that persons would mention if asked what career choices they were considering or other similar questions. In 1969 Dolliver published an article in the *Psychological Bulletin* that compared the predictive validity of expressed and inventoried vocational interests. The review was done against a backdrop of common wisdom that stated that the expressed interests of clients were clearly inferior to inventoried vocational interests, that is, those derived from measures like the Strong Vocational Interest Blank. In contrast to the expectation of the superiority of inventoried interests, Dolliver concluded that expressed interests had predictive validity (in terms of college majors or career choices) that equalled or exceeded that of inventoried interests. This conclusion was based on his review of the research comparing expressed vocational interests and interests taken from the Strong Vocational Interest Blank. Dolliver's conclusion was also supported by a related review by Whitney (1969) and a study by Holland and Lutz (1968). Both papers reached conclusions similar to Dolliver's. In addition, a substantial number of studies conducted since that time, using a variety of subject groups, time intervals, instruments, and methodologies, consistently support the superiority of expressed vocational interests (Bartling & Hood, 1981; Borgen & Seling, 1978; Cairo, 1982; Dolliver & Will, 1977; Gade & Soliah, 1975; Gottfredson & Holland, 1975; Holland & Gottfredson, 1975; O'Neil & Magoon, 1977; Touchton & Magoon, 1977). Clearly this support for the predictive validity of expressed vocational interests also seems to support the usefulness of the sorting of occupations that is central to the vocational card sorts. This relationship between card sorts and expressed interests was noted by Dolliver when he referred to the TVCS as an "expressed-interest method" (Dolliver & Will, 1977, p. 53).

The 1967 paper by Dolliver was quite important in taking the basic outline suggested by Tyler and using it as a basis for developing an intervention for career exploration. The 1969 paper was also extremely important in adding a strong note of legitimacy to the incorporation of expressed vocational interests, via the card sorts, into career counseling. Although Dolliver's contributions have been quite important in the development of the vocational card sort approach to career exploration, he has been quite gracious in attributing credit for the technique to Tyler while being less attentive to the importance of his own contributions.

CURRENTLY AVAILABLE CARD SORTS

Based primarily on the original work of Tyler and the expansions, clarifications, and improvements of Dolliver, a number of additional card sorts have been developed more recently. Five of these are commercially available and, in addition, there is a sixth version which has been used mainly in a series of studies on the approach. The five that are commercially available are the Non-Sexist Vocational Card Sort, (NSVCS); the Missouri Occupational Card Sort, College Form, (MOCS); the Occ-U-Sort, (O-U-S); the Vocational Card Sort that is incorporated into the Vocational Exploration and Insight Kit, (VEIK); and the Missouri Occupational Preference Inventory, (MOPI). These card sorts were reviewed as a group by Dolliver (1981) and more recent reviews of the O-U-S and the VEIK were also located in the Ninth Mental Measurements Yearbook (1985). Interested readers are referred to those reviews. Only some of the more important characteristics and differences in these sorts will be noted here.

Dewey's Non-Sexist Vocational Card Sort

Dewey's paper entitled "Exploring Interests: A Non-Sexist Method," introduced the Non-Sexist Vocational Card Sort, (NSVCS) and was published in 1974. Basically, she followed the steps articulated by Dolliver in administering the card sort although she omitted the use of the Rosenberg checklist and made no mention of Kelly's theory of personal constructs as a rationale. Dewey did include the Holland high point codes of the 76 individual occupations that were presented on the cards. In her article she presented the distribution of the occupations across the Holland types and she stated that the ". . . occupations included in the card sort were chosen as being representative of a wide range of vocational values." However, exactly how they were selected was not described. The distribution of occupations across the Holland types was unequal ranging from 9 occupations in the Conventional category to 21 in the Social category. Beyond the placement of the Holland high point codes on the individual cards, it is unclear how the codes were to be utilized within the sorting procedure or within counseling in general. For example, the programmed materials encourage clients to "scan" the Holland codes. What precisely is involved in scanning or what is expected as a result is not clear. Only 12% of the occupations require only a high school diploma or less while 65% require a college degree or more. Consistent with the title, Dewey implied that the instrument applied equally to men as well as women. Again, how this was determined was not noted.

Dewey based her approach on the work of Tyler and Dolliver but, in calling her instrument the Non-Sexist Vocational Card Sort, she clearly intended to emphasize the non-sexist aspect of the instrument. In this regard Dewey noted that:

> the NSVCS is less sexist than traditional approaches to vocational counseling because (a) the same vocational alternatives are offered to both men and women, (b) the gender of the occupational titles has been neutralized, and (c) the process orientation of the technique allows the counselor to confront and explore sex-role biases as such biases emerge in the counseling session. (p. 311)

Although the first two issues were relevant at the time Dewey wrote her article, these concerns have been virtually eliminated by subsequent revisions of the most widely used commercially published instruments. However, there is some question about the actual effects of these alterations in terms of encouraging women to explore all of their available career alternatives. The remaining rationale for the use of the NSVCS is that the presence of a counselor will allow the issue of sex role bias to be addressed as a part of the counseling session. This possibility is, however, dependent on the sensitivity and perceptiveness of the counselor and does not appear to be inherent in any particular procedure that is a part of the NSVCS. This rationale is also dependent on the assumption that counselors themselves are not sources of sex bias and that they are alert to and can deal effectively with sex bias as it occurs in the session. When clients take the self-directed version there are comments about sex bias in the accompanying materials. No studies on the effectiveness of this material were located. Overall, the importance and effects of the "non-sexist" aspects of the Dewey card sort appear questionable.

The Missouri Occupational Card Sort

The Missouri Occupational Card Sort, College Form, by Krieshok, Hansen, and Johnston (1982) has 90 occupations that are evenly distributed across the six Holland types. The incorporation of the Holland types into the task is rather vaguely described as a "step which could be included" (p. 10). About a quarter of the occupations require a high school degree, 63% require a college degree, and 12% more than a college degree. The MOCS assumes that a counselor will administer it. It is the only one of the commercially available sorts that does not have instructions so clients can take the instrument without the assistance of a counselor. Another difference is that in addition to ranking the top ten "LIKE" occupations the clients also rank-order their bottom ten "DISLIKE" occupations. According to Dolliver, the MOCS occupation cards contain the most occupational information. Whether this information is of significance in the effects the task has on clients is not clear. No empirical studies that investigated or included the MOCS were located.

Occ-U-Sort/ O-U-S

The Occ-U-Sort or O-U-S by Jones includes 60 occupational cards for each of three educational levels labelled "Plus 3 Level," "Plus 4 Level," and "Plus 5 Level." The numbers refer to the General Educational Levels that are taken from the Dictionary of Occupational Titles. "Plus" in the titles indicates that some occupations from higher levels (of required educational background) are also included. The occupations are distributed equally across the six Holland types. In addition to the cards, "A Self Guided Booklet" is included to make the exploration experience self-directed. A specific approach to deriving a Holland Code is provided for the client based on the occupations that are sorted as "Might Choose." A "Guide to Occupations" contains 555 occupations that are organized according to Holland types, subdivided into worker trait groups, and assigned numbers according to the *Dictionary of Occupational Titles* and the *Guide for Occupational Exploration.*

In the review of the O-U-S by Dolliver (1981), he questioned the strategy of not including occupations in which either sex predominated that was adopted by the O-U-S for addressing sex bias. Dolliver suggested that including some of these occupations might make sense because they represented some rather common occupations and their exclusion seemed a bit strange. Jones (1982) wrote a reaction to Dolliver's review that focused on this issue. In response to that reaction Dolliver (1982) wrote yet another commentary. Neither author appeared to be noticeably persuaded by the other's perspective. Labelling the disagreement between Dolliver and Jones a controversy, Westbrook and Mastie (1982) wrote another review of the O-U-S provocatively titled "Shall We Sort the Occ-U-Sort Into the Might-Choose, Would-Not-Choose, or Uncertain Pile?"

Westbrook and Mastie focused their concerns about the O-U-S on five basic issues. First, they stated that they were concerned that "the manual is misleading" (p. 249). They note that the Manual cites four studies under the heading "Occ-U-Sort as an Individual Career-Counseling Tool." They took issue with this title because they pointed out that, of the four studies describing the usefulness of card sorts, none used the O-U-S. They suggested that the O-U-S cannot be recommended until the necessary research is done. Second, they stated that the Manual does not adequately support the claim that the O-U-S is effective as a "self-administered career-counseling experience" (p. 249). They suggested more data on these issues need to be generated. Their third concern was that the data supporting the claim that the O-U-S assesses vocational interests were unclear and/or inadequate. Clarification and more data were called for. A fourth concern was whether the O-U-S codes were sufficiently dependable to serve as measures of vocational interests. Their fifth concern was that the Manual's claims to have eliminated traditionally sex-linked job titles were simply inaccurate. Finally, they were concerned that the reading levels assigned to the cards were also inaccurate. They concluded that

> . . . the Occ-U-Sort is not at this time ready for serious use with students in a career counseling setting. Although the Occ-U-Sort appears to have considerable potential, the lack of empirical evidence to support its recommended uses means that it should be used for research purposes only until the necessary evidence is forthcoming. (p. 252)

Jones (1982) responded to the criticisms and concerns raised by Westbrook and Mastie. He clarified the issues pertaining to reading level by noting that the actual occupational titles were not included in the determination of the levels. Jones also responded to the charge that the Manual had inaccurately implied that sex bias was attended to by eliminating traditionally sex-linked job titles, whereas titles like dental assistant, elementary school teacher, and civil engineer remained. He cited the manual as stating: "To minimize the effect of sex bias, those occupations having strong sex-role stereotypes were excluded whenever possible" (p. 4).

The above responses of Jones seemed responsive to only some of the concerns raised by the reviewers. They did clarify the concerns that were based on a lack of clarity or understanding. However, after citing the Manual on the issue of sex bias, Jones concluded that, in minimizing the effects of sex bias, the O-U-S had succeeded "quite well considering the magnitude of the problem" (p. 255). It seems unclear whether Westbrook and Mastie or the careful reader would agree that The O-U-S has done "quite well" in responding to the issue of sex bias. In fact, the use of imprecise yet positive terms like "quite well" is at least one of the issues for which they take Jones and the Manual to task. It does not seem difficult to imagine them asking what the term "quite well" means precisely and how it was determined that this term was an appropriate summation of the progress achieved in minimizing sex bias. It seems true that the indefinite and imprecise use of language does not help readers to determine what has actually been done with the O-U-S and what was found. In addition, Jones' responses were not directly responsive to some of the other criticisms and concerns raised by the reviewers. It is clear that Jones did not agree with many of the points raised by Westbrook and Mastie. It is less clear that his responses were consistently directed at clarifying the exact status, adequacy, and nature of the data gathered on the O-U-S.

Two additional reviews of the O-U-S appeared in the Ninth edition of the Mental Measurements Yearbook. Cochran raised the interesting point that the method of calculating Holland types by using the primary and secondary codes of the occupations is biased because, although the primary codes are equally distributed across the types, the secondary codes of the occupations are not. He also noted that the requirement of selecting 12 occupations may bias the code because it may force clients to select occupations in which they have no real interests, but which are used in calculating the code. Consistent with other reviews, Cochran noted that "In general, the technical information presented in the Manual is inadequate" (p. 1077). In closing he noted that "The instrument offers much promise for career counseling. Unfortunately, as it stands, the measurement portion of the intervention is not suitable for research or practice" (p. 1077).

Crites (1985) noted, as did Westbrook and Mastie, that "the studies cited for it [i.e., the O-U-S] as an 'Individual Career-Counseling Tool' however, all pertain to other occupational card sorts. None pertains to the Occ-U-Sort" (p. 1078). Crites also raised basic questions about other data that were offered as support for the O-U-S. Beyond this, however, he raised an even more basic issue about whether the approaches to supporting the validity of the O-U-S were not simply misguided. According to Crites:

> The primary reason Tyler (1961) introduced the occupational card-sort was to explore the uniqueness of the individual's responses. These are given in the reasons for the card sorts; they are the source of data not provided by the SDS or interest inventories. Why not concentrate validation and interpretation on them? Otherwise research on the psychometric properties of Occ-U-Sort does not justify its use at this time, unless possibly as an adjunct to career counseling by an experienced counselor. This conclusion does not mean Occ-U-Sort has no promise. It does, but it needs to be validated differently in order to preserve and document its unique qualities. (p. 1078–1079).

All of the above reviews suggested that the data base provided thus far for the O-U-S and presented in the Manual contains inadequacies and, at the very least, more data and clarification are needed. Crites agreed with that general assessment but raised the more intriguing question of whether the more or less conventional approach to gathering data, especially validity data, was not simply irrelevant to the nature of the vocational card sort task and its intended effects. Crites' statements on the issue of validity are reminiscent of the earlier comments of Tyler (1961) and Dolliver (1967) when they suggested that the vocational card sort represents a different type of instrument that is, in essence, an intervention. It appears that the approach to gathering validity data on vocational card sorts may need to be carefully reexamined.

The Vocational Exploration and Insight Kit

The Vocational Exploration and Insight Kit (VEIK) by Holland and Associates (1980), is really a combination of a Vocational Card Sort (VCS), the Self-Directed Search (SDS), and its instructional booklet, "Understanding Yourself and Your Career," the "Occupations Finder," an "Action Plan Workbook," and the "Counselor's Guide." The VCS consists of 84 occupations, equally divided over the six Holland types. About one quarter of the occupations require a high school diploma or less, half require a college degree, and another quarter a postgraduate degree. The occupations are the same as those that are used in the SDS as well as in the Vocational Preference Inventory. The VEIK has, according to Dolliver (1981), "the greatest number and diversity of reflective questions for the client (e.g., In what occupation could I fulfill my hopes? In what occupation would I avoid my weaknesses?)." The client can also include occupations that are not on the cards. The VCS also contains, according to Takai and Holland (1979) "a specific step developed to confront a person with the role that sex, race, religion, or social class may have played in sorting occupational titles" (p. 313). Although the cards have only the occupational titles printed on them, the supplementary materials provide additional information that is relevant to career exploration and thinking about career choices and issues. Instructions are provided for computing a Holland code.

Reviews of the VEIK appeared in the Ninth edition of the Mental Measurements Yearbook (1985). Both reviewers seemed a bit unclear about the issues of reliability and validity as they apply to the VEIK. Daniels noted that: "Evidence about the reliability and validity of the total program are not available, although such evidence for both the VCS and the SDS are available elsewhere" (p. 1675). He did not state where this evidence was available for the VCS nor did he describe its exact nature. Tittle (1985) noted that: "No reliability data are available for the VEIK. Two validity studies have compared the VEIK, the SDS, and the VPI-based VCS" (p. 1676). This latter statement makes it clear that, in referring to validity studies, Tittle is discussing what could also be classified as intervention or outcome studies. This issue has been previously referred to in discussing the validity of the card sort. There is some confusion about whether they are interventions or instruments that should have their items' reliability and validity assessed by using conventional means, that is, test-retest, split half, construct, or concurrent validity. For the VEIK, it seems clear that the package is meant to be an intervention for career counseling. Validity then, it can be argued, needs to be assessed in terms of whether the instrument or package performs or creates the effects that it states or suggests it should. Does it have validity as an intervention? It is important to note that it is far less clear how this determination of validity is to be made than it is when more conventional approaches to validity are considered. Considering the VCS as an embedded component of the VEIK leaves it unclear what implications research results for the VEIK have for the VCS.

Both of the reviewers seemed generally positive about the VEIK. Both also suggested that more research was needed on the package. Daniels (1985) suggested that the VEIK was not significantly more helpful in expanding users' awareness than was the SDS alone. Tittle noted the same effect and cited the studies that led to that conclusion, i.e., Takai and Holland (1979) and Talbot and Birk (1979). In addition Tittle noted that:

> The adaptation of VPI occupations to a card sort format and the particular questions included lack supporting data at present. Counselors following Holland's suggestion to take the VEIK themselves may well judge that only highly motivated and articulate clients are likely to complete this set of activities successfully (p. 1676).

This latter point would appear to refer to the time required to complete the entire VEIK which Dolliver stated is three to four hours. If, as it appears, research does seem to suggest that the total VEIK does not produce any differential additive treatment effects beyond those experienced by clients who take only the SDS, then very basic questions are raised about the advantages of the longer, more involving, and expensive VEIK. At the same time, there is also a question whether the conclusions about the lack of effects for the VEIK are justified based on the limited empirical scrutiny it has received. To conclude that there are no treatment differences between interventions and then lose interest in and discard a treatment on this basis implies that the studies done have asked the right questions. Whether this has occurred for the VEIK is an issue that deserves consideration. Beyond this, the tendency to examine the VCS that is a part of the VEIK, as part of the total package, seems both natural in terms of the VEIK and confusing in terms of the VCS.

The Missouri Occupational Preference Inventory

The final commercially available vocational card sort was the Missouri Occupational Preference Inventory (MOPI) by Moore and Gysbers [with Pamela Carlson] (1980). The MOPI contains a total of 180 occupations, with 60 at each of three educational levels requiring: (a) a high school education or less, (b) high school plus additional training, and (c) a college or postgraduate degree. The

Holland types are not equally represented nor are there equal numbers of occupations at each educational level. However the MOPI includes more occupations at the lower educational level than does any other card sort. The Manual relates occupations to the DOT and illustrates how a Holland code can be determined based on the occupations chosen. In their recent book, entitled *Career Counseling,* Gysbers and Moore devote a chapter to "Occupational Card Sorts." They are quite concrete in their directions for using a card sort in career counseling and they focus on the specific approach used by the MOPI. It is not clear in this chapter that the MOPI is, in fact, quite different from the approaches taken by the other card sorts.

For example, after the client has sorted the cards into the three major groups, each individual card in the "Like" pile is considered individually instead of as a part of a group of related occupations. The instructions, which are to be read or paraphrased, are as follows:

> In order to better consider the reasons (themes) for choosing certain occupational titles, begin by thinking about the first occupational card in the like pile. Explain the reason or reasons why you like it. Do this for each card in the pile. Make sure each reason is specific. (p. 139)

The counselor records the reasons beside each occupation. A slash mark is placed beside each reason on the "Finding Themes" worksheet each time a reason is repeated. When the client has gone through all of the "Like" occupations, the "Dislike" occupations are similarly addressed. The "Undecided" occupations are also addressed individually and the reasons are tabulated. When this task is completed the reasons or themes are rank-ordered, based on frequency, on the "Understanding Themes" worksheet. The "Likes" are rank-ordered first. Then the "Dislikes" column is filled in with attention to placing "Dislikes" that are the opposite of the "Likes" in the rank across the page. The same is done with the "Undecided" column. Finally, those "Likes" for which no opposites were noted are considered to determine what the opposite might be.

Then the client is asked to rank-order the occupations using the "Like" pile. The instructions, which are to be read or paraphrased are:

> Now that you know more about the reasons behind your occupational choices, rank-order them. Look at the cards in the like pile again. Decide which one would be your first choice, your second choice, and so on, for all the occupations that seem to be important to you. (p. 144)

The 3-letter Holland codes of the occupations that are ranked are then used to derive a Holland code for the client. The authors use a weighted scoring system similar to that used as part of the SDS. A code is computed and checked, the Holland classification system is reviewed with the client, and the reasonableness of the code is discussed with the client. Finally, a worksheet entitled ''Your Career Information Summary'' is used to ''help the client focus on what has been learned'' (p. 146). There are five aspects:

1. The themes or the reasons for liking or disliking occupations are summarized.
2. The top five occupations are recorded.
3. The Holland codes are recorded.
4. The Holland code for the client is discussed.
5. A plan of action is formulated.

In the chapter on the ''occupational sorts'' the authors seem to suggest several central functions for which a counselor appears to be necessary. It is not clear how these functions are met when the task is self-directed. There are also several separate sheets to be completed. In Dolliver's review it is noted that the MOPI takes about 30 minutes. The source for this estimate is unclear and, given the apparent complexity of the various operations, this sounds like an extremely conservative estimate of the time requirements for self-administering the MOPI. No studies on the MOPI were located and Gysbers and Moore cite no studies in their recent chapter. In addition, a recent letter from Dolliver (personal communication, 1988) quoted Gysbers as stating that he was not aware of any current research activity. Whether any research at all exists on this instrument is not clear. No reviews of the instrument in addition to the review by Dolliver (1981) were located.

Overall, the MOPI represents a different, if unexamined, approach to the card sort task. It is unclear whether the novel approach to examining the reasons for liking and disliking occupations leads to different effects or if the self-directed version is effective in examining the themes when clients take the MOPI by themselves. Although the total lack of research on this instrument suggests that the answers to such questions cannot be determined at present, potential users should at least be aware of the differences in the approach to the card sort that the MOPI represents.

Slaney's Vocational Card Sort

The final Vocational Card Sort to be discussed is not commercially available and has been used in a series of empirical studies of the VCS as a self administered career intervention (Atanasoff & Slaney, 1980; Croteau, 1986; Slaney, 1978; 1983; Slaney & Dickson, 1985; Slaney & Lewis, 1986; Slaney & MacKinnon-Slaney, 1986; Slaney & Slaney, 1981). Its origins can be clearly traced to the work of Dolliver and Tyler with a few alterations that are of interest. First, the Vocational Card Sort by Slaney included descriptions of the Holland types printed on 5″ × 8″ cards. Subjects were asked to rank-order the cards according to how well each of the Holland types described them. From these rankings, subjects recorded their 3-letter Holland codes. This was, of course, a markedly different approach to getting the Holland types of the subjects than that used by any of the other instruments. These types were later used in making sense of the results of the VCS and, along with "The Occupations Finder" from the Self-Directed Search (SDS), to suggest additional occupations that the subjects might wish to explore. It was suggested, as part of the experimental procedure, that all permutations of the 3-letter Holland codes be used in developing possible leads.

A small number of studies have investigated the rank-ordering of the descriptions of the Holland types. Slaney (1978) derived 3-letter Holland codes based on the rank-ordered Holland types done as part of the Vocational Card Sort and another set of three letter codes taken from the Strong-Campbell Interest Inventory (SCII) for 84 undergraduate women. The agreement between the two codes varied considerably and appeared moderate overall. There were no statistically significant differences in the relationship of the rank-ordered themes and the SCII Holland themes to their respective second themes, the five highest basic interests, or the five highest occupational scales of the SCII. However, when the themes were related to three different measures of expressed vocational choices and college majors, the themes from the rank-ordered Holland types were found to be more highly related to expressed choices and significantly different from the relationships found for the SCII. Given the relationship between expressed choices and actual later choices, those findings are at least of interest and appear supportive of the ranking procedure.

Slaney (1978) had 32 undergraduate women, who were not in the comparative study, rank-order the Holland themes. Three weeks later they returned and rank-ordered the themes again. Spearman rhos, using all six themes, yielded a median rho of .83 and a mean rho of .84. Another sample of 42 undergraduate women was given the Vocational Preference Inventory and rank-ordered the Holland themes as part of the VCS, in that order. The median Spearman rho was .66 and the mean rho was .56. Finally, a third sample of 30 undergraduate women, rank-ordered the Holland themes and two weeks later completed Holland's Self-Directed Search. The median Spearman rho was .77 and the mean rho was .69. Slaney concluded that while the measures of concurrent validity were not as high as might have been desirable, they did indicate that a substantial relationship existed between the rank-ordered Holland themes and other methods of deriving themes. A study by Harmon and Zytowski (1980) also found that when different sources were used for Holland codes, different instruments yielded different codes. Although there is no compelling rationale for preferring one of several possible sources for deriving Holland codes, the relationship between the rank-ordered codes and expressed choices does offer some support for the rank-ordering procedure.

A study by Atanasoff and Slaney (1980) compared the 3-letter Holland themes from the Vocational Card Sort with similar codes derived from the SDS and the SCII. The themes from the SDS and the VCS were both more highly related to the expressed choices of the subjects than were the themes of the SCII. The SDS and VCS were not significantly different from each other. Again, based on the importance of expressed vocational interests, these results seem supportive of the codes derived from rank-ordering the descriptions of the Holland types. This seems particularly true given the wide use of the instruments used as a basis for comparison.

Slaney and Slaney (1981) compared the agreement of the Holland codes derived from the rank-ordering of the Holland types with types derived from the SCII for 50 female and 50 male counseling center clients who requested career counseling. All clients had taken both the VCS and the SCII. The relationships between the two sets of 3-letter Holland codes varied a great deal but were generally moderate. Finally, Slaney and MacKinnon-Slaney (1986) studied 54 undergraduate females who requested career counseling at a university counseling center. Again all of the clients had taken both the VCS and the SCII. The sample was divided based on the agreement of the clients' expressed and inventoried choices, using the occupation on the SCII that had the highest standard score for the latter choice. Slaney and MacKinnon-Slaney found that clients with greater agreement between their expressed and inventoried interests had a stronger relationship between their rank-ordered Holland codes from the VCS and their expressed choices than did clients with low agreement. There were no differences between the SCII themes of clients in their relationship to expressed choices. It appeared that the higher agreement clients were better able to match their Holland personality types with their expressed choices through the rank-ordering task than were the low agreement clients. Given that high agreement clients have been found to be more predictable in a number of studies, these results make intuitive sense and also seem to support the validity of the rank-ordering of the Holland types as incorporated into the Vocational Card Sort. Although more research is clearly needed, the initial studies offer some support for rank-ordering the Holland types as a part of the Vocational Card Sort. Given future support, one clear advantage of the rank-ordering task is that it encourages clients to think of themselves in holistic terms in relationship to the Holland types. These types can also be compared with the types that can be derived from the inspection of the specific occupations chosen on the VCS.

A second addition to the VCS that was made by Slaney (1978), was the incorporation of the Basic Interest categories from the SCII into the VCS. This was done as part of a series of studies that made comparisons between the VCS and the SCII. Again, only a few studies have examined the inclusion of the basic interests into the VCS. Slaney (1978) had subjects sort the basic interest categories into three groups entitled: (a) "I have a strong interest in these activities, (b) I have little or no interest in these activities, or (c) I dislike these activities." Slaney found that there was a clearer and more positive relationship between the basic interests of the SCII and those sorted as part of the VCS than there was, for example, for the occupations that were sorted and also listed on the SCII. Similar results were also found in Slaney and Slaney (1981). The greater similarity between the basic interest scales for the two instruments is quite probably related to the similarity of the methods of deriving the scale items for the SCII and expressed interests. The basic interest scales, in fact, resemble expressed interest scales. Although more recent studies of the VCS have dropped the sorting of the basic interests to reduce the total time needed, the use of the basic interests as a part of career exploration might be a particularly relevant exercise for younger students in junior high school or the lower high school years. Thus far, however, the use of basic interests in career counseling has been largely unexamined.

The occupations used by Slaney were those that appeared on the printout of results of the SCII. This procedure was taken from Dolliver. However, Slaney (1981) added a descriptive pamphlet entitled "The Vocational Card Sort-Understanding Your Results." This pamphlet, first included in the Slaney (1983) study, reviews the VCS and instructs clients in using Holland's "Occupation Finder" to locate occupations based on their rank-ordered Holland codes. Clients are also informed about the *Dictionary of Occupational Titles* and the *Occupational Outlook Handbook.* A particular effort is made to instruct clients on gender stereotyping and to encourage them to explore occupations that appeal to them separate from their sex role stereotypes about those occupations. Other points of emphasis include ways of making sense of their final rank-ordering of their career choices. Finally, "some next steps" to take in the exploration of career choices are presented. Some readings are also suggested and the use of a career counselor is suggested if additional issues or questions need exploration. In the studies on the VCS, subjects or clients were given a copy of their record of their VCS results, a copy of the "Occupations Finder" and a copy of the pamphlet "The Vocational Card Sort-Understanding Your Results." No specific studies of the effects of the pamphlet as a separate part of the VCS have been conducted.

The VCS used by Slaney contains some additions and permutations on the original card sort devised by Dolliver, but clearly the similarities outweigh the differences. The inclusion of the description of the Holland types and their rank-ordering is an addition that has a number of implications. Certainly it presents an interesting task that can make the relationship of the Holland types to careers more involving and interesting for clients (as well as counselors). It also asks the client and the counselor to take a broad, holistic, integrative view of the client as a beginning step in considering career choices. With a counselor present, this task can get clients started in talking about themselves as whole persons and help them to focus on the importance of integrating themselves and their career possibilities.

Additional research is needed but the study by Slaney and MacKinnon-Slaney (1986) suggested, logically enough, that clients whose expressed choices and inventoried choices were in agreement were better able to relate their Holland codes and their expressed choices. One implication of this finding is that low agreement clients might productively spend more time thinking about who they are relative to the Holland types. This idea is reminiscent of a great deal of the conventional trait-factor theorizing on matching which assumes a certain knowledge of self as a necessary precursor to informed matching. Additional research on the rank-ordering of the Holland types would seem to be theoretically important as well as pragmatically useful. The inclusion of the "Occupations Finder" in relation to the rank-ordered Holland types also gives clients who take the VCS an additional important source of possible occupations to explore.

The inclusion of the basic interest category from the SCII was done as a part of the comparative studies with the SCII and the VCS as well as other instruments. Although the use of basic interests in career counseling seems like a potentially productive area of study, the basic interests are no longer included in the VCS because of the additional time required to sort them and their apparent limited relevance for most college and adult or re-entry students. The explanatory booklet that has been developed for the VCS does seem like an important addition to the task, especially when the VCS is taken as a self-administered activity. It appears to add potentially useful information and it attempts to add cautionary notes about the importance of being aware of sex-role stereotyping in thinking about and selecting possible career choices. Although the information contained in the booklet seems helpful to clients, no data on the effects of this booklet have been gathered.

DESCRIPTION OF THE INSTRUMENT

Clients for whom the Instrument seems most Appropriate

The flexibility of the vocational card sort technique makes it an appropriate career intervention for a broad variety of clients:

1. Undecided clients, particularly those who do not yet have a good sense of identity, as well as those who have not yet had an opportunity to explore the world of work
2. Older clients who have the diversity of life and work experiences to draw upon
3. Female clients who limit their career options to stereotyped, pink-collar occupations
4. Clients with psychopathology or handicaps–but the counselor must make the judgment about the severity of pathology or level of comprehension

5. Young clients working on self assessment
6. Intellectually oriented clients who like to control their own decision-making
7. Clients for whom expressed and inventoried choices are not in agreement.

Undecided clients can be difficult to work with, especially when traditional testing does not add to their understanding of career choices. By using the vocational card sort technique, counselors can gain insight into how clients see themselves. Counselors can then note patterns of interests and abilities that make sense in relation to other biographical information (for example, hobbies, extra-curricular activities, courses which the client has enjoyed in school, family patterns, and ways of coping). The process allows the client to integrate self knowledge with knowledge of occupations and, at the same time, allows the counselor to use clinical skills to further the integration process. The vocational card sort technique provides a productive intervention vehicle for both client and counselor, and offers the counselor an interactive treatment mode.

Older clients have varied life experiences that add to their understanding of who they are, and how they see themselves in the work world. Many adults who are reconsidering careers have not had the time to think about turning aspirations into reality. The vocational card sort technique can help adult clients understand the process of career decision-making and yet assist them in considering alternatives in a realistic way. If the client is considering occupations that are not included in the occupation cards, the counselor can encourage the client to add those occupations, so that similarities and differences in all occupational preferences can be examined. Because vocational card sorts are very individual and dependent upon the clinical skills of the counselor, the technique can be helpful with adult clients from all socioeconomic backgrounds, from executives terminated as a result of corporate acquisitions, to impoverished clients barely a step away from welfare.

Women clients may be hampered unwittingly in their career exploration by traditional values and stereotyped perspectives of occupations—even though it now seems clear that very few jobs cannot be performed by either sex. Because gender is not mentioned on vocational card sorts, women do not have to be constrained by outdated conventions. In fact, as clients think out loud about the career selection process, counselors can reflect and explore values, stressing a developmental perspective. The developmental approach can take into consideration ''what if'' questions related to marriage, family, child rearing, divorce, and so forth. Female clients need the freedom to explore all occupations which fit their potential and interests: Career choices can perhaps then be based on rational decision-making and not internal or external sex biases (Slaney, 1983). Indeed in a comparison of a vocational card sort technique and the Strong Campbell Interest Inventory, women using the vocational card sort tended to select occupations which were less female dominated than did women using the SCII (Slaney

& Slaney, 1981). The card sorting system seems to encourage women to consider a wide range of career options.

Clients who have a physical or psychological handicap sometimes feel unnecessarily limited in their career choices. By using the card sort technique in conjunction with clinical skills and judgment, counselors may gain insight into the impact of the disability on the vocational choice: They can monitor the effect of the disability on the client's self understanding and knowledge of occupations. Counselors can raise the issue of how clients might select a career differently if the handicap were not present. From an even more pragmatic perspective, clients with reading difficulties (because of learning disabilities) can be identified, and put at ease by the counselor. Thus the counselor can intervene to relax the client and to broaden the client's career horizons.

Young clients benefit from being in control of the vocational card sort process. It is easy for youngsters who do not have a clear understanding of their own identity to rely on a computer print-out as "the voice of wisdom." Career counselors in the university setting often see young clients who accept, without question, parental advice on the choice of a career or a major. However because the first step of a card sort technique is the selection of the Holland code and an understanding of one's own vocational personality, clients immediately have a framework for understanding themselves as unique individuals—individuals with special configurations of personality traits. Some clients may feel that counselors have "magical" understanding and insight, because the self-selected Holland code makes so much sense and is easily grasped. The framework gives clients insight into the relationship between their own interests, abilities, and personality traits, and their occupational selections.

Intellectually-oriented clients like to direct their own decision-making process. As the vocational card sort technique moves from self-knowledge to individual occupations, the client feels in control and understands the progression of events. The physical manipulation of the cards also places the client in control. Our observation has been that integration of self-knowledge and knowledge of occupations allows the decision-making process to build logically.

Clients for whom expressed choices differ from inventoried choices may not receive the confirmation hoped for (Slaney, 1978). By explaining the research on expressed versus inventoried choices, counselors can allay the fears that clients have when the inventory "says" that their interests are dissimilar to workers employed in that particular occupation. With the card sort technique, counselors can reassure clients that their career choices are either efficacious or perhaps in need of reexamination in light of personal or occupational variables.

Self-Directed versus Counselor Administered

When using vocational card sorts, the counselor has two choices: (a) to monitor the client step by step, or (b) to provide the card sort in a self-directed manner along with instructions (Slaney, 1978) and then process the results with the client later. Time and complexity of presenting issues will determine which method the counselor selects.

If the client is especially undecided or confused, the counselor may opt to facilitate the card sorting process in conjunction with clinical assessment strategies. As the client arranges and sorts the cards, the counselor asks the client to think out loud. By focusing on verbal and nonverbal behavior, the counselor can then clarify or intervene when appropriate. The thoughts elicited may be career-oriented, personal, social, or family information. Thus the counselor can have some understanding of the client's thoughts and the way in which the client makes decisions.

Whether or not the client has a good sense of self, an understanding of occupations, or is undecided about career options, the counselor may assign the card sort technique as a counselor-free intervention. The process itself provides clarification for the client (Slaney, 1978). It also confirms the counselor's confidence that the client will resolve his or her own career choice issues, and focuses the answer to the problem on the client himself or herself. At a later session, the counselor can then question the client's perceptions of the process, as well as the outcome information furnished by the client. This is a less time consuming procedure for the counselor, but not necessarily less clinically revealing. Is is a useful and productive intervention for many clients.

Units and Levels at which Assessment Occurs

A vocational card sort technique allows clients to work at different units and levels of understanding. The movement is from an analysis of the individual occupations (the units) to an examination of the three different groupings or piles (the levels), "Would not choose," "In question," and "Would choose." Within each grouping or level, the client then deals with clusters or "split levels" which are labelled according to commonalities.

With one sweep through the cards, clients can frequently, unequivocally rule out certain occupations, (the "Would not choose" units) and feel a sense of accomplishment as the pile of cards remaining becomes smaller. By examining the "Would not choose" occupation cards for commonalities, clients have evidence that shows that they do know what they are doing: they usually feel that the "Would not choose" occupations really would be inappropriate career choices. The labels on the disliked clusters reinforce the clients' confidence in the task and their ability to succeed in making a reasoned choice. As the "Would not choose" occupational cards are physically shoved aside, clients usually feel a sense of satisfaction.

At this point only "Would choose" and "In question" occupations remain: the occupational card pile is a great deal smaller than it was originally. The client now scrutinizes the individual occupations and then moves them into either the "Would choose" or the "In question" piles. As these two piles are clustered and labelled, the client focuses on important values and attitudes toward occupations. The individual occupations (the units) are thus arranged and organized to build the piles (levels) of "Would choose" or "In question" occupations.

ADMINISTERING VOCATIONAL CARD SORTS

Materials Needed

Vocational card sorts generally consist of three sets of cards, which can be used in conjunction with Directions for the Vocational Card Sort, (Slaney, 1978), The Vocational Card Sort—Understanding Your Results (Slaney, 1981) and The Occupation Finder (Holland, 1985b). The cards are designed to be arranged and manipulated easily, making the career exploration task manageable for clients. Indeed, clients are in control as they sort the cards and monitor their own results, either with or without the direction of a counselor. If the process is counselor-free, then clients will need response sheets that automatically provide a carbon for the client and the original (because it is usually easier to read) for the counselor.

The first set of cards consists of six 5″ × 8″ cards labelled according to the Holland vocational personality types and containing a short description of each. The vocational personality types are Realistic, Investigative, Artistic, Social, Enterprising, and Conventional and are often referred to by their first letter (R, I, A, S, E, C). The Realistic personality type is mechanically inclined and often enjoys working outdoors with heavy machinery; the Investigative personality type is theoretically inclined and enjoys science and math; the Artistic personality is imaginative, as well as creative, and seeks self expression; the Social personality type enjoys helping others; the Enterprising personality type works with others in a persuading or managing way; and the Conventional personality type works well within a defined chain of command and enjoys working with data, rather than with people or things.

The second set of cards consists of 4″ × 6″ cards: the three category cards are labelled (a) I have a strong interest in these activities, (b) I have little or no interest in these activities, and (c) I dislike these activities. The remaining 23 cards have interest areas printed on them, such as Social Service, Religious Activities, Science, and Law or Politics.

The third set of cards consists of three 5″ × 8″ category cards and one hundred and seven 3″ × 5″ occupation cards. The category cards are labelled (a) Might choose, (b) In question, and (c) Would not choose. The occupation cards represent careers such as Reporter, Nursing Home Administrator, Carpenter, Dentist, Geographer, Secretary, and so forth.

Procedures

With a counselor-free version of a card sort, clients are instructed to read the pamphlet, Directions for the Vocational Card Sort (Slaney, 1978). The directions indicate that clients should prepare for the vocational exploration task by focusing on themselves as individuals, so that they can react to a variety of activities and occupations and examine the reasons behind their reactions.

When the counselor opts to administer a vocational card sort to a client, the counselor should first focus on building a relationship with the client. The client must feel comfortable with the counselor—only then will the client feel free to provide all the necessary information related to the vocational exploration task. The vocational card sort technique fosters a holistic approach to career exploration.

In Step 1, clients are instructed to read each of the six descriptions of the Holland vocational personality types and to arrange the descriptions in rank order, from most similar to their own personality to least similar. The ranking should then be recorded for later use.

In Step 2, clients sort the activity cards into three piles, according to the category cards: (a) I have a strong interest in these activities; (b) I have little or no interest in these activities; and (c) I dislike these activities. The cards should be arranged relatively quickly. The client then focuses on the five activities in which he or she had the strongest interest and the five activities which he or she disliked the most. After these selections are recorded, the cards are put aside in their separate piles.

Step 3 instructs the client to look at the third set of cards and organize the occupations in groups: (a) Might choose, (b) In question, and (c) Would not choose.

The client then examines the "Would not choose" pile and arranges the cards into groups that logically go together, in terms of their relationship to each other. For example, people frequently see the occupations of dentist and doctor (physician) as related and group them together. When all the cards in the "Would not choose" pile are arranged into groups, then each group is labelled according to the client's perception of what the occupations have in common. The labels for the clusters may focus on values, aptitudes, fears, family concerns, socio-economic status, educational concerns, money issues, and so forth. The groups and their labels should then be recorded.

Next, the client examines the "In question" pile. Are there any occupations in this group, that on second thought, the client might want to move to the "Would choose" pile? Are there any that the client would like additional information about? Sources of information can be discussed later. Finally, the client is asked to state why these occupations are in question: How relevant is their status to the process of making a career choice? The client and counselor should keep notes on the process.

The client then examines the "Might Choose" pile and arranges the cards into logically related groupings. When all the cards are sorted, the client is asked to give a label to each group and to think of reasons to explain why he or she might choose these occupations. Again groups and labels should be recorded.

From the occupations in the "Might Choose" pile, the client is asked to select the 10 most preferred, in order of preference. The client then examines the groups in which these 10 most preferred occupations reside, and looks for relationships, similarities, and differences. Each occupation can then be examined in light of "real world" issues facilitating or hampering the client from reaching his or her career goal. If the issues make a difference from either a positive or negative standpoint that too should be noted, for later examination.

To be sure that nothing has been omitted, the client should review the list of preferred occupations to make sure that all occupations, whether on the cards or not, are on the list. Any occupation can be added and ranked accordingly.

After the client has completed the self-directed form of administration, he or she may be instructed to read "The Vocational Card Sort—Understanding Your Results" (Slaney, 1981). This pamphlet provides the client with information about the vocational exploration process, suggests sources of occupational information, and raises issues which the client may consider before seeing the counselor the next time.

Variations and Possibilities

Any number of variations on the sorting technique are available to the counselor—the counselor can be creative and imaginative. The counselor can adapt the technique to meet the needs of the client.

The Holland vocational personality type cards are particularly useful for gaining insight into the client's personality and world. After having the client rank order the cards, the counselor may ask the client to point out the words and phrases on each card which are descriptive of him or her. This provides the counselor with additional information about the client. For example, if the client mentions that she enjoys being at the center of a group and taking leadership roles, the counselor can question further about prior experiences, positive and negative, related to that personality trait; or if the client mentions that he is a "people pleaser" the counselor can find out whether that occurs in family settings, work setting, or peer settings, and how the client feels about it. The card sort technique is a flexible tool for the counselor to use.

With the Holland vocational personality type cards, the counselor can focus on self-acceptance, an important aspect of vocational exploration. Does the client like himself or herself? Which qualities would the client like to change? What do family members or friends say about these personality traits? What are the personality types of other family members and what does that do to relationships within the family? With this technique of vocational exploration, many personal and family issues become apparent: such as liking or disliking one's appearance, bulimia, family patterns of abuse, physiological symptoms related to stress, and so forth.

The Holland vocational personality types can also help counselors in the college setting explore with clients why certain majors or college courses are a good fit and others a bad fit. The Holland types help to explain the paradigms, or world views of different fields of study (Kuhn, 1970). For example if a student in computer science selects Social or Enterprising as the first theme in the rank ordering, then it is easy to explain how that particular paradigm may either be different from that student's predominating world view, or may take some extra work for that student to understand. Because the student rank orders all the Holland types, it becomes important to discuss how important each of the themes are to his or her personality. Most careers require multiple and diverse personality traits from just about all of the personality types and most students can point out which of their own personality characteristics are associated with each type. The result for the student is a better understanding of himself or herself and a better understanding of different fields of study and careers.

The basic interest cards and the occupation cards can be sorted in many different ways. The counselor can instruct the client to arrange the cards according to different time periods: How would the client sort the cards today; How would the client have sorted the cards in high school. Different feeling modes provide another variation: When the client is feeling up-beat and positive, how would she sort the cards, in contrast with when feeling depressed. If there are strong parental or family pressures, the cards can be sorted according to how the client would arrange and label them, in contrast with how parents would sort and label. Clients with a physical handicap can be instructed to sort the cards as though the handicap was not an issue. Women may be asked to sort the cards as though they were men. Many variations of the sorting technique are possible, allowing the counselor to tailor the intervention to the perceived needs of the client.

For counselors in a university or college setting, the same sorting technique works with college majors. By dividing the available college majors into three groups (Might choose, In question, and Would not choose) and then providing labels for clusters, students can understand their interests in different majors and do some reality testing by taking courses (or browsing through books in the book store) in each of the Might choose majors. At the same time, the majors can be tied to the occupations and the ranking of the Holland vocational personality types. Because one college major provides the flexibility to enter several occupations—as well as graduate and professional school—the student can keep occupational options open until a choicc is mandated at a later time.

MAKING SENSE OF THE INSTRUMENT

Constructs or Dimensions Assessed by the Instrument

For clients there are three obvious levels at which assessment of constructs occurs: (a) self-understanding of personality traits; (b) likes and dislikes of basic interests; and (c) likes and dislikes of occupations. With the help of the counselor, understanding moves at each step beyond the obvious to explore and integrate values, aptitudes, past experiences, and aspirations.

Because the first step of the vocational card sort technique is the rank ordering of the Holland types, clients usually have a better understanding of their own vocational personality (Slaney, 1978). This can be quite revealing for clients—and almost mystical—as they gain understanding of why certain occupations have appeal and others do not, and why certain courses or majors in school are more interesting for them than others. Strengths and weaknesses, which many clients takc for granted, begin to make sense. Family issues and ways of coping can also be examined.

The second step and second level of assessment involves interest in broad categories of activities. What does the client like to do; what does the client dislike? These interests can then be meshed with the personality traits of the Holland types.

The third level of assessment relates to specific occupations. As the client divides occupations into clusters which seem interesting, and labels the clusters according to logical similarities, consistencies with the vocational personality type and preferred activities become apparent. By examining clusters of occupations that are not on the "Might choose" pile or are "In question," the client begins to understand some of the attitudes about occupations, as well as values which he or she holds. These attitudes and values can then be examined in light of developmental issues and other personal concerns.

Results

The results are produced as clients proceed with the task. Self-understanding occurs with each unit and level of exploration in a reasonable and organized way. Clients even report self-understanding, without counselor intervention (Slaney, 1978; 1983). No formal scoring procedure external to the client is needed.

The process of vocational exploration using a card sort technique provides results in and of itself. From the process, clients seem to have a better understanding of (a) their vocational personality, (b) their interests (both likes and dislikes), (c) the occupations which they like and dislike, and (d) their reasons for liking or disliking.

Because the results are self explanatory, when the counselor facilitates the process or goes over the recorded information with the client, he or she can focus on a holistic view of career counseling. By questioning the categories, groupings and reasons, the counselor helps the client understand why certain choices seem more appropriate than others. The counselor may also encourage the client to keep all options open until additional information is obtained or a first choice is mandated.

Involvement of the Client in the Process

The client is the most important part of the vocational card sort technique. Results are produced by the client, monitored by the client, evaluated by the client, and used by the client without the assistance of a formal scoring procedure.

The counselor-free application of the card sort almost forces clients to be self-reliant and to make sense of the sorting procedure themselves. Although seeking help for their problems related to career choice (a dependent, one-down position), clients are shown that they have the capacity to find the answer to their own problems (an independent, one-up position). The counselor-free application fosters independent decision-making in a logical and organized manner.

Counselor-facilitated card sorting distributes the responsibility for problem solving to some degree to both the client and the counselor. Some clients become somewhat self-conscious as they sort the cards in front of the counselor. However when counselors monitor the card sorting process, they can observe both verbal responses and nonverbal behavior. By facilitating the process, counselors are able to help clients focus on here-and-now issues of decision-making style, as well as historical and future concerns.

Immediacy of Feedback

Card sort techniques provide clients with immediate feedback. The client does not really need the counselor to interpret results and does not need to wait for a computer print-out. The process provides results which are generally quite understandable to the client.

Lack of Technology

The lack of technology involved in the process of manipulating cards takes the mystery out of making career decisions. The process provides a logical and reasoned answer for the client. There is no instant voice of wisdom out of the computer print out telling the client what careers he or she is suited for. In our impatient, pill popping, quick fix, microwave society, this can be seen as a benefit or a draw back.

However, because feedback is immediate but not technological, clients are satisfied. Results come from the client's own efforts and readiness to find an answer to career choice issues.

EFFECTS AND INFLUENCE OF THE INSTRUMENT ON COUNSELORS

Importance of this Issue to Career Counseling

No issue is more important to our clients than sense of identity—and that sense of identity is intimately connected with career choice. We invest time, energy and ourselves in our careers—40 hours in a week, two thousand hours in a year, and a hundred thousand hours or more in a life time. Career selection is of central concern to our clients.

Finding appropriate interventions for clients is not always easy. The card sort technique offers an alternative intervention which is focused on the individual client, is generated by the client, is not reliant on computer technology, and usually makes intuitive sense to the client.

Importance to Counselors in General

Card sort techniques are wonderfully counselor-friendly. Because of the flexibility provided by the manipulation of the cards and the logical progression of the process, counselors can provide as much or as little input as seems appropriate.

The focus of the counselor-client interaction can be geared to any area of concern (family, personal, social, marital, aptitudes, values), which might help the client. Yet the card sorting process itself takes care of the assessment of the individual occupations and provides the client with an answer to his or her presenting problem of career indecision. The process leads to client understanding and not just another test-and-tell-em method of career counseling.

Because the results are self-explanatory, the counselor does not need an intimate knowledge of test construction or statistics to help the client understand the results. Proficient clinical skills will add more to the process than will an understanding of standard scores or norms.

Anecdotal Experience and Prescriptions for Research

In the college or university career counseling center, undecided clients can be particularly difficult to deal with. Young college students do not have an appreciation for the free career counseling service that they receive: yet they are impatient to know what to major in. We have found that a combination of the card sort technique to assess careers, and a similar process to assess college majors can provide interim answers and satisfaction for clients, in concert with reality-testing by taking courses in different fields and reading about occupations. This format provides a productive and satisfying intervention for undecided clients whose expressed interests differ from their inventoried interests. These are the clients who otherwise tend to feel stranded with the unanswered questions.

Returning adult women students, who may select occupations on the basis of traditional female values, are also good candidates for the card sort technique. Research indicates that there are differences in cohort groups of re-entry students: Women in their forties seem to select more female dominated occupations than do women in their thirties or twenties (MacKinnon-Slaney, 1986). Married women tend to select more traditional occupations than either single or divorced women (MacKinnon-Slaney, Barber, & Slaney, 1988).

Because of these proclivities it makes sense to stimulate less stereotyped thinking on the part of reentry women. Because gender differences are not highlighted by the card sort process, adult women students seem to be less limited by thinking of occupations as being either ''male'' or ''female.'' In our experience, these learned attitudes, powerful as they are for adults, seem to be muted by the card sort technique.

CASE EXAMPLE

Description of the Client

Susan was a 19-year-old first semester, college sophomore. She requested career counseling because she was not doing well in the classes that would prepare her for a career in veterinary medicine. She had been interested in veterinary medicine since her freshman year in high school and had worked part-time with a vet during her vacations. Her background was suburban. She described herself as being similar to her father, a computer hardware engineer who enjoyed a country atmosphere and animals.

Susan felt that her dreams had been shattered because her grade-point average in college was barely passing—vet school was impossible. Her reasons for the poor grade-point average centered on family matters that had caused her a great deal of stress during her first year in college; she did not seem to want to elaborate further in the first session.

Because she had been interested in veterinary medicine for so long, Susan could hardly envisage alternative occupations. After being pressed to answer the Occupational Alternatives Question (Zener & Schnuelle, 1976), Susan offered dairy production, animal production, biology teacher, animal scientist, veterinary assistant, and veterinary as her expressed choices. She still saw veterinary medicine as her first choice, even though reality testing was making that a questionable choice. Susan's level of indecision appeared to be between level 2 (first choice with alternatives) and level 3 (alternatives and no real first choice (Slaney, 1980).

Reasons for Using a Card Sort Technique with Susan

For Susan, the use of the vocational card sort technique seemed to make sense for a variety of reasons. Susan's expressed interest in veterinary medicine was of such long standing that any vocational interest inventory would be colored by that choice. Even if inventoried interests agreed with her expressed interests, other interests and abilities needed to be examined. And the nuances of animal science and dairy production were not usually found on an interest inventory. If Susan's interests were not confirmed by the inventory, then she would be discouraged by the results—leaving her more depressed than she already was.

There was something about Susan's manner that indicated some kind of personal problems or stresses that also might be affecting her at college. She had mentioned family concerns and a health problem that had never been fully resolved. The card sort technique offered the flexibility to explore career issues, as well as personal and family issues to the extent that Susan desired.

Results and Effects

Susan rank ordered the Holland vocational personality type cards and discussed her own personality traits. First she selected the Realistic theme because that seemed to her to be the personality type most like her own. She noted that she preferred to deal with things rather than ideas or people. She enjoyed camping and her work with animals. The outdoors gave her peace of mind. She saw herself as being strong and having good physical skills (in high school she had been on the softball team.) She indicated that she was practical and noted that she did have difficulty expressing her ideas and feelings to others. When asked to give an example of a situation in which she had trouble expressing her feelings, she said that there were some family matters during her senior year in high school that had caused her problems, but she did not elaborate.

The Investigative theme came second in Susan's ranking since she saw herself as interested in science, but neither creative nor original in that context. In high school she had always done very well in science; in fact the idea of veterinary medicine as a career had emerged in her sophomore year of high school and her teachers had encouraged her. She indicated that now in college she was not doing well in the sciences and was, in fact, only receiving good grades in biology. She particularly disliked college physics. Again she reiterated that she was not interested in work around people.

She selected the Conventional theme next because she was generally organized and did not seek leadership or power. She acknowledged that she did like to know what was expected of her and could work well within a chain of command.

Susan's ranking of the last three themes was Social, Artistic, and Enterprising. The Social theme came next in her ranking because Susan saw herself as responsible, cheerful, and concerned with the welfare of others. She saw herself as being particularly concerned with her family because she was the oldest of three daughters. Her preference was not to be in the center of a group, but on the fringe. In high school she had been in the French club, the Honor Society, the school newspaper, and the biology club, but she had not played a central role in any of the groups. She described herself as not particularly popular, but able to get along well with others. She indicated again that she did not seek leadership—in fact even when thinking about being a vet, she wanted to be the assistant and not the vet in charge. Susan selected the Artistic theme next because she was sensitive and emotional, but not assertive about her own opinions and capabilities. She saw herself as having some creative tendencies and acknowledged that she was a very independent person. The Enterprising personality type was the one which was least in keeping with her personality. She knew that she did not like economics, sales, or the business fields.

It became clear that Susan's interest in animals might be related in some way to her disappointment in people. During the second session, she disclosed that family issues were complex. Her father was abusive, but it was the for the good of the three daughters in the family. Her mother, she said, "Was a very nice, kind, and gentle person" but unable to stand up for her daughters. Susan's younger sister had turned her father in to the police for child abuse, but the sister was a trouble maker, and so on. Susan's stomach problems had just about disappeared after one and a half years at college. The personal issues were overwhelming—the card sort technique provided a vehicle for those concerns to be placed along side the career issues.

Career and family issues were foremost in Susan's thoughts. At least while Susan was away at school, family problems receded into the background a little. For Susan, resolving career goals and choice of college major could make in immediate difference in her feelings about herself, in the way she approached her college career, and in her view of her total life space.

Because of time limitations at the end of the school year, the basic interest cards were disregarded and Susan was asked by the counselor to sort the occupational cards. Many personal issues impinged on Susan's choice of career and major, so the counselor chose to facilitate the occupation card sort process.

Susan sorted the occupational cards into the three piles, "Would not choose," "In question," and "Might choose." After the "Would not choose" cards were sorted into clusters, Susan labelled the clusters: for example (a) Too much difficult science involved (medicine, dentistry, geology), (b) Too confining (military and public official careers), (c) Too much direct public service (executive housekeeper, food service, beautician), (d) No talent (artist, interior decorator), and (e) Other people's theoretical money (investment, banking).

Next Susan examined the "In question" and "Might choose" piles. The "In question" cards were examined and moved to either the "Might choose," or "Would not choose" piles. Occupations that Susan wanted more information about were moved to a separate pile. Susan then examined the cards in her "Might choose" pile. She rank ordered the cards according to her interest in each occupation and added other occupations which were not listed on the cards (vet assistant, dairy production, animal production, and biology teacher were the occupations which interested her).

After categorizing the occupational cards that reinforced her interest in animals and biology, Susan turned to college majors. As she examined the possible majors at the university, and categorized them according to "Would not choose," "In question," and "Might choose," it became clear that animal science, dairy science, animal production, and even agronomy held some interest for Susan. After carefully examining these options in light of the labels from the "Would not choose" and "In question" card sorting, Susan found that her interests were confirmed. For Susan that information was comforting.

Interpretation

All her life, Susan had been playing a moderating role in her family between her sisters and her mother, between her mother and her father, and between her sisters and her father. So much of her energy had been channelled into family matters that she had not had time to realize that she had been focusing on everyone else's needs but her own. She had managed high school fairly easily under those circumstances, but college was a different matter.

Susan's call for help with career matters was also a call for help with life. She was relieved that counseling took a holistic approach to career issues and examined the personal and family concerns too. But her career plans were very important to her—this was something she could do for herself. She really did not want counseling to focus only on the personal issues. In fact she felt that she could get personal counseling at any time, and already had, but the career issues were much more central to her well-being at this time in her life.

Evaluation by Client and Counselor

The card sorting technique allowed Susan to discuss all aspects of her life while she was concentrating on career issues. She was relieved to have her career interests confirmed and was quite willing to undertake homework assignments to discover more about kindred occupations: reading about careers, talking with faculty who could shed light on her areas of interest, talking to her friends to find out what they liked or did not like about their majors, joining student clubs related to majors which sounded interesting, and so forth. As a sophomore, Susan was beginning to panic about selecting a major, so she was eager to have concrete tasks to undertake in order to help her make a reasoned decision.

From the counselor's perspective, the card sort technique worked well. Susan had made a good beginning on the decision-making process. She had been able to see how personal and family problems impinged on her career decisions. She was now moving ahead to do some things for herself so that she could find her own niche in life, and her own identity as an individual separate from her family. The card sort had provided the vehicle.

RESEARCH ON THE VOCATIONAL CARD SORTS

This section of the chapter will examine the published research available on the vocational card sorts. The first published study located was a dissertation by Cooper (1976). She compared a Vocational Card Sort, which she based on Dewey's Non-Sexist VCS and adapted to be self-administered, with the then recently merged male and female forms of the SCII. Both were either given by themselves or preceded by the Auxiliary Information Material (AIM), which was a brief survey of myths and realities about men and women in the world of work. It was designed to increase awareness of the importance of the eventual career choice. Cooper also included a no treatment control group. The general hypothesis was that the inclusion of the AIM would increase career salience and career exploration in college women. Cooper randomly distributed 120 undergraduate women to one of the five groups. The SCII groups received their results in the form of the interpretive report produced by NCS. The outcome measures were gathered one month after the treatment.

Cooper found that subjects who had taken the VCS were considering more occupational options, more nontraditional options, and were reading occupational information more than were the control group members. There were no differences between the groups on the proportion of nontraditional careers being considered. Only those subjects who had been exposed to the AIM were significantly more career salient than the control group members. The AIM had no effects on increasing career options or information seeking. The effects found for the AIM were mixed but somewhat promising. The results for the VCS were unexpected but seemed promising for expanding the number and type of the occupations being considered as well as the career exploration of college women. The authors did not speculate about the reasons for the differences between the VCS and the SCII.

Dolliver and Will (1977) did a 10-year follow-up of the 67 undergraduate subjects who had participated in Dolliver's dissertation research. Of the original 67, 46 had been clients seeking career counseling and 21 had had career counseling provided as part of a federally funded work-study program for students from low income families. There were 37 males and 30 females. A letter and questionnaire were sent to each subject who could be located. The questionnaire asked the subjects to record their present job, to select the SVIB occupational scale closest to that job, to record their level of job satisfaction, and to state whether they would be willing to fill out a current SCII. The subjects were also asked to sort the SVIB-M scale titles into the three VCS classifications (''Like, Indifferent, Dislike'').

Thirty-seven respondents returned the questionnaire. An additional 7 were contacted by phone, and the occupations of 3 more were established through the alumni office. Altogether, the current occupations of 47 subjects were determined, 28 males and 19 females; 35 had been counseling clients and 12 had been work study students. The results, though complex, suggested to Dolliver and Will that the Tyler Vocational Card Sort was slightly more accurate than the SVIB in predicting occupations that were held 10 years later. Both were accurate for about 50% of the subjects. These and other results suggested that the results of the VCS were quite similar to the results of the widely used SVIB. Dolliver and Will suggested that the two instruments might have differential usefulness depending on the needs of the career client. They wrote:

> Measures of inventoried interests probably help orient clients to new occupational areas that had not previously been considered or to provide a confirmation of what had seemed an appropriate choice. Methods of expressed-interests measurement probably are helpful to clients who have considered a lot of occupational areas but have difficulty in narrowing their choices. Cognitively complex clients, especially, seem to benefit from the chance to sort out their ideas. Expressed-interests measures, by their nature, help the client to take more seriously what they already know about their ideas, values, and goals. The TVCS and NSVCS both promote the clients' consideration of their reasons for being attracted to or repelled from occupations, an aspect of the method that could not be included in the present study. (p. 53)

In concluding their discussion section, Dolliver and Will suggested that counselors should use both an ''expressed-vocational-interests method'' and an inventory and make special note of the areas of agreement. This final suggestion was supported by a conclusion reached by Slaney and Russell (1981). Based on a review of the research comparing the predictive validity of expressed and inventoried vocational interests, they concluded that when expressed and inventoried interests are in agreement, predictive validity is higher than when they are not in agreement. The results of the Dolliver and Will study were quite supportive of the use of the vocational card sort in career counseling.

A study by Slaney (1978), was developed to compare the results and reactions of subjects who took both the VCS and the SCII. He had 84 undergraduate women, who were paid for participation, take both instruments. The subjects were screened to assure that they had not decided on a career choice. In the first session they were given a questionnaire and then asked to complete the SCII. Two weeks later they returned and took the VCS, which was self-administered. When they completed the VCS they were given the printout of their SCII results. After reading these results, they completed a questionnaire that compared the two instruments and were asked to return in three weeks. At this final session, the subjects filled out a final questionnaire, were asked for their reactions to the study, and were paid.

Slaney found moderate agreement between the two sets of Holland themes gathered from the two instruments. There was rather clear agreement between the basic interests of the two instruments and less clear agreement between the occupations as they were presented on the SCII printout and as they were sorted as part of the VCS. Slaney concluded that while there were generally statistically significant relationships between the corresponding Holland themes, basic interests, and occupations of the two instruments, the results of the instruments were not interchangeable for individual clients. He also found that the VCS Holland themes were not less consistent, as Holland defines consistency, than the SCII themes. The VCS themes were more highly related to expressed interests than were the themes of the SCII. The 12 bipolar items of a comparative questionnaire were specifically designed to measure differences between the two instruments based on the suggestions of Dolliver and Will quoted above. None of these differences was statistically significant.

A separate question asked subjects to identify which instrument they would recommend to a friend. One suggested neither, 76 (92%) suggested both, four suggested only the SCII and three suggested only the VCS. Finally, an open ended question asked subjects to write comments that would compare the two instruments. These comments were combined for each instrument and two raters were asked to summarize the comments they had read. The first rater, a female Ph.D., wrote the following:

> My overall impression was that the subjects found the instruments complementary; the VCS was a more personal, thought-provoking experience but the computerized results of the SCII lent validity or provided a challenge to the personal evaluation. While the SCII was sometimes found boring, the VCS, because it questioned the reasons for choices, was more fun to take and kept interest alive.

The second rater, a male Ph.D. summarized the comments he had read as follows:

> The VCS seemed to stimulate more thinking and individual initiative, the SCII seemed to be regarded as more objective and having wider coverage. It was obvious that there is a great deal of individual variance in terms of how the two tests were perceived.

These comments of the raters do seem reminiscent of the earlier comments of Dolliver and Will that suggested that the VCS helps clients by encouraging them to think about their choices and, more specifically, their reasons for these choices.

The results of the study by Slaney seemed supportive of the inclusion of the Holland themes as rank-ordered by the clients, as well as the relation of these themes to measures of expressed interests and college majors. The comparison of some of the psychometric aspects of the two instruments also seemed encouraging for the VCS. The generally positive evaluations of the instrument by the women who had taken both versions, as well as the summary of their comments on the two instruments, were also seen as positive support for the continued investigation of the instrument. Taken together, the results of this study suggested that the VCS held up quite well in comparison to the SCII. Given that the SCII was then, and continues to be, one of the most widely used inventories as well as one of the most carefully developed, these results were seen as encouraging.

Lawler (1979) investigated the effects of the Non-Sexist Vocational Card Sort and the Self-Directed Search when both were self-administered in their standard formats or were revised to conform to the requirements of the NIE Guidelines on Sex Bias and Sex Fairness. She also included an Information-only group and a Waiting-list control group. She studied 198 undergraduate women who were uncertain about their vocational futures and were interested in participating in a study on career exploration. The women were randomly distributed to one of the six groups. Lawler found no differences based on whether the groups received the original or the revised versions of the instruments. There were also no statistically significant differences in the satisfaction with the various treatments or in the amount of vocational exploration that was reported or the vocational information that was requested. She did find that the NSVCS suggested a broader range of career alternatives to the participants than did the SDS. However, although the NSVCS suggested more nontraditional occupations to these women, there were no differences in the traditionality of the careers they were actually considering immediately following treatment and two weeks later. The fact that the NSVCS suggested more nontraditional choices is encouraging. The fact that the choices the women were actually considering were not affected is, of course, less encouraging. Lawler suggested that perhaps a lengthier treatment might have been more effective in influencing the actual choices of these women. Overall, the NSVCS suggested more nontraditional choices to these women and in other respects performed as well as the widely used Self-Directed Search. Although these results are not exciting they were generally supportive of the card sort approach.

Two studies, one by Talbot and Birk (1979) and another by Takai and Holland (1979) investigated different aspects of the then new Vocational Exploration and Insight Kit (VEIK) by Holland and his associates. The VEIK contains the Self-

Directed Search as well as a Vocational Card Sort (VCS) which was modified by Holland. The VCS, according to Talbot and Birk, consisted of 10 steps which,:

> instruct the user to sort occupational titles; explain tentative preferences and exclusions; confront the role that sex, race, social class, or religion may have played in the sorting process; and identify "personal needs, hopes, talents, personal weaknesses, distasteful activities, and unpleasant roles or tasks" related to the user's occupational preferences. (p. 359)

Talbot and Birk assigned 103 undergraduate women to one of four groups: a SDS group, a VCS group, a VEIK group, or a control group. They found that subjects exposed to the SDS and the VEIK were considering significantly more occupations than the VCS or control groups. Later the authors noted that, although the number of occupations being considered has been used in research with some frequency, its meaning is far from clear. They suggested that some subjects would probably be better served, for example, by having less choices as a result of treatment. Talbot and Birk also found no differences on a measure of client satisfaction with the treatments. Although some minor differences between the treatments were found, the expectation that the VEIK would surpass the effects of its component parts was not supported.

Takai and Holland assigned 252 high school girls to one of three treatments: a SDS group, a VCS group, or a VEIK group. Their study yielded even more disappointing findings than did Talbot and Birk's. Despite the expectation that the VEIK would exceed the VCS and the SDS in its effects on a variety of outcome measures, that was not found. Instead, it was found that the SDS had the highest means, though these were not statistically different, the VCS had the next highest means, and the VEIK, generally, had the lowest means. Some speculations were offered on the possible reasons for these results, for example, a ceiling effect is quickly reached and additional treatments add nothing, or there may be an order effect. However, overall it was clear that the results for the more extensive VEIK were extremely disappointing. No other studies on the VEIK were located. In the present context it should be noted that the results of this study as well as the results of Talbot and Birk do add some support to the use of the card sort approach as a career intervention.

Jones and DeVault (1979) compared the Occ-U-Sort (O-U-S) and the SDS. They used 95 high school students from a variety of training programs ranging from welding to advanced placement classes in Spanish. Half of the students took the O-U-S and the other half took the SDS. All took Holland's VPI and filled out a Satisfaction Opinionnaire. Jones and DeVault found one item on the Satisfaction Opinionnaire that favored the O-U-S. They did not, however, use multivariate analyses for the overall scale. The Holland codes derived from the SDS and the O-U-S did not differ significantly in their relationships to the Holland codes of the VPI. Both relationships were moderate. There were no differences in the number of errors made in calculating the Holland codes for each instrument. Jones and DeVault interpreted these results as indicating that the O-U-S had a lot of promise as a method of meeting the career development needs of students. They noted that the possible conclusions that could be derived from their study were qualified "by the limited scope of this investigation" (p. 340).

In a later study, Jones (1983) again compared the O-U-S and the SDS with 578 8th- and 10th-grade students from North Carolina. Although a few minor differences were found, several of these did not hold up after three weeks and, overall, the study was remarkable for the lack of differences, given the large number of subjects. The study also used a rather simplistic approach to the analyses of the results and failed to look for possible gender or race differences. The O-U-S did, however, appear to perform as well as the more widely used SDS on the dimensions measured.

Atanasoff and Slaney (1980) compared the effects of three counselor-free career interventions, the SDS, the interpretive format of the SCII, and the VCS. The subjects were 140 undergraduate women volunteers who were interested in career exploration and had not decided on a career choice. The women were randomly distributed to one of the treatment groups or to a no treatment control group. The effects of treatment were measured three weeks after the subjects received the results from their particular intervention. Using a rather large number of outcome measures, Atanasoff and Slaney found that the relationship between the Holland codes and expressed interests was significantly lower for the SCII than for the SDS and the VCS, which did not differ from each other. This result for the VCS and the SCII replicated the finding of Slaney (1978). All of the treatment group members indicated that they understood the kinds of occupations suitable to their personalities better than did the control group members. Beyond these results, most of the differences did not discriminate the treatment groups from the control group members. In addition, the few interaction effects that were found did not lead to unequivocal interpretations. It is interesting that the rank-ordering of the Holland types in the VCS again seemed to be supported. Overall, however, the clearest findings were that the results of the three treatments were not strikingly different from each other. Given the widespread use of the SDS and the SCII, these results at least suggested that the effects of the lesser known VCS compared quite favorably with the effects of these instruments.

The next study in this series was by Slaney and Slaney (1981) and compared the results of the merged male and female form of the SCII and the VCS for 50 female and 50 male counseling center clients who had received career counseling at a university counseling center. There was moderate agreement between the Holland codes generated by the two instruments. Slightly less than three of the five highest basic interest scales for the 2 instruments overlapped, while for the 5 highest occupational scales slightly less than one overlapped for women and slightly more than one overlapped for men. For women, all of the 5 highest occupations suggested by the SCII were more stereotypically feminine than were the 5 highest occupations of the VCS. All of these results were statistically significant. For the men, there were no statistically significant differences in the sexual composition of the occupations suggested by the two instruments. These results were consistent with the results of Slaney (1978) for the relationships between the Holland codes, basic interests, and occupational scales of the SCII and the VCS. The results for the sexual composition of the occupations suggested by the two instruments were consistent with the findings of Cooper (1976) who also compared the SCII and another version of the VCS on this dimension. Given the amount of attention that was being directed toward expanding the career options of women, this result seemed to provide important support for the VCS although the exact cause of these results was not clear.

Slaney (1983) blocked on three levels of career indecision and randomly distributed 180 undergraduate women (60 per indecision level) into a VCS or SCII treatment group or a control group. Using a large number of outcome measures, Slaney found few treatment differences, although three items of a satisfaction scale indicated that the SCII group members rated that intervention more positively than did the VCS group members. The means for both treatments were quite positive, however. There were also more judged changes in the career choices of the two treatment groups than occurred in the control group. For the VCS the greatest change took place at the most undecided level. For the SCII the changes were concentrated at the most undecided level but were also spread across the more decided levels more equally than occurred for the VCS. There were no differences between the treatments in the sexual composition of the occupations that the women were considering three weeks after treatment, no differences in vocational exploration, and no differences in satisfaction with career. Overall, there was much clearer and consistent support for the importance of career indecision. The subjects who were most undecided showed the greatest change in their career choices and expressed the greatest need for additional vocational services, and the least satisfaction with their career choices.

The results of Slaney (1983) suggested that the level of career indecision of the subjects of career intervention studies was an important consideration for future research. This variable was clearly related to a variety of outcome measures in a convincingly consistent manner. The clarity of the treatment effects was less obvious. It is at least interesting to note that the differences in satisfaction with the two instruments were not found in the Slaney (1978) study where the women took both instruments or in Atanasoff and Slaney (1980). It is also interesting that the occupations being considered by the women three weeks after treatment were not less sexually stereotyped for the VCS group. This finding is inconsistent with the earlier results of Cooper but mirrors what was found by Lawler. Unfortunately this study did not examine the occupations suggested to the subjects by the two instruments. However, even if the VCS suggested less stereotyped occupations, it is difficult to argue for the importance of this effect if the occupations actually considered do not differ. The finding that the SCII led to more changes in the decided subjects is even more intriguing. Atanasoff and Slaney in their (1980) study raised the possibility that the SCII, because it did not confirm the expressed choices of career decided subjects, may have led them to reexamine their choices even when those choices were perhaps appropriate. The present study did, in fact, find that SCII subjects who were decided changed more than did the decided subjects who received the VCS or were in the control group. None of the decided women in the control group changed, two women in the VCS group changed, and eight decided women in the SCII group changed. although these numbers are not large and the case needs to be clearly labelled as a speculative one, the issues raised deserve further exploration.

Slaney and Dickson (1985) studied reentry women, that is, undergraduate women who were over the age of 30, who had responded to a mail survey (N = 985) and expressed a willingness to be involved in a study on career choice (N = 526). Slaney and Dickson blocked in level of career indecision, based on extreme scores (upper and lower 20% of the sample) on the Vocational Identity subscale of the My Vocational Situation scale (Holland, Daiger, & Power, 1980). For the undecided group 87% were willing to participate; for the decided group 35% were willing. For each level of indecision, reentry women were randomly distributed to either a VCS only treatment group, a VCS plus videotape treatment group, or a control group. The videotape was included to attempt to encourage these women to consider more nontraditional careers. The videotape was entitled "The Joy of Choosing" and was developed as a part of Project "Born Free" to "broaden the range of career options for both women and men" (Dege, Warsett, Hansen, & Miles-Novoa, 1980). There were about 20 women per cell and a total of 121 women completed the study. A follow-up was conducted one year after the original study and over 84% of the women responded.

Outcomes were measured across a number of domains including career indecision, satisfaction with career choice, treatment satisfaction, vocational needs, the sexual composition of career choices, and career choice change. The only treatment effects found indicated that the women who had seen the videotape agreed more strongly than those who had not that they would recommend the treatment to a friend. They also agreed more strongly that the experience encouraged them to find information about occupations. Written comments from a number of the women suggested that they had responded positively to the VCS as well as the videotape. One woman wrote, "I particularly liked the 'Joy of Choosing.' My favorite gal . . . was the chemical engineer (an older lady). She will be among women I choose as a professional image." An undecided woman wrote, "In sorting the cards and really thinking about what I like to do, I was able to put more factors together and come up with a decision to research and probably commit to (the above) goals." Other undecided women also found the VCS helpful; for example: "This vocational planning experience helped me sort out my thoughts a little and gave me some ideas I hadn't thought of before. . . .'' Another wrote, ''Being part of this exploration in careers led me to really examine my wants and desires.'' Although the statements represented only a portion of the sample, they were almost entirely positive and supportive of the treatment.

As in Slaney (1983), the clearest effects were found for the variable of career indecision. The undecided women expressed a greater need for additional vocational services, were less satisfied with their career choices, and were clearly more undecided 2 weeks after treatment and 1 year after treatment. For the undecided women, indecision was reduced from pretest to posttest but unchanged from posttest to follow-up. They also had more changes in their career choices. For the satisfaction scale, undecided women agreed that they had clearer ideas about unsuitable occupations and that the experience encouraged them to find career information. They disagreed that the results of the experience had been confusing or unsatisfactory.

These results suggested that career indecision was not a transitory state for these reentry women. One year later the undecided women were still clearly undecided. The treatments for this group were not effective and no spontaneous remission effects were in evidence. Although the possibility exists that these women were experiencing other life difficulties that made them particularly difficult to treat, they do represent a proportion of the reentry population that needs career counseling, will take the time to participate, and clearly need career interventions that attend to their states of career indecision. Minimal treatments, although appreciated by these women, were not adequate in dealing with the degree of career indecision that they were experiencing. It also was clear that the intervention to encourage the exploration of more nontraditional career choices did not have a clear effect on the career choices that these women were considering two weeks or one year after counseling. Although the effects of the VCS compared quite well with the effects of other interventions and did seem to influence the thought that at least some of these women were giving to their career choices, additional attention certainly seems to be needed for the growing population of reentry women. It is also clear as it was in Slaney (1983) that career indecision is an extremely important and explanatory variable to include in future studies of interventions designed to increase career exploration.

Slaney and Lewis (1986) compared the effects of the SCII and the VCS using a different sample of career undecided reentry women. Level of indecision was assessed by the Occupational Alternatives Question (OAQ) which was the criterion measure used in Slaney (1983) for blocking on career indecision. A score of three on the OAQ indicates that a person has some alternative career choices but that there is no first choice. Women with this score in Slaney (1983) had shown the clearest and most dramatic responses to treatment, including career choice changes. Previous research has also linked this OAQ score to being undecided about a career choice (Slaney, 1980; 1983; Slaney & Dickson, 1985; Slaney, Stafford, & Russell, 1981). Slaney and Lewis used a score of three on the OAQ for selecting women. They randomly assigned 34 reentry women (i.e., undergraduate women over the age of 25) to either the VCS or the SCII. The study used a substantial number of outcome measures and included a 6-month follow-up. No statistically significant treatment differences were found on measures of vocational needs or on satisfaction with treatment at posttest. Three measures of career indecision were used and indicated that there were statistically significant reductions in career indecision for both groups three weeks after treatment but not from posttest to follow-up. Changes in career choices were not statistically significant, but post hoc inspection of the data indicated that 14 of the women (41%) had made substantive changes in their career choices, 7 from each group.

Overall, the results of the Slaney and Lewis study seem more supportive of both career interventions with reentry women who appeared to be appropriate candidates for career interventions. Both groups showed what can be considered positive treatment effects. Given that these women were rather clearly undecided and were also interested in being in a study on career exploration, it seems reasonable to suggest that becoming less career undecided equals a positive change. The generally high levels of satisfaction with both interventions is at least consistent with such an interpretation. However, a clear limitation of the study, that also limits the confidence that can be maintained in any interpretation, involves the lack of a control group. Still, these results do seem supportive of the two interventions for career undecided women. The fact that the differences in indecision that occurred after treatment were significant but the differences from posttest to follow-up were not seems to strengthen the argument that the treatments were related to the reductions in career indecision and the changes in career choices. Again, although the VCS compared quite well with the effects of the widely used SCII, the study, per se, provided no compelling rationale for preferring one treatment over the other.

Croteau (1986) compared 95 college men who were randomly assigned to an SCII treatment group or the VCS treatment group. The VCS was self-directed using Slaney's approach (Slaney, 1983). The SCII was interpreted using the individualized self-interpretive format. Croteau reasoned that the previous studies comparing the VCS and the SCII had not really looked for differences based on the possible differential effects that might be expected for each instrument. Croteau included a measure of Career Development Responsibility, an instrument that was seen as related to the Rotter Internal-External Locus of Control scale but specifically aimed at career development responsibility issues. The idea that Croteau attempted to measure was that the SCII might have greater appeal to men with external career development responsibility (who looked outside of themselves for making a career choice) in comparison with men with internal career development responsibility. He also reasoned that the VCS might be more likely to increase scores on the Career Decision Making Self-Efficacy Scale (Betz & Taylor, 1982). Neither hypothesis was supported by the data. He did find that the immediate reactions to the interpretive results of the SCII were more positive than the immediate responses to the VCS. However, these differences faded over time until, two weeks after each group had received the results of treatment, there were no differences in the groups' reactions.

Croteau also had the subjects give written reactions to the two interventions. These reactions were then read and summarized by two experienced counselors. One counselor, an experienced female Ph.D. in Clinical Psychology, seemed to suggest that the subjects who had taken the SCII reacted somewhat more positively than the VCS subjects. She noted that, "The vast majority of the responses . . . were very favorable to the Strong-Campbell." This same counselor began her comments on the VCS by stating that "Reactions to the Card Sort task were more varied than the reactions to the SCII." However, she also noted that, "Many found the task (VCS) led them to want to get more information about particular jobs, and many commented that the task opened up new career choices that they had not previously considered." The second counselor, an experienced male counselor with an Ed.D. in Higher Education, began his comments by stating that "The vast majority of respondents to the questionnaire thought positively about their experience with the VCS." His comments were more consistent with the comments made by the raters in Slaney (1978) and were more consistent with the expectations for the VCS. He wrote:

> For some, it provided new avenues to explore, gave them new insights about careers they hadn't considered and directed their thoughts in new directions. For others it helped them narrow down their focus. . . . Some just indicated that the experience was "easy," "different," "interesting," "fun" . . . . There was the indication from some that it made them think about their values and what was important to them. (p. 156–157)

In commenting on the SCII, the second rater wrote:

> The Strong responses seemed to reflect a greater legitimacy once again because respondents interpreted specific careers as having been identified for themselves. They seemed more positively effusive about the SCII than the Card Sort. . . . There was less mention made of gaining insight about values, likes, and dislikes in the Strong. There seemed to be a greater focus among the responses to the Strong on specific career options and less on values and personal preferences. (p. 157)

Although it is not clear why there was not greater agreement between the raters, the comments of the second rater do seem consistent with the comments gathered earlier by Slaney (1978) and with the expectations of the study. Although this sort of support is well short of compelling, it is suggestive that the VCS makes clients think about the basis for their career decisions more than does the SCII. The other results of Croteau suggest that for future studies that might examine this issue it will be important to consider the best time for gathering this sort of data.

Croteau's expectation of finding differential effects for the SCII and the VCS based on organismic variables, although a good idea, was not productive. Although possible reasons for this failure were examined, there was a very real question about whether the problem was with the measures used or the fact that the treatments were really not very discriminable to the subjects based on the dimensions of internal-external control and self-efficacy. Overall, the findings are consistent with the earlier studies that have compared the SCII and the VCS and found that, for the most part, the lack of treatment differences for the two interventions is much clearer than are the reasons for preferring one over the other based on the research.

EVALUATION AND FUTURE DIRECTIONS

Overall the research on vocational card sorts suggests that their effects on clients and subjects in intervention studies compare quite well with the effects of other widely used and carefully developed instruments. Whether this is encouraging for the card sorts, discouraging for all of the interventions considered, or somewhat encouraging for both, may depend upon one's perspective. Some effects do seem to be reliably measured although the magnitude of those effects is not always impressive. Still, if these interventions are considered as only one part of the career counseling process, the results can be seen as moderately encouraging. The link between the effects of treatment and the degree of career indecision being experienced by the client is a reasonable but important relationship for counselors and researchers to consider. The incorporation of the Holland types in Slaney's version of the card sort also seems like an interesting and promising addition, especially in relation to the research on expressed interests. The relationship of the rank-ordered Holland types to other aspects of the card sorts is also encouraging. Whether the reliability of these types as selected by clients holds up irrespective of career indecision is an interesting issue for future research.

Beyond the work noted above, it seems most accurate and conservative to say that overall little actual research has been done on the vocational card sorts. For most versions of the card sort either very few or no studies at all have been done. It is most striking that of all the studies located, only Dolliver's original study involved a counselor in the administration of the card sort. Although it seems legitimate to argue that the exclusion of the counselor helped to clarify the effects of the instrument, separate from the effects of the counselor, it now seems appropriate to determine whether the card sorts do produce different effects depending on whether a counselor is involved or not. This is a quite important direction for carefully conceived future research and it has pragmatic implications for career counseling. Certainly Goldman (1983) was opposed to making the card sort a self-administered treatment based on his perception of a clear need for a sensitive counselor to observe and interpret the reactions and responses of the client. Dolliver, (personal communication, 1988) in writing about his original work with the TVCS, also seems to agree on the need for a counselor. Our experience with the instrument lends some possible support to this contention. More specifically, this experience raises the question of whether clients do question or think about the reasons for their choices as energetically when the card sort is self-administered. The tendency of clients who are doing the card sort with counselors to give rather simple responses the first time they are asked why they did or did not choose a particular group of occupations suggests that this issue deserves study. Another potentially important role for the counselor might involve being aware of any possible limitations that clients may impose on themselves, especially if these are unrealistic and have an important influence on the careers being considered or excluded from consideration.

If one believes that a primary strength of the card sort resides in its ability to get clients to think about the reasons for their choices then this becomes an important issue. A closely related issue is whether it can be demonstrated that the card sorts actually make clients more thoughtful about their career choices. They do seem to have this effect. There are open ended comments that seem to suggest that at least some clients and counselors see the card sorts as having this effect but a more compelling empirical demonstration of this effect would add important support for the use of the card sort technique. At the same time, the method for demonstrating such an effect unequivocally is not at all clear.

Another central issue that needs to be addressed through research is whether it can be demonstrated that the use of the card sort technique does, as we have suggested, actually increase the interest and involvement of counselors in career counseling. This issue raises the possibility of a series of studies that address a variety of related concerns. More specifically, a few studies might explore whether counselors who use the card sort feel more involved with their clients, like them better, and recall more about their interests, values, Holland types, career choices, and other aspects of their lives. Other related questions do not seem difficult to generate. We would, of course, suspect that the card sort would receive support but these questions raise interesting possibilities for future exploration. Obvious comparisons would be with counselors who use the SCII, the SDS, (Holland, 1985c), one of the many available computer programs, or any of a variety of other instruments or approaches. Similar issues could also be investigated from the perspective of clients. We would also predict that they would be more involved in the process of counseling, like their counselor and career counseling better, be more thoughtful about their choices, reveal more about themselves, miss fewer appointments, and remember their own career interests, values, Holland types, and career choices better than clients who received other interventions. These studies might also begin to explore the importance of the relationship in career counseling. The suggested studies would appear to be quite interesting to perform and the results could have practical implications in terms of what effects are actually best achieved by the card sorts as well as the other approaches investigated.

Another issue that needs to be addressed through research concerns the reliability of the categories that clients use for the classification of the careers that they choose or reject as a part of the card sort. A related question would be whether this reliability is related to other career-relevant variables. The reliability of clients' final hierarchy of choices might also be studied as well as the relationship of the rank-ordered Holland types to the career choices in relation to some other dimensions such as career indecision. For example, are the hierarchies of decided clients more stable than those of undecided clients? Are the relationships between the Holland types and career choices affected by degrees of career indecision? Other investigators have suggested that the number of categories used by clients might be related to the degree of career indecision but thus far no studies have addressed this interesting and easily studied topic. The issue raised by several investigators about the validity of the instrument and how it should be studied also needs to be addressed. Some of the studies suggested above address the unique effects that the card sort may have on clients that might differentiate it from other instruments such as the SDS or the SCII.

In summary, the vocational card sorts seem like a promising approach to include in career counselors' armamentaria of interventions. At this point the enthusiasm and clinical or anecdotal support for the card sorts, from a number of sources, seems to outstrip the research investigations that have addressed this instrument. Indeed, the research has barely begun to investigate the effects of the card sort technique in career counseling. Whether future studies will support the effects that the card sorts are suggested to have on career clients is at this point an open question. Several important and interesting sounding questions have been raised above and a substantial number of additional questions could have been generated. Whether the needed research will be conducted is, at present, unclear. These studies will involve a series of carefully developed investigations that will be expensive and difficult to carry out. The technique does at this point seem promising and worth the needed research effort. Hopefully, that effort will be forthcoming.

ACKNOWLEDGMENT

The authors express appreciation to Professor Paul R. Salomone for his careful and thoughtful comments on an earlier version of this chapter.

REFERENCES

Atanasoff, G. E., & Slaney, R. B. (1980). Three approaches to counselor-free career exploration among college women. *Journal of Counseling Psychology, 27,* 332–339.

Bartling, H. C., & Hood, A. B. (1981). An 11-year follow-up of measured interest and vocational choice. *Journal of Counseling Psychology, 28,* 27–35.

Betz, N. E., & Taylor, K. M. (1982). Concurrent validity of the Strong-Campbell Interest Inventory for graduate students in counseling. *Journal of Vocational Behavior, 29,* 626–635.

Birk, J. M., & Brooks, L. (1986). Required skills and training needs of recent counseling psychology graduates. *Journal of Counseling Psychology, 33,* 320–325.

Borgen, F. H., & Seling, M. J. (1978). Expressed and inventoried interests revisited: Perspicacity in the person. *Journal of Counseling Psychology, 25,* 536–543.

Cairo, P. C. (1982). Measured interests versus expressed interests as predictors of long-term occupational membership. *Journal of Vocational Behavior, 20,* 343–353.

Cochran, L. R. (1985). Review of Occ-U-Sort. *The Ninth Mental Measurements Yearbook,* James Mitchell, Jr., editor. The Buros Institute of Mental Measurements. pp. 1076–1078.

Cooper, J. F. (1976). Comparative impact of the SCII and the Vocational Card Sort on career salience and career exploration of women. *Journal of Counseling Psychology, 23,* 348–352.

Crites, J. O. (1985). Review of Occ-U-Sort. *The Ninth Mental Measurements Yearbook,* James Mitchell, Jr. Editor. The Buros Institute of Mental Measurements, pp. 1077–1079.

Croteau, J. M. (1986). The differential effects of "measured" versus "expressed" interest interventions. Unpublished doctoral dissertation. Southern Illinois University-Carbondale.

Daniels, M. H. (1985). Review of Vocational Exploration and Insight Kit. *The Ninth Mental Measurements Yearbook,* James Mitchell, Jr., Editor. The Buros Institute of Mental Measurements, pp. 1675–1676.

Dege, D., Warsett, S., Hansen, S. L., & Miles-Novoa, B. (1980). *Video viewers' guide no. 4: The Joy of Choosing.* Washington, DC: Office of Education.

Dewey, C. R. (1974). Exploring interests: A non-sexist method. *Personnel and Guidance Journal, 52,* 311–315.

Dolliver, R. H. (1966). The relationship of certain variables to the amount of agreement in inventoried and expressed vocational interests. Unpublished doctoral dissertation, Ohio State University.

Dolliver, R. H. (1967). An adaptation of the Tyler Vocational Card Sort. *Personnel and Guidance Journal, 45,* 916–920.

Dolliver, R. H. (1969). Strong Vocational Interest Blank versus expressed vocational interests: A review. *Psychological Bulletin, 72,* 95–107.

Dolliver, R. H. (1981). Test review: A review of five vocational card sorts. *Measurement and Evaluation in Guidance, 14,* 168–174.

Dolliver, R. H. (1982). Dolliver's response. *Measurement and Evaluation in Guidance, 15,* 170.

Dolliver, R. H., & Will, J. A. (1977). Ten-year follow-up of the Tyler Vocational Card Sort and the Strong Vocational Interest Blank. *Journal of Counseling Psychology, 24,* 48–54.

Fitzgerald, L. F., & Osipow, S. H. (1986). An occupational analysis of counseling psychology: How special is the specialty? *American Psychologist, 41,* 535–544.

Gade, E. M., & Soliah, D. (1975). Vocational Preference Inventory high point codes versus expressed choices as predictors of college major and career entry. *Journal of Counseling Psychology, 22,* 117–121.

Gelso, C. J., Prince, J., Cornfeld, J. L., Payne, A., & Royalty, G., & Wiley, M. O. (1985). Quality of counselors' intake evaluations for clients with problems that are primarily vocational versus personal. *Journal of Counseling Psychology, 32,* 339–347.

Goldman, L. (1983). The Vocational Card Sort Technique: A different view. *Measurement and Evaluation in Guidance, 16,* 107–109.

Gottfredson, L. S. (1981). Circumscription and compromise: A developmental theory of occupational aspirations. [Monograph]. *Journal of Counseling Psychology, 28,* 545–579.

Gottfredson, G. D., & Holland, J. L. (1975). Vocational choices of men and women: A comparison of predictors from the Self-Directed Search. *Journal of Counseling Psychology, 22,* 28–34.

Gysbers, N. C., & Moore, E. J. (1987). *Career counseling: Skills and techniques for practitioners.* Englewood Cliffs, NJ: Prentice-Hall.

Harmon, L. W., & Zytowski, D. G. (1980). Reliability of Holland codes across interest measures for adult females. *Journal of Counseling Psychology, 27,* 478–483.

Holland, J. L. (1985a). *Making vocational choices: A theory of vocational personalities and work environments.* (2nd ed.) Englewood Cliffs, NJ: Prentice-Hall.

Holland, J. L. (1985b). *The occupations finder.* Odessa, FL: Psychological Assessment Resources.

Holland, J. L. (1985c). *The Self-Directed Search: Professional Manual - 1985 edition.* Odessa, FL: Psychological Assessment Resources.

Holland, J. L., & Associates. (1980). *Counselor's guide to the vocational exploration and insight kit* (VEIK). Palo Alto, CA: Consulting Psychologists Press.

Holland, J. L., Daiger, D. C., & Power, P. G. (1980). *My vocational situation.* Palo Alto, CA: Consulting Psychologists Press.

Holland, J. L., & Gottfredson, G. D. (1975). Predictive value and psychological meaning of vocational aspirations. *Journal of Vocational Behavior, 6,* 349–363.

Holland, J. L., & Lutz, S. W. (1968). The predictive value of a student's choice of vocation. *Personnel and Guidance Journal, 46,* 428–434.

Jones, L. K. (1982). A reaction to Dolliver's review of the Occ-U-Sort. *Measurement and Evaluation in Guidance,. 15,* 169.

Jones, L. K. (1983). A comparison of two self-directed career guidance instruments: Occu-Sort and Self-Directed Search. *The School Counselor,* 204–211.

Jones, L. K., & DeVault, R. M. (1979). Evaluation of a self-guided career exploration system: The Occu-Sort. *The School Counselor,* 334–341.

Krieshok, T. S., Hansen, R. N., & Johnston, J. A. (1982). *Missouri Occupational Card Sort Manual (College Form).* Available from the Career Planning and Placement Center, 100 Noyes Hall, University of Missouri-Columbia, Columbia, Missouri.

Kuhn, T. S. (1970). *The structure of scientific revolutions* (2nd ed.). Chicago: University of Chicago Press.

Lawler, A. C. (1979). Career exploration with women using the non-sexist Vocational Card Sort and the Self-Directed Search. *Measurement and Evaluation in Guidance, 12,* 87–97.

MacKinnon-Slaney, F. (1986). Career indecision in reentry and undergraduate women. *Journal of College Student Personnel, 27,* 114–119.

MacKinnon-Slaney, F., Barber, S. L., & Slaney, R. B. (1988). Marital status as a mediating factor on the career aspirations of reentry women students. *Journal of College Student Development, 29,* 327–333.

Moore, E. J., & Gysbers, N. C. (1980). Missouri Occupational Preference Inventory, Columbia, MO.: Human Systems Consultants, Inc.

O'Neil, J. M., & Magoon, T. M. (1977). The predictability of Holland's investigative personality type and consistency levels using the Self-Directed Search. *Journal of Vocational Behavior, 10,* 39–46.

Pinkney, J. W., & Jacobs, D. (1985). New counselors and personal interest in the task of career counseling. *Journal of Counseling Psychology, 32,* 454–457.

Rosenberg, M. (1957). *Occupations and values.* New York: The Free Press.

Slaney, R. B. (1978). Expressed and inventoried vocational interests: A comparison of instruments. *Journal of Counseling Psychology, 25,* 520–529.

Slaney, R. B. (1980). Expressed vocational choice and vocational indecision. *Journal of Counseling Psychology, 27,* 122–129.

Slaney, R. B. (1981). *The Vocational Card Sort—Understanding your results.* Unpublished manuscript (Available from R. B. Slaney, Department of Counseling and Educational Psychology, The Pennsylvania State University, 333 CEDAR, University Park, PA 16802).

Slaney, R. B. (1983). Influence of career indecision on treatments exploring the vocational interests of college women. *Journal of Counseling Psychology, 30,* 55–63.

Slaney, R. B., & Dickson, R. D. (1985). Relation of career indecision to career exploration with reentry women: A treatment and follow-up study. *Journal of Counseling Psychology, 32,* 355–362.

Slaney, R. B., & Lewis, E. T. (1986). Effects of career exploration on career undecided reentry women: An intervention and follow-up study. *Journal of Vocational Behavior, 28,* 97–109.

Slaney, R. B., & MacKinnon-Slaney, F. (1986). Relationship of expressed and inventoried vocational interests of female career counseling clients. *Career Development Quarterly, 34,* 24–33.

Slaney, R. B., & Russell, J. E. A. (1981). An investigation of different levels of agreement between expressed and inventoried vocational interests among college women. *Journal of Counseling Psychology, 28,* 221–228.

Slaney, R. B., & Russell, J. E. A. (1987). Perspectives on vocational behavior, 1986: A review. *Journal of Vocational Behavior, 31,* 111–173.

Slaney, R. B., & Slaney, F. M. (1981). A comparison of measures of expressed and inventoried interests among counseling center clients. *Journal of Counseling Psychology, 28,* 515–518.

Slaney, R. B., Stafford, M. J., & Russell, J. E. A. (1981). Career indecision in adult women: A comparative and descriptive study. *Journal of Vocational Behavior, 19,* 335–345.

Takai, R., & Holland, J. L. (1979). Comparison of the Vocational Card Sort, the SDS, and the Vocational Exploration and Insight Kit. *The Vocational Guidance Quarterly, 27,* 312–318.

Talbot, D. B., & Birk, M. M. (1979). Does the vocational exploration and insight kit equal the sum of its parts?: A comparison study. *Journal of Counseling Psychology, 26,* 359–362.

Tittle, C. K. (1985). Review of Vocational Exploration and Insight Kit. *The Ninth Buros Mental Measurements Yearbook,* James Mitchell, Jr., Editor. The Buros Institute of Mental Measurements, p. 1676.

Touchton, J. G., & Magoon, T. M. (1977). Occupational daydreams as predictors of vocational plans of college women. *Journal of Vocational Behavior, 10,* 156–166.

Tyler, L. E. (1961). Research explorations in the realm of choice. *Journal of Counseling Psychology, 8,* 195–201.

Watkins, C. E. Jr., Lopez, F. G., Campbell, V. L., & Himmell, C. D. (1986). Contemporary counseling psychology: Results of a national survey. *Journal of Counseling Psychology, 33,* 301–309.

Westbrook, B. W., & Mastie, M. M. (1982). Shall we sort the Occu-U-Sort into the might-choose, would-not-choose, or uncertain pile? *Measurement and Evaluation in Guidance, 15,* 259–256.

Whitney, D. R. (1969). Predicting from expressed vocational choice: A review. *Personnel and Guidance Journal, 48,* 279–286.

Williams, S. K. (1978). The vocational card sort: A tool for vocational exploration. *The Vocational Guidance Quarterly, 26,* 237–243.

Zener, T. B., & Schnuelle, L. (1976). Effects of the self-directed search on high school students. *Journal of Counseling Psychology, 23,* 353–359.

12 The Use of Career Choice Process Scales in Counseling Practice

Mark L. Savickas
College of Medicine
Northeastern Ohio Universities

Determining clients' readiness to cope with the career choice process is the principal assessment task in comprehensive career counseling (Crites, 1974b; Super, 1983). The present chapter begins with an explanation of this assertion. The bulk of the chapter describes three psychometric inventories, each of which is designed to measure different variables in the career choice process. The first scale, the Career Decision Scale (Osipow, Carney, Winer, Yanico, & Koschier, 1976), measures difficulties in making a career choice. The second scale, the Career Development Inventory (Super, Thompson, Lindeman, Jordaan, & Myers, 1981), measures adaptability for mastering career development tasks. The third scale, the Career Maturity Inventory (Crites, 1978b), measures dispositions for vocational decision making. Each scale's construction and development is described, and its validity is considered. How psychologists use the scales in counseling practice is discussed and illustrated with a case example. The chapter concludes with an evaluation of career choice process assessment in contemporary counseling practice.

CAREER CHOICE PROCESS

All too often career counselors have worked with clients only to find that they still cannot make a career choice. Counseling that leaves clients unable to choose a career usually deals with choice content, that is, the occupations that fit a client's interests and abilities. Counseling methods that match clients' interests and abilities to occupational positions work well for clients who are ready to make decisions. Decisive clients can use the results of interest inventories and aptitude tests to make realistic career choices. However, other clients who are not ready to make decisions encounter difficulty when they try to make career choices. In fact, after discussing test results and occupational information, they become even more confused about their career choices because they have more data than they are ready to use.

Counselors who are sensitive to variations in clients' readiness to make career choices appreciate Crites' (1974b) distinction between the content and the process of vocational decision making. Content refers to which occupation a client should enter and thus focuses on the client's interests and abilities. Process refers to how a client arrives at an occupational choice and thus focuses on the client's decision-making concerns and coping responses. Crites used the analogy of an assembly line to describe the distinction. He likened career choice to the product and vocational decision making to production activities. Crites explicated the distinction between choice content and choice process in refining Super's (1955) model of vocational development. Crites' model charted two content dimensions and two process dimensions in the maturation of vocational decision making during adolescence (see Figure 12.1). One content dimension, wisdom, deals with the development of fit between clients' occupational preferences and their interests, abilities, and experiences. The other content dimension, consistency, deals with the development of stability and coherence in clients' occupational preferences. The two process dimensions in Crites' model deal with the development of attitudes toward and competencies for vocational decision making. The decisional attitudes are dispositions that influence readiness to choose. The competencies refer to the information, comprehension, foresight, and problem solving required for rational decision making.

The classic matching model for career counseling focuses on the content dimensions of career choice (Bell, 1940; Williamson & Darley, 1937). Content-oriented counselors use matching methods, such as aptitude tests, to identify the occupational level at which a client can best function and interest inventories to identify the occupational field in which the client can find the most satisfaction. Counselors who use the matching model and methods in a pedestrian manner act as if all clients are ready to choose an occupation. Their behavior manifests a test-centered rather than client-centered approach and reflects the belief that all clients can be treated in the same way. For example, it is not uncommon for a student seeking vocational guidance at a college counseling center to be scheduled by the receptionist for an interest inventory prior to the initial appointment with a counselor. Nor is it unusual for a counselor to administer an interest inventory to an entire high school class. Although this practice has been effective and efficient for clients who have been ready to make choices, at best it has been ineffective and inefficient for other clients. The piles of scored interest invento-

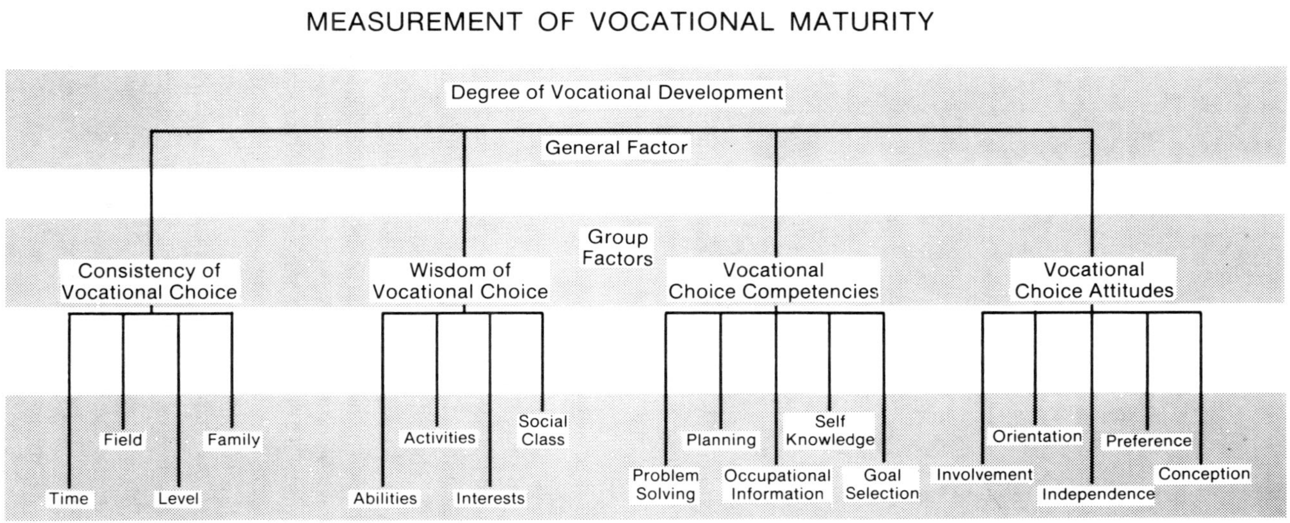

FIG. 12.1. *Crites' Model of Vocational Maturity in Adolescence*

Note. From "Measurement of vocational maturity in adolescence: I. Attitude Scale of the Vocational Development Inventory" by J. O. Crites, 1965, *Psychological Monographs, 79*, page 5. Copyright 1965 by The American Psychological Association. Reprinted by permission of the publisher and author.

ries taken by clients who never reappeared for an interpretation and the only partial success of group guidance with clients who have different career concerns reflect the inapropriateness of the matching model and methods for clients not ready to benefit from them.

To more effectively use the matching model and its content-oriented methods, experienced counselors view career choice as a process that develops over time. Typically, they conceptualize career choice as an adaptive process through which individuals meet and master social expectations (also called developmental tasks) to choose an occupation in which they can fulfill both the job demands and their own needs. The choice process begins with the task or social expectation that individuals orient themselves to work as a salient life role. This work salience or career orientation produces a ''basic readiness'' for vocational decision making, a readiness based on foresight, autonomy, and self-esteem (Super, 1983). When career orientation reaches a critical threshold, people meet the task of crystallizing a career preference. Crystallization involves formulating a general preference for occupations within a particular field and at a particular level. The next task that they encounter is to convert their field and level preferences into specific choices. The specification task includes developing certainty about and comfort with one's occupational choice. The final task in the career choice process is to implement one's choice. Implementation as a developmental task means converting a choice into reality by preparing for and securing a position in the chosen occupation.

In practice, counselors may use the task sequence of orientation, crystallization, specification, and implementation to assess clients' degree of development and vary how they use the matching model and methods. To assess clients' progress in the career choice process, counselors identify the tasks that clients have mastered and are concerned about, the clients' difficulties in coping with the task of concern, and the clients' decision-making attitudes and competencies (Savickas, 1984). Based on this process assessment, counselors can decide whether or not to ask clients to respond to interest inventories and aptitude tests. Clients who do not express work salience or a career orientation may not be mature enough for their interests to have meaning for career choice (Super, 1983). They need life experiences or counseling to induce or strengthen foresight, autonomy, and self-esteem, which support the basic readiness for vocational decision making. If counselors do administer interest inventories to underdeveloped clients, then counselors should not interpret the results relative to clients' crystallizing preferences, specifying choices, or implementing plans. Instead, counselors should use the results to orient clients to the occupational structure in the world of work and to prepare them to investigate several career fields and clarify their work values.

In contrast to clients who are not oriented to career choice, clients who are more highly developed can derive personal meaning from the results of interest inventories and aptitude tests, especially if counselors interpret the scores (data) to them as information (meaning) that eases their coping with the tasks of crystallization, specification, or implementation. In particular, clients who face the crystallization task benefit from information that prompts them to explore several clusters of occupations in related fields and levels. Clients who face the specification task benefit from information that narrows their exploration to occupations in one field and level and helps them choose from among these occupational alternatives. Clients who face the implementation task benefit from information that helps them prepare for and secure positions in their chosen occupations. In short, counselors can assess clients' developmental task mastery and then treat them in accordance with this assessment.

Even the architect of the matching model advised counselors to use developmental assessments to guide differential treatment of clients. In describing the goals of an initial career counseling interview, Parsons advised counselors to classify clients into one of two main classes.

> First, those who have well-developed aptitudes and interest and a practical basis for a reasonable conclusion in respect to the choice of a vocation. Second, boys and girls with so little experience or manifestation of special aptitudes or interests that there is no basis yet for a wise decision. (1909/1967, p. 19)

Following Parsons' example, experienced counselors used interview techniques and clinical judgment to subjectively assess clients' development and select relevant counseling interventions. Early attempts to objectively assess clients' developmental readiness for career choice, such as the "interest maturity" scale of the Strong Vocational Interest Blank (Strong, 1943, Chapter 12), focused on the content of clients' interests. The marginal success of this approach led some counselors to focus on the structure of clients' interests such as "profile homogeneity" (Holland, 1966) or "interest patterning" (Super, 1955) as indices of readiness for decision making. As recently as 1982, Wigington (p. 179) reported a content-derived index of readiness for the Kuder Occupational Interest Survey: "Clients whose highest Occupation score and/or highest College Major score is below 50 would be viewed as less ready to participate in the career decision-making process."

Instead of deriving indices of readiness indirectly from interest inventories, Super (1955) suggested that counselors directly measure variables in the career choice process. After years of research and reflection that identified and defined the important variables in the career choice process, psychometricians devised objective inventories to directly measure these variables. Content-oriented researchers focused on "indecision" as "slow and complex rate of development" (Holland & Nichols, 1964, p. 33). They constructed measures of decidedness and difficulties in vocational decision making such as the Career Decision Scale

(Osipow, Carney, Winer, Yanico, & Koschier, 1976), My Vocational Situation (Holland, Daiger, & Power, 1980), and the Vocational Decision Scale (Jones & Chenery, 1980). In contrast, process-oriented researchers focused on "career maturity" as readiness for vocational decision making (Super & Overstreet, 1960). They constructed measures of vocational development and career choice attitudes and competencies such as the Career Maturity Inventory (Crites, 1978b), the Career Development Inventory (Super, et al., 1981), and Assessment of Career Decision Making (Harren, 1978). Counselors may use these indecision and career maturity scales to directly measure career choice process variables and differentially treat career counseling clients.

Although these scales each measure the career choice process, they differ in one fundamental way. The indecision scales address decision-making difficulties whereas the career maturity scales address decision-making resources. Before comparing and contrasting the indecision and maturity approaches to process measurement, representative measures from each perspective will be presented in detail. Each of the next three sections in the present chapter discusses one of the three prominent career choice process scales. These scales were selected for inclusion in this chapter because they were the only process measures that met three criteria: (a) sufficient research literature to judge their psychometric characteristics, (b) easy availability through commercial publishers or other means, and (c) adequate practitioner lore about appropriate use and clinical interpretation. The three scales which met the criteria are the Career Decision Scale (Osipow, Carney, Winer, Yanico, & Koschier, 1976), the Career Development Inventory (Super, et al., 1981), and the Career Maturity Inventory (Crites, 1978b).

CAREER DECISION SCALE

For decades, researchers used just two categories—*decided* and *undecided*—to classify an individual's adaptation to the career choice process. They extensively investigated the personalities and situations of individuals who had been classified as undecided, but they did not examine how these individuals engaged in vocational decision making (Osipow, 1983). In the mid-1970s, many researchers began to view adaptive status as a continuum of decidedness instead of a dichotomy between undecided and decided. They also became sensitive to the degree of closure among decided individuals and thus started to measure variation in choice satisfaction, choice certainty, commitment to a choice, and even choice implementation. Osipow and his colleagues (1976) helped to popularize the process view of decidedness by providing a scale with which counselors could quickly survey high school and college students' progress in making career choices. The Career Decision Scale (CDS) measures a person's career choice status and identifies difficulties that thwart career choice closure.

Development

The CDS originated as part of a proposed modular system for assisting clients with vocational indecision. Osipow, Winer, Koschier, and Yanico (1975) began by identifying separate components of indecision. They assumed that a finite number of relatively discrete problems thwart adaptation to the choice task. Although they have not written about the criteria used in selecting these problem behaviors, they have explained that they identified the problems in their study of a model relating specific intervention strategies to distinct types of difficulties in the choice process (Osipow et al., 1975). Osipow and his colleagues considered problems they had encountered in their own experience with students as well as problems they found in examining records of students seeking career counseling. From these sources they compiled 14 problem behaviors that thwart progress in reaching closure on a career choice. They asserted that each of the 14 difficulties was a distinct antecedent of or unique reason for being undecided. The antecedents act as barriers to prevent adaptation to the choice task by thwarting progress along the decidedness continuum or by reducing satisfaction with, certainty about, and commitment to a choice that has been made. Because each antecedent differs from the other 13, an individual may experience several difficulties simultaneously or sequentially. People who experience more problems are expected to be more prone to indecision, to make slower progress in advancing along the decidedness continuum, and to be less satisfied with, certain about, and committed to choices they have made.

Each of the 14 types of indecision or reasons for being undecided were expressed in a descriptive item consisting of one to three statements. These 14 items were published originally as the Types Questionnaire (Osipow et al., 1975). Osipow and Carney revised the Types Questionnaire into the Scale of Vocational Indecision (see Osipow, Carney, & Barak, 1976, p. 237). This revision included five new items: two items state additional explanations for indecision, an open-ended item allows respondents to describe unique sources of indecision, and two items measure certainty about career and major choices, respectively. Osipow, Carney, Winer, Yanico, and Koschier (1976) slightly revised the Vocational Indecision Scale and renamed it the Career Decision Scale (3rd Revision). Marathon Consulting and Press published the Career Decision Scale from 1976 to 1987 when Psychological Assessment Resources assumed publication of the scale.

Description

The Career Decision Scale (CDS) was designed for high school and college students and has been used successfully with women returning to college (Slaney, Stafford, & Russell, 1981). It also has been slightly modified for use with graduate students (Hartman, Utz, & Farnum, 1979) and medical students

(Savickas, Alexander, Osipow, & Wolf, 1985). In fact, the CDS probably can be used with any individual crystallizing field and level preferences or specifying a career choice. Individuals can be given the CDS as a part of an intake process or a vocational appraisal test battery. Because it takes only 10 to 15 minutes to administer and is easy to understand and respond to, the CDS also can be used to survey large groups for screening purposes or to evaluate vocational interventions and career education programs.

The CDS is published in a 4-page 8½″ × 11″ booklet. The front page has lines for name, date of birth, age, grade, and sex, as well as instructions to respondents to indicate on a 4-point Likert scale how closely each item describes their thinking about career or educational choices. The response scale ranges from "exactly like me" (4), to "not at all like me" (1). Clients circle on the test booklet the appropriate number for each item. These ratings show how well each item corresponds to sources of clients' indecision.

Scale items appear on the inner two pages. The first two items compose the Certainty Scale. They state that one has already decided on a career (item 1) or a major (item 2) and that one feels comfortable with and knows how to implement that choice. Items 3 through 18 describe reasons for being undecided and compose the Indecision Scale. Item 19 asks clients to describe their unique difficulties if none of the 16 items describe them. Six lines are provided for written responses.

At the bottom of page 3, spaces are provided to record scores, identify normative group, and indicate percentile ranks. Counselors compute the raw score for the Certainty Scale by summing the ratings for items 1 and 2. The scores can range from 2 to 8, with higher scores indicating greater certainty. They compute the Indecision Scale raw score by summing the ratings for items 3 through 18. The scores can range from 16 to 64, with higher scores indicating greater indecision. Item 19 is clinically interpreted. The manual presents four normative groups that can be used to convert raw scores to percentiles: high school students (N = 720 males and 738 females); college students (N = 225 males and 192 females); adults seeking continuing education (N = 81); and women returning to college (N = 67). The back page of the booklet is blank.

Interpretation

To interpret a client's CDS scores, a counselor may begin by assessing the client's progress toward decidedness in general from the Certainty Scale score, and then assess progress toward major and career choice in particular from the two item ratings. Based on experience, I have concluded that significant discrepancies between ratings for the two certainty items require further assessment. If major choice certainty exceeds career choice certainty by two or three points, then the counselor should investigate the possibility that the client has a plan without a clear goal. Often these clients have made pseudo-crystallized choices, that is, "they have not analyzed the essential elements and have not fully accepted the commitments entailed'' (Ginzberg, Ginsburg, Axelrad, & Herma, 1951, p. 108). They may be implementing plans that reflect their parents' dreams rather than commitments to self-chosen goals that manifest their own vocational identities. If career choice certainty exceeds major choice certainty by two or three points, then the counselor should investigate the possibility that the client has a goal without a plan. For example, a high school student may be certain about the goal of being a lawyer but not know, or eventually like, the activities required to become a lawyer. Often such clients have uninformed interests in choices that may be subject to change in light of new experience and information (Strong, 1943, p. 17).

After assessing the Certainty Scale results, counselors may look to the Indecision Scale score to assess degree of indecision, that is, number and intensity of difficulties in the decision-making process. Although the definition of high, average, and low indecision scores depends on the context, Osipow (1987) suggested that scores from the 16th to the 84th percentile be considered middle scores, with scores above the 84th percentile signifying high indecision and scores below the 16th percentile signifying low indecision. Counselors should expect the Indecision Scale score to oppose the Certainty Scale score because theoretically these variables associate inversely and empirically these scales correlate negatively. When both scores are either high or low, the counselor should investigate the possibility that the scores are invalid or that the client is quite unique. When the scores are valid, I have usually found that students with high certainty and high proneness to indecision feel very committed to a series of different choices over short time periods. In contrast, I have usually found that students with low certainty and low indecision feel very comfortable with being undecided and are not yet concerned about making a career choice. If certainty is high and indecision is low, then the counselor should hypothesize that the client may not need an intervention or, at least, that the client does not feel a need for assistance. Because combinations of middle scores on both scales are ambiguous, Osipow suggested that if this occurs counselors should further assess the client's vocational situation. If they need or want an intervention, these clients usually benefit from content-oriented career counseling. If certainty is low and indecision is high, then the counselor should hypothesize that the client would benefit from a process-oriented intervention.

When working with a client who scores low on the Certainty Scale and high on the Indecision Scale, the counselor examines the client's item ratings and considers any response to item 19. By studying the items that the client rated as most self-descriptive, the counselor can learn about the type and intensity of decision-making difficulties that the client experiences in trying to make career choices. With training and experience, a counselor can often discern a coherent pattern of decisional difficulties from the item ratings and then tentatively select a process intervention to address this pattern. To aid clinical judgment in pattern recognition, some counselors consider items in clusters based on factor analyses of the Indecision Scale.

Osipow, Carney, and Barak (1976) reported that four dimensions structure the Indecision Scale. Their factor analysis of 837 college students' responses to the 16 items produced four factors which explained 81.3% of the total variance. They did not report how much variance each orthogonal (uncorrelated) factor explained. They interpreted the factors as:

1. Avoidance of choice: 9 items indicating choice anxiety and lack of structure and confidence in approaching vocational decision making.
2. External barriers: 5 items indicating the presence or perception of external barriers to a preferred choice and questions about alternative possibilities.
3. Approach-approach: 2 items indicating difficulty in deciding from among attractive alternatives.
4. Conflict: 2 items suggesting some kind of personal conflict about how to make a choice.

The items in these four factors total 18 rather than 16 because two items loaded on two factors.

Osipow, Carney, and Barak's (1976) conclusions about the factor analytic results suggest that the items state 16 distinct manifest difficulties in decision making yet they reflect only four unique latent dimensions or basic types of indecision. Some counselors and researchers have taken this to mean that they could score the Indecision Scale for subscales to appraise the client across four major types of indecision. Osipow (1987, p. 7) warned CDS users that the instability of its factor structure does not warrant such a practice. His caution, which is shared by Allis (1984), Harmon (1985), Herman (1985), and Slaney (1985), is based on repeated failures to completely replicate the Indecision Scale factor structure. Kazin (1976), Slaney (1978), and Slaney, Palko-Nonemaker, and Alexander (1981) each replicated only the first factor, whereas Rogers and Westbrook (1983) replicated only the second and third factors.

One explanation for the failure to replicate the original factor analytic results faults the scale items. The complexity of each item, according to Osipow, Carney, & Barak (1976), makes it subject to more than one answer. Recall that some of the items consist of two or three statements. In some cases statements within the same item are independent, so we cannot be sure exactly which statement evoked a respondent's rating. For example, item 7 describes intrapsychic confusion, interpersonal dependency, and an information deficit: "Until now, I haven't given much thought to choosing a career. I feel lost when I think about it because I haven't had many experiences in making decisions on my own, and I don't have enough information to make a career decision right now."[1]

---

[1]Copyright 1987 by Psychological Assessment Resources, Inc. Reprinted by permission of the publisher.

Although these elements may cohere in defining one type of indecision, they do not form an easily interpretable item in psychometric analyses. Slaney et al. (1981) hypothesized that this item complexity may cause the overlap and instability in the Indecision Scale factor structure.

Two other possible explanations for the failure to identify an invariant factor structure underlying the CDS were offered by Shimizu, Vondracek, Schulenberg, and Hostetler (1988): the structure of CDS indecision constructs varies at different levels of career maturity and statistical-methodological artifacts attenuate the extent of factor similarity across the studies. In considering the latter possibility, they reasoned that the most serious problem in CDS factor analytic studies was the selection of Varimax rotation procedures to produce orthogonal factors. To examine this hypothesis, they rotated each of the Varimax solutions presented in seven previous studies to Promax solutions, which produced oblique (correlated) factors. To compare the similarity of the correlated factors across the seven studies, they calculated congruence coefficients. From these comparisons, they concluded that "there are more similarities across the factor analytic studies than have been previously reported" (p. 218). They extended the generalizability of this conclusion with a new sample. Moreover, they suggested further research on four linearly independent subscales that represent the correlated factors in their two studies. They described the four subscales as (a) feelings of indecision, (b) relative decidedness yet desire for reinforcement and support, (c) classic approach–approach conflict, and (d) external and internal barriers to decision making. Despite questions about the factor structure of the Indecision Scale, there is no doubt that it is multidimensional. However, almost all of the studies on the CDS used a single score as a unidimensional measure of decisional difficulties. The single best summary of these studies appears in the CDS manual.

Technical Information

The CDS manual (Osipow, 1987) is thorough and well organized. It summarizes five factor analytic studies of the Indecision Scale and cites reports of test-retest reliability at .90 and .82 for two weeks (Osipow, Carney, & Barak, 1976) and .70 for six weeks (Slaney, et al., 1981). An unpublished master's thesis not cited in the manual reported a 3-week test-retest reliability coefficient of .79 and an internal consistency coefficient of .91 (Williams-Phillips, 1983). Rogers and Westbrook (1983) reported an internal consistency coefficient of .88.

The manual presents different types of validity evidence in four sections. The first section discusses studies that compared demographic groups on the CDS and that related the CDS to other career choice process measures. The second section reviews treatment studies indicating that the CDS is sensitive to pre-test/post-test changes and is an effective outcome measure. The third section discusses studies that demonstrate how the CDS relates to personality variables such as locus of control and fear of success. The fourth and final section summarizes studies that relate the Indecision Scale to demographic variables. Four studies reported no significant sex differences, whereas two studies reported significant sex differences, one favoring females and the other favoring males. The only study that addressed ethnic differences reported greater indecision in blacks than whites.

The CDS manual includes 19 tables containing data about the CDS. The manual refers to 65 works, 51 of which deal with the CDS from its inception through 1986. This amount of literature represents an enthusiastic response by researchers and practitioners to a scale published in 1976. It implies widespread acceptance of the CDS or, at least, positive reaction to the conceptualization of vocational decision making as a process fraught with measurable difficulties.

Reviews

In a review of the CDS, Slaney (1985) concluded that an impressive amount of research had been conducted in the early development of the CDS and that this research "provided substantial support for the reliability of the instrument and for its construct and concurrent validity" (p. 142). Three other reviewers were equally impressed by the CDS. Harmon (1985) concluded that "the CDS is extremely well developed and researched for such a relatively new inventory" and highly recommended its use in career counseling and evaluation. Herman (1985) concluded that its "brevity, comprehensiveness, and extensive research support are important strengths of the inventory." Allis (1984) called support for its construct validity "impressive."

Research Directions

Each review of the CDS and many investigations of it have offered explicit suggestions for research to further develop the Indecision Scale. In sum, reviewers and researchers have called for:

1. Explication of the conceptual rationale for item selection.
2. Continuation of studies to define types of indecision, or patterns of vocational decision-making difficulties.
3. Development of subscales for the Indecision Scale that can be used in differential diagnosis of indecision types.
4. Extension of the inchoate work (e.g., Barak & Friedkes, 1981) on matching intervention methods and materials to types of indecision.
5. Initiation of research on written responses to item 19.
6. Examination of qualitative differences between male and female CDS responses (Hartman, Fuqua, & Jenkins, 1988).

Item revision is a potentially productive suggestion for future research but it requires a significantly greater commitment of time and resources than do the above suggestions. In the first published article dealing with the CDS, Osipow, Carney, & Barak (1976, p. 240) wrote that "because some of the items are complex and may be subject to more than one answer, the items may need further revision." Slaney and his colleagues (1981) suggested that Osipow approach item revision by dividing the logically independent statements in complex items into separate items. Reducing the complexity of item statements and the corresponding ambiguity of item responses may produce a stable factor structure and thus facilitate definition of indecision types, construction of CDS indecision subscales, and development of differential diagnosis systematics.

Experimentation with refining the two Certainty Scale items could elaborate the CDS model of career choice status. Recall that the Certainty Scale represented an innovative and heuristic conception of status in adapting to the developmental tasks of career choice. Rather than categorizing choice status with the undecided-decided dichotomy, Osipow, Carney, & Barak (1976) conceptualized choice status as a continuous variable with levels of decidedness. Jones and Chenery (1980) have demonstrated the merit of elaborating the conception of choice status from a univariate model (i.e., decidedness) into a multivariate model. They investigated four choice status subtypes created by combining the variables of decidedness and comfort with choice. Using the responses to two items of 224 college students in an introductory psychology class, they found that 70.4% were decided-comfortable, 17% undecided-uncomfortable, 3.2% undecided-comfortable, and 9.4% decided-uncomfortable. Each CDS Certainty Scale item combines statements about being decided, feeling comfortable with that choice, and knowing how to implement it. Dividing these statements into three separate items each for major and career choice could stimulate research on a differentiated model of career choice status, which might eventually systematically relate to a differentiated model of vocational decision-making difficulties.

CAREER DEVELOPMENT INVENTORY

Super and his collaborators investigated the maturation of adolescents' coping repertoire for making the pre-vocational and vocational choices required by their school curricula. They conducted the longitudinal Career Pattern Study (Super & Overstreet, 1960) to determine which variables, in addition to socioeconomic status and intelligence, most affect vocational development in adolescents and young adults. The staff of the Career Pattern Study (CPS) postulated that vocational development occurs along five dimensions:

> (1) increasing orientation to vocational choice, (2) increasing amounts of vocational information and more comprehensive and detailed planning, (3) increasing consistency of vocational preferences, (4) the crystallization of traits relevant to vocational choices, and, consequently, (5) increasing wisdom of vocational preferences. (Super, 1955, p. 154)

They originally identified possible measures or indices of vocational maturity and grouped them into these five dimensions: orientation to choice, information about preferred occupation, consistency of preferences, crystallization of traits, and wisdom of preferences (Super, 1955, p. 161). Preliminary empirical work led them to add vocational independence as a sixth dimension and to group 20 indices into the six dimensions (Super, 1974, p. 12). They tested this 6-dimensional model in the CPS. Their research eventually led them to construct a theoretical model of vocational maturity during adolescence (Super, 1974) that has five dimensions:

1. Planful attitudes toward life stages and tasks.
2. Attitudes toward exploration.
3. Educational and occupational information.
4. Knowledge of decision-making principles and practice.
5. Realism.

Although the variables that constitute these dimensions have been modified and refined (Super, 1983), the basic five dimensions in the theoretical model have remained unchanged.

Development

Super and his colleagues constructed the Career Development Inventory (CDI) to measure the first four dimensions of their theoretical model. They chose not to measure the realism dimension because the CPS realism measures did not interrelate with each other or correlate to other vocational maturity variables during adolescence. In this section, I will briefly trace the development of the CDI from its two early predecessors through its three unpublished forms, before describing the published form in the next section. In 1969 Super and his collaborators devised a career development measure called the Student Questionnaire to evaluate a career education project (Myers, Lindeman, Thompson, & Patrick, 1975). It contained 87 items that had been validated in the CPS. They scored the items on six scales. In 1970, they expanded the Student Questionnaire to 216 items grouped into 13 scales and renamed it the Career Questionnaire. Factor analysis (Forrest, 1971) led to item reduction and rearrangement of the 13 scales into three basic scales that contained a total of first 93 and later 91 items. The three scales in Form I of the CDI (Super & Forrest, 1972) corresponded to the first four dimensions in Super's theoretical model of vocational maturity:

1. Scale A, Planning Orientation (33 items): concern with choice, specificity of planning, and self-estimated amount of occupational information

2. Scale B, Resources for Exploration (28 items): quality of the actually-used and potentially-usable resources for educational and occupational exploration
3. Scale C, Information and Decision Making (30 items): amount of educational and occupational information that a student has acquired, together with mastery of the use of information for sound decisions

Super and his collaborators expanded Form I of the CDI to more broadly measure knowledge of the world of work, assess specific types of occupational information, and diagnose cognitive awareness of career development tasks. They used Form II in laboratory research and then modified it to produce Form III which they explicitly organized around a refined model of vocational maturity (Super & Thompson, 1979). Form III contained 191 items grouped into six scales:

1. Extent of Planning (30 items): similar to Form 1, Scale A
2. Use and Evaluation of Resources in Exploration (30 items): largely Form 1, Scale B
3. Career Decision Making (30 items, many new): principles and practice of decision making
4. Career Development Information (30 items, many new): awareness of and concern with developmental tasks
5. World of Work Information (30 items, many new): general occupational information
6. Information about Preferred Occupation (41 new items): knowledge of occupational group selected by student as of interest

Essentially, Form III used the Form I planning orientation (A) and exploration scales (B), split the decision-making and occupational information scale (C) into two scales and expanded each to 30 items, and added a scale to measure developmental task concern and a scale to measure specificity of information.

The test authors quickly concluded that Form III was too long because students required at least two 40-minute class periods to respond to the 191 items. They returned to their original goal of devising a measure of career maturity that could be administered within one class period. Using factor analysis, they reduced the first three scales in Form III to 20 items each, combined the Career Development Information and World of Work Information scales into one 20 item scale, and reduced the Knowledge of Preferred Occupational Group scale from 41 to 40 items. Students require about 60 minutes to complete the 120 items, but by eliminating Knowledge of Preferred Occupational Group Scale, they can complete Form IV of the CDI in a 40-minute class period.

Description

Super and his collaborators (1981) published this fourth version of the CDI in two forms: the Junior/Senior High School Form and the College and University Form. The forms are quite similar in that the authors slightly modified for the college form those high school form items that deal with levels of educational and occupational options to make them more pertinent to college students. The CDI is sold as a reusable 16-page test booklet with separate, computer-scored answer sheets. The front page explains the purpose of the inventory and how to respond to the items on the answer sheet. It also explains that the inventory has two parts: (I) Career Orientation and (II) Knowledge of Preferred Occupation.

Part I begins with Section A, Career Planning. This section measures extent of planning by asking about involvement in thinking about the future and in planning career-related high school and post-high school activities. Section B, Career Exploration, measures willingness to find and use good resources for career planning. Section C, Career Decision Making, measures ability to apply decision-making principles and methods to solve problems involving educational and occupational choices. Section D, World of Work Information, measures knowledge of types of occupations and ways to obtain and succeed in jobs.

Part II, Knowledge of Preferred Occupational Group, measures familiarity with the type of work that students say interests them most. Students select one personally preferred occupational group from 20 groups listed on the back of the IBM answer sheet. Then they answer 40 questions about the kinds of work in that field and the abilities, interests, values, and personal characteristics of workers in that field. The CDI manual states that Part II is most suitable for students in 11th and 12th grades who are about to enter the labor force and for college students who are about to declare a major. Younger students probably need take only Part I.

The CDI must be machine scored using differential item weights which are not reported in the manual. Hand-scoring keys are unavailable. In addition to scores for the five scales, the computer scoring service provides three composite scores: Career Development Attitudes combines planning and exploration scores, Career Development Knowledge and Skills combines decision making and world of work scores, and Career Orientation Total combines the planning, exploration, decision-making, and world of work scores. The composite scores offer increased reliability for individual interpretation because some of the basic scales have reported 3-week test-retest reliability in the low sixties.

The computer test report does not include raw scores. It provides only scale scores that have a mean of 100 and a standard deviation of 20. The basic scoring service offers four reports: (a) standard score and percentile on the five basic and three composite scales for individuals, (b) mean standard scores and standard deviations for the group, (c) percent of students selecting each alternative for the items in Part I, and (d) number and percentage of students in the group preferring each of the 20 occupational fields. The manual presents norms by sex for grades

9 through 12 for each of the eight CDI scores based on the standardization group of 5,039 students, a nation-wide but not demonstrably representative sample. The CDI authors advise users to compile local norms, a process facilitated by the reporting system when N is 100 or more.

Interpretation

Counselors use the CDI to measure students' readiness to cope with the developmental tasks of crystallizing, specifying, and implementing a career choice. Counselors and career educators can administer it within one high school class period to obtain data for diagnosing individual career development attitudes and competencies, planning group guidance programs and career education curricula, and evaluating program outcomes. In addition, counselors can annually readminister the CDI to measure rate of career development and identify, for preventive interventions, those students who are regressing or maintaining rather than developing. After completing an individual diagnosis, group needs assessment, survey, or program evaluation, counselors may use the CDI data to plan individual counseling, structured learning programs, or exploration experiences.

To select an intervention, counselors begin by examining clients' scale scores to identify their assets and deficits. The CDI authors consider scores above the 75th percentile as strengths to build upon and scores below the 25th percentile as weaknesses to remediate. They suggest interpretive hypotheses for each scale and illustrate their approach to interpretation with one case in the *User's Manual* (Thompson & Lindeman, 1981), three cases in the *Technical Manual* (Thompson & Lindeman, 1984), and three cases in an article on the Developmental Assessment and Counseling Model (Super, 1983). These illustrations demonstrate the logical order in which the CDI authors interpret the scales. This order follows the sequence of developmental task mastery. Fundamental to task mastery is awareness that one faces or will face a developmental task. Awareness precedes and prompts concern about and responsibility for task mastery.

Counselors look to scores on the Career Planning scale to assess clients' inclination to look ahead, take a planful approach, and involve themselves in career planning activities. A low score indicates that clients do not foresee their future in the world of work; therefore, they do not feel a need to acquaint themselves with or relate themselves to occupations. Often these clients display low work-role salience (Nevill & Super, 1988; Super & Nevill, 1984), either because they look forward to other life roles (e.g., homemaker) or because they do not look forward at all (Gordon, 1970). Clients who lack a future orientation typically need personal counseling to deal with their lack of optimism, goals, and achievement (Savickas, 1986). Clients who only look forward to other life roles need to learn that they will probably work in the future. A counselor can facilitate both work salience and career orientation by teaching clients about the developmental tasks they face, the implications of ignoring these tasks, and the value of a planful approach in mastering the tasks. If clients' scores indicate a planful and responsible approach to developmental tasks, then the counselor considers clients' career exploration attitudes.

The Career Exploration scale score indicates inclination to use exploration opportunities and resources. It measures attitudes toward information sources and willingness to use and evaluate these sources. Low scores suggest that clients are not concerned with using good sources of data about the fields and levels of work. These clients should learn to distinguish between good and bad information sources and to appreciate how competent sources can facilitate their information gathering. Counselors help these clients increase their awareness of career exploration opportunities. If a client is inclined to use competent sources for career exploration, then the counselor assesses the information that the client has already acquired.

The World of Work Information scale score indicates knowledge about work, occupation, and career. Low scores indicate that clients need to learn about types of occupations, the mores of work, and career development tasks. They probably do not know much about the range of occupations available to them. Thus counselors encourage uninformed clients to survey a wide range of occupations and then explore the fields of work that they find interesting. High scores on this scale suggest that clients are sufficiently knowledgeable to apply occupational information to self and to begin crystallizing field and level preferences.

The Decision Making scale score indicates knowledge of the principles and practices of decision making. Low scores suggest that clients do not know what to consider in making choices. This means that clients are not ready to use the occupational information they have acquired for career planning. Counselors help these clients to understand sound principles of decision making and to apply these principles in matching self to occupations. High scores suggest that clients may be ready to make matching decisions. When decision-making knowledge is supported by an adequate fund of occupational information based on planful exploration, then clients are ready to make tentative career choices. Aptitude tests, interest inventories, and self-reports have meaning for these clients because they already know about the world of work and how to make vocational decisions. In other words, the client displays the dispositions and competencies needed to benefit from content-oriented career counseling.

The development of attitudes and competencies for task mastery does not follow the above sequence for some clients. In these cases, the counselor must rely on common-sense and clinical experience to generate interpretive hypotheses. For example, if the Career Planning scale score is the only low scale score, then the counselor may want to determine if clients relate exploration and information to planning their own future. Or, if the Career Exploration scale score is the only low score, then the counselor may ask clients how they learned about occupations and developed decision-making skill.

Counselors do not need the Preferred Occupational Group scale to form the above interpretive hypotheses, thus it is not included in the Career Orientation Total score. Typically, counselors administer the Preferred Occupational Group scale only to students who are expected to be able to state a thoughtful preference for a career field. Ideally, these students have crystallized a preference for a group of occupations in a particular field and level of work and are beginning to specify a choice from among occupational alternatives in that group.

The Preferred Occupational Group scale score indicates knowledge about the occupational group of most interest to a client. Low scores suggest that clients do not possess accurate knowledge about their stated preferences. These clients need sharply focused exploration within their preferred field to generate and test specific career choices. The counselor must look at the four basic scales to determine if the client is ready for this focused exploration. Interpretation of high scores on the Preferred Occupational Group scale also requires relating the score to the other four basic scales. For example, a high Preferred Occupational Group score along with a low World of Work Information score means that clients know about the preferred field but not its place in the occupational structure. In these cases, the counselor should ask clients how they acquired this selective information and whether they have adequately examined other options. Often it is a case of premature closure in which a client commits self to a parental preference or a glamorous preference. For example, some clients grow up in a family business (e.g., farming or medicine), learn about this one field in great detail, and specify a choice in this field without exploring other fields, perhaps because of parental pressure or financial incentives.

Technical Information

The CDI manual consists of two volumes and a supplement. The 27-page *User's Manual* (Thompson & Lindeman, 1981) presents the rationale, description of item content, administration instructions, scoring procedures, interpretation methods, and recommended uses. The 48-page *Technical Manual* (Thompson & Lindeman, 1984) presents the theory and research supporting the development of the CDI and detailed data on its psychometric characteristics. The 20-page *College and University Supplement* (Thompson & Lindeman, 1982) discusses psychometric characteristics of and normative data for that form.

The manual appropriately cautions users about low test-retest reliabilities for the CDI scales (Career Planning, .79; Career Exploration, .73; Decision Making, .70; World of Work, .67; Preferred Occupation, .61) and encourages them to use the composite scales because of their greater reliability (Career Development Attitudes, .83; Career Development Knowledge, .83; and Career Orientation Total, .84). In light of their reliability, the authors instruct users in how to apply the standard error of measurement to interpret scale scores and score profiles.

The manual reports a respectable amount of validity evidence for an inventory published in 1981. However, Thompson and Lindeman (1981, p. 7) may have been overly enthusiastic when they wrote that much of the research on earlier forms of the CDI directly applies to the current form. The CDI possesses superior content validity because it explicitly operationalizes a model of career maturity that has been refined by four decades of programmatic research. Although the instrument's construct validity needs more empirical support, its factor structure and relations to age, grade, and school curricula provide an adequate base. In regard to criterion-related validity, Thompson and Lindeman (1984) cite three concurrent validity studies that showed the CDI related as expected to ability, work salience, and other career development measures. More predictive-validity evidence is needed, but longitudinal data takes time to accumulate. Until the completion of predictive-validity studies using the published form of the CDI, we may cautiously use evidence collected on earlier forms of the inventory. At least two longitudinal studies by the CDI authors and others are now underway.

Reviews

The CDI's greatest strength derives from its articulation of a cogent model of career development. Although the CDI culminates 30 years of programmatic research on vocational behavior during adolescence, further research is needed to substantiate its tentatively established validity. While waiting for more validity research, CDI users are advised not to inadvertently apply research on earlier forms to the current form and not to overinterpret the scales by confusing the CDI's construct validity for criterion-related validity.

In a review based on the *User's Manual* (Thompson & Lindeman, 1981) and written before publication of the *Technical Manual* (Thompson & Lindeman, 1984), Hansen (1985) called for more reliability and validity research. In particular she recommended criterion-related research to examine the CDI relative to occupational aspiration, career success, and job satisfaction. She concluded that the World of Work Information and Preferred Occupational Group scales were ''sufficiently unreliable over short periods to warrant caution in their use'' (p. 223). She also questioned the need for five scales in light of factor analytic studies that show two factors accommodate the CDI—Career Development Attitudes and Career Development Knowledge. However, in a Rasch analysis of the psychometric characteristics of an Australian adaptation of the CDI, Punch and Sheridan (1985) reported that the two attitudinal scales (Career Planning and Career Exploration) do not constitute one dimension and should be considered as separate components of the CDI. Yet they did conclude, like Hansen, that the Decision Making and World of Work Information scales may represent one factor and added that the CDI authors may have erred in dividing Scale C of Form I into separate decision making and information scales.

Research Directions

The CDI needs criterion-related research to firmly establish its validity and nomological network. In particular, researchers could refine the Developmental Assessment and Counseling Model by linking the CDI to variables commonly studied in developmental and personality psychology. To date, research on the CDI has been conducted in isolation from advances and debates in the behavioral sciences (Heath, 1976; Vondracek & Schulenberg, 1986). Linkages to this body of accumulated basic research would increase practitioners' understanding of career maturity and its facilitation. For example, researchers could relate the CDI variables to future orientation, causal attribution, and self-efficacy to learn if these personality variables determine career planning and exploration attitudes (Super, 1983).

Practitioners would also benefit from research on the interpretative hypotheses suggested for each CDI scale. Although the descriptive interpretations in the manual make sense, they await empirical confirmation. The interpretations of profile patterns also lack empirical support. For example, the interpretation that spiked Career Planning scale and Knowledge of Preferred Occupational Group scale scores reflect the premature closure or early fixation seems cogent but needs empirical confirmation. Validated decision rules for interpreting profiles could stimulate advances in differential treatment of clients.

Some revision of the CDI itself to increase scale reliabilities would support work on scale and profile interpretation. The scale with the lowest reliability, Knowledge of Preferred Occupational Group, is quite innovative and may benefit from research to increase its reliability.

CAREER MATURITY INVENTORY ATTITUDE SCALE

The other prominent inventory that measures variables in the career choice process also evolved from the Career Pattern Study. In fact, the Career Maturity Inventory (CMI; Crites, 1978b) was the first paper-and-pencil measure of vocational development. Crites constructed the CMI to measure two dimensions in his model of vocational development which appears in Figure 12.1. He refined the original CPS model of vocational development by reorganizing and defining its dimensions. Crites accepted the Consistency of Vocational Choice and Wisdom of Vocational Preference dimensions and reorganized the other three dimensions into two dimensions. He proposed that the Orientation to Vocational Choice dimension, the Information and Planning dimension, and certain aspects of the Crystallization of Traits dimension (e.g., increasing independence) could be elaborated as several different kinds of career choice concepts and competencies, that is, attitudes and aptitudes for vocational decision making. Thus, the third and fourth dimensions in Crites' model were called Career Choice Attitudes and Career Choice Competencies. Crites (1965) defined attitudes as dispositional response tendencies that mediate both choice behaviors and competencies. He defined competencies as comprehension and problem-solving abilities that pertain to vocational decision making.

Development

Crites constructed and standardized the CMI to measure the attitudes and competencies dimensions in his vocational development model. The original form of the CMI was called the Vocational Development Inventory. It consisted of a Concept Test and a Competence Test. The Concept Test, which eventually became the CMI-Attitude Scale, measured variables from the work of Ginzberg and Super: bases for choice, reliance upon others in decision making, involvement in the choice process, planful daydreaming and fantasy, time perspective, and means-end cognizance. The Competence Test consisted of five subtests measuring variables that bear on decision-making: self-appraisal, occupational information, goal selection, planning, and problem solving.

Although the Concept Test has gone through four research forms and two published forms, the Competence Test has not been developed beyond the original research edition, probably because of the excessive time required to administer it. Crites subsequently stopped working on the Competence Test and instead has been developing a new scale, the Career Readiness Inventory, to measure career choice competencies. The CMI Competence Test is not dealt with in the present chapter.

The Concept Test consisted of self-descriptive statements about an individual's career choice attitudes and behaviors. Crites drew the subject matter from real life sources. He wrote a pool of 1,000 items based on attitudinal statements made by clients in vocational counseling over a 5-year period. To guide selection of items from the pool for inclusion in the scale, Crites wrote behavioral descriptions and literary definitions for five central concepts in vocational theory and research. The concepts and their definitions appear in Table 12.1.

Two experimental forms of the Concept Test consisted of the same 100 items written in two grammatical formats, first and third person. The two test forms also differed in response format: true/false versus 5-point Likert scales. Crites administered the items to a stratified sample of fifth through 12th-grade students with Ns varying from 500 to 1,000 in each grade. He wanted items that empirically differentiated among these criterion groups because he believed that "any measure of a developmental variable must be systematically related to time" (Crites, 1961). Of the 100 items used in Forms 1 and 2, 86 items differentiated between grade level at or beyond the .01 level. Fifty of the 86 items related monotonically to grade (Crites, 1964, p. 332). Results also indicated that the two item formats and two response scales were essentially equal in differ-

TABLE 12.1
Variables in the CMI-Attitude Scale, Screening Forms A-1 and A-2

Dimension	*Definition*	*Sample Item*
Involvement in the choice process	Extent to which individual is actively participating in the process of making a choice	"I seldom think about the job I want to enter."
Orientation toward work	Extent to which individual is task- or pleasure-oriented in his or her attitudes toward work and the values he or she places upon work	"Work is dull and unpleasant" and "Work is worthwhile mainly because it lets you buy the things you want."
Independence in decision-making	Extent to which individual relies upon others in the choice of an occupation	"I plan to follow the line of work my parents suggest."
Preference for vocational choice factors	Extent to which individual bases his or her choice upon a particular factor	"Whether you are interested in a job is not as important as whether you can do the work."
Conceptions of the choice process	Extent to which individual has accurate or inaccurate conceptions about making an occupational choice	"A person can do any kind of work he wants as long as he tries hard."

Note. From "Measurement of vocational maturity in adolescence: I. Attitude Scale of the Vocational Development Inventory" by J. O. Crites, 1965, *Psychological Monographs, 79,* page 35.

entiating power. He chose to retain both grammatical forms but use only the less time consuming true/false response scale in a 50-item revision of the original Vocational Development Inventory Concept Test which Crites (1971) named the Vocational Development Inventory Attitude Test. Crites published this form in 1973 and renamed it the Career Maturity Inventory Attitude Scale. The name change fit the then current emphasis on career education.

Crites referred to this 1973, 50-item version of the CMI-Attitude Scale as the Screening Form (A-1) to distinguish it from a Counseling Form then being developed. In 1978, he published the Counseling Form (B-1) along with a revised screening form (A-2). Form A-2 differs only slightly from Form A-1. Research indicated that two items needed to be keyed differently. One other item (#46) was replaced with a new item. In addition, Crites reorganized the items to arrange identical scoring keys for forms A-1 and A-2.

Crites constructed the Counseling Form to provide subscales that measure the career choice attitudes variables in his model of career maturity. However, the

Counseling Form subscales do not correspond exactly to the variables listed in Table 12.1. Crites modified them in response to criticism that three of the variables reflected career choice content. He replaced the three variables that dealt with attitudes toward a career choice with three new variables that dealt with attitudes toward vocational decision making. Thus each of the five variables in the revised model, which are listed in Table 12.2, clearly pertains to the decisional process. Compromise replaced choice factors and decisiveness replaced conception. Crites retained the variable named orientation but redefined it.

There is some confusion regarding the Orientation subscale in the Counseling Form (Stowe, 1985). The *Theory and Research Handbook* (Crites, 1978c, p. 10) mistakenly retained the original definition stated in Table 12.1. However, the items scored for it differ substantially from the orientation items in Form A-1. In Form A-1, items 7, 8, 14, 47, 24, 35, 4, and 9 measure orientation to intrinsic or extrinsic rewards in making a career choice. The items state that a job is important because it lets one make money, buy things, get ahead, and become famous. In Form B-1, the items measure orientation to the decision-making process. They deal with how much one thinks about jobs, imagines self in a job, and thinks about preparing for a job. To correct the mistake in the *Handbook,* Savickas and Crites (1981) redefined orientation as the extent to which an individual is familiar with and relates self to the vocational decision-making process.

TABLE 12.2
Variables in the CMI-Attitude Scale, Counseling Form B-1

Dimension	*Definition*	*Sample Item*
Decisiveness in career decision making	Extent to which an individual is definite about making a career choice	"I keep changing my occupational choice."
Involvement in career decision making	Extent to which individual is actively participating in the process of making a choice	"I'm not going to worry about choosing an occupation until I'm out of school."
Independence in career decision making	Extent to which an individual relies upon others in the choice of an occupation	"I plan to follow the line of work my parents suggest."
Orientation to career decision making	Extent to which individual is familiar with and relates self to the career decision-making process	"I have little or no idea of what working will be like."
Compromise in career decision making	Extent to which individual is willing to compromise between needs and reality	"I spent a lot of time wishing I could do work I know I can never do."

Note. From *Theory and Research Handbook for the Career Maturity Inventory* (2nd ed., p. 10) by J. O. Crites, Monterey, CA: CTB/McGraw-Hill, Inc. Copyright 1978 by McGraw-Hill, Inc. Reprinted by permission of CTB/McGraw-Hill.

The 50 items in Form A-1 could not generate subscales to measure the new variables. To solve this problem, Crites added 25 items to the Screening Form A-2. He selected these items, after try-out on a sample of 7,000 students, from 50 items drawn from the original 1,000-item pool. The empirical criterion for selecting these 25 items differed from the criterion used to select the 50 items in the Screening Form. Crites used a less restrictive definition of developmental phenomena based on conceptual refinements (Crites, 1974a; 1978c). The new criteria called for a systematic relationship to grade but not necessarily a monotonic function. In the end, the 47 items in the five subscales used 28 items from Form A-2 and 19 new items. Crites is developing an unrealism subscale with the 28 unscored items.

Description

The Attitude Scale Screening Form (A-2) is published in an 8-page 8½ × 11-inch booklet. The front page states the title and publishing information; the back page is blank. Page 2 explains the purpose of the inventory, and page 3 explains how to answer the items and mark responses on the IBM answer sheet. The items appear on pages 4 through 7.

The Screening Form takes about 20 minutes to administer and the Counseling Form takes about 30 minutes. Both forms have about a 6th-grade reading level. The manual gives clear instructions for individual administration and a script for group administration. The Scale resembles a survey questionnaire more than a test, so the administrator tells students to indicate their feelings about each item rather than attempt to discern the correct answer. The answer sheets can be scored by hand or computer. The Screening Form (A-2) yields only a total score. The Counseling Form (B-1) yields the screening scale total score and five subscale scores. The manual provides interpretive frequency distributions derived from 74,000 student scores collected between the Fall of 1973 and Spring of 1976. Counselors can use these distributions to convert Screening Form and Counseling Form scores to derived scores and percentiles for students in grades 6 through 12. Nevertheless, Crites prefers that counselors compile and use local norms.

Interpretation

The Screening Form score is designed to indicate the maturity of a student's attitudes toward making a career choice. Higher scores indicate more mature attitudes and thus greater readiness to make a career choice. Crites likens readiness for career planning to reading readiness. Clients below a certain threshold of readiness are neither sufficiently mature nor properly disposed to make a realistic choice. These clients need to develop their attitudes more completely to reach the choice threshold. Unfortunately, the threshold point (i.e., raw score) at which attitudes are sufficiently developed to produce choice behavior and realistic career planning has not been empirically identified. Crites does not state what score represents the threshold. Instead, he recommends that counselors consider students who score above the 25th percentile as progressing normally and suggests that counselors offer assistance to students who score in the bottom quartile because they may be delayed or impaired in their career development (Crites, 1978a, p. 32).

In interpreting Screening Form scores, counselors should remember that they represent the original five variables defined in Table 12.1, not the five variables measured by the Counseling Form subscales. It is worth noting that the majority of validity data for the Screening Form total score pertains to Form A-1. The screening scores for Forms A-2 and B-1 differ slightly from A-1 in that they contain one different item, score two items differently, and present the items in a different order. Nevertheless, it is probably safe to assume that the validity data for Form A-1 extends to Forms A-2 and B-1.

In contrast to the screening score, the validity for use of the Counseling Form (B-1) subscales has not been established. Only two validity studies have dealt with the subscales (Lopez-Baez, 1981; Stowe, 1985). Crites (1978a, p. 29) advised that while researchers develop the subscales they be considered a research instrument. Because their interpretative validity has not yet been firmly established, many counselors do not interpret subscale scores to clients.

Teaching the Test Model

Instead of interpreting the subscale scores, many counselors interpret the items because they have content and criterion-related validity. In interpreting the items, counselors can draw upon each item's conceptual rationale and empirical data. As rationally-derived items, they have been linguistically explicated as part of a cogent theoretical model. Moreover, as empirically derived items, they have been operationally defined. This combination of theory and research makes CMI items especially suitable for interpretation to clients.

Crites (1974b) claimed that by discussing the items that they answered in the immature direction, clients can incorporate new ideas into their thinking and develop a more mature approach to vocational decision making. He recommended that counselors "teach the test" to clients in order to bring them up to the choice threshold. Simply stated, the logic for teaching the test is that the items state attitudes that the client should hold.

Some counselors "teach the test" by discussing the items a client missed in the order that the items appear in the Scale. Other counselors discuss all the items that a client missed within one subscale then move in turn to items from another subscale until they have discussed all five subscales. This procedure allows counselors to use the subscale items to explain the five attitudinal variables and relate them to the client's decision making. A few counselors teach the test by organizing the five variables into two groups. Presenting the results in two large chunks helps some clients retain and apply the information. A logical grouping divides the scales into those that deal with planful concern about the future and those that deal with a sense of self-control over one's future.

A concerned approach to decision making is sustained by the attitudes Crites called orientation and involvement. *Orientation* items deal with the client's awareness of the vocational decision-making process. Clients with mature attitudes usually seek to familiarize themselves with how people choose occupations and develop careers. Clients less inclined to orient themselves to how careers develop have vague and inaccurate notions about career choice. When pressed to make a career choice, they feel confused. These clients benefit from consciousness-raising counseling techniques (Skovholt & Hoenninger, 1974) that increase foresight and heighten awareness of career development tasks. When clients have a cognitive schema to sustain career dreams and occupational fantasies, they are ready to involve themselves in the decision-making process.

A client can be familiar with the choice process without getting involved in it. *Involvement* items address whether clients relate themselves to the process of making a choice and actively participate in it. Clients with mature attitudes tend to think about alternative careers and try to relate their present behavior to future goals. Clients who are less inclined to get involved in the vocational decision-making process just do not worry about their future. Often, they prefer to enjoy the present and take life one day at a time. When pressed to make a career choice, they feel anxious. These clients benefit from counseling techniques that help them make their future ''real'' by populating it with anticipated events and goals that give it shape and substance (Oleksy-Ojikutu, 1986). Clients who are concerned about their futures are ready to take control of the vocational decision-making process.

A sense of control over vocational decision making is sustained by the attitudes Crites called independence, decisiveness, and compromise. *Independence* items deal with self-reliance in making career choices. Immature attitudes incline clients to depend on others to choose for them. *Decisiveness* items deal with commitment to making career choices. Immature attitudes incline clients to feel uncertain and to avoid committing themselves to making a choice. *Compromise* items deal with willingness to acknowledge and concede to the demands of reality. Immature attitudes incline clients to distort or deny aspects of reality which may limit or block their need fulfillment. To avoid anxiety or frustration, clients with immature compromise attitudes rigidly maintain their subjectivity rather than increase their objectivity.

Clients who incompletely develop or lack one or more of these attitudes usually display a dependent, uncertain, or rigid approach to career choice that leads to indecision. These clients typically benefit from behavioral counseling techniques (Woody, 1968) that increase their self-esteem and realism or develop their assertiveness and decisional skills. Clients disposed to independence, decisiveness, and compromise approach career choice with a sense of control because these attitudes facilitate self-reliant, confident, and realistic vocational decision making. Thus, they are ready for content-oriented career counseling.

As a transition to content-oriented assessment or counseling, a few counselors augment their discussions of career concern and control dispositions by discussing three more groups of items from the Attitude Scale. They base these item groups on three variables measured by the Screening Form: conception, orientation toward work, and preference for choice factors (see Table 12.1 for definitions).

To use an alliteration with "C," counselors can follow counseling about vocational decision-making *concern* and *control* with counseling about career *concepts, criteria,* and *choice bases.* Six items (5, 18, 21, 32, 41, and 68) in the Counseling Form deal with clients' conceptions of how to make a career choice. The counselor should try to disabuse clients of any misconceptions expressed in their responses to these items. Six items (6, 11, 26, 29, 47, and 50) deal with the criteria one imposes on making a choice. Originally these items were called orientation-toward-work items in that they referred to whether one sought intrinsic or extrinsic rewards from work. Savickas and Crites (1981) referred to these items as criterion items, that is, client's criteria for defining a good career choice. Counselors can use these items to identify clients who use power, prestige, or possessions as choice criteria and encourage them to consider the role of intrinsic rewards in producing job and life satisfaction.

After discussing a client's choice criteria, the counselor can use four items (2, 8, 17, and 35) to explain the intrinsic criteria on which one should base a career choice: needs, interests, abilities, and values. The counselor should try to convince clients to base their choices on a synthesis of these four factors because using any one factor alone can produce an incongruent career choice. Discussions of choice bases make a smooth transition to administration or interpretation of interest inventories and ability tests.

As noted above, critics argued persuasively that content-oriented elements confounded these three variables. Although they do not reflect the decision-making process itself, these variables do define important attitudes toward a career choice; therefore, they can be used validly in teaching the test. Furthermore, if a counselor discusses them after discussing the five attitudes toward the vocational decision-making process, then this discussion of attitudes toward a career choice makes a smooth transition to content-oriented assessment and counseling.

In summary, clients are ready for content-oriented assessment and counseling when they display concern for and a sense of control over the vocational decision-making process, hold an accurate conception of how to make a choice, express intrinsic criteria for their choices, and want to base their choices on a synthesis of their needs, interests, abilities, and values.

Teaching the Test Materials and Methods

To help counselors interpret Attitude Scale items to clients, Crites (1973) wrote programmed instructional materials to use in teaching the test. For each item, he explained the rationale for the more mature responses. Crites and Savickas (1980) revised the Screening Form rationales based on feedback from counselors and their own experience in using the rationales. They also added rationales for the additional items in the Counseling Form. They suggested that counselors use a three-step cycle in discussing item rationales with a client: (a) nondirective exploration, (b) directive shaping, and (c) active learning. Different types of interviewing responses and goals define each phase in this item teaching cycle.

Non-directive exploration. Counselors begin the cycle by reading an item that the client answered in the immature direction and asking the client to explain the reason for the chosen response. This sets the topic and begins the exploration of the client's outlook (Van Riper, 1974). For example, a counselor might say, "On item 54 you agreed that you would feel better if someone chose for you. What did you have in mind when you answered this question?" To draw out the client's attitude and to probe the beliefs, feelings, and behavioral tendencies associated with it, the counselor may use "nondirective" responses such as open questions, restatement of relevant content, reflection of feeling, silence, and clarification of meaning.

Directive shaping. Having explored the client's outlook, the counselor actively uses responses that elicit and shape a more mature view (Flake, Roach, & Stenning, 1975). The counselor teaches the client the rationale for the item and uses values confrontation (Young, 1979) to create dissonance about immature attitudes toward vocational decision making. During the ensuing discussion the counselor may use responses such as instruction, persuasion, verbal modeling, storytelling, and reinforcement to help clients reduce the felt discrepancy by reconceptualizing their beliefs and developing new attitudes. Counselors use their expertness, trustworthiness, and attractiveness to block unproductive paths to dissonance reduction (e.g., discredit counselor, use counterpersuasion, devalue the issue, seek social support), and confirm client attitude change with encouragement and support (Strong, 1968).

Active learning. When the client verbally expresses an improved outlook, the counselor encourages the client to translate it into goal directed vocational behavior. The counselor may use responses such as behavioral modeling, homework assignments, role playing, and feedback to guide instrumental learning. This completes the three phases in the item discussion cycle. Accordingly, the counselor moves to the next item that the client answered in the immature direction and repeats the cycle. In exploring the new item, the counselor listens to hear if the client has integrated and generalized pertinent insights that were learned in discussing a previous item. If the earlier learning has not generalized to the new item, then the counselor proceeds to the directive shaping and active learning steps.

After considering each item, the counselor usually summarizes what the client has learned and restates what the client will do to confirm and enact the new attitudes. The counselor may also draw from the client implications that the new decisional attitudes have for choices the client is trying to make in interpersonal, family, or leisure roles. For example, the counselor might say "I hear you now saying that it is important to make your own career choice. I wonder if you think it is okay to rely on people to make other kinds of choices for you?"

Teaching the Test Variations

A few counselors use the item discussion cycle without administering the CMI to clients. Unlike the test interpretation method, the test teaching method does not require that the client take the test. The counselor may just sit down with a client and begin to discuss the items by asking the client to verbally respond to the first item. If the client offers a mature response, the counselor reinforces it and moves to the next item. If the response shows an immature outlook, then the counselor begins the discussion cycle outlined above.

In addition to teaching the test to individual clients, counselors have used the item rationales in process-oriented career counseling groups. These groups do not address which occupational choice (content) is right for each group member, but instead deal with the approach to decision making (process) that is right for everyone in the group. Teaching the test works even more effectively when the counselor enlists group dynamics in the item discussion cycle. For example, those group members who have already developed a particular attitude receive reinforcement and serve as role models to other group members who are still developing that disposition. The group members can help the counselor confirm or contradict the thinking of a client as well as encourage the client to experiment with new attitudes and behaviors.

Although not widely used, other variants of teaching the test have been effective. Healy (1982, pp. 317–321) suggested that counselors reduce client errors and lessen anxiety associated with "instructional counseling" by teaching the concepts assessed by the scale before administering it and discussing incorrect answers. Savickas and Crites (1981) designed and field tested a course to teach the Counseling Form item rationales to high school students. A teachers' guide for the course includes detailed lesson plans, teaching tips, overhead transparencies, and student handouts. Freeman (1975) wrote and pilot tested ten sociodramas to teach the Screening Form variables to students. The sociodramas are semi-structured; an opening dialogue sets the problem and leaves the conclusion of the drama to the student actors. A community college placement center modified the item rationales for a series of "Dear Abby"-type articles in their newsletter for students. Other innovative ways of teaching the test probably will appear as more counselors use the item rationales.

Technical Information

Because of its extensive use in theoretical research and program evaluation, the Attitude Scale has a well-articulated nomological network and strong support for its validity. The large volume of research reflects the fact that the Attitude Scale was the first objective measure of career maturity and thus widely used during the 1970s to evaluate career education programs and career counseling interventions. At least 400 studies involving the Attitude Scale have appeared as published journal articles or unpublished doctoral dissertations. To approach this voluminous literature, one should begin by reading Crites' (1971) monograph on the Attitude Scale and the *Theory and Research Handbook* (Crites, 1978c). After this introduction, the reader should review a Counseling Form validity study (Stowe, 1985) and several Screening Form validity studies (Alvi & Khan, 1982; Chodzinski & Randhawa, 1983; Hanna & Neely, 1978; Khan & Alvi, 1983; and Neely & Hanna, 1977). So prepared, the reader is ready to consider critiques of the Attitude Scale.

Reviews

After hundreds of studies, four questions about the Attitude Scale's validity remain unanswered. The first question addresses the Attitude Scale's construct validity. Reviewers have disagreed with several decisions that Crites made in constructing the scale. Super (1969) and Katz (1978) criticized the operational definition and validity of the construct measured by the Attitude Scale because 43 of the 50 Screening Form (A-1) items were keyed false, that is, written to reflect what career maturity is not. Westbrook and Mastie (1973) expressed concern about the large number of items with low positive ($< .30$) and high negative biserial correlations with the total score. They argued that, even in a factorially complex instrument, all the items should relate positively to the total score. They wondered what the items with negative biserial correlations contribute to the principal construct measured by the scale. They also questioned whether the true/false response scale adequately reflects respondents' attitudes.

The second question addresses an aspect of the Attitude Scale's criterion-related validity. Hansen (1974) called for longitudinal studies to examine the Attitude Scale's predictive validity. Most of the available criterion-related validity data is concurrent. For example, Westbrook (1976) showed that students with higher Screening Form scores made more realistic vocational choices. Although a few longitudinal studies have been conducted (Collins, 1986; Herr, Good, McCloskey, & Weitz, 1982), we still do not know if students with higher Attitude Scale scores more accurately predict their future occupation or achieve greater job satisfaction and success. Researchers need to empirically investigate the assumption that career maturity during adolescence relates to career adaptability and work adjustment during adulthood.

The third question addresses the Attitude Scale's convergent and discriminant validity. Westbrook and Mastie (1973) have questioned the Attitude Scale's convergent validity because it correlates more strongly with CDI cognitive scales than with CDI attitude scales. Researchers (Palmo & Lutz, 1983; Westbrook, 1982) have also challenged the discriminant validity of the Attitude Scale because it correlates with measures of mental ability. Crites, Wallbrown, and Blaha (1985) have countered these arguments, but the issue remains unresolved.

The fourth question addresses the Scale's validity for use. Hansen (1974) called for research to determine the usefulness of the Scale in career guidance. Katz (1978, p. 1563) expressed "reservations about the strong claims in the handbook and manual of categorical validity for various uses of the Scale in guidance" and Sorenson (1974) considered the validity data for the claimed uses unpersuasive. Zytowski (1978) faulted Crites for not using available data to distinguish the valid uses of the Scale. Cronbach's (1980) idea of validity for use should guide future studies of the diagnostic subscales in the Counseling Form.

Research Directions

At this time, the most pressing research need relative to the Attitude Scale is a literature review. The last literature review appeared in the *Theory and Research Handbook* (Crites, 1978c). A voluminous literature dealing with the CMI has appeared since 1975, the latest reference in the *Handbook* bibliography. A systematic synthesis of the accumulated evidence would allow theorists, researchers, and practitioners to make the fullest use of the varied information offered by the numerous studies. It might also help resolve the controversy surrounding the CMI-Attitude Scale's relationship with intelligence (Crites, et al., 1985; Westbrook, 1982).

The most pressing empirical research need is for studies of the validity of the five subscales. In order for these subscales to be helpful to counselors, their validity for use must be formally established. Research on interpreting the Attitude Scale should identify, if possible, the "threshold" of readiness to make a realistic career choice. It should also investigate the effect of teaching the test on career choice decidedness and realism. If teaching the test increases decidedness and realism, then investigators should examine the relative effectiveness of different instructional methods such as individual counseling, group counseling, programmed learning, and behavioral modeling.

USES OF THE MEASURES

This section deals with the selection and use of career choice process measures. The first part compares and contrasts the three prominent measures and offers guidelines for their use. The second part discusses suggestions on how to interpret scores from process measures to clients. The third part presents a case that illustrates the use of process measures in career counseling.

The Measures Compared

In the introduction to the present chapter, I noted that career choice process scales measure either difficulties or resources. Having reviewed the three most prominent scales, we are now prepared to further distinguish the scales according to their various uses. Obviously the main distinction remains as stated in the introduction. The CDS deals with indecision whereas the CDI and CMI deal with career maturity. More precisely, the CDS addresses adaptation to the tasks involved in developing a career choice. The CDS Certainty Scale helps counselors make a *differential diagnosis* of a client's decisional status, that is, degree of decidedness. The CDS Indecision Scale helps counselors assess the amount and variety of difficulties that delay clients' adaptation to career choice tasks. The CDI and CMI address not adaptation but adaptability, that is, the personal resources one can draw upon to form behavioral responses to the vocational development tasks of crystallization, specification, and implementation. In particular, the CDI measures planning and exploration attitudes and informational and decisional competencies that people use to develop a realistic career choice. Counselors can use the CDI to make a *developmental diagnosis* of clients' readiness for coping with career choice tasks. In contrast, the CMI-Attitude Scale measures attitudes toward career choice (Form A-2 or B-1 total score) and disposition for vocational decision making (Counseling Form B-1 subscales). Counselors can use the CMI to make a *decisional diagnosis* of clients' readiness to make realistic career choices. The differential, developmental, and decisional perspectives on the career choice process focus on distinct variables, yet the variables of difficulties, readiness, and dispositions may eventually be integrated into comprehensive career choice process measures (Jepsen & Prediger, 1981) and diagnostic classification schemes (Rounds & Tinsley, 1984, p. 156).

In addition to informing diagnosis for counseling, each of the career choice process inventories discussed in this chapter has been used in evaluation, research, screening, and surveys. Each inventory has unique characteristics that make it likely to be selected for a particular purpose. This is most true with regard to research and evaluation.

The best documented use of the inventories is in research on treatment outcomes and evaluation of program effects. When selecting an inventory for program evaluation, evaluators should choose the one that most closely coincides with objectives of the program: the CDS to measure decisional status and difficulties, the CDI to measure developmental task mastery attitudes and competencies, and the CMI-Attitude Scale to measure attitudes toward vocational decision making. Although this selection criterion seems obvious, some evaluators have overlooked it because the inventory titles describe in general, not in particular, what they measure. In selecting an inventory for a research study, investigators should choose the one that measures the variables being examined. An empirical comparison of the inventories reported by Jepsen and Prediger (1981) distinguished among the measures and can help researchers make a more informed choice. An article by Hilton (1974) offers suggestions on selecting an evaluation instrument and analyzing evaluation data.

Many counselors select the CDS and CMI Screening Form (A-2) to quickly screen large groups of students. The CMI Screening Form works particularly well with junior and senior high school students. The CDS works better than the CMI with college students (Fretz & Leong, 1982) because it addresses major choice and has a higher ceiling. Students who are identified as needing assistance can be invited to orientation programs and career workshops or informed about opportunities for group guidance and individual counseling. Some college counselors have used the CDS to help students choose between personal and career development courses. They advise students with lower scores to take the personal development course first, whereas they advise students with higher scores to take only the career choice course.

When planning guidance programs and career education curricula, counselors can use career choice measures to survey students' needs. The CDI and CMI Counseling Form (B-1) are particularly useful in this regard. Because they each measure five variables, they provide multidimensional data as a basis for intervention design. With these data, counselors can design guidance programs and career education curricula to address the unique needs of the participants. Survey results can also be used to structure enrichment opportunities. For example, one college has administered the CDI to all incoming freshmen. At the first meeting with their academic advisors, students are given a booklet that explains their CDI results. The advisors engage students in "career conversations" to plan exploration experiences and select elective courses based upon CDI results. During the year, the counseling center staff invites students to different types of career development workshops based on their CDI profiles. The CDS (Savickas, Alexander, Jonas, & Wolf, 1986) and the CMI (Crites, 1978a) have been used similarly.

Using Process Assessments in Counseling

Several writers have discussed the use of career choice process measures in counseling. The architects of the Developmental Assessment and Counseling Model view test interpretation as a prime counseling method. Super (1983) enjoined counselors to make CDI results "part of the active thinking of the client." In a book edited by Super, Jordaan (1974) used four case examples to discuss how interpreting CDI results can help clients "repair developmental deficits" and "build on strengths." In the same book, LoCascio (1974) described problems in using career choice process measures with school dropouts and ethnic minorities, and Richardson (1974) discussed the use of these measures in counseling girls and young women. Crites (1974b; 1981) asserted that counselors should use process measures to enhance clients' self-understanding and improve their thinking and problem solving as a foundation for future coping with career development tasks.

The writers seem to agree that the best counseling use of the measures involves focusing on developmental possibilities and discussing experiences that could facilitate clients' career development. Crites (1981) addressed how to meaningfully communicate this information to clients in an article on "integrative test interpretation." He suggested that counselors use the measures to focus on aspects of career development which are particularly difficult for the client, embed information from the results in discussions of these difficulties, respond to the clients' verbalizations rather than interpreting the profile, and attend to the client's choice process as opposed to the measurement instrument.

A Case Illustration

The following case illustrates one way of using career choice process measures to improve a client's thinking about career choice, identify developmental possibilities, and select maturation experiences. A 20-year-old college student, dissatisfied with school, sought career counseling at the behest of a concerned friend. The student was about to successfully complete the third year of a 6-year accelerated program that led to Bachelor of Science and Doctor of Medicine degrees. However, as he was completing his first year in medical school, he experienced serious misgivings about his decision to become a physician. He felt uncomfortable with his classmates because they had different interests and lonely because school demands precluded time for old friends with similar interests. Although he passed every course, he claimed that it required tremendous willpower to study because he disliked the subject matter. In counseling, he wanted to reconsider his career choice of medicine, consider his specialty choice within medicine (i.e., psychiatry versus family medicine), and identify career alternatives outside of medicine. After a brief intake interview, I told him that I wanted more data about the career difficulties he was experiencing, his resources for resolving these difficulties, and the pattern of his vocational interests. To provide more data, he agreed to take the CDS, CDI, and the Jackson Vocational Interest Survey (JVIS; Jackson, 1977) during the next week and to return for counseling when they had been scored.

I assigned him the CDS to acquire specific information about the difficulties that were thwarting his adaptation to the task of specifying the details of his career choice with certainty and commitment. I assigned him the CDI to learn about the maturation of the attitudes and competencies that he would need to develop his career choice. I did not use the CMI with this client because I was more interested in his readiness for vocational development task coping in general rather than his disposition toward vocational decision making in particular. Based on the intake interview, he impressed me as having a pseudo-crystallized preference for medicine. CDI data is better suited than CMI data to objectively assess this subjective impression. For a case study that illustrates the use of the CMI, counselors may read the case of Karen as presented by Crites (1976).

In hand scoring the CDS, I determined that the client scored three points on the CDS Certainty Scale (i.e., two points for "only slightly like me" for major choice certainty plus one point for "not at all like me" for career choice certainty). The client scored 47 points on the CDS Indecision Scale. This raw score converted to the 99th percentile for decision-making difficulties among college students. In my experience, such an extreme score appears to mean that a person is in a state of career crisis and feels overwhelmed by career concerns. His response to the open-ended question (i.e., CDS item 19) coincided with this interpretation.

> I grew up in hospitals and it was "given" that I was going to be a doctor. I really don't know what a doctor does. It seems that one has to be "perfect" to be an M. D. Therefore, I can't be a good one. I am stuck. I still don't know what I would be good at, if anything. So, if I don't have medicine, I don't have anything. I am concerned and confused by everything.

The client rated five items as "4" or "exactly like me": CDS items 7, 8, 10, 13, and 14. I formed a composite statement of the client's salient decisional difficulties as stated in these items.

> I do not know what my abilities and interests are because I have not given much thought to my career choice until now. I feel lost and discouraged because I am not used to making my own decisions. Everything about choosing seems so uncertain but I want to be absolutely certain that I make the right choice. However, none of the careers I know about seem ideal for me so I need more information about careers.

The CDI results, as prepared by the commercial scoring service, appear in Table 12.3. After considering the CDS data, I turned to the CDI profile to understand how the client's decisional difficulties may have developed and to begin to formulate ideas about what he could do to outgrow the difficulties. Two features of the CDI profile drew my attention. The first feature involved the Career Planning Scale (CP). By itself, the client's extremely low CP scale score indicated that he did not look ahead to foresee himself in the world of work nor

TABLE 12.3
The Career Development Inventory: College Form (CDI)

▶ *NAME:*	▶ *ID:* 00000001	▶ *SEX:* M	▶ *DATE SCORED:* 12/ 4/87

Year : SENIOR
Major : Omitted Items—Part I: 0 Part II: 0
Occupational Group Preference: D Social Science: Research

	Standard Scores	*Percentile Local National*
CP	69	1
CE	99	53
DM	103	46
WW	96	31
CDA	82	7
CDK	99	33
COT	86	10
PO	117	74

Percentile

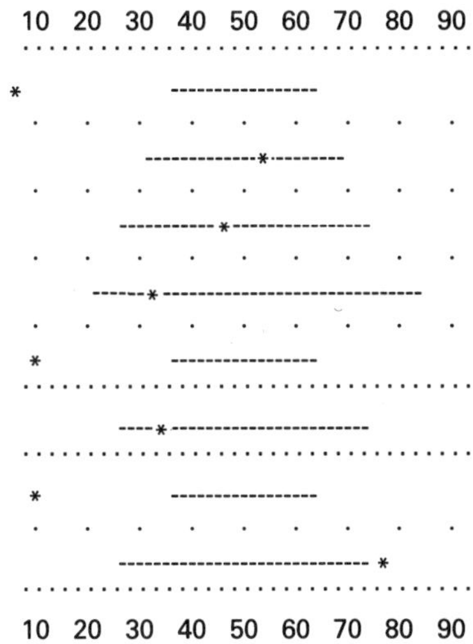

Descriptions of CDI Scales:

Career Planning (CP): How involved you are in thinking about your future and making career plans.

Career Exploration (CE): How able you have been to find and utilize good sources of career planning information.

Career Decision-Making (DM): How able you are to solve problems involving vocational and educational choices.

World-of-Work Information (WW): How much you know about jobs and what it takes to find and succeed at one.

Career Development Attitudes (CDA): A combination of your Career Planning and Career Exploration scores.

Career Development Knowledge and Skills (CDK): A combination of your Career Decision-Making and World-of-Work scores.

Career Orientation Total (COT): A combination of your scores on the CP, CE, DM, and WW scales.

Knowledge of Preferred Occupation (PO): How much you know about occupations in the group to which your preferred occupation belongs.

involve himself in planning his future. The score coincided with his statement during the intake interview that he has trouble seeing himself as a competent physician. In relation to the Career Exploration, World of Work, and Decision Making scores, the CP score suggested that the client may be actively avoiding career planning in that he has not applied available exploration, comprehension, and problem-solving resources to relate himself to the world of work. The second CDI profile feature that draw my attention involved the Preferred Occupational Group Scale (PO). By itself, I was surprised that he had chosen Social Science Research as his preferred field and that he had a good fund of knowledge about this field. I wondered if he had explored occupations in this field. In relation to other CDI scales, I noted that PO exceeded his World of Work score. Apparently, he is somewhat naive about occupations in general but knows about occupations in social science research.

Next I considered the JVIS. The JVIS includes work-style scales along with more traditional interest scales. On work-style scales, the client scored low on independence, planfulness, and interpersonal confidence and high on stamina, job security, and accountability. On vocational interest scales, he scored "high," but not "very high," on life science, social science, medical service, mathematics, technical writing, and social service.

To me the data coincided with a diagnosis of pseudo-crystallized preference preventing specification of a choice with certainty and commitment. The CDS revealed difficulties in developing a clear and stable picture of talents, interests, and goals and difficulty in emotionally accepting a preference he was already implementing. The CDI revealed a naivete about occupations and a lack of involvement in planning his vocational future. The JVIS revealed an unfocused interest pattern and a disposition toward passively following rules rather than assertively choosing and planning his own behavior. As a group, his diffused vocational interests, occupational naivete, and passive work style seemed to explain his self-reported difficulty in specifying the details of his career choice with certainty and commitment. Moreover, as a group they form a pattern, which suggests that specification is not the problem but rather the symptom of an earlier problem. Based on the inventory data, I concluded that the client's career choice of physician was not holding up under pressures to perform in medical school and to elaborate a specialty choice because it followed from a pseudo-crystallized preference for a career in medicine. The preference seems to be pseudo-crystallized in that he had failed to actively involve himself in the career choice process (CP score) and to analyze essential elements of his preference for medicine (PO score exceeded WW score). Furthermore, the JVIS work-style scores suggested the possibility that his preference for medicine may not have been a self-chosen goal. Instead, his preference may have resulted from the "interplay between the emotional needs of two persons—the individual making the choice and the individual who influences him" (Ginzberg, et al., 1951, p. 110).

At our next meeting, I used the integrative interpretation approach described by Crites (1981) to present my assessment of the inventory scores. As recommended by Guardo (1975, 1977) in her writings on developmental existentialism, I used the client's vocational development pattern as a backdrop for understanding and appreciating his unique experiences and opinions. In discussing my assessment with him, I highlighted his developmental pattern to help him articulate the course, pace, and scope of his existential experiences. My goal for this session was to combine our perspectives on his experiences to identify problems in and opportunities for developing a realistic career choice.

After orienting him to this goal, I began the session by discussing his response to CPS item 19. During the discussion, the client orally elaborated his written response and described pervasive feelings of anxiety caused by his desire to be certain about and comfortable with his career choice. Next, we considered the CDS items which he rated as "4" by discussing my composite statement of his decisional difficulties. The student endorsed this statement as "him." He self-explored each of the four components in turn: (a) he lacked self-knowledge and planfulness because he had always passively succumbed to an aggressive father who demanded that he become a physician; (b) he lacked decision-making skill because he relied on his father's decisions; (c) he wanted to make the ideal choice because he saw the bitterness that had resulted from his father being trapped in the wrong career; and (d) he lacked occupational information because of his early fixation on a career in medicine.

I used his self-disclosures about early fixation on medicine as a bridge to the CDI data. I informed him that the CDI indicated that his early fixation explained many of his current career concerns. To resolve these concerns, he might need to increase his foresight, deliberate more about the outcomes of his decisions, use daydreams to conceptualize himself in different kinds of work, explore several fields, and become more self-sufficient in decision making. I weaved the JVIS work-style data into discussing the last idea. He agreed that he needed to take positive steps on his own behalf rather than passively accept his father's career commands. I did not mention the JVIS interest scores because they were not yet pertinent to the discussion. During the remainder of the session, I responded empathically to his anxiety about his future, fear of confronting his father, and disgust with himself for still making decisions like a child. We concluded the session with an agreement to meet again to design a plan to develop his autonomy and career choice.

During the planning session, we concentrated on two themes: transforming the client's relationship with his father and developing his career choice. Because this case is presented to illustrate the use of career choice process measures in counseling, and not interest inventory interpretation or counseling techniques, I will only summarize the plan and its results. The client decelerated his movement through the accelerated B.S./M.D. program by asking to spend seven rather than six years in it. He used the extra year, at the end of his first year in medical school, to implement his growth plan. During this year he took no courses at the medical school while his classmates pursued full-time studies there. Instead, he: (a) completed his B. S. requirements as a half-time student, (b) used electives in his B. S. curriculum to explore careers in clinical psychology, medical sociology, and journalism, (c) worked 20 hours per week for six months as a biochemistry laboratory technician, (d) "shadowed" a psychiatrist for a week, (e) spent the summer away from home working as an intern in a public health program, (f) participated in an assertiveness training course, (g) received short-term counseling to increase his self-esteem and reduce his obsessiveness, and (h) studied judo. These activities enhanced his self-esteem and his ability to make independent decisions. The activities also strained his relationship with his father, yet the client and his father both felt that their relationship was improving. At the end of this year, the client transferred to another university where he enrolled in a graduate program in epidemiology. He planned to become an epidemiologist and possibly teach at a medical school. On follow-up a year later, he reported success in and satisfaction with his graduate program as well as increased certainty about his career in epidemiology.

CONCLUSION

This chapter explained how some counselors view career choice as a sequence of developmental tasks from crystallizing field and level preferences, to specifying a choice, and then implementing that choice. Students must adapt to social expectations that they master these tasks in a viable and suitable manner. To facilitate task mastery, comprehensive career counseling deals with both the process of vocational decision making and the content of career choice.

Counselors begin comprehensive career counseling by making a differential diagnosis of the client's vocational decision-making status, that is, identifying the tasks which a client faces and the difficulties experienced. With clients who are ready to specify a choice, the counselor proceeds to assist the client by using content-oriented counseling methods and materials. For those clients who are not ready, the counselor makes a developmental diagnosis of the client's attitudes and competencies for mastering the tasks of crystallizing preferences and specifying a choice. Furthermore, for those clients who need to develop the maturity to specify a choice, the counselor may make a decisional diagnosis of the client's disposition for vocational decision making.

Three scales that many counselors use to assess clients' career choice process were presented. The three scales may each be used to make all three of the diagnoses, yet each scale is especially useful for a particular assessment: the Career Decision Scale for differential diagnosis, the Career Development Inventory for developmental diagnosis, and the Career Maturity Inventory Attitude Scale for decisional diagnosis. The usefulness of each scale for a particular type of diagnosis probably explains counselors' practice of using the CDS to screen students for decision-making difficulties, the CDI to survey students for needs assessment in program development and evaluation, and the CMI to select students' individual counseling topics.

The instrument authors' ingenuity in theory construction, perseverance in instrument development, and leadership in research production has helped counselors expand occupational guidance to career counseling. In the future, research and reflection on the inventories' use in career counseling will probably result in new career choice process assessment instruments that measure a broader range of variables (Jepsen & Prediger, 1981), offer decision rules for diagnoses, and prescribe differential interventions for clients (Fretz & Leong, 1982; Rounds & Tinsley, 1984). The new instruments will build on the successes of the Career Decision Scale, Career Development Inventory, and the Career Maturity Inventory.

REFERENCES

Allis, M. (1984). [Review of the *Career Decision Scale*]. *Measurement and Evaluation in Counseling and Development, 17,* 98–100.

Alvi, S. A., & Khan, S. B. (1982). A study of the criterion-related validity of Crites' Career Maturity Inventory. *Educational and Psychological Measurement, 42,* 1285–1288.

Barak, A., & Friedkes, R. (1981). The mediating effects of career indecision and subtypes on career counseling effectiveness. *Journal of Vocational Behavior, 20,* 120–128.

Bell, H. M. (1940). *Matching youth and jobs.* Washington, D.C.: American Council on Education.

Chodzinski, R. T., & Randhawa, B. R. (1983). Validity of Career Maturity Inventory. *Educational and Psychological Measurement, 43,* 1163–1172.

Collins, J. E. (1986). Career maturity as a predictor of job adaptation: A longitudinal study (Doctoral dissertation, Kent State University, 1985). *Dissertation Abstracts International, 47,* 357A.

Crites, J. O. (1961). A model for the measurement of vocational maturity. *Journal of Counseling Psychology, 8,* 255–259.

Crites, J. O. (1964). Proposals for a new criterion measure and research design. In H. Borow (Ed.), *Man in a world at work* (pp. 324–340). Boston: Houghton Mifflin.

Crites, J. O. (1965). Measurement of vocational maturity in adolescence: I. Attitude Scale of the Vocational Development Inventory. *Psychological Monographs, 79*(2, Whole No. 595).

Crites, J. O. (1971). *The maturity of vocational attitudes in adolescence.* Washington, D. C.: American Personnel and Guidance Association.

Crites, J. O. (1973). *Rationales for Career Maturity Inventory Attitude Scale (Form A-1) items.* Unpublished manuscript.

Crites, J. O. (1974a). Methodological issues in the measurement of career maturity. *Measurement and Evaluation in Guidance, 6,* 200–209.

Crites, J. O. (1974b). A reappraisal of vocational appraisal. *Vocational Guidance Quarterly, 22,* 272–279.

Crites, J. O. (1976). Career counseling: A comprehensive approach. *Counseling Psychologist, 6,* 2–12.

Crites, J. O. (1978a). *Administration and Use Manual for the Career Maturity Inventory* (2nd ed.). Monterey, CA: CTB/McGraw-Hill.

Crites, J. O. (1978b). *The Career Maturity Inventory.* Monterey, CA: CTB/McGraw-Hill.

Crites, J. O. (1978c). *Theory and research handbook for the Career Maturity Inventory* (2nd ed.). Monterey, CA: CTB/McGraw-Hill.

Crites, J. O. (1981). Integrative test interpretation. In D. H. Montross & C. J. Shinkman (Eds.), *Career development in the 1980s: Theory and Practice* (pp. 161–168). Springfield, IL: Charles C. Thomas.

Crites, J. O., & Savickas, M. L. (1980). *Rationales for Career Maturity Inventory Attitude Scale (Form B-1) items.* Unpublished manuscript.

Crites, J. O., Wallbrown, F. H., & Blaha, J. (1985). The Career Maturity Inventory: Myths and realities—A rejoinder to Westbrook, Cutts, Madison, and Arcia (1980). *Journal of Vocational Behavior, 26,* 221–238.

Cronbach, L. J. (1980). Validity on parole: How can we go straight? *New Directions for Testing and Measurement, 5,* 99–108.

Flake, M. H., Roach, A. J., Jr., & Stenning, W. F. (1975). Effects of short-term counseling on career maturity of tenth-grade students. *Journal of Vocational Behavior, 6,* 73–80.

Forrest, D. J. (1971). Construction and validation of an objective measure of vocational maturity for adolescents (Doctoral dissertation, Columbia University, Teachers College, 1971). *Dissertation Abstracts International, 32,* 3088A.

Freeman, M. (1975). A comparison of the relative effectiveness of two instructional methods for developing attitudinal dimensions of career maturity in adolescents (Doctoral dissertation, Kent State University, 1974). *Dissertation Abstracts International, 35,* 6583A.

Fretz, B. R., & Leong, F. T. L. (1982). Career development status as a predictor of career intervention outcomes. *Journal of Counseling Psychology, 29,* 388–393.

Ginzberg, E., Ginsburg, S. W., Axelrad, S., & Herma, J. L. (1951). *Occupational choice: An approach to a general theory.* New York: Columbia University Press.

Gordon, C. (1970). *Looking ahead: Self-conceptions, race, and family as determinants of adolescent orientation to achievement.* Washington, D.C.: American Sociological Association.

Guardo, C. J. (1975). The helping process as developmental existentialism. *Personnel and Guidance Journal, 53,* 493–499.

Guardo, C. J. (1977). Toward growth of adolescents. *Personnel and Guidance Journal, 55,* 237–241.

Hanna, G. S., & Neely, M. A. (1978). Discriminant validity of Career Maturity Inventory Scales in grade 9 students. *Educational and Psychological Measurement, 38,* 571–574.

Hansen, J. C. (1974). [Review of J. O. Crites, *Career Maturity Inventory*]. *Journal of Counseling Psychology, 21,* 168–172.

Hansen, J. C. (1985). [Review of *Career Development Inventory*]. *Measurement and Evaluation in Guidance, 17,* 220–224.

Harmon, L. W. (1985). [Review of *Career Decision Scale*]. In J. V. Mitchell, Jr. (Ed.), *Ninth Mental Measurements Yearbook* (Vol. 1) (p. 270). Lincoln, NE: The University of Nebraska Press.

Harren, V. A. (1978). *Assessment of Career Decision Making: Counselor/instructor guide.* Unpublished manuscript, Southern Illinois University, Carbondale.

Hartman, B. W., Fuqua, D., & Jenkins, S. J. (1988). Multivariate generalizability analysis of three measures of career indecision. *Educational and Psychological Measurement, 48,* 61–68.

Hartman, B. W., Utz, P. W., & Farnum, S. O. (1979). Examining the reliability and validity of an adapted scale of educational-vocational undecidedness in a sample of graduate students. *Journal of Vocational Behavior, 15,* 224–230.

Healy, C. C. (1982). *Career development: Counseling through the life stages.* Boston: Allyn and Bacon.

Heath, D. H. (1976). Adolescent and adult predictors of vocational adaptation. *Journal of Vocational Behavior, 9,* 1–19.

Herman, D. O. (1985). [Review of *Career Decision Scale*]. In J. V. Mitchell, Jr. (Ed.), *The Ninth*

Mental Measurements Yearbook (Vol. 1) (pp. 270–271). Lincoln, NE: University of Nebraska Press.

Herr, E. L., Good, R. H., III, McCloskey, G., & Weitz, A. D. (1982). Secondary school curriculum and career behavior in young adults. *Journal of Vocational Behavior, 21,* 243–253.

Hilton, T. L. (1974). Using measures of vocational maturity in evaluation. In D. E. Super (Ed.), *Measuring vocational maturity for counseling and evaluation* (pp. 145–159). Washington, D.C.: National Vocational Guidance Association.

Holland, J. L. (1966). *The psychology of vocational choice.* Waltham, MA: Ginn & Company.

Holland, J. L., Daiger, D. C., & Power, P. G. (1980). *My vocational situation.* Palo Alto, CA: Consulting Psychologists Press.

Holland, J. L., & Nichols, R. C. (1964). The development and validation of an indecision scale: The natural history of a problem in basic research. *Journal of Counseling Psychology, 11,* 27–34.

Jackson, D. N. (1977). *Jackson Vocational Interest Survey.* Port Huron, MI: Research Psychologists Press.

Jepsen, D. A., & Prediger, D. J. (1981). Dimensions of adolescent career development: A multi-instrument analysis. *Journal of Vocational Behavior, 19,* 350–368.

Jones, L. K., & Chenery, M. F. (1980). Multiple subtypes among vocationally undecided college students: A model and assessment instrument. *Journal of Counseling Psychology, 27,* 469–477.

Jordaan, J. P. (1974). The use of vocational maturity instruments in counseling. In D. E. Super (Ed.), *Measuring vocational maturity for counseling and evaluation* (pp. 113–121). Washington, D.C.: National Vocational Guidance Association.

Katz, M. R. (1978). [Review of J. O. Crites, *Career Maturity Inventory*]. In O. K. Buros (Ed.), *The Eighth Mental Measurement Yearbook* (Vol. 2) (pp. 1562–1565). Highland Park, NJ: Gryphon Press.

Kazin, R. I. (1976, August). *Educational/vocational indecision questionnaire: Replication of a factor analysis.* Paper presented at the meeting of the American Psychological Association, Washington, D.C.

Khan, S. B., & Alvi, S. A. (1983). Educational, social, and psychological correlates of vocational maturity. *Journal of Vocational Behavior, 22,* 357–364.

LoCascio, R. (1974). The vocational maturity of diverse groups: Theory and measurement. In D. E. Super (Ed.), *Measuring vocational maturity for counseling and evaluation* (pp. 123–133). Washington, D.C.: National Vocational Guidance Association.

Lopez-Baez, S. I. (1981). A study of career consciousness: Temporal experience and career maturity (Doctoral dissertation, Kent State University, 1980). *Dissertation Abstracts International, 41,* 3427A.

Myers, R. A., Lindeman, R. H., Thompson, A. S., & Patrick, T. A. (1975). Effects of educational and career exploration system on vocational maturity. *Journal of Vocational Behavior, 6,* 245–254.

Neely, M. A., & Hanna, G. S. (1977). A study of the concurrent validity of the Career Maturity Inventory. *Educational and Psychological Measurement, 37,* 1087–1090.

Nevill, D. D., & Super, D. E. (1988). Career maturity and commitment to work in university students. *Journal of Vocational Behavior, 32,* 139–151.

Oleksy-Ojikutu, A. E. (1986). The career time-line: A vocational counseling tool. *Career Development Quarterly, 35,* 47–52.

Osipow, S. H. (1983). *Theories of career development* (3rd ed.). Englewood Cliffs, NJ: Prentice-Hall.

Osipow, S. H. (1987). *Career Decision Scale Manual.* Odessa, FL: Psychological Assessment Resources.

Osipow, S. H., Winer, J. L., Koschier, M., & Yanico, B. (1975). A modular approach to self-counseling for vocational indecision using audio cassettes. In L. Simpson (Ed.), *Audio-visual media in career development.* Bethlehem, PA: College Placement Council.

Osipow, S. H., Carney, C. G., & Barak, A. (1976). A scale of educational-vocational undecidedness: A typological approach. *Journal of Vocational Behavior, 9,* 233–243.

Osipow, S. H., Carney, C. G., Winer, J. L., Yanico, B., & Koschier, M. (1976). *The Career Decision Scale* (3rd revision). Columbus, OH: Marathon Consulting & Press and (1987) Odessa, FL: Psychological Assessment Resources, Inc.

Palmo, A. J., & Lutz, J. G. (1983). The relationship of performance on the CMI to intelligence with disadvantaged youngsters. *Measurement and Evaluation in Guidance, 16,* 139–148.

Parsons, F. (1909/1967). *Choosing a vocation.* New York: Agathon Press.

Punch, K. F., & Sheridan, B. E. (1985). Some measurement characteristics of the Career Development Inventory. *Measurement and Evaluation in Guidance, 17,* 196–202.

Richardson, M. S. (1974). Vocational maturity in counseling girls and women. In D. E. Super (Ed.), *Measuring vocational maturity for counseling and evaluation* (pp. 135–143). Washington, D.C.: National Vocational Guidance Association.

Rogers, W. B., & Westbrook, B. W. (1983). Measuring career indecision among college students: Toward a valid approach for counseling practitioners and researchers. *Measurement and Evaluation in Guidance, 16,* 78–85.

Rounds, J. B., Jr., & Tinsley, H. E. A. (1984). Diagnosis and treatment of vocational problems. In S. D. Brown & R. W. Lent (Eds.), *Handbook of counseling psychology* (pp. 137–177). New York: Wiley & Sons.

Savickas, M. L. (1984). Career maturity: The construct and its assessment. *Vocational Guidance Quarterly, 32,* 222–231.

Savickas, M. L. (1986). Career time perspective in special populations. In E. A. Whitfield, H. W. Drier, & D. Hickey (Eds.), *Improving career development through counselor education programs* (pp. 57–62). Columbus, OH: Ohio Department of Education.

Savickas, M. L., Alexander, D. E., Jonas, A. P., & Wolf, F. M. (1986). Difficulties experienced by medical students in choosing a specialty. *Journal of Medical Education, 61,* 467–469.

Savickas, M. L., Alexander, D. E., Osipow, S. H., & Wolf, F. M. (1985). Measuring specialty indecision among career decided students. *Journal of Vocational Behavior, 27,* 356–367.

Savickas, M. L., & Crites, J. O. (1981). *Career decision-making: Teaching the process.* Unpublished manuscript.

Shimizu, K., Vondracek, F. W., Schulenberg, J. E., & Hostetler, M. (1988). The factor structure of the Career Decision Scale: Similarities across selected studies. *Journal of Vocational Behavior, 32,* 213–225.

Skovholt, T. M., & Hoenninger, R. W. (1974). Guided fantasy in career counseling. *Personnel and Guidance Journal, 52,* 693–696.

Slaney, R. B. (1978). *Factor replication of the Career Decision Scale.* Unpublished data, Southern Illinois, Carbondale, IL.

Slaney, R. B. (1985). [Review of S. H. Osipow, C. G. Carney, J. L. Winer, B. Yanico, & M. Koschier, *Career Decision Scale*]. In D. J. Keyser & R. C. Sweetland (Eds.), *Test critiques* (Vol. 2) (pp. 138–143). Kansas City, MO: Test Corporation of America.

Slaney, R. B., Palko-Nonemaker, D., & Alexander, R. (1981). An investigation of two measures of career indecision. *Journal of Vocational Behavior, 18,* 92–103.

Slaney, R. B., Stafford, M. J., & Russell, J. E. A. (1981). Career indecision in adult women: A comparative and descriptive study. *Journal of Vocational Behavior, 19,* 335–345.

Sorenson, G. (1974). [Review of J. O. Crites, *Career Maturity Inventory*]. *Measurement and Evaluation in Guidance, 7,* 54–57.

Stowe, R. W. (1985). Convergent and discriminant validity of Crites's Career Maturity Inventory Attitude Scale, Counseling Form B-1. *Educational and Psychological Measurement, 45,* 763–770.

Strong, E. K. (1943). *Vocational interests of men and women.* Stanford: Stanford University Press.

Strong, S. R. (1968). Counseling: An interpersonal influence process. *Journal of Counseling Psychology, 15,* 215–224.

Super, D. E. (1955). The dimensions and measurement of vocational maturity. *Teachers College Record, 57,* 151–163.

Super, D. E. (1969). Vocational development theory in 1988: How will it come about? *Counseling Psychologist, 1,* 9–14.

Super, D. E. (Ed.). (1974). *Measuring vocational maturity for counseling and evaluation.* Washington, D.C.: National Vocational Guidance Association.

Super, D. E. (1983). Assessment in career guidance: Toward truly developmental counseling. *Personnel and Guidance Journal, 61,* 555–562.

Super, D. E., & Forrest, D. J. (1972). *Career Development Inventory, Form I: Preliminary manual.* (Mimeo). New York: Columbia University, Teachers College.

Super, D. E., & Nevill, D. D. (1984). Work role salience as a determinant of career maturity in high school students. *Journal of Vocational Behavior, 25,* 30–44.

Super, D. E., & Overstreet, P. L. (1960). *The vocational maturity of ninth-grade boys.* New York: Teachers College Press.

Super, D. E., & Thompson, A. S. (1979). A six-scale, two-factor measure of adolescent career or vocational maturity. *Vocational Guidance Quarterly, 28,* 6–15.

Super, D. E., Thompson, A. S., Lindeman, R. H., Jordaan, J. P., & Myers, R. A. (1981). *The Career Development Inventory.* Palo Alto, CA: Consulting Psychologists Press.

Thompson, A. S., & Lindeman, R. H. (1981). *Career Development Inventory: User's manual.* Palo Alto, CA: Consulting Psychologists Press.

Thompson, A. S., & Lindeman, R. H. (1982). *Career Development Inventory college and university form supplement to user's manual.* Palo Alto, CA: Consulting Psychologist Press.

Thompson, A. S., & Lindeman, R. H. (1984). *Career Development Inventory: Technical manual.* Palo Alto, CA: Consulting Psychologists Press.

Tinsley, H. E. A., & Tinsley, D. J. (1987). Use of factor analysis in counseling psychology research. *Journal of Counseling Psychology, 34,* 414–424.

Van Riper, B. W. (1974). From a clinical to a counseling process: Reversing the test appraisal process. *Measurement and Evaluation in Guidance, 7,* 24–30.

Vondracek, F. W., & Schulenberg, J. E. (1986). Career development in adolescence: Some conceptual and intervention issues. *Vocational Guidance Quarterly, 34,* 247–254.

Westbrook, B. W. (1976). The relationship between vocational maturity and appropriateness of vocational choices of ninth-grade pupils. *Measurement and Evaluation in Guidance, 9,* 75–80.

Westbrook, B. W. (1982). Construct validation of career maturity measures. In J. D. Krumboltz & D. A. Hamel (Eds.), *Assessing career development* (pp. 66–112). Palo Alto, CA: Mayfield Publishing.

Westbrook, B. W., & Mastie, M. M. (1973). Three measures of vocational maturity: A beginning to know about. *Measurement and Evaluation in Guidance, 6,* 8–16.

Wigington, J. H. (1982). Career maturity aspects of the Kuder Occupational Interest Survey. *Journal of Vocational Behavior, 20,* 175–179.

Williams-Phillips, L. J. (1983). Five career decidedness scales: Reliability, validity, and factors. Unpublished masters thesis, North Carolina State University, Raleigh, NC.

Williamson, E. G., & Darley, J. G. (1937). *Student personnel work: An outline of clinical procedures.* NY: McGraw-Hill.

Woody, R. H. (1968). Vocational counseling with behavioral techniques. *Vocational Guidance Quarterly, 17,* 97–103.

Young, R. A. (1979). The effects of value confrontation and reinforcement counseling on the career planning attitudes and behaviors of adolescent males. *Journal of Vocational Behavior, 15,* 1–11.

Zytowski, D. G. (1978). [Review of J. O. Crites, *Career Maturity Inventory*]. In O. K. Buros (Ed.), *The eighth mental measurement yearbook* (Vol. 2) (pp. 1565–1567). Highland Park, NJ: Gryphon Press.

13 Contemporary Issues In Testing Use

Nancy E. Betz
Ohio State University

The need for a consideration of contemporary issues in the use of tests in counseling is based on the fact that although tests have tremendous potential utility, they can also be misused. The misuse of tests may stem from characteristics of the test and/or the test user, and it is ultimately the responsibility of the test user to ensure that the test is of high quality and appropriate for use in the population intended. Because of the possibility of misuse of tests and test scores, psychologists and test specialists formulated ethical and professional standards designed to ensure that tests are used appropriately, effectively, and fairly.

First, many of the Ethical Principles of the American Psychological Association (APA, 1981) pertain to the use of psychological tests and assessments. Second, although a general set of ethical statements concerning test use is available, the American Psychological Association (APA), American Educational Research Association (AERA), and National Council on Measurement in Education (NCME) have formulated a much more specific set of professional standards by which the *quality* of psychological tests and assessments may be evaluated and by which the *effectiveness* and *fairness* of test use in specific situations may be judged.

In the first part of this chapter, ethical and professional considerations in the selection and use of psychological tests in counseling are described. The discussion contains sections on: (a) quality of tests and test materials; (b) test user competence; (c) protecting the rights of test takers; and (d) sources of information about tests.

Second, even though a test may be of generally high quality, there may be unique issues involved in using it with some types of clients. In particular, issues in the use of tests with racial/ethnic minorities, women, and cross-culturally are the subject of the second portion of this chapter.

ETHICAL AND PROFESSIONAL STANDARDS IN USING TESTS

Quality of Tests and Test Materials

The first and most fundamental consideration in using tests and assessments is that the tests be of high technical quality and should be accompanied by enough information for a test user to effectively evaluate, administer, use, and interpret the test. Concern about the quality of tests and accompanying test materials dates back to 1895, when the first APA committee on mental measurements was formed. In 1938, the first edition of Buros' *Mental Measurements Yearbook* appeared, providing extensive information about and reviews of the tests available at the time. In 1954, APA published its first set of *Technical Recommendations for Psychological Tests and Diagnostic Techniques,* providing initial guidelines concerning the evaluation of tests (e.g., validity, reliability, use of scales and norms) and stressing the importance of an informative manual accompanying a test. At about that same time, (1955), the Technical Recommendations for Achievement Tests were published by the AERA and the NCME. By 1966, APA, AERA, and NCME were cooperating—the result was the 1966 *Standards for Educational and Psychological Measurement.* Revisions of these standards were published in 1974 and 1985. The 1974 revision was expanded to include a response to the 1970 EEOC Guidelines and other concerns of test misuse and bias and race and sex discrimination. The most recent revision devotes complete chapters to clinical testing, testing in the schools, test use in counseling, employment testing, professional and occupational licensure and certification, program evaluation, and testing people who have handicapping conditions or who are linguistic minorities. These specialty uses will be discussed below as appropriate, but the reader is referred to the 1985 *Standards for Educational and Psychological Testing* for full details.

A first major purpose of the test standards was to provide guidelines for the *quality* of tests and test materials. Standards for test quality must be observed by test developers in constructing the test, by test publishers before distributing the test, and by test users in evaluating and selecting tests. There are a number of dimensions along which test quality may be evaluated. Following the outline used in the current revision of the test standards (AERA, APA, NCME, 1985), the following dimensions of quality may be addressed: (a) Reliability and Errors of Measurement; (b) Validity; (c) Test Development and Revision; (d) Scaling, Norming; Score Comparability, and Equating; and (e) Test Publication, Technical Manuals, and Users' Guides.

In stating the criteria by which to evaluate test quality, the authors of the standards have classified them as either *primary standards* or *secondary standards*. Primary standards are those that should be met by *all* published or marketed tests; the only tests exempt from these standards would be teacher-made tests or tests used only in research. Secondary standards are those which are desirable in some testing situations but may not be feasible to ask with respect to other testing situations.

In general, high quality tests are those for which evidence of both reliability and validity is available. Although methods of test construction and the accumulation of evidence for reliability and validity are beyond the scope of this chapter, a brief summary of the types of evidence needed is provided below. For more detailed information, see sources such as Walsh and Betz (1990) *Tests and Assessment* and Dawis' (1987) article on scale construction in the *Journal of Counseling Psychology*.

Reliability, the extent to which a test measures something in a consistent, stable manner is assessed through such methods as internal consistency reliability, alternate or parallel forms, and test-retest reliability, also known as "stability." With respect to reliability, several key points should be noted. First, there is no *single* reliability coefficient describing a test or scale; the values of obtained coefficients vary somewhat across studies using the *same* population, and with different research methodologies. A test is never said to "be reliable"—rather, we look for an accumulation of evidence supporting test reliability.

Tests to be used for applied purposes, that is, in counseling, selection, or placement, should consistently yield internal consistency reliability coefficients above .80 and, ideally, above .90. Tests for which internal consistency reliability coefficients are in the range of .70 to .80 may be used in research, but those with coefficients below .70 should be further refined before they are used in research, not to mention practice. Test-retest reliability, or stability, coefficients may be lower and still acceptable, particularly as the interval between testings lengthens. Although some researchers may contest these guidelines, the undeniable fact is that scales having reliability coefficients below about .70 are not measuring anything in a consistent manner—the information obtained from some of the items is not consistent with that yielded by other items purportedly measuring the same thing, and the information obtained on one testing is not necessarily the same information that will be yielded by testing one hour or one day later.

The test standards also emphasize that, if possible, the establishment of the reliability of the test should include all of the methods of studying reliability, that is, alternate forms, internal consistency, and test-retest stability. All of these methods of estimating reliability are important to supporting the test's reliability for applied purposes. In addition to evidence for reliability, information regarding the standard error of measurement should be reported in enough scope and detail to enable the test user to judge whether scores are sufficiently dependable for the intended uses of the test.

Along with evidence for its reliability, a test should be shown to possess validity for the intended uses. Validity refers to the extent to which the test actually measures what we intend it to measure. If scores from a test designed to measure career decision-making skills or career maturity actually correlate more highly with verbal ability or socioeconomic status than they do with other career-related variables, we would question the nature of the construct measured by our test. There are several different kinds of evidence pertinent to the establishment of a test's validity—the three basic types of validity evidence are construct validity, content validity, and criterion-related validity.

Construct validity, the most general validity concept, refers to a variety of evidence addressing the question, "Does the test measure the underlying construct or concept we intend it to measure?" Content validity refers to how well the particular sampling of items constituting the test represents the nature and scope of the domain of interest. Evidence for content validity includes expert judgements regarding the rational or logical relationship of an item to the content domain of interest. For example, the item "I enjoy painting flowers" has a clear logical relationship to the construct "Artistic Interests" but would have questionable relationship to, and thus content validity for, the construct "Investigative Interests."

Finally, criterion-related validity is the degree to which test scores are related as predicted to criterion indices. The correlation between scholastic aptitude test scores and performance in college is an example of *predictive* validity evidence (because the predictor data are collected prior to the collection of the criterion data), whereas the relationship between MMPI scores and current DSM-III-R diagnosis would be concurrent validity evidence (because predictor and criterion data are collected concurrently). The test standards emphasize that all three components of validity are important and that, ideally, evidence for a test's validity should include evidence from all three types of validity.

The third group of standards pertaining to test development requires that test developers use both expertise and care in their methods of test construction and that they revise their tests periodically to ensure that test content continues to be relevant and appropriate for the purposes for which the test is used. In addition, these standards specify that the test developers and publishers are responsible for the provision of a test manual describing the methods of construction and revision, data regarding reliability and validity, and normative and other information needed for effective and accurate test interpretation.

The fourth dimension of test quality pertains to the availability of scales, norms, and other means of interpreting test scores. Methods of scoring the test should be carefully described, and normative, criterion-referenced, or other methods of comparative interpretation of test scores should be provided. In addition, as new forms of a test are developed, information concerning methods of comparing or equating scores across forms may be necessary. The normative data provided should be clearly described in terms of the population from which they come and should be the same groups of people with whom the test is designed to be used.

Finally, standards regarding test publication, technical materials, and user guides emphasize the importance of published or at least widely available *information* about a test. Further, that information should provide a clear description of the extent to which and in what manner the test has met the other test standards; the information should be sufficient to allow the potential user to evaluate the quality and potential utility of the test. This complete information is best provided in a manual for the test; the manual should be revised as new data regarding the test's reliability, validity, norms, and use become available. Not only should test information be adequate to evaluate the test's quality, but it should provide detailed instructions for the administration and scoring of the test.

Ideally, these dimensions of test quality should be addressed *before* the test is distributed for use. More realistically, however, test manuals are expected to provide information by which the user can evaluate the extent to which the standards *have* been met, should mention areas in which technical support is lacking, and should describe the current research efforts which will increase the base of technical support for the quality of the instrument. Test manuals should also make it clear that extra caution in test use and interpretation is necessary in cases where there is as yet insufficient evidence supporting the test's quality. Also, tests not yet meeting quality standards should probably be reserved for needs for which there are no better alternative tests or assessment devices.

Finally, it should be emphasized that because test use occurs with a specific individual in a specific setting for a particular reason, the *ultimate* basis for judging the utility of a test is the good judgment, sound knowledge, and professional integrity of the counselor. Thus, the professional competence and integrity of the test *user* are the subject of the next section.

Test User Competence

It is of course essential that tests be of high quality, but it is also essential that test *users* be qualified to use them. A major principle of the APA ethical code is that psychological knowledge and techniques, including tests, are used only by those *qualified* to use them and, conversely, that individuals practice only within the bounds of their own knowledge and competence. As related specifically to the use of tests, the principle states that psychologists who use test results have an understanding of "psychological or educational measurement, validation problems, and test research" (APA, 1981, p. 636).

Qualifications for test use vary according to the types of tests in question but, in general, are stricter with tests having greater potential for harm and misinterpretation. One of the earliest systems by which user qualifications were specified, provided by the first APA test standards (APA, 1954, pp. 146–148), classified tests according to three levels of complexity. *Level A* tests were those which can be administered, scored, and interpreted by responsible nonpsychologists who have carefully read the test manual and are familiar with the overall purposes of testing. Educational achievement tests would fall into this category.

Level B tests require technical knowledge of test construction and use and appropriate advanced coursework in psychology and related courses, for example, statistics, individual differences, and counseling. Vocational interest inventories, group intelligence and special aptitude tests, and some personality inventories are generally considered Level B tests. For example, Consulting Psychologists' Press limits purchase of such tests as the Strong-Campbell Interest Inventory, State-Trait Anxiety Inventory, Myers-Briggs Type Indicator, and Bem Sex Role Inventory to individuals who have completed university courses in tests and measurements or equivalent training. Similar requirements for access to such tests as the Jackson Vocational Interest Inventory, Personality Research Form, and Jackson Personality Inventory are stated by their publisher, Research Psychologists Press.

Finally, Level C tests require an advanced degree in psychology or licensure as a psychologist *and* advanced training/supervised experience in the particular test. Level C tests generally include individually-administered intelligence tests and personality tests, for example, the Stanford-Binet, Wechsler Adult Intelligence Scale-Revised (WAIS-R), and Minnesota Multiphasic Personality Inventory (MMPI). Graduate students may be qualified to purchase and use Level B or Level C tests *if* they are being supervised in that work by someone who possesses the appropriate user qualifications.

Although the A, B, C system has some face validity, it has never been widely and consistently adopted nor, more importantly, have specific guidelines for defining test user qualifications been addressed in either the APA Ethical Principles or Test Standards.

In a recent attempt to discern if and how test publishers were restricting the sale of tests, the Test User Qualifications Working Group (TUQWOG) of the Scientific Affairs Office of the APA conducted a study of test publishers (see Eyde, 1986; Moreland, 1986; Robertson, 1986). All of the 13 major test publishers placed some restriction on the sale of tests to individuals based on their professional qualifications, but there was wide variability in the nature and extent of the criteria used to screen potential test buyers. In response to this lack of uniformity, Eyde (1986) proposed a method for the development of an improved and voluntary system based on test ethics. First, a classification system for tests was proposed; the categories include Personality and Interest Tests, Tests of Separate Abilities: Occupational, Educational and Achievement Tests, Neuropsychological Tests, Speech, Language, and Hearing Tests, Tests of General Intellectual Level, and Development Scales. The TUQWOG is now working on defining essential qualifications needed by purchasers of various types of tests. The results of their work should be available soon.

In addition to user competence, there are several major principles of responsible, ethical test use. In the 1985 test standards, several of these principles are outlined. They include the following primary standards:

1. Test users should evaluate the available written information on the reliability and validity of the test for the uses intended;
2. When a test user makes a change in a test (e.g., in format, mode of administration, etc.), he/she should revalidate the test for the changed conditions;
3. When a test is to be used for a purpose for which it has not been previously validated, the user is responsible for providing evidence for validity;
4. Test users should accurately portray the relevance of a test to the assessment and decision-making process and should not use test scores to justify a decision that has been largely made on some other basis;
5. Test users should be alert to and avoid possible unintended consequences of test use, for example, the tendency of lay people to attribute surplus meaning or absolute "truth" to test scores;
6. Test users *should not* attempt to evaluate test takers whose special characteristics, for example, ages, handicapping conditions, linguistic, generational, or cultural backgrounds, are outside their range of academic training or supervised experience. If faced with such a request, the test user should seek consultation.
7. A test taker's score should not be accepted as a reflection of a lack of some type of ability without consideration of alternative explanations for the person's inability to perform well on that test.

In summary, a test user *must* be aware of possible misuses of tests and test scores, must be informed about both the psychometric quality and practical utility of a test, and must use tests with care, good judgment, and concern for the people being tested.

Protecting the Rights of Test Takers

Principle #5 of the APA ethical code and Chapter 16 of the Test Standards describe psychologists' obligations in maintaining the confidentiality of information obtained from individuals, through testing or any other formal or informal means of gathering information. The maintenance of confidentiality means protecting the individual's right to privacy and involves the principles of informed consent, constraints on the provision of individual information to other parties, and care in the storage and disposal of information.

The first responsibility of the test user is to minimize, as far as possible, the extent to which testing may invade a person's right to privacy. The extent to which the use of tests constitutes an invasion of individual privacy is a complex issue with a number of considerations involved. It should be noted that test data are no more invasive of privacy than are other kinds of information obtained about people. With any kind of personal information, *including* test data, the use of the data should be characterized as far as possible by the principles of *relevance* and *informed consent* (Anastasi, 1982).

The concept of "relevance" means that test scores are collected and used only if they are relevant to some valid set of purposes—collecting a set of test scores for no other purpose than "curiosity" would constitute an unnecessary invasion of an individual's privacy. The principle of informed consent means that, as far as possible, the individual is informed concerning both the *nature* of the information collected and the purposes for which the information will be used. This principle does not imply that test takers (or their parents) necessarily have a right to information that would invalidate the use of the test or which is beyond the sophistication of the consumer, for example, test items or methods of scoring, but that the test taker is informed as fully as possible concerning the nature and uses of the test scores.

Although the principle of informed consent is intended to provide to the test taker at least some opportunity for *choice* in the matter of how much information to reveal and in the uses to which that information will be put, the extent to which the individual actually *does* have a choice varies across different situations. For a client in counseling, revealing personal information is important to the process of getting help; unwillingness to be open with the counselor or therapist may make treatment very difficult and client improvement less likely. As an extreme example, a client wishing help with vocational decision-making who refused to talk about his/her vocational interests or take a vocational interest inventory would be very difficult for a counselor to help.

In essence, the issue of invasion of privacy means finding a compromise between the *need* for meaningful, relevant information to guide problem solving in counseling situations and the individual's *right* to personal privacy and freedom of choice. This compromise is best achieved when respect for the individual is combined with sound professional judgment concerning the kinds of information needed for the purposes at hand.

Confidentiality issues pertain to decisions about access to test results on the part of those other than the original test user. For example, a psychologist may have given his/her client an MMPI, scores from which are later requested by another psychologist. Ethical and test standards mandate that, in general, the confidentiality of test results is to be protected by the *original test user* unless the test taker gives his/her consent for test results to be provided to someone else.

The original informed consent should have covered all intended test uses and *additional consent* is necessary for any use beyond those originally agreed to. In the example given, the client would need to release his/her MMPI scores to the second psychologist.

A final responsibility of test users involves the secure storage of test results and, when test results are too old to be useful, for the permanent disposal of test data. Keeping test results in places where they are accessible to anyone but the original test user is irresponsible, as is disposing of test scores in such a way that they could be easily retrieved by unauthorized individuals. And the test user is responsible for judgments concerning the continued utility of test results collected previously. According to the test standards, test scores should be kept in a person's file only as long as they serve a useful purpose.

Sources of Information by Which to Evaluate Tests

Given the large amount of information needed by an informed, responsible user of psychological test data, it is fortunate that many sources of information are available.

The most important source of information about a test is the *test manual.* Test manuals may be ordered from the test publisher, and information about the test publisher is available in Buros' *Mental Measurements Yearbook Series* (the Ninth Edition, which appeared in 1985, is the most recent) or *Tests in Print* (1961, 1974). The catalogs distributed by test publishers provide information about ordering test booklets, answer sheets, scoring keys, and other interpretive aids, as well as the manual itself. Many test publishers now make available several manuals, for example, a technical manual, a manual for administration and scoring, and an interpretive manual. A particularly noteworthy example of this is the comprehensive *Manual for the SVIB-SCII* (Hansen & Campbell, 1985) and the excellent *User's Guide* for the SVIB-SCII (Hansen, 1984b).

Beyond the test manual(s), test users should review the test reviews, as published periodically in the Mental Measurements Yearbook (MMY). Now in its ninth edition (Mitchell, 1985) the yearbook series provides descriptions of all published tests and reviews a number of tests in each edition. Because the MMY does not review every test in every edition, a potential user may need to go back to the eighth or even the seventh yearbook if, for example, the test in question is not reviewed in the most recent yearbook.

Other sources of information about tests are books on testing and test use. Books like Watkins and Campbell's *Testing in Counseling Practice,* in which this chapter appears, and Walsh and Betz' *Tests and Assessment* are particularly useful since they provide interpretive information such as examples of test profiles and case studies. Major tests such as the MMPI have entire books written about them. An important new series entitled Advances in Vocational Psychology (edited by Walsh and Osipow and published by Lawrence Erlbaum Associates) has begun with two very helpful volumes: *Volume I: The assessment of interests* (Walsh & Osipow, 1986) and Volume II: *The assessment of career-decision making* (Walsh & Osipow, 1988). Finally, many journals contain test reviews and articles about tests. Counselors using tests should closely monitor the articles in *Measurement and Evaluation in Counseling and Development* and *Educational and Psychological Measurement,* as well as those in such journals as the *Journal of Counseling Psychology, Journal of Vocational Behavior, Career Development Quarterly,* and the *Journal of Counseling and Development.*

Summary

The ethical and professional standards for tests and test use are designed to ensure that tests and assessment devices themselves are of high technical, informative, and interpretive quality, and that they are used by qualified, knowledgeable, ethical people who care deeply about the rights and welfare of the individuals they serve. High quality, effective, and fair test use is dependent on the quality of *both* the tests and the users. Even the highest quality test can be misused by an unqualified or careless person, and the most highly skilled test user in the world is ineffective without carefully developed, well-standardized, reliable and valid tests. As test users, therefore, we are responsible for ensuring both our own competence and the quality of the tools we use. Ethical test use is knowledgeable, informed, careful, and critical test use.

USING TESTS WITH SPECIAL GROUPS

General Issues in Using Tests with Special Groups

A major recent focus within the counseling field has been whether or not traditional counseling methods are useful with women, minorities, and other special groups of individuals. A parallel and a closely related concern within the more general field of mental measurement and individual differences has been fairness in testing. Although the issues regarding test use differ depending on the type of test involved (e.g., intelligence and aptitude tests, vocational interest inventories, personality inventories) and on the "special group" with which the test is to be used (e.g., women, racial and/or ethnic minorities, the disabled, etc.), there are some common bases for the concerns about special groups.

At the most fundamental level is the fact that tests are, at least to some extent, culture-bound. It is difficult, if not impossible, to construct a test independently of a cultural context. For example, a test of verbal aptitude is constructed in a given language and is based on what may well be culture-specific item content. Even though test constructors may not purposely favor a given culture, it's difficult to avoid this. Most intelligence and aptitude tests in use were constructed in the context of a White, middle-class value system. Thus, non-White or lower-class examinees would possibly be less familiar with the test content than would examinees representing the white middle class. A picture of a deciduous tree on a picture vocabulary test of intelligence for children would be an unfair item for a Navaho child raised in the Arizona desert. An item representing a farm animal might be unfamiliar to a Black child raised in a ghetto.

The issue of test item familiarity affects interest measurement as well as ability measurement. For example, basic dimensions of vocational interest have been measured using content differentially characteristic of the experiential backgrounds of males versus females. To ask a female whether she's interested in auto mechanics when she's never had the chance to experience activities related to it is an example of how item content can be sex-biased. The use of sexist occupational titles (e.g., policeman, cleaning woman) or, as was the case in one inventory for children, pictures of Whites in higher status and Blacks in lower status occupations, provide further examples of content bias.

Finally, when measuring dimensions of personality, cross-cultural differences in the perceived appropriateness of different behaviors may affect measurement. For example, the sometimes conflicting values of cooperation/community versus competition/individuality are differentially valued in different cultures. In some cultures, for example the Japanese, assertiveness vìs a vìs one's elders may be viewed as a sign of disrespect and, therefore, as highly inappropriate. In some cultures men are free to publicly express affection to other men, whereas in other cultures such displays would be frowned upon. Different views of social appropriateness cannot help but influence self-reports of behavior and personality.

In addition to the cultural relativity of test item content is the nature of the standardization or norm groups. A basic principle of test interpretation is that test scores should be interpreted with reference to *appropriate* norm groups, that is, norm groups consisting of individuals comparable to the individual being tested. If norm groups are predominantly or totally White, the scores of a Black or Hispanic individual are of reduced interpretability. Similarly, using a test cross-culturally is unwise until both necessary translations of the test and collection of norms in the new population have been accomplished.

Thus, responsible test constructors and users no longer automatically assume the usefulness of a test for any examinee. Thanks to this widespread criticism of possible biases in test content and of the predominance of Whites or, in some cases, White males only, in norm groups, revisions in tests and collection of new, more diverse normative samples have occurred. However, differences in the *outcomes* of testing still occur. That is, even after revisions to both test content and normative procedures have been undertaken, group differences, such as race differences in intelligence and some abilities, continue to occur. What to do about differences in test *outcomes* is a social policy issue rather than a measurement issue, as will be further discussed in the next section.

ISSUES IN USING TESTS WITH RACIAL/ETHNIC MINORITIES

Introduction

The fundamental issue in using tests with racial/ethnic minority groups is interpretation and use of ability and intelligence test scores that are, among Blacks and other U.S. minorities, consistently lower on the average than are the average scores of White individuals. Bringing this issue to widespread public and professional attention was Arthur Jensen, who in 1969 published an article entitled "How much can we boost IQ and scholastic achievement?" in the *Harvard Educational Review*. In this article, Jensen asserted that genetic factors were the cause of observed differences between Blacks and Whites in performance on standardized intelligence tests. Research data had fairly consistently indicated that on standardized tests of intelligence, the performance of Whites as a group generally exceeded the performance of Blacks as a group. To illustrate, the mean IQ of Whites on a given intelligence test might be 105, in contrast to a mean IQ of 95 for a group of Blacks. Jensen took this *observed* difference in intelligence test performance and attributed that difference primarily to heredity rather than environment. In other words, it would be possible to interpret this score difference as the result of some inherent differences between Blacks and Whites, and/or it would be possible to attribute the difference to the fact that in U.S. culture, Blacks are disadvantaged relative to Whites in terms of their socioeconomic status, their educational and occupational opportunities, and so on. So although the *existence* of the test score difference was not necessarily being debated, the *reasons* for this difference were an important focus of controversy.

Jensen's article led to widespread public outrage and to numerous alternative explanations. First of all, there is no question that Blacks and Whites in this country grow up in drastically different environments—Black people have been of generally lower socioeconomic status than have White people and have in general been culturally disadvantaged. Any group that suffers cultural disadvantage may be expected to perform less well on tests that are constructed within and reflect the majority culture or the middle class culture. Thus, any discussion of race differences in IQ test performance must account for the fact that Blacks and Whites develop in drastically different socioeconomic, cultural, and educational environments. Second, it is always essential to recall the point that even if we observe group differences in intelligence, we cannot make any statements about the performance of a given individual.

Probably the most frequently offered argument, and that which has been the subject of most *current* controversy, is that intelligence and aptitude tests are by their nature and their content biased against Blacks and other individuals not representative of the "majority" culture. This argument suggests that because Blacks and others represent a cultural as well as economic minority, tests constructed by and for the cultural majority (i.e., the White middle-class) are simply inappropriate and unfair.

This section begins with a brief review of the issue of potential racial bias in testing and goes on to discuss the problems of using tests with minority groups for purposes of employment selection and scholastic aptitude testing. Although counselors may not themselves use tests for these purposes, they will deal with individuals for whom such scores may be available and part of the individual decision making process. Further, it is essential that *all* psychologists and all counselors using tests be knowledgeable about these issues—their implications for organizations and individuals, and for society, are staggering.

Cultural Bias in Testing

As has been mentioned, one major possible explanation for the generally poorer performance of blacks and other minority groups on standardized aptitude and intelligence tests is that tests discriminate against minority groups through cultural bias. This argument is based on the charge of cultural bias in both the nature and content of intelligence and aptitude tests. It is assumed that tests developed by and for the White middle-class stress *those* values and areas of knowledge, rather than the values and areas of knowledge within the black or other minority cultures. Cultural bias has been postulated to be manifested in tests themselves in one of three ways: *content* bias, bias in *internal structure,* and *selection* bias.

Content bias can occur if a test contains content more familiar to White, middle-class examinees than to members of other racial or socioeconomic groups. Specifically, content bias may involve test questions that would be more familiar to one cultural group than another. As was mentioned in the introduction to this section, questions about rural life and farm animals would be less familiar to a ghetto child than would questions about urban life, for example, traffic. Another type of content bias is found in the item format and item presentation. For example, pictorial material that shows only White males and never females nor Blacks is biased, as would be test materials and pronouns always using "he."

Test constructors have addressed the problem of content bias by obtaining expert judgments of the degree to which item content is culturally-loaded and soliciting item contributions from test professionals representing other cultural groups. The construction of most scholastic aptitude and achievement tests is now done by panels of experts which include a representative balance of men and women, whites, blacks, hispanics, and so forth, and members of higher versus lower socioeconomic status groups. These panel members both contribute items and evaluate the item pool with the objective of minimizing gender, race, cultural, and class bias. Tests not originally constructed in this manner should be revised to remove content bias as far as possible. Test users should include in their evaluations of tests the extent to which issues of gender and cultural diversity were incorporated into test development.

A second type of test bias postulated is that in the internal structure of the test. If the internal or factor structure of a test and/or the behavior of items in relationship to each other (i.e., internal consistency) are found to differ across cultural groups, then the test is measuring different things across groups. In other words, factor structure and item interrelationships contribute to the explication of the construct being measured by the test, and tests should not be used for the same purposes in different groups unless they are measuring the same construct as well.

Accordingly, test developers and publishers have done research investigating and comparing factor structure and item characteristics across groups. In general, available studies of factor structure (e.g., Humphreys & Taber, 1973; Jensen, 1980) have reported similarity across groups in factor structure and patterns. Studies of such characteristics of individual test items as item difficulty and item total score correlations have generally shown at least some group differences, but consistent patterns of difference suggesting test revisions which could reduce race differences have not yet been found (see Cole, 1981). More research comparing tests' internal structural characteristics across groups is needed.

The final type of test bias postulated is a large category of bias that can be summarized as *selection* bias. Selection bias would be a bias caused if a test has different predictive validity across groups. A scholastic aptitude test that predicts the performance of White middle-class students should not automatically be assumed to predict the performance of Blacks or lower-class individuals. It is erroneous to assume that what we know about predictive validity in one group also characterizes other groups, and if a test has not been shown to predict well for Blacks or members of other groups then it shouldn't be used for that purpose in those groups. Selection bias is examined through the comparison of regression equations and regression lines obtained within different groups. If the regression lines differ significantly across groups, then some type of selection bias is occurring.

Studies of selection bias suggest that the majority of tests predict about as well for minority group members as they do for majority group members. If anything, use of the overall regression lines leads to overprediction rather than underprediction of the criterion performance of minority group members (Breland, 1979; Cole, 1981; Hunter, Schmidt, & Hunter, 1979). In general, findings that the use of overall-group regression lines benefits Blacks are also true for lower SES groups and, in general, for groups obtaining lower *mean* test scores. (See Linn, 1982, for a review of pertinent research). Thus, there is little, if any, evidence that psychological tests discriminate against Blacks in a predictive sense and, in fact, the use of total group regression lines is likely in some cases to benefit the Black applicant.

Overall, then, charges of test bias have been met by many constructive changes in methods of test construction designed to remove content bias as far as possible. Research investigating bias in internal structure and selection bias has not led to much evidence for either their existence or their effects.

Unfortunately, addressing and hopefully correcting at least some of the biases in *tests* have not, nor will they ever, ameliorate the problem of the negative impact that testing has on Blacks and members of other minority groups. In other words, a test can be valid and relatively free of bias yet still produce scores having negative results for blacks, scores which lead, for example, to the rejection of proportionately more Black than white applicants for a college or a job. The quality of a test and the *uses* of test scores are separate issues—the quality issue, the subject of the previous section, appears to have been largely resolved through test revisions, but the issues surrounding the *uses* of tests are social policy issues which cannot be addressed psychometrically. (Gottfredson's, 1986a discussion of these issues provides an excellent additional source of information).

Social Policy Issues

Tests in Employment Selection. The controversy surrounding the use of tests in employment selection may be summarized as the problem of *adverse impact.* Adverse impact means that even when standardized aptitude tests are not used with *intent* to discriminate against minorities, their use has led to the hiring of proportionately *fewer* minorities. Thus, whether or not discrimination was intended, the *impact* of using standardized tests in employment selection has been *negative* or *adverse* in terms of the representation of minorities.

Race and sex discrimination in employment selection, regardless of *how* it occurs (e.g., from outright refusal to consider black or female applicants to selection procedures, which make it difficult or impossible for blacks or women to qualify and compete) has been an important, indeed crucial, civil rights issue which was first addressed by federal legislation beginning in 1964. The Equal Employment Opportunity Act, based on Title VII of the 1964 Civil Rights Act, prohibited discrimination on the basis of race, color, religion, sex, or national origin in selection procedures leading to employment decisions within employers (both private or governmental), labor organizations, employment agencies, and licensing and certification boards. The Equal Employment Opportunity Commission (EEOC) was formed to implement and enforce the act, and in 1970 the EEOC developed a set of guidelines for that purpose.

These guidelines developed by the EEOC specified, among other things, that properly validated and standardized employment selection procedures can *contribute* to rather than detract from fair personnel practices because they are objective and "blind" to someone's race, gender, national origin, and so forth. The guidelines also stated, however, that tests that adversely affect the hiring, promotion, and so forth, of protected groups such as racial minorities and women must be shown to possess validity for the selection *and* the employer must demonstrate that alternative selection procedures *not* having adverse impact are not available. In 1978 a revised and simplified set of guidelines, the "Uniform Guidelines on Employee Selection Procedures," was issued by the EEOC.

The major concept currently underlying the justification for using tests or other selection methods that have adverse impact is that of *job-relatedness,* that is, the tests or selection procedures used must be convincingly demonstrated to be related to job performance. If a test or selection requirement has little or nothing to do with job performance then its use is illegal and unfair. The concept of job-relatedness is closely related to that of content validity.

A classic legal case related to job-relatedness was that of *Griggs v. Duke Power Company,* in which the Supreme Court ruled that the use of a general intelligence test, a mechanical aptitude test, and the requirement of possession of a high school diploma were illegal in the selection of common laborers, as they resulted in the selection of far fewer Blacks than Whites and *were not job-related.*

Although paper-and-pencil aptitude and intelligence tests most often result in adverse impact on Blacks, performance tests, such as those required for selection into the police and fire services, more often affect female candidates adversely and, again, job-relatedness must be demonstrated. For example, if a height of 5′8″ were to be required for selection as a police officer (a selection criterion which would have adverse impact for women versus men as a group), that requirement must be shown to be necessary for adequate job performance. As an example of the possible invalidity of height requirements, a discriminatory height requirement for selection as a police officer in New York was stated to be necessary so that officers could stand and fire guns over the top of their police cars. The court ruled that this requirement was illegal because the "performance" for which height was supposedly needed (i.e., firing over the top of the car) was actually *contrary* to established police procedure in the state!

Although the concept of job-relatedness seems like a reasonable basis on which to justify versus challenge the use of tests or other selection devices, the continuing problem in court cases centers around the definition of job-relatedness (Bersoff, 1981). Job-relatedness can be interpreted to mean content similarity, that is, the similarity of the test's content to the job itself. As an example, a test of typing speed and accuracy has obvious relatedness to, or content validity for, the job of typist or secretary. In contrast, a test of intelligence would be less obviously related to the job duties so its use would have to be justified. And, in contrast, using physical requirements such as height, weight, and/or body build to select secretaries would be clearly discriminatory and, therefore, illegal because employers would be hard-pressed to show how these were related to job content.

Job-relatedness can also be interpreted in terms of criterion-related validity. For example, if scores on a test of finger dexterity are positively related to the number of "widgets" the employee can produce per hour, then the finger dexterity test has criterion-related validity, and is fair testing practice.

A significant set of research findings regarding the validity of tests for employment selection is that from research on "validity generalization." A variety of research evidence, summarized by Schmidt and Hunter (1977; 1981), and Schmidt, Hunter, Pearlman, & Shane (1979), suggests that cognitive ability tests (including tests of verbal, quantitative, spatial and mechanical ability, perceptual speed, reasoning abilities) are valid predictors of performance both on the job and in training across a *variety* of jobs and job settings and are equally valid for majority and minority applicants.

The implications of research on "validity generalization" and other research on the use of tests in selection is that the use of most tests of cognitive abilities, no matter how valid, and "job-related," will continue to have adverse impact on many racial minorities, particularly blacks, in employment selection. In other words, although federal legislation has undoubtedly had tremendous positive effects in terms of reducing the use of discriminatory or adverse selection procedures, the possibility of adverse impact simply cannot be totally eliminated unless it is decided to "outlaw" tests *and* any other valid selection criteria which also have adverse impact. What this points out is that the basic issue is not the validity of tests but how selection decisions should be made—again we see that troublesome social policy issues continue to exist even after measurement problems have been addressed.

Scholastic Aptitude Testing. One of the bitterest controversies has involved criticisms of the use of scholastic aptitude tests. In a widely-read and commented-upon 1980 report ("The Reign of ETS: The Corporation That Makes Up Minds", authored by Allen Nairn and often called the Nairn/Nader report), Ralph Nader's research group charged that scholastic aptitude tests like the SAT and LSAT were not only biased against minority-group and lower-income students but they were not *helpful* because they did not predict success in college, not to mention success in pursuits following completion of formal education. The report was particularly critical of the Educational Testing Service, the publisher of many widely used scholastic aptitude tests; the report implied that ETS' only concern was the profits that could be gained through scholastic aptitude testing rather than with either the educational utility of testing or the scientific basis or social implications of testing. As may be expected, the Nairn/Nader report elicited considerable reaction and many responses to the charges from the scientific and professional community.

In response to charges questioning the quality of the SAT and tests like it, it was stressed that the SAT is, psychometrically, one of the most impressive tests available. It is highly reliable (values of KR-20 average .91 for SAT-V and .92 for SAT-M) and possesses a respectable degree of validity for predicting grades in the first year of college. Although validity coefficients vary across academic majors, they range from the teens to the .60s and for liberal arts students average in the mid .40s for women and the .30s for men (Kaplan, 1982).

With respect to the alleged *lack* of predictive validity of these tests, the Nairn/Nader conclusions were based on frequent misinterpretation of validity data, for example, regression coefficients. In addition, the Nairn/Nader report failed to acknowledge the effects of restriction in range of aptitude test scores in samples constituted by individuals whose aptitude test scores are high enough to be selected and of the only moderate reliability of the criterion itself, that is, grades during one's freshman year in college, in suppressing relationships between variables. Anyone who has been a freshman in college can attest to the challenges of adjustment and their potential effect on performance in classes. Given these considerations the SAT and tests like it do a rather impressive job of prediction. (And, in fact, Schrader's (1977) review of studies of the relationship of LSAT scores to grades in law school showed a strong positive relationship between the *variability* in students' LSAT scores and the obtained validity coefficient—the more variable, that is, the *less* restriction in ranges, the higher the predictive validity coefficient.)

In their challenge of racial bias, Nairn/Nader defined bias as any test that results in a disproportionate selection of minorities, in other words what has been referred to as "adverse impact." As has been mentioned, adverse impact is difficult to eradicate without throwing out tests altogether, and it *can* be addressed by simply including race as a variable in selection decisions. As long as there are group differences on standardized tests of cognitive abilities, any selection procedure *not* explicitly taking race into account will lead to the disproportionate selection of minority applicants.

Other recommendations of the Nairn/Nader report restated guidelines already stated in the SAT manual. For example, they (Nairn/Nader) insist that SAT scores should not be the only factor in selection, but the SAT manual has *always* recommended against such practices. Any selection policy based solely on one test score would be inappropriate and irresponsible. Even as scholastic aptitude tests *are* excellent predictors of both grades and persistence in higher education, it is essential to remember that there are a number of other important variables that scholastic aptitude tests simply do not measure. Variables such as motivation, social skills, common sense, perseverance, sense of humor, sensitivity and caring, and talent in a variety of areas are not measured by these tests. Certainly scholastic aptitude is helpful in terms of achieving goals of higher education, but there are many other personal and motivational qualities that are important to people's ability to be successful in and contribute to our society.

The responsibility of ETS, which has been met, is to continue to ensure correct use through the manual's clear and detailed guidelines concerning use and interpretation of test scores. It is the responsibility of college and university personnel to ensure that testing practices follow these guidelines but, beyond that, it is not the responsibility of ETS to ensure that Harvard or Yale, for example, institute a particular type of *selection* policy. As stated by Kaplan (1982): "Psychometricians and test constructors have an ethical responsibility to develop fair selection devices, and with the help of these devices, college administrators have the responsibility to assure that the available spaces are filled in a fair and just manner" (p. 22).

In fact, many colleges and graduate and professional schools clearly are using much more than test scores in admissions decisions. Law schools admit a far higher proportion of Blacks than Whites at LSAT score levels below 600 (Evans, 1977). For example, 62% of black versus only 27% of white students scoring between 450 and 500 on the LSAT were admitted to at least one law school (Evans, 1977).

Whether or not test scores are used may not even be important to admission to college. Kaplan (1982) and Linn (1982) demonstrate that tests like the SAT have very little effect on whether or not a given individual will go to college. According to Hartnett and Feldnesser (1980), a third of all colleges accept 90% or more of those applying and only 10% of schools select fewer than 50% of their applicants. Although SAT's may be too low for acceptance to Harvard or Princeton they rarely stand in the way of a college education. Further, there are many institutions which selectively accept and reject people without ever using tests at all (see Hartnett & Feldnesser, 1980, cf., Linn, 1982). Thus, the hostility of the Nairn/Nader group seems to suggest a crisis in college admissions which, in fact, does not exist.

Summary of Issues in Cultural Bias. In summary, critics of standardized tests point to the well-established test score differences between Blacks and Whites and the numerous instances where low test scores have restricted the educational and/or occupational opportunities of blacks and other low status groups. They contend that standardized tests do not accurately measure the abilities of low-status groups and that they should be used, if at all, only with middle-class groups. Tests proponents, on the other hand, counter with psychometric and statistical arguments. They point, for example, to the equivalent predictive validity across racial groups and to the fact that objective, well-standardized tests should be the most "race-blind" selection technique available. But the dialogue has not led to resolution of the controversy.

Most likely the *reason* why all the argument, debate, statistical innovations, and research data have neither resolved nor quieted the controversy is that it is not a technical, statistical, methodological controversy nor one which is specific to testing. Rather, it is a *value* controversy and the values questions concern the merits of traditional methods of *selection* versus demands for equal opportunity (e.g., see Gordon & Terrell, 1981). In other words, the issue is really not the tests *used* in selection, but the existence of selection policies which, by their very nature and definition, select some and reject others.

Testing in education and industry is based on the assumptions and values of a meritocracy, that is, that ability, talent, and achievement should be developed and rewarded regardless of social class, family background, or other background characteristics. And although the idea of a *meritocracy* has been thought to be a great improvement over privilege status based on wealth, family name and ancestry, or race, it is in principle a problematic concept because measured ability and past opportunity are related. A true concept of equal opportunity in the future really necessitates some control over opportunity in the past. Blacks and other disadvantaged groups may argue that past inequities in educational and occupational opportunity leave them at a disadvantage in terms of the meritocratic *ideal* of competition for present and future opportunities. Tests, therefore, continue to result in adverse impact when traditional methods of selection are used.

In summary, it seems self-evident that tests should not be the only basis on which to decide access to educational and occupational opportunities in our society. Concerns about past inequities and their possible continuing effects on blacks and other disadvantaged groups must be part of any decision which controls access to opportunities. Test users must familiarize themselves with the technical and interpretive considerations and cautions necessary in testing minority group members and, most importantly, must confront the reality of inherent contradictions between some aspects of the institutional value system, for example, selection, and the societal value of equal opportunity. It probably makes most sense to attempt to develop decision models which can consider and evaluate quantitative data obtained from various assessment procedures in the context of institutional objectives of equal opportunity and affirmative action. Also, where possible, tests should serve a developmental function; they help to clarify in what directions and *how* the individual's talents can be further developed and utilized.

To argue that tests should not be used at all is as extreme and untenable a position as that of total unresponsiveness to issues of discrimination and cultural bias. Rather, tests must be used in ways which, as far as possible, take advantage of the tremendous *utility* of test and other assessment data while also making sure that all segments of our society are given the chance for self-development and for educational and occupational success.

Individual Counseling Issues

One of the most important things to recall in using ability or aptitude tests with minority group members is the APA/AERA/NCME Test Standard mentioned in the first part of this chapter, that is: "A test taker's score should not be accepted as a reflection of a lack of ability with respect to the characteristic being tested without alternative explanations for the test taker's inability to perform on that test at that time" (p. 43).

In interpreting the ability test scores of a minority group member, the likelihood that that individual has come from a socioeconomically deprived background or a less privileged school system *must be* kept in mind. Consider these two students, each having ACT scores at the 30th percentile.

First, Jill is an 18-year-old White female who has just graduated from the top suburban high school in your city. Because this school is outside of the city school district, it was not subject to busing to alleviate defacto segregation in the city's schools, and middle-class White families moved to this suburb with great haste once busing was enforced in the city district. Not surprisingly, the suburban school's resources are rich, providing students with excellent educational opportunities.

Joan, on the other hand, is an 18-year-old Black female who has just graduated from a city high school. She is from a relatively poor family, and the school itself was minimally equipped with books and equipment.

Thus, it can be contended that Jill grew up in a "enriched" environment (at least in terms of support for academic pursuits), whereas Joan grew up in a "deprived" environment. Jill and Joan have the same ACT scores, but it would be reasonable to interpret them differently. Although we don't know if there are other factors which limited Jill's intellectual development, we can assume that Joan's background was not conducive to the full development of her intellectual potential and that, given environmental enrichment, she may be able to do substantially better academically than her current test scores would indicate. Certainly there are many reasons, such as lack of motivation, why students of all races and SES backgrounds might underutilize their intellectual potential, but minority students usually start with a less advantaged educational background. Thus, experiences that can help to enrich that background are vital.

GENDER ISSUES IN TEST USE

Gender issues in test use and counseling focus around the problems of sex restrictiveness in interest inventories and aptitude batteries and sex bias in the nature of aptitude test item content.

Sex Restrictiveness in Vocational Interest Inventories

The concept of sex restrictiveness in interest inventories is based on the pervasive and strong influence in our society of gender role socialization and the continuing existence of occupational sex segregation (see Betz, in press; and Betz & Fitzgerald, 1987, for detailed reviews of research on these concepts and Cook's, 1985, review of research on androgyny.)

Gender role socialization is the phenomenon by which girls are socialized into traditionally female roles, personality characteristics, competencies, and interests, and, likewise, boys are socialized into traditionally-male areas of competency and interest. Occupational sex segregation refers to the continuing overrepresentation of women in a small number of "pink-collar" jobs such as waitress and secretary and in the traditionally female professions, including nursing, teaching, social work, and so forth, and their continuing underrepresentation in traditionally male areas such as the sciences, engineering, academia, business, and the skilled trades.

Vocational interest inventories have, at least until recently, unintentionally emphasized socialized sex differences and, consequently, have perpetuated occupational sex segregation and limited the options of individual men and women. To understand the process by which this has occurred some background may be helpful.

Historically, the interests of the two sexes were measured separately (Campbell, 1977, Hansen, 1984a). The construction of separate forms of the Strong Vocational Interest Blank for men (SVIB-M; 1927) and for women (SVIB-W; 1933) was based on the different item responses of men and women and on the marked differences between men and women in the extent and nature of their employment (Campbell, 1977). For decades this system was generally accepted, although career-oriented women were frequently administered the SVIB-M rather than the SVIB-W because of the former's greater utility in suggesting professional level careers (Campbell, 1977).

Although the more recent criticisms of sex bias and restrictiveness in interest inventories have largely eliminated the use of separate forms for males and females (see expanded discussion below), males and females continue to respond differentially to many interest inventory items. Generally, women are more likely than men to indicate interests in social and artistic activities, whereas men are more likely than women to indicate interest in scientific, technical, and mechanical activities.

The existence of sex differences at the item level has resulted in different overall score patterns for the two sexes (Cole & Hanson, 1975; Prediger & Hanson, 1976). Raw scores on interest tests are computed by simply summing the number of "yes" or "like" responses to the items representing each domain of interest, for example, the six Holland themes measured in the Self-Directed Search (SDS; Holland, 1985b; Holland & Rayman, 1986) or the ACT Unisex Interest Inventory (UNIACT; Lamb & Prediger, 1981). Combined sex norms compare a person's scores on each theme or interest scale to those of a standardization sample consisting of both males and females. Because most interest scales are composed of items differentially reflective of the experiences of males versus females (the items "I like to build things with wood" and "I like to take care of children" are illustrative), it is not surprising that when raw or combined sex norms are used females obtain higher mean scores on the Social, Artistic, and Conventional themes, whereas males obtain higher means on the Realistic, Investigative, and Enterprising themes (Gottfredson, Holland, & Gottfredson, 1974; Prediger & Hanson, 1976). Similar findings have resulted using the Vocational Interest Inventory (VII; Lunneborg, 1980), a measure of Roe's eight fields of occupational interest. Findings of sex differences on basic dimensions of vocational interest are most evident and durable for Social and Realistic (Technical) interests. Social interests are far more predominant among females, while Realistic interests are found far more frequently among males (e.g., Lunneborg, 1979, 1980; Prediger, 1980).

One major implication of differential raw score patterns among males and females is that when these scores are taken to the interpretive guides accompanying interest inventories (such as The Occupations Finder accompanying the SDS, Holland, 1985b), the resulting occupational suggestions tend to reinforce the existing segregation of females and males in our society into traditionally female and traditionally male occupations. High scores on the Social and Conventional themes suggest traditionally female educational and social welfare and office and clerical occupations (e.g., Holland, 1973). In contrast, females' lower scores on the Realistic, Investigative, and Enterprising themes result in less frequent suggestion of traditionally male professions, for example, medicine, engineering, science, and of occupations in management and the skilled trades (Holland, 1973). Thus, socialized patterns of interest lead to interest inventory results which perpetuate females' overrepresentation in traditionally female occupations and their underrepresentation in occupations traditionally dominated by males.

Such divergent and sex-stereotypic suggestions of occupational alternatives to males and females were the basis for the criticisms of sex bias and sex-restrictiveness in interest inventories, extensively documented and discussed in reports funded by the National Institute of Education (Diamond, 1975; Tittle & Zytowski, 1978). According to this and other discussions of sex bias, the use of separate forms for men and women, sexist language in occupational titles (e.g., policeman versus police officer), and raw scores or combined-sex normative scores, among other things, contributed to the failure of interest inventories to result in fairness in the suggestion of occupational alternatives to males and females. In other words, interest inventories served to maintain and perpetuate the limited range of occupations considered appropriate for and usually pursued by women.

In response to the criticisms of sex bias, many test developers have addressed these issues by combining the men's and women's forms, e.g., the Strong-Campbell Interest Inventory, by eliminating sexist language, and by discussing issues of sex-role socialization in interpretive materials (Association for Measurement & Evaluation in Guidance Commission on Sex Bias in Measurement, 1977). In revisions of the SDS, sexist occupational titles were changed and items with vastly different endorsement percentages for the two sexes were omitted.

In addition to changes such as those mentioned above, other test developers have focused on reducing the sex-restrictiveness of interest inventory scores. The two major approaches to reducing sex-restrictiveness in the scores provided for basic dimensions of vocational interest are the use of same-sex normative scores and the use of sex-balanced items. Same-sex normative scores compare a person's scores on basic dimensions of vocational interest, for example, the Holland themes or the Basic Interest scales of the SCII, to those of persons of the same-sex. Thus, women are compared to other women, whereas men are compared to other men. The use of same-sex norms increases the likelihood that the background socialization experiences of the comparison sample are more similar to those of the examinee, and this in turn tends to highlight interests that have developed in spite of the limiting effects of sex-role socialization. The SCII provides same-sex normative scores for both the General Occupational (i.e., Holland) Themes and the Basic Interest Scales (see Hansen, 1984b, 1986 for guidelines regarding their use).

The second approach to reducing sex-restrictiveness in interest inventories is the use of sex-balanced item sets. A sex balanced inventory scale, for example one of the Holland themes, would be constructed to include items more likely to characterize male sex role socialization and others more common in female socialization; the desired end result is interest scales on which the sexes obtain similar raw scores. The Unisex Edition of the ACT-IV (UNIACT, Lamb & Prediger, 1981) and the revised version of the Vocational Interest Inventory (VII, Lunneborg, 1980, 1981) are based on this strategy of scale construction, and both result in more equivalent distributions of scores across the six Holland themes (UNIACT) or Roe's eight fields (VII) for the two sexes. Thus, on the UNIACT for example, the Realistic scale contains items pertaining to sewing and cooking, that is, *content* areas more often emphasized in the backgrounds of females, in addition to items more reflective of males' socialization experiences, for example, the skills learned in high school shop courses. The UNIACT, incidentally, is available for administration in both standardized and self-directed formats and thus provides an alternative to well known scales such as the SCII and the SDS for the measurement of the Holland themes.

The use of same-sex normative scores and sex-balanced interest scales is intended to increase the probability that females who could potentially be interested in Realistic, Investigative, or Enterprising occupations will obtain interest inventory profiles suggesting those areas. Thus, such methods of constructing and scoring interest inventories are designed to facilitate females' exploration of the full range of occupational alternatives and to minimize the extent to which women continue to be directed toward traditionally-female occupations.

Counselors are strongly urged to use either same-sex normative scores in interpreting scales such as the Holland themes or to use sex balanced interest inventories. Arguments against such uses (e.g., Gottfredson, 1986b; Holland, 1985b) have included the rationale that we should not attempt to reverse the effects of socialization because they are durable and important. This argument has also been described as the "socialization dominance hypothesis" (Cole & Hansen, 1975), which contends that we should take a laissez faire approach and leave people to go in the directions in which prior socialization experiences have led them. In contrast, the "opportunity dominance hypothesis" (Cole & Hansen, 1975) suggests that individuals can develop new interests if exposed to new learning experiences and, as a corollary, that we cannot accurately assess the potential for interest development if a person's previous learning experiences and opportunities have been limited in some way, for example, by sex role socialization.

In other words, attempting to assess interest in science or carpentry or nature or cooking is premature if the person has not been exposed to background experiences in those areas. We can only conclude a lack of interest if the person has seriously tried the activity. It may be useful to again recall the APA Test Standard, mentioned in the sections on test use and on racial/ethnic minorities, concerning the danger of interpreting low test scores as indicative of a lack of ability prior to exhausting alternative explanations for the low scores. I would suggest that interpreting low scores on interest scales as indicative of lack of interest be deferred until alternative explanations such as lack of background exposure to the area have been considered and addressed.

In essence the use of same sex norms and sex balanced interest inventory scales allows counselors to be alert for areas in which the person has developed interests *in spite of* sex role socialization—there seems no good reason why such interests should not be encouraged by suggesting further, or in some cases initial, opportunities for exploration. Most counselors would resist the suggestion that it is too late for them as individuals to develop new interests, so it would be inconsistent and unfair to endorse a view of clients as irrevocably limited by the shaping of sex role socialization.

Thus, although attempts to remove sex-restrictiveness from interest inventories are important and useful, the more direct solution to the problem of sex-stereotypic vocational interests involves increasing the range of experiences relevant to the development of those interests. Until girls and women have the opportunity to engage in activities relevant to, for example, Realistic and Investigative as well as Social and Artistic interest areas, interests in nontraditional areas will not develop in the majority of women. Encouraging a wider variety of activities and experiences for young girls and, for women, encouraging involvement in jobs or job-related experiences beyond the limits of socialized interests and experiences is necessary; women's vocational interests and, consequently, their career choices, should derive from a rich background of experience and knowledge rather than from a background exposing them only to stereotypically-female areas of activity and interest.

Gender Issues in Aptitude Testing

Regarding employment selection, the major issue facing women has not been that of intelligence testing, as it has been for racial minorities, but physical requirements, for example, height and weight, on which there are sex differences. For example, there are often height and weight requirements for jobs such as police officer and fire fighter. Although such requirements can be highly discriminatory against women, this problem is not generally one in which counseling psychologists would be directly involved. Counselors should, however, always be alert to the possible barriers that may confront a client in her/his pursuit of her/his career goals. An understanding of Federal, state, and local regulations concerning the use of tests in employment selection, and in particular the importance of demonstrating that a physical requirement is job-related if it is to be used in selection, are vital.

Counselors should also be concerned about the fact that in the areas of aptitude and ability testing, males have often obtained higher scores than females on tests representative of stereotypically male domains, for example, mechanical reasoning, spatial ability, and mathematical ability. Such score differences, when used in educational or occupational planning, may serve to further restrict females' educational and career options.

To some extent, aptitude test score differences, like interest test score differences, are due to differential patterns of male and female socialization in our society. For example, males have been encouraged to take math, science, and shop courses, and females have been encouraged to take English, home economics, and typing. But tests themselves have worsened the problem through bias in item content and wording. In aptitude tests, for example, use of predominantly male characters in word problems, the use of sexist language, and sex biased content have frequently been used (see Betz & Fitzgerald, 1987, for numerous examples).

Examples of sex biased content may be drawn, for example, from the General Aptitude Test Battery (GATB) ''Tool Matching'' Test, which is a measure of the ability of Form Perception. In the GATB Numerical Reasoning Test, male characters and objects predominate—the word problems focus on amounts of lumber and electrical wire rather than on fabric or recipe ingredients. Tools, lumber, and electric wire are far more common in the background experiences of boys than girls growing up in our society. Test items could be written to use content such as sewing patterns to measure form perception and amounts of food or fabric in spatial test items or mathematics word problems—this content would probably tap more into the socialization experiences of females and yet be equally appropriate in the measurement of spatial and math abilities.

In an illuminating recent study, Betz and Hackett (1983) measured the perceived self-efficacy expectations or confidence of college women and men with respect to a variety of math tasks and problems. There were 18 math tasks, 16 math-related college courses, and 18 math problems, or a total of 52 items. As predicted, males reported higher expectations of self-efficacy on 49 of the 52 math-related items. There were only *three* out of 52 items on which females reported higher expectations of self-efficacy than males—those three items were as follows: 1) figure out how much material to buy in order to make curtains; 2) estimate your grocery bill in your head as you pick up items; and 3) calculate recipe quantities for a dinner for 41 when the original recipe was for 12 people.

Given these data, one wonders what the effects would be of testing math ability, as well as math self-efficacy, using a more balanced set of items. If the sex differences in self-efficacy expectations can be eliminated by asking questions based on content familiar to women, it seems that ability measurement should also be revised. A similar conclusion has been made by Lunneborg and Lunneborg (1986) in their research exploring the experiential bases for the development of spatial ability. (It should be noted that revisions of test content should not be taken as a sufficient answer to the limiting effects of sex role socialization on the development of both males and females, and it is hope that broadened childhood experiences for both boys and girls would be facilitated by parents, the schools, the media, etc. But until socialization practices change for the majority of girls and women, testing them using content underemphasized in their background experiences is unfair).

Even if a test profile is not used in selection, it may be used by a client and her counselor to make educational and career decisions. And in this respect it is vital to again recall that we cannot accurately measure an ability, or an interest, if the person's background experience has provided only limited exposure to that domain of competency—again, the APA standard cautioning against inferences of lack of ability prior to exhausting other explanations should be recalled. For example, the literature suggests that sex differences in math performance begin to appear only as girls stop taking math, and that the differences disappear when math background is controlled for or partialled out (see Betz & Fitzgerald, 1987, for an extensive review). Thus, lack of potential must not be inferred in the absence of ample opportunity to develop that potential.

There are several ways to address these issues. First, counselors should be well-informed regarding the nature and occurrence of sex bias in ability tests. In an important recent study, Selkow (1984) evaluated the extent of bias and sex role stereotyping in 74 major tests of ability, personality, and school achievement and readiness. Familiarity with the methods and findings of this study would facilitate informed test use.

Second, it is critical that counselors, when interpreting differential aptitude test scores, for example, mathematics versus verbal ability, remember that gender-role socialization shapes girls and boys differently, that girls are not encouraged to continue taking math, and that girls may need more help in building confidence and reducing anxiety with respect to math. The amount of math taken in high school and college is strongly related to the degree to which educational and career options remain open or closed to the individual. A counselor examining a pattern of aptitude test scores should not overlook alternative explanations for low scores, particularly in the context of overall high ability.

Finally, use of same-sex norms in interpreting ability test scores, urging test publishers to include test items from the backgrounds of both sexes, and cognizance of the overall tendency of females to under-utilize their abilities in educational and career pursuits are among the possible ways of addressing the sex bias in ability test items.

CROSS CULTURAL ISSUES IN TEST USE

There are at least two major issues to be considered in the cross cultural use of tests. First, when using tests with ethnic minorities or foreign-born examinees in this country, the possible influences of different cultures on both test performance and the meanings of various attributes and behaviors must be considered. As was mentioned in the introduction to this section, tests of behavioral capabilities and personality tests may be of particular concern because they inevitably involve assumptions about appropriate or psychologically healthy versus less appropriate or healthy behaviors and characteristics. The example given in the introduction pertained to the behavior of assertiveness which, in some cultures, might be viewed as inappropriate vis a vis at least some types of people, for example, one's elders.

The issue of how culture affects views of psychological health and of the usefulness of counseling and therapy has received little or no study, but it is safe to say that there *are* cross-cultural differences in these views. This issue must be considered in counseling as well as assessment—the counselor who wishes to encourage assertive behavior in a Japanese client may need to proceed more carefully and slowly than he/she would with an Anglo client. Although the present chapter cannot provide solutions to this more general problem, counselors must always remember the cultural relativity of their assumptions about appropriate individual behavior and about therapeutic goals and methods. Counseling, like any other field of endeavor, develops within a given set of cultural beliefs and norms, and we must constantly guard against assumptions that our theories and methods, including tests, are automatically helpful for or appropriate to all of our clients.

The second issue regarding the use of tests cross-culturally centers around whether or not a test has been translated into other languages or cultural usages (e.g., making sure that a U.S.-developed test is revised to incorporate language usages common in Great Britain or Australia) and, if it is available in other cultures, the extent to which there are data pertaining to the reliability, validity, and utility of the test scores in that culture.

The extent to which a test satisfies these criteria varies markedly across tests, although most tests provide little or no information about cross-cultural usage. It is the responsibility of the test user to make sure that a test to be used in another country or with people from another culture has been supported for those uses. For example, the cross-cultural utility of the SCII has been investigated in a series of studies (Fouad, 1984; Fouad, Cudeck, & Hansen, 1984; Fouad &

Hansen, 1987; Fouad, Hansen, & Arias, 1986). In a particularly important study, for example, the utility of the SCII with bilingual Hispanic high school students was investigated (Fouad et al., 1984). Super's Career Development Inventory (CDI) has also been the subject of considerable cross-cultural research, and several editions for use in foreign countries have been developed. For example, the CDI has been revised for use in such countries as Australia, Portugal, and Great Britain (see also Betz, 1988 for an extensive discussion of recent innovations in the measurement of career development and maturity). Holland (1985a, 1985b) discusses research investigating the applicability of the SDS in other countries.

Although the SCII and the CDI represent exemplars in this area, most tests have not been examined for cross-cultural uses. At this point three statements can be made with confidence: (a) use of a test which has not been validated in the population in which it is to be used is highly problematic and should be avoided unless no locally validated alternatives are available; (b) there has been very little research investigating the cross-cultural or cross-national utility of well-known U.S.-developed tests (but see Hansen, 1984; for a review of what is available); and (c) additional research in this area is sorely needed and would have the potential of contributing substantially to the utility of tests in counseling.

SUMMARY

In summary, this chapter has reviewed ethical and social issues concerning the use of tests in counseling. It is hoped that test users will become familiar with the uses, misuses, and limits of any test they are considering for use—an informed test user will be well on his/her way to ethical and socially responsible test use. Also important is further research on specific uses of tests, with, for example, ethnic minorities and individuals from other cultures. Counselors who use tests in their work should be continually alert to possible research hypotheses stemming from their actual counseling use of tests. Finally, respect for the individual and continuing awareness of the fact that tests are fallible sources of information (even if clients think they are infallible) is vital to ethical test use.

REFERENCES

American Psychological Association (1954). *Technical recommendations for psychological tests and diagnostic techniques*. Washington, D.C.: Author.

American Educational Research Association, American Psychological Association, National Council on Measurement in Education (1985). *Standards for educational and psychological testing*. Washington, D.C.: American Psychological Association.

American Psychological Association (1981). Ethical principles of psychologists. *American Psychologist, 36,* 633–638.

American Psychological Association (1986). *Test purchaser qualifications: Present practice, professional needs, and a proposed system.* Paper prepared under the auspices of the Scientific Affairs Office, APA. Washington, D.C.: Author.

Anastasi, A. (1982). *Psychological testing* (5th edition). New York: Macmillan.

Association for Measurement and Evaluation in Guidance. Commission on Sex Bias in Measurement. (1977). A case history of change: A review of responses to the challenge of sex bias in interest inventories. *Measurement and Evaluation in Guidance, 10,* 148–152.

Bersoff, D. N. (1981). Testing and the law. *American Psychologist, 36,* 1047–1056.

Betz, N. E. (in press). Sex and gender as individual differences variables: New concepts and findings. In R. Dawis & D. Lubinski (Eds.), *Assessing individual differences in human behavior: New concepts, methods, and findings.* Minneapolis, MN: University of Minnesota Press.

Betz, N. E. (1988). Advances in the assessment of career development and maturity. In W. B. Walsh & S. H. Osipow (Eds.), *Advances in vocational psychology: Volume II: The assessment of career decision making* (pp. 77–136). Hillsdale, NJ: Lawrence Erlbaum Associates.

Betz, N. E., & Fitzgerald, L. F. (1987). *The career psychology of women.* New York: Academic Press.

Betz, N. E., & Hackett, G. (1983). The relationship of mathematics self-efficacy expectations to the selection of science-based college majors. *Journal of Vocational Behavior, 23,* 329–345.

Breland, H. M. (1979). *Population validity and college entrance measures.* New York: The College Board.

Buros, O. K. (Ed.). (1961). *Tests in print.* Highland Park, N.J.: Gryphon Press.

Buros, O. K. (Ed.). (1974). Tests in print: II. Highland Park, NJ: Gryphon Press.

Campbell, D. P. (1977). Manual for the SVIB-SCII Strong Campbell Interest Inventory (2nd ed.). Stanford, CA: Stanford University Press.

Cole, N. S. (1981). Bias in testing.*American Psychologist, 36,* 1067–1077.

Cole, N. S., & Hanson, G. R. (1975). Impact of interest inventories on career choice. In E. E. Diamond (Ed.), *Issues of sex bias and sex fairness in career interest measurement* (pp. 10–25). Washington, D.C.: National Institute of Education.

Cook, E. P. (1985). *Psychological androgyny.* New York: Pergamon.

Dawis, R. V. (1987). Scale construction. *Journal of Counseling Psychology, 34,* 481–489.

Diamond, E. E. (1975). Guidelines for the assessment of sex bias and sex fairness in career interest inventories. *Measurement and Evaluation in Guidance, 8,* 7–11.

Evans, F. R. (1977). Applications and admissions to ABA accredited law schools. In Law School Admissions Council (Ed.), *Reports of LSAC sponsored research: 1975–1977.* (Vol. 3). Princeton, NJ: Law School Admissions Council.

Eyde, L. D. (1986). Test purchaser qualifications: A proposed voluntary system based on test ethics. In APA (Eds.), *Test purchaser qualifications* (pp. 14–29). Washington, D.C.: APA Office of Scientific Affairs.

Fouad, N. A. (1984). Comparison of interests across cultures. *Dissertation Abstracts International, 4503A* (84–13): 777.

Fouad, N. A., Cudeck, R., & Hansen, J. C. (1984). Convergent validity of the Spanish and English forms of the SCII for bilingual Hispanic high school students. *Journal of Counseling Psychology, 31,* 339–348.

Fouad, N. A., & Hansen, J. C. (1987). Cross-cultural predictive accuracy of the Strong-Campbell Interest Inventory. *Measurement and Evaluation in Counseling and Development, 20,* 3–10.

Fouad, N. A., Hansen, J. C., & Arias, F. G. (1986). Multiple discriminant analysis of cross-cultural similarity of vocational interests of lawyers and engineers. *Journal of Vocational Behavior, 28,* 85–96.

Gordon, E. W., & Terrell, M. D. (1981). The changed social context of testing. *American Psychologist, 36,* 1167–1171.

Gottfredson, L. S. (1986a). Societal consequences of the "g" factor in employment. *Journal of Vocational Behavior, 29,* 379–410.

Gottfredson, L. S. (1986b). Special groups and the beneficial use of vocational interest inventories. In W. B. Walsh & S. Osipow (Eds.), *Advances in vocational psychology: Vol. 1. The assessment of interests.* (pp. 127–198). Hillsdale, NJ: Lawrence Erlbaum Associates.

Gottfredson, G. D., Holland, J. L., & Gottfredson, L. S. (1975). The relation of vocational aspirations and assessments to employment realities. *Journal of Vocational Behavior, 7,* 135–148.

Hansen, J. C. (1984a). The measurement of vocational interests: Issues and future directions. In R. B. Lent & S. D. Brown (Eds.), *Handbook of counseling psychology* (pp. 99–136). New York: Wiley.

Hansen, J. C. (1984b). *User's guide for the SVIB-SCII.* Stanford, CA: Stanford University Press.

Hansen, J. C. (1986). Strong Vocational Interest Blank/Strong Campbell Interest Inventory. In W. B. Walsh & S. H. Osipow (Eds.), *Advances in vocational psychology. Volume I: The assessment of interests* (pp. 1–30). Hillsdale, NJ: Lawrence Erlbaum Associates.

Hansen, J. C., & Campbell, D. P. (1985). *Manual for the SVIB-SCII* (4th ed.). Stanford, CA: Stanford University Press.

Hartnett, R. T., & Feldmesser, R. A. (1980). College admissions testing and the myth of selectivity. *AAHE Bulletin, 32,* 3–6.

Holland, J. L. (1973). *Making vocational choices: A theory of careers.* Englewood Cliffs, NJ: Prentice Hall.

Holland, J. L. (1985a). *Making vocational choices: A theory of vocational personalities and work environments.* Englewood Cliffs, NJ: Prentice Hall.

Holland, J. L. (1985b). *Professional manual for the Self-Directed Search—1985 Edition.* Odessa, FLA: Psychological Assessment Resources.

Holland, J. L., & Rayman, J. R. (1986). The Self-Directed Search. In W. B. Walsh & S. H. Osipow (Eds.), *Advances in vocational psychology. Volume I: The assessment of interests* (pp. 55–82). Hillsdale, NJ: Lawrence Erlbaum Associates.

Humphreys, L. G., & Taber, T. (1973). Ability factors as a function of advantaged and disadvantaged groups. *Journal of Educational Measurement, 10,* 107–115.

Hunter, J. E., Schmidt, F. L., & Hunter, R. (1979). Differential validity of employment tests by race: A comprehensive review and analysis. *Psychological Bulletin, 86,* 721–735.

Jensen, A. R. (1969). How much can we boost I. Q. and scholastic achievement? *Harvard Educational Review, 39,* 1–123.

Jensen, A. R. (1980). *Bias in mental testing.* New York: Free Press.

Kaplan, R. M. (1982). Nader's raid on the testing industry: Is it in the best interests of the consumer? *American Psychologist, 37,* 15–23.

Lamb, R. R., & Prediger, D. J. (1981). *Technical report for the unisex edition of the ACT interest inventory (UNIACT).* Iowa City: American College Testing Program.

Linn, R. L. (1982). Admissions testing on trial. *American Psychologist, 37,* 279–291.

Lunneborg, P. W. (1979). Service versus technical interest: Biggest sex difference of all? *Vocational Guidance Quarterly, 28,* 146–153.

Lunneborg, P. W. (1980). Reducing sex bias in interest measurement at the item level. *Journal of Vocational Behavior, 16,* 226–234.

Lunneborg, P. W. (1981). *The Vocational interest inventory manual.* Los Angeles: Western Psychological Services.

Lunneborg, P. W., & Lunneborg, C. E. (1986). Everyday Spatial Activities Test for studying differential experience and vocational behavior. *Journal of Vocational Behavior, 28,* 135–141.

Mitchell, J. V., Jr. (Ed.). (1985). *The ninth mental measurements yearbook.* Highland Park, NJ: Gryphon Press.

Moreland, K. L. (1986). An introduction to the problem of test user qualifications. In APA (Eds.), *Test purchaser qualifications* (pp. 2–5). Washington, D.C.: APA Office of Scientific Affairs.

Nairn, A. (1980). *The reign of ETS: The corporation that makes up minds.* Washington, D.C.: Nader.

Prediger, D. P. (1980). The determination of Holland types characterizing occupational groups. *Journal of Vocational Behavior, 16,* 33–42.

Prediger, D. P., & Hanson, G. R. (1976). A theory of career applied to men and women: Analysis of implicit assumptions. *Journal of Vocational Behavior, 8,* 167–184.

Robertson, G. D. (1986). Establishing test purchaser qualifications: Present practices and future needs. In APA (Eds.), *Test purchaser qualifications* (pp. 7–12). Washington, D.C.: APA Office of Scientific Affairs.

Schmidt, F. L., & Hunter, J. E. (1977). Development of a general solution to the problem of validity generalization. *Journal of Applied Psychology, 62,* 529–540.

Schmidt, F. L., & Hunter, J. E. (1981). Employment testing: Old theories and new research findings. *American Psychologist, 36,* 1128–1137.

Schmidt, F. L., Hunter, J. E., Pearlman, K., & Shane, G. S. (1979). Further tests of the Schmidt-Hunter Bayesian validity generalization procedures. *Personnel Psychology, 32,* 257–281.

Schrader, W. B. (1977). Summary of law school validity studies 1948–1975. In Law School Admissions Council (Ed.), *Reports of LSCA sponsored research 1975–1977* (pp. 1–24). Princeton, NJ: Law School Admissions Council.

Selkow, P. (1984). *Assessing sex bias in testing.* Westport, Connecticut: Greenwood Press.

Tittle, C. K., & Zytowski, D. G. (Eds.). (1978). *Sex fair interest measurement: Research and implications.* Washington D.C.: National Institute of Education.

Walsh, W. B., & Betz, N. E. (1990). *Tests and assessment.* (2nd Ed.). Englewood Cliffs, NJ: Prentice Hall.

Walsh, S. H., & Osipow, S. H. (Eds.). (1986). *Advances in psychology. Volume I: The assessment of interests* (whole). Hillsdale, NJ: Lawrence Erlbaum Associates.

Walsh, S. H., & Osipow, S. H. (Eds.). (1988). *Advances in vocational psychology. Volume II. The assessment of career decision making.* Hillsdale, NJ: Lawrence Erlbaum Associates.

14 Computer Applications and Issues in Using Tests in Counseling

James P. Sampson, Jr.
Florida State University

INTRODUCTION[1]

Computer applications in testing and assessment have now been in use for over three decades. Experience with the application of this technology has resulted in the creation of a substantial body of knowledge. The goal of this chapter is to synthesize this literature to provide practitioners and researchers with an understanding of the potential benefits and problems associated with computer-assisted testing and assessment, within the context of past, present, and future use of this technology.

The chapter begins with a brief review of the historical development of computer-assisted testing and assessment, followed by a description of the state of the art. The necessity of keeping terminology related to computer applications congruent with actual professional practice is then examined. The benefits associated with computer applications are explored in light of how appropriate use of technology can potentially enhance: (a) the validity and reliability of testing and assessment, (b) client integration of assessment data in counseling, (c) staff efficiency and cost-effectiveness, and (d) the development of new testing and assessment practices. The problems associated with computer applications are then explored in light of how inappropriate use of technology can potentially compromise: (a) the validity and reliability of testing and assessment; and (b) effective implementation of services. Finally, the future use of computer applica-

[1]The term practitioner in this chapter refers to counselors, psychologists, and other mental health professionals who are qualified by virtue of their training and experience to engage in testing and assessment functions as one component of the counseling and behavior change process.

tions in testing and assessment is examined in terms of hardware developments, software developments, and professional practice.

Evolution of Computer-Assisted Testing and Assessment

The use of computer applications in assessment began with quantitative features of the testing and assessment process and has now progressed to include many verbal features as well. Examples of early quantitative features included keyboard entry from existing answer sheets, optical scanning of specialized answer sheets, scoring of traditional paper-and-pencil tests, scores printed with scale labels, and graphic presentation of score profiles. With improvements over time in the cost-effectiveness of data processing, verbal features became available, for example, the administration of test items and the development of narrative interpretive reports. As telecommunications improved, users could enter data and print reports at remote locations (via a modem that allows communication between computers) with scoring centralized in another location. The emergence of the personal computer (microcomputer) provided substantial cost-effectiveness improvements and a shift in locus-of-control that brought test administration, scoring, profiling, and interpretive report generation into actual service delivery settings, as opposed to remote computer centers. Advancements in the integration of audio-visual (first videotape and now videodisc) technology with the computer have resulted in the presentation of generalized test interpretations directly to the client (Hansen, 1986, 1987; Sampson, 1983). Fowler and Butcher (1987) provided a comprehensive historical account of the evolution of computer-assisted psychological assessment.

State of the Art

The following is a description of state-of-the-art computer-assisted testing and assessment.

1. *Test administration* via:
   - (a) keyboard input by the client from items presented on the computer display, with alternative input options available for physically disabled clients; or
   - (b) client completion of a specially prepared test answer sheet that is then optically scanned for computer input; or
   - (c) client completion of a traditional test answer sheet with keyboard input by a clerical staff person.
2. *Test scoring* via the computer (local or remote).
3. *Test score profile generation* via the computer.

4. *Narrative interpretive report generation* via the computer with reports available for both the client and practitioner if appropriate (the narrative report may also include the test profile).
5. *Videodisc-based generalized test interpretation* provided to the client immediately following test administration.

Prior to test administration, computer-assisted instruction may be used to help clients understand: (a) the role of assessment in the counseling and behavior change process, and (b) the procedures to be involved in testing (Sampson, 1986a).

Moreland (1987), Madsen (1986) and Roid and Gorsuch (1984) provided detailed descriptions of the specific options available for computer-assisted test administration, scoring, and report generation. Refer to Bridges (1988), Butcher (1987a), Krug (1987b), and Sampson, Tenhagen, Ryan-Jones, & Koeteeuw (1987) for information on computer versions of specific tests.

Computer-Assisted vs. Computerized: Keeping Terminology Congruent with Recommended Practice

It appears that the terms "computer-assisted" and "computerized" are used with nearly the same frequency in describing the use of computer technology as an aspect of the assessment process (Sampson, 1987). Using "computerized" instead of "computer-assisted" may create problems, because it may foster misunderstanding of the role of the computer in the testing and assessment process. Practitioners who misunderstand the role of the computer are likely to reject technology because they view the computer as performing inappropriate functions that lead to dehumanization or they are likely to view the computer as effective in performing functions not intended by the developer, such as compensating for a lack of professional skill. The former is likely to lead to *underuse* of the computer, the latter to *misuse*.

Using the term "computerized" implies that labor previously completed by humans is now completed by the computer; in essence the testing and assessment process is now automated. The testing and assessment process is not, however, as automated as the term "computerized" implies. First, although a computer may actually administer individual items, the *APGA Policy Statement: Responsibilities of Users of Standardized Tests* (APGA, 1980) and the *Standards for Educational and Psychological Testing* (AERA, APA, & NCME, 1985) require that a trained professional be available for orientation, providing appropriate assistance and observing the client in order to ensure the validity of the results. Second, while the computer often performs all scoring tasks, potential errors in optical scanning devices and scoring programs necessitate regular human intervention to evaluate the accuracy of test results. The verification of scoring accuracy of computer applications has been included in the *Ethical Standards* (American Association for Counseling and Development, 1988), the *Guidelines for Computer-Based Tests and Interpretations* (American Psychological Association, 1986), and the *Code of Ethics* (National Board for Certified Counselors, 1987). Third, even though a computer may generate a narrative test interpretation, the *Guidelines for Computer-Based Tests and Interpretations* (American Psychological Association, 1986, p. 12) state that the professional should judge the validity of computer-generated interpretive reports based on his or her "knowledge of the total context of testing and the test taker's performance and characteristics." Thus the term "computerized" is an inaccurate and potentially misleading depiction of the actual use of computer technology in the testing and assessment process.

The term "computer-assisted," as used by Bleuer and Walz (1983), Walz (1984), and Loesch (1986), and "computer-as-assistant" as used by Altemose and Williamson (1981), implies that the computer is being used to facilitate another more complex process. In this way the major emphasis is placed on testing and assessment, with the computer fulfilling a support role; improving, as opposed to replacing, the human element. This perspective is more likely to avoid practitioner or client underuse or misuse of computer applications. This perspective is also congruent with the professional standards described above.

RATIONALES FOR COMPUTER-ASSISTED TESTING AND ASSESSMENT

Both rationales for using computer technology to support the assessment process are directed toward improving the quality of counseling services. The first rationale focuses on assigning to humans and computers the tasks best suited to the respective capabilities of each. For example, *computers* are better at computational and repetitive instructional tasks, whereas *practitioners* are better at interpersonal tasks, such as helping clients understand how testing and assessment supports the counseling process, helping clients fully understand test results, and helping clients integrate the self-knowledge obtained in assessment into a broader plan for behavior change. Sampson (1986b) provides a detailed literature review concerning common assumptions about the use of computer applications in counseling.

The second rationale involves developing previously unavailable techniques that result in improved quality of test instruments and procedures. For example, adaptive devices allow disabled individuals to independently complete test items that previously would have required the assistance of an attendant (Burkhead & Sampson, 1985; Krug, 1987a; Merrell, 1986; Sampson, 1983).

POTENTIAL BENEFITS ASSOCIATED WITH COMPUTER APPLICATIONS

The potential benefits of using computer applications in support of testing and assessment can be conceptualized into four general areas: (a) enhanced validity and reliability (administration and scoring as well as test interpretation), (b) enhanced client integration of assessment data in counseling, (c) enhanced staff efficiency and cost-effectiveness, and (d) development of new testing and assessment practices.

Enhanced Validity and Reliability

Computer applications have the potential to enhance the validity and reliability of testing and assessment. This affects administration and scoring as well as interpretation.

Administration and Scoring. The greater degree of standardization inherent in computer functioning results in increased validity and reliability of test administration and scoring (Denner, 1977; French, 1986). Test items and response sets are presented in the same way for each test taker, thus achieving more standardization than is available with paper-and-pencil-tests. Krug (1987a) notes that measurement errors are reduced because the computer can present very complex stimuli and maintain precise time limits for item presentation. Byers (1981) states that in paper-and-pencil testing the test taker often errs by getting out of sync between the answer sheet and test item printed in a booklet. Because items are administered one at a time on the computer, extraneous errors of this type are eliminated. Furthermore, the rapid feedback available from computer administered and scored tests has improved client attitudes toward testing (Byers, 1981).

Disabled individuals can now complete a test with only minimal assistance from staff members. The many adaptive devices that allow this flexibility grew out of the numerous computer options for data input (Burkhead & Sampson, 1985; Krug, 1987a; Merrell, 1986; Sampson, 1983). Because staff members have a reduced opportunity to influence test administration, the results are more likely to be a valid representation of the disabled person's perceptions, knowledge, and behavior. In terms of test scoring accuracy, the computer is both faster and more accurate in comparison to paper-and-pencil methods (French, 1986; Hansen, 1977).

In addition to standardized tests, the computer can be used to effectively administer interviews and checklists. In differentiating between standardized tests and psychosocial histories (one type of interview), Giannetti (1987) states:

> Tests provide standardized estimates on a set of personality, intellectual, or symptomatic variables. They inform us about the person's internal characteristics, re-

> sources, and patterns of behavior in a normative framework. The psychosocial history, on the other hand, provides information on the long series of external stimuli, events, and individuals with which the person has interacted, including the consequences of those interactions. It describes how internal characteristics, resources, and patterns of behavior measured by psychological tests have been externally applied and shaped. (p. 124–125)

Computer administration offers some important advantages over more traditional interviews. In comparison with human interviewers, the computer-assisted interviews provided more comprehensive and consistent topic coverage of important issues (Giannetti, 1987; Schwartz, 1984) and were less affected by time of day and interview sequencing (Slack & Slack, 1977). Clients were more honest in responding to the computer (Lucas, Mullins, Luna & McInroy, 1977). Giannetti (1987) reported that clients reacted positively to computer-assisted interviews and that a majority of clients were capable of completing the computer-assisted interviews with minimal assistance.

Despite initial concerns that clients would perceive the use of computer technology as ''impersonal'' or ''mechanistic'' and react negatively to the computer, actual experience has shown that clients respond positively to both computer-assisted testing (Allen & Skinner, 1987; Byers, 1981; French & Beaumont, 1987; Johnson & Johnson; 1981) and computer-assisted interviewing (Byrnes & Johnson, 1981; Giannetti, 1987; Lockshin & Romanczyk, 1986; Space, 1981; Stout, 1981). It is important to note, however, that clients do not always perceive computer use as a positive experience. Allen and Skinner (1987) reported that five percent of clients assigned to use a computer-assisted interview refused to complete the procedure. Cruickshank (1982) states that nervous or highly stressed clients were less likely to accept the use of computer technology.

Test Interpretation. Computer-Based Test Interpretation (CBTI) is designed to enhance the validity and reliability of testing by providing the practitioner with an expanded and consistent knowledge base to assist in the interpretation of the test data of an individual client. The knowledge base available to the practitioner is expanded as a function of the research data and clinical experience of other practitioners that is typically included in CBTI programs. Consistency in the knowledge base available for test interpretation is achieved as a function of the standardized nature of computer functioning. *Descriptive interpretations* typically include descriptive sentences related to specific scales (Roid & Gorsuch, 1984). Moreland (1987) states that in descriptive interpretations, scales are interpreted independently of each other and are typically cryptic in nature. *Clinician-modeled interpretations (renowned clinician type)* are designed to replicate the interpretive judgments of a single clinician who has had the most experience with the test being used (Roid & Gorsuch, 1984). *Clinician-modeled interpretations (statistical model type)* are designed to replicate the interpretive judgments of a group of experienced clinicians by creating a statistically valid model that incorporates the best consensus possible among the experts (Roid & Gorsuch, 1984). *Clinical actuarial interpretations* are designed to provide "narrative descriptions and clinical hypotheses based on the clinical research findings for particular score patterns" (Roid & Gorsuch, 1984, p. 145). Karson and O'Dell (1987) provide an example of a clinician-modeled interpretation (renowned clinician type) for the 16PF. Butcher (1987b) provides a description of clinical actuarial interpretation of the MMPI. Fowler (1987) presents a detailed discussion of the factors involved in developing a valid CBTI system.

Used appropriately, CBTI serves in a consulting role, with the practitioner integrating data from a variety of sources in the creation of an assessment report (Krug, 1987a; Sampson, 1986b). Butcher (1987b, p. 167) states, "It is important that computerized interpretive reports be used only in an adjunct or 'advisory' way and not as the final word . . ."

There are several potential benefits associated with using CBTI. First, CBTI is not subject to interpreter bias or extraneous circumstances (Butcher, 1987c). Second, CBTI is being more frequently used as an outside opinion in forensic settings, due to the perception that CBTI is generally free of bias (Butcher, 1987c). Third, CBTI systems can be used by the practitioner to organize and systematically access the rapidly growing and often extensive data bases related to popular instruments (Krug, 1987a). Fourth, CBTI systems can be easily updated as new research becomes available (Krug, 1987a; Vale & Keller, 1987).

Enhanced Client Integration of Assessment Data in Counseling

Computer applications related to objective personality assessment (Butcher, 1987b), projective personality assessment (Exner, 1987), intellectual performance (Fisher & Jenkins, 1986), and neuropsychological functioning (Adams & Heaton, 1987) are intended to be used by qualified mental health professionals as one aspect of the psychotherapeutic process. In most cases the actual CBTI report is not given to the client. The tradition in career counseling, however, has been to provide interpretive reports directly to the client. The *Interpretive Report* for the *Strong Interest Inventory* (SII) (Hansen, 1987) is an example of a CBTI report designed for direct use by clients. The report is intended to synthesize the vast amount of interpretive data on the SII, providing the client with a basic understanding of the results, steps in the decision-making process, and suggested follow-up resources. This allows the practitioner to spend additional time exploring more complicated issues. The *Self-Directed Search* (Holland, 1985) was created to be self-administered, scored, and interpreted. The *Self-Directed Search: Computer Version* (Reardon, Psychological Assessment Resources & Holland, 1987) attempts to improve the administration, scoring, and interpretation process, as well as extend the instrument by adding additional diagnostic and analytical components (Reardon, 1987). The client and the practitioner both potentially benefit by having information that is more reliable and more comprehensive. The client is also better prepared for test interpretation. DISCOVER for Colleges and Adults (American College Testing Program, 1987) provides a self-assessment process, prior to searching for occupational alternatives. Clients have the option of either completing an on-line administration of the *UNIACT Interest Inventory,* or inputting scores for previously administered and scored instruments. This approach directly infuses assessment into the broader career counseling process.

Generalized test interpretations further integrate assessment data into the counseling process by adding video-based technology to test interpretation. "Clients who view a generalized interpretation of test results can improve their preparation for counseling by being aware of basic terminology, concepts, and the general nature of their scores" (Sampson, 1983, p. 294). A computer-controlled videodisc is used to embed the SII in a comprehensive career guidance system (Hansen, 1986; 1987). PATHFINDER (Interactive Videosystems, Inc., 1985) incorporates the SII into a 4-step career exploration and decision making process for individuals or groups.

Enhanced Staff Efficiency and Cost-Effectiveness

In comparison with traditional methods, computer-assisted testing and assessment tends to be more cost-effective (Butcher, 1987c; Byers, 1981; Byrnes & Johnson, 1981; Elwood, 1972; Klinger, Miller, Johnson, & Williams, 1977; Johnson & Johnson, 1981; Space, 1981; Stout, 1981). Krug (1987a) estimates that 15 to 50% of total testing time may be saved as a result of using computer technology. Computer applications generally can improve the time utilization of support staff, and thus contribute to increased cost-effectiveness, by increasing the number of tests and structured interviews that can be administered. Practitioners can also prepare for a test interpretation with a client or write a test report in a more timely manner.

Optical scanning or clerical staff input of item responses may result in the greatest cost-effectiveness when large numbers of tests are administered. Duthie (1984), Moreland (1987) and Space (1981) caution that on-line test administration reduces the availability of the computer to support other functions such as record keeping or word processing.

Development of New Testing and Assessment Practices

Several computer-based testing and assessment practices have evolved in addition to the innovations for disabled individuals described previously in this chapter. Adaptive testing reduces administration time because the computer only administers the items that are necessary to produce statistically valid results

(Johnson & Johnson, 1981; Hofer & Green, 1985; Johnson, 1984; Space, 1981; Vale, 1981; Ward, 1984; Weiss & Vale, 1987). The numerous options for computer input, for example, keyboard, joystick, finger-tapping device, and so forth, have resulted in the development of computer-assisted neuropsychological assessment (Golden, 1987). The computer can collect data on the manner in which clients respond to items, as well as recording specific responses. This ancillary data, which can include random rapid response patterns, testee fatigue, and changes in response latencies for items comprising a specific scale, can be analyzed and included in CBTI reports in such a way that testing validity is improved (Hofer & Green, 1985; Standing Committee on Test Standards, 1984; Stout, 1981). It is also possible to use the computer as a research tool (Space, 1981). The computer can automatically collect and analyze data on how clients behave in relation to various computer-assisted administration strategies and client perceptions regarding the assessment process.

POTENTIAL PROBLEMS ASSOCIATED WITH COMPUTER APPLICATIONS

The potential problems of using computer applications in support of testing and assessment can be conceptualized into two general areas: (a) threats to validity and reliability (administration and scoring, test interpretation, ethical issues as well as ethical standards), and (b) ineffective implementation.

Threats to Validity and Reliability

Factors related to administration and scoring, test interpretation, and ethics have the potential to undermine the validity and reliability of the testing and assessment process.

Administration and scoring. Although a number of studies have demonstrated the equivalence of results obtained from paper-and-pencil and computer-assisted administration (Beaumont & French, 1987; Hansen, 1987; Reardon & Loughead, 1988; Wilson, Thompson & Wylie, 1982), other studies have shown that the difference in administration modalities affects the results obtained (Allred & Harris, 1984; Beaumont & French, 1987). The validity of the testing and assessment process is compromised when the norms developed from paper-and-pencil administrations are applied to computer-assisted administration, when in fact the method used may influence the results obtained (Duthie, 1984). In general, the existing literature suggests that traditional and computer administration tend to be equivalent more often than not (Hofer & Green, 1985; Moreland, 1987; Roid, 1984). The fact, however, that some data exist to the contrary suggests that each instrument needs to be examined individually to clearly establish equivalency and that blanket assumptions of equivalency are unwarranted

(French, 1986). Hofer and Green (1985) provide guidelines for determining equivalency.

Another threat to validity and reliability involves scoring errors. Although it is true that computer-assisted testing has the *potential* to virtually eliminate scoring errors, it would be inappropriate to assume that this is *automatically* the case. Most (1987) stated, "The computer itself does not contribute error, but the complex nature of computer programming and the difficulty involved in reading computer programs or code makes it easy to make program errors which are difficult to find" (p. 377). Specific problems include incorrect weighting of items into scales, incorrect scoring of correctly weighted items, inaccurate algorithms, and cutting-scores that are so far apart that real differences are masked (Most, 1987). These problems are confounded by the common public perceptions of the infallibility of computers (Ben-Porath & Butcher, 1986; Eberly & Cech, 1986; Elwork & Gutkin, 1985; Herr & Best, 1984; Lister, 1970; Matarazzo, 1983; Turkington, 1984). It is often automatically assumed that if the output is computer-generated, then it is necessarily accurate when in fact this may not be true.

Still another threat to validity and reliability involves inadequate provision for human factors in test administration. Human factors study seeks to understand the optimum interface between human beings and machines (Hirsch, 1981). The term "user friendly" has been applied to describe a condition where the human factors associated with using computer hardware and software contribute to ease of use. The human factors associated with administration of tests via the computer are *not* universally adequate. Specific human factors that may cause problems include misunderstanding computer-based test instructions, wording of error messages, screen layout, inappropriately difficult reading level, and the lack of an error correction feature (French, 1986; Johnson & Johnson, 1981). Beaumont (1982) provides a description of the elements involved in effective computer-assisted test administration.

Test Interpretation. Research validating CBTI has typically involved customer satisfaction studies and external criterion studies (Moreland, 1985). In one external criterion study, Eyde and Kowal (1987) found differences among MMPI CBTI reports from different software developers, as well as differences between the CBTI reports and the conclusion reached by a clinical interviewer. Eyde, Kowal and Fishburne (1987) presented comparative data from seven MMPI CBTI reports that varied considerably in the type of output produced. Matarazzo (1986a) questioned the appropriateness of CBTI due to validity questions. Eyde and Kowal (1987) stated

> Buyers should be aware of the limitations of computer products and remind themselves that computer output is only as good as the data behind the decision rules used to produce the interpretation. In the final analysis, these computer test in-

> terpretations cannot be expected to function as more than a signal to the test user regarding possible psychological problems or as corroboration of problems detected by other means (p. 407).

For a detailed analysis of the issue of CBTI validity see Eyde (1987), Eyde and Kowal (1985; 1987), Eyde, Kowal and Fishburne (1987), Fowler and Butcher (1986), Matarazzo, (1983; 1985; 1986a; 1986b; 1987), Moreland (1985), Murphy (1987), and Vale and Keller (1987).

Another important ethical issue involves the qualifications necessary for appropriate use of CBTI (Butcher, 1987c; Eyde & Kowal, 1987; Fowler, 1987; Zachary & Pope, 1984). This issue is directly related to the broader question of who should have access to tests, irrespective of the type of technology in use. The American Psychological Association is currently reviewing policies related to test user qualifications (Moreland, 1986). Proposals for revised standards have been formulated by Robertson (1986), Eyde and Primoff (1986) and Eyde, Moreland, Robertson, Primoff, and Most (1988).

Ben-Porath & Butcher (1986, p. 173–174) suggested the following criteria for evaluating CBTI:

1. To what extent has the validity of this report been studied?
2. To what extent does this report rely on empirical findings in generating its interpretation?
3. To what extent does this report incorporate all of the currently validated descriptive information?
4. Does the report take demographic variables into account?
5. Are different versions available for various referral questions?
6. Is the report internally consistent?
7. Does the report include practical suggestions?
8. Is the report periodically revised to reflect newly acquired information?

Farrell (1984) also provided specific criteria for determining when a CBTI system is ready for general use. The *Guidelines for Computer-Based Tests and Interpretations* (American Psychological Association, 1986) and Eyde, Kowal and Fishburne (1987) include similar evaluative criteria. In conducting validation research and preparing software reviews, it is essential that the purpose, theoretical basis, design assumptions, and formative analysis of the software serve as an evaluation standard (see Butcher, 1987b; Hansen, 1987; Giannetti, 1987; Krug, 1987a; Reardon, 1987; for examples of this type of literature). Krug (1987a) and Moreland (1985) presented additional suggestions for conducting CBTI validation studies.

The best way to improve the quality of CBTI reports is to exert economic pressure on developers and publishers. If practitioners consistently apply the evaluative criteria suggested by the *Guidelines for Computer-Based Tests and Interpretations* (American Psychological Association, 1986), Ben-Porath & Butcher (1986) and Farrell (1984) as a condition of purchase, then the general quality of CBTI would gradually improve in response to market dynamics.

Ethical Issues. The potential for misuse of psychological testing has existed for some time (Ben-Porath & Butcher, 1986). The difficulties inherent in comprehending obtuse score profile forms, voluminous code books, and complicated decision rules previously served as an inherent deterrent to misuse of assessment instruments, such as the MMPI (Sampson, 1986b). These inherent deterrents have been removed with the advent of CBTI reports that explain the meaning of various test results in relatively clear unambiguous language. Practitioners may now erroneously conclude that CBTI systems can be used to ''expand'' the range of services they provide by offsetting their lack of training and experience. This type of misuse is likely to involve unqualified users, for example, individuals lacking training and experience in psychological assessment (Goodyear & Sinnett, 1984; Zachary & Pope, 1984) and unsophisticated users, e.g., individuals who have general training in assessment but lack background in a specific test (Zachary & Pope, 1984). Meier and Geiger (1986) further explored the relationship between training issues and professional competence.

An issue related to the misuse described above involves practitioner dependence on expert system elements of computer-assisted testing and assessment (Sampson, 1986b). Expert and decision support systems provide an important opportunity to gain ''second opinions.'' Vale and Keller (1987, p. 66) stated that, ''An expert system is a knowledge-based reasoning program that emulates the work of a human expert to solve complex problems in a narrow domain.'' An important characteristic of an expert system is the capacity to interactively explain to the user the process used to reach a particular decision (Eyde, 1987; Waterman, 1986). As stated above, the computer serves a consulting function with the practitioner having final responsibility for communicating test results (Butcher, 1987b; Krug, 1987a; Sampson, 1986b). This author has previously stated (Sampson, 1986b):

> Practitioners who are confident of their skills and who wish to extend their abilities and the quality of the services that they provide will likely make good use of this technology. Practitioners who are inadequately trained, overworked, or unsure of their skills will be more likely to use this technology to compensate for their lack of training, time, or ability and, as a result, retard their growth as therapists and further detract from their self-concept as a competent counseling psychologist. It is also quite likely that the quality of services provided by such practitioners will be inadequate because of the inability of computer applications to compensate for the human aspects of the counseling process (p. 571).

As with traditional paper-and-pencil testing and assessment, not all clients are capable of providing valid item responses or integrating assessment data into the counseling and behavior change process due to intellectual, emotional, or neurological limitations. For example, an individual in crisis may not be able to adequately respond to items presented at the computer (Cruickshank, 1982; Johnson, Godin, & Bloomquist, 1981). Even if clients have the capabilities for completing a test or structured interview, they may have unrealistic expectations as to the potential power of the computer to provide absolute "answers" (Elwork & Gutkin, 1985; Eyde & Kowal, 1985; Lister, 1970). This particular issue is more problematic for computer-based than traditional assessment approaches. For the above reasons, inadequate practitioner intervention may result in inappropriate clients using computer technology due to a lack of prescreening, and client inability to effectively and realistically integrate assessment data into the counseling and behavior change process.

Additional ethical issues having a potentially negative impact on the validity of testing in the broadest sense include the confidentiality of client records stored electronically (French, 1986; Lister, 1970; Meier & Geiger, 1986; Sampson & Pyle, 1983; Space, 1981), the lack of equality of access by all members of our society to computer technology (Elwork & Gutkin, 1985; Hofer & Green, 1985; Ibrahim, 1985) and unauthorized duplication of copyrighted software (Butcher, 1987c, Fowler, 1987; French, 1986).

Ethical Standards. As a result of the increased awareness of potential ethical problems related to computer applications in testing and assessment, numerous ethical standards have been proposed and adopted. The most comprehensive standards proposed to date are the *Guidelines for Computer-Based Tests and Interpretations* (American Psychological Association, 1986). These standards include statements regarding the practitioner's responsibilities related to computer administration and interpretation of tests, as well as statements regarding the software developer's responsibilities related to the human factors, psychometric properties, classification, validity of computer interpretation, and review of computer applications. Prior to the publication of the above guidelines, individual state psychological associations provided guidance on the appropriate use of computer applications in psychological assessment, e.g., *Guidelines for the Use of Computerized Testing Services* (Colorado Psychological Association, 1982) and *Principles for Dealing With Ethics Cases Involving Computerized Assessment* (Ohio Psychological Association, 1983). The British Psychological Society (Standing Committee on Test Standards, 1984) has made recommendations regarding the equivalence of computer-based and traditional testing and the staff qualifications necessary for using CBTI systems.

The 1988 revision of the *Ethical Standards* of the American Association for Counseling and Development and the *Code of Ethics* of the National Board for

Certified Counselors (1987) includes specific statements regarding the confidentiality of electronically stored data, the role of the counselor in relation to client use of a computer application, professional qualifications for CBTI use, equality of access to computer technology in counseling, the role of the counselor in developing self-help software, verification of the accuracy of computer-assisted scoring programs, and verification of the validity of CBTI systems. Ethical standards have also been proposed by Roid and Gorsuch (1984), Sampson & Pyle (1983) and Walker & Myrick (1985). In addition to ethical standards, standards of preparation need to include computer related issues to increase the likelihood that entry level professionals will be competent in the use of computer technology (Sampson & Loesch, 1985). The 1988 revision of the *Accreditation Standards* of the Council for the Accreditation of Counseling and Related Educational Programs includes the requirement that counselors-in-training have the opportunity to obtain knowledge and skills related to computer technology in counseling.

The development of ethical standards represents a crucial step forward in maximizing the appropriate use of computer technology. The above standards need regular review and revision as computer hardware and software evolve and as practitioners gain additional research data and service delivery experience. Mental health professionals need to develop the attitudes and skills alluded to in the standards during their initial training. These attitudes and skills then need to be reinforced by colleagues in professional practice and further supported by continuing professional education.

Ineffective Implementation

Staff resistance is the most significant barrier to effective implementation of testing and assessment software (Space, 1981). Butcher (1986) stated

> One salient roadblock to progress in the computerized assessment area is inertia among clinical practitioners when it comes to applying novel technology. Novelty and change are scary to many people. Many individuals are comfortable with the ways and methods they learned in graduate school and they resist change (p. 7).

One of the primary factors contributing to staff resistance involves the lack of staff participation in decision making regarding hardware and software selection. This author has previously stated (Sampson, 1983, p. 297), "The potential benefits to be gained from a system that is theoretically sound are negated when, as a result of inadequate planning and implementation, professionals resist the use of such a system." Another factor contributing to staff resistance involves anxiety related to changes in service delivery methods (Kiresuk, Davis & Lund, 1980; Taylor, 1981). In extreme cases, staff members may develop "cyberphobia." Romanczyk (1986, p. 1) defines cyberphobia as, "an irrational refusal to become acquainted with and to utilize a computer or computer-related services." Romanczyk goes on to state that issues of perceived control are closely related to cyberphobia. Pinkerton and Raffoul (1984) state that as much as one-third of the workforce in the United States may be affected by some degree of cyberphobia.

Hammer and Hile (1985) conceptualize practitioner resistance to computer applications as involving structural or process variables. Structural variables include: (a) interaction of individuals with computers (cognitive style differences, perceptions of client resistance, efficacy questions, and value conflict); (b) interaction among individuals as a result of automation (goal conflict, threats to power and status, and fears of evaluation), and (c) transactions with the environment (potential legal liability and ethical concerns). Process variables include: (a) initial involvement of end-users, (b) acquisition problems related to time and effort, (c) time required for implementation, (d) timing of implementation, (e) training required, (f) poor quality program documentation, and (g) value conflicts and organizational preparedness.

Experience in a variety of mental health settings has shown that poor staff support for computer applications is related to insufficient organizational readiness, lack of a planned change strategy, and an inadequate methodology for effectively dealing with staff concerns (Byrnes & Johnson, 1981). A lack of communication during implementation also generally results in reduced acceptance of computer applications (Johnson & Williams, 1980). The significant time investment necessary to implement computer technology and the confusing abundance of available software (Butcher, 1987c) also contribute. Allen and Skinner (1987) report that staff acceptance of computer technology increases as a result of direct experience with computers.

It seems clear that the major barrier to effective implementation of computer technology involves interpersonal dynamics and not issues directly related to hardware and software. Careful planning, group input in decision making and a reasonable rate of change increase the likelihood of success. Alberts (1984), Pinkerton and Raffoul (1984), and Sampson (1984) provide specific suggestions for effective implementation of computer technology.

THE FUTURE

Hardware Developments

The most intriguing and potentially significant development in the evolution of computer hardware involves the practical application of voice input and output to testing and assessment. Butcher (1986) contends that computer-human interaction by human voice will become the dominant method for test administration. In addition to the obvious advantages for persons with many physical disabilities, natural language processing will likely make it easier for anxious clients to use the technology as well as those clients with limited reading skills. Considerable research, however, will be necessary to equate voice and visually administered tests.

Although at present the computer can realistically generate the sound of a human voice, it is not possible for the computer to "recognize" the human speech of several individuals at the speed of normal conversation. The complexity involved in understanding even a simple spoken sentence is enormous when the diversity of dialects, cultural influences, speech characteristics, and the multiple meanings of individual words are taken into account. Vale (1986, p. 3) states, "Speaker-independent recognition of continuous speech will require several more years of research and development."

A more likely development will involve continued improvements in the cost-performance of computer hardware (Vale, 1986). This development will be important for two reasons. First, computer technology will be inexpensive enough that cost will not be a significant barrier to the availability of computer applications in testing and assessment. Second, performance improvements in processing speed, memory size, and disk storage capacity will facilitate the design of tests and assessment techniques that would not be possible with traditional paper-and-pencil methods. Examples would include the extensive use of adaptive testing, fully integrated CBTI reports, and comprehensive structured interviews.

Software Developments

Computer applications in testing and assessment have most commonly involved objective personality assessment, vocational interest assessment, and structured interviews. Applications in projective personality assessment, intellectual performance, and neuropsychological functioning have been somewhat less prevalent. In the future, assessment software will diversify with more applications designed to measure specifically defined content areas. Computer-assisted marriage and family assessment (Atkinson, McKenzie, & Keeney, 1985; Gerson, 1985; Lehtinen & Smith, 1985; Olson, 1985); represents an example of this trend.

Current computer applications in testing and assessment have also tended to involve the development of computer versions of traditional paper-and-pencil tests and interviews (French, 1986). In order to fully utilize the potential of the computer, tests will need to be designed from the beginning to be administered, scored and interpreted via the computer. Examples include the presentation of items via video-based stimuli (Butcher, 1986; Hofer & Green, 1985; Johnson, 1984) and the integration of data from multiple instruments into a comprehensive report (Butcher, 1986; Roid, 1984; Schinka & Smith, 1984).

Testing and assessment are not an isolated event, but rather exist within the context of the counseling and behavior change process. An elegant computer-based test interpretation is ultimately useless if the client or the practitioner cannot apply the knowledge they have obtained. Videodisc-based generalized test interpretations (Hansen, 1986; 1987; Sampson, 1983; 1988) and computer-assisted instruction that provides the client with clarification of the role of assessment and the procedures involved in testing (Sampson, 1986a) can help the client to make better use of testing and assessment data.

Expert and decision support systems have the potential to make a significant impact in terms of the delivery of assessment services and the training of mental health professionals (Sampson, 1986c). Expert systems will likely be integrated into testing and assessment in three ways. First, new tests will be designed with expert system elements as an integral aspect of system design, e.g., Krug (1987a). Second, expert systems will be included as an integral aspect of the assessment components of computer-assisted career guidance systems (Ballantine, 1986). Third, instruments that are supported by extensive research data bases, such as the MMPI, will gradually add expert system elements to existing computer-based test interpretations. Vale (1986) proposes a specific agenda for fully integrating expert systems into CBTI. Expert and decision support systems more fully provide for the consultant role envisioned for CBTI by Butcher (1987b) and Krug (1987a). These systems can also be used as a powerful training resource by allowing professionals the opportunity to query the computer as to the rationale for a particular interpretive statement.

Professional Practice

The current literature generally reflects two basic positions on CBTI. One position tends to focus on the potential for CBTI to improve the validity and reliability of assessment. The variable quality of the "typical" traditional assessment by a practitioner is contrasted with the current and potential future quality of computer-assisted assessment. A second position tends to focus more on the present limitations of CBTI and the potential quality of traditional assessment services provided by competent practitioners. The issue of the quality of services provided by the average practitioner is just as important as the issue of the quality of current CBTI in deciding the extent to which computer technology should be used in the assessment process. An incompetent practitioner who prepares a substandard psychological assessment is likely to be no better or worse than an incompetent practitioner who misuses a CBTI report (with the possible exception that there may be greater uncritical acceptance of CBTI reports by unqualified professionals [Butcher, 1987c]). The end result is poor quality service in both cases. Similarly, quality assessment services can currently be provided by competent practitioners with or without computer assistance. The practitioner remains the key element in determining the quality of the assessment process, irrespective of the use of computer technology.

In my opinion, CBTI research and development should continue given the potential for this technology to improve services. At the same time, practical application of CBTI in the current delivery of services should proceed with considerable caution, monitored by practitioners who are aware of current CBTI standards. In this way, actual practice can enrich the research and development process while at the same time making available the highest quality services possible. As a result of this potent mixture of research, development, and practice, computer applications involving expert system techniques can evolve that will produce computer-assisted assessment services that will indeed surpass the skills of the competent individual therapist using traditional methods.

CONCLUSION

In one sense, computer technology has had a profound impact on the testing and assessment process. Most popular instruments used by practitioners can now be administered and scored by computer, with many of these instruments having CBTI features. The computer is now an important design consideration in the creation of new tests. In another sense, however, little empirical evidence is available to suggest that the computer is being used on any widespread basis to do a better job of helping clients understand and apply personal data to the behavior change process.

Whether or not the computer actually helps practitioners to substantially improve the quality of the test administration, scoring, and interpretation process depends more on practitioner attitudes and skills in using this technology, than on future advances in computer hardware and software. The discovery of fire by early humans would have been a meaningless footnote in history, if something important had not been done to make effective use of what was then "new" technology.

REFERENCES

Adams, K. M., & Heaton, R. K. (1987). Computerized neuropsychological assessment: Issues and applications. In J. N. Butcher (Ed.), *Computerized psychological assessment: A practitioner's guide* (pp. 355–365). New York: Basic Books.

Alberts, F. L. (1984). Microcomputers in clinical practice: Preparing and involving office personnel. In M. D. Schwartz (Ed.), *Using computers in clinical practice: Psychotherapy and mental health applications* (pp. 69–73). New York: Haworth Press.

Allen, B., & Skinner, H. A. (1987). Lifestyle assessment using microcomputers. In J. N. Butcher (Ed.), *Computerized psychological assessment: A practitioner's guide* (pp. 108–123). New York: Basic Books.

Allred, L. J., & Harris, W. G. (1984). *The non-equivalence of computerized and conventional administrations of the Adjective Checklist.* Unpublished manuscript, Johns Hopkins University, Department of Psychology, Baltimore, MD.

Altemose, J. R., & Williamson, K. B. (1981). Clinical judgment vs. the computer: Can the school psychologist be replaced by a machine? *Psychology in the Schools, 18,* 356–363.

American Association for Counseling and Development. (1988). *Ethical Standards*. Alexandria, VA: Author.

American College Testing Program. (1987). *DISCOVER for Colleges and Adults*. Hunt Valley, MD: Author.

American Educational Research Association, American Psychological Association, & National Council on Measurement in Education. (1985). *Standards for educational and psychological testing*. Washington, D.C.: American Psychological Association.

American Personnel and Guidance Association. (1980). *APGA policy statement: Responsibilities of users of standardized tests*. Washington, D.C.: Author.

American Psychological Association. (1986). *Guidelines for computer-based tests and interpretations*. Washington, D.C.: Author.

Atkinson, B. J., McKenzie, P. N., & Keeney, B. P. (1985). The Multiple Vantage Profile: A computerized assessment of social organization in family therapy. *Computers and Family Therapy, 1*(1/2), 117–131.

Ballantine, M. (1986). Computer-assisted careers guidance systems as decision support systems. *British Journal of Guidance and Counselling, 14*, 21–32.

Beaumont, J. G. (1982). System requirements for interactive testing. *International Journal of Man-Machine Studies, 17*, 311–320.

Beaumont, J. G., & French, C. F. (1987). A clinical field study of eight automated psychometric procedures: The Leicester/DHSS Project. *International Journal of Man-Machine Studies, 26*, 661–682.

Ben-Porath, Y. S., & Butcher, J. N. (1986). Computers in personality assessment: A brief past, an ebullient present and an expanding future. *Computers in Human Behavior, 2*, 167–182.

Bleuer, J., & Walz, G. R. (1983). *Counselors and computers*. Ann Arbor: ERIC/CAPS, University of Michigan.

Bridges, M. (Ed.). (1988). *Guidance and counseling directory of microcomputer software* (Vols. 1–2). San Jose, CA: Department of Career/Vocational Education and Guidance, Santa Clara County Office of Education.

Burkhead, E. J., & Sampson, J. P., Jr. (1985). Computer-assisted assessment in support of the rehabilitation process. *Rehabilitation Counseling Bulletin, 28*, 262–274.

Butcher, J. N. (1986). Future directions in computerized psychological assessment procedures: The psychological clinic in the year 2001. In J. N. Butcher (Chair), *Future directions in computerized psychological assessment: Psychological clinics—Year 2000*. Symposium conducted at the meeting of the American Psychological Association, Washington, D.C.

Butcher, J. N. (1987a). Commercially available computerized psychological software and services. In J. N. Butcher (Ed.), *Computerized psychological assessment: A practitioner's guide* (pp. 367–412). New York: Basic Books.

Butcher, J. N. (1987b). Computerized clinical and personality assessment using the MMPI. In J. N. Butcher (Ed.), *Computerized psychological assessment: A practitioner's guide* (pp. 161–197). New York: Basic Books.

Butcher, J. N. (1987c). The use of computers in psychological assessment: An overview of practices and issues. In J. N. Butcher (Ed.), *Computerized psychological assessment: A practitioner's guide* (pp. 3–14). New York: Basic Books.

Byers, A. P. (1981). Psychological evaluation by means of an on-line computer. *Behavior Research Methods & Instrumentation, 13*, 585–587.

Byrnes, E., & Johnson, J. H. (1981). Change technology and the implementation of automation in mental health care settings. *Behavior Research Methods & Instrumentation, 13*, 573–580.

Colorado Psychological Association. (1982). *Guidelines for the use of computerized testing services*. Denver: Author.

Council for the Accreditation of Counseling and Related Educational Programs. (1988). *Accreditation procedures manual*. Alexandria, VA: Author.

Cruickshank, P. J. (1982). Patient stress and the computer in the consulting room. *Social Science and Medicine, 16,* 1371–1376.

Denner, S. (1977). Automated psychological testing. *British Journal of Social and Clinical Psychology, 16,* 175–179.

Duthie, B. (1984). A critical examination of computer-administered psychological tests. In M. D. Schwartz (Ed.), *Using computers in clinical practice: Psychotherapy and mental health applications* (pp. 135–139). New York: Haworth Press.

Eberly, C. G., & Cech, E. J. (1986). Integrating computer-assisted testing and assessment into the counseling process. *Measurement and Evaluation in Counseling and Development, 19,* 18–26.

Elwood, D. L. (1972). Test-retest reliability and cost analyses of automated face-to-face intelligence testing. *International Journal of Man-Machine Studies, 4,* 1–22.

Elwork, A., & Gutkin, T. B. (1985). The behavioral sciences in the computer age. *Computers and Human Behavior, 1,* 3–18.

Exner, J. E., Jr. (1987). Computer assistance in Rorschach interpretation. In J. N. Butcher (Ed.), *Computerized psychological assessment: A practitioner's guide* (pp. 218–235). New York: Basic Books.

Eyde, L. D. (1987). Computerised psychological testing: An introduction. *Applied Psychology: An International Review, 36*(3/4), 223–235.

Eyde, L. D., & Kowal, D. M. (1985). Psychological decision support software for the public: Pros, cons, and guidelines. *Computers and Human Behavior, 1,* 321–336.

Eyde, L. D., & Kowal, D. M. (1987). Computerised test interpretation services: Ethical and professional concerns regarding U.S. producers and users. *Applied Psychology: An International Review, 36*(3/4), 401–417.

Eyde, L. D., Kowal, D. M., & Fishburne, Jr., F. J. (1987), September). Clinical implications of validity research on computer-based test interpretation of the MMPI. In A. D. Mangelsdorf (Chair), *Practical test user problems facing psychologists in private practice.* Symposium conducted at the meeting of the American Psychological Association, New York.

Eyde, L. D., Moreland, K. L., Robertson, G. J., Primoff, E. S., & Most, R. B. (1988). *Test user qualifications: A data-based approach to promoting good test use.* Washington, D.C.: Scientific Affairs Office, American Psychological Association.

Eyde, L. D., & Primoff, E. S. (1986). *Test purchaser qualifications: A proposed voluntary system based on test ethics.* Washington, D.C.: Scientific Affairs Office, American Psychological Association.

Farrell, A. D. (1984). When is a computerized assessment system ready for distribution? Some standards for evaluation. In M. D. Schwartz (Ed.), *Using computers in clinical practice: Psychotherapy and mental health applications* (pp. 185–189). New York: Haworth Press.

Fisher, G. L., & Jenkins, S. J. (1986). Computer software: An aid in interpreting the Wechsler Intelligence Scale for Children–Revised. *Measurement and Evaluation in Counseling and Development, 19,* 53–59.

Fowler, R. D. (1987). Developing a computer-based test interpretation system. In J. N. Butcher (Ed.), *Computerized psychological assessment: A practitioner's guide* (pp. 50–63). New York: Basic Books.

Fowler, R. D., & Butcher, J. N. (1986). Critique of Matarazzo's views on computerized testing: All sigma and no meaning. *American Psychologist, 41,* 94–96.

Fowler, R. D., & Butcher, J. N. (1987). International applications of computer-based testing and interpretation. *Applied Psychology: An International Review, 36*(3/4), 419–429.

French, C. F. (1986). Microcomputers and psychometric assessment. *British Journal of Guidance and counselling, 14,* 33–45.

French, C. F., & Beaumont, J. G. (1987). The reaction of psychiatric patients to computerized assessment. *British Journal of Clinical Psychology, 26,* 267–278.

Gerson, R. (1985). Teaching systems psychotherapy with microcomputers: A creative approach. *Computers and Family Therapy, 1*(1/2), 179–190.

Giannetti, R. A. (1987). The GOLPH Psychological History: Response-contingent data acquisition and reporting. In J. N. Butcher (Ed.), *Computerized psychological assessment: A practitioner's guide* (pp. 124–144). New York: Basic Books.

Golden, C. J. (1987). Computers in neuropsychology. In J. N. Butcher (Ed.), *Computerized psychological assessment: A practitioner's guide* (pp. 344–354). New York: Basic Books.

Goodyear, R. K., & Sinnett, E. R. (1984). Current and emerging ethical issues for counseling psychologists. *The Counseling Psychologist, 12*(3), 87–98.

Hammer, A. L., & Hile, M. G. (1985). Factors in clinicians' resistance to automation in mental health. *Computers in Human Services, 1*(3), 1–25.

Hansen, J. C. (1977). Evaluation of accuracy and consistency of machine scoring of the SCII. *Measurement and Evaluation in Guidance, 10,* 141–143.

Hansen, J. C. (1986). Computers and beyond in the decision-making process. *Measurement and Evaluation in Counseling and Development, 19,* 48–52.

Hansen, J. C. (1987). Computer-assisted interpretation of the Strong Interest Inventory. In J. N. Butcher (Ed.), *Computerized psychological assessment: A practitioner's guide* (pp. 292–321). New York: Basic Books.

Herr, E. L., & Best, P. (1984). Computer technology and counseling: The role of the profession. *Journal of Counseling and Development, 63,* 192–195.

Hirsch, R. S. (1981). Procedures of the Human Factors Center at San Jose. *IBM Systems Journal, 29,* 123–171.

Hofer, P. J., & Green, B. F. (1985). The challenge of competence and creativity in computerized psychological testing. *Journal of Consulting and Clinical Psychology, 53,* 826–838.

Holland, J. L. (1985). *Self-Directed Search.* Odessa, FL: Psychological Assessment Resources.

Ibrahim, F. A. (1985). Human rights and ethical issues in the use of advanced technology. *Journal of Counseling and Development, 64,* 134–135.

Interactive Videosystems, Inc. (1985). *PATHFINDER: A career decision process.* Minneapolis, MN: Author.

Johnson, J. H. (1984). An overview of computerized testing. In M. D. Schwartz (Ed.), *Using computers in clinical practice: Psychotherapy and mental health applications* (pp. 131–133). New York: Haworth Press.

Johnson, J. H., Godin, S. W., & Bloomquist, M. L. (1981). Human factors engineering in computerized mental health care delivery. *Behavior Research Methods & Instrumentation, 13,* 425–429.

Johnson, J. H., & Johnson, K. N. (1981). Psychological considerations related to the development of computerized testing stations. *Behavior Research Methods & Instrumentation, 13,* 421–424.

Johnson, J. H., & Williams, T. A. (1980). Using on-line computer technology to improve service response and decision-making effectiveness in a mental health admitting system. In J. B. Sidowski, J. H. Johnson, & T. A. Williams (Eds.), *Technology in mental health care delivery systems* (pp. 237–249). Norwood, NJ: Ablex.

Karson, S., & O'Dell, J. W. (1987). Computer-based interpretation of the 16PF: The Karson Clinical Report in contemporary practice. In J. N. Butcher (Ed.), *Computerized psychological assessment: A practitioner's guide* (pp. 198–217). New York: Basic Books.

Kiresuk, T. J., Davis, H. R., & Lund, S. H. (1980). Knowledge utilization and planned change in the mental health services. In J. B. Sidowski, J. H. Johnson, & T. A. Williams (Eds.), *Technology in mental health care delivery systems* (pp. 295–325). Norwood, NJ: Ablex.

Klinger, D. E., Miller, D. A., Johnson, J. H., & Williams, T. A. (1977). Process evaluation of an on-line computer-assisted unit for intake assessment of mental health patients. *Behavior Research Methods & Instrumentation, 9,* 110–116.

Krug, S. E. (1987a). Microtrends: An orientation to computerized assessment. In J. N. Butcher (Ed.), *Computerized psychological assessment: A practitioner's guide* (pp. 15–25). New York: Basic Books.

Krug, S. E. (1987b). *Psychware sourcebook: 1987–1988.* Kansas City, MO: Test Corporation of America.

Loesch, L. C. (1986). Computer-assisted assessment: A reaction to Meier and Geiger. *Measurement and Evaluation in Counseling and Development, 19,* 35–37.

Lehtinen, M. W., & Smith, G. W. (1985). MATESIM: Computer assisted marriage analysis for family therapists. *Computers and Family Therapy, 1*(1/2), 117–131.

Lister, C. (1970). Privacy and large-scale personal data systems. *Personnel and Guidance Journal, 49,* 207–211.

Lockshin, S., & Romanczyk, R. G. (1986). Assessment and diagnosis. In R. G. Romanczyk (Ed.), *Clinical utilization of microcomputer technology* (pp. 57–69). New York: Pergamon Press.

Lucas, R. W., Mullins, P. J., Luna, C. B. X., & McInroy, D. C. (1977). Psychiatrists and a computer as interrogators of patients with alcohol-related diseases: A comparison. *British Journal of Psychiatry, 131,* 160–167.

Madsen, D. H. (1986). Computer applications for test administration and scoring. *Measurement and Evaluation in Counseling and Development, 19,* 6–14.

Matarazzo, J. D. (1983, July). Computerized psychological testing. *Science, 221,* p. 323.

Matarazzo, J. D. (1985). Clinical psychological test interpretations by computer: Hardware outpaces software. *Computers in Human Behavior, 1,* 235–253.

Matarazzo, J. D. (1986a). Computerized clinical psychological test interpretation: Unvalidated plus all mean and no sigma. *American Psychologist, 41,* 14–25.

Matarazzo, J. D. (1986b). Response to Fowler and Butcher on Matarazzo. *American Psychologist, 41,* 96.

Matarazzo, J. D. (1987). Response to Murphy on Matarazzo. *American Psychologist, 42,* 193–194.

Meier, S. T., & Geiger, S. M. (1986). Implications of computer-assisted testing and assessment for professional practice and training. *Measurement and Evaluation in Counseling and Development, 19,* 29–34.

Merrell, K. W. (1986). Computer use in psychometric assessment: evaluating benefits and potential problems. *Computers in Human Services, 1*(3), 59–67.

Moreland, K. L. (1985). Validation of computer-based test interpretations: Problems and prospects. *Journal of Consulting and Clinical Psychology, 53,* 816–825.

Moreland, K. L. (1986). *Test purchaser qualifications: Present practice, professional needs, and a proposed system. Washington, D.C.: Scientific Affairs Office, American Psychological Association.*

Moreland, K. L. (1987). Computerized psychological assessment: what's available. In J. N. Butcher (Ed.), *Computerized psychological assessment: A practitioner's guide* (pp. 26–49). New York: Basic Books.

Most, R. (1987). Levels of error in computerized psychological inventories. *Applied Psychology: An International Review, 36*(3/4), 375–383.

Murphy, K. R. (1987). The accuracy of clinical versus computerized test interpretations. *American Psychologist, 42,* 192–193.

National Board for Certified Counselors. (1987). *Code of Ethics.* Alexandria, VA: Author.

Ohio Psychological Association (1983). *Principles for dealing with ethics cases involving computerized assessment.* Columbus: Author.

Olson, D. H. (1985). Microcomputers for couple and family assessment: ENRICH and other inventories. *Computers and Family Therapy, 1*(1/2), 105–115.

Pinkerton, G. L., & Raffoul, P. R. (1984). Professional colleagues: Confronting the attitudes of professionals toward microcomputers. In M. D. Schwartz (Ed.), *Using computers in clinical practice: Psychotherapy and mental health applications* (pp. 61–66). New York: Haworth Press.

Reardon, R. C. (1987). Development of the computer version of the Self-Directed Search. *Measurement and Evaluation in Counseling and Development, 20,* 62–67.

Reardon, R. C., Psychological Assessment Resources, & Holland, J. L. (1987). *Self-Directed Search: Computer Version.* Odessa, FL: Psychological Assessment Resources.

Reardon, R. C., & Loughead, T. A. (1988). A comparison of paper-pencil and computer versions of the Self-Directed Search. *Journal of Counseling and Development, 67,* 249–252.

Robertson, G. J. (1986). *Establishing test purchaser qualifications: Present practices and future needs.* Washington, D.C.: Scientific Affairs Office, American Psychological Association.

Roid, G. H. (1984). Computer technology in testing. In B. S. Plake & J. C. Witt (Eds.), *The future of testing: The Second Buros-Nebraska Symposium on Measurement and Testing. Hillsdale, NJ: Lawrence Erlbaum Associates.*

Roid, G. H., & Gorsuch, R. L. (1984). Development and clinical use of test-interpretive programs on microcomputers. In M. D. Schwartz (Ed.), *Using computers in clinical practice: Psychotherapy and mental health applications* (pp. 141–149). New York: Haworth Press.

Romanczyk, R. G. (1986). *Clinical utilization of microcomputer technology.* New York: Pergamon Press.

Sampson, J. P., Jr. (1983). Computer-assisted testing and assessment: Current status and implications for the future. *Measurement and Evaluation in Guidance, 15*(4), 293–299.

Sampson, J. P., Jr. (1984). Maximizing the effectiveness of computer applications in counseling and human development: The role of research and implementation strategies. *Journal of Counseling and Development, 63,* 187–191.

Sampson, J. P., Jr. (1986a). The use of computer-assisted instruction in support of psychotherapeutic processes. *Computers in Human Behavior, 2,* 1–19.

Sampson, J. P., Jr. (1986b). Computer technology and counseling psychology: Regression toward the machine? *The Counseling Psychologist, 14,* 567–583.

Sampson, J. P., Jr. (1986c). Computer-assisted testing and assessment: Matching the tool to the task. *Measurement and Evaluation in Counseling and Development, 19,* 60–61.

Sampson, J. P., Jr. (1987). "Computer-assisted" or "computerized": What's in a name? *Journal of Counseling and Development, 66,* 116–118.

Sampson, J. P., Jr. (1988, August). Computer-assisted testing and the goals of counseling psychology. In C. E. Watkins, Jr., & V. L. Campbell (Co-chairs), *Testing and assessment in counseling psychology: Contemporary developments and issues.* Symposium conducted at the American Psychological Association Convention, Atlanta, GA.

Sampson, J. P., Jr., & Loesch, L. C. (1985). Computer preparation standards for counselors and human development specialists. *Journal of Counseling and Development, 64,* 31–33.

Sampson, J. P., Jr., & Pyle, K. R. (1983). Ethical issues involved with the use of computer-assisted counseling, testing and guidance systems. *Personnel and Guidance Journal, 61,* 283–287.

Sampson, J. P., Jr., Tenhagen, C. A., Ryan-Jones, R. & Koeteeuw, R. I. (1987). *Guide to microcomputer software in testing and assessment.* Alexandria, VA: Association for Measurement and Evaluation in Counseling and Development, American Association for Counseling and Development.

Schinka, J. A., & Smith, R. B. (1984). The computer in the psychotherapist's office: Present and future applications. In M. D. Schwartz (Ed.), *Using computers in clinical practice: Psychotherapy and mental health applications* (pp. 7–17). New York: Haworth Press.

Schwartz, M. D. (1984). People in the organization: The effects of computer-mediated work on individuals and organizations (a review). In M. D. Schwartz (Ed.), *Using computers in clinical practice: Psychotherapy and mental health applications* (pp. 55–59). New York: Haworth Press.

Slack, W. V., & Slack, C. W. (1977). Talking to a computer about emotional problems: A comparative study. *Psychotherapy: Theory, Research and Practice, 14,* 156–164.

Space, L. G. (1981). The computer as psychometrician. *Behavior Research Methods & Instrumentation, 13,* 595–606.

Standing Committee on Test Standards. (1984). Note on the computerization of printed psychological tests and questionnaires. *Bulletin of the British Psychological Society, 37,* 416–417.

Stout, R. L. (1981). New approaches to the design of computerized interviewing and testing systems. *Behavior Research Methods & Instrumentation, 13,* 436–442.

Taylor, J. B. (1981). *Using microcomputers in social agencies.* Beverly Hills, CA: Sage Publications.

Turkington, C. (1984). The growing use, and abuse, of computer testing. *APA Monitor, 15,*(1), 7, 26.

Vale, C. D. (1981). Design and implementation of a micro-computer based adaptive testing system. *Behavior Research Methods & Instrumentation, 13,* 399–406.

Vale, C. D. (1986, August). The computer technology of psychology in the year 2000. In J. N. Butcher (Chair), *Future directions in computerized psychological assessment: Psychological clinics—Year 2000.* Symposium conducted at the meeting of the American Psychological Association, Washington, D.C.

Vale, C. D., & Keller, L. S. (1987). Developing expert computer systems to interpret psychological tests. In J. N. Butcher (Ed.), *Computerized psychological assessment: A practitioner's guide* (pp. 64–83). New York: Basic Books.

Walker, N. W., & Myrick, C. C. (1985). Ethical considerations in the use of computers in psychological testing and assessment. *Journal of School Psychology, 23,* 51–57.

Walz, G. R. (1984). The computer: Counselor enhancement or eclipse? *CAPS Capsule,* No. 2.

Ward, W. C. (1984). Using microcomputers to administer tests. *Educational Measurement: Issues and Practice, 3*(2), 16–20.

Waterman, D. A. (1986). *A guide to expert systems.* Reading, MA: Addison-Wesley.

Weiss, D. J., & Vale, C. D. (1987). Computerized adaptive testing for measuring abilities and other psychological variables. In J. N. Butcher (Ed.), *Computerized psychological assessment: A practitioner's guide* (pp. 325–343). New York: Basic Books.

Wilson, S. L., Thompson, J. A., & Wylie, G. (1982). Automated psychological testing for the severely physically handicapped. *International Journal of Man-Machine Studies, 17,* 291–296.

Zachary, R. A., & Pope, K. S. (1984). Legal and ethical issues in the clinical use of computerized testing. In M. D. Schwartz (Ed.), *Using computers in clinical practice: Psychotherapy and mental health applications* (pp. 151–164). New York: Haworth Press.

15 An Integration and Perspective on Using Tests in Counseling

C. Edward Watkins, Jr.
University of North Texas

In this concluding chapter, I would like to provide some integration of and perspective on the use of tests in counseling. This chapter presents 10 basic statements about the material considered in this book. Although there are numerous statements that could be made about the rich material the various contributors have provided, 10 integrative statements or postulates that I regard as particularly salient are put forth subsequently. The different statements, although quite fundamental, seem worthy of attention and consideration here; they consistently apply to most, if not all, of the reviewed instruments and methods.

SOME POSTULATES ABOUT THE USE OF TESTS IN COUNSELING

1. *Test use in counseling should be guided by a model and method that considers both process and outcome variables.* Consistent with the material considered in Chapter 1, the use of tests in counseling should not be a random, purposeless, haphazard process. Instead, the use of tests in counseling should be purposeful, with a goal, direction, and objective in view. To render the testing process most meaningful to counseling, counselors should follow some model or method of test use that informs their practice. Such a model (like the model presented in Chapter 1) considers both process and outcome variables and provides the counselor with an overall perspective on how to use tests and their place in the counseling process.

A model of test use takes into account such process and outcome variables as: the purposes of assessment, client needs, the tests available to provide the most useful information, the effective integration of test information into the counseling process, and means by which to maximize the benefit of test information to the client, among others. The model of test use, by considering these and other relevant variables, would provide direction to both the counselor's intrasession behavior (e.g., gauging a client's readiness to use the test information) and extrasession behavior (e.g., reviewing several tests to decide which one or ones would best meet the client's needs). An effective model of test use would seemingly apply to the various forms of assessment (e.g., personality, intellectual, vocational) in which the counselor may engage. Although providing direction, a good model is also a flexible schema that enables the counselor to accommodate to new information and needed changes.

2. *Tests can be integrated into and can be facilitative of the counseling process.* If anything, the chapters in this book demonstrate that tests can be facilitative of the counseling process. Tests can provide helpful information about client issues, stimulate client insights, confirm working hypotheses, and provide possible directions for clients to consider. Too often, it seems that tests are not seen as valuable tools that can assist in the work of counseling. It also seems that tests, when used, are often not integrated smoothly and effectively into the counseling process. Instead, tests are used in a rather awkward and disjointed manner that may hinder rather than help the counselor and client.

In some work settings, it is not uncommon for clients to be given a battery of tests at the outset of counseling. Such a procedure can be very useful and provide much valuable information for the counseling relationship. Conversely, if such a procedure merely involves the routine administration of tests without appropriate follow-up or fails to actively involve clients in the assessment process (e.g., by not sharing test information with clients), the potential value of testing for the counseling relationship remains unrealized. Similarly, if testing is done only as an afterthought to the work of counseling, its potential value is again compromised. For tests to be used most effectively, counselors must first realize that tests indeed can be facilitative of the counseling process and then seriously focus on how best to integrate them into the work of counseling. The degree to which assessment instruments and information are useful to clients, in large part, depends on the counselor's effective utilization of them.

3. *Tests are designed to be of benefit to the client and should be used accordingly.* The purpose of testing is to assist the client in some way. Therefore, tests should be seen as a means by which clients can be helped. The question for the counselor then becomes, "How might the use of tests be of potential benefit to this client?" Before using tests in counseling, this is a question counselors should always ask themselves. It also is a question counselors may wish to directly pose to their clients as well.

Consistent with the focus on benefiting the client, tests as viewed throughout this book are considered to be aids or tools to stimulating personal development. Tests are thought of in terms of their facilitative, constructive potential. Tests are not regarded as static instruments (i.e., they do not merely reflect the current status of the person, environment, and so on). Rather, they are regarded as process instruments. In other words, tests are looked upon for their ability not only to reflect the present but to give some means by which the future can be approached and considered.

4. *Tests can be used to help individuals identify strengths, assets, and opportunities for growth.* If tests are thought of in terms of their facilitative, constructive potential, how is this done? For one, as this postulate indicates, counselors approach tests from a position of strength rather than weakness. That is, counselors attempt to use tests to identify client strengths, assets, and opportunities for growth. Such an approach does not deny client weaknesses or deficiencies. Weaknesses or deficiencies are recognized, but counselors want to know how they can build upon available strengths and assets to assist the client.

Perhaps a rather simplistic way of summarizing the preceding paragraph is that counselors, in using tests, look for what is right with clients instead of what is wrong. Unfortunately, this approach to using tests is often seemingly misunderstood, being labeled as naive and uninformed about psychopathology. Such misunderstanding, however, is more often based on a lack of knowledge about counselors' conceptualization of tests than otherwise. A focus on client strengths, assets, and constructive potentials, in both theory and practice, does not exist exclusive of client deficiencies and obstacles blocking growth. The approach to helping clients adopted by counselors evolves from a hygiological (health-orientation; Super, 1955) rather than pathological (disease-orientation) perspective (Watkins, 1989). Counselors do not think of tests as a method to identify what is "wrong" with the client. From the perspective adopted here, such a mindset is defeatist and unhelpful.

In reflecting on the rise and fall of psychodiagnosis, Cleveland (1976) seems to capture well much of the thinking I am trying to communicate.

> Our test reports tend to emphasize pathology and to ignore assets, constructive characteristics, and healthy mechanisms used by the client. As testers, we must be as diligent in our search of test data for the positive features of a respondent's personality as we are in our invocation of pathology. Psychological test findings should serve as forecasts for useful and constructive potentials as well as for unfavorable portents. (p. 314)

5. *Tests can be used to enhance the functioning of well-adjusted or relatively well-adjusted individuals.* As indicated in the preface, the focus of this book has been on using tests with individuals characterized by such descriptors as well-functioning, relatively well-functioning, mild to moderately distressed, and non-psychiatrically disturbed. A not uncommon question, particularly with the current attitude prevailing in mental health care, is asked as follows: If individuals are functioning well or adequately, why do we then need to engage them in a

testing/counseling relationship? In answer to this question, the old addage, "If it ain't broke, don't fix it," is often invoked. From a purely cost-effectiveness perspective, this question and addage are highly appropriate and defensible. However, in terms of enhancing personal satisfaction and happiness, the previously asked question and addage may not be in the public's best interest.

Just as the poorly functioning client can benefit from a testing/counseling process, the well-functioning client can also benefit from such a process. The chapters in this book, which largely focused on using tests with a non-psychiatrically disturbed clientele, illustrate this point well. Personality and vocational tests and related assessment methods (e.g., cognitive and behavioral methods) can all be used toward this end. Tests and related assessment methods, in being used with well-functioning or relatively well-functioning clients, can have a number of positive process and outcome effects: (a) provide insight into current behavioral patterns and thought processes; (b) narrow a seemingly vast field of possibilities to a manageable number; (c) provide life/career alternatives for consideration and review; (d) identify resources and abilities upon which one can build; (e) identify areas needing further examination, analysis, or remediation; and (f) enhance self and life satisfaction. Thus, tests indeed can be viably and very effectively used with a well-functioning or relatively well-functioning clientele. The benefits of using tests with such clients are many, with one important potential benefit being the development of even more and better life functioning for clients in counseling.

6. *Tests provide a framework or schema for organizing, understanding, and integrating seemingly disparate types of information about clients.* The tests considered in sections one and two are methods by which various forms of information about clients can be organized. The tests bring a sense of coherence and order to what at first glance may seem to be irreconcilable pieces of data. The tests, then, provide a framework or schema through which organization can occur. In one respect, the framework or schema derives from the test scales themselves. Each test scale can provide selected information on certain forms of behavior, affect, or aspects of personality. When different test scales of an instrument (e.g., the Minnesota Multiphasic Personality Inventory) are considered collectively, the configuration of scales can provide a comprehensive picture of the client's current functioning across a number of areas. Thus, test scales, when taken separately and collectively, provide a method for organizing, understanding, and integrating seemingly disparate types of information about clients.

In many of the tests covered in this book, a higher-order framework or schema is also used to organize the test data. Such higher-order schemas can be seen, for example, in Gough's cuboid model (Chapter 3), the concept of "types" in the Myers-Briggs Type Indicator (MBTI; Chapter 5), and the integration of Holland's type theory (Holland, 1985) into the use of the Strong-Campbell Interest Inventory, Self-Directed Search, and vocational card sorts (Chapters 7, 10, and

11, respectively). These higher-order schemas provide a means of understanding test data at the macro-level of analysis, whereas a test scale in and of itself provides a means of understanding test data at a micro-level of analysis. The higher-order schemas are more molar and comprehensive in scope, whereas lower-order schemas (i.e., test scales) are more molecular and specific in nature. Higher-order and lower-order schemas, although both being potentially important when approached as independent sources of data, are really complementary forms of understanding, organizing, and integrating test information and are most meaningful when used as such.

7. *Tests are multipurposed instruments.* As is clear from the test chapters, the tests considered here can provide both counselor and client with rich information across a variety of areas. In considering the different information these tests can provide, it also is important to regard them as multipurposed instruments. (On an abstract level, the ultimate purpose of a test is to benefit the client. However, the term, "multipurposed," is used quite concretely in this postulate to indicate the different uses to which tests can be put.) In sections one and two, we divided the test instruments and assessment methods into personality and vocational. The division we made is accurate and consistent with the primary foci of the tests (i.e., being primarily oriented toward either personality or vocational assessment). But, as several of the contributors pointed out, some of the personality instruments can be useful in vocational counseling. For example, certain traits (16 Personality Factor Questionnaire) or personality types (MBTI) may be more consistent with particular jobs or careers. Conversely, some of the vocational instruments can be useful in personal counseling (cf. Lowman, 1988). After all, Holland's theory of vocational types is a theory of personality types (see Holland, 1985). The counselor would do well to not exclusively consider a test instrument (at least in terms of the ones covered here) as unidimensional and singular in focus. Instead, where appropriate, the counselor should consider the possible uses to which a test can be put and its potential multipurposed, multidimensional nature.

If a test is multipurposed and multidimensional in nature, then it follows that the counselor would also examine the multiclient and multisetting uses of it. What are the different types of clients for which the test is appropriate and could be helpful? What are the different settings in which the test could be viably used? The point here is not to consider a test as serving all purposes for all clients, but to critically evaluate how a test can assist certain types of clients who present with different types of issues and who come for counseling in different types of settings. These concerns relate back to point one, the counselor's model or method for using tests, and the material presented in Chapter 1.

8. *Counselors should be familiar with various assessment instruments and, when appropriate, consider a multimethod approach to using tests in counseling.* Although a test can be multipurposed in focus, the use of tests in combination with one another sometimes will be the best approach to obtaining the desired

information for counseling. In considering the use of several tests in combination, the idea is not that "more is better." Instead, the question to be asked is as follows: Would two (or more) instruments complement one another in more effectively answering the questions that now present themselves in counseling? Again, the answer to such a question is guided by a model or method of test use and must be informed by the counselor's knowledge of the tests being considered and how they would work together. The chapter by Savickas (Chapter 12), for example, provides a good illustration of how different instruments can be combined and used effectively.

If a multimethod approach to assessment is to be considered, then the counselor must have the requisite information available to evaluate this option. As indicated in the preceding paragraph, the counselor's knowledge base about the tests is critical. Perhaps this goes without saying but, too often, it seems that different test instruments are used either separately or in conjunction with each other without the counselor possessing sufficient understanding of or knowledge about them. Any consideration of the multimethod approach (or, for that matter, a single-method approach) must be solidly grounded in a critically informed perspective.

9. *Effective test use requires a sound knowledge base that is informed by contemporary assessment issues, test user guidelines and qualifications, and familiarity with the particular assessment methods being used.* This postulate as well as the preceding postulate are clearly interrelated. Effective test use is not a matter to be taken lightly, as the chapter by Betz (Chapter 13) well illustrates. If tests are to be used effectively, then there are a number of issues to which the test user must be sensitive. A sound knowledge about ethical and professional standards in using tests, reliability and validity of the tests being used, and the qualifications needed to use different test instruments, among other areas, is critical to possess. Also, it is important to be knowledgeable about the concept of bias in testing and how this issue relates to women, racial/ethnic minorities, and cross-cultural testing applications.

If the counselor is to develop the knowledge base needed to use tests effectively, then it pays to be ever-mindful of the various sources that provide contemporary test information or bear upon the use of tests. These sources include the *Standards for Educational and Psychological Testing* (AERA, APA, NCME, 1985) and ethical principles that guide the practice of counselors and psychologists (AACD, 1988; APA, 1981). Equally important are test reviews, which can be found in such sources as the *Mental Measurements Yearbook* and in issues of the *Journal of Counseling and Development* and *Measurement and Evaluation in Counseling and Development*. Test reviews provide a valuable source of critical, evaluative information and their importance in appraising a test is well in evidence in several of the chapters presented here (e.g., see Slaney, Chapter 11; Savickas, Chapter 12). For other valuable sources of test information, the reader is referred back to the excellent chapter written by Betz. As mentioned in postulate two, the degree to which assessment instruments and information are useful to clients largely depends on the counselor's effective utilization of them. In agreement with this statement, the effective utilization of assessment instruments and information largely depends upon the soundness and thoroughness of the counselor's knowledge base about them.

10. *The computer-assisted testing and assessment services now available to the counselor represent an increasingly burgeoning technology, which should be approached favorably but with an awareness about the positive and negative features accompanying it.* The computer-assisted testing and assessment services now available for counselor use have mushroomed in growth in recent years. Indeed, the computer services available to the counselor have grown so rapidly that it is often difficult to remain abreast of contemporary developments. The counselor would do well, however, to be familiar with some of these developments because, as Sampson (Chapter 14) indicates, a number of benefits can accompany the use of computer-assisted assessment services. Some of these benefits, which include better integrating assessment data into counseling, enhanced test reliability and validity, and the saving of counselor time, cut to the heart of some important assessment/counseling issues and have the potential for rendering the assessment/counseling process more effective.

As Sampson further points out, just as there are potential benefits to the use of computer-assisted assessment services in counseling, there are also potential problems. The potential problem areas he identifies—threats to test reliability and validity and ineffective implementation—are by no means minor. The threats to test reliability and validity that Sampson mentions are certainly of concern and merit attention. As with much work in assessment and counseling, the problem area of ineffective implementation of computer services appears to be attitudinally based. Thus, the person/machine interface is and probably always will be an issue in the use of assessment services in counseling. With these limitations acknowledged, however, computer-assisted assessment services seemingly can contribute positively to the counseling experience. Counselors should become knowledgeable about these services but should be ever-familiar with the potential benefits and problems that accompany them.

CONCLUSION

These 10 integrative, summative statements can be considered postulates about the use of tests in counseling. Although quite fundamental and limited in scope, these postulates seem worthy of attention here because they provide some perspective on the material presented in this book. As has been evident in this chapter and preceding chapters, testing is a complex process that involves such variables as forethought, planning, knowledge, and effective utilization. Testing is not a haphazard, random process that can be done in a "quick and dirty" way.

Like counseling, testing requires a commitment on the parts of the counselor and client.

Although effective test use requires commitment and other variables as mentioned above, it is a process well worth the effort. The potential gains from using tests in counseling far outweigh the effort invested. The chapters in this book attest again and again to the value of tests and their many uses. The different chapter contributors have put together some highly valuable information on the state-of-the-art and state-of-the-science of the place of tests in counseling. I hope that counselors may often find this information of value to them as they prepare to use tests in counseling practice.

REFERENCES

American Association for Counseling and Development. (1988). Ethical standards of the American Association for Counseling and Development. *Journal of Counseling and Development, 67,* 4–8.

American Educational Research Association, American Psychological Association, and National Council on Measurement in Education. (1985). *Standards for educational and psychological testing.* Washington, D.C.: American Psychological Association.

American Psychological Association. (1981). Ethical principles of psychologists. *American Psychologist, 36,* 633–638.

Cleveland, S. E. (1976). Reflections on the rise and fall of psychodiagnosis. *Professional Psychology, 7,* 309–318.

Holland, J. L. (1985). *Making vocational choices: A theory of vocational personalities and work environments.* Englewood Cliffs, NJ: Prentice-Hall.

Lowman, R. L. (1987). Occupational choice as a moderator of psychotherapeutic approach. *Psychotherapy, 24,* 801–808.

Super, D. E. (1955). Transition: From vocational guidance to counseling psychology. *Journal of Counseling Psychology, 2,* 3–9.

Watkins, C. E., Jr. (1989, April). Can we really assess strengths and positive dynamics? The role of interpretive language. In A. M. O'Roark (Chair), *The sunny side of the street: Assessing strengths and positive dynamics.* Symposium conducted at the annual meeting of the Society for Personality Assessment, New York.

Author Index

C

D

E

H

N

S

T

U

V

Subject Index

K

M

S

T

V